Global environmental change is one of the most pressing international issues of the next century. There is a need to monitor the Earth's vital signs, from atmospheric ozone to tropical deforestation to sea level change. Satellite data sets will be vital in addressing global change issues, in determining natural variability and monitoring global and regional changes. This highly illustrated and accessible volume demonstrates the variety of satellite-derived global data sets now available, their uses, advantages and limitations, and the range of variation that has already been observed with these data.

Atlas of satellite observations
related to global change

Atlas of satellite observations related to global change

R. J. GURNEY

NERC Unit for Thematic Information Systems,
University of Reading, UK

J. L. FOSTER

Hydrological Sciences Branch,
Laboratory for Hydrospheric Processes,
NASA/Goddard Space Flight Center, Greenbelt, Maryland, USA

C. L. PARKINSON

Oceans and Ice Branch,
Laboratory for Hydrospheric Processes,
NASA/Goddard Space Flight Center, Greenbelt, Maryland, USA

CAMBRIDGE
UNIVERSITY PRESS

Published by the Press Syndicate of the University of Cambridge
The Pitt Building, Trumpington Street, Cambridge CB2 1RP
40 West 20th Street, New York, NY 10011-4211, USA
10 Stamford Road, Oakleigh, Melbourne 3166, Australia

First published 1993

Printed in Great Britain at Butler & Tanner,
Frome and London

A catalogue record for this book is available from the British Library

Library of Congress cataloguing in publication data

Gurney, R. J. (Robert J.)
Atlas of satellite observations related to global change/R. J. Gurney, J. L. Foster, C. L. Parkinson.
p. cm.
Includes index.
ISBN 0–521–43467–X
1. Climatic changes – Observations. 2. Earth sciences – Observations.
3. Astronautics in earth sciences. I. Foster, J. L. (James L.) II. Parkinson,
C. L. (Claire L.) III. Title. QC981.8.C5G87 1993
551.5 – dc20   92–29559
CIP

ISBN 0 521 43467 X hardback

Contents

List of Contributors

P. A. Arkin, Climate Analysis Center, NOAA/NWS/NMC, Washington, DC 20233.

R. Atlas, Laboratory for Atmospheres, NASA/Goddard Space Flight Center, Greenbelt, MD 20771.

W. Bandeen, Hughes STX Corporation, 7601 Ora Glen Drive, Greenbelt, MD 20770.

B. R. Barkstrom, Atmospheric Sciences Division, NASA Langley Research Center, Hampton, VA 23665.

S. C. Bloom, Universities Space Research Association, Laboratory for Atmospheres, NASA/Goddard Space Flight Center, Greenbelt, MD 20771.

O. B. Brown, RSMAS/MPO, University of Miami, Miami, FL 33149.

A. J. Busalacchi, Laboratory for Hydrospheric Processes, NASA/Goddard Space Flight Center, Greenbelt, MD 20771.

A. T. C. Chang, Hydrological Sciences Branch, NASA/Goddard Space Flight Center, Greenbelt, MD 20771.

B. J. Choudhury, Hydrological Sciences Branch, NASA/Goddard Space Flight Center, Greenbelt, MD 20771.

H. J. Christian, Earth Science and Applications Division, NASA/Marshall Space Flight Center, Huntsville, AL 35812.

W. Esaias, Information Systems Development Facility, Oceans and Ice Branch, NASA/Goddard Space Flight Center, Greenbelt, MD 20771.

G. Feldman, Information Systems Development Facility, Oceans and Ice Branch, NASA/Goddard Space Flight Center, Greenbelt, MD 20771.

J. L. Foster, Hydrological Sciences Branch, NASA/Goddard Space Flight Center, Greenbelt, MD 20771.

P. W. Francis, Planetary Geosciences Division, Department of Geology and Geophysics, School of Ocean and Earth Science and Technology, University of Hawaii, Honolulu, HI 96822.

G. G. Gibson, Lockheed Engineering and Sciences Company, Hampton, VA 23665.

P. Gloersen, Oceans and Ice Branch, NASA/Goddard Space Flight Center, Greenbelt, MD 20771.

S. J. Goodman, Earth Science and Applications Division, NASA/Marshall Space Flight Center, Huntsville, AL 35812.

S. N. Goward, Laboratory for Global Remote Sensing, Department of Geography, University of Maryland, College Park, MD 20742.

R. Greenstone, Hughes STX Corporation, 7601 Ora Glen Drive, Greenbelt, MD 20770.

R. J. Gurney, NUTIS, University of Reading, PO Box 227, Reading RG6 2AB, UK.

D. K. Hall, Hydrological Sciences Branch, NASA/Goddard Space Flight Center, Greenbelt, MD 20771.

E. F. Harrison, Atmospheric Sciences Division, NASA/Langley Research Center, Hampton, VA 23665.

R. C. Harriss, Institute for the Study of Earth, Oceans & Space, University of New Hampshire, Durham, NH 03824.

J. R. Heirtzler, Laboratory for Terrestrial Physics, NASA/Goddard Space Flight Center, Greenbelt, MD 20771.

R. N. Hoffman, Atmospheric and Environmental Research Inc., Cambridge, MA 02139.

J. E. Janowiak, Climate Analysis Center, NOAA/NWS/NMC, Washington, DC 20233.

J. A. Kaye, NASA Headquarters, Code SED, Washington, DC 20546.

C. J. Koblinsky, Oceans and Ice Branch, NASA/Goddard Space Flight Center, Greenbelt, MD 20771.

K.-M. Lau, Climate and Radiation Branch, NASA/Goddard Space Flight Center, Greenbelt, MD 20771.

S. P. Leatherman, Laboratory for Coastal Research, Department of Geography, University of Maryland, College Park, MD 20742.

W. T. Liu, NASA/Jet Propulsion Laboratory, California Institute of Technology, Pasadena, CA 91109.

C. R. McClain, Information Systems Development Facility, Oceans and Ice Branch, NASA/Goddard Space Flight Center, Greenbelt, MD 20771.

M. P. McCormick, Atmospheric Sciences Division, NASA/Langley Research Center, Hampton, VA 23665.

P. Minnis, Atmospheric Sciences Division, NASA/Langley Research Center, Hampton, VA 23665.

P. J. Mouginis-Mark, Planetary Geosciences Division, Department of Geology and Geophysics, School of Ocean and Earth Science and Technology, University of Hawaii, Honolulu, HI 96822.

E. G. Njoku, NASA/Jet Propulsion Laboratory, California Institute of Technology, Pasadena, CA 91109.

C. L. Parkinson, Oceans and Ice Branch, NASA/Goddard Space Flight Center, Greenbelt, MD 20771.

D. C. Pieri, NASA/Jet Propulsion Laboratory, California Institute of Technology, Pasadena, CA 91109.

W. B. Rossow, NASA/Goddard Institute for Space Studies, New York, NY 10025.

M. R. Shoeberl, Atmospheric Chemistry and Dynamics Branch,

NASA/Goddard Space Flight Center, Greenbelt, MD 20771.

R. W. Spencer, NASA/Marshall Space Flight Center, Huntsville, AL 35812.

K. Sullivan, Office of the Chief Scientist, NOAA, Herbert Hoover Building, 14th and Constitution Avenue, NW, Washington DC, 20230 (formerly Astronaut Office, NASA/Johnson Space Center, Houston, TX).

J. Susskind, Laboratory for Atmospheres, NASA/Goddard Space Flight Center, Greenbelt, MD 20771.

R. H. Thomas, NASA Headquarters, Code SEC, Washington, DC 20546.

J. R. G. Townshend, Laboratory for Global Remote Sensing, Department of Geography, University of Maryland, College Park, MD 20742.

C. J. Tucker, Biospheric Sciences Branch, NASA/Goddard Space Flight Center, Greenbelt, MD 20771.

R. S. Williams, Jr., US Geological Survey, Quissett Campus, Woods Hole, MA 02543.

R. C. Willson, NASA/Jet Propulsion Laboratory, California Institute of Technology, Pasadena, CA 91109.

Foreword

The latter half of the twentieth century has been an amazing era for everyone interested in the Earth and its wonders. The dawning of the Space Age in the late 1940s heralded the arrival of technologies that soon would provide us with a revolutionary, global perspective on our planet. These global views in turn stimulated the development of an exciting new conceptual framework among Earth scientists, and are widely credited with catalysing a new level of international public concern about global environmental issues. Our home planet is an intricate ensemble of interacting systems, whose workings are as yet understood poorly. The confluence of technologies and concepts that comprise the space age has let us see more clearly the fragility of this home, as well as the magnitude of human impacts upon it. Our need to learn more about Earth systems and to be wise stewards of them has perhaps never been clearer. These are exciting and important times for the Earth sciences, and ones in which satellites have a central role to play.

I have had the extraordinary privilege of seeing our planet from orbit with my own eyes—something most Earth scientists only dream of. This is an awe-inspiring experience that virtually defies description. On the one hand, the vista below is familiar: shapes well-known from years spent poring over maps; features and places remembered from prior, Earth-bound travels. On the other hand, though, it is all quite unlike anything one could ever imagine. Added to the visual wonder is the absolutely magic feeling of floating over this vast panorama at an apparently stately pace, with none of the sounds or sensations we normally associate with great speeds. Pretty astounding perceptions, given that the scenery is really racing past at about 18 000 miles per hour!

There is added wonder in this experience for an Earth scientist, I think, because so many places and phenomena that pass below evoke thoughts of today's environmental concerns and controversies. Excited, gleeful moments of recognition—'There's the Amazon—and it's clear over the river!'—are followed by a mixture of amazement, wonder and worry as a landscape scrolls beneath the Shuttle that clearly shows the far-reaching impacts of human activity upon the Earth. Sediment plumes, electrical storms, smoke palls, fire scars, hurricanes, volcanoes, and myriad signs of human activities all glide past the windows, visually striking examples of the many processes that continually modify the Earth, oceans and atmosphere. The scientist at the window also ponders the many unseen but critical phenomena occurring simultaneously, such as the atmospheric processes that control the abundance and distribution of the stratospheric ozone. The 'ozone hole' seems quite remote to most of us in daily life. As we go about our business here on Earth, the atmosphere seems to be a vast ocean of air. From orbit, however, one quickly sees that the atmosphere is more like the thin shell of an egg than a deep ocean. This thin layer is all that protects life on Earth—including us!—from the harshness of space. This eggshell is the dynamic system we know as weather, climate and the breath of life. Looking through the spacecraft window, one's lasting impression is of fragility, and one wonders whether mankind can, and will, learn enough about the planet to safeguard its vital systems. In the end, the experience is at once inspiring, motivational and frustrating: spectacularly beautiful sights, many questions, no immediate answers.

The vital questions raised by this experience cannot be answered with the sort of personal views I've described, illustrative and moving though these may be. Instead, an entirely different sort of satellite view is needed, along with data from ground-based, ship-borne and air-borne sensors, plus powerful computing techniques. Painstaking care must be taken to understand the significance and limitations of all the measurements and the analytical methods before one can construct sound hypotheses about Earth processes and model important phenomena with any confidence. Such detailed studies are the subject matter of this volume.

The Editors have undertaken a tremendous job, gathering representative works from a broad array of Earth science disciplines that are centrally involved in the study of global change processes. In each subject area, they have endeavored to provide a compendium of the satellite data and imagery relevant to the problem, a description of the key scientific methodologies, and an overview of significant results. All these elements are useful to a very wide audience, from specialists in other Earth science disciplines seeking to broaden their horizons, to the general public and government decision-makers, who may be trying to sort out the reliability and limitations of the myriad studies they have before them today. This Atlas will serve each of these groups quite well, and will contribute greatly to the growing understanding of Earth's complex systems that is being attained through scientific analysis of satellite observations.

KATHRYN D. SULLIVAN, PhD
NASA ASTRONAUT
EARTH SCIENTIST

Preface

The idea for this volume arose out of numerous preparatory meetings held at NASA's Goddard Space Flight Center on Mission to Planet Earth and the forthcoming Earth Observing System (EOS). Interspersed with discussion of potential new observations possible after the launch of EOS were frequent discussions of existent data sets and the information derivable from them. The number and quality of these data sets were much greater than many people had realized. At the same meetings it became very clear that climate modelers were in general not confronting their models with the range of data that was currently available, either through assimilating the data into the models, initializing the models with the data, or checking the results of the models by using the data. This book attempts to bridge some of the information gap by allowing scientists instrumental in deriving or analyzing these sets of observations to describe what they show, give an idea of their limitations, and indicate where further information may be obtained in the literature. The list of variables included is not exhaustive, but aims to be fairly comprehensive.

The chapter authors are almost exclusively from the United States, because it is from here that most of the long-term data sets have originated as a result of sustained investment in aerospace technology. As other nations proceed also to produce long-term sets of global observations, this bias will undoubtedly disappear. Investigators on the European Space Agency's Earth Resources Satellite (ERS-1) are already starting to produce global data sets that will considerably extend those described in this volume.

As will be clear upon reading the various chapters in the book, the same variable is often examined from the data of several different instruments and, conversely, an individual instrument is often used for examining a wide variety of geophysical variables. Remote sensing instruments measure only radiation, but the range of geophysical algorithms that can be derived is very great. As a consequence, the book contains some repetitious information about the satellite instruments, but this is necessary to maintain the cohesiveness of each chapter and to reduce cross-referencing to a useful amount.

Changes in the Earth's environment are constantly occurring, so that no book can be totally up to date by the time of its publication. Some important phenomena which were observed too recently to be adequately addressed in this volume nevertheless deserve mention. The eruption of Mt Pinatubo in the Philippines in June 1991, the deepening of the Antarctic ozone hole in October 1991 and 1992, and the dramatic decrease of total ozone in sub-Arctic regions in 1992 are all significant on at least a regional and perhaps a global basis. The nexus between the Earth–atmosphere system is demonstrated by noting that surface events such as volcanic eruption may produce far-ranging consequences in the stratosphere in terms of aerosol loading. Conversely, the ozone hole is a stratospheric event that results in increases in ultraviolet radiation at the surface.

In order to ensure scientific standards, the individual chapters have all been peer reviewed by experts in their respective fields, and the authors have incorporated the majority of the reviewers' comments into their revised texts. In addition, the entire manuscript was reviewed as a whole by anonymous referees selected by Cambridge University Press.

Many people deserve thanks for their help in bringing this book to fruition. The people who gave of their time and expertise to serve as reviewers for individual chapters were: Mark R. Abbott, Oregon State University; Eric Barrett, University of Bristol; Carl S. Benson, University of Alaska; Craig F. Bohren, Pennsylvania State University; Kevin Burke, US National Research Council; Moustafa T. Chahine, Jet Propulsion Laboratory; A. T. C. Chang, Goddard Space Flight Center; Bhaskar Choudhury, Goddard Space Flight Center; William P. Chu, Langley Research Center; Mary Cleave, Goddard Space Flight Center; Brian R. Dennis, Goddard Space Flight Center; Inez Fung, Goddard Institute for Space Studies; Marvin A. Geller, State University of New York at Stony Brook; Marti Hallikainen, Helsinki University of Technology; Robert C. Harriss, University of New Hampshire; Dennis L. Hartmann, University of Washington; Chris Justice, University of Maryland; E. Philip Krider, University of Arizona; Tom Lachlan-Cope, British Antarctic Survey; William K. M. Lau, Goddard Space Flight Center; Stephen P. Leatherman, University of Maryland;

Robert B. Lee, Langley Research Center; W. Timothy Liu, Jet Propulsion Laboratory; Edward Maltby, University of Exeter; Seelye Martin, University of Washington; Massimo Menenti, Winard Staring Centre, Netherlands; J. Peter Muller, University College London; Eni Njoku, Jet Propulsion Laboratory; Albert Rango, Beltsville Agricultural Research Center, US Department of Agriculture; Harry H. Roberts, Louisiana State University; William B. Rossow, Goddard Institute for Space Studies; Susan Solomon, Environmental Research Laboratories, US National Oceanic and Atmospheric Administration; Joel Susskind, Goddard Space Flight Center; Robert H. Thomas, NASA Headquarters; Anne M. Thompson, Goddard Space Flight Center; Geoffrey Wadge, University of Reading; Alta Walker, US Geological Survey; John Walsh, University of Illinois; Bruce A. Wielicki, Langley Research Center; Thomas T. Wilheit, Texas A & M University; Earl Williams, Massachusetts Institute of Technology; Richard S. Williams, Jr., US Geological Survey.

In addition, the consistent support of many NASA/Goddard and NASA Headquarters personnel is much appreciated. These include particularly Stan Wilson, Greg Wilson, and Ralph Brescia of NASA Headquarters and Jerry Soffen of NASA/Goddard. We also thank Nancy Firestine of W. T. Chen and Company for her assistance at several points during the project. Finally, we would like to thank Alan Crowden of Cambridge University Press for his patience, his amiability, and his many useful suggestions.

Robert Gurney
James Foster
Claire Parkinson

Greenbelt, Maryland
January 1992

Introduction

The twentieth century has been a time of impressive techno-logical developments, among which has been the technology that has allowed observations from space of the planet Earth, thereby revolutionizing our ability to observe our planet and the changes occurring on it. In this book we present a sample of satellite observations of many variables that, together, allow us to monitor important aspects of our planet, with explana-tions and analyses of the methods involved and the results obtained.

Space observations are an important step toward recording and understanding Earth changes sufficiently to enable use of that understanding to benefit the Earth and the species inhabiting it. Scientists in the twenty-first century will, of necessity, have to be concerned about addressing and redres-sing the problems associated with natural and man-made changes on the planet. Natural changes and fluctuations in the atmosphere, oceans, and on the continents have been occurring since the formation of the Earth billions of years ago. These changes have affected the biosphere in the past and will do so in the future, with short-term effects on individual species being sometimes detrimental and sometimes beneficial. Only recently has mankind been recognized as a further significant agent of environmental change. The internal variability of the climate system needs to be understood before the effects of human-induced changes can be fully clarified.

Amongst the benefits of a deeper understanding of past and present changes on the Earth would be the increased ability to predict changes and thus to provide ample warnings and the possibility of adequate preparation for probable changes on both regional and global scales. The advent of remote sensing technology and spaceborne sensors is a critical advance, mak-ing it possible to monitor from space a large number of the Earth's vital signs, from atmospheric ozone to vegetation cover to sea level and glacial ice, and therefore to provide a background for prediction studies.

Advances in satellite instruments and their calibration and in methods of processing and archiving remotely sensed data have led to the creation of numerous time series of geophysi-cal data relevant to studies of global change. Many of these

data sets involve complicated retrieval methods and are not yet widely understood or used. Nevertheless, these data will be essential in addressing global change issues, in determin-ing natural variability in the climate system, and in monitoring global and regional changes. Many more data sets are pro-posed to be collected over the next several decades by the US National Aeronautics and Space Administration (NASA), the European Space Agency (ESA), the Japanese National Space Development Agency (NASDA) and others as part of the Earth Observing System (EOS). It is therefore timely that a volume be published illustrating the variety of satellite-derived global data sets now available and discussing the methods used to retrieve these data, their uses, advantages and limitations, and the range of geophysical, chemical, and biological variations that these data have already revealed. Information presented in this volume shows some of the variability of Earth processes and should help scientists both to understand global processes and interactions better and to predict future changes.

Remote sensing affords the opportunity to view the Earth synoptically as an entity. Although variations can often be detected from ground-based observations, these variations tend to be site-specific and fail to provide a convincing global or even regional view. Ground-based stations have an uneven spatial density and varying observational quality compared with the more consistent and broader coverage possible from satellites. However, there are some variables, including many within the deep ocean that cannot yet be observed from space platforms, and it would be naive to think that the availability of space observations eliminates the need for ground-based observations. Rather, the advent of satellite technology means that a wider range of scientific questions can now be addressed.

Satellite sensors record and transmit data about electro-magnetic radiation observed at various wavelengths or wavelength ranges. These data are then interpreted into geophysical information through various quantitative or quali-tative models. The most important components of the Earth's radiation budget that enter into remote sensing calculations are direct solar radiation reflected off the Earth, radiation emitted or scattered by the atmosphere downward to the surface and then reflected upward to the sensor, radiation emitted from the surface, and radiation emitted or scattered towards the sensor by the atmosphere. Sensors are designed to utilize the electromagnetic properties unique to the particular substance or material being examined. When using ultra-violet, visible, and near infra-red wavelengths, the detector measures reflected solar energy, so that the reflectance properties of the substance are particularly important, whereas when using the infra-red and microwave portions of the spectrum, emitted energy is measured, so that the emittance of the substance is most relevant. These properties are related, so some retrievals described in this book use observations of both reflectance and emittance.

Complementing the advances made in the understanding of the Earth system from remote sensing have been the advances made from numerical models. Since the 1960s, computer models of the atmosphere and oceans have become increasingly important and have been made more realistic for simulating and analyzing many global processes. Much has been learned about predictability, especially of climate systems. Models of the Earth's atmosphere and oceans are being used to predict global changes and particularly the likelihood of global warming and its consequences. Modelling experiments allow insight into physical processes and have been useful for generalizing the results of local or limited observations. This information, in turn, is helpful in defining ways to improve the performance of the models. However, the models are only crude approximations, simplifying the real world, and have not yet fully utilized global observational data sets. When the observational data are incorporated into the models, considerable progress can be expected.

Few models, however, are capable of accepting new kinds of input data readily. Unless designed specifically to accept them, all models have significant problems in using new data of any type. To overcome these difficulties and enable appropriate incorporation of data from new technologies, the models must be modified. Efforts put into modifying or designing models to be compatible with remote sensing data are generally easily justified on the basis of potential improved simulation accuracies and a better understanding of physical processes. Advances in the observations themselves are also needed, as is made clear at many points throughout this book.

Descriptions of satellite-derived data sets and the information revealed by them constitute the bulk of this volume. The second to the penultimate chapters deal with specific variables and existent remotely sensed data sets relevant to them, while the final chapter discusses future data sets and provides some prospects and conclusions. An appendix gives a list of many of the most important satellites that have sensed information about the Earth and its atmosphere from the initiation of satellite sensing to the end of 1991.

Because of differences in the data sets and in writing styles, chapters vary somewhat in length and organization. However, most of the chapters include an introduction or background section, an explanation of the methodology used to develop the algorithm from which the geophysical information is derived, data analysis and results, including an indication of any trends in the data, a discussion of the accuracy, reliability, and limitations of the data, and a concluding section containing, among other things, information on where the user can obtain the data and possible applications. Chapters are arranged into groupings on the radiation balance, stratosphere, troposphere, oceans, land, and cryosphere. These groupings are arbitrary to some extent, and some of the chapters deal with variables that relate to more than one grouping and hence could have been placed in alternative sections. There is also, of necessity, some repetition of technical information, in order to allow each chapter to be reasonably self-contained. For instance, a particular instrument, what it senses, its orbital characteristics, resolution, etc., may be described in more than one chapter. Although several of the chapters deal with human-induced changes in the environment, there are many additional such changes observable from space, and we have included a chapter entitled 'Indications and effects of human activities' illustrating a variety of these.

A quintessential concern regarding our understanding of the well-being of our environment and the health of our planet is the determination of how the Earth is changing. Many decades of observations are needed to determine with some degree of certainty if what is being observed is actually changing in a long-term climatic sense, above and beyond seasonal and inter-annual fluctuations. The data sets that comprise this volume can serve as benchmarks so that the family of sensors on the next generation of satellites can be better used to assess the rates and magnitudes of the changes occurring in the Earth system, their allocation to inter-annual or long-term variabilities, and their significance to human societies.

PART I

RADIATION BALANCE

Solar irradiance

RICHARD C. WILLSON

Introduction

The desire to detect possible variations of the total solar irradiance, the total amount of power supplied to the Earth from the Sun by radiative means, has been a goal of mankind for more than a century. The interest in this quantity arose from a realization that it is a primary determining factor for the Earth's climate. At any time in the Earth's history, the atmospheric composition and the distribution of oceans and land masses combine with the solar irradiance to determine the radiative balance, and hence the climate, of the Earth.

As science uncovered evidence that the Earth's climate has varied in the past, the possibility that variations in total solar irradiance might be a cause of climate change has stimulated research aimed at detecting solar variability. Experiments from ground-based observatories, most notably those of the Smithsonian Astrophysical Observatory which extended over more than 50 years beginning in the first decade of the twentieth century, and from aircraft and balloons during the third quarter of the twentieth century, were unable to detect total irradiance variations that were unambiguously solar in origin (Frohlich, 1977; Hoyt, 1979; Newkirk, 1983) (See Table 1.). These early

efforts were frustrated by two principal limitations: uncertainties due to 1) instrument calibration and 2) atmospheric attenuation whose combined effects were larger than intrinsic solar variability over the timescales of the observations.

Two developments following the end of the Smithsonian ground-based program in the early 1960s have facilitated exploration of solar total irradiance variations. First, a new generation of instruments was developed that could provide space-borne observations of high accuracy and precision. And secondly, space platforms capable of supporting sustained solar observations for solar monitoring became commonplace. The first decade of high precision solar total irradiance variability has now been measured, documented and archived, and an active program for sustaining a multi-decadal total irradiance database is now in place.

Interest in measuring the solar spectral irradiance has evolved along with interest in total irradiance. Spectral observations were ancillary to the early efforts to monitor total irradiance, since they were necessarily made from the ground, and correction for atmospheric attenuation was required to deduce extra-atmospheric values of total flux (Abbot & Fowle, 1908). During the last half of the twentieth century, the

Table 1. *Early solar total irradiance monitoring experiments. None was able to detect intrinsic solar variability for various reasons. The results shown (except for the Smithsonian) have been corrected to the World Radiometric Reference*[1]

Year(s)	Experiment or investigator	Instrument and (sensor type)*	Calibration approach**	Platform	Results (W/M2)
1902–62	Smithsonian	Water Flow (1)	ESCC	Ground	1346
1962–68	Kondratyev	Yanishevsky (2)	RS	Balloon	1376
1967–68	Murcray	Eppley (2)	RS	Balloon	1373
1967	Drummond	Eppley (2)	RS	Aircraft	1387
1967	McNutt	Cone (1)	ESCC	Aircraft	1375
1968	Kendall	PACRAD (1)	ESCC	Aircraft	1373
1968	Willson	ACR II (1)	ESCC	Balloon	1370
1969	Plamondon	TCFM (1)	ESCC-P	Spacecraft	1362
1969	Willson	ACR III (1)	ESCC	Balloon	1368
1975	Hickey	Nimbus 6/ERB (2)	RS	Spacecraft	1389

Sensor type: (1) – cavity, (2) – flat surface.
**Calibration approach (in order of decreasing accuracy): ESCC: electrically self-calibrated cavity, ESCC-P: partial implementation of electrically self-calibrated cavity, RS: relative sensor, no cavity, self-calibration, relies on pre-flight calibration.
[1]Frohlich (1972).

accessibility of aircraft, balloon, rocket and satellite experimental platforms has provided opportunities to explore the entire solar spectrum from X-rays through the infra-red. These extra-atmospheric platforms facilitated exploration of the near-to-mid ultra-violet spectrum that is so important to upper atmospheric physics and chemistry. In particular, the variability of ultra-violet solar flux in the wavelength range affecting ozone production has become a significant focus in recent years with the discovery of the 'ozone hole' phenomenon.

Despite exploration of portions of the solar spectrum with significance for particular atmospheric or solar physics investigations, the spectral irradiance over a wavelength range encompassing most of the total irradiance has not, unfortunately, been a research goal during the first two decades of space research. The principal experiments contributing to the last such compilation were made from a combination of aircraft and a ground-based observatory observations, well below significant atmospheric absorbing and scattering media, and suffered non-trivially in the areas of calibration and data interpretation (Arveson, Griffin & Pearson, 1969; Labs & Neckel, 1968; Willson, 1985). The variations observed in total irradiance during the past decade, however, have stimulated renewed interest in the spectral variability of the visible and infra-red regions which contain 90% of the total flux.

Methodology

Development of space-based solar irradiance monitoring experiments

A new generation of total irradiance measurement instrumentation was developed during the 1960s and 1970s. These new electrically self-calibrating cavity (ESCC) solar pyrheliometers were capable of addressing both the principal problem areas of earlier irradiance experiments. They had higher precision and accuracy than their predecessors and could be operated automatically in space flight environments.

The ESSC pyrheliometer with many of the essential features in use today was developed by the Smithsonian Astrophysical Observatory (SAO) in the first decade of the twentieth century (Abbot & Fowle, 1908). The instrumentation advances that have facilitated space-based solar monitoring observations with useful accuracy and precision today are the result of implementing SAO instrumentation concepts with modern technology, plus the introduction of two operational features: the so-called 'active cavity' operational mode and the differential measurement approach. The 'active cavity' operational mode is one in which the same

thermodynamic state is sustained for the sensor in both the solar viewing (shutter open) and reference (shutter closed) phases of a measurement. The differential measurement approach utilizes only the differences between solar viewing and reference values. The 'active cavity' operation is achieved by an electronic servosystem that provides electrical heating for the cavity detector at all times, adjusting the amount to sustain constant relative instrument temperatures in the two phases of the measurement. The measurement is thereby reduced to relating the cavity heating power in the two measurement phases and several other key sensor parameters to the International System of Units (SI). Operation does not depend significantly on the International Practical Temperature Scale and the observational uncertainties are reduced to differences between small terms in the two phases of measurement. The combination of these techniques greatly decreases the overall measurement uncertainty (Willson, 1971, 1973, 1979; Brusa & Frohlich, 1972).

There have been improvements in solar spectral instrumentation as well: holographic diffraction gratings, detectors and the development of 'flyable' calibration sources, such as deuterium lamps for the ultra-violet wavelength range. A promising approach to high precision long-term monitoring of the UV using a group of stellar references is being attempted for the first time by the SOLSTICE experiment on the Upper Atmosphere Research Satellite (Rottman, 1988).

Early space-based solar observations

The availability of space-based observation platforms did not produce immediate success in detecting intrinsic solar variability. A summary of early solar monitoring attempts shown as Table 1 includes two space-based total solar irradiance experiments that were unable to detect solar variability. The first was the Nimbus-6 Earth Radiation Budget (ERB) experiment launched in 1975 (Hickey et al., 1980). There were several reasons for its failure: its sensor was not an ESCC device, it had limited data resolution and suffered large, uncalibratable sensor degradation. The second was the Thermal Control Flux Monitor (TCFM) flown on the Mariner 6 and 7 spacecrafts to Mars in 1969 (Plamondon, 1970). The TCFM represented a substantial contribution in being the first spaceflight utilization of an ESCC sensor (although this capability was utilized only at the end of its mission), yet limited resolution in the digital data stream and sensor drift prevented the detection of true solar variability.

Table 2. *Results from the NASA total solar irradiance rocket flight experiments*

Investigator	Instrument* (type)	And calibration approach	1976 (w m^{-2})	1978	1980	1984	1985
Willson	ACR402A (1)	ESCC	1368.1	1367.1	1367.8	1367.4	1367.1
Kendall	PACRAD (1)	ESCC-P	1364	1373	1373		
Hickey	ESP (1)	ESCC-P	1369	1387	1377		
Hickey	ERB CH3 (2)	RS	1389	1387	1377		
Hickey	HF (1)	ESCC-P			1376		
Frohlich	PMOD (1)	ESCC				1366.7	1366.8

*Instruments: (See Table 1 for sensor type description): ACR = Active Cavity Radiometer, PACRAD = Passive Absolute Cavity Radiometer and Detector, ESP = Eclectic Solar Pyrheliometer, ERB CH3 = engineering backup model of Nimbus 6/ERB thermopile radiometer, HF = Hickey-Friedan radiometer, PMOD = Physical Meteorological Observatory of Davos radiometer.

Sounding rocket experiments

The first full implementation of ESCC solar pyrheliometry in a space flight environment occurred as part of a series of sounding rocket flights. In 1976 an active cavity radiometer (ACR) on the maiden flight of NASA's solar irradiance sounding rocket program made the first such solar observations (Willson & Hickey, 1977). Both the ACR and other cavity pyrheliometers have since been flown in the series with full or partial ESCC implementation. (See Table 2.) The rocket program's principal purpose was to provide independent calibrations of satellite solar irradiance sensors over the 1976 to 1986 period (Duncan *et al.*, 1977). The series was terminated when a new NASA program to accomplish the same objective was initiated using the Space Shuttle.

The Nimbus-7/ERB experiment

The first long-term space flight solar monitoring experiment utilizing a cavity sensor capable of electrical self-calibration was the Earth Radiation Budget (ERB) experiment on the Nimbus-7 spacecraft. The solar database from this experiment, launched in late 1978 and continuing into the present, is the longest currently available (Hickey *et al.*, 1980; Hoyle & Kyle, 1990).

The objective of the Hickey–Freidan (HF) solar sensor in the ERB experiment was to provide solar total irradiance insolation observations for the Earth radiation budget experiment with an accuracy better than ±0.5%. This and more has certainly been achieved, yet the full potential of ESCC sensors like the Nimbus-7/ERB cannot be realized on this type of 'nadir-staring', polar orbiting platform without an independent solar pointing subsystem. The lack of such a subsystem for the ERB produced one of its principal sources of uncertainty: limited observational opportunities (a few minutes per orbit while the sun swept through its field-of-view) and uncertainties resulting from off-axis irradiation of the cavity.

Another major source of measurement uncertainty arose from temperature-dependent calibration errors – the result of infrequent operation in the ESCC mode (once every two weeks). These factors combined to sustain a noise level in the Nimbus-7/ERB database that inhibited recognition of intrinsic solar variability features until detected by another solar monitoring experiment (see next section). Once discovered, however, clear evidence of solar variability on active region and solar cycle timescales were found in the ERB results. The corroborative function of the ERB data has been of great significance in verifying solar variability on solar cycle timescales. Results of the most recent revision of the ERB database, compiled by Hoyt (Hoyt & Kyle, 1990) and available from the National Space Science Data Center Archives (NSSDCA), NASA/Goddard Space Flight Center, Greenbelt, MD 20771 are included in Fig. 1.

The SMM/ACRIM I solar monitoring experiment

The active cavity radiometer irradiance monitor (ACRIM I) experiment launched on the Solar Maximum Mission (SMM) in early 1980 was specifically designed to provide the start of a long term, high precision solar total irradiance climate database (Willson *et al.*, 1981). The first in a series of satellite experiments in the solar monitoring program of the NASA Jet Propulsion Laboratory (JPL), the ACRIM I experiment produced a high precision database throughout the 9.75 years of the Solar Maximum Mission, including a period between late 1980 and early 1984 affected by solar pointing limitations. Its observations ceased in October, 1989 when the SMM satellite re-entered the Earth's atmosphere. The results of the ACRIM I experiment are included in Fig. 1. These results

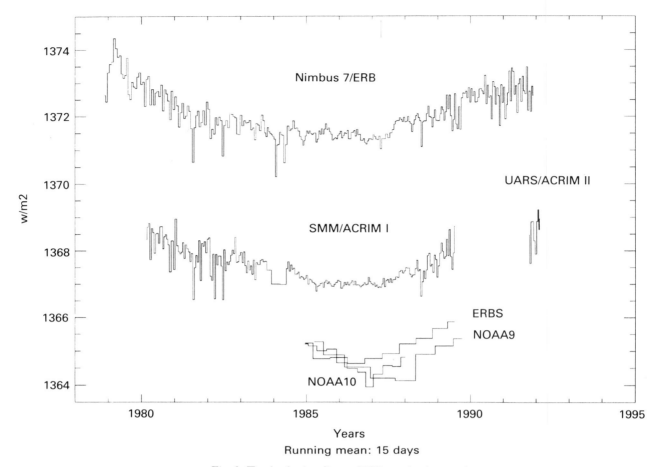

Fig. 1. Total solar irradiance (TSI) monitoring results.

are available from the National Space Science Data Center archives.

The high precision and accuracy of the ACRIM I results are attributable to its continuous 'active cavity' ESCC mode of operation, its degradation self-calibration capability and the SMM's full-time solar pointing. Its shutters opened or closed every 65 seconds, providing electrical self-calibration before and after each solar observation. It employed three independent ACR sensors with different duty cycles to provide internal calibration of cavity optical degradation (See Fig. 2). Precision references calibrated its electrical measurement system continuously. The solar pointing of the SMM provided acquisition of large numbers of daily observations (10^4 during normal operations, 10^2 during the 1981–84 'spin mode' of solar pointing), providing small statistical uncertainties of average daily values.

The ACRIM I results of early 1980 provided the first unequivocal evidence of intrinsic solar variability (Willson, 1980). Solar variations have since been detected on every observable timescale, from the experiment's 1.024 second

sampling interval, to the duration of the mission (Willson *et al.*, 1981, 1986; Willson, 1980, 1982, Willson & Hudson, 1981, 1988, 1991; Hudson *et al.*, 1982; Hudson & Willson, 1982).

Solar monitoring by ERBE experiments on ERBS, NOAA-9, and NOAA-10 satellites

The successor experiments to the Nimbus-7/ERB are the Earth Radiation Budget Experiment (ERBE) instruments on the Earth Radiation Budget Satellite (ERBS) and the NOAA-9 and NOAA-10 satellites (Barkstrom, Harrison & Lee, 1990, Hickey *et al.*, 1982). Most of the operational constraints of the Nimbus-7/ERB experiment affect the ERBE experiments as well. While they use ACR-type sensors in a fully implemented ESCC mode during solar observations, the quality of their results is fundamentally limited by minimal solar viewing opportunities, on the order of minutes per orbit during one day every second week. They acquire observations that are more than adequate for the earth radiation budget

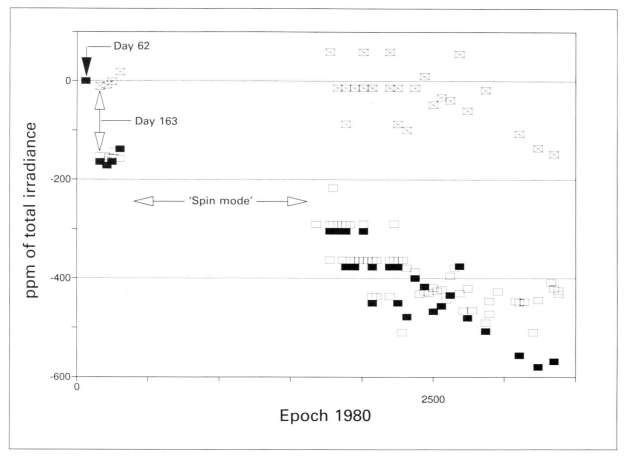

Fig. 2. ACRIM 1 Degradation calibrations. Ratios of sensors A, B and C.

modeling objectives but have insufficient precision for the climate solar monitoring database, as can be seen in Fig. 1. The ERBS, NOAA-9 and NOAA-10 results show larger scatter than those of the ERB and ACRIM I, a direct consequence of the paucity of observations and the constraints imposed by the 'nadir-staring' platforms on which they reside without independent solar pointing. Some significant differences can be seen between the ERBS, NOAA-9 and NOAA-10 results. Those of ERBS generally reflect the characteristics of the ACRIM I and ERB results. The NOAA-9 and NOAA-10 results demonstrate substantial differences relative to both the ERBS results and between themselves.

The ACRIM II experiment on the upper atmosphere research satellite

The ACRIM II experiment was launched on the Upper Atmosphere Research Satellite (UARS) in September, 1991. Observations by the ACRIM II experiment began in early October and are continuing at present. Approximately 100 days of overlapping observations were made with the Nimbus-7/ERB during late 1991 and early 1992 prior to a cessation of ERB operation caused by instrumental electronic problems. These have facilitated relating the results of ACRIM I, ERB and ACRIM II with high precision as described later in this chapter and will make a significant contribution toward constructing the long-term climate TSI database.

Results of solar monitoring during solar cycles 21 and 22

Variability on solar cycle timescales (years to decades)

The results of solar monitoring to date have proved significant for both solar physics and climate research. On the longest timescale, about one solar (sunspot) cycle, the database is just of the length of only the shortest climate cycle on record.

The ACRIM I and ERB results shown in detail in Fig. 1

are 15 day running mean values constructed from daily mean observations, normalized to the mean earth–sun distance. It can be seen that the gross features of the two sets of results, the decline from solar cycle 21 maximum to solar minimum and the increase to solar maximum of cycle 22, are basically the same. There are some detailed differences, most of which are assumed to be remaining solar pointing or thermally induced errors in the ERB results. These are most noticeable during the solar minimum period (1985–87).

The apparent abrupt change in the level of fluctuation of ACRIM I results following the gap in early 1984 is an artefact of the transition from spin mode to precision pointed mode following repair of the SMM satellite's pointing system by the Space Shuttle, and the decreasing levels of solar activity during the period. The gap resulted from a paucity of data samples, caused by satellite data acquisition restrictions during the four months prior to the Shuttle repair mission. Had the SMM pointing system not failed, and the gap not occurred, a more gradual transition in variability of the database from the peak solar activity levels of 1980–81 to the 1986 activity minimum would likely have been recorded. In support of this, a relatively gradual transition can be seen in the uninterrupted ERB results during 1984 (See Fig. 1). An interesting side note to this is that the last major activity occurred just prior to the solar minimum period and just during the gap in ACRIM I results.

The average irradiance declined systematically from launch through mid-1986 at an average rate of 0.015% per year. The irradiance minimum in 1986 occurs near the near cycle magnetic minimum in September. The rapid increase, corresponding to the build-up of solar activity in cycle 22, becomes clearly visible in 1988, continuing to the end of the SMM/ACRIM I results in mid-1989, and on through the peak of solar cycle 22, as can be seen in the continuing results from the ERB and UARS/ACRIM II experiments.

The general character of the solar cycle variation is clearly shown in the results of both the ACRIM and ERB experiments, as can be seen in Fig. 1. The only major divergence occurs after 1988 where the rate of irradiance increase in ACRIM I results exceeds that of ERB. The explanation for this may be uncorrected degradation of ERB after 1988 as the level of high energy solar particles and flux increased. This was the same period in which significant degradation was observed to occur in ACRIM I comparison sensor B.

The direct correlation of luminosity and solar activity is a major discovery from the solar cycle results. It agrees in sense with that predicted from the coincidence of the 'Little Ice Age' climate anomaly and the 'Maunder Minimum' of solar activity during the sixteenth and seventeenth centuries (Eddy, 1977). The average temperature decreased by about 1.5 °C in

response to what models indicate was a total irradiance decrease of about 0.5–1%. The 0.1% peak-to-peak amplitude of the total irradiance during solar cycle 21 would correspond to a cooling of 0.15–0.30 °C on that basis, probably an undetectable climate change during a single solar cycle.

Another major discovery from these results is the apparent asymmetry of the solar cycle total irradiance variation relative to solar minimum, with a long gradual decrease from the maximum levels of solar cycle 21 to the minimum in 1986, followed by the rapid increase to the solar maximum of cycle 22. This is consistent with the shape of other, more traditional solar activity indices such as the Zurich sunspot number and the 10.7 cm radio flux.

Level of significance of the long-term database

The long-term precision of the ACRIM I, ERB and ACRIM II databases is critically important to understanding the significance of their solar cycle results. The principal source of systematic error for ESCC sensors during flight is degradation of their solar absorbing surfaces caused by exposure to solar flux. Of these three experiments, only the ACRIMs are capable of self-calibrating cavity degradation.

Degradation of ACRIM I's continuously monitoring sensor (A) over the mission was found to be a bit less than 600 parts per million (ppm) of the total irradiance. (See Fig. 2.) Its effect on the results was removed by the internal degradation calibration capability with a residual uncertainty smaller than 50 ppm. The period of missing data points in Fig. 2 corresponds to the SMM spin mode when the average uncertainty of observations was larger than the total degradation during the period. Eventual degradation of sensor B is seen as well after about day 2500 (epoch 1980), as its solar exposure time accumulated and the level of high energy, degradation-inducing solar fluxes produced by the rising activity phase of cycle 22 increased. The linearity of the A/C ratio and the complementarity of the A/B and B/C ratios during the last 1000+ mission days combine to indicate that: 1) there was no significant sensor C degradation, 2) the B/C ratio continued to be related predictably to the prior observations, and 3) the assumption that the degradation of all sensors was proportional to exposure time and the level of solar activity was confirmed.

Degradation is proportional to solar exposure, so ERB's short solar observing time each orbit (~5 minutes/orbit compared to 50 for ACRIM I) should experience degradation at a slower rate than ACRIM I. The relative rates of degradation cannot be computed precisely based on exposure time, however, since the cavity designs are sufficiently different that their degradation sensitivity to exposure cannot be the same. The 'inverted cone' cavity design of the ERB places more of its absorbing surfaces closer to the instrument's aperture than for the ACRIM I design, which would increase its rate of degradation by solar exposure.

No corrections have been applied for degradation of the ERB sensor to the results shown in Fig. 1, so the generally good agreement between its results and those of ACRIM I is probably an indication that significant degradation did not occur during the majority of its mission. The increasing divergence of ACRIM I and ERB results (and of ERBS and ERB as well) following solar minimum may indicate the accrual of significant degradation by the ERB sensor during the rising activity portion of solar cycle 22. If this is the case, the relationship between ACRIM's I and II and the quality of the long-term climate TSI database will be adversely affected.

Variability on solar active region timescales (days–months)

The sunspot 'deficit' effect

An inverse relationship between sunspot area and solar total irradiance was discovered using ACRIM I results early in the SMM (Willson *et al.*, 1981; Willson, 1980, 1982; Willson & Hudson, 1981; Hudson *et al.*, 1982; Hudson & Willson, 1982). The larger such features can be seen in the Nimbus-7/ERB results as well (Hickey *et al.*, 1982). As active regions containing sunspot area rotate onto, and/or form and grow on the Earth side of the Sun, a corresponding decrease in total irradiance is detected. These decreases last the duration of the transit of the sunspots and have been observed with amplitudes of up to −0.25% of the total irradiance. These decreases, so-called 'sunspot deficits', can be seen clearly in Fig. 3, a plot of the average results from each orbit's observations of ACRIM I in early 1980. The irradiance deficit shown there, the first recognized as clearly caused by sunspot area, is well defined relative to the standard errors of the individual orbital means (the vertical extent of each tic mark). This pattern was repeated many times, with varying detail, throughout 1980, as shown in Fig. 4.

Facular 'excess' effect

A direct relationship between active region faculae and total irradiance was found in the ACRIM I results (Willson, 1982; Oster, Schatten & Sofia, 1982; Sofia, Oster & Schatten, 1982; Schatten *et al.*, 1985; Chapman, 1983; Chapman, Herzog & Lawrence, 1986). Irradiance peaks were found to

occur during the transit of active regions known to contain large facular areas. On other occasions the presence of large active region faculae were observed to decrease the net irradiance deficit produced by sunspots, relative to deficits produced by comparable sunspot area when less faculae were present. The facular effects can be most clearly seen in Figs. 3 and 4 as 'wings' on either side of the prominent sunspot 'deficits'. Active region faculae have generally larger areas than sunspots and are more widely distributed around the periphery of active regions. This results in their being the first radiative component of an active region to be seen as it rotates onto our side of the sun, and the last to be seen as it rotates off the opposite limb. The other effect, reduction in the sunspot 'deficit', is always present but more subtle. It can be seen in mid-July, 1980 (Fig. 4) where the relatively shallow 'deficit' corresponds to the 'deficit' effect of large sunspot area being partially offset by very large facular area.

Energy balance in active regions

The evolution and energy balance in active regions has been investigated using solar active region area measurements and the ACRIM I results. No two active regions behave in the same way, but a general pattern was observed during sunspot maximum in solar cycle 21. Sunspot area, with its high contrast relative to the undisturbed photosphere (−0.5), peaked quickly and subsided within several solar rotations (about 81 days). Faculae have less contrast relative to the 'quiet photosphere' ($\sim +0.03$) and have slower development, but have larger areas and longer persistence than sunspots (up to six solar rotations). Several studies indicate that initial sunspot 'deficit' appears to be substantially made up by excess emission within the 'lifetime' of an individual active region, and the balance is dissipated into the solar atmosphere in the form of the 'active network' (Willson, 1982; Chapman 1983; Chapman *et al.*, 1986).

Short-term variability – solar global oscillations (minutes to days)

Solar global oscillations of low degree have been detected in the ACRIM I total irradiance data, including pressure modes (timescales of minutes) and gravity modes (timescales of hours to days) (Woodard & Hudson, 1983; Frohlich & Delache, 1984; Woodard & Noyes, 1985; Woodard, 1984). Pressure mode oscillations of low degree ($L = 0, 1, 2$) and orders 15–25 have been derived from ACRIM I shutter cycle observations (averages over 32 seconds spaced every 131.072 seconds) as shown in Fig. 5. Peak amplitudes of these '5 minute' oscillations are 3 ppm of the total irradiance signal.

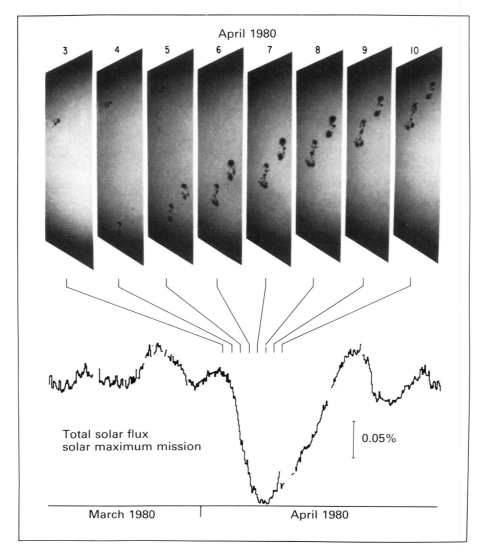

Fig. 3. 'Sunspot deficit' effect in ACRIM I results.

Results of 'P-mode' analysis of ACRIM I data have provided new physical insights on the properties of the convection zone and the outer solar core. The most significant of these are: 1) support for the relativistic interpretation of Mercury perihelion observations; 2) an upper limit to the radial variation of solar rotation of 2.2 times that of the photospheric rate; 3) coherence times for oscillation modes of 1–2 days; 4) a frequency shift of the modes of the results for the 1980 (solar active) and 1984–86 (solar quiet) periods that may be related to the solar cycle luminosity trend (Woodard, 1984).

There are preliminary indications that detectable gravity mode (G-mode) oscillation signatures exist in the ACRIM I results (Frohlich & Delache, 1984). Preliminary analysis by one group claims to have isolated G-mode signals in the 10–80 μHz frequency range (one day to several hours period-

icity). If true, the G-mode signal structure can provide information on the physics of deep solar layers, extending to the solar core. A G-mode periodicity of 29.85 minutes derived from ACRIM I data supports the weakly interactive massive particle (WIMP) model of the solar core. If this or another 'cool' solar core model is supported by further analysis, it could explain the observational 'neutrino deficit' of 'hot' solar core models.

Empirical models of the solar cycle irradiance variation

Once total irradiance variability on solar active region and sunspot cycle timescales was established, empirical irradiance

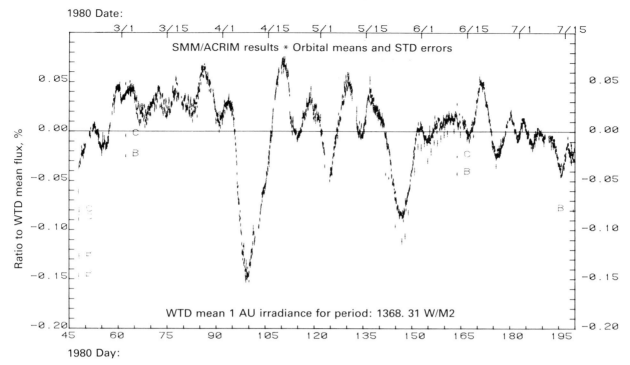

Fig. 4. ACRIM I results during 1980.

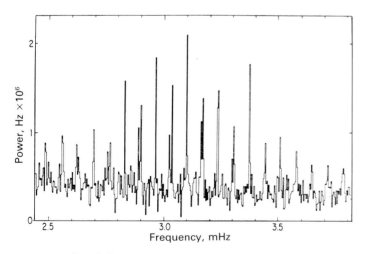

Fig. 5. P-modes derived from ACRIM I results.

models were developed with the desire to explore the physical causes of the variability and to extrapolate the variability to past solar cycles. Most models were based on linear regression between the ACRIM I and/or ERB results and several solar activity indices, such as the Zurich sunspot number, the 10.7 cm radio flux and the time series of solar emission lines observed in both satellite and ground-based experiments.

Active region timescales

Variability on solar active region timescales was the focus of the first simple models. The total irradiance deficit effect of sunspots, the so-called photometric sunspot index (PSI), was calculated from the area and contrast of sunspots, taking into account the limb darkening (Hudson *et al.*, 1982; Hudson & Willson, 1982). Hoyt and Eddy developed a model using their sunspot blocking function and the Zurich sunspot index to predict the total irradiance variability as far back as 1874 (Hoyt & Eddy, 1982). However, irradiance models based only on the sunspots could explain just about half of the total irradiance variation observed by ACRIM I.

The next obvious step was to incorporate faculae into the models. Active region faculae were recognized as significant contributors of excess flux, relative to the undisturbed photosphere, and as the probable means of offsetting the energy deficit of sunspots in active regions, from early studies of the total irradiance measured by ACRIM I (Willson, 1982; Oster *et al.*, 1982; Sofia *et al.*, 1982; Schatten *et al.*, 1985; Chapman, 1983). Similar conclusions were derived from UV observations made by the Solar Mesosphere Explorer (SME) mission (Lean *et al.*, 1982; Pap *et al.*, 1990). More recently, precision ground-based photometry of the solar disk has convincingly demonstrated these effects for faculae (Chapman, 1991).

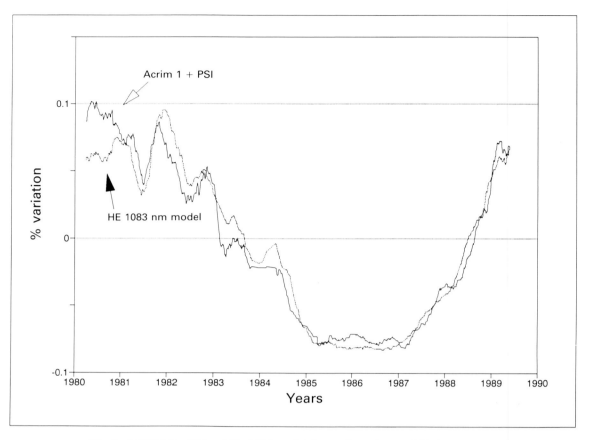

Fig. 6. ACRIM I+ PSI and He 1083 model fluxes. % variation of 81 day means.

Solar cycle timescales

As the length of the ACRIM I and ERB database extended from the maximum of solar cycle 21 to the minimum marking the end of cycle 21 and the beginning of cycle 22, the interest of modelers shifted to the solar-cycle timescale. The results of models by several investigators indicated that the distributed, faculae-like, 'active network' provides a significant contribution to the total irradiance variation on solar cycle timescales (~11 years) (Willson & Hudson, 1988, 1991; Foukal & Lean, 1988, 1990). The active network is thought to be populated by residual faculae from old, decaying active regions and/or faculae-like features deriving from general solar magnetic activity. Many of the major features of the irradiance data during the latter part of solar cycle 21 and at the beginning of cycle 22 were reproduced successfully by linear regression models using the full disk equivalent width of the He-line at 1083 nm and 10.7 cm radio flux.

Shortcomings of linear regression models

The success of irradiance models developed by linear regression analysis did not extend to the maximum of solar

cycle 21 preceding 1981, where they produced estimated fluxes significantly lower than the results of ACRIM I and ERB observations (see Fig. 6). The reason for this is not presently understood. It has recently been shown, however, that a regression model based on one particular time series of the full disk CaK line (Livingston, Wallace & White, 1989) provides better agreement prior to 1981, relative to the models based on the He-line or 10.7 cm radio flux. The CaK time series is, unfortunately, significantly undersampled (several data points per month) compared to the ACRIM I data and may therefore provide only a general proxy of solar cycle irradiance variations.

Multi-variate spectral analysis

Clearly, linear regression analysis can provide useful but only broad insight into the physics of total irradiance variations (Frohlich & Pap, 1989). Another approach referred to as multivariate spectral analysis has been shown to be an effective tool in studying the combined effect of various solar events on the solar irradiance (Frohlich & Pap, 1989; Pap & Frohlich, 1989). Results of multivariate spectral analysis

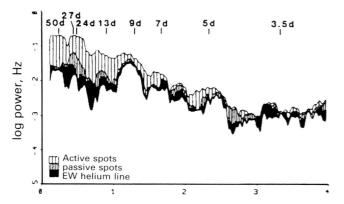

Fig. 7. Multi-variate analysis of 1984–85 ACRIM I results.

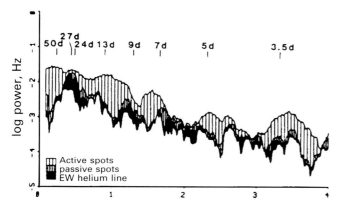

Fig. 8. Multi-variate analysis of 1980 ACRIM I results.

(Figs. 7 and 8) show that, during the maximum of solar cycle 21 in 1980, most of the power spectral density of ACRIM I's time series was explained by sunspots. During solar minimum (1984–85) more than 80% of the power spectral density at the average solar rotation period (~27-day) was caused by faculae and the active network. Multivariate analysis also shows power spectral peaks that are not explained by sunspots, faculae or the bright magnetic network near periods of 27 and 9 days, indicating that yet to be discovered solar events are modifying total solar irradiance.

Total solar irradiance monitoring plans – implications for the climate database

The detection of solar luminosity variability during solar cycles 21 and 22 thus far underscores the need to extend the irradiance database indefinitely with maximum precision. There may be other luminosity variabilities with longer periodicities and/or proportionately larger amplitudes that could have significant climatic implications. Subtle trends in the total irradiance of as little as ±500 ppm per century could eventually produce the extreme range of climates known to

have existed in the past, from warm periods without permanent ice, to the great ice ages (Eddy, 1977). Accumulation of a database capable of detecting such trends will necessarily require the results of many individual solar monitoring experiments. If these experiments last an average of a decade each, about the maximum that can be expected from today's technology, they will have to be related with a precision smaller than 50 ppm.

A careful measurement strategy will be required to sustain adequate precision for the database since the uncertainty of current satellite instrumentation on an absolute basis is inadequate for this purpose (no better than ±0.1% of the total solar irradiance). An approach must be used that relates successive solar monitoring experiments at a precision level defined by the operation of the instrumentation. The method of choice is the overlapping and comparison of successive solar monitoring experiments, the so-called 'overlap strategy'. Relative precision of less than 5 ppm is achievable for the data from overlapped solar monitors with the current state-of-the-art, given sufficient samples. The principal remaining uncertainty for the 'overlap strategy' is the degradation of solar monitor sensors over decade-long missions. Calibration of such degradation should be possible for future solar monitoring experiments at the 10 ppm level.

The 'overlap strategy' is the only currently available approach capable of providing precision approaching 5 ppm. The next best strategy is the intercomparison of successive solar monitors using independent ('third party') flight experiments. There are several possibilities. One is the ACRIM and/or SOLCON experiments to be flown annually as part of the Atmospheric Laboratory for Applications and Science (ATLAS) missions beginning in 1992. Another is the solar monitors planned for deployment on the shuttle-deployed European recoverable platform (EURECA). Results achievable using the 'third party' strategy will depend on the specific experiments involved and the number of data points, but should be able to provide precision levels of 50 ppm.

Constructing the long-term climate TSI database

Relating SMM/ACRIM I and UARS/ACRIM II results

The 'overlap strategy' was to have been used to relate the SMM/ACRIM I and UARS/ACRIM II experiments but the UARS launch delay to 1991 and the termination of the SMM in late 1989 made this impossible. Connection of the ACRIM I and ACRIM II databases with useful precision has been accomplished using a 'third party' comparison with the Nim-

Table 3. *Slopes of SMM/ACRIM 1 and Nimbus-7/ERB results during solar cycles 21 and 22*

Database	Time frame (y)	Slope (%/y)	Std. dev. of Slope (±%/y)	Number of observations
Nimbus 7/ERB	1979–80	−0.023	0.004	584
SMM/ACRIM 1	1980	−0.057	0.017	296
Nimbus 7/ERB	1980	−0.043	0.015	276
SMM/ACRIM 1	1981–85	−0.016	0.001	1573
Nimbus 7/ERB	1981–85	−0.013	0.001	1550
SMM/ACRIM 1	1988–89	+0.043	0.007	555

The slope standard deviations are for 1 sigma. Results obtained from the National Space Science Data Center. Results for ERB not available for 1988–89 at time of writing.

Table 4. *Ratios of SMM/ACRIM I, UARS/ACRIM II and Nimbus-7/ERB daily mean observations*

Years	Average ratio (ACRIM/ERB)	Standard error (1 sigma)	Number of daily means
ACRIM I/ERB			
1980–89 (All observations)	0.996871	0.000004	3098
1980–84 (SMM 'spin mode')	0.996982	0.000010	1518
1985–87 (Solar minimum)	0.996765	0.000009	1027
1989 (last comparison year)	0.996958	0.000005	192
ACRIM II/ERB			
Oct – Nov., 1992	0.995203	0.000008	60
ACRIM I/ACRIM II			
(based on 1989)	1.001763		

bus-7/ERB experiment. The ACRIM I and the ERB results were compared for the duration of the ACRIM I experiment. The ACRIM II and ERB were compared for their first two months of overlapping observations in January, 1992. The results of these comparisons are shown in Tables 3 and 4.

Additional results will soon be available through mid-January, 1992 from both ACRIM II and ERB experiments that should further improve ACRIM I/ACRIM II relative precision. A remaining issue is the apparent change in slope between the ERB results and those of ACRIM I and ERBS after 1988. Establishment of the most correct relationship between the two sets of ACRIM results will require further analysis.

Another possibility for a 'third-party' comparison involves two total solar irradiance experiments developed for the Space Shuttle: an ACRIM instrument (the prototype for the UARS/ACRIM II) and the European Space Agency (ESA) SOLCON. Both were flown on the Spacelab 1 Mission in 1983 in what was to have been the first of a program of annual flights to provide just such backup 'third party' comparison experiments for satellite solar monitoring. Unfortunately, both ACRS and SOLCON failed to achieve many of their measurement goals in the Spacelab 1 Mission, and subsequent flights during the SMM were canceled or postponed.

Some observations in comparison with ACRIM I were obtained, and these data will be re-evaluated in light of their potential importance to the solar monitoring program, to discover whether usefully precise comparisons were obtained. The same two solar experiments will begin making flights as part of the ATLAS program in 1992 and should provide a reliable backup or 'third party' comparison capability for solar monitoring during the mid-to-late 1990s.

The potential TSI deficit of the 1990s

Following the launch of UARS/ACRIM II, there is a deficit in solar monitoring opportunities between 1994 and 2002. While the resources available on UARS will provide the capability for sustaining an orbital lifetime substantially in excess of its $2\frac{1}{2}$ year 'minimum mission', the probability of its lasting until 2002 is small. Three ACRIM experiments have been included in the NASA Earth Observation System program for flights of opportunities at five year intervals starting in about 2002. In the interim, ESA will contribute to the total solar irradiance database with an experiment on the Solar Heliospheric Observer (SOHO) Mission in the latter 1990s. SOHO may begin, however, after observations by the ACRIM II cease and the duration of the mission is unknown.

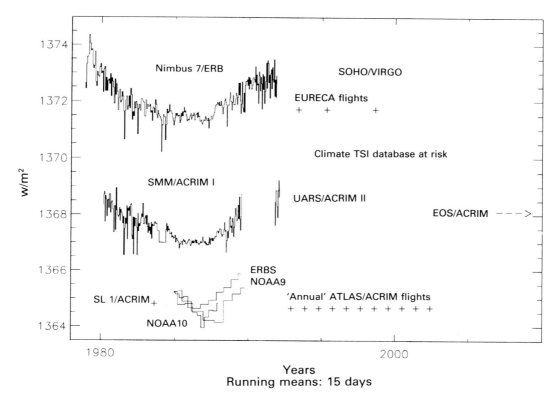

Fig. 9. Total solar irradiance (TSI) monitoring program.

The long-term solar monitoring scenario showing past, present and planned future experiments is shown as Fig. 9. Deployment of additional solar monitoring instrumentation, possibly on new, small satellites, at the midpoint and near the end of the 1990s, will be required to guarantee continuity of the climate TSI database until the advent of the Earth Observation System in the early twenty-first century.

Eventually, research geostationary platforms, proposed as an adjunct to the EOS, will provide the optimum near-earth observation opportunity for solar irradiance monitoring. The high solar observing duty cycle provided by geostationary platforms (99% annually), high data rates and possible on-orbit instrument retrieval and serviceability will provide the strategic elements for a long-term solar monitoring program of maximum precision and accuracy. A continuing backup program of Space Shuttle-based 'third-party' experiments should be retained, however, to guard against worst case scenarios of prematurely failed solar monitors and satellites.

The new cryogenic radiometric technology should be considered for deployment on the shuttle platform (Quinn & Martin, 1982; Foukal, Hoyt & Miller, 1985). Cryogenic radiometers, operating near liquid He temperatures, can define the radiation scale with accuracy approaching 100 ppm of the total solar irradiance. They require expendable cryogens at present, limiting their use to recoverable or serviceable plat-

forms. And while they are not competitive with the precision of overlapping flight instrument or 'third-party' shuttle-based comparisons, they could provide a useful backup position for the climate TSI database in a worst case scenario.

Data availability

The results of the Nimbus-7/ERB, SMM/ACRIM I, ERBS, NOAA9 & 10 and UARS/ACRIM II experiments are available from the National Space Science Data Center, NASA Goddard Space Flight Center, Greenbelt, MD 20771, USA. 20771, USA.

References

Abbot, C. G. & Fowle, F. E. (1908). *Ann. Astrophys. Observ. Smithsonian Inst.*, **II**.

Arveson, J. C., Griffin, R. N. & Pearson, B. D. (1969). *J. Appl. Optics*, 8, 2215.

Barkstrom, B. R., Harrison, E. F. & Lee, R. B. (1990). *Trans. Am. Geophys. Union*, 71(9), 279.

Brusa, R. W. & Frohlich, C. (1972). Entwicklung eines neuen absolutradiometers, Technical Note 1., World Radiation Center, Davos, Switzerland.

Chapman, G. A. (1983). Ground-based measurements of solar irradiance variations. In *Solar Irradiance Variations on Active*

Region Timescales, Pasadena, CA, June, 1983, NASA Conference Publication 2310, pp. 73–89.

Chapman, G. A., Herzog, A. D. & Lawrence, J. K. (1986). *Nature*, 76, 211–19.

Chapman, G. (1991). Photometry of sunspots at San Fernando Observatory. Proc. Solers 22 1991 Workshop, Ed. J. Pap, in press.

Crommelynck, D. A. (1981). Fundamentals of absolute pyrheliometry and objective characterization. Notes Techniques 46, Royal Meteorological Institute of Belgium.

Duncan, C. H., Harrison, R. G., Hickey, J. R., Kendall Sr., J. M., Thekaekara, M. P., Willson, R. C. (1977). *Appl. Opt.*, 16, 2690.

Eddy, J. A. (1977). In *Solar Output and its Variation*, O. R. White, ed., pp. 51–71, Univ. of Colo. Press, Boulder, CO.

Foukal, P. A. & Lean, J. L. (1988). *Astrophys. J.*, 328, 347.

Foukal, P. A. & Lean, J. (1990). *Science*, 246, 556–8.

Foukal, P., Hoyt, C., Miller, P. (1985). In *Advances in Absolute Radiometry*, P. V. Foukal, ed., Atmospheric and Environmental Research, Inc., Cambridge, MA, p. 52.

Frohlich, C. (1977). *Solar Output and Its Variation*, O. R. White, ed., University of Colorado Press, Boulder, Colorado.

Frohlich, C. & Delache, P. (1984). Solar gravity modes from ACRIM/SMM irradiance data. In *Solar Seismology from Space*, R. K. Ulrich, J. Harvey, E. J. Rhodes and J. Toomre, eds., JPL Publ., Pasadena, pp. 183–94.

Frohlich, C. & Pap, J. (1989). *A&A*, 220, 272.

Hickey, J. R., Alton, B. M., Griffin, F. J., Jacobowitz, H., Pellegrino, P., Smith, E. A., Vonder Haar, T. H. & Maschoff, R. H. (1982). *Solar Energy*, 29, 125.

Hickey, J. R., Griffin, F. J., Jacobowitz, H., Stowe, L., Pellegrino, P., Maschoff, R. H. (1980) *Eos* (*Trans. American Geophysical Union*), 61, 355.

Hickey, J. R., Stowe, L. L., Jacobowitz, H., Pellegrino, P., Maschoff, R. H., House, F. & Vonder Haar, T. H. (1980). Initial determinations from Nimbus-7 cavity radiometer measurements, *Science*, 208, 281.

Hoyt, D. V. (1979). The Smithsonian Astrophysical Observatory solar constant program. *Rev. Geophys. Space Phys.* 17, 427.

Hoyt, D. V. & Eddy, J. A. (1982). An atlas of variations in the solar constant caused by sunspot blocking and facular emissions from 1874 to 1981. NCAR Tech. Note, National Center for Atmospheric Research/TN 194+ STR.

Hoyt, D. & Kyle, L. (1990). An alternative derivation of the Nimbus-7 total solar irradiance variations. *Proc. Climate Impact of Solar Variability*, NASA Conf. Rpt. 3086.

Hudson, H. S., Silva, S., Woodard, M. & Willson, R. C. (1982). *Solar Physics*, 76, 211.

Hudson, H. S. & Willson, R. C. (1982). Sunspots and solar variability. In *The Physics of Sunspots, Proc. Conference on Sunspots*, L. Cram and J. Thomas, eds., Sacramento Peak Observatory, Sunspot, AZ.

Labs, D. & Neckel, H. (1968). *Zeitschrift für Astrophysik*, 69, 1.

Lean, J., White, O. R., Livingston, W. C., Heath, D. F., Donnely, R. F., Skumanich, A. (1982). *J. Geophys. Res.* 87, 10307.

Livingston, W. C., Wallace, L. & White, O. R. (1989). *Science*, 240, 1765–7.

Newkirk, G. Jr. (1983). Variations in solar luminosity, *Ann. Rev. Astron. Astrophys.*, 21, 382.

Oster, L. F., Schatten, K. H. & Sofia, S. (1982). *Astrophys. J.*, 256, 768.

Pap, J., Frohlich, C. (1988). *Adv. Space Res.*, 8(7), p. (7) 31.

Pap, J., Hudson, H. S., Rottman, G. J., Willson, R. C., Donnely, R. F. & London, J. (1990). In *Climate Impact of Solar Variability*, Schatten, K. H. and Arking, A., eds., NASA Conference Pub. 3086, 189.

Plamondon, J. A. (1969). TCFM Solar Observations on Mariner 6, JPL Space Programs Summary, 3, p. 162, Jet Propulsion Laboratory, Pasadena, CA, USA.

Quinn, T. & Martin, J. (1982). In *Temperature, Its Measurement and Control in Science and Industry*, American Institute of Physics, New York, NY, vol. 5, p. 169.

Rottman, G. J. (1988). *Adv. Space Res.*, 8(7), 53.

Schatten, K., Miller, N., Sofia, S., Endal, A. & Chapman, G. A. (1985). *Ap. J.*, 294, 689–96.

Sofia, S., Oster, L. & Schatten, K. (1982). Solar irradiance modulation by active regions during 1980. *Solar Physics*, 80, 87.

Willson, R. C. (1971). The active cavity radiometric scale, the international pyrheliometric scale and the solar constant, *J. Geophys. Res.*, 76, 4325.

Willson, R. C. (1973). Active cavity radiometer. *J. Appl. Optics*, 12, 810.

Willson, R. C. (1979). Active cavity radiometer type IV. *J. Applied Optics*, 18, 179.

Willson, R. C. (1980). Solar irradiance observations from the SMM/ACRIM experiment, American Geophysical Union, Toronto, Canada, May.

Willson, R. C. (1982). *J. Geophys. Res.*, 86, p. 4319.

Willson, R. C. (1985). Solar total irradiance and its spectral distribution. In *The Encyclopedia of Physics*, 3rd Edn. R. M. Besancon, ed., Van Nostrand Reinhold, pp. 1135–43.

Willson, R. C. & Hudson, H. S. (1981). *Astph. J. Lett.*, 24, 185.

Willson, R. C. & Hudson, H. S. (1988). *Nature*, 332, (6167), 810.

Willson, R. C. & Hudson, H. S. (1991). *Nature*, 351, 42–4.

Willson, R. C. (1977). Hickey, J. R. (1977). 1976 rocket measurements of the solar constant and their implications for variation in the solar output in cycle 20. In *The Solar Output and Its Variation*, O. R. White, ed., Colorado Associated University Press, Boulder, CO, USA.

Willson, R. C., Gulkis, S., Janssen, M., Hudson, H. S., Chapman, G. A. (1981). Observations of solar irradiance variability, *Science*, 211, 700.

Willson, R. C., Hudson, H. S., Frohlich, C. & Brusa, R. W. (1986). *Science*, 234, 1114.

Woodard, M. (1984). Short-period oscillations in the total solar irradiance. Thesis, U. Calif. at San Diego, La Jolla, CA.

Woodard, M. & Hudson, H. (1983). *Nature*, 305, 589.

Woodard, M. & Noyes, R. (1985). *Nature*, 318, 449.

Radiation budget at the top of the atmosphere

EDWIN F. HARRISON, PATRICK MINNIS,
BRUCE R. BARKSTROM AND GARY G. GIBSON

Introduction

Climate is defined as the average weather over various time periods ranging from a few weeks to decades to geological timescales. Weather, described by temperature, humidity, winds, and precipitation, is ultimately determined by location, topography, and the exchange of radiant energy between the Sun, Earth, and space. For the Earth as a whole, this energy transfer must be constant when averaged over annual timescales. Otherwise, the mean temperature of the Earth–atmosphere system must change to establish the equilibrium dictated by thermodynamics. The uneven heating of the Earth–atmosphere system by the Sun coupled with Earth's rotation causes regional and zonal temperature gradients which drive atmospheric circulations and ocean currents. The incident solar energy heats the atmosphere and surface, evaporating water to form clouds and produce rain. Earth maintains the equilibrium with the absorbed solar radiation by emitting longwave (LW) radiation back to space. The Earth radiation budget accounts for the balance of incoming shortwave (SW) radiation from the Sun and LW radiation exiting from the Earth–atmosphere system at various temporal and spatial scales. This balance, the net radiation at the top of the atmosphere, is the absorbed SW radiation minus the outgoing LW radiation.

An approximation of the annual mean radiation balance of the Earth–atmosphere system is illustrated in Fig. 1. About 30% of the sun's radiant energy incident on the Earth is reflected back toward space. The fraction of reflected solar radiation is defined as the albedo. Most of the albedo is due to clouds which are highly variable in space and time. Reflection by the atmosphere varies primarily with dust concentration and the zenith angle of the Sun. Although surface reflectance comprises a relatively small portion of the total albedo, its variation from dark forests to bright deserts to blinding snow has a significant impact on the distribution of absorbed solar radiation. Approximately half of the incident solar energy is absorbed at the Earth's surface, 20% is absorbed by the atmosphere, and 30% is reflected back to space. Radiation absorbed by the surface heats the land and oceans and causes evaporation. The warm surface heats the atmosphere by conduction and radiation. Some of the radiation emitted by the surface passes through the atmosphere into space. The atmosphere redistributes the heat through convection, advection, and radiation. Some of the atmosphere's energy is radiated back to the surface; thus, the surface is made warmer due to the presence of the atmosphere. This process is the greenhouse effect. The atmosphere also radiates energy to space, resulting in a nearly balanced energy budget for the globe during a year.

To understand, simulate, and predict climate, one must first account for the processes by which the atmosphere, land, and oceans transfer energy to achieve the necessary global radiative equilibrium. Thus, the components of the radiation budget comprise a first-order set of parameters which must be accurately calculated by any given climate model. Though not sufficient by itself, a radiation budget which matches the observations is a necessary condition for verification of a climate model. Earth radiation budget measurements, therefore, play an essential role in the effort to monitor and predict climate.

Fig. 1 greatly simplifies the complexity of the radiation budget. Since the components in any given system tend toward thermal equilibrium through various energy transfer processes, the schematic in Fig. 1 only represents the globally averaged effect of all of these processes. The value of each component varies greatly from one place and time to another. Thus, as the accuracy of the models improves it becomes more important to measure the radiation budget at finer temporal and spatial resolutions and to measure it for different components in the Earth–atmosphere system. This concern for a more detailed and accurate description of the Earth radiation budget has been and continues to be a fundamental goal in the design and execution of the satellite radiation budget measurements.

Earth radiation budget measurements

The goal of Earth radiation budget (ERB) missions is to make measurements of the energy emission and reflection by the

Earth radiation budget processes

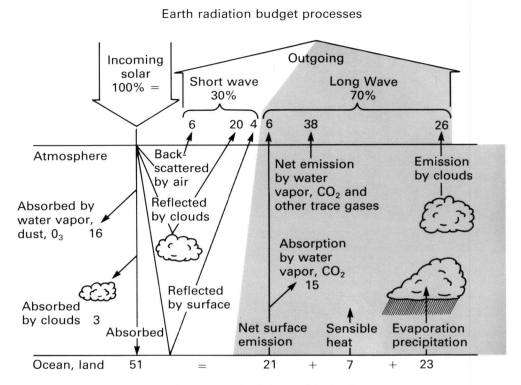

Fig. 1. The radiation balance of the Earth.

Earth that are not sensitive to the particular frequencies at which the energy is carried, except that it is desirable to separate solar and terrestrial radiation. In addition, it is desirable to maintain absolute calibration to facilitate monitoring and model validation. These considerations lead to the use of thermal detectors and the provision of redundant methods for absolute calibration, which are what make ERB data unique. The Earth Radiation Budget Experiment (ERBE), consisting of three satellites launched in the mid-1980s, is currently the most comprehensive and best resolved source of ERB measurements. Results from ERBE constitute the primary source of the ERB data presented later in this chapter. First, a brief discussion of some past satellite missions is presented to illustrate the evolution of ERB measurements. Reviews of radiation budget studies can be found in Stephens *et al.* (1981), Kandel (1983), Ohring and Gruber (1983), Vonder Haar (1983), Hartmann *et al.* (1986), and House *et al.* (1986).

Suomi (1957) proposed the first experimental satellite dedicated to the measurement of the ERB. The success of early ERB orbital missions was limited not only because of relatively unsophisticated radiometers and calibrations, but also by spacecraft spin stabilization requirements. During the following years, the evolution of ERB observational systems paralleled the overall advancement of space technology. The development of multi-channel scanning radiometers and new

spacecraft attitude control systems paved the way for a new generation of ERB missions. The Television and Infra-Red Observational Satellite (TIROS) series in the late 1960s, followed by the Improved TIROS Operational Satellite (ITOS), and the National Oceanic and Atmospheric Administration (NOAA) series during the 1970s marked a new era in weather satellite technology. These satellites, not intended for ERB use, measured visible and infra-red window radiances to form images of weather patterns. Albedos and longwave fluxes were inferred from the narrow spectral radiances (Gruber, 1978). Despite these spectral limitations and the lack of on-board calibrations, these early observations provided a wealth of information for diagnostic studies of the climate.

The Scanning Medium Resolution Infra-red Radiometer on the Sun-synchronous Nimbus 2 and 3 satellites (see Raschke & Bandeen, 1970; Raschke *et al.*, 1973) provided the first measurements of the ERB for the entire globe. Although data were taken for only a few months, these early observations provided new insights for ERB instrument design concepts as well as model development and methods for data analysis. Beginning in about 1975, a dedicated ERB experiment (Smith *et al.*, 1977) was included in the payloads of the Nimbus 6 and 7 satellites which also operated in sun-synchronous orbits with near-noon equatorial crossing times. The Nimbus instruments measured all three components of the ERB: direct solar irradiance, reflected SW radiation, and emitted LW radiation. The instruments employed both fixed wide field-of-view and biaxial scanning radiometers to view the Earth. The successful Nimbus-7 ERB experiment has amassed 9 years of WFOV data for long-term climate studies (see Kyle *et al.*, 1990), and 20 months of scanner data that have been used in regional climate analyses.

With the increasing concern over potential climate change and its effects on agricultural and urban areas, the need for more accurate measurements of regional-scale radiation budgets was recognized (e.g. JOC, 1975). The largest sources of uncertainty in the radiation budget results arose from errors due to calibration and stability, sampling, and data analysis methods. Better understanding of instrument operation and reliable calibration sources were needed to obtain better measurement accuracy. Studies utilizing the NOAA (e.g. Hartmann & Short, 1980) and geostationary satellites (e.g. Minnis & Harrison, 1984*b*) revealed widespread semi-regular diurnal variations in cloudiness which could cause substantial errors in regional radiation budgets derived with single sun-synchronous satellite measurements (Brooks & Minnis, 1984*a*; Minnis & Harrison, 1984*c*). Examination of the Nimbus-7 scanner data (Taylor & Stowe, 1984) exposed inadequacies in the models used to account for the angular dependence of the measured radiances. These and other shortcomings in previous ERB measurement systems led to the development of the multiple-satellite Earth Radiation Budget Experiment (ERBE; Barkstrom, 1984; Barkstrom & Smith, 1986).

The ERBE satellite system, consisting of a mid-inclined (57° inclination) Earth Radiation Budget Satellite (ERBS) and two sun-synchronous NOAA spacecraft, provides measurements nearly covering the complete diurnal cycle over the course of a month for most regions over the globe. The ERBE instrument package consists of both scanning and nonscanning radiometers. The scanning instruments provide high-resolution regional-scale measurements necessary for most scientific studies of current interest, while the wide field-of-view non-scanners continue the long-term, continent-scale monitoring of the radiation budget begun with Nimbus-6. An ERBE scanner (Kopia, 1986) has three spectral channels, 0.2–5.0 μm (SW), 5–50 μm (LW), and 0.2–50 μm (total), to provide consistency checks and redundancy. The scanner spatial resolution at nadir, the point on the Earth directly below the spacecraft, is about 40 km. The non-scanner (Luther *et al.*, 1986) comprises a wide field-of-view radiometer which views the Earth from limb to limb, and a medium field-of-view sensor which sees a field of view about 1000 km in diameter. Ground calibration sources consist of a reference blackbody and an integrating sphere in a vacuum

chamber. In flight, an internal blackbody, evacuated tungsten lamps, and observations of the Sun are used to check the stability and precision of the instruments. There is no method of measuring the Earth's radiation budget that is independent of the satellite measurements; thus, inter-comparisons between the various ERBE measurements are the primary source of validation information (Green *et al.*, 1990).

Data analysis methodologies were also improved for ERBE. Results from earlier satellite ERB studies were utilized to produce a more comprehensive set of LW and SW angular dependence models (Suttles *et al.*, 1988, 1989) than previously available. A method for separating and identifying clear-sky and cloud-contaminated measurements (Wielicki & Green, 1989) was constructed to improve radiance interpretation for selecting the correct angular model and to understand the effects of clouds on the ERB better. Geostationary satellite data were used to develop a more accurate technique for averaging the data over the diurnal cycle (Brooks & Minnis, 1984*b*). All of these improvements were included in the ERBE data processing system which performs three major tasks: 1) to convert telemetry data to calibrated radiation measurements at the instruments, 2) to relate the satellite measurements to radiative flux at the top of the Earth's atmosphere using angular dependence models (Smith *et al.*, 1986), and 3) to average the measurements over various space and time scales (Brooks *et al.*, 1986). Together, the improved instrument and sampling capabilities and the data processing system allow ERBE to meet the near-term goals of the climate community.

ERB data analysis

Regional

The ERBE output products include monthly averages of radiative parameters in 2.5° latitude × 2.5° longitude regions for the scanner instrument, and in 5° × 5° and 10° × 10° resolutions for non-scanners. ERBE scanner products have received special emphasis for scientific analysis because of their high spatial resolution and the availability of both total-scene and clear-sky radiative parameters.

Figures 2–4 show the geographical distributions of monthly average ERBE scanner total-scene and clear-sky albedo, LW flux, and net radiation for January 1986. The data are shown on a Hammer-Aitoff projection, which provides an elliptical, equal-area representation of the entire Earth and also minimizes distortion of continent shapes. The significant climatological features of the Earth can be seen in these maps. Clear-sky albedo distributions reflect the differences in the radiative properties of snow, vegetated land surfaces, deserts,

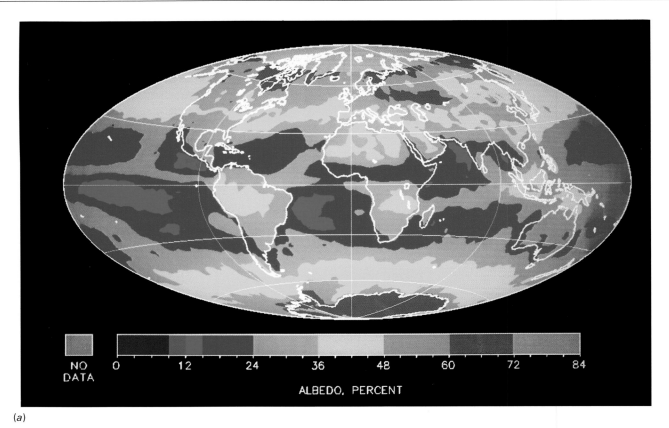

(a)

(b)

Fig. 2. ERBE regional monthly average (*a*) total-scene and (*b*) clear-sky albedo for January 1986.

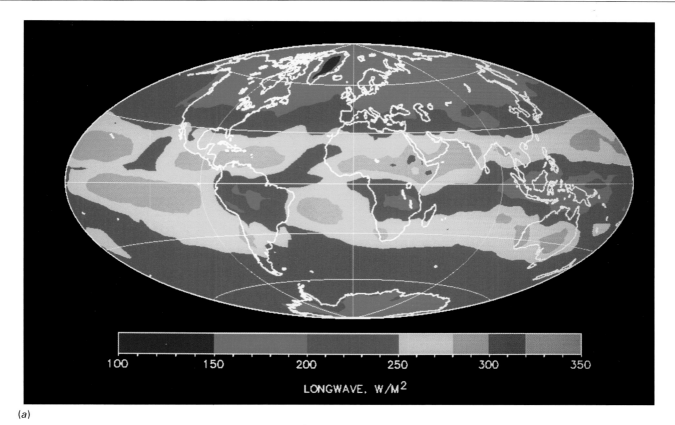

(a)

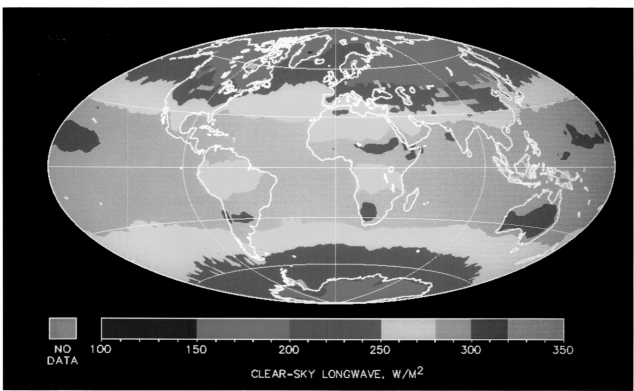

(b)

Fig. 3. ERBE regional monthly average (a) total-scene and (b) clear-sky LW flux for January 1986.

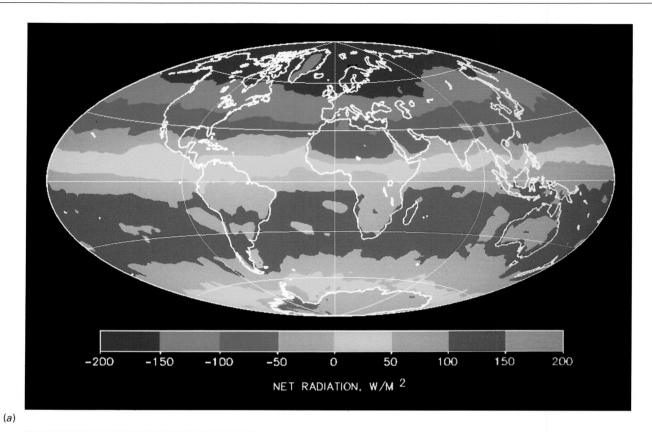

(a)

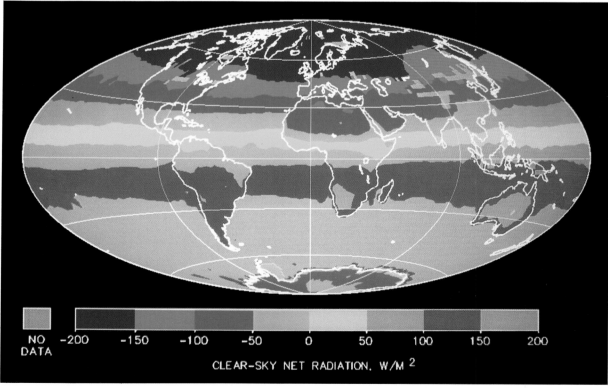

(b)

Fig. 4. ERBE regional monthly average (*a*) total-scene and (*b*) clear-sky net radiation for January 1986.

and the oceans. The increase in clear-sky ocean albedo near the wintertime pole results from the effects of the high solar zenith angles at those latitudes (Briegleb *et al.*, 1986). Deserts, persistently cloudy regions, and snow-covered areas have the highest albedos in the total albedo map. Cloud-free ocean areas are relatively dark. Longwave radiation is more zonal in appearance with broad maxima in the tropics and minima at the poles. Major cloud systems over the eastern subtropical oceans are apparent in the albedo data, but are not as prominent in the LW data since the clouds are at low altitude (e.g. Minnis & Harrison, 1984*b*). Regions which experience intense convective activity resulting in higher, thicker clouds appear as bright, cool areas (e.g. central South America, Congo Basin, and Indonesia). The intertropical convergence zone (ITCZ) is evident in the LW data as a relative minimum over the oceans at about 15° S. The total-scene data are in good qualitative agreement with similar, lower resolution results from the Nimbus-7 ERB scanner (Kyle *et al.*, 1990; Hartmann *et al.*, 1986).

Zonal

The zonal variation of radiation is useful for understanding the global climate system. Figs. 5 and 6 show the annual cycle of monthly averaged latitudinal zonal means of albedo and LW flux, respectively, from ERBE scanners. Albedo (Fig. 5) minima from 20–23% occur at about 12° latitude in the winter hemisphere. On average, minima in the north are slightly less than those in the Southern Hemisphere. Maximum albedos occur in the snow-covered regions at the poleward latitudes. There is a trend toward increasing albedo with latitude due to the solar zenith angle effect. Albedo is also higher in the summer hemisphere, probably owing to an increase in cloud cover and cloud optical depth. This effect is more pronounced in the northern latitudes due to the greater area of land masses.

The LW zonal fluxes (Fig. 6) show a systematic pattern for all months. Maximum LW flux occurs in the tropics and decreases toward the poles. The relative minimum near the equator coincides with the location of the ITCZ and the continental convection areas, where persistent, relatively high, cloud cover dramatically reduces LW radiation at the top of the atmosphere. During the year, LW flux experiences a slow increase toward the summer hemisphere, with higher peaks in the northern latitudes. Antarctica remains much cooler all during the year than corresponding northern latitudes. The high-albedo Antarctic snow cover persists year-round, while some breakup of the Arctic ice pack occurs each summer.

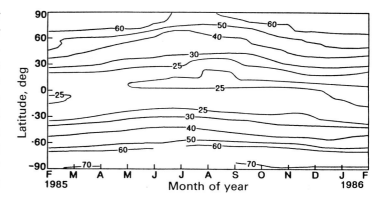

Fig. 5. Annual cycle of monthly mean zonal albedo (%) from ERBE.

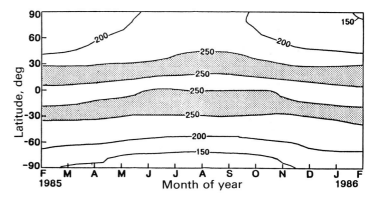

Fig. 6. Annual cycle of monthly mean zonal LW (Wm⁻²) from ERBE.

Global

Estimates of globally averaged radiative parameters have varied little since the first observations of Earth from satellites. Table 1 shows globally and annually averaged albedo

Table 1. *Annual average global albedo and LW flux from ERB satellites (early data adapted from Jacobowitz* et al., *1984)*

Source	Albedo %	Longwave emission W m⁻²
Pre-1972 experiments (Ellis & Vonder Haar, 1976)	30.4	236
Pre-1972 experiments plus Nimbus 6 ERBE (Campbell & Vonder Harr, 1980)	30	232
Nimbus 6 ERB wide field of view (Jacobowitz *et al.*, 1979)	31	234
Nimbus 6 ERB narrow field of view (Campbell & Vonder Haar, 1980)	31	230
Nimbus 7 ERB wide field of view	31	229
Nimbus 7 ERB narrow field of view	31	233
NOAA scanning radiometers (Ohring & Gruber, 1983)	31	244
ERBE (Harrison & Gibson, 1991)	30	234

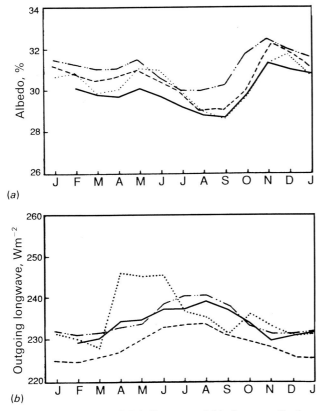

(a)

(b)

Fig. 7. Annual variation of globally averaged (a) planetary albedo and (b) LW flux. ERBE data (solid lines) are from Gibson *et al.* (1990); other results are adapted from Hartmann *et al.* (1986): Data from Ellis and Vonder Haar (1976) (dotted lines), Nimbus-7 ERB wide field of view (WFOV) (dashed curves), and Nimbus-6 ERB WFOV (dotted–dashed curves).

and LW flux derived from ERB satellites. The earlier data were adapted from Jacobowitz *et al.* (1984), the Nimbus-7 results from Kyle *et al.* (1990), and the ERBE estimates from Harrison and Gibson (1991). The large value of LW flux derived from NOAA measurements is most likely due to the difficulties of estimating the ERB from narrowband data. The ERBE values (albedo = 29.9%, LW = 234 W m^{-2}) currently represent the best estimate of the global annual averages for these parameters. For a mean solar irradiance of 1365 W m^{-2}, the ERBE measurements are out of balance by almost 6 W m^{-2}, which is similar to the uncertainty in the global, annual average net radiation (Barkstrom *et al.*, 1990).

The global solar insolation, planetary albedo, and emitted LW flux all vary during the year. Annual changes in global radiative parameters are due to the eccentricity of the Earth's orbit about the Sun, and geographical differences between the northern and southern hemispheres. Global average annual variations have been measured with several ERB observing systems, and selected results adapted from Hart-

mann *et al.* (1986) are shown in Fig. 7 along with ERBE data (Gibson *et al.*, 1990). Planetary albedo (Fig. 7(a)) shows similar annual trends for all of the data sets, although the actual albedo values vary for a given month. The ERBE albedos are somewhat lower than the earlier Nimbus results. Albedo reaches a maximum in November, a secondary maximum in May, and a sharp minimum just before the September equinox. This albedo variation reduces the effect of the annual variation in incoming solar radiation on the net radiation. The range of LW emission during the year (Fig. 7(b)) is about 10 W m^{-2}. Maximum values occur during the period from June through August. During this time, the extensive land areas in the Northern Hemisphere experience substantial temperature increases resulting in higher LW emissions. Since ocean temperatures are less variable with season, summer in the hemisphere with the most land produces the greatest global emissions of LW radiation. ERBE data compare closely with the Nimbus-6 results. The Nimbus-7 data have been reprocessed since this comparison was made and are now in much closer agreement with ERBE (Kyle *et al.*, 1990).

Scientific data analysis using radiation budget data

In addition to developing improvements to ERB measurement systems, the most frequent uses of ERB data fall into two categories: climate model validation and climate monitoring. Climate modellers use the ERB measurements in either direct comparisons with model-computed albedos, LW fluxes, or net fluxes at different temporal and spatial scales or in indirect comparisons of model-computed parameters with similar quantities derived from the ERB measurements. Assorted aspects of climate are observed in time series of various ERB parameters to detect statistical trends and to use the trends for prediction. Brief periods of ERB data are also used as diagnostic tools to understand regional-scale episodic events better.

Climate models

Energy transport

Estimation of net energy transport is one of the primary uses of ERB measurements (e.g. Vonder Haar, 1968; Bryan, 1982; Hartmann *et al.*, 1986; Masuda, 1988). The net energy transport is the amount of thermal and latent heat which must be moved by the atmosphere and oceans from one latitude to another to achieve thermal equilibrium over the Earth. This quantity is used as a constraint for climate and circulation

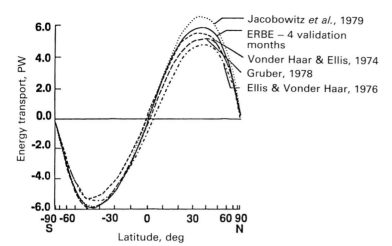

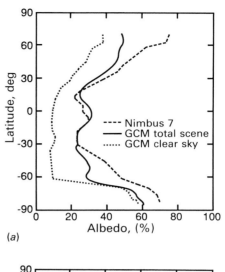

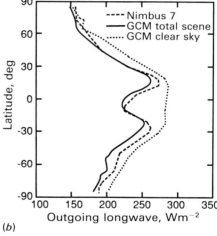

Fig. 8. Net energy transport from ERB measurements (adapted from Barkstrom *et al.*, 1990).

models which calculate the transfer of heat by the oceans and atmosphere. Integration of the mean zonal net radiation from the North Pole to the South Pole yields the required energy transport through a given latitude. Fig. 8 shows estimates of the net energy transport determined from various satellite observations (Jacobowitz *et al.*, 1979; Gruber, 1978; Ellis & Vonder Haar, 1976; Vonder Haar & Ellis, 1974; and Barkstrom *et al.*, 1990). A negative value in this figure indicates that southward transport is required. Since the net radiation is positive near the equator and negative at the poles, the ocean and atmosphere must move heat away from the tropics as seen in all of the measurements. The differences in the values in Fig. 8 result from inter-annual variability in the radiation budget and from the evolution in measurement systems and analysis techniques from 1974 to the ERBE.

Climate-model radiation validation

General circulation models (GCM's), which are often used for climate analysis and prediction studies, account for many of the physical processes within the atmosphere by using simple parameterizations of very detailed, complex mathematical formulations of those processes. The properties of important components of the Earth–atmosphere system are specified as variables or constants in these models, the sun is 'turned on' to heat the system in a realistic fashion, and the parameterization equations are solved in progressive time steps until an equilibrium climate is reached. The time averaged values of the model variables in this final state represent the climate for the conditions and processes specified in the models. Radiative processes are simulated with computer algorithms which include input variables such as surface albedo and temperature, atmospheric temperature and water vapor,

Fig. 9. Comparison of model-computed and satellite-observed (*a*) albedo and (*b*) outgoing LW radiation (adapted from Harshvardhan *et al.*, 1989).

cloud fractional coverage and height, and sometimes cloud optical depth. The radiation budget at the top of the atmosphere is one set of climate parameters which is generally produced by the GCM calculations. Comparison of the model-generated results to satellite observations gives the modeller one means to determine if the process has been reasonably simulated. Differences in the computed and observed values facilitate adjustments to the parameterizations and to the values of specified constants.

Fig. 9 presents results adapted from Harshvardhan *et al.* (1989) which compare some modeled albedos and LW fluxes to the same quantities derived from Nimbus-7 data. Although the model values follow the same general zonal trends as the data, significant differences are evident especially in the mid- and polar latitudes. Other modelling groups have also made similar comparisons using Nimbus-6 (e.g. Hense & Heise,

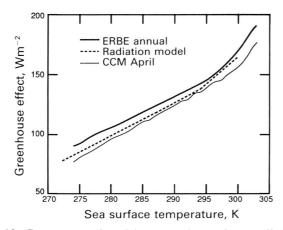

Fig. 10. Comparison of model-computed greenhouse effect with annual mean computed over ocean from clear-sky ERBE measurements (adapted from Raval and Ramanathan, 1989). The CCM (National Center for Atmospheric Research Community Climate Model) values refer to those for a perpetual April. The dashed line refers to an explicit line-by-line model which uses climatological profiles of temperature and humidity.

1984) and Nimbus-7 data. The calculated clear-sky variables in Fig. 9 have no counterpart in the Nimbus-7 data. Clear-sky conditions provide the simplest cases for intercomparison since they lack complex cloud effects. They allow the modellers to test various specifications of surface albedo and temperature in addition to the parameterizations of radiative transfer in the atmosphere. For example, Raval and Ramanathan (1989) used the clear-sky LW fluxes over oceans to validate a climate model's calculations of the greenhouse effect. Fig. 10, adapted from their results, shows the greenhouse effect, or warming of the Earth–atmosphere system by atmospheric gases, as related to sea surface temperature. The ERBE data verify the magnitude and variation of the greenhouse effect with sea surface temperature. The upturn of the curves at high temperatures indicates that the model's estimate of a rapid increase in atmospheric warming at high sea surface temperatures is confirmed by the ERBE results. Future modelling studies will make additional use of the ERBE-derived clear-sky results for verification.

Cloud-radiative forcing

The inadequate handling of clouds is the single largest shortcoming of current GCM's (Cess *et al.*, 1989). A convenient way of summarizing the effects of clouds on heating and cooling the Earth is to compute the cloud-radiative forcing (e.g. Charlock & Ramanathan, 1985). This quantity is the flux value at the top of the atmosphere measured for all conditions minus that for clear-sky conditions. Although cloud radiative forcing depends on a combination of various factors (e.g.

cloud amount, cloud altitude), it provides a first-order constraint on the contributions of clouds to the radiation budget. The ERBE system is the first to make global measurements of clear-sky and total-scene fluxes permitting direct calculations of cloud radiative forcing (Ramanathan *et al.*, 1989a, b).

Figs. 11 and 12 show the geographical distributions of LW and SW cloud-radiative forcing, respectively, for January 1986. In general, clouds tend to cause a LW warming (greenhouse effect) and a SW cooling (albedo effect) of the Earth–atmosphere system. In the tropics, these two competing effects of clouds tend to cancel each other as seen in the net cloud forcing results shown in Fig. 13. The largest negative net cloud forcing is found over the storm tracks at middle to high latitudes in the summer hemisphere where the cloud albedo impact outweighs the greenhouse effect. The most extreme values occur over marine areas since the contrast in albedo between clear and cloudy conditions is greatest over oceans.

Harrison *et al.* (1990a) quantified the seasonal variation of cloud-radiative forcing over the globe from ERBE data. Zonally averaged LW, SW, and net cloud-radiative forcing for April, July, and October, 1985 and January 1986 are shown in Fig. 14. The LW component remains fairly constant during the year, but SW cloud forcing varies dramatically with the changing seasons. Table 2 summarizes the global and hemispherical differences in seasonal cloud forcing. On average, clouds have a net cooling effect on the Earth for all seasons.

Zonal means of cloud forcing are compared with results from two GCMs for January in Fig. 15 (see Harrison *et al.*, 1990a). The model results are from the modified National Center for Atmospheric Research community climate model (modified NCAR CCM) (see Charlock & Ramanathan, 1985) and the Oregon State University/Lawrence Livermore National Laboratory (OSU/LLNL) GCM (see Cess & Potter, 1987). In general, the ERBE values of LW cloud forcing lie between the results from the two models (see Fig. 15(*a*)). The latitudinal variation of LW cloud forcing from the OSU/LLNL GCM is more extreme than the observations, while the modified NCAR CCM results are relatively insensitive to latitude. The substantial discrepancies over the deep convective centers at about 10° S suggest the need for improvements in the characterization of tropical cloudiness in the models. Similar differences are found in the comparisons of SW cloud forcing in Fig. 15(*b*), except that both models tend to overestimate the magnitude of the negative SW cloud forcing in the tropics. Comparison of the net cloud forcing (Fig. 15(*c*)) between ERBE and the models shows good agreement north of 40° N, overestimation of cooling by the models in the tropics, and underestimation of net cooling in

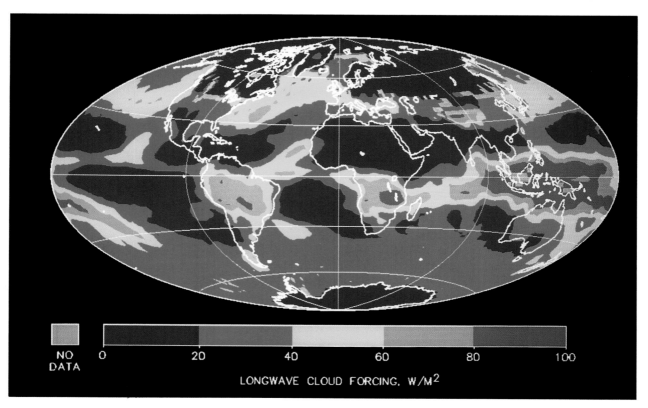

Fig. 11. Regional LW cloud–radiative cloud forcing from ERBE for January 1986.

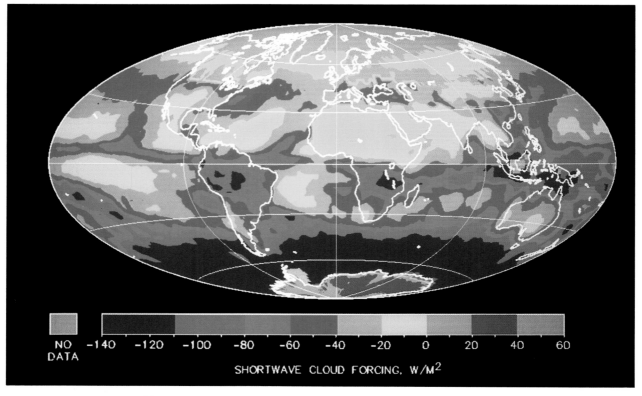

Fig. 12. Regional SW cloud–radiative cloud forcing from ERBE for January 1986.

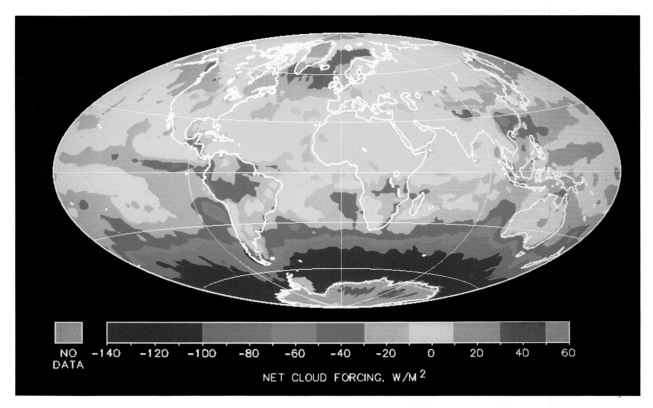

Fig. 13. Regional net cloud–radiative cloud forcing from ERBE for January 1986.

Table 2. *Hemispherical and global summary of seasonal cloud-radiative forcing variations (Harrison* et al., *1990*a)

Date	Geographical extent	Cloud forcing, W m^{-2}		
		Long wave	Short wave	Net
April 1985	Northern Hemisphere	31.2	−49.8	−18.6
	Southern Hemisphere	31.5	−40.4	−8.9
	Global	31.3	−45.1	−13.8
July 1985	Northern Hemisphere	33.8	−66.3	−32.5
	Southern Hemisphere	26.4	−27.2	−0.8
	Global	30.1	−46.7	−16.6
Oct. 1985	Northern Hemisphere	34.1	−40.1	−6.0
	Southern Hemisphere	30.2	−60.2	−30.0
	Global	32.2	−50.1	−17.9
Jan. 1986	Northern Hemisphere	26.6	−26.7	−0.1
	Southern Hemisphere	34.7	−76.8	−42.1
	Global	30.6	−51.7	−21.1
Annual	Northern Hemisphere	31.4	−45.7	−14.3
	Southern Hemisphere	30.7	−51.1	−20.4
	Global	31.1	−48.4	−17.3

the southern midlatitudes. The global mean net forcing agrees to within 2 W m^{-2} for the three data sets.

A summary comparison of the global cloud forcing parameters derived from the ERBE data and from several GCM calculations (Cess & Potter, 1987) is presented in Table 3. This comparison includes model results from Herman *et al.* (1980), Charlock and Ramanathan (1985), Ramanathan (1987), Randall and Harshvardhan (1986), Slingo and Slingo (1988), and J. F. B. Mitchell (unpublished data, but included in Cess & Potter, 1987). The ranges in the modeled values for LW, SW, and net cloud forcing are 32, 29, and 35 W m^{-2}, respectively. The ERBE data fall in the middle of the model results.

It is evident from these results that the differences in the modeled and observed ERBs (e.g. Fig. 9) are due to inadequate parameterizations of cloud amount, type, and optical properties in current GCMs. Improvements in these model cloud schemes await further advances in the basic understanding of cloud processes through combined cloud and radiation measurement programs.

Diurnal variations

Many cloud processes, especially those related to convection, depend on the amount of solar heating of the surface and the clouds. The magnitude of the absorbed SW flux and, therefore, cloud processes, ultimately depend on the available solar radiation determined by the Sun's zenith angle (related to day, local time, and latitude). Thus, there is a significant

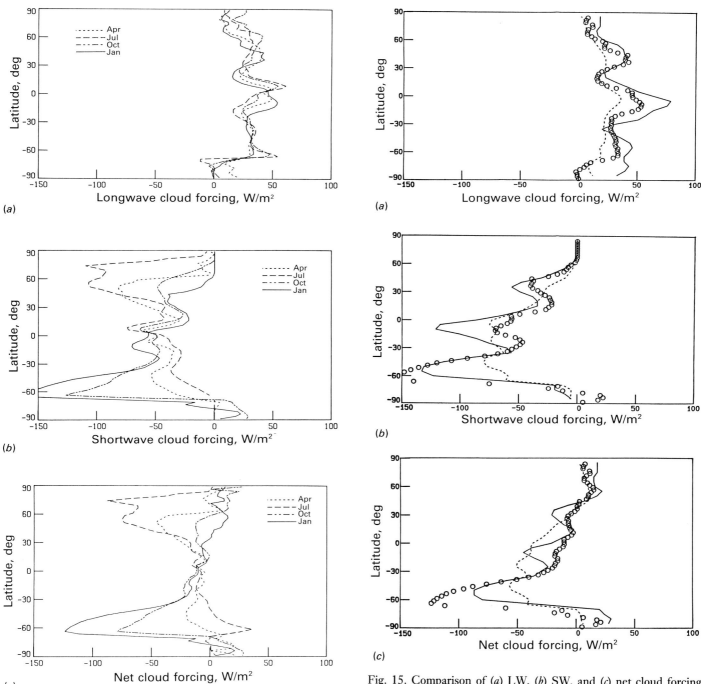

Fig. 14. Seasonal variation of zonally averaged (*a*) LW, (*b*) SW, and (*c*) net cloud radiative forcing from ERBE.

Fig. 15. Comparison of (*a*) LW, (*b*) SW, and (*c*) net cloud forcing from ERBE (circles) with calculations from two GCMs for January (solid line is from Cess and Potter, 1987; dashed line is from Charlock and Ramanathan, 1985).

diurnal dependency in the ERB and in the atmospheric energetics which respond to the Sun. A classic example of this diurnal variation is the afternoon thunderstorm common in the tropics and during the spring and summer months in temperate climes. Parameterizations which simulate the daily

heating of the ground (e.g. Bhumralkar, 1975) and atmosphere and the cloud response to it (e.g. Turton & Nicholls, 1987) have been developed to account for diurnal variations in GCMs. Recognizing the importance of the diurnal cycle, climate researchers (e.g. Cess & Potter, 1987; Slingo *et al.*,

Table 3. *Comparison of ERBE cloud-radiative forcing with GCM predictions (GCM results adapted from Cess and Potter, 1987)*

Reference	Model	Cloud radiative forcing W m^{-2}		
		Longwave	Shortwave	Net
Herman *et al.* (1980)	GLAS GCM, Jan.	40	−54	−14
Charlock and Ramanathan (1985)	Modified NCAR CCM, Jan.	23	−45	−22
Ramanathan (1987)	NCAR CCM, Jan.	35	−57	−22
Randall and Harshvardhan (1986)	UCLA/Goddard GCM, Jan.	55	−57	−2
	UCLA/Goddard GCM, July	53	−52	+1
J.F.B. Mitchell (in Cess & Potter, 1987)	UKMO GCM, Jan.	40	−74	−34
	UKMO GCM, July	42	−69	−27
Cess and Potter (1987)	OSU/LLNL GCM, Jan.	42	−62	−20
	OSU/LLNL GCM, July	39	−52	−13
Slingo and Slingo (1988)	NCAR CCM1, Jan.	30	−51	−21
Harrison *et al.* (1990a)	ERBE, Jan.	31	−52	−21
	ERBE, July	30	−47	−17

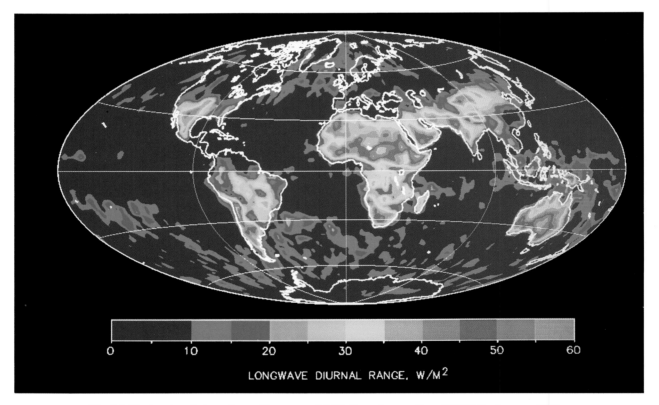

Fig. 16. Regional variation of monthly averaged LW diurnal range from ERBE for January 1986.

1987) are increasingly including such parameterizations in their models.

Progress in diurnal process modelling has coincided with advances in the measurement of the diurnal variations in the ERB. Determination of the diurnal phases and amplitudes of the ERB components has typically relied on estimates derived from geostationary satellites (e.g. Minnis & Harrison, 1984*a*, *c*, Duvel & Kandel, 1985, Minnis *et al.*, 1987) which are limited in spectral and spatial coverage and from sun-synchronous satellites (Hartmann & Recker, 1986; Liebmann & Gruber, 1988) that are constrained temporally and spectrally. The multi-satellite ERBE provides significant improvements in temporal and spatial sampling capability over these earlier measurement systems (e.g. Harrison *et al.*, 1983). Diurnal variations in the LW flux derived from ERBE have been analyzed by Harrison *et al.* (1988) and Harrison *et al.* (1990*b*). Fig. 16 shows the global distribution of LW diurnal range for January 1986. The observed patterns can be related not only to the heating and cooling of the surface, but also to changes in cloud amount and vertical structure during a typical day. Because surface temperatures are relatively constant over oceans, diurnal variations in LW are primarily due to changes in cloudiness. The largest diurnal range of LW occurs in desert regions (50–60 W m^{-2}) and over land areas, such as the Amazon Basin, that experience intense convective activity. Typically, vegetated land regions have moderate (20–40 W m^{-2}) diurnal ranges. Seasonal analyses (Harrison *et al.*, 1990*b*) reveal consistency in the relative magnitude of the diurnal range of LW flux as a function of surface type. The ERBE results will be extremely useful for better understanding and modelling of the diurnal variability of the ERB.

Surface radiation budget

The exchange of energy at the surface–atmosphere interface determines the amount of evaporation and sensible heating of the atmosphere. This heat transfer is constrained by the surface radiation budget (SRB). The balance of radiation at the surface cannot be measured directly with satellites, so it must be inferred from satellite data. To date, little use of broadband ERB data (e.g. Raschke & Preuss, 1979) has been made to estimate components of the global SRB. Most schemes for SRB determination have relied on the narrowband sensors on meteorological satellites such as the NOAA series (for review see Schmetz, 1989). The value of using broadband ERB data for SRB studies was illustrated by Cess and Vulis (1989). The suggested methods have since been applied to ERBE SW data with very satisfactory results (Cess *et al.*, 1991). Inferences of SRB from ERB data are likely to become more common in the future.

Climate monitoring

Time series analyses

Long time series of data are needed to detect changes in climate and to determine statistical relationships between events at different times and locations. A 12-year data set has been compiled from wide field-of-view ERB sensors on board the Nimbus 6 and 7 satellites (Kyle *et al.*, 1990). These data include 3 years of Nimbus-6 measurements starting in 1975 and 9 years of Nimbus-7 results starting in 1978. Cess (1990) detected a downward LW trend with time in his analysis of an 8-year record of Nimbus-7 wide field-of-view long wave measurements. He showed that the trend was not a result of greenhouse warming due to increasing atmospheric carbon dioxide, but instead was strongly correlated with observed variability of global-mean surface air temperature. A

short period of global cooling was detected for part of the last two decades that have, overall, been a time of global warming. Thus, ERB data provide an independent means of appraising global climate variability.

The Nimbus measurement period encompasses the El Niño/Southern Oscillation (ENSO) events of 1976/1977, 1982/1983 (Ardanuy & Kyle, 1986), and 1986/1987. The Southern Oscillation is a fluctuation in the intensity of the inter-tropical general atmospheric and hydrospheric circulation over the Indo-Pacific region, the fluctuation being dominated by an exchange of air between the southeast Pacific subtropical high and the Indonesian equatorial low. El Niño is an anomalous warming of ocean surface waters off South America. ENSO is a large-scale perturber of the climate system with strong effects reaching far beyond the equatorial Pacific. ENSO has been linked to changes in atmospheric circulations which cause disastrous floods and droughts well into the mid-latitudes. Bess *et al.* (1989) used a 10-year segment of the Nimbus outgoing LW data set to study radiative features associated with ENSO events. Fig. 17 shows the non-ENSO pattern of weak negative LW anomalies over Indonesia, and weak positive anomalies over the central Pacific and to the east. For ENSO years, this pattern reverses and strengthens with negative anomalies in the central Pacific and positive anomalies over Indonesia. Although the 1976/1977 ENSO was not as strong as the 1982/1983 event, it was very persistent, consistent with broad-peaked Tahiti-Darwin pressure anomalies observed at that time.

The 1986/1987 ENSO observed by ERBE sensors on the Earth Radiation Budget Satellite showed LW anomalies nearly as strong as those for the 1982/1983 event. Fig. 18 shows a time series of LW flux from 1985 through 1987 for a 2.5°-wide latitude strip at the equator. The high-resolution scanner data clearly show the build-up and peak of the LW anomaly associated with the ENSO event.

These examples demonstrate the importance of obtaining a long-term data set of radiation budget parameters. The last of the ERBE scanners ceased operation in late 1989. Data from the wide field-of-view instruments continue to be obtained in an attempt to maintain a continuous ERB record until the launch of the Earth Observing System (EOS) satellites in the late 1990s.

Climate diagnostics

Radiation budget data have also been used in various studies to understand better the dynamics of a particular event or phenomenon. For example, Chen *et al.* (1985) used Nimbus-7 data to help quantify the summertime atmospheric heat

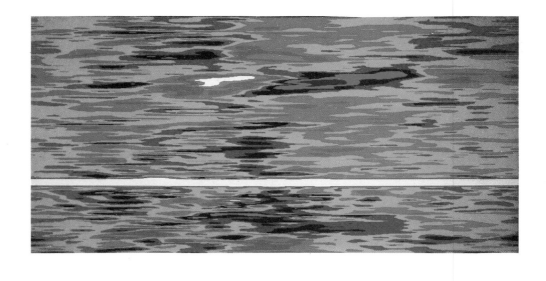

Fig. 17. Ten-year time series (1975–1985) of LW flux at the equator from Nimbus 6 and 7 (from Bess *et al.*, 1989).

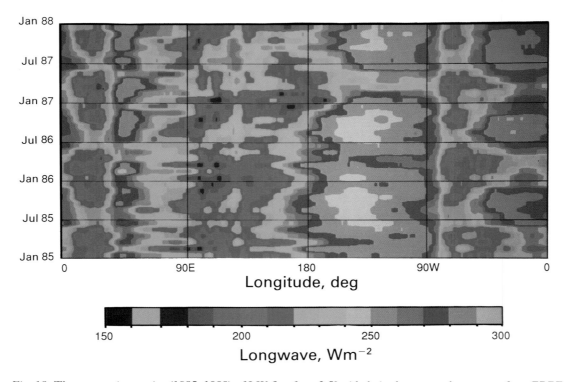

Fig. 18. Three-year time series (1985–1988) of LW flux for a 2.5° wide latitude zone at the equator from ERBE.

source over the extensive Tibetan Plateau. Interpretation of jetstream oscillations was facilitated by analyses of NOAA LW fluxes (e.g. Weickmann *et al.*, 1985). Statistical examinations of LW fluxes have also been useful for discerning teleconnection patterns in meteorological data (e.g. Charlock *et al.*, 1990).

The utility of ERB data has been growing with the increased availability and accuracy of the satellite products. The applications presented here clearly demonstrate the value of Earth radiation budget measurements for scientific studies of the Earth's climate.

Limitations of ERB data

Some of the major limitations and sources of uncertainty in the various ERB missions have been mentioned previously. Early missions had severe time-space sampling deficiencies as well as instrumentation of questionable accuracy and stability. The Nimbus ERB instruments shared some of their predecessors' problems, but benefited from sensor design improvements and a multiple-sensor experiment concept. The accuracy of these earlier measurements, however, has not been well understood due to limited knowledge of the sensors and the system being measured.

A comprehensive assessment of the accuracy of the results was fundamental in the design of ERBE. For ERBE, the most significant errors still arise from calibration uncertainties, the application of angular dependence models, and from sampling deficiencies (Barkstrom *et al.*, 1989). Scene identification errors result in the selection of the wrong anisotropic models and the incorrect categorization of a given measurement. The anisotropic models also have some inherent uncertainties which may not be entirely eliminated through averaging. Incorrect categorization may result in biases in the average fluxes for a given scene type. Sampling errors result from variations in meteorology and optical properties not taken into account in the procedures which compute monthly average fluxes from measurements taken at four or five times during each day. Without additional satellites or the use of auxiliary information from geostationary satellites, such sampling deficiencies will persist in future studies. Several researchers (e.g. Diekmann & Smith, 1989; Stuhlmann & Raschke, 1987; Barkstrom *et al.*, 1990; Hartmann & Doelling, 1991; Harrison *et al.*, 1990*a*) have addressed the problem of quantifying the uncertainty in ERBE results. Barkstrom *et al.* (1989) estimated the uncertainties in monthly average, regional scanner data to be about ± 5 W m^{-2} for both SW and LW. The uncertainty in global, annual average net radiation is about ± 5 W m^{-2}.

One of the most useful results of the ERBE is the estimate of cloud radiative forcing. The value of this parameter, while essential, is only one part of the equation needed to understand the radiative interaction of clouds with climate. Knowledge of the spatial distribution of clouds and their optical properties which give rise to the observed cloud forcing is also needed. Although detailed cloud properties were not measured simultaneously as part of ERBE, complementary global cloud data were taken by the International Satellite Cloud Climatology Project (Schiffer & Rossow, 1983; Rossow *et al.*, 1991) during the ERBE mission. Analysis of the combined results of the two projects will be of significant value in deciphering the radiative role of clouds in the climate.

Many of the sampling and accuracy limitations of current data sets will be improved with the launch of the Clouds and the Earth's Radiant Energy System (CERES; Wielicki & Barkstrom, 1991) in the late 1990s. Instrument design, calibration, and data processing lessons learned from ERBE are being factored into the CERES mission. Simultaneous, detailed cloud properties will be included for each scanner measurement using high spatial and spectral resolution cloud imager data. The launch of CERES on EOS and other satellites as part of the Mission to Planet Earth will mark the beginning of the next long-term ERB measurement program to provide vital data for improving predictive climate models. The synergistic use of the wide variety of climate measurements obtained simultaneously by EOS will allow the study of not only cloud radiative forcing, but also cloud feedback processes in the climate system.

Data availability

The primary top-of-the-atmosphere radiation budget satellite data sets from ERBE and Nimbus 6 and 7 are available to the scientific community through the National Space Science Data Center (NSSDC). Within the United States, the address is National Space Science Data Center, Code 633.4, Goddard Space Flight Center, Greenbelt, Maryland 20771. For scientists outside the United States, the address is World Data Center A, Rockets and Satellites, Code 630.2, Goddard Space Flight Center, Greenbelt, Maryland 20771, USA.

References

Ardanuy, P. E. & Kyle, H. L. (1986). El Niño and outgoing long-wave radiation: Observations from Nimbus-7 ERB. *Mon. Wea. Rev.*, **114**, 415–33.

Barkstrom, B. R. (1984). The Earth Radiation Budget Experiment (ERBE). *Bull. Am. Meteor. Soc.*, **65**, 1170–85.

Barkstrom, B. R. & Smith, G. L. (1986). The Earth Radiation Budget Experiment: Science and implementation. *Rev. Geophys.*, **24**, 379–90.

Barkstrom, B. R., Harrison, E. F. & Lee, R. B. (1990). Earth Radiation Budget Experiment, Preliminary seasonal results. *Eos Trans., Am. Geophys. Union*, **71**, February 27.

Barkstrom, B. R., Harrison, E., Smith, G., Green, R., Kibler, J., Cess, R. & ERBE Science Team (1989). Earth Radiation Budget Experiment (ERBE) archival and April 1985 results. *Bull. Am. Meteor. Soc.*, **70**, 1254–62.

Bess, T. D., Smith, G. L. & Charlock, T. P. (1989). A ten-year monthly data set of outgoing longwave radiation from Nimbus-6 and Nimbus-7 satellites. *Bull. Am. Meteor. Soc.*, **70**, 480–9.

Bhumralkar, C. M. (1975). Numerical experiments on the computation of ground surface temperature in an atmospheric general circulation model. *J. Appl. Meteorol.*, **14**, 1246–58.

Briegleb, B. P., Minnis, P., Ramanathan, V. & Harrison, E. F. (1986). Comparison of clear-sky albedos inferred from satellite observations and model computations. *J. Climate Appl. Meteorol.*, **25**, 214–26.

Brooks, D. R. & Minnis, P. (1984a). Comparison of longwave diurnal models applied to simulations of the Earth Radiation Budget Experiment. *J. Climate Appl. Meteor.*, **23**, 155–60.

Brooks, D. R. & Minnis, P. (1984b). Simulation of the Earth's monthly average regional radiation balance derived from satellite measurements. *J. Climate Appl. Meteor.*, **23**, 392–403.

Brooks, D. R., Harrison, E. F., Minnis, P., Suttles, J. T. & Kandel, R. S. (1986). Development of algorithms for understanding the temporal and spatial variability of the Earth's radiation balance. *Rev. Geophys.*, **24**, 422–38.

Bryan, K. (1982). Poleward heat transport by the ocean: observations and models. *Ann. Rev. Earth Planet. Sci.*, **10**, 15–30.

Campbell G. G. & Vonder Haar, T. H. (1980). Climatology of radiation budget measurements from satellites. *Atmos. Sci. Paper 323*, Colorado State University, Fort Collins.

Cess, R. D. (1990). Interpretation of an 8-year record of Nimbus-7 wide-field-of-view infrared measurements. *J. Geophys. Res.*, **95**, 16653–7.

Cess, R. D., DeLuisi, J. J., Dutton, E. G. & Jiang, F. (1991). Determining surface solar absorption from broadband satellite measurements: Comparison with surface measurements. *J. Climate*, **4**, 236–47.

Cess, R. D., Potter, G. L., Blanchet, J. P., Boer, G. J., Ghan, S. J., Kiehl, J. T., Le Treut, H., Li, Z.-X., Liang, X.-Z., Mitchell, J. F. B., Morcrette, J.-J., Randall, D. A., Riches, M. R., Roeckner, E., Schlese, U., Slingo, A., Taylor, K. E., Washington, W. M., Wetherald, R. T. & Yagai, I. (1989). Interpretation of cloud- climate feedback as produced by 14 atmospheric general circulation models. *Science*, **245**, 513–16.

Cess, R. D. & Vulis, I. L. (1989). Inferring surface solar absorption from broadband satellite measurements. *J. Climate*, **2**, 974–85.

Cess, R. D. & Potter, G. L. (1987). Exploratory studies of cloud radiative forcing with a general circulation model. *Tellus*, **39A**, 460–73.

Charlock, T. P. & Ramanathan, V. (1985). The albedo field and cloud radiative forcing produced by a general circulation model with internally generated cloud optics. *J. Atmos. Sci.*, **42**, 1408–29.

Charlock, T. P., Rose, F. G., Bess, T. D. & Smith, G. L. (1990). The relationship of extratropical outgoing longwave radiation to monthly geopotential teleconnection patterns. *J. Climate*, **3**, 1390–9.

Chen, L., Reiter, E. R. & Feng, Z. (1985). The atmospheric heat source over the Tibetan Plateau: May–August 1979. *Mon. Wea. Rev.*, **113**, 1771–90.

Diekmann, F. J. & Smith, G. L. (1989). Investigation of scene identification algorithms for radiation budget measurements. *J. Geophys. Res.*, **94**, 3395–412.

Duvel, J. P. & Kandel, R. S. (1985). Regional-scale diurnal variations of outgoing radiation observed by Meteosat. *J. Climate Appl. Meteor.*, **24**, 335–49.

Ellis, J. S. & Vonder Haar, T. H. (1976). Zonal average Earth radiation budget measurements from satellites for climate studies. *Atmos. Sci. Paper 240*, Colorado State University, Fort Collins, 58pp.

Gibson, G. G., Denn, F., Young, D., Harrison, E., Minnis, P., Barkstrom, B., Smith, O. & Travers, D. (1990). Characteristics of the Earth's radiation budget derived from the first year of data from the Earth Radiation Budget Experiment. *SPIE Proceedings, Long-Term Monitoring of the Earth's Radiation Budget* (B. R. Barkstrom, ed.), **1299**, 253–63.

Green, R. N., House, F. B., Stackhouse, P. W., Wu, X., Ackerman, S. A., Smith, W. L. & Johnson, M. J. (1990). Intercomparison of scanner and non-scanner measurements for the Earth Radiation Budget Experiment. *J. Geophys. Res.*, **95**, 11785–98.

Gruber, A. (1978). Determination of the Earth–atmosphere radiation budget from NOAA satellite data. *NOAA Tech. Rep. NESS 76*, Washington, DC, 28pp.

Harrison, E. F. & Gibson, G. G. (1991). Seasonal cloud-radiative forcing over land and ocean derived from ERBE satellites. *AIAA Paper No. 91–0052, 29th Aerospace Sciences Meeting*, Reno, NV, Jan. 7–10.

Harrison, E. F., Brooks, D. R., Minnis, P., Wielicki, B. A., Staylor, W. F., Gibson, G. G., Young, D. F., Denn, F. M. & ERBE Science Team (1988). First estimates of the diurnal variation of longwave radiation from the multiple-satellite Earth Radiation Budget Experiment (ERBE). *Bull. Am. Meteorol. Soc.*, **69**, 1144–51.

Harrison, E. F., Minnis, P., Barkstrom, B. R., Ramanathan, V., Cess, R. D. & Gibson, G. G. (1990a). Seasonal variation of cloud radiative forcing derived from the Earth Radiation Budget Experiment. *J. Geophys. Res.*, **95**, 18687–703.

Harrison, E. F., Minnis, P., Barkstrom, B. R., Wielicki, B. A., Gibson, G. G., Denn, F. M. & Young, D. F. (1990b). Seasonal variation of the diurnal cycles of Earth's radiation budget determined from ERBE. *AMS 7th Conf. Atmos. Radiation*, San Francisco, CA, July 23–27, 87–91.

Harrison, E. F., Minnis, P. & Gibson, G. G. (1983). Orbital and cloud cover sampling analyses for multisatellite Earth radiation budget experiments. *J. Spacecraft and Rockets*, **20**, 491–5.

Harshvardhan, Randall, D. A., Corsetti, T. G. & Dazlich, D. A. (1989). Earth radiation budget and cloudiness simulations with a general circulation model. *J. Atmos. Sci.*, **46**, 1922–42.

Hartmann, D. L. & Doelling, D. (1991). On the net radiative effectiveness of clouds. *J. Geophys. Res.*, **96**, 869–91.

Hartmann, D. L. & Short, D. A. (1980). On the use of Earth radiation budget statistics for studies of clouds and climate. *J. Atmos. Sci.*, **37**, 1233–50.

Hartmann, D. L. & Recker, E. E. (1986). Diurnal variation of outgoing longwave radiation in the tropics. *J. Climate Appl. Meteor.*, **25**, 800–12.

Hartmann, D. L., Ramanathan, V., Berroir, A. & Hunt, G. E. (1986). Earth radiation budget data and climate research. *Rev. Geophys.*, **24**, 439–68.

Hense, A. & Heise, E. (1984). A sensitivity study of cloud parameterizations in general circulation models. *Beitr. Phys. Atmosph.*, **57**, 240–58.

Herman, G., Wu, M.-L. & Johnson, W. T. (1980). The effects of clouds on the Earth's solar and infra-red radiation budgets. *J. Atmos. Sci.*, **37**, 1251–61.

House, F. B., Gruber, A., Hunt, G. E. & Mecherikunnel, A. T. (1986). History of satellite missions and measurements of the Earth radiation budget (1957–1984). *Rev. Geophys.*, **24**, 357–77.

Jacobowitz, H., Tighe, R. J. & Nimbus 7 ERB Experiment Team (1984). The Earth radiation budget derived from the Nimbus-7 ERB experiment. *J. Geophys. Res.*, **89**, 4997–5010.

Jacobowitz, H., Smith, W. L., Howell, H. B., Nagle, F. W. & Hickey, J. R. (1979). The first 18 months of planetary radiation budget measurements from the Nimbus 6 ERB experiment. *J. Atmos. Sci.*, **36**, 501–7.

JOC (Joint Organizing Committee) (1975). The Physical Basis of Climate and Climate Modelling. *Global Atmospheric Research Program Publication No. 16*, ICSU and WMO Report of the International Study Conference in Stockholm, 29 July–10 August, 1974, 265pp.

Kandel, R. S. (1983). Satellite observation of the Earth radiation budget. *Beitr. Phys. Atmosph.*, **56**, 322–40.

Kopia, L. P. (1986). Earth Radiation Budget Experiment scanner instrument. *Rev. Geophys.*, **24**, 400–6.

Kyle, H. L., Mecherikunnel, A., Ardanuy, P., Penn, L., Groveman, B., Campbell, G. G. & Vonder Haar, T. H. (1990). A comparison of two major Earth radiation budget data sets. *J. Geophys. Res.*, **95**, 9951–70.

Liebmann, B. & Gruber, A. (1988). Annual variation of the diurnal cycle of outgoing longwave radiation. *Mon. Wea. Rev.*, **116**, 1659–70.

Luther, M. R., Cooper, J. E. & Taylor, G. R. (1986). The Earth Radiation Budget Experiment non-scanner instrument. *Rev. Geophys.*, **24**, 391–9.

Masuda, K. (1988). Meridional heat transport by the atmosphere and the ocean: Analysis of FGGE data. *Tellus*, **40A**, 285–302.

Minnis, P. & Harrison, E. F. (1984a). Diurnal variability of regional cloud and clear-sky radiative parameters derived from GOES data, I, Analysis Method. *J. Climate Appl. Meteor.*, **23**, 993–1011.

Minnis, P. & Harrison, E. F. (1984b). Diurnal variability of regional cloud and clear-sky radiative parameters derived from GOES data, II, November 1978 cloud distributions. *J. Climate Appl. Meteor.*, **23**, 1012–31.

Minnis, P. & Harrison, E. F. (1984c). Diurnal variability of regional cloud and clear-sky radiative parameters derived from GOES data, III, November 1978 radiative parameters. *J. Climate Appl. Meteor.*, **23**, 1032–51.

Minnis, P., Harrison, E. F. & Gibson, G. G. (1987). Cloud cover over the equatorial eastern Pacific derived from July 1983 International Satellite Cloud Climatology Project data using a hybrid bispectral threshold method. *J. Geophys. Res.*, **92**, 4051–73.

Ohring, G. & Gruber, A. (1983). Satellite radiation observations and climate theory. *Adv. Geophys.*, **25**, 237–304.

Ramanathan, V. (1987). The role of Earth radiation budget studies in climate and general circulation research. *J. Geophys. Res.*, **92**, 4075–95.

Ramanathan, V., Barkstrom, B. R. & Harrison, E. F. (1989a). Climate and the Earth's radiation budget. *Physics Today*, May, 22–32.

Ramanathan, V., Cess, R. D., Harrison, E. F., Minnis, P., Barkstrom, B. R., Ahmad, E. & Hartmann, D. (1989b). Cloud-radiative forcing and climate: Results from the Earth Radiation Budget Experiment. *Science*, **243**, 57–63.

Randall, D. A. & Harshvardhan (1986). Cloud radiative forcing in a general circulation model. *AMS 6th Conf. Atmos. Radiation*, Williamsburg, VA., May 13–16, 31–4.

Raschke, E. & Bandeen, W. R. (1970). The radiation balance of the planet Earth from radiation measurements of the satellite Nimbus II. *J. Appl. Meteorol.*, **9**, 215–38.

Raschke, E. & Preuss, H. J. (1979). The determination of the solar radiation budget at the Earth's surface from satellite measurements. *Meteor. Rundsch.*, **32**, 18–28.

Raschke, E., Vonder Haar, T. H., Bandeen, W. R. & Pasternak, M. (1973). The annual radiation balance of the Earth atmosphere system during 1969–1970 from Nimbus 3 measurements. *J. Atmos. Sci.*, **30**, 341–64.

Raval, A. & Ramanathan, V. (1989). Observational determination of the greenhouse effect. *Nature*, **342**, 758–61.

Rossow *et al.* (1993). Clouds, this volume.

Schmetz, J. (1989). Towards a surface radiation climatology: retrieval of downward irradiances from satellites. *Atmos. Res.*, **23**, 287–321.

Schiffer, R. A. & Rossow, W. B. (1983). The International Satellite Cloud Climatology Project (ISCCP): The first project of the World Climate Research Programme. *Bull. Am. Meteorol. Soc.*, **64**, 779–84.

Slingo, A. & Slingo, J. M. (1988). The response of a general circulation model to cloud longwave radiative forcing. I: Introduction and initial experiments. *Quart. J. Roy. Meteorol. Soc.*, **114**, 1027–62.

Slingo, A., Wilderspin, R. C. & Brentnall, S. J. (1987). Simulation of the diurnal cycle of outgoing longwave radiation with an atmospheric GCM. *Mon. Wea. Rev.* 115, 1451–7.

Smith, G. L., Green, R. N., Raschke, E., Avis, L. M., Suttles, J. T., Wielicki, B. A. & Davies, R. (1986). Inversion methods for satellite studies of the Earth's radiation budget: Development of algorithms for the ERBE mission. *Rev. Geophys.*, 24, 407–21.

Smith, W. L., Hickey, J., Howell, H. B., Jacobowitz, H., Hilleary, D. T. & Drummond, A. J. (1977). Nimbus-6 Earth Radiation Budget Experiment. *Appl. Opt.*, 16, 306–18.

Stephens, G. L., Campbell, G. G. & Vonder Haar, T. H. (1981). Earth radiation budgets. *J. Geophys. Res.*, 86, 9739–60.

Stuhlmann, R. & Raschke, E. (1987). Satellite measurements of the earth radiation budget: Sampling and retrieval of shortwave exitances – a sampling study. *Contrib. Phys. Atmos.*, 60, 393–410.

Suomi, V. E. (1957). The radiation balance of the Earth from a satellite. *Ann. Int. Geophys. Year*, 6, 331–40.

Suttles, J. T., Green, R. N., Minnis, P., Smith, G. L., Staylor, W. F., Wielicki, B. A., Walker, I. J., Young, D. F., Taylor, V. R. & Stowe, L. L. (1988). Angular radiation models for Earth–atmosphere system, vol. I, Shortwave radiation. *NASA RP-1184*.

Suttles, J. T., Green, R. N., Smith, G. L., Wielicki, B. A., Walker, I. J., Taylor, V. R. & Stowe, L. L. (1989). Angular radiation models for Earth–atmosphere system, vol. II, Longwave radiation. *NASA RP-1184*.

Taylor, V. R. & Stowe, L. L. (1984). Reflectance characteristics of uniform earth and cloud surfaces derived from Nimbus-7 ERB. *J. Geophys. Res.*, 89, 4987–96.

Turton, J. D. & Nicholls, S. (1987). A study of the diurnal variation of stratocumulus using a multiple mixed layer model. *Quart. J. Roy. Meteorol. Soc.*, 113, 969–1009.

Vonder Haar, T. H. (1968). Variations of the Earth's Radiation Budget. Phd. Thesis, Dept. of Meteorology, Univ. of Wisc., Madison, 118pp.

Vonder Haar, T. H. (1983). Climate studies from satellite observations: Special problems in the verification of Earth radiation balance, cloud climatology, and related climate experiments. *Adv. Space Phys.*, 2, 3–10.

Vonder Haar, T. H. & Ellis, J. (1974). Atlas of radiation budget measurements from satellites. *Atmos. Sci. Paper 231*, Colorado State University, Fort Collins, 180pp.

Weickmann, K. M., Lussky, G. R. & Kutzbach, J. E. (1985). Intraseasonal (30–60 day) fluctuations of outgoing longwave radiation and 250 mb streamfunction during northern winter. *Mon. Wea. Rev.*, 113, 941–61.

Wielicki, B. A. & Green, R. N. (1989). Cloud identification for ERBE radiative flux retrieval. *J. Appl. Meteorol.*, 28, 1133–46.

Wielicki, B. A. & Barkstrom, B. R. (1991). Clouds and the Earth's radiant energy system (CERES): an earth observing system experiment. *AMS 2nd Symposium on Global Change Studies*, New Orleans, LA.

PART II

STRATOSPHERE

Stratospheric chemistry, temperature, and dynamics

JACK A. KAYE

Introduction

The stratosphere, the region of the Earth's atmosphere between roughly 12 and 50 km (8 and 30 miles) above the surface, is a crucial component in the Earth's environment. Much of the importance of the stratosphere stems from its absorption of the bulk of solar ultra-violet radiation in the 290–320 nm wavelength regions. Since these wavelengths are particularly harmful to life owing to their absorption by nucleic acid in cells, their penetration to the surface would have harmful environmental consequences. In particular, there would be a dramatic increase in human skin cancers (not to mention a whole host of other biological effects) if appreciably larger amounts of solar ultra-violet radiation were to reach the Earth's surface. These effects have been summarized in a book edited by Bower and Ward (1982) and also in a report by Makhijani, Makhijani & Bickel (1988).

The component in the stratosphere absorbing the bulk of the ultra-violet radiation is ozone (O_3), which is formed from molecular oxygen (O_2) by ultra-violet and extreme ultra-violet photolysis followed by recombination of atomic oxygen (O) with O_2:

$$O_2 + \text{UV light} \rightarrow O + O \qquad (1)$$

$$O + O_2 + M \rightarrow O_3 + M \qquad (2)$$

where the third body (M) is present to allow for conservation of energy and momentum. O_3 amounts are small in the stratosphere, with its mixing ratio (the ratio of the number of O_3 molecules per unit volume to the total number of molecules in that volume) rarely exceeding 10 parts per million by volume (ppmv). The total amount of O_3 in the stratosphere is such that if brought to the surface it would form a layer between 1 and 5 mm thick. Stratospheric O_3 comprises some 90% of the O_3 in the atmosphere. These amounts, though small, are highly important.

In fact, it is these small amounts of O_3 which help define the stratosphere, as may be clearly seen in Fig. 1, in which the variation of the temperature and ozone density (number of molecules of ozone per unit volume of air) with altitude in the atmosphere is shown. The two major characteristics of the stratosphere – a temperature which increases with altitude (as opposed to the lowest 15 km of the atmosphere, the troposphere, where temperature decreases substantially with increasing altitude) and the large amounts of O_3 – are related. This relationship occurs because the absorption of ultra-violet radiation by O_3 leads to heating of the stratosphere when the energy of the ultra-violet radiation is converted to kinetic energy of atmospheric molecules:

$$O_3 + \text{UV light} \rightarrow O + O_2 \qquad (3)$$

$$O + O_2 + M \rightarrow O_3 + M \qquad (2)$$

The net result of processes (3) and (2) is only radiative; there is no net chemical effect.

The increase of temperature with altitude in the stratosphere has important consequences for the meteorology there. These areas of increasing temperature with height are more stable with respect to vertical mixing than is the troposphere. Thus, there can be large vertical gradients in the trace constituent compositions there. Instead of being mixed vertically by overturning or other convective motions, trace constituents can only be mixed vertically by either the large-scale dynamics of the stratosphere (for example, rising vertical motion in the tropics balanced by descent at high latitudes), by features associated with large planetary-scale wave disturbances, or by smaller-scale gravity waves. The planetary wave activity is located primarily in the winter hemisphere. In the summer hemisphere, mixing by random motion of air parcels (eddy diffusion) becomes increasingly important. Stratospheric meteorology has recently been reviewed by Schoeberl (1987).

The distribution of O_3 in the stratosphere is strongly affected by the meteorology there. Most production and destruction of O_3 occurs in the tropical upper stratosphere, where ultra-violet amounts are largest. Dissociation of O_3, however, extends lower in the stratosphere and to higher latitudes than does production; transport processes must obviously play an important role in controlling the distribution of a species whose production and destruction are not in local balance everywhere.

The reason for the separation between the production and

Ozone number density, 10^{12} cm^{-3}

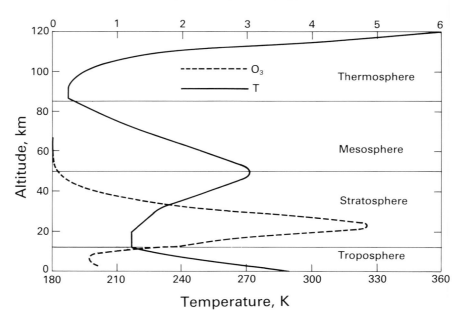

Fig. 1. Vertical profile of temperature (yellow) and ozone number density (red) in the atmosphere. Regions of the atmosphere are labeled with approximate location of divisions between them indicated in blue. Data are from the US Standard Atmosphere [1976].

destruction regions of O_3 is that the processes resulting in O_3 destruction differ markedly from those resulting in its production. O_3 production is driven by ultra-violet and extreme ultra-violet photolysis of O_2 (wavelengths below 240 nm), while O_3 loss typically involves production of atomic oxygen (reaction 3) which occurs at longer wavelengths in the ultra-violet (up to 320 nm) and, to a lesser extent, in the visible. Since longer wavelength photons penetrate deeper into the atmosphere, this difference between production and destruction regions of O_3 can occur.

Some O_3 is destroyed by a process involving only oxygen atom chemistry

$$O_3 + UV, \text{ visible light} \rightarrow O + O_2 \qquad (3)$$

$$O + O_3 \rightarrow O_2 + O_2 \qquad (4)$$

but most O_3 destruction occurs by catalytic processes involving free radical species containing either hydrogen, nitrogen, chlorine, or bromine atoms. These may usually be represented by a two-step cyclic pathway involving the free radical X:

$$O_3 + X \rightarrow XO + O_2 \qquad (5)$$

$$O + OX \rightarrow X + O_2 \qquad (6)$$

The most important radicals X include hydroxyl (OH), nitric oxide (NO), chlorine (Cl), and bromine (Br). These are themselves formed in the stratosphere by the decomposition of various atmospheric source gases, which can be of either natural or anthropogenic origin. For example, OH comes

from decomposition of water (H_2O) or methane (CH_4), NO comes from nitrous oxide (N_2O), Cl comes from naturally occurring methyl chloride (CH_3Cl) or anthropogenically emitted chlorofluorocarbon (CFC) molecules, such as dichlorodifluoromethane (CF_2Cl_2), and Br comes from either methyl bromide (CH_3Br, which may have natural and anthropogenic sources), or various bromine-containing halocarbons (Halons), such as the fire extinguishant trifluoromethylbromide (CF_3Br). A complete description of stratospheric chemistry has been given in several books, including those of Brasseur and Solomon (1984), Shimazaki (1985), and Wayne (1985).

Stratospheric chemistry is quite complicated because the chemistry of the various compounds of all these chemical elements (oxygen, hydrogen, nitrogen, chlorine, and bromine, in which the compounds of each of these elements are often referred to as 'families') is occurring simultaneously. In addition, the different families' chemistries interact. For example, catalytically active constituents in two different families may recombine to form a so-called 'reservoir' molecule, which is unreactive towards O_3. Thus, in the case of the hydrogen and nitrogen families, the reservoir species nitric acid (HNO_3) can form:

$$OH + NO_2 + M \rightarrow HNO_3 + M \qquad (7)$$

Because these reservoir molecules are fairly stable (being only slowly photolyzed by ultra-violet radiation and having a lifetime on the order of days to weeks), they can build up in large concentrations. For example, for HNO_3, concentrations of up to 10 parts per billion by volume (ppbv) are not uncommon in the winter; the largest concentrations of OH (a very reactive radical) ever observed, on the other hand, are approximately 1 ppbv. Since these reservoir molecules are long-lived, they can also undergo appreciable transport. They therefore provide a mechanism by which the 'raw materials' for O_3 destruction can be transported from one region of the stratosphere to another. A complete review of observations of the distribution of source gas, reservoir, and catalytically active compounds has been prepared by the World Meteorological Organization (WMO, 1986).

The stratospheric system, then, is a complex one, whose composition, winds, and temperature are all related. If the amounts of O_3 in the stratosphere changed, ultra-violet heating rates could as well, which would lead to changed stratospheric temperatures. Since winds form in response to temperature gradients, changes in wind fields would also result, and these would then, in turn, affect the transport of O_3 and the chemical source and reservoir species in the stratosphere. The concentration of radical species derived from these species would then change, and these would affect the O_3 distribution, completing a cycle of interconnected physical processes.

The recognition that mankind is dramatically affecting the composition of the Earth's atmosphere has led to substantial interest in stratospheric composition and meteorology in the last 20 years. Changes in temperature due to increasing amounts of carbon dioxide (CO_2, increasing by 0.4%/year) and other greenhouse gases are expected to occur, and there are measurable increases in the amounts of stratospheric hydrogen (due primarily to increasing amounts of CH_4, growing at approximately 1%/year), nitrogen (due to N_2O increasing by 0.2–0.3%/yr), and chlorine and bromine (due to increasing amounts of CFCs and halons). In 1986, the increase in the amounts of the most abundant CFCs was 4%/year, with less abundant ones increasing more rapidly. Annual increases of the most important halons were greater than 10%. Thus, changes in the composition and meteorology of the stratosphere are expected.

Observations of ozone amounts over the last two decades suggest that there have been reductions in ozone amounts. Ground-based measurements (measurement techniques are described in the following section) showed decreases in the total column ozone amount of 1.7 to 3.0% over the period from 1969 to 1986 between 30° and 64° N, with larger decreases occurring in the winter than in the summer. Ground- and satellite-based measurements of ozone at 40 km suggest decreases by 3 and 9% respectively from 1979 to 1986. Much larger decreases in ozone have occurred over the Antarctic in Austral spring (50% decreases in total ozone in October from 1979 to 1987). Stratospheric temperatures in the 45–55 km region have also decreased by approximately 1.7 K since 1979. There have also been increases in the concentrations of certain reservoir molecules, most notably hydrogen chloride (HCl) and hydrogen fluoride (HF). A summary of known changes to atmospheric composition and a review of predictions of future changes in stratospheric O_3 amounts has been prepared recently by Watson, Prather & Kurylo (1988).

In order to understand better the future of the stratosphere, it is important that its current state be understood. If accurate models for stratospheric change are to be developed, models and observations of the current stratosphere need to be validated. Stratospheric science is global in nature, and observations over the entire Earth are needed for a complete understanding of the stratosphere. Remote sensing from satellites provides an important tool for the study of the stratosphere, both because of its global nature and because of the ability of long-duration satellite missions to obtain data over a long enough period of time for the major components of the natural variability of the stratosphere to be observed.

Methodology

A variety of techniques is available for studying the composition and meteorology of the stratosphere. These include *in situ* measurements (made from aircraft, balloons, and rockets) and remote measurements (made from balloon-, ground-, aircraft-, space shuttle-, and satellite-based platforms). Since the emphasis here is on the spatial and temporal variability of the global stratosphere, this section emphasizes those techniques which can best give information about these features. The other techniques are also useful, especially in a 'research mode', in that they help define a climatology of stratospheric composition and dynamics and also provide guidelines for development of future instruments and measuring techniques for these quantities. They can also be important in localized campaigns, such as the recent missions to study the stratosphere in the Antarctic (the Airborne Antarctic Ozone Experiment, AAOE, in August–September 1987) and the Arctic (the Airborne Arctic Stratospheric Expedition, AASE, in January–February, 1989).

In situ measurements

Information about the temperature, winds, and composition of the stratosphere can be obtained by sending instruments into the stratosphere and making direct measurements of the desired quantity in the immediate vicinity of the instrument (*in situ* measurements). Small balloons routinely reach the lower and even the middle stratosphere, but very large balloons and rockets are needed to reach the upper part of the stratosphere. For example, stratospheric temperatures have long been measured with balloon-borne (radiosonde) thermometers. Winds may also be measured by the tracking of balloons. Similarly, the more abundant trace constituents may also be measured. Amounts of O_3 may be measured by chemical techniques, typically with electrochemical sondes (which make use of the oxidation of iodide to iodine accompanied by the reduction of oxygen in ozone). Similarly, H_2O, typically present in the stratosphere at the 2–6 ppmv range, may be observed with balloon-borne frost point hygrometers or by the detection of hydrogen atoms produced in the photolysis of water. Most other stratospheric trace constituents, which are present at the ppbv level, are not well suited for relatively simple *in situ* measurement with on-board analysis. Thus, other techniques must be employed for their measurement, and these must be suitable for frequent use from multiple sites if they are going to be useful in studying trace constituent variability in the stratosphere.

Ground-based remote sensing techniques

Remote sensing techniques appropriate for studying stratospheric composition and meteorology make use of a broad region of the electromagnetic spectrum. The applications of ground-based remote sensing to studies of stratospheric composition and its change with time have been summarized in the National Plan for Stratospheric Monitoring 1988–1997 (Federal Coordinator, 1989).

The best studied of these techniques is the ultra-violet method used for determining the total column amount of O_3 in the atmosphere (Dobson method). This technique uses the fact that O_3 has a series of bands in its ultra-violet absorption spectrum and that by measuring the solar UV radiation transmitted to the surface at several pairs of wavelengths (one close to an absorption maximum, one away from it), the total column amount may be calculated even in the presence of aerosols. A variation of this technique (Umkehr) uses measurement made as the sun sets to determine information about the vertical distribution of O_3 in the stratosphere. These techniques have been used extensively over several decades. In particular, there is a large network of Dobson stations which produces a daily data set of total column ozone distributions and these have been used extensively in studying stratospheric composition and dynamics. For example, the Antarctic Ozone Hole (see following chapter by M. R. Schoeberl) was first observed from the Dobson station at the Halley Bay Station in Antarctica, which is run by the British Antarctic Survey.

Absorption of solar infra-red radiation can be used to determine the total column amount of a large number of stratospheric trace constituents. These include the halides, hydrogen chloride (HCl) and hydrogen fluoride (HF), which are important reservoir species formed on the breakdown of CFCs. The monitoring of increasing concentrations of these molecules is important because it provides a test of atmospheric models which suggest that they should be increasing as CFC amounts increase. Other species studied include H_2O (both normal variety and several of its isotopic variants), various nitrogen-containing compounds (including NO, NO_2, HNO_3, and $ClONO_2$), CH_4, and carbon monoxide (CO), among others. Ultra-violet and visible absorption techniques have been used for several compounds as well, notably NO_2, NO_3, OClO, and OH.

Emission techniques to measure trace constituent amounts from the ground can also be used. Ground-based microwave emission measurements have been used most extensively for ClO, the important active free radical in the chlorine-catalyzed cycle for O_3 destruction, and O_3. Other molecules also observed in this way include the free radical hydroperoxyl (HO_2, a key intermediate in the hydrogen-catalyzed cycle for O_3 destruction), hydrogen peroxide (H_2O_2), and hydrogen cyanide (HCN).

LIDAR (light detection and ranging) techniques have been used recently to determine both the temperature and ozone content of the stratosphere. In these techniques, laser radiation is shot upward into the atmosphere, and information about composition and temperature in the stratosphere is obtained by analyzing the radiation scattered back downward to the ground. Radar techniques (using radio frequencies) can also provide some information about winds in the upper atmosphere; this technique is known as MST radar after the regions of the atmosphere (mesosphere, stratosphere, troposphere) about which it can determine wind velocities.

A disadvantage of all these ground-based techniques is that they are limited to measurements from land areas, which means that the stratosphere above some 70% of the Earth's surface cannot be studied in this way. Many trace constituent measurements are best made from high altitudes (above at least 2 km), further restricting the range of locales from which measurements can be made to mountainous areas. Finally, many of the instruments used for making these measurements are fairly complicated, and require skilled personnel for operation. Thus, it becomes expensive to set up multiple sites with trained personnel making comparable measurements from well-calibrated (and frequently intercompared) instruments.

Satellite-based remote sensing techniques

Satellite-based platforms have been used for the measurements of stratospheric temperature and ozone amounts for more than 20 years. These have been discussed extensively in the book by Houghton *et al.* (1984). Information on stratospheric temperatures is required for weather forecasting, since numerical models are sensitive to what happens near their upper boundaries. The correct treatment of stratospheric meteorology is therefore needed for accurate models to be developed. Space-based measurement of temperature may be nearly global in nature (the exact viewing range depending on the orbit of the satellite and the viewing pattern of the instrument). It can determine temperatures for the full altitude range of the stratosphere and, depending on the instrument, also into the mesosphere (the region of the atmosphere from approximately 50 to 85 km, see Fig. 1). Both infra-red and microwave techniques are used for stratospheric temperature determination. Infra-red techniques usually involve measurement of radiation emitted by vibrationally excited CO_2 molecules, while microwave ones measure radiation emitted by rotationally excited O_2.

Infra-red emission instruments include the Selective Chopper Radiometer (SCR) on Nimbus-4, the Stratospheric Sounding Unit (SSU) and the High Resolution Infra-red Sounder (HIRS) on TIROS N and the series of satellites flown by the National Oceanic and Atmospheric Administration (NOAA) for providing meteorological data, and the Limb Infra-red Monitor of the Stratosphere (LIMS) and Stratospheric And Mesospheric Sounder (SAMS) on Nimbus-7. Microwave instruments include those on the Microwave Sounding Unit (MSU) on the TIROS N and NOAA series satellites. The LIMS and SAMS instruments measured temperature well into the mesosphere as well as in the stratosphere.

O_3 measurements have used an even wider variety of spectral techniques. The first used was an occultation technique, in which O_3 profiles at selected latitudes are determined by measurement of the absorption of visible or ultra-violet light during sunrise and sunset as well as by starlight. This technique is still used today by the Stratospheric Aerosol and Gas Experiment (SAGE) series of instruments. The second of these (SAGE-II) was launched on the Earth Radiation Budget Satellite (ERBS) in October 1984 and is still taking data. The solar occultation technique is particularly attractive in that it is very stable, as it is 'self-calibrating' (each occultation event goes from looking directly at the Sun to looking through the atmosphere, so that a 'baseline' is determined as well). An important limitation of this technique is that it only provides data at limited latitudes, which vary in time depend-

ing on the orbit of the satellite and the position of the Sun.

The largest amount of satellite-based O_3 measurements comes from the Back-scattered Ultra-Violet (BUV) technique. In this method, the ratio of sunlight scattered back to the spacecraft from the Earth–atmosphere system to that incident at the top of the atmosphere (measured by deploying a diffuser plate in the spacecraft) is used to determine ozone amounts. The basic principle is very similar to that used in the ground-based ultra-violet techniques in that pairs of wavelengths on and off absorption maxima are used. This technique only works during daytime. Both total column ozone amounts (the total amount of ozone in a column of air from the surface to the top of the atmosphere) and vertical distribution of ozone in the middle and upper stratosphere have been measured with this technique. Total column ozone was studied with both the Solar Backscattered Ultra-Violet (SBUV) and Total Ozone Mapping Spectrometer (TOMS) instruments on Nimbus-7, while the latter was studied with SBUV instrument. The total column ozone measurements are made with much greater horizontal resolution by the TOMS instrument than the SBUV one, and the TOMS column data have therefore been much more extensively analyzed.

The BUV technique can also be used to infer information about the concentration of other trace species which absorb in the same wavelength region; till now both mesospheric NO and tropospheric sulfur dioxide (SO_2) have been studied in this way. The latter is seen following eruptions of large volcanoes, while the former is seen year-round, but particularly strongly following periods in which the sun produces an uncharacteristically large amount of protons (solar proton events). Correct application of the BUV technique requires correction for the presence of stratospheric aerosols, which are also produced following volcanic eruptions.

Disadvantages of the BUV technique are that it cannot be used at night, including in the polar night, about which there has been much interest following the discovery of the Antarctic ozone hole, and that the diffuser plate used to measure the solar irradiance at the top of the atmosphere can become 'dirty' after years in space as a result of outgassing from plastics and other material in the satellite. Since the changes in the optical characteristics of the diffuser plate over a period of years have been impossible to determine precisely, it has been difficult to extract unambiguous long-term trends solely from the BUV data record. The SBUV-2 instruments now being flown on NOAA satellites have been improved by the addition of an on-board calibration lamp which should allow for improved determination of diffuser plate characteristics and thus long-term trend determination. Also, a shuttle-based version of this instrument (SSBUV) has been flown and will continue to be flown at approximately one-year intervals in the future. Because this instrument may be carefully calibrated in the laboratory between flights, its use should also help in improving absolute accuracy and long-term precision of BUV measurements of O_3 amounts. The program for space-based measurement of ozone outlined here has been presented in more detail in the recently published National Plan for Stratospheric Monitoring (Federal Coordinator, 1989).

The third technique for O_3 measurement which has been used from satellites is that of detection of infra-red emission. This is similar in spirit to that used for temperature described above, both with a 9.6 micron band of O_3 used (radiation measured is from vibrationally excited O_3 instead of CO_2). The technique was used on HIRS and on the LIMS instrument (Gille & Russell, 1984) on Nimbus-7. The LIMS instrument obtained nearly global fields of O_3 (and temperature and other constituents–see below) with good vertical resolution (approximately 2.5 km) throughout the stratosphere and lower mesosphere for a seven-month period in 1978–79. A solid cryogen was used to cool the detector, and after it became depleted the instrument was no longer usable. A related emission technique for measuring upper stratospheric and mesospheric ozone was made by the Solar Mesosphere Explorer (SME) satellite. This measured far infra-red emission at 1.27 microns from electronically excited O_2, produced primarily as a result of the ultra-violet photolysis of O_3 (reaction 3). The inference of O_3 amounts from the radiance at 1.27 microns is somewhat less straightforward than that from 9.6 microns, however.

Concentrations of other stratospheric trace constituents, most notably NO_2, H_2O, HNO_3, CH_4, and N_2O, have been made from satellites as well. The LIMS instrument obtained information about NO_2, H_2O, and HNO_3 by measuring infra-red emission in the 1580–1613, 1396–1527, and 859–900 cm^{-1} wavelength regions, respectively. The SAMS instrument measured amounts of CH_4 and N_2O by measuring infra-red emission at 7.7 microns. NO_2 measurements have been made by visible solar occultation from the SAGE instrument and also from SME, while H_2O amounts have been observed by the SAGE II instrument.

Results

Examples of the spatial dependence of stratospheric temperatures, dynamics, and composition are shown in Fig. 2, in which the zonally averaged temperature (a), zonal wind (b), O_3 mixing ratio (c), and HNO_3 mixing ratio (d) are shown as a function of latitude and altitude for the month of January 1979. These figures were prepared using data from the LIMS instrument on the Nimbus-7 satellite (see previous section). Data cover the latitude range from 64° S to 84° N and the pressure range of 100 to 0.05 mb (approximately 15–70 km above the surface). Where the mesospheric data are available, they are included in the figures to help put the stratospheric measurements into a broader atmospheric perspective.

There are several key features in the temperature distribution (Fig. 2(a)). First, notice the increase in temperature with increasing altitude throughout the stratosphere from very low temperatures (below 200 K, colored black) near the tropical tropopause and the high latitude winter lower stratosphere (200 K at 80° N, 30 mb) to very high temperatures (above 285 K, colored yellow) near the summer stratopause (60° S, 1 mb). Secondly, there is a marked seasonal asymmetry in temperature throughout the stratosphere. For example, at 10 mb (roughly 35 km above the surface) and 60° latitude, the January average temperature is 245 K (dark blue color) in the summer (southern) hemisphere, while it is slightly below 200 K (white color) in the winter (northern) one. Third, one sees that the decrease in temperature with altitude in the mesosphere can be quite strong.

The latitude–altitude cross section of the mean zonal wind (the average around a latitude circle of the wind blowing in an easterly or westerly direction), shown in Fig. 2(b), was not measured by the LIMS instrument but was instead calculated using the geostrophic approximation. This assumes that the force associated with a horizontal pressure gradient in the atmosphere is balanced by the Coriolis force due to the Earth's rotation. This approximation breaks down in the tropics, which is why no wind values are shown there (note the black area, indicating no data, covering all altitudes in the tropics). The major features in the calculated zonal wind are a large westerly jet (shown by the large pink area) reaching speeds of 54 meters per second (m/s) in the northern (winter) hemisphere, centered at 1 mb, and a large region of strong easterlies in the summer (southern) hemisphere, indicated by the white and black areas. The zero wind line is calculated to fall between approximately 10° and 30° N throughout the stratosphere and into the lower mesosphere (green areas represent easterlies, while blue ones represent westerlies). These velocities lead to large-scale longitudinal transport in the stratosphere. A 50 m/s zonal wind corresponds to a value of some 4000 km/day; at 60° N, where the latitude circle is only approximately 20 000 km long, this suggests that the mean wind blows around the whole Earth over a five-day period.

Mixing ratios of O_3 and HNO_3 are shown in Fig. 2(c) and 2(d), respectively. O_3 reaches its maximum mixing ratio (slightly above 9 ppmv, yellow color) near 10 mb and 10° S,

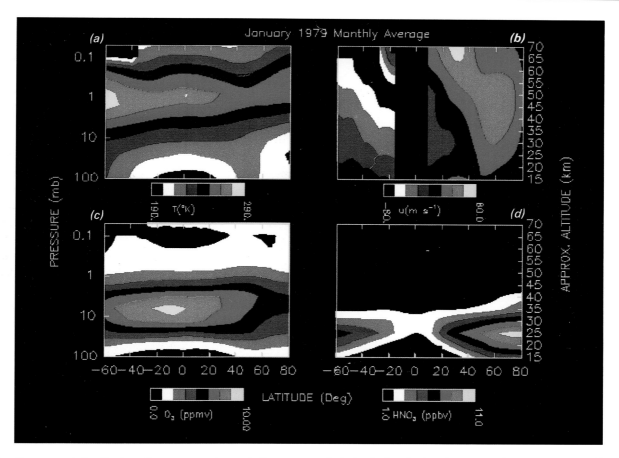

Fig. 2. Zonally averaged distribution of temperature (*a*, top left), mean zonal wind calculated using the geostrophic approximation (*b*, top right), mixing ratio of O₃ (*c*, bottom left), and mixing ratio of HNO₃ (*d*, bottom right) for January 1979 as calculated with data from the LIMS instrument on the Nimbus-7 satellite. Color scheme for each panel is indicated in the corresponding color bar. Note black is used both as color for lowest values and to represent regions of missing data (top left corner of panel (*a*), bar in center of panel (*b*), and area of panel (*d*) above 2 mb).

with reasonably, but not totally, symmetric seasonal (hemispheric) behavior. In the lower stratosphere, O_3 amounts are smaller in the tropics than they are at high latitudes, while in the middle stratosphere, the opposite is true. In the upper stratosphere and lower mesosphere, the largest O_3 mixing ratios are found to occur in the northern mid-latitudes. The origins of these features are a complicated function of both the chemical processes for production and destruction described earlier and of transport processes due to stratospheric winds.

The distribution of HNO_3 is quite different, however, from that of O_3, even though both are chemically long-lived in the lower stratosphere. Maximum HNO_3 mixing ratios (colored yellow) occur in the high latitude low-mid stratosphere (30 mb) with a marked seasonal asymmetry. In the summer (southern) hemisphere, values slightly below 7 ppbv are found, while in the winter (northern) hemisphere, values in

excess of 10 ppbv are observed. HNO_3 has a very strong meridional gradient throughout the lower and middle stratosphere as well as poleward of 50° N. The differing distributions of HNO_3 and O_3, which must arise from differences in their chemical sources and sinks (because both are subject to transport by the same wind fields), will have important effects on how they respond to periods of strong dynamical activity in the stratosphere.

Some sense of the annual cycle in temperature for the stratosphere may be seen in Fig. 3, in which we plot the average temperature throughout the year over locations near Kiruna, Sweden (68° N, 21° E), Nairobi, Kenya (1° S, 37° E), and Lauder, New Zealand (45° S, 71° W) over the time period from 12/1/78 to 11/30/88. These are calculated using the temperature fields produced by the Climate Analysis Center of the National Meteorological Center (NMC) and archived by the Goddard Space Flight Center. The data are

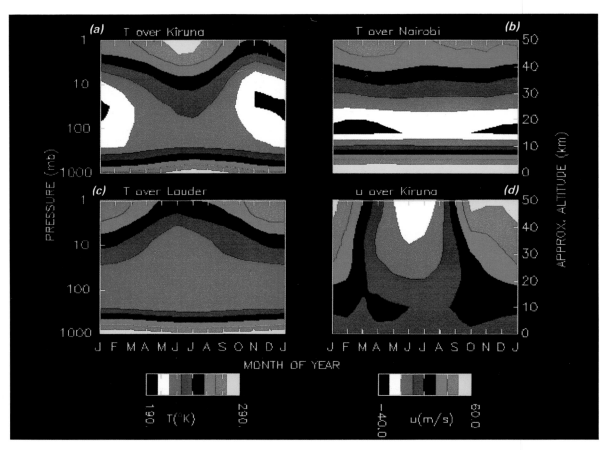

Fig. 3. Annual cycle of monthly averaged temperatures over data grid point closest to Kiruna, Sweden (*a*, top left), Nairobi, Kenya (*b*, top right), and Lauder, New Zealand (*c*, bottom left) averaged over the period 12/1/78–11/30/88 calculated with temperature data from the National Meteorological Center and average monthly mean zonals wind over Kiruna (*d*, bottom right) for this period calculated using the geostrophic approximation. Color bar for temperature is given at lower left while that for wind is at lower right.

archived on a grid of 5 degrees in longitude and 2.5 degrees in latitude, and data shown are for the grid points nearest the indicated locations. Tropospheric data are included for comparison.

A clear annual cycle in stratospheric temperatures is evident in both the Kiruna (Fig. 3(*a*)) and Lauder (Fig. 3(*c*)) data with an annual cycle whose amplitude is approximately 30 K (highest values in the summer). The seasonal variation in the lower stratosphere over Lauder is much smaller than it is over Kiruna (or than it is over Lauder in the upper stratosphere). Note the absence of very low temperatures (white and black colors) in the stratosphere over Lauder. The width of the region of little or no vertical temperature gradient over Lauder is much larger in the winter (June–July) than it is in the summer, while the opposite is true over Kiruna. There is an approximately six month phase shift between the Kiruna and Lauder temperatures, consistent with the shift in seasons between the hemispheres. Very different behavior is observed for the temperatures over Nairobi (Fig. 3(*b*)), however. The

region of minimum temperature is narrower and has little seasonal variation in width or temperature throughout the year. There is also very little variation in temperature anywhere in the stratosphere, even as high as at 1 mb. An example of the high latitude seasonal cycle in the zonal wind is shown for Kiruna in Fig. 3(*d*); the clearest signature is the variation from westerlies (blue, pink, yellow colors) in the stratosphere in the fall and winter to easterlies (white, red, green colors) in the summer.

The annual cycle in total column ozone is shown as a function of latitude and season in Fig. 4. The data in this Figure were obtained by the TOMS instrument on the Nimbus-7 satellite, and represent the average over 10 years of data. Column amounts range from approximately 220 to 460 Dobson units (DU), where 1 DU corresponds to 2.69×10^{16} molecules per square centimeter, or alternatively to the amount of gas which at 1 atmosphere pressure and 273 K would form a layer 0.001 cm thick.

The total column amount of O_3 is a strong function of both

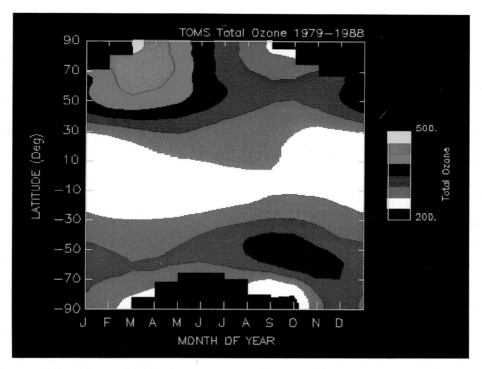

Fig. 4. Latitudinal and seasonal dependence of total column ozone over the period 1979–1988 as measured by the TOMS instrument on Nimbus 7. Color scheme is indicated in the color bar at right. Black indicates both lowest ozone amounts and, more commonly, regions of no data due to absence of sunlight.

latitude and season, as shown in Fig. 4. The largest amounts are observed at high northern latitudes in the late winter and early spring (there are no data at high northern latitudes during much of winter because those regions are in darkness then and, as pointed out above, the BUV technique only works where there is sunlight). The smallest amounts (small region of black color at right end of the regions in which there are no data, which also are represented in black) are observed in October in the Antarctic; small amounts (colored white) are also observed in the tropics over much of the year. The amplitude of the annual cycle in total ozone is quite large (some 200 DU) at high northern latitudes but is much smaller in the tropics. There are important differences between the ozone distribution between the Northern and Southern Hemispheres as well. In particular, the highest amounts of ozone in the Northern Hemisphere occur at the highest latitudes in late winter and spring, while in the Southern Hemisphere they occur away from the pole (closer to about 55° S) in the spring (October–November). One important aspect of ozone distributions at high latitudes in the Southern Hemisphere spring is the Antarctic ozone hole described in the following chapter.

The spatial and temporal variability of temperature, winds, and trace constituent composition in the stratosphere may be studied by looking at particular examples from the winter of

1979, when the LIMS instrument on Nimbus-7 returned information. Attention is focussed on a constant pressure surface at 30 mb (corresponding approximately to 24 km above the Earth's surface). On this surface, constituents such as O_3 and HNO_3 are long lived and should serve as good tracers of stratospheric motion. An example of a more or less typical undisturbed winter day is January 15, 1979. On this day, there was a large cold polar vortex centered more or less over the north pole (see Fig. 5(a)) with a region of warm temperature (the Aleutian anti-cyclone), indicated by the pink area, centered off the Kamchatka Peninsula. In the Northern Hemisphere, wind fields tend to blow clockwise around a high pressure region and counterclockwise around a low pressure region on a constant altitude surface, and, in many cases (including this one) this corresponds to clockwise motion around high temperatures and counterclockwise motion around low temperatures on a constant pressure surface. This may be seen in Fig. 5(b), in which the zonal (east–west) component of the wind is plotted. Positive values (green, blue, pink colors) imply westerly winds (blowing from west to east). It is seen that westerly winds are observed in most locations poleward of 30° N, with velocities of above 60 m/s being found over western Siberia and above 70 m/s near Hudson Bay in Canada. Easterlies, as seen by the red areas, occur almost completely only south of 30 degrees N.

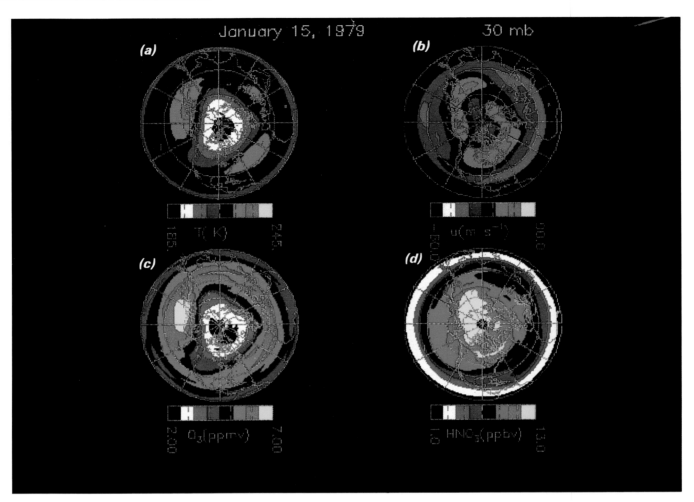

Fig. 5. Distribution on the 30 mb pressure surface for 1/15/79 of temperature (*a*, top left), zonal mean wind calculated with the geostrophic approximation (*b*, top right), mixing ratio of O$_3$ (*c*, bottom left), and mixing ratio of HNO$_3$ (*d*, bottom right). Color scheme for each panel is indicated in the accompanying color bar. Black is used both to indicate lowest values and for regions of no data. The same color schemes are used in Figs. 6 and 7.

The ozone distribution reflects this nearly symmetric pole-centered vortex accompanied by a well-defined Aleutian anti-cyclone, as may be seen in Fig. 5(*c*). Low ozone amounts (shown in black and white) are found near the pole (mixing ratios below 3 ppmv), while high values (pink and yellow colors) are found (greater than 6 ppmv) near the Kamchatka Peninsula. For HNO$_3$ one similarly sees in Fig. 5(*d*) high values (greater than 10 ppbv, shown in yellow) throughout much of the polar region. In addition, the region of high meridional gradient (transition from white to blue) is more or less zonally symmetric, except over the North Atlantic ocean, where there is a small region of strong gradient over which the mixing ratio changes from about 7 to 10 ppbv.

During the winter of 1979 there were two so-called 'strato-spheric warming events' in which unusually warm tem-peratures were observed at high latitudes in the Northern

Hemisphere and there was a shift of the prevailing winds away from their normal westerly sense. The first of these, which occurred in late January, was associated with the motion of the vortex well off the pole and the formation of an unusually large and warm Aleutian anticyclone. This may be seen in Fig. 6(*a*), in which the temperature distribution at the 30 mb pressure level on January 25, 1979 is shown. The contrast with January 15, 1979 is quite striking. For example, on January 25, the region of lowest temperature (white region) at 30 mb includes most of Scandinavia, which was at least 10 degrees cooler than it had been ten days earlier. On the other hand, the temperature over northern Greenland increased during those ten days by up to 20 degrees, as evidenced by the color change in that region from black to red.

The wind fields shifted enormously as well (Fig. 6(*b*)).

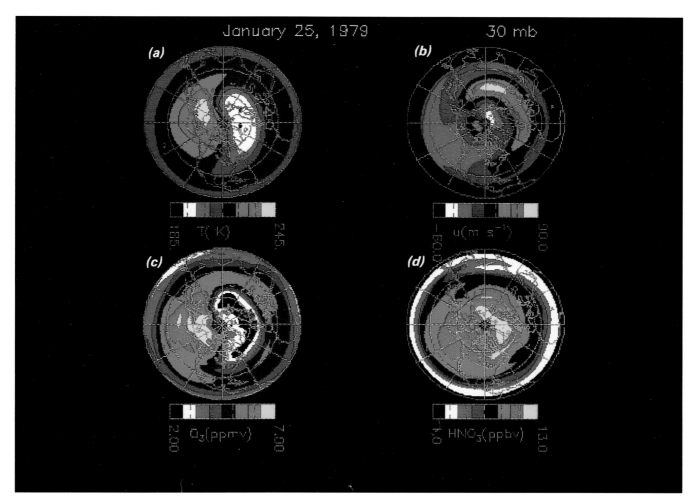

Fig. 6. As Fig. 5 but 1/25/79.

There were regions of strong westerlies (pink and yellow areas) over Siberia and the north Atlantic Ocean, but there were also regions of easterlies (red and white areas) inside the Arctic circle and also over much of North America and the Pacific Ocean (red areas); these latter ones were associated with the clockwise motion around the well-developed Aleutian anticyclone.

The constituent distributions reflected this asymmetric vortex. On January 25, 1979, the lowest O_3 mixing ratios (black areas) were now found along the northern coast of Russia near Scandinavia (Fig. 6(c)), but low values are seen also over southern Scandinavia and the British Isles, as well as off the coast of northeastern Canada. High values of ozone are seen over Alaska as well as over the northern Pacific as was seen on January 15. The HNO_3 distribution (Fig. 6(d)) also changed. One major change was the formation of a region of low mixing ratios (light blue color) over the Arctic Ocean north of Alaska, where the values had been larger

earlier in the month. There was also an increase in HNO_3 values over the eastern United States, as shown by the change in color of the Gulf Coast region from green (Fig. 5(d)) to light blue (Fig. 6(d)). Changes are seen even equatorward of 30° N. Note also the formation of kinks in the HNO_3 contours (blue, green, red, and white colors) between approximately 80 and 130° E over southeast Asia. Such kinks were far less conspicuous on January 15 (see Fig. 4(d)).

A very different situation occurred in late February, when a strong stratospheric warming event occurred. In this event, the zonal mean winds over much of the high northern latitudes reversed themselves completely from westerly to easterly. For example, at 60° N, zonal mean easterlies of up to 25 m/s were calculated geostrophically at 5 mb at the end of February; 10 days earlier westerlies of approximately 20 m/s were calculated for that location.

The meteorology of the situation may be seen in Fig. 7(a), in which the 30 mb temperature distribution on February 22,

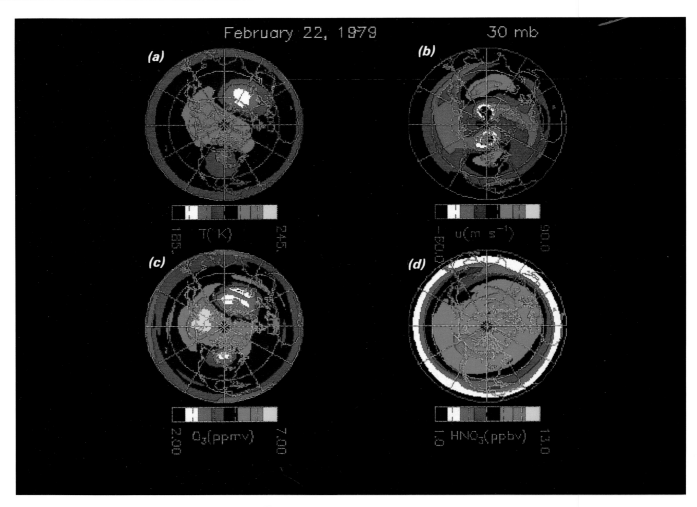

Fig. 7. As for Fig. 5 but 2/22/79.

1979 is shown. On this day, the polar vortex has split, with two lows, a strong one (colored red and white) centered approximately over central Russia and a weaker one (the small region of red) centered over central Canada. The Aleutian anticyclone has been distorted to cover much of the area inside the Arctic circle, with temperatures above 230 K (pink color) observed above much of Greenland and also northwestern Siberia. The effect of this temperature distribution on the zonal wind field is shown in Fig. 7(b). This split vortex produced strong easterlies (white and black regions) inside much of the Arctic circle; velocities of some 60 m/s were calculated over longitudes in both the Western and Eastern Hemispheres. Weaker easterlies (red areas) were found for considerably lower latitudes over the Pacific Ocean. Strong westerlies (light blue and pink regions) are still calculated for lower latitudes over continental North America and central Asia.

The split nature of the vortex is also reflected in the O_3

distribution (Fig. 7(c)). Low O_3 values (red and white regions) centered over both northern Canada and central Russia are observed, with high values (pink and yellow areas) over the western tip of the Soviet Union and also western Greenland. HNO_3 values (Fig. 7(d)) reflect the split vortex less clearly. There are regions of high mixing ratios (pink) over the northern Pacific Ocean and east of Greenland, similar to those observed for O_3, but there are several other small highs as well. There is an increase in the mixing ratio over southern Europe and the Mediterranean Sea, a region of lower mixing ratios earlier (color change from dark to light blue between Figs. 6(d) and 7(d)). The kink in the mixing ratio distribution over southeast Asia has also been magnified and moved northward and eastward.

The existence of spatially well-defined but evolving structures in stratospheric temperatures, winds, and composition means that there can be substantial day-to-day variability in these quantities above a particular location on Earth. Further,

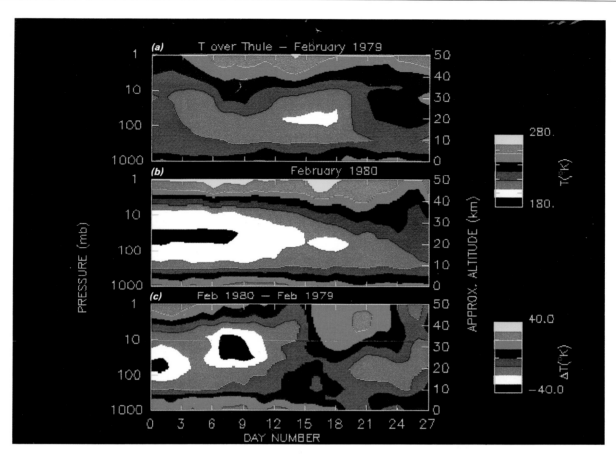

Fig. 8. Temperature distribution over data grid point closest to Thule, Greenland during February 1979 (*a* top) and 1980 (*b* center) as a function of time of the month and the difference 1980–1979 (*c*, bottom). Color scheme for panels (*a*) and (*b*) is given on the upper right, while that for panel (*c*) is at the lower left.

since strong dynamical features which produce distorted fields such as those shown in Figs. 6 and 7 are not everywhere reproducible from year to year, substantial year-to-year variability in these quantities is expected as well.

As an example, consider the temperature above Thule, Greenland (76° N, 68° W) in the month of February. In Fig. 8 we plot the temperature as a function of altitude and day number for February 1979 (*a*) and February 1980 (*b*), together with the difference between the two (1980–1979, (*c*)). Although there is a broad similarity between the two years, numerous important differences exist as well. In 1979 (Fig. 8(*a*)) the dominant feature is a strong warming in the lower and middle stratosphere occurring between about 2/18 and 2/22 as seen by the color change from white to dark blue; a temperature increase in excess of 20 K was observed. An increase of similar magnitude was observed earlier in the month in the middle stratosphere, followed by cooling a few days later. The lowest temperatures observed during the month were below 205 K between 2/14 and 2/19 (white region). In 1980 (Fig. 8(*b*)), on the other hand, there were no

rapid changes in temperature; instead, there was a gradual warming over the lower and middle stratosphere throughout the month as seen by the color change from white to blue. The lowest temperatures occurred early in the month (2/3–2/8) and have values below 190 K. The differences between the two years (Fig. 8(*c*)) were quite large, ranging from more than 35 degrees cooler in 1980 (2/9, 10 mb) to 25 degrees warmer in 1980 (2/21, 2 mb). We thus see that temperatures measured during a particular time one year may not be at all appropriate to the following year in the winter at high latitudes (in other locations and seasons, the day-to-day differences and inter-annual variability will be considerably smaller).

There are a number of other types of variability which affect stratospheric temperatures, winds, and trace constituent compositions, although these are typically weaker than the seasonal and meteorological variability discussed above. One of the more unusual of these is the so-called quasi-biennial oscillation (QBO), which is an approximately 26-month long alternation in the shift of the zonal winds in the tropical lower stratosphere. A more or less regular pattern of shifts between easterlies and westerlies is observed there. This has been shown to have an effect both on the temperature and on the total ozone distribution. For example, in the Tropics one typically finds a difference of approximately 10 DU between the total ozone column in the easterly and westerly phases of the QBO (smaller amounts are observed during periods of easterlies than during westerlies). At higher latitudes, on the other hand, the opposite is true; higher ozone amounts are associated with easterly winds in the tropics. The QBO-O_3 connection and, in particular, its effect at high latitudes has recently been reviewed by Lait, Schoeberl & Newman (1989). There is also some evidence from balloon measurements that the QBO may have an effect on stratospheric water vapor amounts.

Changes in temperature and trace constituent distribution can also be associated with changes in solar output. The Sun has an approximately 11 year solar cycle, in which there is a fairly regular variation in the flux of ultra-violet photons from the Sun. Calculations suggest that during solar maximum there should be slightly more ozone (averaged over the Earth's surface) than during solar minimum. The difference in globally averaged ozone amounts between solar maximum and solar minimum is calculated to be on the order of 0.5–2%. This difference is similar in magnitude (but slightly smaller) than the decrease in total ozone measured in recent years, demonstrating the importance of determining the smaller natural variabilities if one is to understand anthropogenically induced ozone changes. The solar cycle–ozone connection has been described in the recent report by Watson *et al.* (1988).

Changes in stratospheric composition can also occur in response to dramatic changes in solar radiation, notably solar proton events (SPEs), in which the Sun emits an atypically large flux of protons for brief periods of time. Because of the Earth's magnetic field, the effects of charged particle precipitation are felt most strongly in the polar regions. During SPEs, O_3 changes in excess of 25% have been observed; these are usually largest when the Sun is close to the horizon with O_3 loss due to chemical processes being quite small. The altitude at which this O_3 loss occurs depends on the energies of the protons emitted in the SPE; higher energy protons penetrate deeper into the atmosphere and produce effects lower down. Strongest effects typically occur in the topmost part of the stratosphere and the lower mesosphere. The mechanism by which SPEs produce O_3 depletion involves the production of hydrogen-containing or nitrogen-containing free radicals as a result of ion–molecule reactions (the ions are produced by collisions of protons with atmospheric molecules). Direct confirmation of increases in nitric oxide (NO)

following the SPE of 13 July, 1982 have been made with the SBUV instrument on Nimbus-7. The effect of SPEs on atmospheric composition has been reviewed by Jackman and McPeters (1987).

The possibility also exists that major volcanic eruptions can have important effects on stratospheric trace constituent composition. It is certain that such eruptions can directly inject constituents into the stratosphere; clear evidence of SO_2 and HCl injections exists. An effect on O_3 has also been reported. Satellite measurements made by the SBUV instrument as well as ground-based Dobson measurements show strong evidence of O_3 decreases following the eruption of the El Chichón volcano in 1982 (this was a particularly strong eruption which injected an unusually large volume of material directly into the stratosphere). Observations and models of the effects of the El Chichón eruption on stratospheric chemistry and temperature have been reviewed by Michelangeli, Allen & Yung (1989).

Future applications

Satellite-based remote sensing is to play an increasingly important role in studying the meteorology and composition of the stratosphere in the years ahead. There are three major missions which will provide new data in the coming years; these are summarized below.

Future TOMS, SBUV flights and shuttle-based measurements

The TOMS instrument on the Nimbus-7 satellite has been producing daily global maps of the total column ozone distribution for more than 14 years now. This is well beyond the planned life-time of the instrument, so plans are being made for new TOMS instruments to be flown in the future. One is part of a Soviet satellite (TOMS-METEOR) launched in 1991, a second is to be launched by NASA, and a third is to be part of a Japanese satellite (TOMS-ADEOS) scheduled for launch in 1996. This set of spacecraft will assure the future availability of the daily total ozone maps which have proved to be so useful in studying a variety of questions in atmospheric chemistry and dynamics (especially in high latitude ozone depletion as discussed in the next chapter).

NOAA will continue to have improved versions of the BUV instruments on its operational meteorological satellites, which will provide information about the vertical distribution of stratospheric O_3 (but with much lower horizontal resolution than obtained by the TOMS instruments). NASA are also making periodic flights of the shuttle-borne version of this instrument (SSBUV) to allow for improved calibration of the

SBUV-2 instruments. The BUV-type instruments should help especially in understanding O_3 changes in the 40 km region of the atmosphere, where response to increases in chlorine is expected to be largest.

SSBUV flights are made as part of a package of instruments (the Atmospheric Laboratory for Applications and Science, or ATLAS, project) making observations of the atmosphere (NASA, 1989). These also include a number of instruments studying atmospheric composition and solar radiation. One of great relevance to the stratosphere is the atmospheric trace molecule spectroscopy (ATMOS) instrument, which measures infra-red absorption at occultation. It flew previously on the NASA Space Shuttle in May 1985 and provided a wealth of information about the vertical distribution of a variety of atmospheric trace constituents (see for example Russell *et al.*, 1988). Another ATLAS instrument of relevance to the stratosphere is the millimeter wave atmospheric sounder (MAS) instrument, which measures O_3 and H_2O in the stratosphere and mesosphere and ClO from 30–45 km using microwave emission techniques. The ATLAS payload flew on the Space Shuttle in March, 1992, and is scheduled to fly again in March, 1993, and October, 1994.

The upper atmosphere research satellite (UARS)

The Upper Atmosphere Research Satellite (UARS) is a NASA satellite that was launched in September 1991. This satellite has six instruments designed to measure temperature, composition, and winds in the stratosphere and above. UARS provides the most complete set of observations of the stratosphere ever produced. These are described in more detail in a report edited by Reber (1985). The instruments included on UARS are the following:

1. *Cryogenic Limb Array Etalon Spectrometer (CLAES).* This is an infra-red emission spectrometer (very much in the spirit of the LIMS instrument on Nimbus-7) which uses a solid cryogen for detector cooling, and as a result is planned for only a 20-month lifetime. Trace constituents measured by CLAES include O_3, NO, NO_2, N_2O, HNO_3, N_2O_5, H_2O, CH_4, $CFCl_3$, CF_2Cl_2, $CFCl_3$, and $ClONO_2$. The CLAES also measures temperature in the stratosphere and lower mesosphere.

2. *Improved Stratospheric And Mesospheric Sounder (ISAMS).* This is an improved version of the SAMS instrument which also flew on Nimbus-7. It uses a mechanical refrigerator for detector cooling, and as a result does not have a limited design life-time. Spe-

cies to be measured include O_3, NO, NO_2, N_2O, HNO_3, N_2O_5, H_2O, CH_4, and CO. It has also measured temperature in the stratosphere and mesosphere.

3. *Microwave Limb Sounder (MLS).* This is a microwave emission spectrometer that measures O_3, H_2O, and ClO in the stratosphere; it also measures O_3 and H_2O in the mesosphere.

4. *Halogen Occultation Experiment (HALOE).* This is an infra-red absorption measuring experiment which only takes data at occultations (sunrises, sunsets) and as a result only obtains data at two latitudes per day (instead of the more global coverage obtained by the three instruments above). Since the UARS satellite is in an inclined orbit, the viewing region of the HALOE instrument moves with time, so that HALOE has global coverage of the stratosphere after a sufficient time period. Species measured with HALOE include O_3, NO, NO_2, H_2O, CH_4, HCl, and HF.

5. *High Resolution Doppler Interferometer (HRDI).* This instrument makes measurements of temperature and horizontal wind components in much of the stratosphere and most of the mesosphere (with a gap in the upper stratosphere). It works by measuring the Doppler shift (the perceived wavelength change when the source of an emission is moving with respect to the observer) of scattered sunlight in the stratosphere and airglow emissions in the mesosphere.

6. *Wind Imaging Interferometer (WINDII).* This instrument makes measurements of temperature and horizontal winds in the thermosphere. It does this by measuring Doppler widths and shifts of spectral lines emitted by airglow and aurora.

In addition, there are other instruments, including two which measure the flux of ultra-violet solar radiation into the Earth's atmosphere and one which measures the flux of X-rays and charged particles into the atmosphere. By having solar UV and particle flux simultaneous with the temperature, constituent, and wind measurements, better understanding of the interrelationships of these quantities should become possible.

The Earth Observing System (EOS)

The next major flight project planned to study the Earth's upper atmosphere is the Earth Observing System (EOS). This is being planned as a multi-platform mission extending over 15 years, with instruments on each available to study numerous aspects of the whole 'Earth system' including the solid earth, the oceans, ice, and the atmosphere. The first American platform is scheduled for deployment in 1998 with an additional one in 2000. Copies of these platforms would then be reflown at two successive five-year intervals. There will also be other platforms produced by other agencies; in particular, one being produced by the European Space Agency is expected to have several instruments measuring stratospheric temperature, and composition.

A number of candidate instruments, described more fully in the EOS Reference Document (EOS, 1989) for the NASA platforms, will make measurements of the stratosphere. The candidate instruments (final payload selection is yet to be made) of most interest to the stratosphere include:

1. *High Resolution Dynamics Limb Sounder (HIRDLS)*. This will be an infra-red emission instrument (similar again to LIMS and SAMS) but will have the capability to scan in the horizontal direction instead of just making one vertical profile measurement per latitude range as the satellite moves along its orbit. As a result, HIRDLS will provide high spatial resolution about the distribution of temperature, trace constituent (O_3, HNO_3, N_2O, NO_2, CH_4, $CFCl_3$, CF_2Cl_2, N_2O_5, $ClONO_2$, and H_2O), and aerosol amounts in the stratosphere.

2. *Microwave Limb Sounder (MLS)*. This instrument will be an improved version of the version planned for UARS (see above). It will make measurements of atmospheric temperature throughout the stratosphere and mesosphere and even into the lower thermosphere (up to about 100 km). Constituents to be measured include O_3, NO, NO_2, HNO_3, N_2O, HO_2, H_2O, H_2O_2, ClO, HCl, $HOCl$, $OClO$, CH_3Cl, BrO, HCN, and SO_2.

3. *Spectroscopy of the Atmosphere using Far Infra-red Emission (SAFIRE)*. This instrument will measure infra-red and far infra-red emission. By extending the previous infra-red emission technique (used on LIMS and SAMS) into the far infra-red (80–390 cm^{-1}), information about a number of trace constituents difficult to study in the past may be obtained. Constituents to be observed by SAFIRE (in addition to temperature) include O_3, $^{50}O_3$, $O(^3P)$, OH, HO_2, H_2O_2, H_2O, HDO, CH_4, NO_2, HNO_3, N_2O_5, HCl, $HOCl$, HBr, and HF. Particularly important is the ability to observe the free radicals OH and HO_2 which are central to the hydrogen-catalyzed destruction of O_3.

4. *Stratospheric aerosol and gas experiment III (SAGE III)*. This is an improved version of the SAGE II instrument currently being flown. It will again measure aerosols, O_3, NO_2, and H_2O in the stratosphere. It will also have the capability to study lunar occultations; these may be used to determine amounts of stratospheric NO_3 (a constituent nearly completely absent in daytime due to its rapid photolysis), and $OClO$ where its concentrations are large.

5. *Tropospheric emission spectrometer (TES)*. Although this instrument is primarily to measure trace constituent composition in the troposphere, it will also provide substantial information about the chemical composition of the lower stratosphere. Constituents to be studied in the stratosphere include O_3, CO, N_2O, H_2O, NO, HNO_3, and CH_4.

In addition to these instruments, there will be numerous instruments measuring temperature, O_3, solar radiation, radiation from the Earth's surface, and particle flux into the atmosphere. As in the case of UARS, the simultaneous measurement of these quantities with temperatures, winds, and composition should help in improving our understanding of the role the atmosphere plays in the whole Earth system.

Summary and conclusions

Space-based remote sensing has played an important role in defining the climatology of stratospheric temperatures and trace constituent amounts. From measured temperatures, information about wind fields has been derived as well. Satellite data show that there is important variability in stratospheric temperature, winds, and trace constituent composition on a variety of spatial scales, including seasonal cycles, short-term planetary-scale meteorological variability, and several others (the quasi-biennial oscillation, solar cycles, response to solar proton events and volcanic eruptions). These natural variabilities need to be understood if accurate measurement of anthropogenically induced trends in stratospheric ozone, temperature, and other trace constituents are to be unambiguously determined. Satellite-based studies of the stratosphere are to continue in this decade with the recent launch of a second TOMS instrument to study O_3 distributions and the launch of UARS. They will continue in the next century with the EOS program. With these data, a good global picture of any changes in the stratosphere in response to human influence (global warming, O_3 depletion, etc.) should become clear.

References

Bower, F. A. & Ward, R. B. eds. (1982). *Stratospheric Ozone and Man* (2 volumes), CRC Press, Boca Raton, Florida.

Brasseur, G. & Solomon, S. (1984). *Aeronomy of the Middle Atmosphere*, Reidel Publ., Boston, Mass.

EOS Program and Project Office (1989). *Eos Reference Information, 1989*, NASA/Goddard Space Flight Center, Greenbelt, Maryland, 1989.

Federal Coordinator for Meteorological Services and Supporting Research (1988). *National Plan for Stratospheric Monitoring 1988–1997*, Report FCM-P17-1988, US Department of Commerce, Washington, DC.

Gille, J. C. & Russell III, J. M. (1984). The limb infra-red monitor of the stratosphere: experiment description, performance and results. *J. Geophys. Res.*, **84**, 5125–40.

Houghton, J. T., Taylor, F. W. & Rodgers, C. D. (1984). *Remote Sounding of Atmospheres*, Cambridge Univ. Press, London.

Jackman, C. H. & McPeters, R. D. (1984). Solar proton events as tests for the fidelity of middle atmosphere models. *Physica Scripta*, **T18**, 309–16.

Lait, L. R., Schoeberl, M. R. & Newman, P. A. (1989). Quasi-biennial modulation of the Antarctic ozone depletion, *J. Geophys. Res.*, **94**, 11, 559–71.

Makhijani, A., Makhijani, A. & Bickel, A. (1988) *Saving Our Skins: Technical Potential and Policies for the Elimination of Ozone-Depleting Chlorine Compounds*, Environmental Policy Institute and Institute for Energy and Environmental Research, Takoma Park, Maryland.

Michelangeli, D. V., Allen M. & Yung, Y. L. (1989). El Chichón volcanic aerosols: impact of radiative, thermal, and chemical perturbation, *J. Geophys. Res.*, **94**, 18, 429–43.

NASA (1989). *ATLAS Spacelab*: Research to Understand our Earth, our Sun, our Atmosphere, NASA Marshall Space Flight Center, Alabama.

Reber, C. A. (1985). *Upper Atmosphere Research Satellite (UARS) Mission*, NASA/GSFC Report 430–1003–001, Greenbelt, Maryland.

Russell, J. M. III, Farmer, C. B., Rinsland, C. P., Zander, R., Froidevaux, L., Toon, G. C., Gao, B., Shaw, J. & Gunson, M. (1988). Measurement of odd nitrogen compounds in the stratosphere by the ATMOS experiment on Spacelab 7. *J. Geophys. Res.*, **93**, 1718–36.

Schoeberl, M. R. (1987). 'Meteorology, stratospheric' in *Encyclopedia of Physical Science and Technology*, vol. 8, pp. 261–80, Academic Press, Orlando, Florida.

Shimazaki, T. (1985). *Minor Constituents in the Middle Atmosphere*, Reidel Publ., Boston, Mass.

US Standard Atmosphere (1976). NOAA-S/T 76–1562, Superintendent of Documents, Washington, DC.

Watson, R. T., Prather, M. J. & Kurylo, M. J. eds. (1988). *Present State of Knowledge of the Upper Atmosphere 1988: An Assessment Report*, NASA Ref. Publ. 1208, Washington, DC.

Wayne, R. P. (1985). *Chemistry of Atmospheres*, Oxford Univ. Press (Clarendon), London.

WMO (1986). *Atmospheric Ozone, 1985*, WMO Report 16, Geneva, Switzerland.

Stratospheric ozone depletion

MARK R. SCHOEBERL

Introduction

Few changes in the global environment have excited as much concern as the unexpected appearance of the Antarctic spring ozone depletion or 'ozone hole'. The ozone hole phenomenon was first noticed by Farman *et al.* (Farman, Gardiner & Shanklin, 1985) in the ground-based total ozone measurements taken at Halley Bay Station on the Antarctic coast. These measurements were subsequently confirmed by satellite.

Large changes in the total column of ozone imply ozone loss in the lower stratosphere (10–30 km). At the time the ozone hole was discovered, stratospheric scientists were expecting anthropogenic ozone loss to take place first in the upper stratosphere (30–50 km) so the signal in total column ozone would be weak. Thus the spring depletion in Antarctic ozone was a major surprise.

An important contribution to understanding the Antarctic ozone hole has come from the total ozone observations made by the Total Ozone Mapping Spectrometer (TOMS) on board the polar orbiting Nimbus-7, launched in November 1978. At this writing, TOMS has made over 4100 daily maps of the global total ozone distribution and the instrument is still in operation eleven years beyond its planned life-time. Not only has this instrument been valuable in understanding the Antarctic ozone hole, but it has been used to map out non-polar changes in the ozone layer (Report of International Ozone Trends Panel, 1988) as well.

The TOMS instrument

The TOMS instrument measures ultra-violet sunlight back-scattered from clouds or the ground to measure the total ozone amount. Thus the instrument cannot measure night time ozone or make measurements in the winter polar darkness. The TOMS instrument consists of a single monochronometer which scans through the subsatellite point perpendicular to the orbital plane. Back-scattered sunlight is sampled sequentially at six ultra-violet (UV) wavelengths from 312.5 nm to 380 nm. The UV absorption of ozone varies significantly over these wavelengths. Thus, the total amount

of ozone between a scattering surface (the ground or a cloud) and the satellite can be determined by comparing the UV intensity at these wavelengths. Six wavelengths (three pairs) are used for redundancy.

In-flight calibration of TOMS is attempted through the use of a diffuser plate. This plate is deployed so that the instrument can measure the solar UV directly as a reference for the detectors. The diffuser plate is used since the detectors would saturate if they sampled the direct solar beam. In principle, all the instrument drifts can be removed once a direct solar measurement is made. However, contamination of the diffuser plate can change its reflectivity and lead to an apparent instrument drift. Reduced reflectivity of the diffuser plate (beyond that expected) means that the back-scattered UV radiation reaching the spacecraft from Earth will thus 'seem' brighter compared to the diffuser plate reflected radiation. This would incorrectly suggest a decrease in the ozone amount between the surface and the spacecraft.

The Ozone Trends Panel (1988) carefully examined the calibration of the TOMS instrument and the solar backscatter ultra-violet instrument (SBUV) on Nimbus-7 which uses the same diffuser plate. After comparison to ozone measurements made by the Stratospheric Aerosol and Gas Experiment I and II (SAGE I and II) and the ground based Dobson total ozone network, trends of decreasing global ozone estimated by TOMS were found to be too large by roughly a factor of two. The diffuser plate was evidently darkening at a faster rate than expected.

To adjust for diffuser plate changes, a new calibration scheme has been recently developed. This scheme examines the changes in the diffuser plate at the different UV wavelengths used by TOMS. The new TOMS Version 6 data is now in very good agreement with the Dobson network data (Herman *et al.* 1991).

Analysis

Seasonal cycle of ozone

Total ozone on a seasonal timescale is controlled by both the transport of ozone within the stratosphere and photochemical

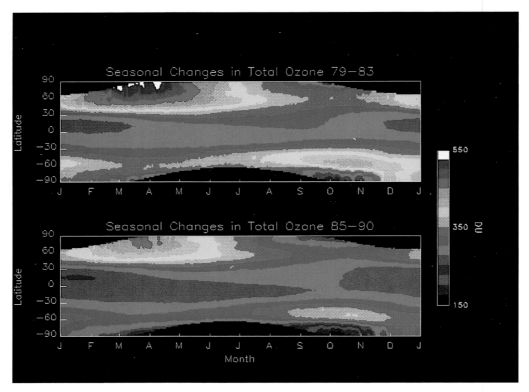

Fig. 1. The zonal mean seasonal cycle from TOMS observations. Units are Dobson Units or atmosphere cm of ozone. Dark areas indicate regions of polar darkness where the instrument cannot measure. Part a, 1979–1983 average; part b, 1985–1990 average.

processes. There is net ozone production in the tropical upper stratosphere. This ozone is transported poleward and downward, particularly in late winter. In the lower stratosphere, the lifetime of ozone is long during the spring and winter, so as ozone is transported downward it begins to build up at high latitudes. The transition from winter to summer circulation in the stratosphere dramatically slows the build-up of ozone and the summer total ozone decreases due to increased photochemical destruction.

Fig. 1, top, shows the zonal mean seasonal cycle of total ozone averaged for 1979–1983. Late winter, polar build-ups of total ozone are seen in both hemispheres with roughly a six-month seasonal difference. However, the build-up in the Northern Hemisphere is greater and more poleward than the build-up in the Southern Hemisphere. Also the Northern Hemisphere increase in ozone takes place in late winter (January–April) while the Southern Hemisphere increase takes place in June–November. The differences between the two hemispheres are somewhat surprising and are thought to result from the relative lack of planetary wave activity in the Southern Hemisphere stratosphere. In the stratosphere, it is the planetary waves, forced by the continents and oceanic thermal sources, which are responsible for most of the north–south transport of ozone and heat. Since the Southern Hemi-

sphere lacks the significant orographic features found in the Northern Hemisphere, such as the Himalayan Plateau, planetary wave activity is weaker. Thus the winter Antarctic stratosphere is on the average more than 10 K colder than the Arctic stratosphere, the Antarctic polar vortex lasts longer, and the winter build-up of ozone is weaker. It is, in fact, these differences which have allowed the more rapid development of the ozone hole in the Antarctic stratosphere rather than the Arctic.

Fig. 1, bottom, shows the seasonal cycle averaging years 1985–1989. The ozone hole can be seen to form at the end of the winter dark period in the Southern Hemisphere. No ozone hole is evident at the end of the Northern Hemisphere winter.

The Antarctic ozone hole

The Antarctic ozone hole develops with the return of spring sunlight to the south polar stratosphere. The total ozone amount, which has stayed relatively constant during the winter dark period, begins to decline in early September and continues to decline until about the end of the first week in October. In 1987 and 1989 about half of the total column of ozone over Antarctica was lost during this period (Krueger *et*

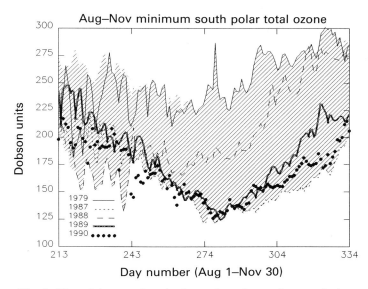

Fig. 2. The minimum values in Antarctic spring total ozone during the Antarctic spring season for the years 1979, 1987, 1988 and 1990. The range of values recorded for other years is indicated by the cross hatching.

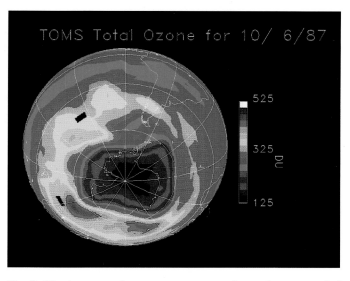

Fig. 3. The lowest total ozone amount ever observed was recorded for October 6, 1987 at the height of the 1987 ozone depletion. The satellite map shows the extent of the ozone hole for that day.

al., 1988). Balloon ozonesondes show that virtually all of the ozone disappears from the region between (about) 12 and 26 km at this time (Hoffman *et al.*, 1989).

Fig. 2 shows the change in the minimum amount of total ozone over Antarctica from TOMS from August through November for 1979, 1987, 1988, and 1989. (The satellite cannot 'see' to the pole until after the equinox as shown in Fig. 1, so August values are from the edge of the continent.) The range of values for other years is also shown. The figure clearly indicates the rapid decrease in column ozone in September. After the minimum value is reached, usually in the first two weeks of October, ozone increases at first slowly then more rapidly. This is the period when the south polar vortex begins to break up. Ozone is mixed in from low latitudes and above, increasing the total. The polar vortex has usually completely dissipated by December and the stratosphere reverts to a summer-time circulation.

Fig. 2 also shows the remarkable differences between the years 1987, 1988 and 1989 as far as ozone hole development. This difference is not unexpected considering the conditions required for the development of the ozone hole as discussed below.

The area of the largest ozone hole (1987) was about 5% of the area of the Southern Hemisphere. Fig. 3 shows an orthographic projection of the ozone hole near the peak of the depletion of 1987. The hole is sharply bounded by a steep ozone gradient. The region defined by the ozone hole is roughly coincident with the coldest regions of the Antarctic stratosphere where polar stratospheric clouds (PSC's) form

(McCormick, Trepte & Pitts, 1989). PSCs are of two types: Type I is the nitric acid trihydrate, which forms at about $-78\,°C$. Type II PSC is water ice which forms at about $-88\,°C$ in the dry stratosphere.

The formation of PSCs is key to the heterogeneous chemical reactions which give rise to the ozone hole (Solomon, 1990). During the winter, PSCs form in the polar darkness as the Antarctic stratosphere radiatively cools. The clouds begin to appear over extensive regions around June. Chemically, the surfaces of the PSCs allow the reaction of chlorine nitrate ($ClONO_2$) and hydrochloric acid to form nitric acid (HNO_3) and chlorine gas (Cl_2). Both chlorine nitrate and hydrochloric acid are relatively long lived byproducts of choloro-fluorocarbon photolysis. They are sometimes referred to as chlorine reservoir species. The chlorine gas is released from the ice during the heterogeneous reaction while the nitric acid remains in the crystal. The removal of reactive nitrogen compounds from the stratosphere by condensation of trihydrate PSCs is also important. If reactive nitrogen remained, then once ClO formed it would react with the nitrogen to form chlorine nitrate which in effect returns the chlorine to the reservoir.

When sunlight returns to the Antarctic stratosphere, the molecular chlorine gas produced by PSC reactions photolizes to chlorine atoms which in turn attack ozone (O_3), forming chlorine monoxide and molecular oxygen. If sufficient chlorine monoxide is present it can react with itself to form the dimer Cl_2O_2 which photolizes into chlorine and molecular oxygen after several steps. The chlorine is now free to attack ozone again. This cycle is catalytic since it has the net effect of

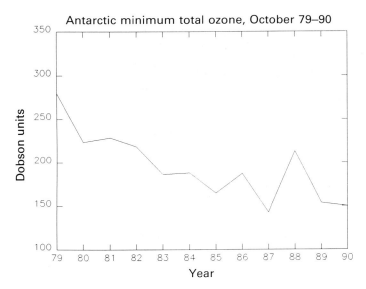

Fig. 4. The monthly mean, October mean minimum values of total ozone for each year since 1979. The decreasing overall trend is clearly shown although it is superimposed on significant inter-annual variability.

converting ozone to molecular oxygen without loss of chlorine. Bromine also plays an important role in this catalytic destruction of ozone in the polar vortex. Since about 80% of the chlorine in the stratosphere has originated with man-made chemicals, the ozone hole can be viewed as a man-made phenomenon.

Year-to-year variation

There is surprising year-to-year variability in the spring Antarctic ozone decrease. This variability is mostly associated with the year-to-year variability of the Antarctic stratospheric temperatures and variability in the isolation of the polar air. If planetary scale activity is great, then the polar stratosphere is warmer and fewer PSCs form. As a result, there will be relatively more reactive nitrogen, so the ClO catalytic cycle would shut down before a large fraction of ozone is lost. Fig. 4 shows the October monthly mean, minimum total ozone from 1979 to 1989. Superimposed upon the overall decrease is the considerable year-to-year variability which corresponds almost exactly to mean stratospheric temperature fluctuations in September and October. For example, with respect to the large change in spring ozone loss between 1987, 1988, and 1989, in September 1988 the lower stratosphere was 10–15 °C warmer than in the neighboring years. The mechanism for the year-to-year variability in planetary wave activity is poorly understood, but seems to be connected to the phase of the tropical quasi-biennial oscillation in stratospheric winds (Lait, Schoeberl & Newman, 1989).

Taking October 7 for some of the lowest years in the 1979–1989 sequence, Fig. 5 shows the development and growth of the ozone hole over the years since 1979.

Global trends

The TOMS instrument can be used to map the long-term global trends. Since the year-to-year fluctuations are large, a simple way to estimate the overall trend is to difference pairs of years. Year pairs are used to minimize the effect of the quasi-biennial fluctuation in total ozone seen in Fig. 4. Fig. 6 shows the percent change in total ozone for March, October and November and the mean values using 1989 plus 1990 average data minus 1979 plus 1980 average data. The ozone hole is dramatically revealed in the October picture, and the breakup of the ozone hole is shown by the smaller decrease region over a wider area in November. Interestingly enough, a decreasing trend is indicated in the Northern Hemisphere in March, the usual month of the break-up of the north polar vortex.

Limitations

The TOMS instrument has been extremely important for measuring and mapping the change in the ozone layer. The drawback in the solar back-scatter technique is that it is a daylight only instrument; measurements cannot be made at night time, nor during polar winter. The TOMS instrument also relies upon a diffuser plate for calibration. The optical changes in this plate must be known precisely for long-term trends to be computed without the aid of ground-based measurements. In addition, stratospheric clouds and retrieval problems at high solar zenith angles create problems with the processing algorithms. Despite these drawbacks, the TOMS instrument has been shown to be extremely useful and unusually reliable.

Conclusions

The Nimbus-7 TOMS has been functioning continuously for 14 years. During that period, TOMS has quantified the growth of the Antarctic ozone depletion and mapped out other significant changes in the ozone layer. Probably no other single satellite instrument has observed such dramatic man-made changes to our environment on the global scale.

NASA plans to build additional TOMS instruments to monitor the global changes in total ozone. The first new instrument was launched upon a Soviet Meteor satellite as part of a joint USSR–USA effort in 1991. Plans are also being made to place a TOMS instrument aboard the

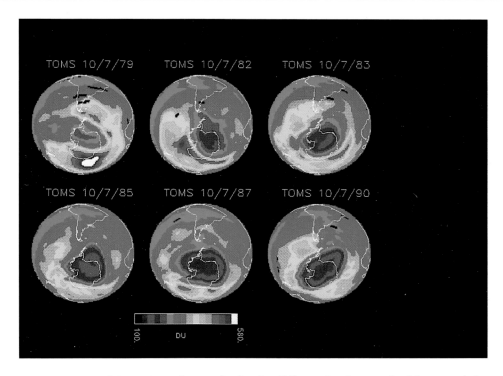

Fig. 5. Six years of Antarctic total ozone for October 7 illustrating the growth of the ozone hole.

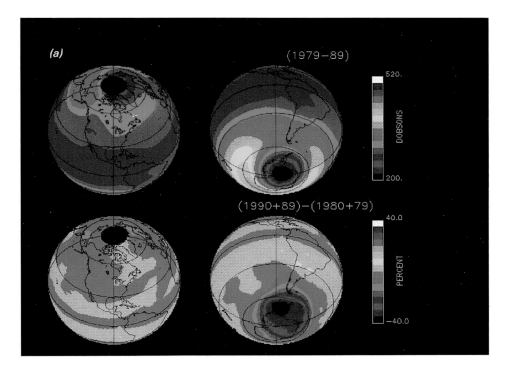

Fig. 6. Ozone difference plots showing the trend in total ozone. Pair averages (1979 plus 1980) and (1989 plus 1990) are used to reduce the effect of the quasi-biennial oscillation. The zero percent contour is the border between bright green and darker green. Fig. 6(a), October; 6(b), November; 6(c), March.

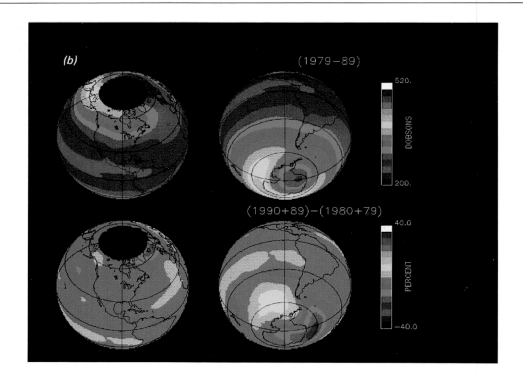

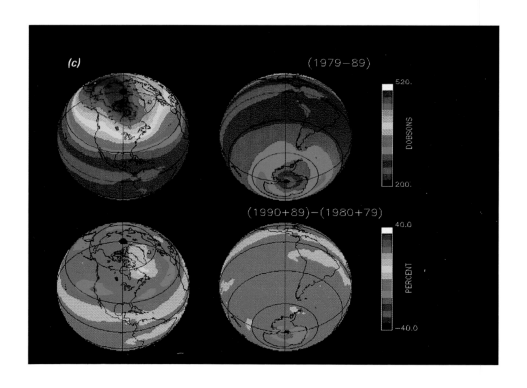

Fig. 6 (*cont.*).

Japanese ADEOS satellite, and a third instrument will be launched as part of the NASA's Earth Probes program.

Availability of data

TOMS data are available on compact disk from Rich McPeters, Code 916, NASA Goddard Space Flight Center, Greenbelt, Maryland 20771, USA.

References

Farman, J. C., Gardiner, B. G. & Shanklin, J. D. (1985). Large losses of total ozone in Antarctica reveal seasonal ClO_x/NO_x interaction, *Nature*, **315**, 207–210.

Herman, J., Hudson, R., McPeters, R., Stolarski, R. Ahmad, Z., Gu, X-Y, Taylor, S. & Wellemeyer, C. (1991). A new self calibration method applied to TOMS/SBUV back-scattered ultraviolet data to determine long-term global ozone change, *J. Geophys. Res.*, **96**, 7531–45.

Hoffman, D. J., Rosen, J. M., Harder, J. W. & Hereford, J. V. (1989). Balloon-borne measurements of aerosol, condensation nuclei and cloud particles in the stratosphere at McMurdo Station, Antarctica, during the spring of 1987, *J. Geophys. Res.*, **94**, 11253–70.

Krueger, A. J., Schoeberl, M. R., Stolarski, R. S. & Sechrist, F. (1988). The 1987 Antarctic ozone hole: a new record low, *Geophys. Res. Lett.*, **15**, 1365–8.

Lait, L. R., Schoeberl, M. R. & Newman, P. A. (1989). Quasi-biennial modulation of the Antarctic ozone depletion, *J. Geophys. Res.*, **94**, 11559–72.

McCormick, M. P., Trepte, C. R. & Pitts, M. C. (1989). Persistence of polar stratospheric clouds in the southern polar region, *J. Geophys. Res.*, **94**, 11241–53.

Report of the International Ozone Trends Panel, (1988). World Meteorological Organization, Geneva, Switzerland, Report #18.

Solomon, S. (1990). Progress towards a quantitative understanding of Antarctic ozone depletion, *Nature*, **347**, 347–54.

Stratospheric aerosols

M. P. McCORMICK

Introduction

Since the discovery of the stratospheric aerosol layer about 30 years ago by Jung, Chagnon & Manson (1961), the characteristics and radiative and chemical effects of stratospheric aerosols have been an area of increasing concern and research. Aerosols (particles in air suspension) can directly and indirectly influence the radiation budget of the atmosphere and, thus, affect climate (Gerber & Deepak, 1984; Hobbs & McCormick, 1988). Their direct radiative effect is due to their scattering, absorption, and emission properties (Hansen, Rossow & Fung, 1990). Their indirect effect is the result of their ability to act as condensation nuclei in the formation of clouds; thus, aerosols affect the resulting concentration, size distribution and optical properties of cloud particles (Twomey, 1977; Twomey, Piepgrass & Wolfe, 1984; Coakley, Bernstein & Durkee, 1988). Recent investigations indicate that polar stratospheric clouds (PSCs) produced from co-condensation of HNO_3 and H_2O on stratospheric aerosols at very low temperatures (polar winter) play a major role in ozone depletion at high latitudes (Solomon et al., 1986; McElroy, Salawitch & Wofsy, 1986; Toon et al., 1986; Hamill, Toon & Turco, 1986; Poole & McCormick, 1988). Moreover, and on a global scale, the potential effect on ozone depletion of heterogeneous chemistry occurring on volcanic and background stratospheric aerosols has been suggested (Hofmann & Solomon, 1989; Mather & Brune, 1990). Since stratospheric ozone also plays an important role in determining the temperature distribution of the Earth's atmosphere, changes in stratospheric aerosols and PSCs may further modify the radiation budget through their effects on the global ozone distribution. In situ changes in stratospheric temperature caused by high aerosol concentrations such as those produced from volcanic eruptions have been well documented (Newell, 1970; Labitzke, Naujokat & McCormick, 1983). Finally, especially after volcanic eruptions, aerosols can produce artifacts in the remotely sensed signals of key atmospheric constituents like H_2O and O_3, rendering their quantitative measurement impossible (Bandeen & Fraser, 1982; Fleig et al., 1990; DeLuisi et al., 1989).

Unlike stratospheric gaseous species, which can be fully characterized by determining their concentration or mixing ratio, a complete description of aerosols would require information about their composition, refractive index, size distribution, and shape. Only with such a complete set of information can the radiative and chemical effects of aerosols be quantified in detail. Fortunately, there is sufficient evidence that the bulk of stratospheric aerosols can be described reasonably well by assuming that they are spherical liquid droplets of approximately 75% H_2SO_4 and 25% H_2O by weight (implying an index of refraction of about 1.42 at stratospheric temperatures and visible wavelengths) (Rosen, 1971; Standard Radiation Atmosphere, 1984) and whose size distribution is log-normal (Pinnick, Rosen & Hofmann, 1976; Russell et al., 1981). Immediately after a volcanic eruption, however, the average size increases and the size distribution becomes more complex, perhaps multi-modal (Oberbeck et al., 1983).

Current understanding of the sources, sinks, and distributions of stratospheric aerosols has been reviewed by Turco et al. (1982). Perhaps, the most important chemical reaction in their formation is the oxidation of SO_2 in the stratosphere

$$SO_2 + OH + M \rightarrow HSO_3 + M$$

where M is a third body, and subsequent formation of H_2SO_4 molecules, which is followed by aerosol nucleation and condensation. Advection, sedimentation, coagulation and growth determine the distribution of the stratospheric aerosols. Perhaps, the most significant sources of stratospheric aerosols are from major volcanic eruptions which can inject large amounts of SO_2 into the stratosphere. Crutzen (1976) suggested that the persistence of the aerosol layer during prolonged periods without major volcanic eruptions is due to tropospheric carbonyl sulfide (OCS), from biogenic or anthropogenic sources, which diffuses into the stratosphere and eventually forms the background aerosols.

Since the discovery of the stratospheric aerosol layer, in situ measurements by particle counters have provided valuable data, most notably the long-term balloon-borne dustsonde data set of the University of Wyoming (Hofmann, 1990).

Dustsondes make measurements using a photoelectric device that counts particles of radius greater than a given amount; over 20 years of these data are available for radii greater than 0.15 μm and 0.25μm. The most recent dustsonde instrument developed by Wyoming is capable of measuring the integrated aerosol number density for all particles greater than six different radii: 0.01, 0.15, 0.25, 0.95, 1.20, and 1.80 μm (Rosen & Hofmann, 1986). Also, there exists a long-term aircraft data set of *in situ* particle characteristics (e.g. size and composition) obtained by the NASA Ames Research Center using a wire-impactor technique (Farlow *et al.*, 1979). Since 1964, lidar systems have been used for remote sensing of stratospheric aerosols (Fiocco & Grams, 1964). Currently, there are at least six stratospheric aerosol lidar stations around the world (McCormick, 1989). The long-term records which extend back 10 to 16 years are from the lidar systems at Hampton, Virginia, Mauna Loa, Hawaii, and Garmisch-Partenkirchen, Germany.

These *in situ* aerosol instruments and lidar systems can provide detailed local and regional information. Continuous monitoring of stratospheric aerosols globally, however, requires remote measurements from satellites. NASA launched a series of such satellite instruments beginning in October 1978. The first was the Stratospheric Aerosol Measurement II (SAM II) instrument aboard Nimbus-7. SAM I was a very simple proof-of-principle device flown on Apollo during the Apollo–Soyuz mission. The second long-term instrument was the Stratospheric Aerosol and Gas Experiment I (SAGE I) launched aboard the Applications Explorer Mission 2 spacecraft (AEM 2) in February 1979, followed by SAGE II launched aboard the Earth Radiation Budget Satellite (ERBS) in October 1984. An advanced instrument of the SAGE series, SAGE III, is proposed for the Earth Observing System (EOS). The SAGE III instrument is expected to be launched in the late 1990s. A spaceborne lidar called LITE (for Lidar In-space Technology Experiment) is being built by NASA for a series of flights aboard Shuttle beginning in mid-1993. In this chapter, the discussion will focus on the measurements from SAM II, and SAGE I and II, with some supporting lidar data.

Methodology

The SAM II instrument is a single channel sunphotometer designed for measuring aerosol extinction at 1.0-μm wavelength in the polar regions. SAGE I was placed in an orbit tailored to complement the SAM II geographical coverage by providing mid- and low-latitude data. The SAGE I sensor operated from February 1979 to November 1981 and was a four-channel sunphotometer providing aerosol extinc-

tion profiles at 0.45 and 1.0 μm wavelengths. Details of the SAM II and SAGE I observations have been reported by McCormick *et al.* (1979). The SAGE II instrument, in a similar orbit to SAGE I, has seven channels and is an improved version of SAGE I (Mauldin *et al.*, 1985). It provides aerosol extinction profiles at 0.385, 0.453, 0.525, and 1.02 μm wavelengths. Like SAGE I, it also measures profiles of ozone and nitrogen dioxide. SAGE II, in addition, measures water vapor, which is of particular importance in understanding aerosol microphysical processes and feedbacks in climate change (Rind *et al.*, 1991). Table 1 summarizes those missions, their latitudinal coverage, wavelengths, and the retrieved species for each. It also includes information on SAGE III (McCormick, 1991).

These satellite instruments all use the solar occultation technique to measure attenuated solar intensity as a function of tangent height at assigned wavelengths during each sunrise or sunset event encounted by the satellite (Fig. 1). Because of the bright source, the instrument can use a very small field-of-view to scan the solar disk vertically during these events to achieve a vertical resolution at the limb tangent of about 0.5 km. The elevation scan rate is such that the sun can be scanned many times during each sunrise or sunset period, which provides up to six measurements of the atmosphere at a given tangent altitude. The measurement of unattenuated solar irradiance, I_0, corresponding to a tangent altitude of approximately 120 km or greater, is used as a reference from which all atmospheric transmittances are determined, thus making the occultation technique self-calibrating. These limb transmissions determined at each instant are grouped into 60 to 70 consecutive 1-km altitude increments, beginning at the lowest measurement altitude. For each event the arithmetic means of the measured transmission at each tangent altitude are computed. The estimated uncertainty in the transmission is given by the square root of the variance divided by the number of independent measurements. Thus, the SAM II, SAGE I and II instruments belong to a unique class of satellite-borne sensors which are self-calibrated, contain continuous estimates of the precision of the measurements, and produce highly resolved vertical profiles. This feature is particularly important for instruments designed to provide multi-year long-term data records for determination of trends or global change.

Scattering by aerosols and air molecules are the main contributors of the attenuation of solar irradiance at 1.0 μm. Air density information provided by the National Meteorological Center (NMC) is used to calculate the amount of molecular scattering for each event and, thus, to remove this contribution from the SAM II measured transmission. The aerosol extinction profile is then derived using a non-linear inversion

Table 1. *Satellite limb extinction measurements*

Experiment	Satellite	Launch	Latitude coverage	Wavelength (µm) (Primary species)
SAM II (Solar)	NIMBUS-7	Oct. 1978*	64°–80° N 64°–80°S	1.0 (Aerosol)
SAGE I (Solar)	AEM-2	Feb. 1979**	79° N–79° S	0.385 (NO$_2$) 0.450 (Aerosol) 0.600 (O$_3$) 1.0 (Aerosol)
SAGE II (Solar)	ERBS	Oct. 1984*	80° N–80° S	0.385 (Aerosol) 0.448 (NO$_2$) 0.453 (Aerosol) 0.525 (Aerosol) 0.600 (O$_3$) 0.940 (H$_2$O) 1.02 (Aerosol)
SAGE III (Solar)	EOS/NPOP†	1999	55°–70° N 60°–90° N	0.290 (O$_3$ above 50 km) 0.385 (Aerosol) 0.430–0.450 (NO$_2$), Aerosol) 0.525 (Aerosol) 0.600 (O$_3$ below 65 km) 0.740–0.780 (O$_2$/T, Aerosol) 0.920–0.960 (H$_2$O, Aerosol) 1.02 (Aerosol) 1.55 (Aerosol)
(Lunar)			90° S–90° N	0.380–0.420 (OCIO) 0.430–0.450 (NO$_2$) 0.640–0.680 (NO$_3$) 0.740–0.780 (O$_2$/T) 0.920–0.960 (H$_2$O)

* Presently operational.
** Obtained data through November 1981.
† NASA polar orbiting platform.

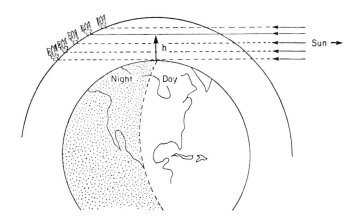

Fig. 1. Geometry for satellite solar occultation measurements.

algorithm. Similar procedures are also used in deriving the 1.0 µm aerosol extinction from SAGE I and II limb transmission data. In the case of aerosol extinction at the SAGE I and II shorter wavelengths, the retrieval algorithm is more complicated because of extinction contributions due to ozone, water vapor and nitrogen dioxide absorption. As a result, the

retrievals involve sequential removal of those components. Readers interested in the details of the retrieval algorithm are referred to the article by Chu *et al.* (1989). Satellite remote sensing requires coordinated validation programs at various global locations and seasons over an extended period. Extensive correlative measurements were conducted for validation of the SAM II, SAGE I and II aerosol observations and are summarized in Table 2.

Analysis and results

As mentioned in the previous sections, the SAM II instrument has been providing measurements in the polar regions since October 1978, the SAGE I instrument collected 34 months of data with global coverage for a period between February 1979 and November 1981, and the SAGE II sensor has been operating since October 1984. Considerable efforts have been devoted to analyzing these multi-year data sets, and to using these data for various atmospheric and radiative studies. Here, some of the results available at this time will be described.

Table 2. *Sensors used in SAM II, SAGE I and II validation studies*

Satellite instrument	Correlative sensor	Particle parameter	Platform/Site
SAM II[1]	Dustsonde (2 channels)	Number	Balloon
	Lidar	Back-scatter (0.694 μm)	P-3
	QCM*	Number, mass, composition	Sabreliner
SAGE I[2,3]	Dustsonde (2 channels)	Number	Balloon
	Lidar	Back-scatter (0.694 μm)	P-3
	Multifilter	Sulfate/mass	U-2
	Wire impactor (75 μm)	Number/mass	U-2
	QCM	Number, mass, composition	Sabreliner, U-2
	Integrating plate	Absorption (~0.55 μm)	U-2
	Nephelometer	Scatter phase function	Sabreliner
SAGE II[4]	Dustsonde (3/6 channels)	Number	Balloon
	Lidar	Back-scatter (0.523, 0.69 μm)	P-3
	Wire impactor (75 μm, 0.5 mm)	Number/mass	U-2
	PMS†	Number/mass	U-2
	Multifilter	Sulfate/mass	U-2
	QCM	Number, mass, composition	U-2
	Lidar**	Back-scatter (0.694 μm)	Garmisch, FRG
		Back-scatter (0.532 μm)	OHP, France
		Back-scatter (0.532 μm)	Frascati, Italy
		Back-scatter (0.532 μm)	Florence, Italy
	Limb photography**	Scatter radiance (0.84, 0.44, 0.375 μm)/Ext.	Balloon/Belgium
	Polarimetry**	Polarization diagram (0.85, 1.65 μm)/Size parameters	Balloon/France

Papers on stratospheric aerosol validation:
1. Russell, P. B. *et al.*, 1981.
2. McCormick, M. P. *et al.*, 1981.
3. Russell, P. B., 1984.
4. Russell, P. B. and M. P. McCormick, 1989.
* QCM, quartz crystal microbalance.
† PMS, particle measurement system incorporated laser probes.
** European correlative measurement sensor.

Aerosols in the polar stratosphere

The SAM II data, with a record of more than 11 years, can be used to study the long-term variations in polar aerosols. Fig. 2 presents 11 years of weekly averaged aerosol optical depth at a wavelength of 1.0 μm (calculated from the tropopause +2 km upwards through 30 km). The times of various volcanic eruptions, which are thought to have injected material into the stratosphere during this 11-year period are noted. Fig. 2 shows an optical depth value of approximately 1.4×10^{-3} in early 1979. Since the stratosphere was unperturbed by volcanic events in the late 1970s, this value has come to be regarded as the background stratospheric aerosol optical depth. The subsequent large increases of optical depth in response to volcanic eruptions are clearly evident. The most remarkable change is the rapid increase after the eruption of El Chichón (17.3° N; 93.2° W), which erupted in late March and early April 1982. A conservative maximum optical depth of about 5×10^{-2} occurred in March 1983 as the volcanic material peaked in the Arctic region due to gas-to-particle conversion and transport processes. It is conservative because

the heavy loading of aerosol at this time prevented SAM II observations from reaching down to 2 km above the tropopause. See McCormick and Trepte (1987) for a complete description of this effect. The maximum value is approximately 40 times that of the background values of early 1979. Note that the time for the El Chichón volcanic material to reach the high latitude regions is different in the two hemispheres. Some of the material (primarily that below about 21 km) appeared in the Arctic region shortly after the eruption, but it took almost 7 to 8 months before it was first observed in the Antarctic region. See the review by Kent and McCormick (1988) for details of the measurements and effects of this eruption.

During the entire 11 years of SAM II Antarctic measurements, periods of increased optical depth occur during each austral winter. These increases are due to the formation of PSCs. Note also, the minimum optical depth value immediately after each PSC seasonal event. It has been suggested that subsidence within the polar vortex and sedimentation of PSCs are the likely mechanisms causing these minima. By examining the corresponding temperatures during the period

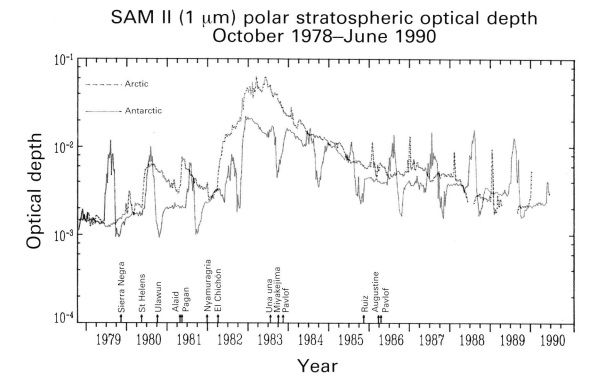

SAM II (1 μm) polar stratospheric optical depth
October 1978–June 1990

Fig. 2. Time series of SAM II weekly averaged stratospheric aerosol optical depths (1·0 μm) at high latitudes calculated from 2 km above the tropopause and upward.

with PSCs, it is found that their occurrences are correlated with temperatures below about 195 K (McCormick & Trepte, 1986).

During the years from 1983 to 1990, the optical depth or stratospheric aerosol loading shows a recovery from the disturbances due to the El Chichón eruption. This recovery is the result of natural cleansing processes of the stratosphere, such as exchanging air through tropopause folds and downwelling in the polar region. The occurrence of PSCs immediately after the El Chichón eruption is not as distinct as in the later years, and is due to the high level of background aerosol. In individual profiles on a given day, however, PSCs are very easy to distinguish. Since the discovery of the Antarctic ozone hole, PSCs have been shown to be key ingredients in the initiation and sustenance of ozone depletion.

Optical depth in late 1989 and early 1990 (about 8 years after the El Chichón eruption) is 2.2×10^{-3}, which is a factor of about 1.6 that measured in 1979. This apparent increase is also supported by long-term records of integrated aerosol back-scatter measured by various lidars throughout the world. Fig. 3 is the lidar record of integrated back-scatter from NASA Langley Research Center, Hampton, Virginia (37° N, 76° W), which is roughly proportional to aerosol optical depth or column aerosol loading. Fig. 3 shows an increase of

integrated backscatter by a factor of 40 over the 1979 value due to the 1982 El Chichón eruption. Note that the 1989 values remain higher than the 1979 values. Either the number of aerosols, their size distribution or composition have not returned to the 1979 values. Recently, Hofmann (1990) suggested that there has been a change in the background stratospheric aerosol over the past 10 years indicating a possible increase in OCS from the troposphere. Since the data on which this suggestion is based are the observations from only a relative short time period, the question of increased background aerosols is still open. More measurements in the coming years are needed in order to answer this important question.

Another way to present the long-term data set from SAM II is to plot isopleths of monthly averages of profiles of extinction ratio versus altitude and time. The extinction ratio is defined as the ratio of the sum of aerosol and molecular extinction to the molecular extinction alone. A value of one, therefore, represents no aerosol content. It is an approximately conserved quantity for transport studies. This ratio minus one is the fractional amount of aerosol to molecular extinction and is plotted in Fig. 4(a) for the Arctic region and in Fig. 4(b) for the Antarctic region. The average tropopause altitude supplied by the NMC for each SAM II measurement

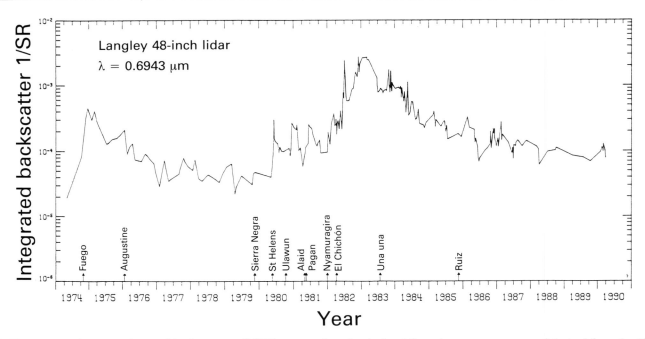

Fig. 3. Time series of integrated aerosol backscatter at 0·6943 μm wavelength calculated from the tropopause upward derived from the 48-inch lidar system at the NASA Langley Research Center (37°N, 76°W).

location is plotted as a solid black line. The most obvious enhancement in Fig. 4(a) is the El Chichón-produced volcanic increase. At these latitudes (64°–80°) the greatest increases are between 12 and about 19 km. The Mt. St. Helens enhancement caused by the May 18, 1980, eruption is much smaller in magnitude and lower in altitude. The eruption of Alaid in Alaska produced the enhancement in mid-1981. Each increase is followed by a slow decay as the stratosphere cleanses itself. Fig. 4(b) also shows increases due to El Chichón but are of lesser amplitude than in the Arctic region. A repetitive seasonal variation is evident in both hemispheres also. Minima or maxima occur at higher altitudes and appear to move down in altitude with progressing time probably due to dynamics and temperature effects. Increased extinction due to PSCs is especially evident in the Antarctic region where they occur more frequently than in the Arctic region since the Antarctic stratosphere is generally much colder than the Arctic stratosphere.

Seasonal behavior of stratospheric aerosol

To study global aerosol seasonal variations, the SAGE I and II aerosol data are used to derive zonal means of the extinction ratio at 1.0 μm for each season. Fig. 5(a) shows the results for the seasons March–April–May (1979), June–July–August (1979), September–October–November (1979), and December (1979)–January–February (1980). These zonal means show a maximum extinction ratio between 3 and 4.5

located near an altitude of 25 to 30 km in the tropics, which is indicative of a source region for stratospheric aerosols, perhaps from OCS being transported upward into the stratosphere by the Hadley Cell flow. Fig. 5(a) also shows a sloping of this aerosol layer with latitude following more or less a constant altitude above the local tropopause. The zonal mean tropopause obtained from the NMC is indicated by a plus sign. The data for 1979 show a gradual diminishing of the ratio maximum from a value just above 4 in the spring to just above 3 in the winter. The maximum below the tropical tropopause is presumably due to high clouds in that region. The results for 1980 are presented in Fig. 5(b). The tropical maximum of the extinction ratio in the stratosphere is further reduced, possibly indicative of a quasi-biennial oscillation affecting temperature and dynamics, or due to cleansing. An enhancement of the stratospheric aerosol layer (bulge in green area) in the northern mid-latitude region from the spring to the summer is clearly evident, and is due to the volcanic eruption of Mt. St. Helens (46.2° N, 122.2° S). During the period from summer to winter, the material from Mt. St. Helens in the northern mid- and high-latitudes decayed with a simultaneous build-up of the aerosol layer near 20 km in the tropics.

SAGE II measurements in 1985 are shown in Fig. 6(a). The stratospheric aerosol was globally enhanced compared to the SAGE I period. A peak extinction ratio greater than 15 at 20 km above the equator is shown in the spring. This is about a factor of 4 greater than that in 1979 and reflects the effects

(a)

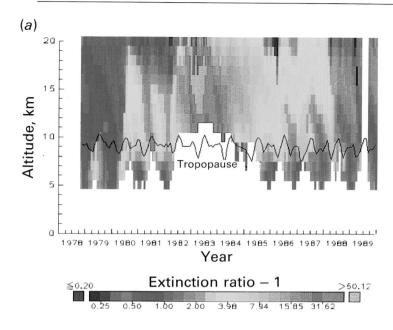

Extinction ratio − 1

≤0.20   >50.12

0.25 0.50 1.00 2.00 3.98 7.94 15.85 31.62

(b)

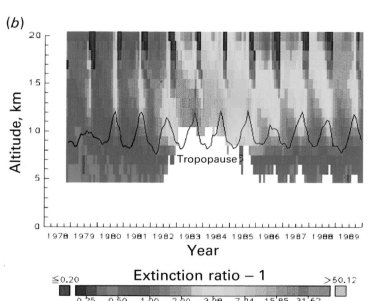

Extinction ratio − 1

≤0.20   >50.12

0.25 0.50 1.00 2.00 3.98 7.94 15.85 31.62

Fig. 4. Isopleths of monthly-averaged profiles of extinction ratio minus one versus altitude and time for the (a) Arctic region, and (b) the Antarctic region.

(a) SAGE I stratospheric aerosols

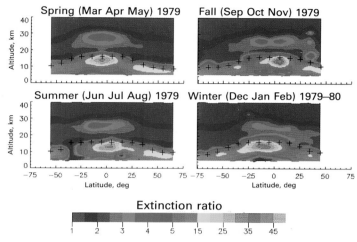

Extinction ratio

1 2 3 4 5 15 25 35 45

(b) SAGE I stratospheric aerosols

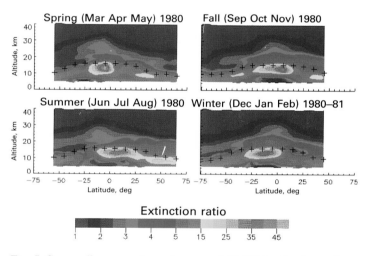

Extinction ratio

1 2 3 4 5 15 25 35 45

Fig. 5. Seasonally averaged zonal means of SAGE I extinction ratio at 1.0 μm for (a) 1979, and (b) 1980. The zonally averaged tropopause height supplied by the NMC is indicated by +.

of the massive 1982 eruptions of El Chichón, estimated to have placed 24 times more aerosols into the stratosphere than Mt. St. Helens (Kent & McCormick, 1988). By the winter of 1985, however, a new disturbance occurred above 22-km altitude in the tropics as a result of the volcanic eruption of Ruiz (4.9° N; 75.4° W) on November 13, 1985. Fig. 6(b) shows that by 1989 the stratospheric aerosol loading almost recovered to the background values of 1979. Roughly, the

stratosphere cleanses itself with an e-folding time of about 1 year.

The ratio of aerosol extinction at two wavelengths provides an estimate of the mean aerosol size (Yue & Deepak, 1983). Similarly, an aerosol size representative of the stratospheric aerosol column can be estimated from the ratio of optical depth at two different wavelengths. Fig. 7 shows the SAGE II optical depth ratio for 0.525 μm to that at 1.0 μm for the period from 1985 to 1988 for the Southern and Northern Hemispheres. Except in the tropics, both hemispheres show a monotonic increase of this ratio, indicating that the mean column aerosol size in the stratosphere was decreasing during

(a) SAGE II stratospheric aerosols

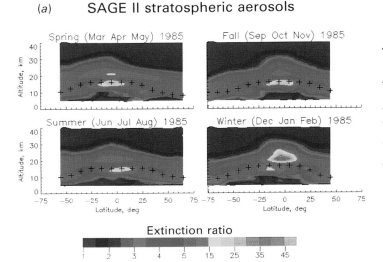

Extinction ratio

(b) SAGE II stratospheric aerosols

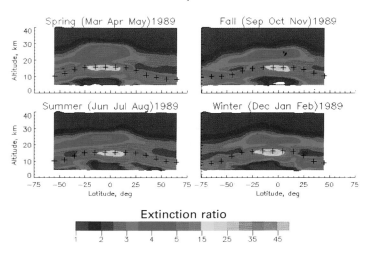

Extinction ratio

Fig. 6. Seasonally averaged zonal means of SAGE II extinction ratio at 1·02 μm for (a) 1985, and (b) 1989.

that period. This is to be expected as larger particles settle out of the atmosphere faster than smaller ones and the processes that generate new aerosols from OCS produce smaller-sized aerosols with an approximate mode radius of 0.08 μm. In the tropics, Fig. 7 shows a distinct decrease of the optical depth ratio in January 1986 indicating an increase of the mean particle size due to the volcanic eruption of Ruiz. Note, Fig. 7 also shows a spread of the Ruiz effects to higher latitudes likely due to transport processes. The reason for the sudden increase in this ratio at higher northern latitudes immediately after the eruption is unknown. The ratio does not change very much from mid-1986 to mid-1988, and then appears to increase slowly to higher values by the end of 1988. As more

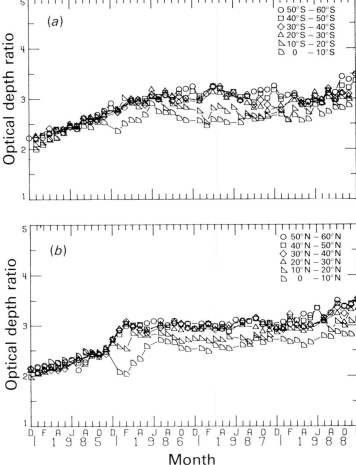

Fig. 7. Ratio of aerosol optical depths at 0·525 μm and 1·02 μm from SAGE II calculated from 2 km above the tropopause upward for the period from 1985 to 1988.

data become available and a climatology emerges, this ratio will help tell us if the background aerosol characteristics or amounts are truly changing.

Trend (1979–1989)

As indicated earlier, global long-term increases in the stratospheric aerosol loading could induce changes in atmospheric circulation and climate. McCormick and Wang (1989) have estimated a global mean aerosol extinction profile for 1979 based on SAGE I measurements. The result is reproduced in Fig. 8. The altitude given here is the height above the mean tropopause height. Similar analyses are also applied to the 1989 SAGE II measurement with the result shown also in Fig. 8 for comparison. In the lower stratosphere, the extinction values from the 1989 profile are as much as a factor of 1.6 larger than those from 1979. Although these differences

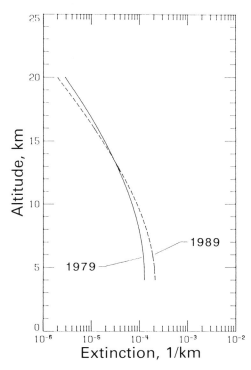

Fig. 8. Estimated global mean aerosol extinction at 1·0 μm from SAGE I for 1979 (solid line), and from SAGE II for 1989 (dashed line). The altitude shown is the height above the mean tropopause height.

SAGE II water vapor measurements are used to constrain the aerosol composition and for estimating the refractive index assuming a sulfuric acid aerosol. The extinction at four wavelengths (see Table 1 for the specific wavelength) are used to retrieve an aerosol model size distribution. Because of the SAGE II extinction at four different wavelengths, a single mode size distribution with up to four model parameters (Russell *et al.*, 1981) can be derived. Since the extinction measurements at a given wavelength are sensitive to a specific particle size range, the quality of the retrieved size distribution depends on the particular wavelength of that channel. Therefore, it is usually desirable to increase the number of aerosol channels so that more information on size distribution can be retrieved from these satellite measurements. In the recently proposed SAGE III instrument, there will be seven aerosol channels with a wider range of wavelength coverage (Table 1). Thus, better information about the fundamental aerosol parameters is expected from the SAGE III measurements. As to the inference of aerosol shape, little has been done so far and additional work is required.

Applications

One of the key objectives of NASA's series of solar occultation experiments is to provide global aerosol observations of sufficient accuracy for use in various studies and in the determination of long-term trends and global change. Because aerosols modify the atmospheric radiation field in many ways, aerosol data are needed to understand their influence on atmospheric circulation and climate through the use of predictive models. Thus, a goal should certainly be the incorporation of the observed aerosol data into general circulation and climate models for global change and climate prediction. In addition, aerosols may be important as are PSCs for heterogeneous chemistry and ozone depletion. Also, volcanic aerosols have been shown to have deleterious effects on most remote sensors, and it has been suggested that stratospheric aerosols could affect the number and optical properties of cirrus clouds. Clearly, the satellite data from SAM II, SAGE I and II have provided valuable information regarding the temporal and spatial characteristics of stratospheric aerosols and PSCs. The SAGE II aerosol results are further shown to be useful for deriving fundamental aerosol parameters. Although other techniques will no doubt be forthcoming, instruments like SAGE II and its successor SAGE III, which are self-calibrating, robust, and relatively inexpensive, should be flown in the near term in several satellite orbit inclinations so that all latitudes will be adequately covered in the shortest time possible. Techniques to enhance sampling per revolution of the spacecraft such as using lunar

may suggest that background aerosols are increasing, or possibly that their size distribution or other optical properties have changed, volcanic effects may still be enhancing the background level. The decreases of extinction from 1979 to 1989 at altitudes above 14 km could also be due to optical property changes or they may be due to errors in the retrievals at these altitudes, where signal-to-noise ratios are much less. As mentioned earlier, future observations are necessary before any trend analysis can be conclusive. Increases could be important to stratospheric chemical and radiative processes and possibly even to the frequency of cirrus clouds and PSCs.

Limitations

A complete description of stratospheric aerosols requires information about fundamental aerosol parameters including aerosol composition, refractive index, size distribution, and shape. Satellite remote sensing of stratospheric aerosols at this time can acquire only information on aerosol optical properties such as extinction at the wavelengths measured. Therefore, it is necessary to infer those aerosol fundamental quantities from the satellite-measured optical properties. Progress has been made recently in the development of algorithms for this purpose (Wang *et al.*, 1989), where the occultation, limb scattering and lidar back-scattering should also be investigated.

Data availability

For more information concerning how to access this data set, contact the National Space Science Data Center at NASA Goddard Space Flight Center, Greenbelt, Maryland 20771, USA, or the author.

References

Bandeen, W. R. & Fraser, R. S. (1982), Radiative effects of the El Chichón volcanic eruption, preliminary results concerning remote sensing. *NASA TM-84959.*

Chu, W. P., McCormick, M. P., Lenoble, J., Brogniez, C. & Pruvost, P. 1989: SAGE II inversion algorithm, *J. Geophys. Res.*, 94, 8339–51.

Coakley, J. A., Jr., Bernstein, R. L. & Durkee, P. A. (1988). Effect of shipstack effluents on the radiative properties of marine stratocumulus: Implications for man's impact on climate. In *Aerosols and Climate*, Hobbs and McCormick, eds., Deepak Publishers 253–60.

Crutzen, P. J. (1976). The possible importance of OCS for the sulfate layer of the stratosphere. *Geophys. Res. Lett.*, 3, 73–6.

Deluisi, J. J., Longenecker, D. U., Mateer, C. L., Mateer & Wuebbles, D. J. (1989). An analysis of northern middle-latitude Umkehr measurements corrected for stratospheric aerosols for 1979–1986. *J. Geophys. Res.*, 94, 9837–46.

Farlow, N. H., Ferry, G. V., Lem, H. Y. & Hayes, D. M. (1979). Latitudinal variations of stratospheric aerosols. *J. Geophys. Res.*, 84, 733–43.

Fiocco, G. & Grams, G. (1964). Observation of aerosol layer of 20 km by optical radar. *J. Atmos. Sci.*, 21, 323–4.

Fleig, A. J., McPaters, R. D., Bhartia, P. K., Schlesinger, B. M., Cebula, R. P., Klenk, K. F., Tayler, S. L., Wellemeyer, C. G. & Heath, D. F. (1990). *Nimbus-7 Solar Backscatter Ultra-violet (SBUV) Ozone Products User's Guide*, NASA/RP-1234, NASA Goddard Space Flight Center.

Gerber, H. E. & Deepak, A. (eds.). (1984). *Aerosols and Their Climatic Effects*, Deepak Publishers, 297pp.

Hamill, P., Toon, O. B. & Turco, R. P. (1986). Characteristics of polar stratospheric clouds during the formation of the Antarctic ozone hole. *Geophys. Res. Lett.*, 13, 1288–91.

Hansen, J., Rossow, W. & Fung, I. (1990). The missing data on global change. *Issues in Science and Technology*, 62–9.

Hobbs, P. V., & McCormick, M. P. (eds.) (1988). *Aerosols and Climate*, Deepak Publishers, 483pp.

Hofmann, D. J. & Solomon, S. (1989). Ozone destruction through heterogeneous chemistry following the eruption of El Chichón, *J. Geophys. Res.*, 94, 5029–41.

Hofmann, D. J. (1990). Increase in the stratospheric background sulfuric acid aerosol mass in the past 10 years, *Science*, 248, 996–1000.

Jung, C. E., Chagnon, C. W. & Manson, J. E. (1961). Stratospheric aerosols, *J. Meteorol.*, 18, 81–108.

Kent, G., & McCormick, M. P. (1988). Remote sensing of stratospheric aerosols following the eruption of El Chichón, *Optic. News*, 5, 11–19.

Labitzke, K., Naujokat, B. & McCormick, M. P. (1983). Temperature effects on the stratosphere of the April 4, 1982, eruption of El Chichón, Mexico, *Geophys. Res. Lett.*, 10, 24–6.

Mather, J. H. & Brune, W. H. (1990). Heterogeneous chemistry on liquid sulfate aerosols: A comparison of in situ measurements with zero-dimensional model calculations, *Geophys. Res. Lett.*, 17, 1283–6.

Mauldin, L. E., III, Zaun, N. H., McCormick, M. P., Guy, J. H. & Vaughn, W. R. (1985). Stratospheric aerosol and gas experiment II instrumentation: A functional description, *Optical Engineering*, 24–2, 307–12.

McCormick, M. P. (1989). *International Lidar Researcher's Directory*, (Available from the author, NASA/Langley Research Center, Hampton, VA 23665).

McCormick, M. P. (1991). SAGE III capabilities and global change, AIAA 29th Aerospace Sciences Meeting, January 7–10, 1991, Reno, Nevada.

McCormick, M. P. & Trepte, C. R. (1986). SAM II measurements of Antarctic PSCs and aerosols, *Geophys. Res. Lett.*, 13, 1276–9.

McCormick, M. P. & Trepte, C. R. (1987). Polar stratospheric optical depth observed between 1978 and 1985, *J. Geophys. Res.*, 92, 4297–306.

McCormick, M. P. & Wang, Pi-Huan (1989). Background stratospheric aerosol reference model, *Handbook for MAP*, 31, 115–22.

McCormick, M. P., Hamill, P., Pepin, T. J., Chu, W. P., Swissler, T. J. & McMaster, L. R. (1979). Satellite studies of the stratospheric aerosol, *Bull. Am. Meter. Soc.*, 60, 1038–46.

McCormick, M. P., Chu, W., McMaster, L., Grams, G. W., Herman, B. M., Pepin, T. J., Russel, P. B. & Swissler, T. J. (1981). SAM II aerosol profile measurements, Poker Flat, Alaska; July 16–19, 1979, *Geophys. Res. Lett.*, 8, 3–4.

McElroy, M. B., Salawitch, R. J. & Wofsy, S. C. (1986). Antarctic ozone: Chemical mechanisms for the spring decrease, *Geophys. Res. Lett.*, 13, 1296–9.

Newell, R. E. (1970). Modification of stratospheric properties by trace constituent changes, *Nature*, 227, 697–9.

Oberbeck, V. R., Danielsen, E. F., Snetsinger, K. G. & Ferry, G. V. (1983). Effect of the eruption of El Chichón on stratospheric aerosol size and composition, *Geophys. Res. Lett.*, 10, 1021–4.

Pinnick, R. G., Rosen, J. M. & Hofmann, D. J. (1976). Stratospheric aerosol measurements, III: Optical model calculations, *J. Atmos. Sci.*, 33, 304–14.

Poole, L. R., & McCormick, M. P. (1988). Polar stratospheric clouds and the Antarctic ozone hole, *J. Geophys. Res.*, 93, 8423–30.

Rind, D., Chiou, E.-W., Chu, W., Larsen, J., Oltman, S., Lerner, L., McCormick, M. P. & McMaster, L. (1991). Positive water vapour feedback in climate models confirmed by satellite data, *Nature*, **349**, 500–3.

Rosen, J. M. (1971). The boiling point of stratospheric aerosols, *J. Appl. Meteorol.*, **10**, 1044–6.

Rosen, J. M. & Hofmann, D. J. (1986). Optical model of stratospheric aerosol: Present status, *Appl. Opt.*, **25**, 410–19.

Russell, P. B. & McCormick, M. P. (1989). SAGE II aerosol data validation and initial data use: An introduction and overview, *J. Geophys. Res.*, **94**, 8335–8.

Russell, P. B., McCormick, M. P., Swissler, T. J., Chu, W., Livingston, J. M., Fuller, W. H., Rosen, J. M., Hofmann, D. J., McMaster, L., Woods, D. C. & Pepin, T. J. (1981). Satellite and correlative measurements of the stratospheric aerosol, II: Comparison of measurements made by SAM II, dustsondes and an airborne lidar, *J. Atmos. Sci.*, **38**, 1295–312.

Russell, P. B., Swissler, T. J., McCormick, M. P., Chu, W., Livingston, J. M. & Pepin, T. J. (1981). Satellite and correlative measurements of the stratospheric aerosol, I. An optical model for data conversion, *J. Atmos. Sci.*, **38**, 1279–94.

Russell, P. B., McCormick, M. P., Swissler, T. J., Rosen, J. M., Hofmann, D. J. & McMaster, L. (1984). Satellite and correlative measurements of the stratospheric aerosol, III: Comparison of measurements by SAM II, SAGE, dustsondes, filters, impactors and lidar, *J. Atmos. Sci.*, **41**, 1791–800.

Solomon, S., Garcia, R. R., Rowland, F. S. & Wuebbles, D. J. (1986). On the depletion of Antarctic ozone, *Nature*, **321**, 755–8.

Standard Radiation Atmosphere Radiation Commission of IAMAP (1984). A preliminary cloudless standard atmosphere for radiation computation, Boulder, Colorado, USA.

Toon, O. B., Hamill, P., Turco, R. P. & Pinto, J. (1986). Condensation of HNO_3 in the winter polar stratosphere, *Geophys. Res. Lett.*, **13**, 1284–7.

Turco, R. P., Whitten, R. C. & Toon, O. B. (1982). Stratospheric aerosols: Observation and Theory, *Rev. Geophys. and Space Phys.*, **20**, 233–79.

Twomey, S. A. (1977). The influence of pollution on the shortwave albedo of clouds, *J. Atmos. Sci.*, **34**, 1149–52.

Twomey, S. A., Piepgrass, M. & Wolfe, T. L. (1984). An assessment of the impact of pollution on cloud albedo, *Tellus*, **36B**, 356–66.

Wang, Pi-Huan, McCormick, M. P., Swissler, T. J., Osborn, M. T., Fuller, W. H. & Yue, G. K. (1989). Inference of stratospheric aerosol composition and size distribution from SAGE II measurements, *J. Geophys. Res.*, **94**, 8381–93.

Yue, G. K. & Deepak, A. (1983). Retrieval of stratospheric aerosol size distribution from atmospheric extinction of solar radiation at two wavelengths, *Appl. Optics*, **22**, 1639–45.

Monitoring of global tropospheric and stratospheric temperature trends

ROY W. SPENCER

Introduction

With the potential for man-induced global warming and resultant regional climate changes, there is an increasing need to understand how the Earth's climate system currently operates. One of the fundamental variables that needs to be measured is temperature. From satellites it is possible to observe the thermal emission of radiation by relatively deep atmospheric layers with radiometers. These instruments measure either infra-red or microwave radiation, the intensity of which can be related to atmospheric temperature. While these instruments have been devoted almost exclusively to monitoring daily changes in weather patterns, which are quite large, the precision demands of temperature monitoring for climate studies requires high sensitivity and long-term stability of the satellite sensors. As an example, the 0.5 °C warming reportedly observed by the global thermometer network over the last 100 years amounts to an average of only 0.05 °C per decade. Can satellites be called upon to make such precise measurements? Two criteria first must be satisfied.

1. The satellite instrument calibration must not vary with time, to within some level of precision which is higher than the climate signal.
2. The satellite measurement must be dominated by air temperature variations when compared to other contaminating influences (e.g. clouds, surface, CO_2 or O_2 abundance), or these other elements must be accounted for by other accurate measurements.

Microwave radiometers have two advantages for such a task. Because of the transparency of cirrus clouds at microwave frequencies below about 100 gigahertz (GHz), temperature sounding radiometers operating near the 60 GHz oxygen absorption complex have a relatively unobstructed view of the thermal emission of radiation from molecular oxygen in the atmosphere. In contrast, infra-red sounding radiometers are very sensitive to cirrus clouds and their use requires careful cloud screening techniques. Also, because oxygen is an abundant gas (20.95% by volume) its atmospheric concentra-

tion remains very stable in space and time (Warnek, 1988; Machta & Hughes, 1970) making it an ideal temperature tracer for satellite monitoring. Infra-red sounders, however, measure thermal emission by CO_2, which has about 1/600th the concentration of oxygen and is much more variable in space and time. While infra-red measurements will no doubt make useful contributions to the temperature monitoring problem, here only the microwave monitoring of global temperatures will be addressed.

Since late 1978, the TIROS-N series of National Oceanic and Atmospheric Administration (NOAA) polar orbiting satellites have been making continuous observations of thermally emitted microwave radiation with a series of scanning radiometers called Microwave Sounding Units (MSUs). These instruments are externally calibrated, with periodic views of the cosmic background (2.7 K), and instrument warm targets whose temperatures are monitored with redundant platinum resistance thermometers. Interpolation of the Earth-viewing measurements between these two extremes yields a brightness temperature, T_b. The MSUs operate at four frequencies near 60 GHz which have different sensitivities to the vertical distribution of atmospheric temperature (Fig. 1). Of these four channels, MSU channel 2 is best suited to monitor tropospheric temperatures, with relatively little sensitivity to surface emission and clouds (Spencer *et al.*, 1990). A procedure for eliminating the stratospheric contribution to channel 2 is addressed below. Channel 4 is well positioned to monitor lower stratospheric temperatures, with only a very small influence from the troposphere, and essentially no contamination from clouds or from the Earth's surface.

Methodology

Philosophy

Individual satellite temperature sounding channels, whether infra-red or microwave, are rarely used by themselves to retrieve temperature information. The traditional use of the MSU instruments, in combination with the High Resolution Infra-Red Sounder 2 (HIRS2, also on TIROS-N), has been

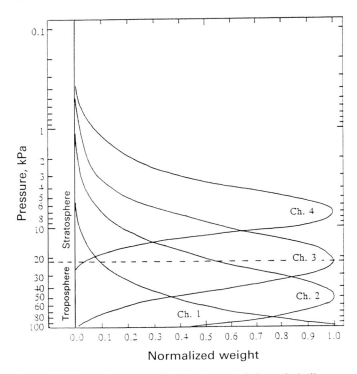

Fig. 1. Weighting functions of MSU channels 1 through 4, illustrating the MSU's sensitivity to temperature as a function of height in the atmosphere. Also shown is the average location of the boundary between the troposphere and the stratosphere.

the retrieval of the vertical temperature and moisture structure of the atmosphere for input into numerical weather prediction models. Fortunately, satellite sounders can resolve finer vertical structure than is suggested by the individual weighting functions in Fig. 1. The fundamental basis of satellite retrieval schemes is the fact that overlapping weighting functions can be combined (i.e. 'deconvolved') into an 'averaging kernel' which has higher vertical resolution than the individual weighting functions themselves (see Conrath, 1972; Grody, 1980). Because this procedure essentially magnifies small differences between two or more large numbers, errors in the satellite measurement also become magnified. Thus there exists a practical limit to deconvolution to an arbitrarily thin atmospheric layer which is set by the instrumental measurement noise, as well as the total number of available channels and their mutual vertical overlap. However, traditional temperature retrieval procedures go one step further. Most methods use some sort of 'first guess' based upon ancillary (e.g. radiosonde) data for the vertical structure because there is insufficient vertical resolution, even in the averaging kernels, to resolve vertical structure important to weather monitoring and prediction.

It is at this point where departure is made from this tradition. Periodic inclusion of ancillary (i.e. radiosonde) data as a

first guess makes the satellite monitoring capability non-independent because changes in the radiosonde system can find their way into the satellite retrievals. Also, first guess statistics do not enhance the satellites' ability to sense climate trends at vertical resolutions finer than what the satellite can observe in the first place, which are deep layer averages.

As a result of these considerations, raw channel 2 and 4 measurements will be emphasized for demonstration of instrument stability, and radiosonde data used as an independent check of the channel 2 results. Raw channel 4 data will be used for monitoring of lower stratospheric temperatures. However, for monitoring of tropospheric temperatures, a tropospheric retrieval suitable for global monitoring of the lower troposphere is described next.

A lower tropospheric retrieval

Because its weighting function is very deep (Fig. 1), channel 2 includes not only the entire troposphere, but also has some influence from the lower stratosphere. To the extent that the stratosphere undergoes temperature changes which are different from tropospheric changes, it would be a mistake to interpret channel 2 anomalies as entirely tropospheric in origin. As discussed above, the deconvolution of overlapping weighting functions to provide a sharper averaging kernel is the logical next step to providing a product useful for climate monitoring. Because channel 3 has information on the lower stratosphere, it would be a natural choice to remove the stratospheric influence. Unfortunately, as shown later in Fig. 5, channel 3 experienced calibration drift.

Fortunately, because the MSU is a cross-track scanner, channel 2 by itself provides slightly different weighting functions at each scan angle owing to the greater atmospheric path length the radiation must travel as the instrument scans away from nadir toward Earth's limb. It has been found that combination of eight of these eleven scan angle measurements in a simple linear retrieval (Fig. 2) provides a much sharper weighting function than channel 2 alone, with removal of the stratospheric influence, and much of the upper tropospheric influence. Since this retrieval requires the entire 2000 km swath width of the MSU to obtain a single retrieval temperature, it can not capture daily synoptic scale temperature gradients very well, and so its use is probably limited to climate monitoring. The retrieval represents an average of the entire 2000 km wide scan line, with errors in that average arising only if significant non-linearities in the temperature gradient exist across the swath. These errors would, of course, average out to zero for large areas (hemispheric and global).

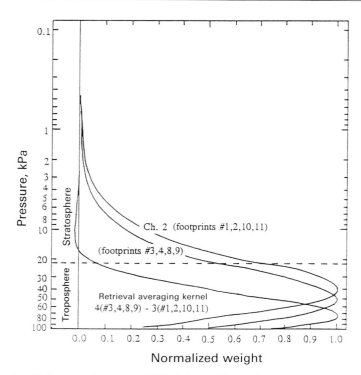

Fig. 2. Scan-angle averaged MSU channel 2 weighting functions for scan positions #1, 2, 10, 11, #3, 4, 8, 9, and a retrieval averaging kernel (channel 2R) computed from their weighted difference.

Satellite intercalibration and anomaly calculation

Much climate research of multi-year data time series involves changes about some long-term mean state. These are termed anomalies, and are analogous to daily weather reports of 'above normal' or 'below normal' temperatures. To compute temperature anomalies at different times of the year throughout a long period of record, we first remove the average annual cycle from the satellite data. If there had been only one MSU operating since 1979, this would be a simple procedure of computing, say, the average for 13 years of Januarys and subtracting it from January 1991 to obtain the anomaly

for that month. If global anomalies are required, the averaging can be on a global basis; if local anomalies were required, averaging and annual cycle removal would be on a local basis. Unfortunately, the MSUs present a couple of complications. First, not one, but eight MSUs have been in operation at various times between 1979 and 1991. Each instrument has a calibration bias relative to the others of up to a few tenths of a degree Celsius which must be accounted for. Overlaps between successive satellites' periods of operation (Fig. 3) allow computation of these offsets. Secondly, the satellites are distributed over two different sun-synchronous orbit times, 7:30am and pm (the 'morning' satellites) and 2:30am and pm (the 'afternoon' satellites). Because the atmosphere and the surface of the Earth undergo a diurnal change in temperature throughout these times, intercalibration of the satellites must account for this effect as well.

While details of the satellite calibration and intercalibration are contained in Spencer, Christy & Grody (1990) and Spencer and Christy (1991a), respectively, they will be summarized briefly here for completeness. After calibration of the raw MSU measurements in terms of T_b, an empirical 'limb correction' is performed which adjusts the off-nadir T_b to match (on the average) the nadir-viewing T_b. This adjusts for the fact that the near-limb weighting functions are somewhat higher in the atmosphere than the near-nadir weighting functions, and so produce different T_b. Although the off-nadir measurements still represent a slightly higher layer than the nadir measurement, this procedure avoids errors caused by month-to-month variations in the relative number of nadir and off-nadir footprints falling in any given grid square. Next, any bad data are screened for, as well as deep convective (thunderstorm) ice scattering signatures which can produce localized temperature depressions of up to several degrees. Channel 2 and 4 data which pass these tests are then binned into the appropriate 2.5° latitude/longitude grid square. A monthly average for each grid square is computed and stored for all operating satellites separately. At each 2.5° latitude/longitude grid square the net offset between the cur-

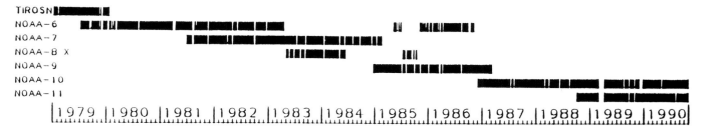

Fig. 3. Periods of operation of MSU channel 2 for individual TIROS-N series satellites during 1979–90. NOAA-8 data were not used in this study due to poor quality. Periods when two satellites are simultaneously operating were used for the satellite inter-calibration in order to obtain a complete time series for 1979–1991.

rent satellite's MSU and (arbitrarily) the NOAA-6 MSU is adjusted for, the offset also depending on whether the satellite is a morning or afternoon satellite. Finally, subtraction of the average of 13 years of each month's T_b from the individual month's T_b removes the 13-year mean annual cycle to arrive at the monthly anomalies. The above procedure is also used for computation of channel 2R anomalies, except the limb correction is not performed and the 2R T_b for a single MSU scan is assigned to all 11 scan locations along the scan line.

Limitations

The magnitude of the errors in air temperature anomalies estimated from the MSU measurements primarily depends upon four factors: 1) how much of the satellite signal is directly due to air temperature versus other geophysical sources, 2) the level of calibration drift of the individual MSUs, 3) the precision with which the satellites can be intercalibrated, and 4) how frequently the region of interest is sampled in space and time.

The contamination of the air temperature signal by several other geophysical signals was evaluated theoretically in Spencer *et al.* (1990). While MSU channel 2 (and especially channel 4) are dominated by air temperature signals, monthly gridpoint errors in the channel 2 anomalies could reach 0.2 °C, although, on a global basis, this is reduced to less than 0.01 °C. This would most likely occur with large inter-annual variations in thunderstorm activity, which cannot be perfectly screened out. Sensitivity analysis of our screening procedure (Fig. 4) shows that, in the case of a small oceanic region experiencing a very large year-to-year change in thunderstorm activity, a residual error of 0.1 °C is probably present, although averaging over a 10° zonal (latitude) band reduces this to a negligible 0.01 °C.

The lack of drift in MSU channels 2 and 4 is evidenced in Fig. 5, where plots of the sum and differences of concurrently operating satellites' daily T_b anomalies show no drift of one MSU versus the other at about the 0.01 °C level. This lack of drift was true of all satellite overlaps, and is addressed in more detail by Spencer and Christy (1991a). If all satellites have small, random drifts, this source of error should be much smaller than the 0.2°–0.3 °C average decadal warming expected for the next several decades from CO_2 increases in the atmosphere. Also, since the NOAA-6 operational period spans more than six years (Fig. 3), a comparison to radiosondes can be performed to evaluate the stability of this instrument. Channel 2 T_b is computed from individual radiosonde data with the radiative transfer equation for 42 radiosonde stations over the eastern United States. This was done for two identical 15-month periods during 1980–81 and

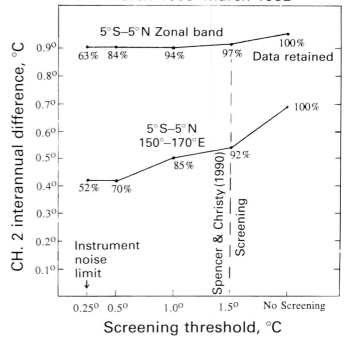

Fig. 4. Sensitivity of MSU channel 2 anomalies to various levels of thunderstorm screening for two tropical regions experiencing large inter-annual changes in deep convection between March 1982 and 1983. As stricter screening is performed and more data are excluded as 'contaminated', an inter-annual temperature difference limit is reached which is assumed to be representative of 'complete' storm screening.

1985–86 and the average difference between the satellite and radiosondes was computed for the two periods separately. The change in this difference over five years was only 0.014 °C, suggesting a lack of noticeable drift in the NOAA-6 MSU channel 2 (as well as the radiosonde system).

The combined effects of error sources 3 and 4 (above) have been evaluated with monthly intercomparisons between concurrently operating satellites' gridpoint anomalies (Spencer & Christy, 1991a, 1991b). These show that single-satellite gridpoint sampling errors for channel 2 are better than 0.05 °C in the tropics to 0.1 °C at some high latitude locations. Globally, this value is about 0.01 °C. For channel 4, the statistics are about the same. For the tropospheric retrieval, the gridpoint errors range from about 0.1 °C in the tropics to occasionally worse than 0.3 °C at higher latitudes, while the globally averaged errors are about 0.02 °C.

Since the satellite anomalies have been computed without any kind of radiosonde first guess, the satellite measurements can be compared to radiosonde calculations for an independent measure of the total satellite skill. The monthly

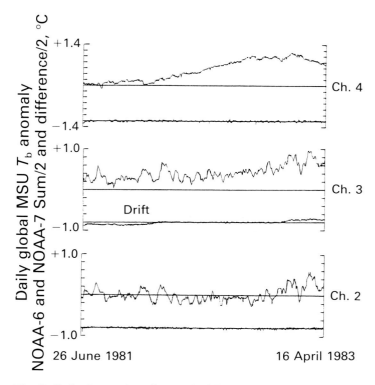

Fig. 5. Daily time series of sums (widely varying traces) and differences (slightly varying traces) of NOAA-6 and NOAA-7 MSU T_b anomalies for channels 2, 3, and 4. The difference time series has been offset for legibility. Calibration drift in one of the MSU's channel 3 data is evident.

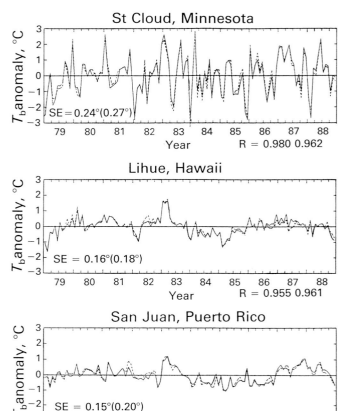

Fig. 6. Time series of monthly anomalies in satellite measured (solid line) and radiosonde calculated (dashed line) MSU channel 2 T_b for three radiosonde station locations. Monthly correlations (R, first number) and yearly correlations (second number) are listed at the lower right of each graph. Monthly standard errors of estimate (SE) of the radiosonde anomalies with the satellite are listed at the lower left: the first number is for radiosonde T_b calculations using the full radiative transfer equation with both temperature and water vapor profiles; the second number is for a simple vertically weighted average of the radiosonde temperature profile.

satellite 2.5° gridpoint anomalies were compared to synthesized channel 2 anomalies computed from radiosonde stations at over 100 United States-controlled stations. The radiosonde-based computations were done in two ways. The first involved the full radiative transfer equation (e.g. Grody, 1983) computed with the radiosonde temperature and water vapor profiles, assuming a constant surface emissivity and a surface temperature equal to the lowest radiosonde level temperature. A second, simplified method utilized only a static weighting function (Fig. 1) applied to the radiosonde temperature profile alone. The results for three radiosonde stations are shown in Fig. 6: St Cloud, Minnesota; Lihue, Hawaii; and San Juan, Puerto Rico. It can be seen that there is excellent agreement at all three stations, with monthly and yearly anomaly correlation coefficients above 0.95 and monthly standard errors of estimate ranging from 0.24 °C at St Cloud to 0.15 °C at San Juan. The standard errors for the static weighting function calculations (in parentheses) reveal an average degradation of only 0.02° to 0.03° in the monthly agreement between satellite and radiosondes. The differences in decadal trends was usually on the order of 0.1 °C and randomly distributed from station to station.

When several radiosonde stations within the same region are composited together, the comparisons to the satellite estimates improve further. For Alaska, the Great Lakes, US West Coast, Caribbean, and tropical west Pacific (Table 1) it is found that regionally averaged channel 2 standard errors fall to about 0.1° to 0.2 °C. Note that contained within these errors (which are partly due to the radiosonde system) are the contaminating influences of variations in surface emissivity, cloud water, thunderstorm ice signatures, etc. Thus, it appears that, on a regional basis, the effect of these influences on channel 2 must be very small compared to the air temperature signal. The radiosonde comparisons to the lower tropospheric retrieval (channel '2R'), are presented with the

Table 1. *Station composite correlations and standard errors of satellite versus radiosonde monthly anomalies in MSU channels 2 and 2R during 1979–88. Numbers in parentheses are the best single-station values from individual stations in these regions*

#Stns/Region	Channel 2	
	R	SE
15 Alaska	.98(.97)	.17°(.24°)
6 Great Lakes	.98(.98)	.22°(.24°)
6 West Coast	.97(.95)	.18°(.25°)
4 Caribbean	.97(.95)	.10°(.15°)
7 West Pacific	.94(.85)	.09°(.14°)

#Stns/Region	Channel 2R	
	R	SE
15 Alaska	.97(.94)	.31°(.50°)
6 Great Lakes	.98(.97)	.37°(.48°)
4 US West Coast	.95(.91)	.35°(.54°)
6 Caribbean	.91(.84)	.16°(.29°)
7 West Pacific	.83(.74)	.11°(.16°)

channel 2 results in Table 1. The agreement is somewhat degraded compared to channel 2, especially for single station comparisons at high latitudes. However, once again, compositing of several stations together results in marked improvement in the results. Of course, hemispheric and global averages would be expected to be correspondingly better since most of the gridpoint degradation in the channel 2R accuracy is the result of loss of temperature gradient information across the 2000 km width of the MSU swath.

Analysis and results

Lower troposphere: 1979–1991

A low-pass filtered time series of the daily anomalies in channel 2R for 1979–91 (Fig. 7) shows significant inter-annual variability, with warming and cooling of several tenths of a degree sometimes occurring within one or two months. The three warmest years were 1987, 1988, and 1980, followed by 1990. The net decadal trend for this 13-year period is +0.07 °C. Because this is small compared to the inter-annual variability, the trend is very sensitive to the addition of one cool or warm year, and so little significance can be attached to the trend value. Changes consistent with global warming projections on the order of 0.3 °C/decade, however, should be much easier to observe if they materialize.

An image of the average global distribution of lower tropospheric channel 2R T_b for January and July (Fig. 8) shows the warmth of the Tropics and the coolness toward the poles, especially in the winter hemispheres. (These average T_b have a cold bias over elevated snow-covered terrain, but this effect

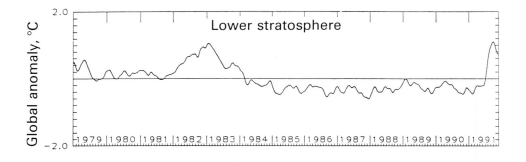

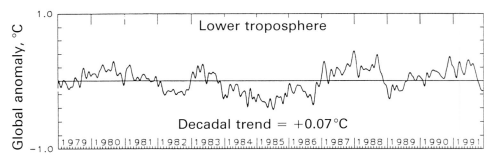

Fig. 7. Satellite inter-calibrated MSU lower tropospheric (channel 2R, bottom) and lower stratospheric (channel 4, top) T_b anomalies for 1979 through 1991. These anomalies were computed on a daily basis and low-pass filtered to emphasize variations on monthly and longer time scales.

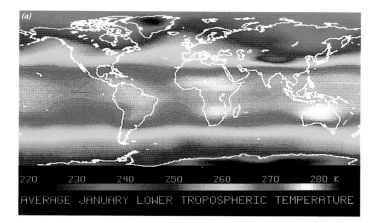

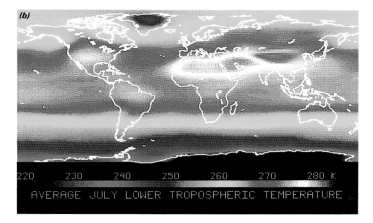

Fig. 8. Geographical distribution of average January (*a*) and July (*b*) MSU channel 2R T_b (lower troposphere). These T_b are dominated by air temperature, except over elevated terrain where a cold bias exists in snow-covered areas.

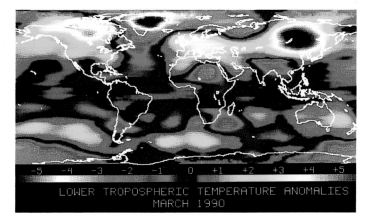

Fig. 9. Lower tropospheric T_b anomalies for March 1990, reported by surface thermometers to be the warmest month of the last 100 years.

does not adversely affect the anomaly calculations since it cancels out.)

An image of the geographical distribution of the March 1990 channel 2R anomalies (Fig. 9) shows strong warm anomalies over North America, Europe, and Russia. Based upon surface thermometer records, this month was widely reported as being easily the warmest month in the last 100 years. However, Fig. 9 seems to suggest the possibility that the chance superposition of the warmest anomalies over those regions having the best surface thermometer monitoring capabilities might have resulted in a thermometer sampling bias which was unrepresentative of globally averaged conditions. The globally averaged anomaly from the MSU was warmer than the 13-year average, but not unusually warm.

Lower stratosphere: 1979–1991

The globally averaged anomalies for MSU channel 4 (Fig. 7) reveal larger variations in the stratosphere than channel 2

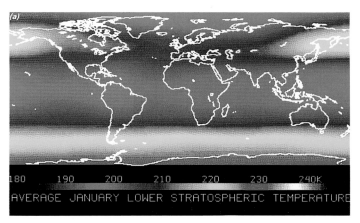

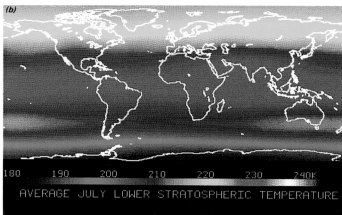

Fig. 10. Geographical distribution of average January (*a*) and July (*b*) MSU channel 4 T_b (lower stratosphere). Because this channel is sensitive only to air temperature, they can be interpreted directly as thermometric temperature.

Fig. 11. Lower stratospheric T_b anomalies for March 1990.

measured in the troposphere. The major feature was extreme warmth during 1982–83 when two volcanoes, Nyamuragria in Africa and El Chichón in Mexico, injected material into the stratosphere. Either solar heating of this material, or trapping of upwelling infra-red radiation by the material, are thought to be responsible for the elevated temperatures. After this warm episode, a seven-year period of cooler and almost constant temperatures has prevailed up until the eruption of Mt Pinatubo in the Philippines, which again caused rapid warming of the lower stratosphere. There is currently some debate about whether the volcanic aerosols contribute to ozone depletion, which leads to cooler temperatures after the eruptions. It will be interesting to see if the Pinatubo warm event is followed by still colder temperatures.

The average January and July lower stratospheric temperature fields (Fig. 10) show that the high latitudes of the winter hemisphere are colder than the summer hemisphere

high latitudes, but the tropics are cold as well. The March 1990 anomalies (Fig. 11) reveal a particularly intense cold anomaly centered on the North Pole, and warmth over most of the tropics.

References

Conrath, B. J. (1972). Vertical resolution of temperature profiles obtained from remote radiation measurements. *J. Atmos. Sci.*, **29**, 1262–71.

Grody, N. C. (1980). Analysis of satellite-based microwave retrievals of temperature and thermal winds: effects of channel selection and *a priori* mean on retrieval accuracy. *Remote Sensing of the Atmosphere and Oceans*, A. Deepak, ed., Academic Press, pp. 381–410.

Grody, N. C. (1983). Severe storm observations with the Microwave Sounding Unit. *J. Climate Appl. Meteor.*, **22**, 609–25.

Machta, L. & Hughes, G. (1970). Atmospheric oxygen in 1967 to 1970. *Science*, **168**, 1582–4.

Spencer, R. W. & Christy, J. R. (1990). Precise monitoring of global temperature trends from satellites. *Science*, **247**, 1558–62.

Spencer, R. W., Christy, J. R. & Grody, N. C. (1990). Global atmospheric temperature monitoring with satellite microwave measurements: Method and results, 1979–84. *J. Climate*, **3**, 1111–28.

Spencer, R. W. & Christy, J. R. (1991a). Precision and radiosonde validation of satellite gridpoint temperature anomalies, part I: MSU channel 2. *J. Climate*, in press.

Spencer, R. W. & Christy, J. R. (1991b). Precision and radiosonde validation of satellite gridpoint temperature anomalies, part II: A tropospheric retrieval and trends 1979–90. *J. Climate*, in press.

Warnek, P. (1988). *Chemistry of the Natural Atmosphere*. Academic Press, Inc., San Diego, California.

PART III

TROPOSPHERE

Water vapor and temperature

JOEL SUSSKIND

Introduction

Global numerical general circulation models of the atmosphere have become quite sophisticated and can make accurate multi-day weather predictions given accurate global initial estimates of the three-dimensional atmospheric structure. Over most of the globe, estimates can only come from satellite observations. The improvement of weather prediction capability by initialization of numerical general circulation models was the initial reason for development of satellite borne atmospheric sounders. These sounders measure passive radiation leaving the Earth's atmosphere in a number of spectral intervals in the infra-red and microwave spectral regions. Depending on the spectral absorption characteristics of the atmosphere and the viewing geometry, these radiances depend to varying degrees on the surface temperature, surface emissivity, and surface reflectivity; vertical temperature, humidity, and ozone profile; and a number of cloud parameters. Radiance in atmospheric windows in the 11 μm and 3.7 μm regions are most sensitive to surface parameters. Radiances in the 15 μm and 4.3 μm CO_2 absorption bands and the microwave 56 GHz O_2 band are primarily sensitive to atmospheric temperature in different portions of the atmosphere. Radiances in the 6.7 μm water vapor absorption band depend significantly on both the water vapor and temperature distributions of the atmosphere, and can be used to determine information about the moisture distribution once the temperature distribution is determined. Lastly, radiances in the 9.6 μm O_3 band depend significantly on O_3 distribution as well as on all the other parameters mentioned.

Satellite sounding instruments generally employ one of two types of viewing geometry: nadir viewing or limb viewing. Nadir viewing instruments look down at the Earth at radiances in a small solid angle centered about a given spot on the Earth. Spatial coverage is maintained by a scanning system (generally cross track or conical) as the satellite moves. Nadir viewing instruments can provide high horizontal spatial resolution on the ground, but are potentially limited in vertical resolution, especially in the stratosphere.

Limb viewing instruments scan up and down in positions beneath the horizon, so as to see the Earth's atmosphere primarily in horizontal paths at different altitudes. Limb viewing geometry allows for very high vertical resolution and ability to sound higher in the atmosphere than do nadir sounding instruments. The horizontal viewing geometry limits the horizontal resolution of the observations, however. In addition, it increases the likelihood of clouds interfering with the observations. For these reasons, limb observations are primarily used for sounding the stratosphere and lower mesosphere, though upper tropospheric measurements are also available in areas where only low clouds are present.

The best measurements of upper atmospheric water vapor profiles have been made by limb sounders. The LIMS (Limb Infra-red Monitor of the Stratosphere) instrument on Nimbus-7 produced global water vapor data extending from the tropopause to the lower mesosphere for a period of 7 months between 1978 and 1979. The SAGE II (Stratosphere Aerosol and Gas Experiment II) instrument, which has been operating since 1985, has a spectral channel that has been used to produce water vapor profiles from cloud top to about 40 km altitude. In order to limit the scope of this chapter, neither limb sounding techniques nor results will be discussed. Only the work which has been done from nadir viewing instruments and concentrate on tropospheric phenomena will be dealt with.

The earliest satellite instruments designed for remote sensing of atmospheric temperature profiles were SIRS A (Satellite Infra-red Spectrometer A), a nadir-viewing 15 μm infra-red radiometric sounder, and IRIS (Infra-red Interferometer Spectrometer), a nadir viewing Michelson interferometer, both on Nimbus-3. Subsequent satellites carried ITPR (Infra-red Temperature Profile Radiometer), VTPR (Vertical Temperature Profile Radiometer), HIRS (High Resolution Infra-red Radiation Sounder) and HIRS2 (High Resolution Infra-red Radiation Sounder 2). These nadir-viewing sounders have represented improvements in spatial coverage and spatial resolution, and, with the addition on HIRS and HIRS2 of 11 μm, 9.6 μm, 6.7 μm, 4.3 μm and 3.7 μm channels, spectral coverage. HIRS2 was first launched on TIROS-N in 1978 and has flown on all low earth orbiting operational meteorological satellites since then. It is accompanied by MSU (Microwave Sounding Unit), a microwave sounder with four channels in the 56 GHz region. These microwave channels not only add more information about the atmospheric temperature profile to that obtained from the infra-red channels, but allow for better treatment of the effects of clouds on the infra-red radiances. HIRS2 and MSU are part of the TOVS (Tiros Operational Vertical Sounder) system. Use of HIRS2 data, together with that of MSU, has resulted in greatly improved atmospheric temperature–humidity profile retrievals and also allowed for the first global determination of sea–land surface temperature, as well global cloud fields and estimates of ice and snow cover (Susskind et al., 1984; Susskind & Reuter, 1985; Susskind, Reuter & Chahine, 1987; Reuter, Susskind & Pursch, 1988). Assimilation of atmospheric temperature profiles retrieved from HIRS2/MSU have led to significantly improved 3–6 day forecast skill (Baker et al., 1984, Kalnay, Jusem & Pfaendtner, 1985, Susskind & Pfaendtner, 1989). Susskind and Pfaendtner (1989) also show fields of total O_3 derived from HIRS2/MSU data and precipitation estimated from HIRS2/MSU soundings which give good qualitative agreement with expectations based on retrieved atmospheric soundings for the same synoptic period. Wu and Susskind (1990) derive outgoing long-wave radiation (OLR) and long-wave cloud radiative forcing from the HIRS2/MSU sounding products.

The data from HIRS2/MSU give the potential of producing a multi-year (starting from 1979) global data set of atmospheric and surface parameters derived in a self-consistent manner. Such a data set is now being produced at the NASA Goddard Space Flight Center Laboratory for Atmospheres (GLA) and is being used for monitoring climate variability and trends, as well as the interrelationship between inter-annual differences in a number of atmospheric and surface parameters. Some preliminary results of this study will be shown later in this chapter.

Methodology

The satellite radiances in different channels depend on geophysical parameters via integral equations given below. There are basically two different types of approaches that can be used to relate satellite radiances to atmospheric temperature and moisture profiles. The first are statistical approaches, in which empirical relationships are found between satellite radiances and atmospheric parameters measured in situ by collocated reports such as radiosondes. Such an approach (Smith & Woolf, 1976) had been used operationally by NOAA NESDIS until very recently. It has

the advantages of being computationally inexpensive and not requiring accurate knowledge of the physics of the radiative transfer equations relating satellite observations to geophysical parameters. It has certain disadvantages, however, such as having a tendency to smooth out large deviations from characteristic profiles and not being able to account adequately for other factors affecting radiances such as surface parameters and reflected solar radiation.

The other basic methodology for determining temperature and moisture profiles from observed radiances involves use of physical inversion approaches which attempt to find geophysical solutions consistent with the radiances and radiative transfer equations. This methodology is becoming popular now and has been adopted operationally by NOAA (Fleming, Goldberg & Crosby, 1988). There are many ways to perform physical retrievals from satellite data, which differ primarily in details such as constraints on the solution, removal of systematic computation errors, and treatment of the effects of clouds on the radiances. As an example, the methodology of Susskind and co-workers which is being used to produce the multi-year data set will be used. This methodology is an extension of the relaxation method developed by Chahine (1970). Only a brief overview of the methodology of analysis will be given here, with details given in the cited references.

Radiative transfer equation

Under cloud-free conditions, the monochromatic radiance leaving the Earth's atmosphere at infra-red and microwave wavelengths at zenith angle θ can be well approximated by the equation

$$R_v = \varepsilon_v(\theta)B_v(T_s)\tau_v(p_s, \theta) + \int_{\ell n p_s}^{\ell n \bar{p}} B_v(T(p))\frac{d\tau_v(p, \theta)}{d\ell n p}d\ell n p \\ + (1 - \varepsilon_v(\theta))R_v\downarrow\tau_v(p_s) + \varrho_v(\theta, \theta_{sun})H_v\tau_v(\theta, \theta_{sun}) \quad (1)$$

where $\varepsilon_v(\theta)$ is the surface emissivity at frequency v and angle θ, $B_v(T)$ is the Planck black body function describing the radiance emitted by a black body with temperature T at frequency v, $\tau_v(p, \theta)$ is the atmospheric transmittance (fraction of radiation transmitted) along a path from pressure p to pressure $\bar{p}$ (the effective top of the atmosphere) at zenith angle θ, $R_v\downarrow$ is the downwelling radiation emitted by the atmosphere, $\varrho_v(\theta, \theta_{sun})$ is the surface bidirectional reflectance for radiation striking the surface at solar zenith angle θ_{sun} and reflected at angle θ, H_v is the incoming solar flux, $\tau_v(\theta, \theta_{sun})$ is the transmittance of solar radiation along the path from the Sun to the surface and then reflected to the satellite, and the subscript s refers to values at the surface. In Equation 1, the first term represents radiation emitted by the surface and transmitted to the satellite. This term is the dominant term at window frequencies in which $\tau_v(p_s) \approx 1$. The second term represents radiation emitted and subsequently transmitted by the atmosphere in the upward direction at zenith angle θ. This term is dominant at frequencies in which the atmosphere is relatively opaque and $\tau_v(p_s)$ is small. The term $\frac{d\tau_v(p, \theta)}{d\ell np}$ is often called the weighting function, $W_v(p, \theta)$, and indicates the weight $B_v(T(p))$ receives in the integral. These weighting functions are typically single peaked functions with a maximum at the pressure in which $\tau_v(p, \theta)$ is about e^{-1}. Radiances in opaque spectral regions of the atmosphere are therefore measures of the average temperature in the vicinity of the peak of the weighting functions. These peaks increase in height at frequencies with stronger absorption coefficients. The peaks of the weighting functions for a given frequency also increase in height at larger atmospheric zenith angles, for which the atmospheric path contains more molecules and is more opaque. The remaining two terms in Equation 1 represent radiation reflected by the surface, arising either from atmospheric emission itself or from incoming solar radiation. These terms are not dominant in the spectral regions of interest, but neither are they insignificant at frequencies in which the surface is seen by the satellite. The solar reflection term increases in importance with decreasing wavelength and is particularly significant at wavelengths below 5 μm.

Radiances are not measured monochromatically but in spectral channels in which R_i, the radiance for channel i, is given by

$$R_i = \int f_i(v) R_v \, dv \tag{2}$$

where $f_i(v)$ is the normalized spectral response function for channel i. A channel is usually categorized by a characteristic frequency v_i, which is the centroid of $f_i(v)$, and the band pass Δv_i, representative of the half-width of the response function. Channel averaged radiances can be expressed as a function of geophysical parameters in an analogous manner to that of monochromatic radiances, replacing v by v_i in all variables and evaluating the functions by appropriate frequency averaging. For example,

$$\tau_{v_i}(p) = \int \tau_v(p) f_i(v) dv \tag{3}$$

Later references to Equation 1 refer to channel averaged quantities, and the subscript v_i is replaced by i.

Of particular significance to the determination of atmospheric temperature and moisture profiles are the channel average weighting functions of the HIRS2 and MSU instruments. These are shown in Figs. 1(a) and 1(b) for a select set of HIRS2 temperature sounding channels in the 15 μm and 4.3 μm regions, and in Fig. 1(c) for MSU temperature sounding channels. The weighting functions shown were computed for a spring mid-latitude temperature moisture profile at nadir viewing. Fig. 1(d) shows weighting functions for the four HIRS2 channels used in humidity sounding. These weighting functions are shown for both a spring mid-latitude profile and a tropical profile, to demonstrate the dependence of the atmospheric regions sounded by moisture channels on moisture profile.

Physical methods involve finding atmospheric and surface parameters which when substituted in the channel radiative transfer equations, match the observations R_i to expected accuracies. A critical element in the success of such methods is the ability to compute accurate atmospheric transmittances and radiances as a function of the geophysical parameters. Susskind *et al.* (1983) provide details about how these calculations are done in the GLA approach.

All retrieval methods involve an equation of the form

$$\{P_j - P^o_j\} = F\{R_i - R^o_i\} \tag{4}$$

where $\{P_j\}$ is the set of geophysical parameters one is solving for, $\{P^o_j\}$ is an initial estimate of their values, $\{R_i\}$ are observed radiances, $\{R^o_i\}$ are radiances associated with the initial estimate, and F is a transfer operator related to the weighting functions. In the case of physical retrievals, R^o_i are the radiances computed from P^o_j using the radiative transfer equations. If discrepancies exist between computed values of R^o_i, given P^o_j, and those observed by the satellite under the same conditions, the initial estimate of P^o_j will be assumed to be incorrect and modifications to the guess will be made according to the operator in Equation 4. If in fact, P^o_j were the truth but R^o_i did not agree with R_i, erroneous results would be retrieved. Biases between observed and computed radiances can be particularly detrimental as they will result in biased fields of geophysical parameters. Biases are particularly damaging from the point of view of monitoring climate variability and trends, as these biases will differ from satellite to satellite and spurious trends may result. Therefore, it is critical that potential satellite dependent biases be removed from the sounding products.

Systematic errors between observed and computed radiances are accounted for in the GLA system as part of the retrieval process. All retrievals begin with a first guess field obtained from a 6 hour forecast from the GLA general circulation model generated from an analysis which has utilized all sounding data and *in situ* data in the last 6 hour period (Baker, 1983). The global forecast field is assumed to have local errors but be globally unbiased. Radiances are computed from the first guess and compared to those observed under conditions which are determined to be clear. Systematic differences between observed and computed

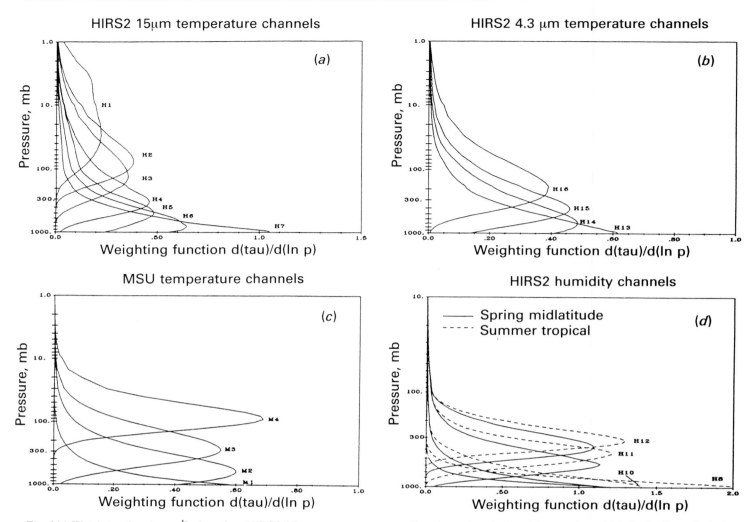

Fig. 1(a) Weighting functions $\frac{d\tau}{d\ln p}$ for select HIRS2 15 μm temperature sounding channels, calculated for a spring mid-latitude climatological profile at nadir viewing. (b). As in Fig. 1(a) but for HIRS2 4·3 μm temperature sounding channels. (c). As in Fig. 1(a) but for MSU temperature sounding channels. (d). Weighting functions $\frac{d\tau}{d\ln p}$ for HIRS2 water vapor sounding channels. Results shown at nadir for two profiles, spring mid-latitude (solid) and summer tropical (dashed).

brightness temperatures (the brightness temperature Θ_i is the temperature of a black body which would give the radiance R_i at frequency ν_i) are kept track of as a function of latitude and satellite zenith angle and modeled in the form

$$\Delta\Theta_i = A_i + B_i \cos(\text{lat}) + C_i \cos(\text{zen}) + D_i \sin(\text{lat}) + E_i \sin(\text{zen}) \quad (5)$$

where $\Delta\Theta_i$ is the systematic correction to computed brightness temperatures, $A_i \ldots . E_i$ are time dependent coefficients for channel i, and lat and zen represent latitude and satellite zenith angle respectively. The coefficients are computed routinely (about one time per orbit) and updated when changes in coefficients of over 0.3 °C occur (see Susskind & Piraino, 1985 for details). The corrections $\Delta\Theta_i$ are added to all computed brightness temperatures used in Equation 4 for the determination of geophysical parameters. This removes,

to first order, biases arising from uncertainties in the calculation of radiances, as well as instrument calibration errors and drifts.

Cloud correction to observed radiances

The previous discussion has dealt with clear conditions. Infra-red radiances are affected significantly by clouds which absorb radiation from below and emit radiation according to their temperature, transmissivity and emissivity. To a reasonable approximation, for a scene which is partially cloud covered with fractional cloud cover α, the observed radiance is given by

$$R_i = (1 - \alpha\varepsilon_i)R_{i,\text{CLR}} + \alpha\varepsilon_i R_{i,\text{CLD}} \quad (6)$$

where ε_i is the cloud emissivity at frequency v_i, $R_{i,\,\text{CLR}}$ is the radiance which would be seen by the satellite if the entire scene were clear (as expressed by Equation 1), and $R_{i,\,\text{CLD}}$ is the radiance which would be seen by the satellite if the entire field of view were covered by an otherwise equivalent cloud but with unit emissivity.

There are three ways to deal with the effects of clouds on the radiances. The simplest way is to identify scenes that are completely clear and only do retrievals in those cases, assuming the radiances are unaffected by clouds. This method has two potential shortcomings. First, some cases identified as clear may have some clouds and erroneous retrievals will occur. Second, and more important, there will be a significant sampling bias when only clear conditions are used which can give an erroneous picture of temperature and moisture distribution and trends.

The second approach to handling the effects of clouds on the IR radiances is to attempt to estimate or 'reconstruct' the radiances which would have been observed by the satellite if the entire scene was identical to the clear portion of the observed scene. This approach involves using observations in two adjacent fields of view, with the assumption that the fields of view have the same clear scene radiances and the same cloudy scene radiances, but differ only in the amount of cloud cover α. Under these assumptions, the clear column radiance for channel i can be reconstructed according to

$$\hat{R}_i = R_{\text{CLR},i} = \eta(R_{i,1} - R_{i,2}) \qquad (7)$$

where $R_{i,j}$ is the observed radiance for channel i in field of view j and $\eta = \alpha_1/(\alpha_2 - \alpha_1)$ (Chahine, 1974). Given η, Equation 7 allows for the reconstruction of all clear column radiances. The GLA interactive run uses the method of Susskind and Reuter (1985) to determine η from combined use of infra-red and microwave radiances.

Equation 7 cannot be used to extrapolate clear column radiances from the observations if the observations in both fields of view are very close to each other. Under these conditions, it is assumed that either both fields of view are completely clear, in which case the clear column radiances are taken as the average of the radiances in each field of view, or the fields of view are overcast, in which case no retrieval is performed. Retrievals are also not performed if η is determined to be large or if no solution can be found which matches the reconstructed clear column radiances to within a given criterion. Susskind *et al.* (1984) give more details about how these decisions are made.

This method has some obvious limitations. In particular, errors will be made if the fields of view have different types of clouds or surfaces. Multi-level cloud formations will produce an error in the estimate of clear column radiances but only to the extent that the multi-level cloud structure is different in both fields of view. Such a case is often rejected because a satisfactory solution cannot be found. Low level overcast can sometimes be taken as clear conditions by the criteria used in the method but this happens infrequently. Chahine and Susskind (1989) show that successful retrievals are performed under conditions of up to 80% cloudiness and retrieval accuracy does not degrade significantly with increasing cloud cover. For climate monitoring purposes, this still introduces a bias in sounding products toward clearer conditions, but it is much less serious than that obtained using method 1. This sampling bias does not occur for retrieved cloud parameters and precipitation estimate because these are retrieved under all conditions.

A more sophisticated method for accounting for cloud effects on the radiances is to attempt to find geophysical parameters for both the clear and cloudy portions of the scene which enable the computation of R_i via computation of $R_{i,\text{CLR}}$, $R_{i,\text{CLD}}$, and $\alpha\varepsilon_i$. This approach does not need the assumption of uniformity of conditions in adjacent fields of view but does require the ability to accurately model cloud radiative transfer properties. This approach is being attempted by some groups but its success has yet to be demonstrated.

Retrieval of geophysical parameters

Geophysical parameters are retrieved in an iterative fashion in the GLA approach. Table 1 shows the channels on HIRS2/MSU and indicates their absorption characteristics and use in the GLA scheme. Channels used primarily for temperature and moisture profiles are indicated as $T(p)$ and $q(p)$ respectively. The peaks of the weighting functions for the water vapor sounding channels are variable, decreasing in pressure with increasing moisture as shown in Fig. 1(d), and nominal values are given in the table. In the case of channels seeing significant amounts of the surface, the main atmospheric absorbing species is indicated. Using the first guess temperature and moisture profile, all terms in Equation 1 are known or can be calculated except for T_s, ε_i, and ϱ_i. The infra-red surface emissivity ε_i is currently prescribed as a function of frequency for land and water. Radiances in channels 8, 18, and 19 are used to give a best estimate of T_s and ϱ_i (assuming one value of ϱ for all channels) during the day, and are used to determine only T_s at night, when there is no reflected solar radiation (Susskind & Reuter, 1985). The retrieved ground temperature and reflectivity are then used, together with the initial guess temperature and moisture profile, to compute radiances for the temperature sounding channels shown in Table 1. The channels used for temperature sounding are all relatively insensitive to moisture

Table 1. *HIRS2 and MSU channels*

Channel	Frequency (cm^{-1})	Peak of dτ/d lnp (mb)	Function
H1	668.4	30	Not used
H2	679.2	60	$T(p)$
H3	691.1	100	Not used
H4	703.6	280	$T(p)$, clouds
H5	716.1	475	Clouds
H6	732.4	725	Clouds
H7	748.3	Surface	Clouds
H8	897.7	Window (water)	Surface temp., q(p), clouds
H9	1027.9	Window (ozone)	Ozone burden
H10	1217.1	(v) 1000	$q(p)$
H11	1363.7	(v) 600	$q(p)$
H12	1484.4	(v) 400	$q(p)$
H13	2190.4	Surface	$T(p)$, cloud correction
H14	2212.6	650	$T(p)$, cloud correction
H15	2240.1	340	$T(p)$
H16	2276.3	170	Not used
H17	2310.7	15	Not used
H18	2512.0	Window (nitrogen)	Surface temperature
H19	2671.8	Window (water)	Surface temperature
M1	50.30 GHz	Window (oxygen)	Surface emissivity
M2	53.74	500	Cloud correction
M3	54.96	300	$T(p)$
M4	57.95	70	$T(p)$

so errors in the initial guess moisture profile do not produce serious errors in the computed brightness temperatures for these channels. The differences between observed and computed brightness temperatures for these channels are used, together with the computed sensitivity of the channels to changes in temperature profiles, to produce an updated estimate of temperature profile (Susskind *et al.* 1984). The new estimate of $T(p)$ is used to update the estimates of T_s and ϱ because the radiances in the window channels do depend somewhat on temperature profile. The entire procedure is then iterated until convergence is reached between $\hat{\Theta}^N_i$, the Nth estimated clear column brightness temperatures, and $\hat{\Theta}^N_i$, the brightness temperatures computed (corrected for

systematic errors) from the Nth estimate of T_s and $T(p)$. The retrieval is accepted if a solution is found matching observations to an RMS difference of less than 1 °C. Otherwise, it is rejected as non-convergent.

Moisture profiles are now updated for the accepted solution using radiances computed for the four moisture channels, using Equation 1 in conjunction with the retrieved ground temperature and temperature profile, but with the first guess humidity profile. The humidity profile is then modified according to the difference between the observed and computed brightness temperature and the computed sensitivity of each channel to changes in moisture profile, given the temperature profile and surface temperature (Reuter, Susskind & Pursch, 1988). The moisture retrieval is iterative but is performed after the temperature retrieval. Total atmospheric O_3 burden, cloud parameters, outgoing longwave radiation and longwave cloud radiative forcing, and precipitation estimate are derived in subsequent steps.

Results

The HIRS2/MSU instruments were first launched on TIROS-N in November 1978 and have subsequently flown on NOAA-6 through NOAA-11. NOAA attempts to maintain a two-satellite system, collecting data at 2:30am, pm and 7:30am, pm local time. Ideally, data from both satellites are obtained simultaneously, giving four times daily observations at both 2:30am, pm local time and 7:30am, pm local time. Many gaps exist in two satellite coverage, and even sometimes in one satellite coverage. Table 2 indicates the time periods for which satellite data exist.

Table 2 also indicates the periods which have been processed using the GLA interactive system. All of TIROS-N data have been processed. Unfortunately, the HIRS2/MSU instruments on TIROS-N performed well for only slightly more than 1 year. NOAA-6 data have been processed from its

Table 2. *Satellite data*

Satellite	Data base	Processed
TIROS-N (2:30)	Dec. 1, 1978–Jan. 20, 1980	Dec. 1, 1978–Jan. 20, 1980
NOAA 6 (7:30)	November 1, 1979–April 16, 1983 13 day gap March 26–April, 1981	Nov. 1, 1979–June 11, 1981
NOAA 7 (2:30)	July 1, 1981–Feb. 5, 1985 6 day gap Sept. 24–29, 1982	July 1, 1983–July 31, 1983
NOAA 8 (7:30)	April 26, 1983–June 20, 1984	—
NOAA 9 (2:30)	Dec. 4, 1984–Feb. 2, 1987	
NOAA 10 (7:30)	Jan. 7, 1987–present	Aug. 2, 1987–Oct. 4, 1987 May 1, 1988–July 15, 1988 Sept. 1, 1988–Oct 15, 1988
NOAA 11 (2:30)	Nov. 1, 1988–present	—

beginning to June 21, 1981. There is about a $2\frac{2}{3}$ month overlap between NOAA-6 and TIROS-N data. The month July 1983, which is the first International Satellite Cloud Climatology Program (ISCCP) month, was also processed using NOAA 7 data. Finally, NOAA 10 data have been processed for the following periods: August 2, 1987–October 4, 1987, in conjunction with the Antarctic ozone hole experiment; May 1, 1988–July 15, 1988, in conjunction with a forecast impact experiment with the National Meteorological Center (NMC); and September 1, 1988–October 15, 1988 to study the period surrounding hurricane Gilbert. The summer of 1988 corresponds to an extensive North American heat wave and drought, and is in a year acknowledged to be extremely warm globally. In fact, some have used this year as evidence that the enhanced greenhouse effect, caused by increases in concentration in greenhouse gases, already has produced a noticeable effect on the climate.

The multi-year data set being produced should prove very useful in addressing questions such as detection of signatures of the enhanced greenhouse effect, as well as studying normal climate variability and interrelationships of the inter-annual differences in the behaviour of different geophysical parameters. Of primary interest in greenhouse effect studies is a possible warming trend in the Earth's temperature. This has been looked at in two ways: the surface skin temperature and the layer average atmospheric temperature between 500 and 1000 mb.

Annual mean fields

Before examining inter-annual variability, it is informative to examine the characteristics of a given year. Fig. 2(a) shows the 1979 annual mean (2:30am, 2:30pm average) 500–1000 mb layer mean temperature determined from TIROS-N data. The area weighted global mean value of the field (273.89 °C) is indicated on the Figure as well as the spatial variance of the field about the global mean (11.26 °C). This field is primarily zonal in structure, with the warmest values at the equator, and values decreasing toward the poles. The lower atmosphere to the west of the continents in the subtropics is in general cooler than that over the adjacent land areas however. Latitudes in the Northern Hemisphere are in general warmer than the corresponding latitudes in the Southern Hemisphere. Fig. 2(b) shows the annual mean surface skin temperature for the same period. The thin red line indicates the 0 °C contour. This field shows considerably more structure than the 500 mb–1000 mb layer mean temperature field, especially in the tropics. The most remarkable structure appears in the tropical oceans. These areas are marked by cold currents off the west coast of the continents in both the

Northern and Southern Hemispheres. The cold currents to the west of South America and Africa result in a considerable asymmetry about the equator of oceanic temperatures in the eastern Pacific and Atlantic Oceans. The small effects of these cold currents on atmospheric temperature have already been noted in Fig. 2(a), but are much weaker and more subtle than in Fig. 2(b). In the Northern Hemisphere extratropics, the Atlantic and Pacific oceans have warm currents to the west of Europe and North America and these warm areas also appear, again more weakly, in the annual 500–1000 mb layer mean atmospheric temperature field. An obvious correlation appears between the coldest land areas and coldest atmospheric areas in the extratropics as well. Tropical land areas show significant features in surface skin temperature which bear little relationship to those of air temperature, however. Spatial correlations of the annual mean fields of T_s with T_{500} are shown in Tables 3 and 4 for land and ocean areas in the tropics and extratropics respectively. Correlations of all other parameters to be discussed are also included in Tables 3 and 4, as well as correlations of fields of their inter-seasonal and inter-annual differences.

Figs. 3(a) and 3(b) show annual mean values of two additional fields determined from analysis of HIRS2/MSU data which are indirectly related to the distribution of surface and atmospheric temperatures and moisture, both by cause and effect. The cloud top pressure, shown in Fig. 3(a), is indicative of atmospheric circulation, with red areas showing low cloud top pressure (high cloud top altitude) being indicative of areas of preferred convection, and blue areas of high cloud top pressure being indicative of preferred subsidence. Comparison of Fig. 3(a) with Fig. 2(b) shows that in tropical oceans, areas of cold currents west of the continents correspond closely with areas of subsidence, and convective areas correspond to warmer oceanic areas. As with the sea surface temperature, the areas of preferred convection are roughly symmetric about the equator in the western Pacific and Indian oceans, but north of the equator in the eastern Pacific Ocean and the Atlantic Ocean. Over tropical land, the relationship of convective activity with surface skin temperature is often reversed, however. Here, areas of preferred convection in South America, Africa, and Indonesia correspond to local minima in annual mean surface skin temperature. The region of preferred convection near the equator is referred to as the intertropical convergence zone (ITCZ).

Figure 3(b) shows the annual mean field of precipitation estimate from HIRS2/MSU sounding products. A number of features are evident from this figure. The precipitation shows very sharp structure in the Tropics over both land and ocean and is closely related to the circulation as depicted in the

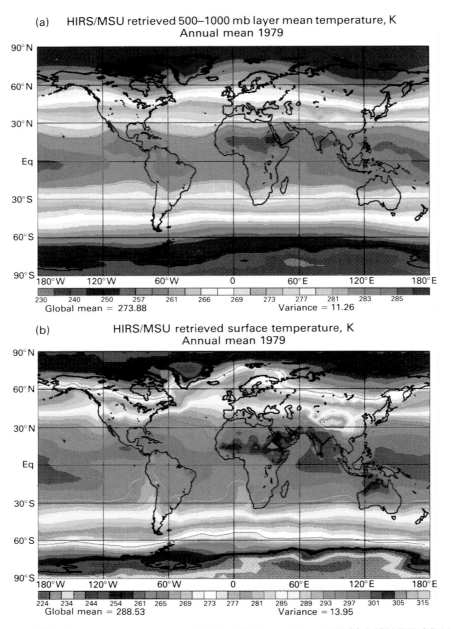

(a) HIRS/MSU retrieved 500–1000 mb layer mean temperature, K
Annual mean 1979

230   240   250   257   261   266   269   273   277   281   283   285
Global mean = 273.88   Variance = 11.26

(b) HIRS/MSU retrieved surface temperature, K
Annual mean 1979

224   234   244   254   261   265   269   273   277   281   285   289   293   297   301   305   315
Global mean = 288.53   Variance = 13.95

Fig. 2(*a*). Annual mean 500 mb–1000 mb layer mean temperature (K) for 1979 derived from HIRS2/MSU TIROS-N sounding data averaged for 2:30 am and 2:30pm soundings. Results are plotted on a 4°×5° latitude longitude grid. The area weighted global mean and area weighted spatial variance about the mean are indicated on the figure. (*b*). As in Fig. 2(*a*) but for surface skin temperature. The 273 K contour is indicated by a thin red line.

cloud top pressure field. Areas of high precipitation in the equatorial oceans correspond to large convective activity and warm ocean areas. These are bordered to the north and especially to the south by extremely arid oceanic areas. Pronounced south Pacific and south Atlantic convergence zones appear with moderate amounts of precipitation. Storm tracks are also evident in the Northern and Southern Hemisphere extratropical oceans. In tropical land areas, there is a strong

out-of-phase relationship between surface skin temperature and precipitation, with more arid areas being warmer, in general, and wetter areas being cooler.

Table 3 shows fairly high correlations of annual mean T_s with p_c (negative correlation means high temperature correlates to lower pressure, or higher altitude, cloud top) and precipitation over tropical ocean, while modest reverse correlations occur over tropical land. Annual mean correlations

Table 3. *Tropical spatial correlations of geophysical parameters*

Ocean

Annual mean

	T_{500}	W	W_{500}	P_c	Precip
T_S	.74	.80	.67	−.73	.61
T_{500}		.81	.71	−.62	.56
W			.93	−.89	.86
W_{500}				−.91	.92
P_C					−.92

July–Annual mean

	T_{500}	W	W_{500}	P_c	Precip
T_S	.56	.51	.36	−.47	.21
T_{500}		.78	.63	−.37	.24
W			.87	−.69	.62
W_{500}				−.73	.73
P_C					−.73

April–Annual mean

	T_{500}	W	W_{500}	P_c	Precip
T_S	.72	.63	.25	−.43	.28
T_{500}		.66	.31	−.29	.24
W			.73	−.63	.64
W_{500}				−.63	.68
P_C					−.72

May 1981–May 1980

	T_{500}	W	W_{500}	P_c	Precip
T_S	.05	.10	.02	−.12	.06
T_{500}		.24	.01	.16	−.06
W			.54	−.41	.51
W_{500}				−.46	.51
P_C					−.63

Land

Annual mean

	T_{500}	W	W_{500}	P_c	Precip
T_S	.62	.13	−.32	.36	−.43
T_{500}		.29	.33	−.19	.07
W			.75	−.54	.82
W_{500}				−.82	.83
P_C					−.72

July–Annual mean

	T_{500}	W	W_{500}	P_c	Precip
T_S	.75	.29	.10	.02	−.16
T_{500}		.75	.62	−.43	.36
W			.91	−.79	.79
W_{500}				−.87	.85
P_C					−.87

April–Annual mean

	T_{500}	W	W_{500}	P_c	Precip
T_S	.66	−.43	−.54	.34	−.53
T_{500}		.05	−.17	−.02	−.14
W			.71	−.69	.63
W_{500}				−.67	.75
P_C					−.70

May 1981–May 1980

	T_{500}	W	W_{500}	P_c	Precip
T_S	.37	−.11	−.18	.33	−.46
T_{500}		.33	.17	.22	−.12
W			.41	−.21	.33
W_{500}				−.33	.51
P_C					−.55

Table 4. *Extratropical spatial correlations of geophysical parameters*

Ocean

Annual mean

	T_{500}	W	W_{500}	P_c	Precip
T_S	.98	.89	.84	−.23	−.42
T_{500}		.90	.86	−.20	−.44
W			.94	−.46	−.16
W_{500}				−.48	−.08
P_C					−.63

July–Annual mean

	T_{500}	W	W_{500}	P_c	Precip
T_S	.85	.80	.67	−.08	−.17
T_{500}		.89	.77	−.15	−.15
W			.92	−.40	.05
W_{500}				−.47	.11
P_C					−.70

April–Annual mean

	T_{500}	W	W_{500}	P_c	Precip
T_S	.86	.81	.66	−.13	.42
T_{500}		.76	.69	−.18	.41
W			.76	−.27	.49
W_{500}				−.28	.38
P_C					−.68

May 1981–May 1980

	T_{500}	W	W_{500}	P_c	Precip
T_S	.28	.05	.00	−.01	−.17
T_{500}		.50	.44	−.05	.05
W			.58	−.35	.37
W_{500}				−.38	.28
P_C					−.72

Land

Annual mean

	T_{500}	W	W_{500}	P_c	Precip
T_S	.97	.89	.75	.45	.57
T_{500}		.91	.85	.32	.48
W			.81	.25	.50
W_{500}				−.03	.32
P_C					.28

July–Annual mean

	T_{500}	W	W_{500}	P_c	Precip
T_S	.97	.81	.52	.49	.31
T_{500}		.84	.59	.46	.34
W			.78	.13	.53
W_{500}				−.05	.64
P_C					−.33

April–Annual mean

	T_{500}	W	W_{500}	P_c	Precip
T_S	.74	.42	.07	−.15	.42
T_{500}		.74	.41	−.48	.52
W			.66	−.54	.60
W_{500}				−.43	.39
P_C					−.60

May 1981–May 1980

	T_{500}	W	W_{500}	P_c	Precip
T_S	.78	.36	.14	.07	−.02
T_{500}		.53	.36	.06	.10
W			.34	−.12	.27
W_{500}				−.27	.25
P_C					−.59

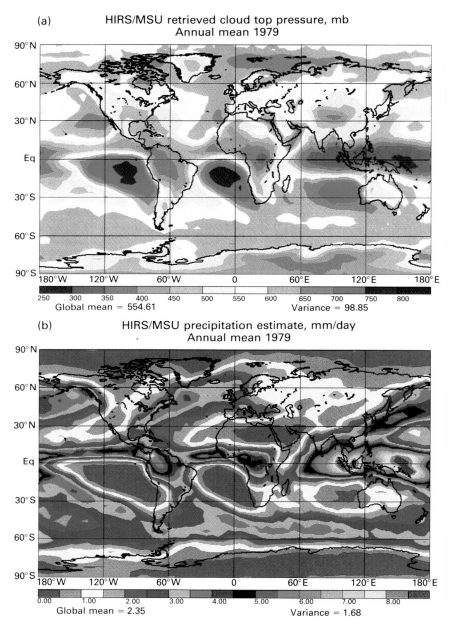

(a) HIRS/MSU retrieved cloud top pressure, mb
Annual mean 1979

250 300 350 400 450 500 550 600 650 700 750 800
Global mean = 554.61   Variance = 98.85

(b) HIRS/MSU precipitation estimate, mm/day
Annual mean 1979

0.00 1.00 2.00 3.00 4.00 5.00 6.00 7.00 8.00
Global mean = 2.35   Variance = 1.68

Fig. 3(a). As in Fig. 2(a) but for cloud top pressure (mb). (b). As in Fig. 2(a) but for precipitation estimate (mm/day).

of tropical cloud top pressure and precipitation with T_{500} are lower than those with T_s.

Figs. 4(a) and 4(b) again show annual mean surface skin temperatures, but separated into 2:30am and 2:30pm values. Over ocean, there are no significant differences between afternoon and night time measurements of surface skin temperature. Over land, very significant diurnal temperature differences occur however. Land is considerably colder than the surrounding oceans at night. During the day, the annual mean land temperature is similar to that of the surrounding ocean, except in particularly arid regions, as indicated in Fig.

3(b). In these regions, land heats up considerably during the day to values considerably higher than those of the surrounding oceans. On the day–night average, these arid areas are of comparable temperature to the surrounding oceans, while the moist tropical land areas are colder than the surrounding oceans, as shown in Fig. 2(b), because they did not heat up significantly during the day.

It is convenient to examine the water vapor distribution of the atmosphere in terms of lower tropospheric moisture and upper tropospheric moisture. Fig. 5(a) shows the annual mean field of total precipitable water, W, in the atmosphere.

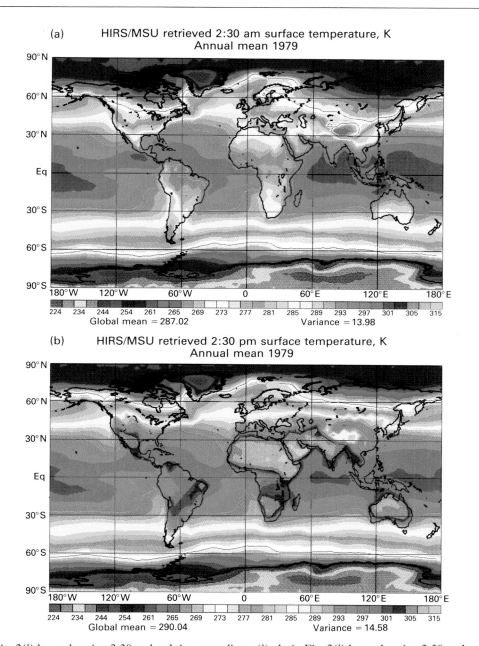

(a) HIRS/MSU retrieved 2:30 am surface temperature, K
Annual mean 1979

224 234 244 254 261 265 269 273 277 281 285 289 293 297 301 305 315
Global mean = 287.02   Variance = 13.98

(b) HIRS/MSU retrieved 2:30 pm surface temperature, K
Annual mean 1979

224 234 244 254 261 265 269 273 277 281 285 289 293 297 301 305 315
Global mean = 290.04   Variance = 14.58

Fig. 4(a). As in Fig. 2(b) but only using 2:30am local time soundings. (b). As in Fig. 2(b) but only using 2:30pm local time soundings.

This represents the integrated water vapor content of the clear atmosphere in units of g/cm^2 (density times distance) or equivalently, in units of precipitable centimeters of water, because 1 cm^3 of water weighs 1 g. Most of the integrated water vapor is in the lowest 1.5 km of the atmosphere. This Figure represents values retrieved only in the clear portion of the field of view, as obtained by the sounding system. There-fore, completely cloudy scenes are excluded from the sample, as are the portions of the scene containing clouds in partially cloudy areas. The features in the field of W in the tropics are quite similar to those of cloud top pressure, with areas of

higher clouds (lower pressures) corresponding to areas with more total precipitable water. Over tropical ocean, W is also quite correlated with sea–surface temperature, with warmer ocean having larger amounts of total precipitable water. This relationship is not surprising, as warmer oceans have higher water vapor pressures. An examination of Figs. 2(b) and 5(a) shows that in going from about 2° S, 150° E to 22° S, 80° W, surface temperatures drop from about 302 K to 292 K and W drops from about 5 g/cm^2 to 1.4 g/cm^2, corresponding to a factor of 3.5. The ratio of the vapor pressure of water at 302 K to that at 292 K is about 1.8. Clearly, there is more to the

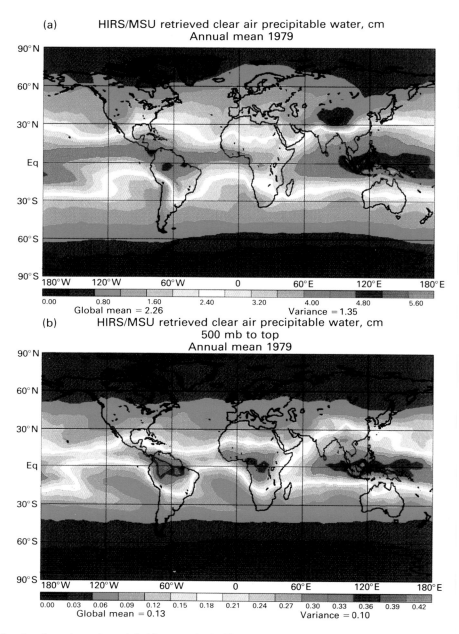

(a) HIRS/MSU retrieved clear air precipitable water, cm
Annual mean 1979

Global mean = 2.26   Variance = 1.35

(b) HIRS/MSU retrieved clear air precipitable water, cm
500 mb to top
Annual mean 1979

Global mean = 0.13   Variance = 0.10

Fig. 5(a). As in Fig. 2(a) but for clear air total precipitable water (cm). (b). As in Fig. 2(a) but for clear air precipitable water above 500 mb (cm).

spatial variation of total precipitable water than variations in the saturation vapor pressure of the ocean surface, though that plays a significant role.

Fig. 5(b) shows the annual mean field of total precipitable water above 500 mb, W_{500}, representing water vapor in the mid-upper troposphere. In the tropical oceans, the features resemble those of total precipitable water and sea surface temperature. The features are much sharper than those of W, however. For example, in the same locations as mentioned earlier, W_{500} drops from 0.38 g/cm^2 to 0.06 g/cm^2, or a factor

of about 6. This indicates that the spatial variability of upper level moisture is much greater than that of moisture in the boundary layer. This greater variability is also indicated by the relative values of the global means and spatial variances shown in Figs. 5(a) and 5(b), as the variance of total precipitable water is 60% of the mean, while the ratio is 77% for W_{500}.

Upper level moisture is driven by convective processes and atmospheric circulation. The correlation of W_{500} to convective areas in the tropics is clearly seen by comparison of Fig. 5(b) with Figs. 3(a) and 3(b), showing cloud top pressure and precipitation. It is apparent from Table 3 that upper level moisture, given by W_{500}, is highly correlated with cloud top pressure and precipitation in both tropical land and tropical ocean areas. The correlations are still substantial, but lower, with regard to low level water vapor, as indicated by W. The correlation of low level water vapor with tropical ocean surface temperature is also substantial, while higher level water vapor is less correlated with sea surface temperature. Precipitable water at all levels is uncorrelated with tropical land surface temperatures. Table 4 shows that annual mean extratropical temperatures and water vapor are highly correlated over land and ocean. This correlation occurs primarily because of the equator to pole gradients in temperature and moisture. Correlations of cloud pressure and precipitation with temperature and moisture in the extratropics are relatively low.

Annual cycle of geophysical parameters

In order to get a feeling for the annual cycle of temperature, moisture, convective activity and precipitation, it is useful to examine zonal mean quantities as a function of time. These are shown in Figs. 6–8 for surface and lower atmospheric temperature; total precipitable water and precipitable water above 500 mb, and cloud top pressure and precipitation. The values are derived from TIROS-N data and are averaged and plotted every 1/3 month from December 11, 1978 through December 10, 1979.

Fig. 6(a) shows the annual cycle of day–night average surface skin temperature. The largest amplitude is observed in the Northern Hemisphere extratropics, where most of the land exists. A similar annual cycle pattern is observed with regard to lower tropospheric temperature, shown in Fig. 6(b), but with reduced amplitude. Fig. 7(a) shows the annual cycle of total precipitable water. The features of the total precipitable water cycle closely follow those of surface and air temperature with warmer periods having greater amounts of total precipitable water. In all cases, the largest annual cycles occur in the Northern Hemisphere extratropics. The annual cycle of total precipitable water above 500 mb (Fig. 7(b)) is similar to that of total precipitable water in the extratropics and is closely tied to thermal effects. In the tropics, however, there are features which are much sharper than those of temperature or total precipitable water, and also are of a pulsating nature. Figs. 8(a) and 8(b) show the patterns of cloud top pressure and precipitation. The north–south motion of the intertropical convergence zone, with maximum convection at 8° N in June–July, and 8° S in December–January, is readily observed in Figs. 8(a) and 8(b). These same

features also appear in Fig. 7(a), and more strongly Fig. 7(b). The pulsation maxima of W_{500} in the tropics also appear in the precipitation field. In the extratropics, the precipitation cycle shows substantial maxima in the fall and winter of both Hemispheres. These maxima do not correlate with features in the temperature or moisture fields.

Figs. 3(b) and 5(b) clearly indicate that averaged over the year, precipitation and upper tropospheric water vapor each behave quite differently in the Eastern and Western Hemispheres, being roughly symmetric about the equator in the Eastern Hemisphere (defined here as 30° E eastward to 150° W) and with maxima north of the equator in the Western Hemisphere (150° W eastward to 30° E). One may therefore expect different annual cycles in each Hemisphere. Figs. 9(a), 9(b) and 10(a), 10(b) show the annual cycle of hemispheric zonal mean values of W_{500} and precipitation for the Eastern and Western Hemispheres respectively. A number of features are evident from these figures. Perhaps most striking is the close relationship between the temporal behavior of precipitation and upper level water vapor in the tropics in each hemisphere. In addition, the behavior in each hemisphere is quite different from the other. In the tropical Eastern Hemisphere, there is considerably more precipitation and upper level moisture than in the Western Hemisphere and a fairly uniform annual cycle is observed. This results in the approximate symmetry about the equator of the annual mean fields in the Eastern Hemisphere shown in Figs. 3 and 5. In the Western Hemisphere, significant convective activity is found over a narrower range of latitudes, located mostly north of the equator, and the maximum south of the equator in the Northern Hemisphere winter is weak and diffuse.

A gross indication of the relationships seen in Figs. 9 and 10 is given in Figs. 11(a) and 11(b) which show area average values of precipitation and upper level moisture as a function of time. Fig. 11(a) shows values of 10 day mean area mean values of precipitation and W_{500}, each averaged separately over the eastern and western tropics (24° N to 24° S latitude). Thirty-day periods are indicated by the vertical dashed lines. It is apparent from Fig. 11(a) that precipitation in the eastern tropics is of pulsating nature with a variable spacing of 30–50 days, which is highly correlated in time with similar features in eastern tropical W_{500}. Moreover, the features in the eastern tropics are out of phase with similar, but weaker, features in the western tropics. The pulsating nature of the fields is particularly strong in the period April through October 1979. The time series of precipitation has a correlation with that of W_{500} of 0.75 in the western tropics and 0.72 in the eastern tropics. In the period April to October, the correlations rise to 0.75 and 0.83. These correlations are considerably higher than those of the time series of hemispheric tropical precipi-

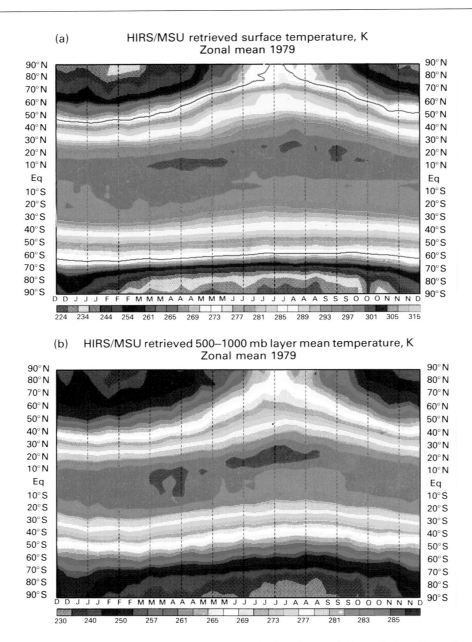

Fig. 6(a). Zonal mean 2:30am, 2:30pm average surface skin temperature (K) plotted every 1/3 month from December 11, 1978 to December 10, 1979. The thin vertical lines are at the middle of the month. (b). As in Fig. 6(a) but for 500 mb–1000 mb layer mean temperature. Black areas in this and subsequent Figures indicate insufficient data.

tation with hemispheric tropical total precipitable water. Eastern tropical precipitation has a correlation of −.68 with western tropical precipitation during April to October, indicating a strong out of phase time relationship of Eastern Hemispheric and Western Hemispheric precipitation.

Fig. 11(b) shows similar statistics, this time divided into northeast and southeast tropics. A north–south annual cycle is clearly observed in all fields. The pulsating nature of both precipitation and upper level moisture is considerably more pronounced in the northeast tropics than in the eastern tropics overall. The southeast tropics has pulsations of smaller magnitude than the northeast tropics, which appear to be out of phase with those of the northeast tropics, though lagged about 10 days. The time correlation of precipitation with W_{500} are 0.92 and 0.96 in the northeast and southeast tropics respectively. Much of this comes from the similarity in the annual cycles of each field, but the fine structure is clearly related as well. In the period April to October, the correla-

(a) HIRS/MSU retrieved clear air precipitable water, cm
Zonal mean 1979

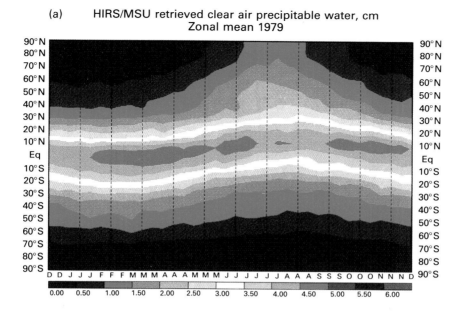

(b) HIRS/MSU retrieved clear air precipitable water, cm
500 mb to top
Zonal mean 1979

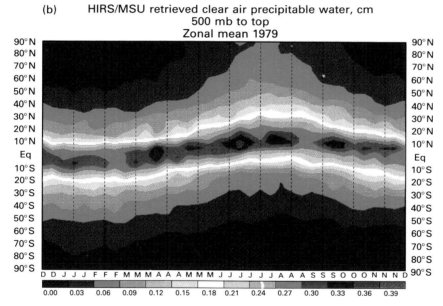

Dig. 7(*a*). As in Fig. 6(*a*) but for total clear air precipitable water (cm). (*b*). As in Fig. 7(*a*) but for precipitable water above 500 mb.

tions still are 0.93 and 0.92, though half the annual cycle has been removed.

An indication of the spatial distribution of the annual cycle is given by the difference of the monthly mean fields from the annual mean. It is interesting to examine two sets of these differences, July and April. These are generally indicative of the largest and smallest differences from the annual averages. Figs. 12(*a*), (*b*) show the difference from the 1979 annual mean of the July 1979 monthly mean values of surface skin temperature (Fig. 12(*a*)) and 500–1000 mb layer mean atmo-

spheric temperature (Fig. 12(*b*)). The largest values of the annual cycle of surface skin temperature occur over extra-tropical land and in areas where the ocean is frozen at some time of year. Oceanic areas have a much smaller annual cycle of surface temperature, and their peak differences from the annual mean come later in the summer in mid-latitudes. It is interesting to note the relatively small, but out of phase, pattern of surface skin temperatures in tropical land areas, where summer (winter) temperatures are cooler (warmer) than the annual mean. These out-of-phase differences are even larger

(a) HIRS/MSU retrieved cloud top pressure, mb
Zonal mean 1979

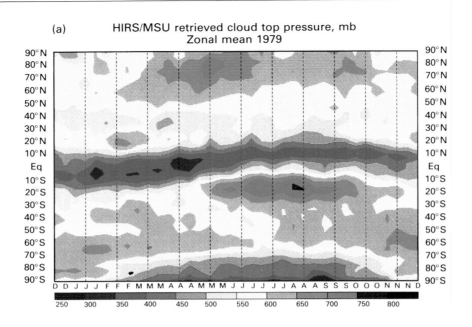

(b) HIRS/MSU precipitation estimate, mm/day
Zonal mean 1979

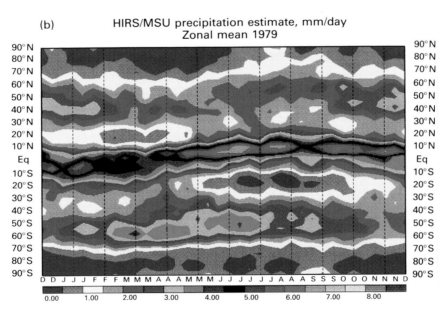

Fig. 8(*a*). As in Fig. 6(*a*) but for cloud top pressure (mb). (*b*). As in Fig. 6(*a*) but for precipitation estimate (mm/day).

when only 2:30pm temperatures are considered, and disappear when only 2:30am temperatures are looked at.

The patterns of the annual cycle of 1000–500 mb layer mean atmospheric temperature indicated in Fig. 12*b* are generally similar to those of surface air temperature, especially over extratropical land areas, in which the correlations of these two fields are 0.84 and 0.87 in the Northern and Southern Hemispheres respectively. The magnitude of the annual cycle of lower atmospheric temperature is less by about a factor of 2 in some inland areas than that of surface

temperature. On the other hand, lower atmospheric temperature over extratropical oceans changes much more significantly than sea surface temperature, with annual cycle magnitudes as great as those over land areas. This increase in atmospheric signal over ocean raises the amplitude of the global mean lower atmospheric temperature annual cycle to about 0.70 of that of the surface skin temperature. Spatial correlations of July–annual mean fields are shown for the tropics and extratropics in Tables 3 and 4. The land extra-tropics correlation of 0.97 between T_s and T_{500} is significantly

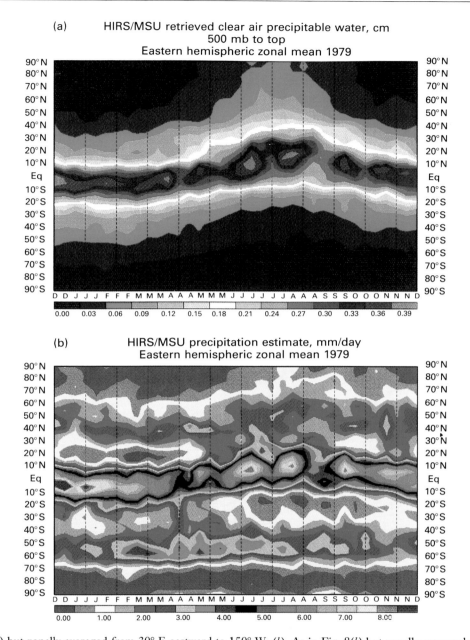

(a) HIRS/MSU retrieved clear air precipitable water, cm
500 mb to top
Eastern hemispheric zonal mean 1979

(b) HIRS/MSU precipitation estimate, mm/day
Eastern hemispheric zonal mean 1979

Fig. 9(a). As in Fig. 7(b) but zonally averaged from 30° E eastward to 150° W. (b). As in Fig. 8(b) but zonally averaged from 30° E eastward to 150° W.

greater than the individual Northern and Southern Hemisphere values because of the pronounced north–south annual cycle at high latitudes.

Figs. 13(a) and 13(b) show July minus annual mean fields of total precipitable water and W_{500}. These fields show large similarities, and are marked by excess moisture in the summer hemisphere and decreased moisture in the winter hemisphere, compared to the annual mean. In the case of total precipitable water, there is a sharp dividing line at about 10° N between areas where July is moist and dry compared to the annual mean. The annual cycle is also reduced considerably over some oceanic areas in the tropics and subtropics. The annual cycle of W_{500} is much more pronounced in the tropics compared to the extratropics than that of total precipitable water. In addition, those oceanic areas showing reductions of the annual cycle of total precipitable water have no signal in upper level moisture. In the extratropics, the July–annual mean values of W are highly correlated with analogous fields of T_s and T_{500} over both land and ocean. The correlation of W with T_s is weak in the tropics, especially over land where some

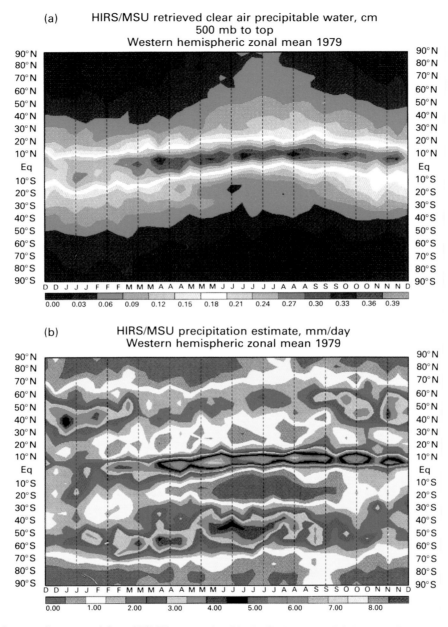

(a) HIRS/MSU retrieved clear air precipitable water, cm
500 mb to top
Western hemispheric zonal mean 1979

(b) HIRS/MSU precipitation estimate, mm/day
Western hemispheric zonal mean 1979

Fig. 10(*a*). As in Fig. 7(*b*) but zonally averaged from 150° W eastward to 30° E. (*b*). As in Fig. 8(*b*) but zonally averaged from 150° W eastward to 30° E.

features are out of phase. W is more highly correlated with T_{500} than it is with T_s in all areas, while W_{500} has lower correlations with both T_s and T_{500} than does W.

Figs. 14(*a*) and 14(*b*) show July–annual mean fields of cloud top pressure (red means lower pressure, higher cloud tops in July) and precipitation. Features in these two fields are somewhat more complex than in the temperature and moisture fields. In particular, the sign of the difference from the annual mean does not show a simple hemispheric dependence. With regard to cloud top pressure, the largest

differences are in the tropics in areas of moderate (450–550 mb) annual mean cloud top pressure. The area of pronounced annual mean convective activity in the equatorial Indian and western Pacific Ocean does not show a significant annual cycle, but convection to the north is greatly enhanced in July while it is suppressed to the south. A similar pattern occurs with regard to the major convective area in the Western Hemisphere in northwest South America, which results in a July maximum in convection in the Gulf of Mexico and surrounding Atlantic and Pacific Ocean areas which cor-

106

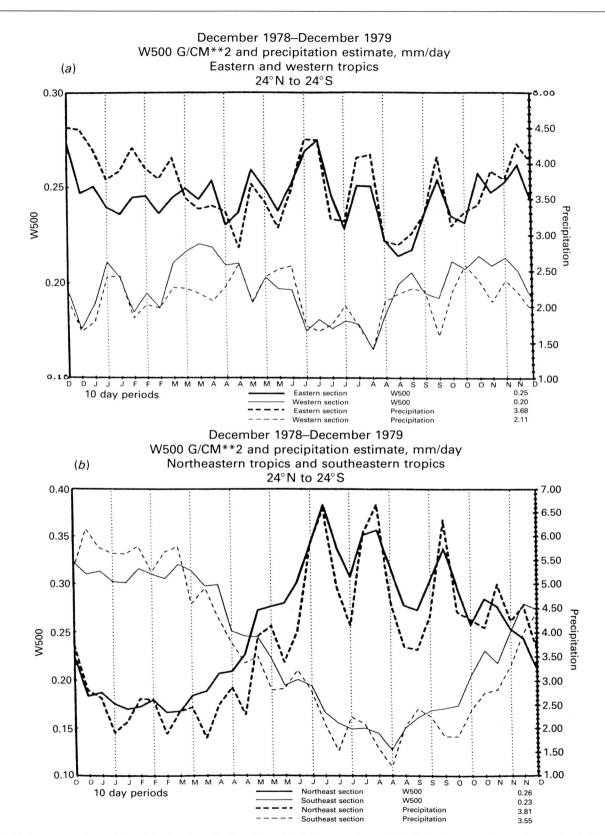

Fig. 11(*a*). 10 day mean values of precipitation (mm/day) and precipitable water above 500 mb (cm) averaged over the tropics in both Eastern (heavy) and Western (light) Hemispheres. Area mean annual mean values are indicated on the figure. (*b*). As in Fig. 11(*a*) but for northeast tropics (0–24° N) and southeast tropics (0–24° S).

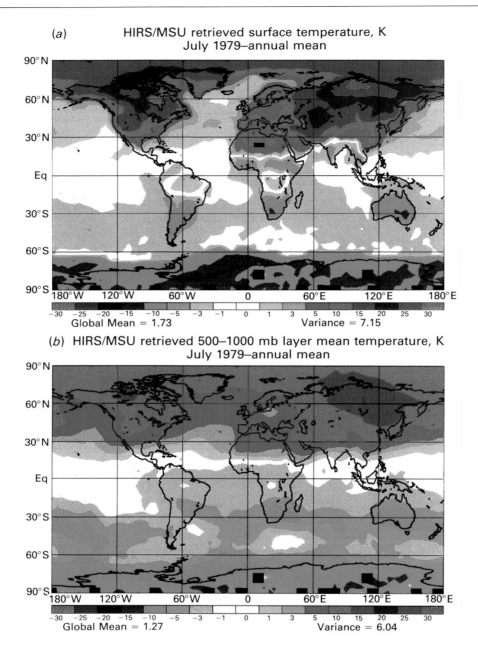

Fig. 12(*a*). Difference between July 1979 surface skin temperature (°C) (average of 2:30am and 2:30pm) and that of 1979 annual mean. Red means July 1979 was warmer than annual mean. (*b*). As in Fig. 12(*a*) but for 500 mb–1000 mb layer mean temperature. (*a*).

respond to moderate annual mean cloud heights. A pattern of opposite sign occurs in the adjacent north Atlantic and western north Pacific Ocean areas, which correspond to lower annual mean cloud top pressures. In these areas, cloud cover is due primarily to large-scale storm activity which is more pronounced in the winter than the summer. A weaker, but analogous feature is found in the extratropical Pacific and Atlantic Oceans near South America.

The precipitation patterns in Fig. 14(*b*) show great

similarity to those of cloud top pressure, but the features are considerably sharper, both with regard to convective precipitation in the tropics, and large scale precipitation in the extratropics. Precipitation fields are sharper and more coherent than cloud top pressure fields because not all high clouds cause precipitation. In particular, convective clouds produce a significant outgrowth of high cirrus clouds which do not produce large amounts of precipitation. Particularly noteworthy is the sharp negative feature in the equatorial Atlantic

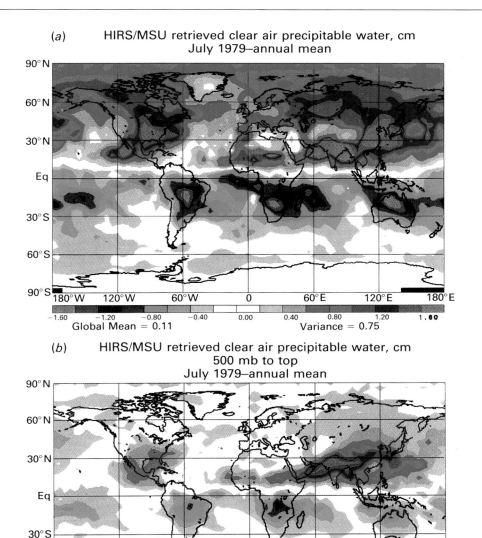

Fig. 13(*a*). As in Fig. 12(*a*) but for clear air precipitable water (cm). Red means July 1979 had more precipitable water than annual mean. (*b*). As in Fig. 13(*a*) but for precipitable water above 500 mb.

Ocean connecting larger negative features in the major convective areas in Africa and South America. This feature is much more diffuse over the ocean in the cloud top pressure field. In addition, changes in low cloud levels, such as found in the eastern equatorial Pacific Ocean, are also not associated with precipitation changes.

Patterns of July minus the annual mean cloud top pressure and precipitation are not in general highly correlated with either surface or atmospheric temperature patterns. Areas of

decreased summer surface skin temperature in the tropics correspond to areas of increased precipitation, which inhibits warming of the land temperatures during the day. This results in the small negative correlation between July–annual mean T_s and precipitation in tropical land areas, as shown in Table 3. This effect was alluded to earlier when it was noted that the out-of-phase signal was particularly strong with regard to afternoon surface temperatures and did not occur with nighttime temperatures. There is a high correlation in the tropics

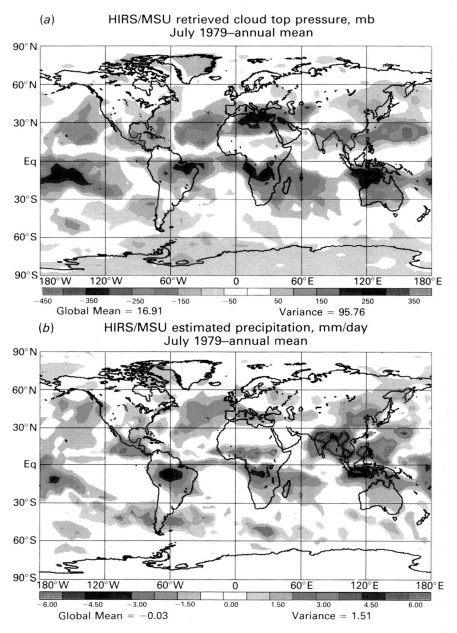

Fig. 14(a). As in Fig. 12(a) but for cloud top pressure (mb). Red means lower cloud top pressure (higher cloud top altitude) in July 1979 compared to annual mean. (b). As in Fig. 12(a) but for precipitation (mm/day). Red means more precipitation in July 1979 compared to annual mean.

of upper level moisture patterns with those of precipitation and cloud top pressure. This spatial correlation is analogous to the temporal correlations shown in Fig. 11. In the tropics, the spatial distribution of seasonal differences of W_{500} is highly correlated with those of p_c and precipitation, over both land and ocean, with values almost as high as those of W_{500} with W. The correlations of W_{500} with p_c and precipitation for July minus the annual mean in tropical land areas are, in fact, even larger than those for the annual mean. July–annual mean

values of W are also highly correlated in the tropics with those of p_c and precipitation, but less so than those of W_{500}.

In general, the difference of July (or January) fields from the annual mean represent the maximum differences, in terms of global spatial variance, found in the annual cycle. April (or October) minus the annual mean fields generally show minimum differences. Figs. 15–17 show April minus annual mean fields analogous to those in Figs. 12–14. Correlation statistics for these fields are included in Tables 3 and

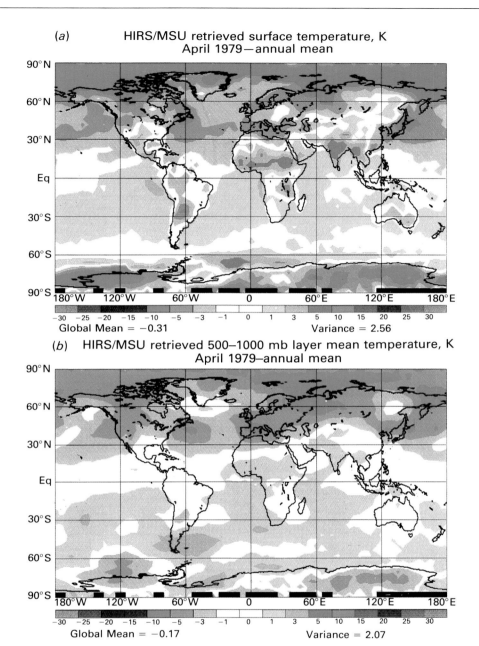

(a) HIRS/MSU retrieved surface temperature, K
April 1979—annual mean

Global Mean = −0.31   Variance = 2.56

(b) HIRS/MSU retrieved 500–1000 mb layer mean temperature, K
April 1979–annual mean

Global Mean = −0.17   Variance = 2.07

Fig. 15(a). As in Fig. 12(a) but for April 1979. (b). As in Fig. 12(b) but for April 1979.

4. Even though the spatial variances of the patterns in Figs. 15–17 are smaller than those in Figs. 12–14, similar relationships and spatial correlations exist between different variables. These correlations are in general lower than those of the July differences because the seasonal differences are also smaller. It is interesting to note that in April–annual mean, the single highest correlation in the tropics is between W_{500} and precipitation over tropical land, and a substantial correlation exists between these fields over tropical ocean as well. Another important point to note is the in-phase relationship between the cycle of precipitation patterns in northern South America and central Africa, again connected by a sharp equatorial Atlantic Ocean feature of the same phase. This connection is a common phenomenon which occurs in interannual difference fields as well.

Inter-annual differences

A main objective of analyzing multi-year surface and atmospheric temperature and moisture structure is to understand

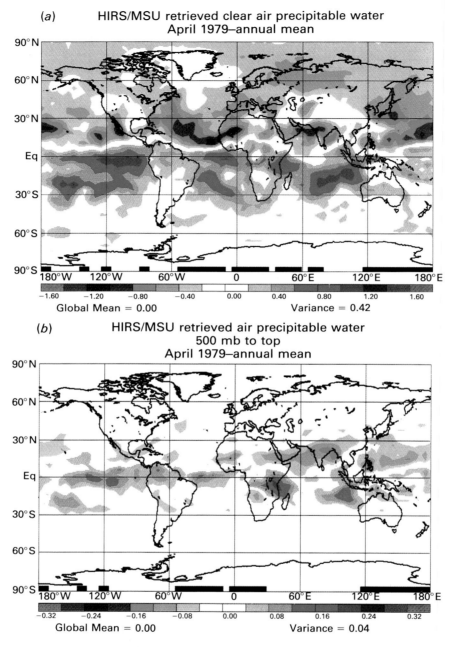

Fig. 16(*a*). As in Fig. 13(*a*) but for April 1979. (*b*). As in Fig. 13(*b*) but for April 1979.

the natural variability of fields of geophysical parameters and their interrelationships. Another goal is to determine if any apparent trends exist in the data, such as global warming. Clear relationships between spatial patterns of surface skin temperature and lower atmospheric temperature in extra-tropical land, and upper level moisture and precipitation in the tropics, are seen to exist in both annual mean fields and seasonal differences from the annual mean. In studying climate, it is of greater interest to examine if such correlations

exist in inter-annual differences of fields for the same month in different years. The following section shows results comparing May 1981 and May 1980.

Relationship between inter-annual differences of surface and atmospheric fields

Figs. 18(*a*) and 18(*b*) show the difference of monthly mean surface skin temperature and lower atmospheric temperature between May 1981 and May 1980 (red means May 1981 was

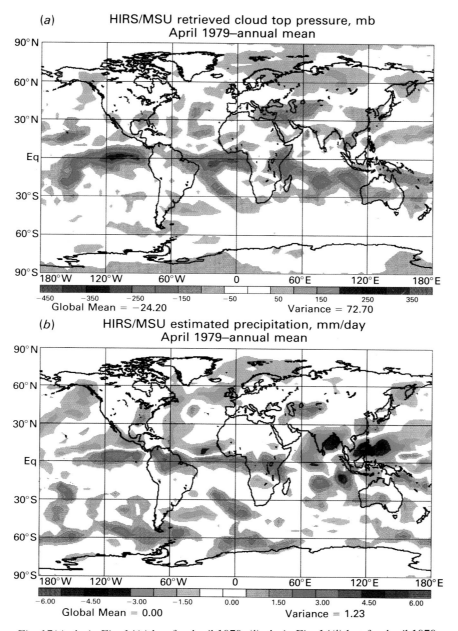

(a) HIRS/MSU retrieved cloud top pressure, mb
April 1979–annual mean

Global Mean = −24.20   Variance = 72.70

(b) HIRS/MSU estimated precipitation, mm/day
April 1979–annual mean

Global Mean = 0.00   Variance = 1.23

Fig. 17(*a*). As in Fig. 14(*a*) but for April 1979. (*b*). As in Fig. 14(*b*) but for April 1979.

warmer). Globally, May 1981 is found to be colder than May 1980 with regard to surface skin temperature (−.08 °C) and lower tropospheric temperature (−.15 °C). The spatial variance of both fields is about 1.35 °C, which is considerably smaller than that of April–annual mean (~2.3 °C) or July–annual mean (~6.5 °C). In order to enhance the inter-annual spatial differences, the color scale on Figs. 18(*a*) and (*b*) is expanded compared to those on Figs. 12 and 15. While the amplitudes are smaller, the features in Figs. 18(*a*) and (*b*) are quite spatially coherent. As in the other fields examined, inter-annual surface skin temperature changes are very heavily correlated with those of lower atmospheric temperature in extratropical land areas, and even have very similar magnitudes. The atmospheric temperature features continue into the extratropical ocean, with comparable amplitude to the values over land, while the surface temperature features do not show a significant oceanic temperature signal. For these two months, there were no appreciable temperature changes in the tropics. Correlation statistics for difference fields between May 1981 and May 1980 are included in Tables 3 and 4. Over extratropical land, the correlation between T_s and T_{500} is 0.78, which is even

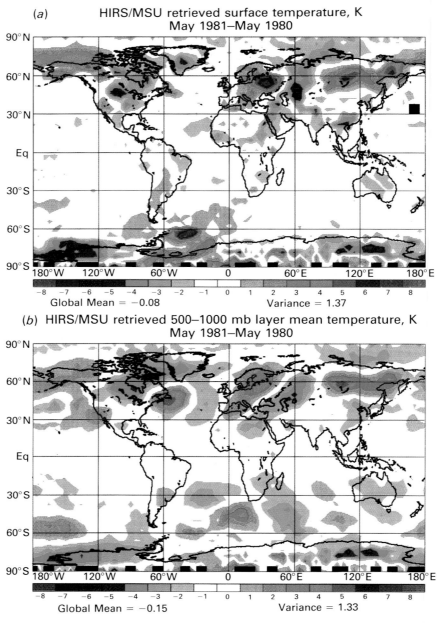

Fig. 18(a). Inter-annual difference of surface skin temperature (7:30am, 7:30pm average) for May 1981 and May 1980. Red means May 1981 was warmer. Black areas indicate insufficient data. (b). As in Fig. 18(a) but for 500 mb–1000 mb layer mean temperature.

larger than its value for April–annual mean. This high correlation is a common feature found in inter-annual differences.

Figs. 19(a) and (b) show May 1981–May 1980 values of total precipitable water and precipitable water above 500 mb. There was little change in global mean moisture between the two months. As with temperature, the spatial variances of the inter- annual differences are lower than those of April–annual mean, though the percentage reduction is not as great. The largest inter-annual changes of moisture are in the tropics,

where most of the moisture exists. Significant changes in total precipitable water patterns also occurred in the mid-latitudes, with a positive correlation with atmospheric temperature differences. Significant negative correlations of moisture with tropical land surface temperatures occur in some areas (note, for example, Indochina). Inter-annual changes in moisture above 500 mb have more coherent spatial patterns than those of total precipitable water and they are confined primarily to the tropics. The most prominent feature is a significant increase in upper level moisture in May 1981, compared to

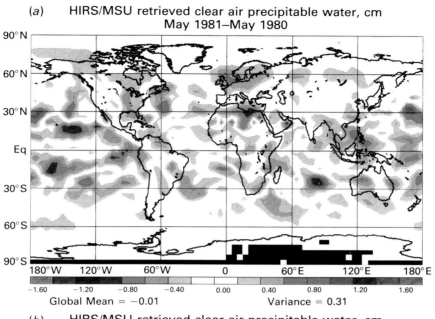

(a) HIRS/MSU retrieved clear air precipitable water, cm
May 1981–May 1980

Global Mean = −0.01   Variance = 0.31

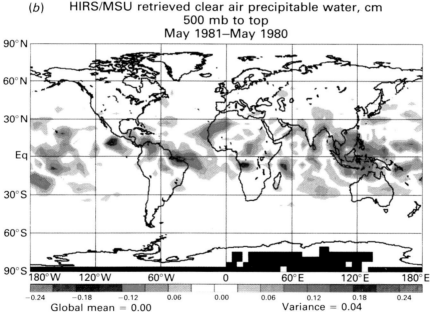

(b) HIRS/MSU retrieved clear air precipitable water, cm
500 mb to top
May 1981–May 1980

Global mean = 0.00   Variance = 0.04

Fig. 19(a). As in Fig. 18(a) but for clear air precipitable water (cm). Red means more precipitable water in May 1981. (b). As in Fig. 19(a) but for clear air precipitable water above 500 mb.

May 1980, in the tropics centered at 120° E, with a decrease in the region from 150° E eastward to 150° W. An analogous pattern also appears in total precipitable water, but no appreciable changes in surface or atmospheric temperatures occurred in these regions.

Figs. 20(a) and 20(b) show the inter-annual difference in cloud top pressure (red means May 1981 had lower pressure and higher cloud top altitude than May 1980) and precipitation (red means more precipitation in May 1981). It is inter-

esting to note in these figures that in the spatial variance sense, two Mays are as different from each other as April is from the annual mean. As with moisture distribution, the patterns are more of an east–west oscillating nature, as opposed to the more north–south orientation in the April–annual mean fields. The patterns of precipitation difference near the equator closely resemble those of the upper level clear air precipitable water differences. The correlation of the inter-annual difference of W_{500} with precipitation is the

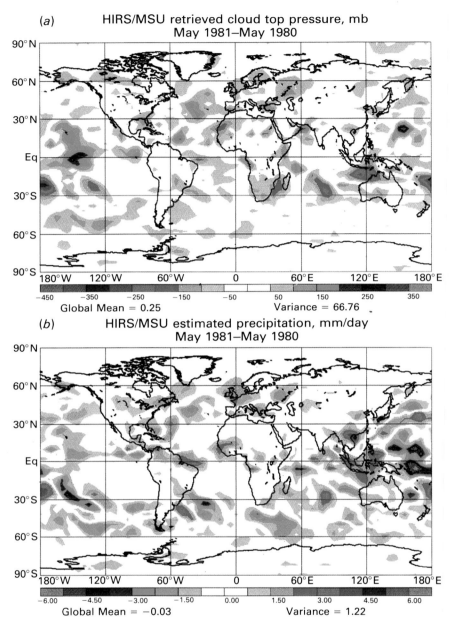

Fig. 20(a). As in Fig. 18(a) but for cloud top pressure (mb). Red means lower pressure (higher altitude) clouds in May 1981. (b). As in Fig. 18(a) but for precipitation (mm/day). Red means more precipitation in May 1981.

second highest of any two fields over tropical land and is equally high over tropical ocean. Thus the close relationship exhibited in space and time during a given year holds for inter-annual differences as well.

Variability and trends in global temperatures

A topic of considerable concern of late is whether a warming trend exists in global temperatures. To discern this, one must be able to measure temperatures accurately and without biases which may arise from using data from different satel-

lites, which may also be measuring at different times of day. Figs. 18(a) and 18(b) obtained using data from NOAA 6 for May 1981 and May 1980, both indicate a slight cooling of May 1981 compared to May 1980. Most of the inter-annual differences are of an east–west variety, expected for normal inter-annual variability. The global mean differences of the order of 0.1 °C are not particularly significant and are well within normal variability.

Figs. 21(a) and 21(b) show global mean values of surface skin temperature and 500–1000 mb layer mean temperatures

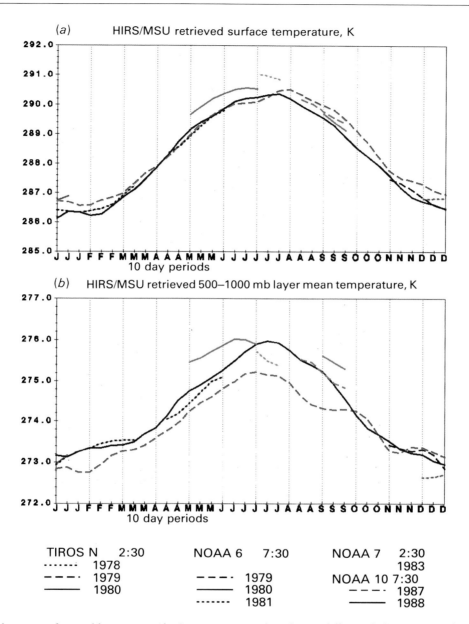

Fig. 21. Retrieved global mean surface and lower atmospheric temperatures plotted every 1/3 month for time periods processed. Satellites and corresponding local observing times are indicated on the Figure.

averaged over 1/3 month periods in each of the time periods processed. Results from different satellites are indicated in different colors, with different years for a given satellite shown in different patterns. The time of day of all the measurements is shown in the Figure and is important to bear in mind because of possible temporal sampling differences. Data from both the am and pm observations have been averaged together in producing the statistics.

A number of observations are evident from these Figures. The most obvious feature is the pronounced annual cycle of global surface and lower tropospheric temperatures. The

global surface skin temperature annual cycle has a seasonal variation of about 4 °C, with maximum values in late July–early August, and minimum values in late January–early February. The magnitude and phase of the annual cycles obtained from TIROS-N 1979 data and NOAA-6 1980 data are quite similar. An analogous phenomenon is observed in the 1000–500 mb layer mean temperature, with roughly 3/4 the amplitude and roughly a 1/2 month phase shift of the maxima and minima to earlier in the year. The annual cycle of global temperature is a result of the Northern Hemisphere, with more land, having a larger (out of

Table 5. *Inter-annual time averaged temperature differences (°C)*

Period	Years	Sat/Sat	ΔT Surface	ΔT 500–1000 mb
Jan. 1–Dec. 31	1980–1979	NOAA 6*/TIROS-N	−0.22	0.36
Nov. 1–Jan. 20	1979,80–1979,80	NOAA 6*/TIROS-N	−0.37	−0.00
Nov. 1–Dec. 30	1980–1979	NOAA 6*/NOAA 6*	−0.12	−0.04
Jan. 1–Feb. 28	1981–1980	NOAA 6*/NOAA 6*	0.12	−0.01
April 11–June 10	1981–1980	NOAA 6*/NOAA 6*	−.09	−.21
April 11–June 10	1981–1979	NOAA 6*/TIROS-N	−.01	0.26
July 1–July 31	1983–1979	NOAA 7/TIROS-N	0.68	0.39
July 1–July 31	1983–1980	NOAA 7/NOAA 6*	0.56	−0.38
Aug. 2–Sept. 30	1987–1979	NOAA 10*/TIROS-N	−0.16	0.82
Aug. 2–Sept. 30	1987–1980	NOAA 10*/NOAA 6*	0.26	0.06
May 1–July 15	1988–1979	NOAA 10*/TIROS-N	0.53	0.99
May 1–July 15	1988–1980	NOAA 10*/NOAA 6*	0.44	0.49
Sept. 1–Sept. 30	1988–1979	NOAA 10*/TIROS-N	−0.35	1.15
Sept. 1–Sept. 30	1988–1980	NOAA 10*/NOAA 6*	0.14	0.50

phase) annual cycle than that of the Southern Hemisphere.

Aside from a pronounced annual cycle, Fig. 21 also shows a considerable inter-annual variability of global mean temperatures. Fig. 21(b) indicates that lower atmospheric temperatures in periods in 1988 were about 1 °C warmer than in similar periods in 1979, but 1980 was also considerably warmer than 1979, as were the periods in 1983 and 1987 which were measured. Comparison of differences of time mean temperatures for different years is summarized in Table 5. The period November 1, 1979–January 20, 1980, which was observed by both TIROS-N and NOAA 6, was found to have almost identical lower tropospheric temperatures from the two satellites. While this may not appear to be noteworthy, it does indicate that artifacts in retrieved atmospheric temperatures, arising from use of two different satellites, with somewhat different instrumentation and observing at different times of day, do not appear to contribute significant errors in retrieved lower atmospheric temperatures, at least for this time period.

In contrast, the retrieved global surface skin temperature, averaged over the period November 1, 1979–January 20, 1980, is 0.37 degrees cooler as determined from NOAA 6 than it is from TIROS-N. The difference in surface skin temperature averaged over this period, as retrieved from data from the two satellites, is shown in Fig. 22(a). Oceanic temperatures, as retrieved from both satellites, are nearly identical, but NOAA 6 (7:30am, pm) land temperatures are considerably cooler than those from TIROS-N (2:30am, pm), especially in arid areas which have large diurnal differences. The difference between the 2:30pm and 2:30am local time surface skin temperature measurements as determined from TIROS-N data for the same time period, is shown in Fig. 22(b). It is apparent that the significant local differences in surface skin temperature, as seen from

TIROS-N and NOAA 6 for the same 2½ months period, are related closely to differences in the sampling times of day of the morning and afternoon satellites. A plot similar to Fig. 22(a), but for lower tropospheric temperatures, showed no significant sampling difference between TIROS-N and NOAA 6.

The effect of time of day sampling on the global mean surface skin temperature and 500–1000 mb layer mean temperature is shown in Figs. 23(a) and 23(b). Annual mean values of temperatures at each time of day for both 1979 and 1980 are indicated in the Figure. Part of the differences between the values shown in 1979 and 1980 is a result of the two years having different characteristics, but another source of differences is the different sampling times. To isolate the second factor, statistics are also given for global mean temperatures averaged only in the overlap period November 1, 1979 to January 20, 1980.

Global mean surface skin temperatures at 2:30pm are greater than those at 2:30am on the average by 3.0 °C and vary from about 2.5 °C–3.5 °C, depending on the time of year. The difference between 7:30pm and 7:30am global mean surface skin temperatures is much smaller, as expected, and has a more complex behavior, with 7:30pm being almost 1 °C warmer in the Northern Hemisphere winter, and 0.4 °C warmer in the Northern Hemisphere summer, but having almost identical global mean temperatures to those at 7:30am in late spring and early fall. Clearly, much care must be taken in interpreting inter-annual differences of surface skin temperatures when obtained from different satellites at different observing times. This is complicated by the fact that diurnal global surface temperature differences are dependent on the season.

Diurnal variations of global lower tropospheric temperature are considerably less than those of surface skin

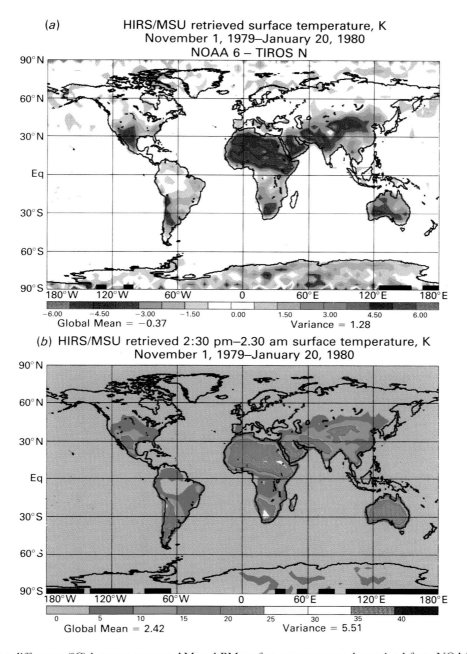

(a) HIRS/MSU retrieved surface temperature, K
November 1, 1979–January 20, 1980
NOAA 6 – TIROS N

Global Mean = −0.37   Variance = 1.28

(b) HIRS/MSU retrieved 2:30 pm–2.30 am surface temperature, K
November 1, 1979–January 20, 1980

Global Mean = 2.42   Variance = 5.51

Fig. 22(a). Retrieved mean difference (°C) between average AM and PM surface temperatures determined from NOAA 6 and TIROS-N for the period November 1, 1979 to January 20, 1980. Blue indicates NOAA 6 surface temperatures are colder. (b). Retrieved mean difference (°C) between 2:30pm and 2:30am surface skin temperatures for the period November 1, 1979 to January 20, 1980 determined from TIROS-N data.

temperature. The difference in global mean 2:30pm–2:30am lower tropospheric temperatures is about 0.5 °C, roughly independent of season, while at 7:30am, pm, the difference is about 0.4 °C. In the overlap period between NOAA 6 and TIROS-N, 2:30am and 7:30pm temperatures are very close together, as are the 2:30pm and 7:30pm temperatures. Sampling differences for atmospheric temperatures appear to be less significant than for surface skin temperatures, but one should still exercise caution in comparison of atmospheric temperatures from different years observed at different times of day.

Table 5 includes differences in temperature of periods observed in other years from those of comparable periods in 1979 and 1980. Periods observed by morning satellites are indicated by *. The most direct inter-annual comparisons are from periods observed both by morning or afternoon satel-

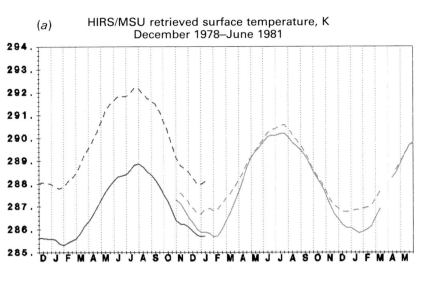

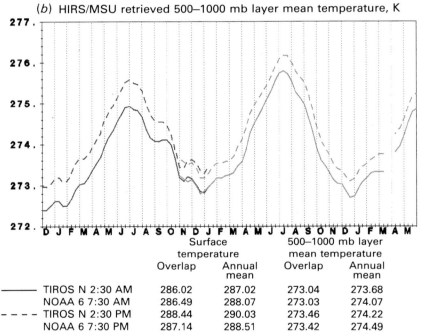

		Surface temperature		500–1000 mb layer mean temperature	
		Overlap	Annual mean	Overlap	Annual mean
——	TIROS N 2:30 AM	286.02	287.02	273.04	273.68
	NOAA 6 7:30 AM	286.49	288.07	273.03	274.07
– – –	TIROS N 2:30 PM	288.44	290.03	273.46	274.22
	NOAA 6 7:30 PM	287.14	288.51	273.42	274.49

Fig. 23. Twice daily global mean values of surface temperature and 500 mb–1000 mb layer mean temperature, plotted every 1/3 of a month, for data processed from TIROS-N and NOAA 6. Annual mean values for 1979 and 1980 are indicated, as well as values for the overlap period November 1, 1979 to January 20, 1980. The vertical dashed lines indicate the first 1/3 of a month.

lites, especially with regard to surface skin temperature. In these time periods, the difference in surface skin temperature is always the same sign as that of 500–1000 mb temperature when a significant difference exists. The atmospheric temperature difference is about 60% as great as the surface temperature difference in the one afternoon case, and about 10% larger than the surface temperature difference in the mean of the three morning cases involving 1987 and 1988.

The summers of 1988 and 1980 both had strong droughts in North America and are interesting to compare with each other. Results show that the summer of 1988 was about 0.5 °C warmer than that of 1980. Figs. 24(a) and 24(b) show the differences in retrieved surface skin temperature and 500–1000 mb temperature, between the periods June 1988 and June 1980. As was found with regard to the inter-seasonal difference fields, inter-annual differences of

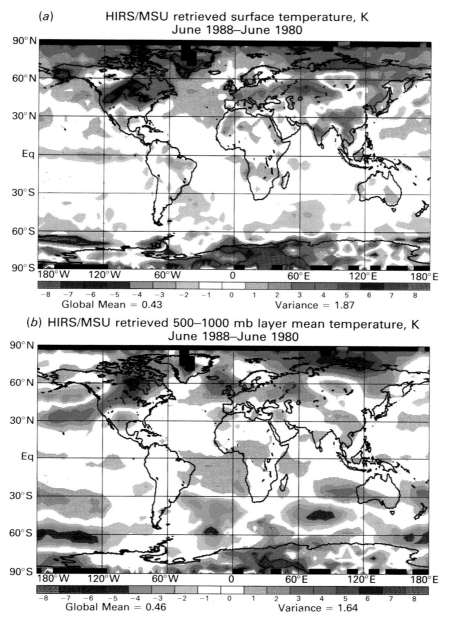

(*a*) HIRS/MSU retrieved surface temperature, K
June 1988–June 1980

Global Mean = 0.43   Variance = 1.87

(*b*) HIRS/MSU retrieved 500–1000 mb layer mean temperature, K
June 1988–June 1980

Global Mean = 0.46   Variance = 1.64

Fig. 24(*a*). Difference of monthly mean surface skin temperature (°C) retrieved for June 1988 and June 1980. Red indicates June 1988 is warmer than June 1980. (*b*). As in Fig. 24(*a*) but for 500 mb–1000 mb layer mean temperature.

monthly mean surface and atmospheric temperatures are also closely related to each other in extratropical land and sea–ice areas, with similar patterns and magnitudes. The correlation of the two fields in extratropical land is 0.91 in the Southern Hemisphere, 0.69 in the Northern Hemisphere, and 0.83 globally. Thus correlations in retrieved inter-annual differences of land atmospheric and surface temperatures, in periods observed from two different satellites, are as great as those of inter-seasonal differences or inter-annual differences observed from the same satellite. Over ocean, large

spatially coherent inter-annual differences are also found in lower atmospheric temperatures, which appear to be closely related to inter-annual differences in adjacent land areas. The anomalously cold sea–surface temperatures in the equatorial Pacific Ocean in 1988 did not appear to induce, or result from, a cold atmospheric anomaly in this area, however.

The agreement in pattern and amplitude of inter-annual surface and lower atmospheric temperatures, derived from years observed by two different satellites, is a very encouraging sign. Retrieval of surface and lower atmospheric

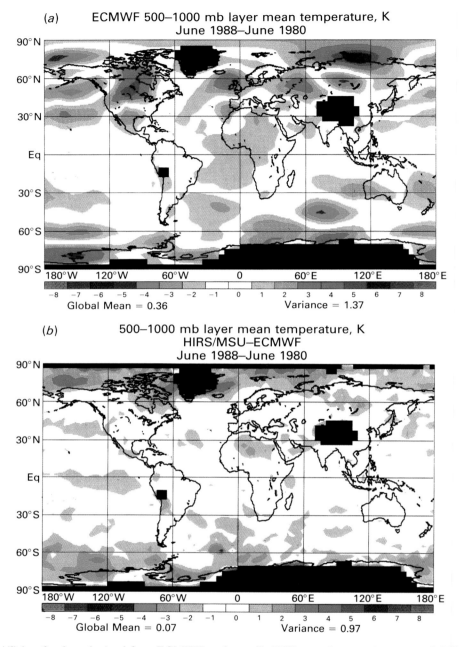

(a) ECMWF 500–1000 mb layer mean temperature, K
June 1988–June 1980

Global Mean = 0.36   Variance = 1.37

(b) 500–1000 mb layer mean temperature, K
HIRS/MSU–ECMWF
June 1988–June 1980

Global Mean = 0.07   Variance = 0.97

Fig. 25(a). As in Fig. 24(b) but for data obtained from ECMWF analyses. (b). Difference between inter-annual difference of June 1988–June 1980 500 mb–1000 mb layer mean temperature as determined from HIRS data and ECMWF. Red means HIRS has June 88–June 80 more positive (or less negative) than ECMWF.

temperatures are basically independent of each other, as they use different sets of channels. It is unlikely that similar spurious biases should occur in both sets of channels. Moreover, systematic errors are indirectly correlated in a negative way, in that spuriously retrieving too warm a surface skin temperature would result in the atmospheric temperature becoming spuriously too cold, as some of the radiance in the temperature sounding channels would be attributed to excess

radiance coming from the surface. This is suggestive that both the patterns and the overall global difference in temperatures between June 1988 and June 1980 of 0.4–0.5 °C is reasonable and is not a result of instrumental artefacts and biases.

Another measure of inter-annual differences in global temperatures can be obtained from taking the difference of ECMWF (European Center for Medium-range Weather

Table 6. *HIRS2/MSU and ECMWF T_{500} differences for June 1988–June 1980*

Area	HIRS Mean	ECMWF Mean	HIRS-ECMWF Mean	HIRS Variance	ECMWF Variance	HIRS-ECMWF Variance	Correlation Coefficient
North America	1.76	1.71	0.04	2.44	2.19	0.73	0.95
Europe	0.87	0.62	0.25	1.46	1.58	0.40	0.97
Australia	1.01	0.97	0.04	1.02	0.84	0.36	0.94
Combined	1.22	1.10	0.12	1.81	1.73	0.54	0.95
Global*	0.43	0.36	0.07	1.61	1.37	0.97	0.76

* Areas in common.

Forecasting) analyses produced during June 1988 and June 1980. This field is shown in Fig. 25(a). These analyses are based almost exclusively on *in situ* radiosonde reports in land areas such as North America, Europe, and Australia. Over ocean, the analyses are based mostly on satellite soundings produced operationally in the appropriate year by NOAA NESDIS. Since these retrievals were not done in an identical fashion in 1988 and 1980, caution must be used in comparing Fig. 25(a) with Fig. 24(b). In addition, ECMWF used different methodology in 1980 and 1988, which is especially noticeable in the extrapolation of atmospheric temperatures to 1000 mb in areas with elevated terrain. Therefore, areas of elevated terrain have been eliminated from Fig. 25(a).

Because the ECMWF results are based on radiosonde reports over most of North America, Europe, and Australia, these areas can be used as an independent evaluation of the quality of the HIRS2/MSU sounding data. Figs. 24(b) and 25(a) show great similarity in both pattern and amplitude over these areas, though the features appear slightly stronger in the HIRS field than in the ECMWF, which is smoother in general. The two fields are, in fact, quite close globally, other than in elevated areas, but the HIRS differences are generally of somewhat larger amplitude. The difference between Figs. 24(b) and 25(a) is shown in Fig. 25(b) (red means the HIRS value of differences of T_{500} between June 88 and June 80 is greater than that of ECMWF). While significant differences between the two fields exist in many locations, differences are generally less than 1.0 °C in areas where considerable radiosonde data exists.

Table 6 shows values of the mean and variance of HIRS and ECMWF June 1988–June 1980 inter-annual difference of T_{500} over select areas, as well as the mean and variance of the difference field (HIRS–ECMWF) of the inter-annual differences and the area correlation coefficients of the difference patterns. Results are shown separately for North America (32° N–56° N, 122.5° W–72.5° W), Europe (36° N–56° N, 12.5° W–52.5° E), Australia (36° S–16° S, 112.5° E–52.5° E) and the combined area of all three locations. In addition, global statistics are given, excluding areas of surface pressure

less than 850 mb which were eliminated from the ECMWF fields.

The global mean of difference of 0.07 °C, and variance of 0.97 °C, shown in Table 6 are the same values shown in Fig. 25(b). The largest differences between the two fields occur at high latitudes and in areas of high elevation. In these areas, the consistency between the HIRS inter-annual surface temperature difference and the lower atmospheric temperature difference is an indication of the reasonableness of the HIRS field.

Global agreement between the two totally independent fields (ECMWF used radiosondes and operational retrievals) is encouraging. The most significant areas to compare are those based only on radiosonde reports (ECMWF did not use satellite retrieval data over land in their analyses). Table 6 shows excellent agreement between the monthly mean difference of HIRS soundings and analyses over North America, Europe, and Australia. Each of these land areas was considerably warmer in June 1988 than June 1980. On the average, ECMWF had a 1.10 °C warming for these land areas, while the HIRS inter-annual difference was 10% larger. The spatial variance, according to ECMWF, was 1.73 °C, while the variance of the difference of the two fields was 0.54 °C and the correlation coefficient was 0.95. This indicates the absolute accuracy of the inter-annual difference of HIRS2/MSU soundings, obtained from two different satellites, is the order of 0.1 °C. In addition, the spatial details of inter-annual differences are highly accurate. There is no reason to expect HIRS2 soundings to be less accurate in other regions of the globe as equivalent processing is done and 500–1000 mb layer mean temperatures have been shown to be highly independent of first guess fields (Reuter *et al.* 1988).

Fig. 26 shows the zonal mean surface skin and lower atmospheric temperatures for June 1988 and June 1980, as well as their differences. It is apparent from Fig. 26, as well as Fig. 24, that most of the warming in 1988 took place at the high latitudes, in regions which are predominantly land. The zonal mean patterns in surface and lower atmospheric temperature

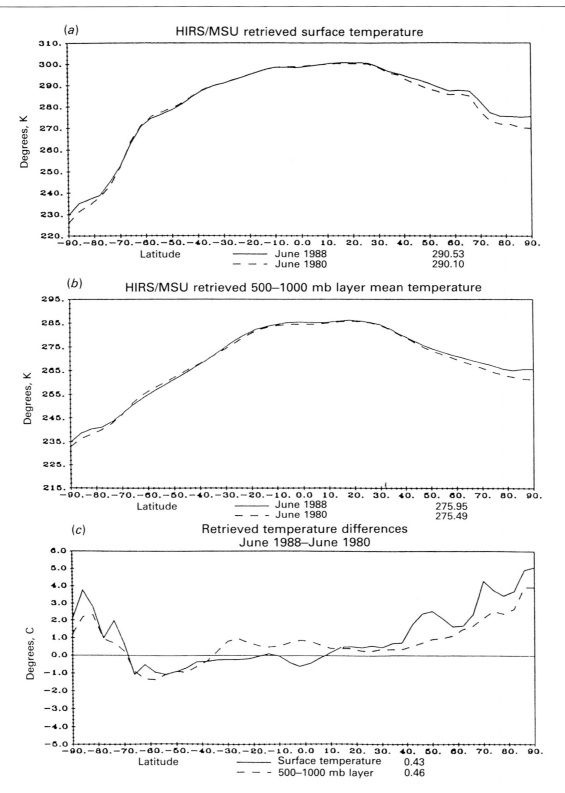

Fig. 26(*a*). Zonal mean surface temperature (K) for June 1988 and June 1980. Global mean values are shown on the Figure. (*b*). As in Fig. 26(*a*) but for 500 mb–1000 mb layer mean temperature. (*c*). The differences in zonal mean surface skin temperatures, and 500 mb–1000 mb layer mean temperatures, between June 1988 and June 1980. Positive values mean June 1988 was warmer.

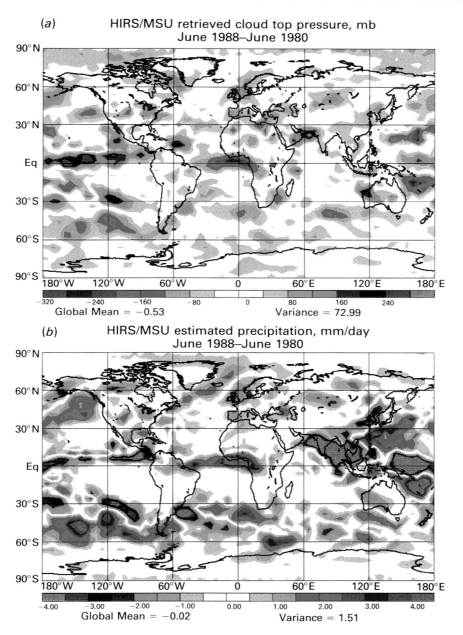

Fig. 27(a). As in Fig. 24(a) but for cloud top pressure (mb). Red indicates lower pressure (higher altitude) clouds in June 1988. (b). As in Fig. 24(a) but for precipitation estimate (mm/day). Red indicates more precipitation in June 1988.

differences are very similar in these latitudes, with surface temperature differences being about 50% larger than lower atmospheric temperature differences. The tropical oceanic areas, influenced by the large negative sea surface temperature anomaly in 1988, were somewhat colder in 1988 than 1980. On the other hand, tropical atmospheric temperatures were slightly warmer in June 1988. This accounts for the global mean surface temperature difference between June 1988 and June 1980 being somewhat lower than the atmospheric temperature difference.

While the cold tropical Pacific sea surface temperature did not appear to have a major effect on tropical atmospheric temperatures, it did play a major role in altering the atmospheric circulation patterns. Fig. 27(a) shows the difference in monthly mean cloud top pressure between June 1988 and June 1980. Lower pressure in 1988 (higher altitude) clouds are depicted in red. The global mean difference in cloud top pressure between the two years is less than 1 mb. This is encouraging as it does not point to the existence of a significant bias in retrieved cloud top pressure arising from use of instrumentation on two different satellites. The spatial variance is quite large, however, with the largest differences occurring in the tropical oceans. Fig. 27(*a*) shows a significant decrease in cloud top pressure over the area of decreased sea surface temperature in the equatorial Pacific Ocean. The decreased convective activity in these areas is augmented by increased convection eastward in the equatorial Atlantic Ocean, and northward and southward in the Pacific Ocean in the vicinity of the dateline. This increase in convection in the north Pacific Ocean extends into the western United States. This is suggestive that the major change in circulation patterns in the United States, with higher clouds in June 1988 in the west, and lower clouds in the east, may well be related to the changes in tropical sea–surface temperature.

This change in atmospheric circulation patterns caused significant differences in the distribution of precipitation in June 1988 and June 1980, as shown in Fig. 27(*b*). It is interesting to note that the spatial variance of precipitation differences in June of two different years is as great as that of the difference between July 1979 and the 1979 annual mean, shown in Fig. 14(*b*). The major inter-annual differences in precipitation are in the tropics, with patterns closely following those of the cloud top pressure difference field. There is very little difference in precipitation between the two years along the equator west of South America because very little rain ever occurs in June in this region. Fig. 27(*b*) also shows some significant changes in precipitation patterns in the extra-tropics, which may be related to changes in the tropical circulation. Note, for example, the track of increased precipitation in June 1988 which originates in the east China Sea and appears to move northwestward into northwest Canada. The path of this track east of about 140° W follows closely the region of warmer oceanic temperatures in 1988. Once land is reached, however, the area of increased precipitation in northwest Canada corresponds to an area of lower surface skin temperature. This out-of-phase relationship of precipitation with surface skin temperature is analogous to the out-of-phase annual cycle of tropical surface temperature and precipitation, and is observed in many land areas in the summer hemisphere. In addition, it appears to hold for equatorial South America as well, although not for Africa. While both June 1988 and June 1980 were periods of heat wave and droughts in the central and eastern United States, the heat wave and drought in 1988 is shown to be both stronger, and located further to the north, than in 1980. This is consistent with *in situ* temperature and rainfall observations.

Limitations

Results obtained thus far from analysis of the HIRS2/MSU data have been encouraging. Evidence from the limited data suggests that inter-annual global temperature changes can be monitored reasonably accurately from the soundings, even when data obtained from different satellites are used. In addition, the data indicate significant correlations between parameters obtained in very different ways, such as extra-tropical land and lower atmospheric temperatures, tropical upper level moisture and precipitation, and inter-annual differences of tropical sea surface temperature and precipitation patterns when these differences are significant (June 1988–June 1980). These correlations both lend credence to the satellite derived results and enable us to learn more about the interrelationship between inter-annual differences of surface and atmospheric behavior.

On the other hand, there are a number of limitations to the data. Perhaps most significant is limited time sampling. At best, soundings are obtained only four fixed times daily. Moreover, soundings of temperature and moisture are only obtained under clear or partially cloudy (up to about 80% cloudiness) conditions. During significant time periods, data exist only twice daily, at 7:30am, pm or 2:30am, pm. Sampling at different times of day results in significant biases in land surface skin temperatures, and possibly small seasonal dependent biases in atmospheric temperatures (see Fig. 23). These have to be better understood to interpret trends observed in temperatures observed at different times of day. Results of the inter-annual difference of June 1988–June 1980 seem to indicate that limited satellite sampling only at 7:30am, pm local time under clear and partially cloudy conditions is not causing a significant sampling error, when compared to results from radiosonde reports 2 times daily (0000 UTC and 1200 UTC) every day. Results might be poorer when data from satellites at different times of day, or even both at 2:30am, pm are used. Diurnal sampling problems may be even more serious for clouds and precipitation, especially in the tropics.

In addition, there are limitations in the products themselves. The vertical resolution of the temperature and moisture soundings is poor and surface skin temperatures are somewhat sensitive to assumptions of the surface emissivity. The accuracy of retrieved cloud parameters is degraded by errors in surface and atmospheric parameters. In addition, in the case of multi-layer clouds, only a radiatively effective cloud pressure and cloud fraction are obtained.

Considerable improvements in sounding capability will be obtained when AIRS (Atmospheric Infra-red Sounder) flies on the NASA polar platform as part of EOS (Earth Observing

System) in the late 1990s. AIRS has roughly 3400 pieces of spectral information from 600 cm^{-1} to 2700 cm^{-1} with a resolving power $v/\Delta v$ of 1200 (0.5 cm^{-1} spectral resolution at 600 cm^{-1}; 2.0 cm^{-1} resolution at 2400 cm^{-1}) and contiguous spectral coverage. AIRS represents a considerable improvement on all the capabilities of HIRS2. AIRS will fly together with AMSU (Advanced Microwave Sounding Unit) A and AMSU B, which are multi-channel microwave radiometers providing additional information about atmospheric temperature and moisture structure. The complement is expected to provide atmospheric temperature structure with an accuracy of 1 °C in 1 km layers throughout the troposphere, and 1 °C in 4 km layers in the stratosphere, under up to about 70% cloudiness. Accuracies in the lowest 1–2 km of the atmosphere will degrade to the order of 3 °C under more extensive cloud cover, however, when AIRS data become less usable. Water vapor profiles are expected to have an accuracy of 10% in 2 km layers in the troposphere. In addition, the spectral surface emissivity of the surface and clouds can be inferred from the data and this will allow for determination of improved surface and cloud parameters. Unfortunately, the temporal sampling problem will remain.

Data from the EOS time period will provide a more accurate description of inter-annual variability and trends. Even with its limitations, much can be learned about using data from the current satellite system. In order to prepare for the EOS time frame, and learn as much as possible about climate variability over the last decade, NASA and NOAA have embarked on a joint effort to produce Pathfinder data sets of geophysical parameters based on multi-year analysis of data from operational satellites, produced in a consistent manner. One of these data sets will be based on analysis of TOVS (HIRS2, MSU, and SSU) data. The Pathfinder TOVS Science Working Group has identified three valid approaches to produce climate data sets from TOVS data and three independent data sets may be produced. Data for the period 1979–1994 is expected to be analysed and available at the end of 1994.

The first approach involves an interactive forecast–retrieval–analysis system along the lines discussed in this chapter. Incorporation of a model forecast as first guess for retrievals is useful in predicting vertical fine structure not resolved by the instruments. Potentially more significant is the use of the forecast to help account for effects of clouds on HIRS2 observations, as well as to identify systematic differences between observed and computed brightness temperatures. This is critical in accounting for satellite instrument calibration drifts and inter-satellite calibration differences. On the other hand, there is a valid concern that use of a forecast model in any way in production of a climate data

set could influence the results toward the climatology of the model. The likelihood of this is small however because the model is initialized by data, including radiosondes, every 6 hours and only short forecasts are performed.

To avoid possible contamination by influence of a general circulation model, a second set of retrievals will be done which uses statistical information relating radiances to a large ensemble of atmospheric profiles to produce the first guess for the soundings. This approach will also produce detailed soundings of temperature and moisture profiles as well as the other geophysical parameters discussed.

A third approach to monitoring climate was to attempt to add no information to that of the radiances, and only use the observations themselves as climate trend indicators, describing behavior in coarse atmospheric layers. Such an approach has been advocated by Spencer, Christy & Grody (1990). The magnitude of inter-annual variability, found by Spencer et al. (1990) is considerably lower than that found in this work. In addition, differences in sign exist in some cases (Spencer's data indicate that the lower troposphere is colder globally in June 1988 than June 1980). More study is needed to understand these differences, which will be aided by the production of the three long-term data sets.

References

Baker, W. E. (1983). Objective analysis and assimilation of observational data from FGGE. *Mon. Wea. Rev.*, **111**, 328–42.

Baker, W. E., Atlas, R., Halem, M. & Susskind, J. (1984). A case study of forecast sensitivity to data and data analysis techniques. *Mon. Wea. Rev.*, **112**, 1544–61.

Chahine, M. T. (1970). Inverse problems in radiative transfer: Determination of atmospheric parameters. *J. Atmos. Sci.*, **27**, 960–7.

Chahine, M. T. (1974). Remote sounding of cloudy atmospheres, I: the single cloud layer. *J. Atmos. Sci.*, **31**, 233–43.

Chahine, M. T. & Susskind, J. (1989). Fundamentals of the GLA physical retrieval method. Report on the Joint ECMWF/EUMETSAT Workshop on the Use of Satellite Data in Operational Weather Prediction: 1989–1993. A. Hollingsworth, ed., vol. 1, 271–300.

Fleming, H. E., Goldberg, M. D. & Crosby, D. S. (1988). Operational implementation of the minimum variance simultaneous retrieval method. Preprints 3rd Conference on Satellite Meteorology and Oceanography, 31 Jan.–5 Feb., Anaheim, California, *Am. Met. Soc.*, Boston, pp. 16–19.

Kalnay, E., Jusem, J. C. & Pfaendtner, J. (1985). The relative importance of mass and wind data in the FGGE observing system. *Proceeding of the NASA Symposium on Global Wind Measurements*. Columbia, Maryland, W. Baker, ed., July 29–August 1, pp. 1–5.

Reuter, D., Susskind, J. & Pursch, A. (1988). First guess

dependence of a physically based set of temperature humidity retrievals from HIRS2/MSU data. *J. Atmos. Ocean Tech.*, **5**, 70–83.

Smith, W. L. & Woolf, H. M. (1976). The use of eigenvectors of statistical covariance matrices for interpreting satellite sounding radiometer measurements. *J. Atmos. Sci.*, **33**, 1127–40.

Spencer, R. W., Christy, J. R. & Grody, N. C. (1990). Global atmospheric temperature monitoring with satellite microwave measurements, 1979–84. *J. Climate*, **3**, 1111–28.

Susskind, J. & Pfaendtner, J. (1989). Impact of interactive physical retrievals on NWP. Report on the Joint ECMWF/EUMET-SAT Workshop on the Use of Satellite Data in operational weather prediction: 1989–1993. A. Hollingsworth, ed., vol. 1. 245–270.

Susskind & Piraino, P. (1985). Automated temperature retrieval bias correction. Global Modeling and Simulation Branch Research Review. GSFC, Greenbelt, MD 20771, pp. 71–76.

Susskind, J. & Reuter, D. (1985). Retrieval of sea-surface temperatures from HIRS2/MSU. *J. Geophys. Res.*, **90C**, 11602–8.

Susskind, J., Reuter, D. & Chahine, M. T. (1987). Cloud fields retrieved from HIRS2/MSU data. *J. Geophys. Res.*, **92D**, 4035–50.

Susskind, J., Rosenfield, J. & Reuter, D. (1983). An accurate radiative transfer model for use in the direct physical inversion of HIRS2 and MSU temperature sounding data. *J. Geophys. Res.*, **88**, 8550–68.

Susskind, J., Rosenfield, J., Reuter, D. & Chahine, M. T. (1984). Remote sensing of weather and climate parameters from HIRS2/MSU on TIROS-N. *J. Geophys. Res.*, **89**, 4677–97.

Wu, M.-L. C. & Susskind, J. (1990). Outgoing longwave radiation computed from HIRS2/MSU soundings. *J. Geophys. Res.*, **95D**, 7579–602.

Surface wind velocity over the oceans

R. ATLAS, R. N. HOFFMAN AND S. C. BLOOM

Introduction

Consistent oceanic surface wind data of high quality and high temporal and spatial resolution are required to understand and predict the large scale air–sea interactions which are thought to significantly influence both the atmosphere and ocean. Such observations are needed to provide initial data and verification data for numerical weather prediction models, drive ocean models and surface wave models, calculate surface fluxes of heat, moisture and momentum, and construct surface climatologies.

Surface wind stress provides the most important forcing of the ocean circulation, while the fluxes of heat, moisture and momentum across the air–sea boundary are important factors in the formation, movement, and modification of water masses and the intensification of storms near coasts and over the open oceans. In addition, air–sea interaction plays a major role in theories of ENSO and the 50-day oscillation, as well as in the initiation and maintenance of heat waves and drought and other persistent anomalies.

Prior to the launch of satellites capable of determining surface wind from space, observations of surface wind velocity were provided primarily by ships and buoys. Such conventional observations are extremely limited and are not adequate for performing detailed studies of atmospheric and oceanic phenomena. For example, reports of surface wind by ships are often of poor accuracy, cover only very limited regions of the world's oceans, and occur at irregular intervals in time and space. Buoys, while of higher accuracy, have extremely sparse coverage. Due to these deficiencies, analyses of surface wind often misrepresent atmospheric flow over large regions of the global oceans, and this contributes to the poor calculation of wind stress and sensible and latent heat fluxes in these regions.

In response to the wind blowing across it, the ocean surface responds with waves ranging in wavelength from short capillary waves to ocean swell. This response provides a mechanism for the microwave remote sensing of ocean surface wind from space. The active sensing of the radar backscatter of centimeter scale capillary waves allows the retrieval of ocean

surface wind vectors with some ambiguity in direction. The Seasat, NSCAT and ERS-1 scatterometers were designed to take advantage of this phenomenon. Seasat data are available for only the third quarter of 1978 (Atlas et al., 1987). ERS-1 scatterometer data are not yet available (as of the first quarter of 1992); NSCAT is planned for launch in 1996. Passive microwave remote sensing of the ocean surface also has the capability of retrieving ocean surface wind speeds through the response of the microwave emissivity to the surface roughness. Several instruments – SMMR, SSM/I, and Geosat – have provided large data sets of ocean surface wind speed. Of these, SSM/I has the best coverage and resolution, although the lack of wind directions in these data have limited their utility in scientific studies to date.

In an effort to make the SSM/I data more generally useful, the SSM/I data have been combined with conventional surface observations and ECMWF analyses (Atlas et al., 1991). In essence these three types of data are combined in a filtering procedure. The resulting analysis is used to assign directions to the SSM/I winds. One year of SSM/I data has been processed in this manner beginning with the operational phase of SSM/I in July 1987.

In this chapter, this unique ocean surface wind data set is described. The methodology used and examples of the results are presented. These data are available through the NASA Ocean Data System (NODS) and can be used in atmospheric and oceanic modeling studies as well as in the calculation of surface fluxes and studies of air–sea interaction.

Methodology

The methodology used is similar to that described by Hoffman (1984) with modifications to accommodate the special attributes of the SSM/I data as well as some additional tuning of the data quality checking and filter weights.

A variational analysis method (VAM) was applied to surface wind data available during the first year of SSM/I operation (July 1987 through June 1988). The numbers of observations for the different data types are listed in Table 1. The only data not included in the analysis are data withheld for the

Table 1. *Inputs to the variational analysis*

Type	N (average obs/analysis)
ECMWF analysis (background)	13 104
Conventional wind data	900
SSM/I wind speeds	16 000

purpose of verification. The analyses were performed every 6 hours on a 2° latitude by 2.5° longitude grid.

Variational analysis method

The variational analysis generates a gridded surface wind analysis by minimizing an objective function **F**, which is a measure of the misfit of the analysis to the background, the data and certain *a priori* constraints. More explicitly, the following expression is used for **F**:

$$F = \lambda_1 S_C + \lambda_2 S_B + \lambda_3 S_S + \lambda_4 S_{VEL} + \lambda_5 S_{DIV} + \lambda_6 S_{VOR} + \lambda_7 S_{DYN}$$

where the λs are weights controlling the amount of influence each constraint has on the final analysis. Table 2 contains a summary of the constraints used in F; note that these constraints are weak constraints; the λs are not Lagrange multipliers.

In the present case, the ECMWF surface wind analysis is used as the background. The data consist of SSM/I wind speeds, ship and buoy wind vectors, and 1000 mb rawindsonde wind reports. The *a priori* constraints are: 1) the analysis should be close to the background field, 2) the differences between the analyzed and background wind, vorticity, and divergence should be smooth, and 3) the estimated time rate of change of the vorticity of the analysis should be small. These constraints control the degree to which the analysis can use the SSM/I data to modify the background field.

The wind data used in the variational analysis are subject to a relatively simple two-step quality control procedure. In each step, differences of the data from a reference field are checked in terms of these: 1) vector velocity magnitude, 2) speed and 3) direction. In the first step, data values far from the background field are flagged and withheld from the analysis procedure. The second step uses the first analysis as the basis for accepting the flagged data; in this case, the previously flagged data are reexamined against the first analysis using the above three criteria. Data passing the three checks in the second pass must have smaller differences from the first analysis than they did from the background in the first pass.

In order to use the SSM/I data, several changes to the

Table 2. *Summary of the penalty terms used in the variational analysis. Subscript 'A' refers to the analyzed value (eg V_A is the analyzed wind vector). All other subscripts are defined below*

Penalty term	Expression	Description
	Penalty terms measuring departures	
S_C	$\Sigma (V_C - V_A)^2$	From conventional data
S_B	$\Sigma (V_B - V_A)^2$	From background field
S_S	$\Sigma (\lvert V_S \rvert - \lvert V_A \rvert)^2$	From SSM/I wind speeds
	Smoothness constraints	
S_{VEL}	$\Sigma (\nabla^2 (u_B - u_A))^2 +$ $\Sigma (\nabla^2 (v_B - v_A))^2$	Velocity component
S_{DIV}	$\Sigma (\nabla^2 (\chi_B - \chi_A))^2$	Divergence smoothing (χ=velocity potential)
S_{VOR}	$\Sigma (\nabla^2 (\psi_B - \psi_A))^2$	Velocity smoothing (ψ=streamfunction)
	Dynamical constraint	
S_{DYN}	$\Sigma (\delta \zeta_A / \delta t)^2$	Analyzed vorticity tendency

VAM were implemented. For Seasat, high values of nadir wind speed were suspect. Wind speed errors for SSM/I have no well-defined dependence on the wind speed. Consequently the weight given to the constraint measuring the departure of the analyzed wind from the SSM/I wind speeds is a constant independent of the value of the SSM/I wind speed. In addition, a series of calibration experiments were performed for the period August 4–9, 1987, from which the appropriate constraint weights for the SSM/I analyses were determined. Three verification data sets were used for the calibration tests: 1) all conventional surface data used in the VAM, 2) a withheld buoy data set, 3) an independent tropical buoy data set.

From these tests, it was determined that the background (ECMWF analysis) should be given much more weight than the first guess fields were given in the Hoffman (1984) study. Similarly, it was found that the constraint on the SSM/I speeds should be the same magnitude as the constraint on the conventional data; the Hoffman (1984) study gave twice as much weight to the Seasat wind speeds as to the conventional data.

Data sets and products

The SSM/I wind speed data were obtained from Remote Sensing Systems, Santa Rosa, California. An algorithm developed by F. Wentz was used to infer the SSM/I wind speeds from surface microwave emissivity. The algorithm relates wind speed (w, in m s^{-1}) at 19.5 m above the sea surface both to the brightness temperatures obtained from two channels of the SSM/I instrument (37 GHz, vertical and horizontal polarizations) and to the radiative transfer and absorption between the sea surface and the satellite. The wind speed and atmospheric transmittance along the path between the sea surface and the satellite (τ) are obtained by the iterative solution of the two equations involving the brightness temperatures ($T_B^{h,v}$):

$$T_B^{h,v} = T_{Bu} + \tau[E^{h,v}T_s + (1 - E^{h,v})(1 + \omega^{h,v}m)(T_{Bd} + \tau T_{B-cold})]$$

$T_{Bu,d}$ are the upwelling/downwelling brightness temperatures due to atmospheric emission and absorption; and they can be related to the sea surface temperature T_s. T_{B-cold} is the 2.8 degree cosmic background radiation. $\omega^{h,v}$ are constants related to surface scattering. $E^{h,v}$ are the emissivities of the sea surface for 37 GHz radiation; they are parameterized in terms of the surface wind speed, surface temperature and the incidence angle. The specifics of the parameterizations of $E^{h,v}$ and other details of the Wentz algorithm can be found in Halpern *et al.* (1991). The process was assumed to have converged when the surface wind speed changed by less than .05 m/s. In cases where no convergence was attained in ten iterations, the brightness temperatures were considered to have been erroneous or rain-contaminated. The wind speed data generated by this method have an effective accuracy of ±2 m/s over the range 3–25 m/s.

The conventional data used in the analyses were obtained from the Scientific Division of the National Center for Atmospheric Research (NCAR). These consisted of all ship and buoy observations of surface wind and rawinsonde observations of 1000 mb wind that were available in real time.

The background fields were obtained from ECMWF surface analyses. In these analyses, conventional observations from land stations, ships and buoys, cloud-tracked winds from geostationary satellites, and temperature profiles from polar orbiting satellites are blended with model forecast fields. The data assimilation procedure used in creating these analyses is described in Hollingsworth *et al.* (1986); and a summary of ECMWF analysis updates is given by Trenberth, Olson & Large (1989). The ECMWF analyses were interpolated to a 2° latitude by 2.5° longitude grid to provide first guess fields for the analyses.

An additional data set, used only for verification, was obtained from the Pacific Marine Environmental Laboratory (PMEL) Ocean Climate Research Division. These data consisted of moored Atlas buoys and island wind stations in the tropical Pacific for the period 1 July 1987 to 30 June 1988.

Several data sets were generated from the analyses. The primary data set, denoted Level 3.0, is the gridded analyses. The SSM/I winds with their assigned directions, binned in 6 hour periods are denoted Level 2.5 data. The Level 2.5 data are binned and averaged in various ways to prepare Level 3.5

Table 3. *NODS SSM/I wind vector data sets*

Description	Level	Frequency	Size (MBytes)
SSM/I winds	2.5	6 hours	450
Gridded winds	3.0	6 hours	450
Gridded, binned winds	3.5	5 days	10
Gridded, binned winds	3.5	30 days	2

wind products. The Level 2.5, 3.0 and two sets of 3.5 data have been deposited in NODS and are available to interested investigators.

The Level 2.5 and 3.0 data sets include 11 months of data: July 1987–June 1988 (with roughly a month-long data gap from December 1987 to January 1988). The two Level 3.5 data sets include SSM/I wind vectors, binned and averaged every 5 days and every month, respectively. A summary of these data sets is given in Table 3.

Validation

In order to validate the methodology and estimate the accuracy of the results, the results were verified against independent withheld data sets. The analyses were also compared to the input conventional data to show how closely these data fitted. Colocation statistics were generated for all SSM/I wind vectors that were within 100 km and ±3 hours of a ship or buoy report. All of the conventional data used in the validation were required to first pass a very weak quality control test.

Table 4 presents the mean absolute error and bias for the SSM/I winds verified against both dependent and independent data. From the table, it can be seen that the SSM/I winds fit the dependent data very closely. Both the SSM/I speeds and assigned directions agree very well with the input ships and buoys and have negligible bias.

Table 4. *SSM/I wind vector colocation statistics using dependent data (the ships and buoys used in the analysis) and independent data (withheld and PMEL buoys). All statistics are for the entire July 1987–June 1988 period, except for statistics of the withheld buoys which are for the July–October 1987 period. In the table, MAE denotes the mean absolute error*

Colocation data	Sample size	Speed (m/s)		Direction (degrees)	
		MAE	Bias	MAE	Bias
Analyzed ships	200 981	2.4	−0.7	18.8	0.9
Analyzed buoys	14 582	2.1	0.5	15.7	1.5
Withheld buoys	3 870	1.7	0.2	21.7	−0.1
PMEL buoys	514	1.3	−0.6	24.8	−10.1

The verification against independent data, shown in Table 4, was performed first using withheld buoys that were primarily located in the Northern Hemisphere extratropics. An average of eight preselected buoys were withheld from each analysis during the first two and one half months of processing. 3870 collocations were made for the period from July to October 1987. These showed a mean absolute error of less than 22° in direction and 2 m/s in speed, with negligible bias.

A second verification was performed using the Atlas buoys that were deployed by PMEL in the tropical Pacific. These buoys were not available in real time and were not used in our analyses. 514 collocations were made from July 1987 through June 1988. These showed a somewhat poorer agreement than the preceding evaluation of direction assignment, with a mean absolute error of 24.8° and a bias of −10.1°; the SSM/I speeds agreed very well with these buoys.

Patterns of marine surface wind vectors

Here some representative results are presented, including monthly averaged data which depict the annual cycle, and annual averaged data. The data are presented in a single uniform format of streamlines (in black) overlaid on vector magnitudes (color filled). For these data, wind components were averaged separately and then the associated vector magnitude calculated. These vector magnitudes will be referred to as speeds in what follows, although it is noted that these values are generally less than the average wind speed. The color coding convention is decreasing speed for yellow to green to blue to violet. Data drop-outs due to ice are colored white and the land masses are colored black.

Unfortunately, with only one year of data, inter-annual trends in the SSM/I winds can not be established. Furthermore, trends from other data sets are problematical: analysis products can be contaminated by trends due to constant improvement in operational procedures. *In situ* observations lack global coverage and observing practices have evolved with time.

General features

The annual average and monthly average data clearly show the surface manifestations of the atmospheric general circulation. These features are most clearly seen in the annual average, which most effectively filters transient phenomena (Fig. 1). Interpretation of annual average results in areas close to the pole is limited by the heavy weighting of the averages towards the summer conditions; there are almost no data over

ice in the conventional data base and absolutely no data over ice in the SSM/I data.

The center of the ascending branch of the Hadley circulation is located just north of the equator, at 5–10° N. Associated with that circulation is the ITCZ (inter-tropical convergence zone), which can be clearly seen in the surface wind field in the Atlantic and Pacific basins as a line of convergence and lower wind speeds. The ITCZ is far from uniform zonally even in this annual average depiction. For example, in the Indian Ocean, the ITCZ is absent most months. Further, even where it is well defined, the average wind speed varies significantly along the ITCZ, from less than 2 m/s in areas like the eastern continental boundaries (note especially the frontal node in the east Atlantic) to 4–5 m/s in the central Pacific.

At roughly 30° from the equator, the main descending branch of the Hadley circulation is associated with the quasi-stationary large-scale subtropical high pressure areas (such as the Bermuda High), which are apparent in Fig. 1 as well defined basin-scale anticyclonic circulations. Surface winds are generally equatorward and westward between the ITCZ and subtropical highs. These are the trade winds or tropical easterlies. Poleward of the subtropics, the surface flows are generally northward and eastward (i.e. the westerlies). The mid-latitudes and polar latitudes are characterized by much more transience, but in the annual average the flow is basically westerly. In the Northern Hemisphere, where there is more topography, there is also more deviation from a purely eastward flow at these latitudes. These are the surface manifestation of the topographically induced stationary waves.

The seasonal cycle

Monthly averaged wind vectors show how the surface circulation over the world ocean is affected by the march of the seasons. Monthly averaged maps are shown for one month from each season in Figs. 2 through 5.

The ITCZ tends to follow the sun, since it is a direct response to the maximum in solar heating. In the eastern Pacific it is near 10° in the Northern Hemisphere summer and near the equator in the Northern Hemisphere winter. These variations seem smooth from monthly data. In the western Pacific, on the other hand, the variations over the year are larger and the location of the ITCZ seems to jump in steps of 10° of latitude. Its most southern position occurs in February at about 15° S.

In the northern oceans there is a lot of month to month variability. The one constant is that, in every month, in the North Atlantic, there is a well-formed anticyclonic circulation

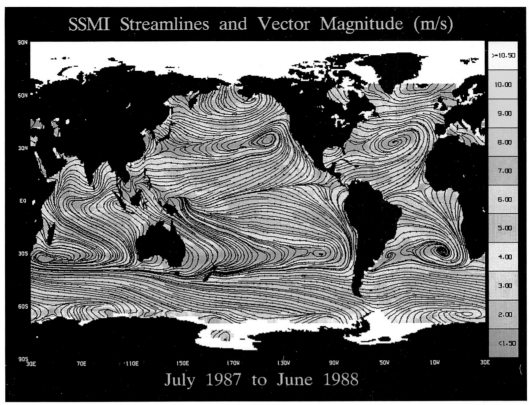

Fig. 1. Average SSM/I surface wind streamlines and vector magnitude (m/s) for July 1987 through June 1988.

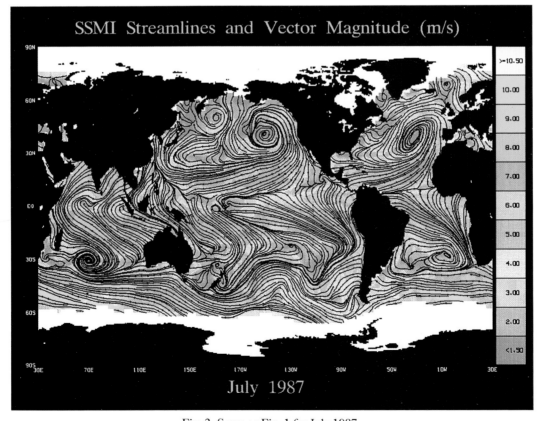

Fig. 2. Same as Fig. 1 for July 1987.

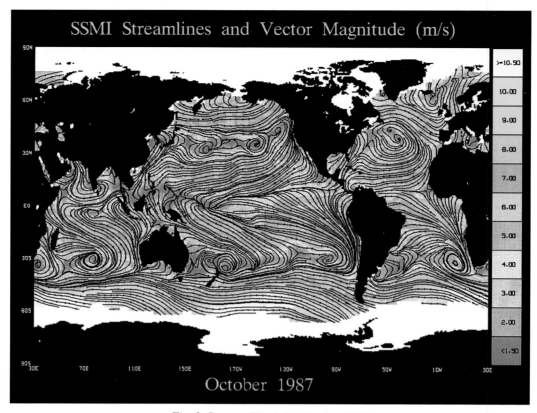

Fig. 3. Same as Fig. 1 for October 1987.

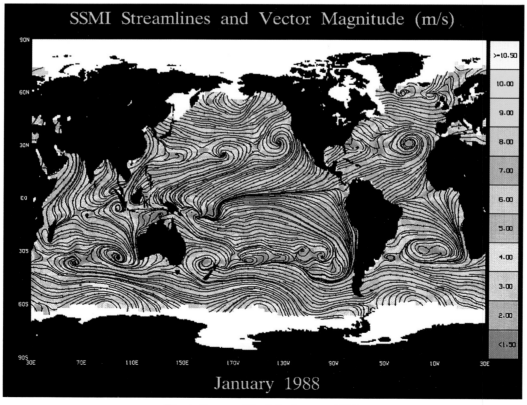

Fig. 4. Same as Fig. 1 for January 1988.

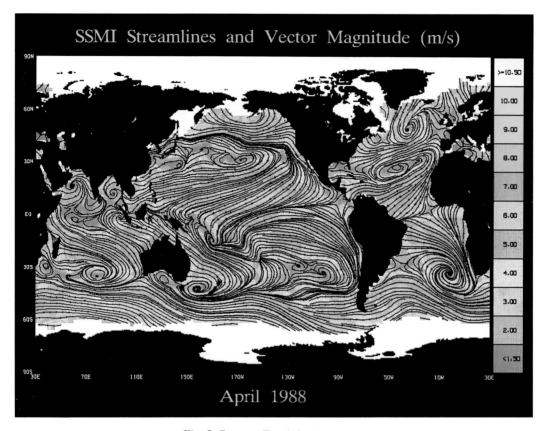

Fig. 5. Same as Fig. 1 for April 1988.

in the subtropical divergence zone. The location and other details of this feature do, however, vary considerably.

During the months of July and August in the Northern Hemisphere, the lowest values of wind speed are observed, while during January and February the highest values occur. The mean vector wind magnitudes displayed here are influenced by the steadiness of the wind direction. That is, very high wind speeds might result in a low value of mean vector wind magnitude if the wind direction varied significantly on timescales of less than a month. However, averaged SSM/I wind speeds show the same cycle as depicted here (Halpern *et al.*, 1991).

The Southern Hemisphere subtropical divergence zone tends to stay near 30°, except for January and February when it is displaced southward by roughly 5°. This latter displacement is in concert with that described for the ITCZ.

In the Southern Hemisphere extratropics, poleward of 40°, the flow is generally zonal. However, in the austral winter, there is often a noticeable standing wave in the eastern Pacific sector with a pronounced trough near the tip of South America. In May 1988, there is also a well-developed trough centered on Tasmania.

Relative to the northern oceans, the distribution of wind speed generally varies little from month to month in the South Pacific and Atlantic. In the tropical Indian Ocean however, wind speeds vary considerably in conjunction with the Monsoon. Speeds are generally high from May through August and then trend downward until April when calm conditions exist over large areas.

Interannual variability

With only 12 months of data the best that can be done in depicting interannual variability is to compare the first and last months of the data set, namely July 1987 (Fig. 2) and June 1988 (Fig. 6). Although there is a general agreement in the overall pattern of the atmospheric general circulation as seen in the surface winds, the two figures do reveal a number of important differences. Wind speeds are generally lower in the July data. The location of the ITCZ for these two months is in close agreement; however, in the Pacific in June 1988, the tropical flow is more zonal and stronger. In the North Atlantic, the subtropical anticyclonic circulation is very similar in June 1988 and July 1987, but in the Pacific the center of this circulation is displaced 10° southward in June 1988. The details of the waves in the Southern Hemisphere subtropical

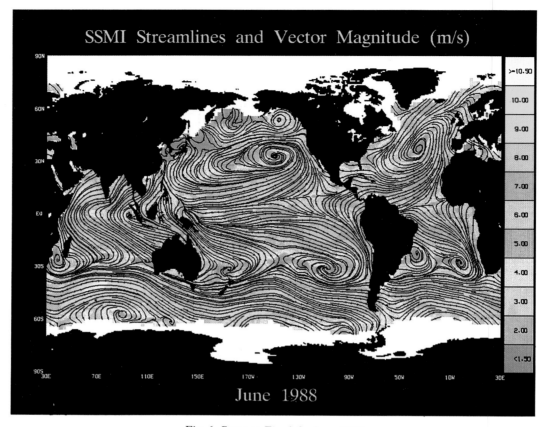

Fig. 6. Same as Fig. 1 for June 1988.

divergence zone and the mid-latitude westerlies are for the most part different for these two months.

Comparison to ECMWF analyses

The difference between the variational analysis and the ECMWF background field is a measure of the impact of the SSM/I data. These differences tend to be coherent and substantial. The differences averaged over the month of July 1987 between the binned SSM/I data (Level 2.5) and ECMWF analyses are shown for the Indian Ocean in Fig. 7(a). In this figure, differences below 2 m/s are not shown. While other areas of the world ocean have smaller differences there are substantial differences on scales similar to those evident in the Arabian Sea in all the oceans. In the Arabian Sea the SSM/I winds are more southwesterly. In the southern Indian Ocean, the differences display a very large-scale cyclonic circulation centered around 30° S, that is, the SSM/I winds are more anticyclonic in the Indian Ocean subtropics than the ECMWF analyses. In general, the differences seen in Fig. 7(a) are opposite to the prevailing July winds in this region (cf. Fig. 4 of Hellerman and Rosenstein), except for the area south of Madagascar where the SSM/I

winds are more northerly than the ECMWF winds but the climate winds are westerly. Thus, the SSM/I data tend to weaken the low level winds of the ECMWF analysis in this area.

From Fig. 7(a) alone it cannot be concluded that there is any impact on the analyzed wind directions. In fact, the average ECMWF and SSM/I winds agree very well in direction in most locations. However, there are compact areas, particularly in the Southern Hemisphere and in regions of low wind speed, where the wind direction is quite different. For example, in the Indian Ocean there are substantial differences south of Madagascar as seen in Fig. 7(b), where the cosine of the angle between the ECMWF and SSM/I winds has been plotted. Similarly, large differences also cover coherent regions of the Atlantic and Pacific oceans where the wind speed is low. This result is not unexpected. The analysis methodology ensures that differences between the ECMWF and SSM/I wind vectors are minimized in an rms sense. Consequently, the rms differences will tend to be of similar magnitude over all areas. Rms differences of the same size will generally result in larger directional differences in regions of low wind speed. For instantaneous fields, noticeable directional differences between SSM/I and ECMWF winds occur

Vector differences between SSM/I and ECMWF winds

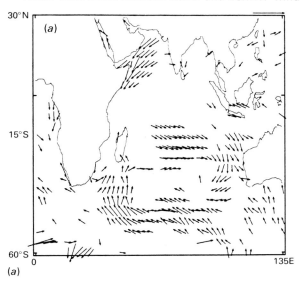

(a)

Cosine of the angle between SSM/I and ECMWF winds

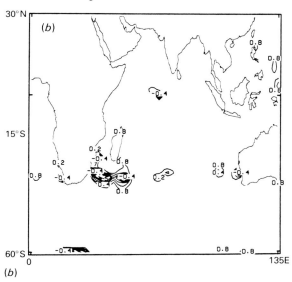

(b)

Fig. 7. The difference between the SSM/I binned winds and the ECMWF analyzed winds for the month of July 1987 in the Indian Ocean. (a) Vector wind difference. Here the length of the arrows is proportional to wind speed and the smallest arrow plotted is 2 m/s. (b) Cosine of the angle between the SSM/I and ECMWF winds.

where the SSM/I wind speeds differ appreciably from the ECMWF wind speeds.

There are some significant differences in wind speed between the ECMWF and SSM/I monthly averaged wind vectors. In July 1987, the ECMWF speeds are generally larger. This is seen almost everywhere, but the magnitude of the difference is small (1 m/s or less). The shape of the wind speed fields are very similar. Similar remarks may be made for

October. However, in January and April the ECMWF and SSM/I speeds are similar in most areas. There are a few notable areas during these periods, where the SSM/I winds are higher. In January, in the southeast portion of the tropical Pacific (90° W–160° W and 0°–30° S) and generally over much of the North Pacific, the SSM/I winds are stronger by 1–2 m/s. In April, in the Bering Sea, SSM/I winds are stronger by 2–3 m/s in some places.

Comparison to climatology

Comparisons between analyses and climatologies based on long-term averages of conventional data reveal differences due to interannual variability and to data differences. The SSM/I winds have been compared to directions from the HR (Hellerman & Rosenstein, 1983) wind stresses. The binned winds are for the single year studied, while the HR winds are for the 106-year period from 1870–1976.

In the North Atlantic and parts of the North Pacific, the quality of the data is quite good and the differences may be taken as an inter-annual variation. In other areas, the quantity of conventional data is low and there are substantial data gaps especially near Antarctica. Consequently, the climatology and ECMWF analyses are of poorer quality in these regions. The directions of the SSM/I binned data are also expected to be adversely impacted by the sparsity of conventional data and the poorer quality of the ECMWF analyses in these regions.

Comparisons with the published climatologies are difficult, because different quantities have been averaged in time. Results are based on time-averaged wind vectors, while the results of HR are based on time-averaged surface stresses. Here only differences in direction will be discussed.

There are significant differences between the HR and SSM/I wind directions. In terms of the annual average, the SSM/I winds are more zonal and the HR winds are more meridional in much of the Southern Hemisphere, especially in the Indian Ocean and southwards to Antarctica. The large-scale anticyclonic circulations of the Northern Hemisphere from the two sets of wind data are noticeably different. In the North Atlantic the SSM/I circulation has rounded, almost closed streamlines, while the HR streamlines describe a large loop from west to east in the extratropics, turning around in the subtropics and then heading from east to west in the tropics. Similar differences are present in the Pacific. As a result of these different patterns, winds from these two data sets are generally perpendicular in the western North Pacific and North Atlantic. Smaller but similar differences can be seen in the South Pacific. In the South Atlantic, the patterns are similar, but the SSM/I center of circulation is positioned considerably towards the east relative to that of the HR winds.

Finally, it is noted that between the Canadian maritimes and Greenland the SSM/I winds are more westerly, while the HR winds are mostly northerly.

While the annual averages contain similar scales, the monthly averaged SSM/I data show more small-scale features. These features may be peculiar to the SSM/I data period. It is more likely that similar features are generally present in monthly average data but with inter-annual differences in position and intensity. Such differences would be enough in a multi-year average (such is the case in the HR data) to considerably smooth and attenuate these features.

Some differences which are noted in the monthly averaged data are the following: in July the Northern Hemisphere anticyclones are displaced northward in the SSM/I winds relative to the HR winds. The SSM/I winds also show cyclonic circulations in the extratropics which are not present at all in the HR winds. In the monthly data, the SSM/I winds are also generally more zonal in the extratropics. For example, in both January and July, the HR winds having a distinct northerly component in the area near Japan and south of Madagascar.

Data limitations

There are two very important limitations to this data set. First it is limited in time to only one year. However, the SSM/I data record is continuous from July 1987 until the present and this limitation can be corrected. Current plans call for processing a second year of SSM/I wind vectors and this may be extended for the entire SSM/I data record. The second major limitation is that the SSM/I data contain no inherent wind directional information. Analysis methods and the ECMWF analyses can account only partially for this limitation. However, the validation results, reported on pp. 131–132, are encouraging.

Additional applications

At the time of this writing, limited applications of the SSM/I wind vectors to atmospheric and oceanic modeling have been made and calculations of surface fluxes of heat, moisture, and momentum are planned.

In the area of atmospheric modeling, a preliminary data assimilation and numerical weather prediction (nwp) experiment was conducted (Bloom & Atlas, 1991). In this experiment, the Goddard Laboratory for Atmospheres (GLA) analysis/forecast system was used to assign directions to SSM/I wind speed observations and assimilate the resulting surface wind vectors. Four 5-day assimilations and a 5-day numerical forecast from each were performed to provide a preliminary assessment of the impact of SSM/I wind vectors on nwp. These included assimilations in which either SSM/I or low-level cloud-track winds were included or excluded, as well as a test of the importance of vertically extending the influence of the surface wind data. The results of this experiment showed a positive impact of the SSM/I surface wind vectors on both analyses and weather forecasts in the Southern Hemisphere, when the influence of the surface data extended to at least 850 mb. While this result is encouraging, it must be considered preliminary. Further experimentation will be required to firmly establish the impact of SSM/I and other satellite surface wind data on weather prediction.

In the area of ocean modeling, Busalacchi, Atlas & Hackert 1993a, Busalacchi, Hackert & Atlas, 1993b have used the one-year of SSM/I surface wind velocity data described here to force a tropical ocean model and have compared the results to similar experiments using other model and subjectively determined surface wind vector data sets. While one year of data is not sufficient to provide a definitive evaluation, the results from these experiments showed the SSM/I wind vectors to be at least comparable to the best of the other data sets and indicated considerable potential for these data for ocean modeling applications.

References

Atlas, R., Bloom, S. C., Hoffman, R. N. Ardizzone, J. & Brin, G. (1991). Space-based surface wind vectors to aid understanding of air–sea interactions. *Eos*, **72**, 201–8.

Atlas, R., Busalacchi, A. J., Ghil, M., Bloom, S. & Kalnay, E. (1987). Global surface wind and flux fields from model assimilation of Seasat data. *J. Geophys. Res.*, **92**, 6477–87.

Bloom, S. C. & Atlas, R. (1991). Assimilation of satellite surface wind speed data and its impact on nwp. *Proceedings of the Ninth Conf. on Numerical Weather Prediction*, October 14–18, Denver, CO.

Busalacchi, A. J., Atlas, R. & Hackert, E. C. (1993a). Comparison of SSM/I vector wind stress with model-derived and subjective products for the Tropical Pacific. *J. Geophys. Res.*, in press.

Busalacchi, A. J., Hackert, E. C. & Atlas, R. (1993b). Impact of space-based wind speed observations on Tropical Pacific ocean simulations. *J. Geophys. Res.*, in press.

Halpern, D., Zlotnicki, V., Newman, J., Brown, O. & Wentz, F. (1991). An atlas of monthly mean distributions of sea surface height, SSMI surface wind speed, AVHRR/2 sea surface temperature, and ECMWF surface wind components during 1988. *JPL Publication 91–8*, 110pp.

Hellerman, S. H. & Rosenstein, M. (1983). Normal monthly wind stress over the world ocean with error estimates. *J. Phys. Ocean.*, **13**, 1093–104.

Hoffman, R. N. (1982). SASS Wind ambiguity removal by direct minimization. *Mon. Wea. Rev.*, **110**, 434–45.

Hoffman, R. N. (1984). SASS Wind ambiguity removal by direct minimization, Part II, Use of smoother and dynamical constraints. *Mon. Wea. Rev.*, **112**, 1829–52.

Hollingsworth, A., Shaw, D. B., Lonnberg, P., Illari, L. & Simmons, A. J. (1986). Monitoring of observation and analysis quality by a data assimilation system. *Mon. Wea. Rev.*, **114**, 861–79.

Trenberth, K. E., Olson, J. E. & Large, W. G. (1989). A global ocean wind stress climatology based on ECMWF analyses.

NCAR Technical Note NCAR/TN-338. National Center for Atmospheric Research, Boulder, CO. 93pp.

Wentz, F. J., Mattox, L. A. & Peteherych, S. (1986). New algorithms for microwave measurements of ocean winds: applications to Seasat and the special sensor microwave imager. *J. Geophys. Res.*, **91** (C2), 2289–307.

Clouds

WILLIAM B. ROSSOW

Introduction

Latitudinal, daily and seasonal changes in the heating of Earth by the Sun cause atmospheric motions that are called weather; the sum of this weather and its seasonal variations are called the climate. Changes of weather, particularly the coming of precipitation, are signalled by, and associated with, changes in clouds. Clouds are the locus of the conversion of water vapor, evaporated from the oceans, to the rain and snow that provide the water that sustains life on land, including humans. Thus, it has long been understood that knowledge of cloud behavior is important to survival.

Variations of clouds and their interaction with sunlight also produce dramatic variations in the appearance of the sky that have long fascinated humans; but only recently has it come to be understood that this entertaining sky display is the herald of a more important role of clouds. The total amount of sunlight absorbed by the Earth's surface and the amount of thermal radiation that escapes it are determined, in large part, by the properties of the clouds (Hartmann *et al.*, 1986); so, in addition to the supply of water, clouds affect the average temperature. Thus, clouds are a key link in both the water and energy cycles and between these cycles that determine climate.

Since variations in solar heating and thermal cooling cause the weather which controls the clouds, there is a crucial feedback loop in the energy exchanges of the climate. Consequently, the sensitivity of the response of the climate to perturbations is affected by the nature of this cloud–radiation–dynamics interaction. Natural sources of climate perturbation, such as variations in the amount of sunlight, the amount of volcanic activity, biospheric and geological changes of atmospheric composition and geography, act on very long timescales; but now, humans are rapidly changing the composition of the atmosphere, producing an unprecedentedly fast climate perturbation. Predicting how the climate will respond requires that it is understood, among other things, how the clouds will change, and how their changes will alter the radiation balance of Earth.

That careful visual observations of clouds were made more

than two centuries ago can be documented by the realism of paintings from that time (Gedzelman, 1989). However, detailed agricultural records from more ancient civilizations in the Americas and western and eastern Asia suggest that good empirical knowledge of cloud forms and their relation to weather may have been available for at least a millennium. In the 1930s to 1950s, these visual 'measurements' by weather observers were standardized (WMO, 1975) and collected to produce the first systematic and nearly global surveys of the variety of clouds (for a review of early cloud climatologies see Hughes, 1984). These data are still being collected and analyzed to extend the length of the climate record (Warren *et al.*, 1986, 1988); however, these data describe only the amount of various cloud types that occur and not their physical properties.

The advent of artificial satellites almost immediately led to instruments designed expressly to observe global weather patterns by making images of clouds: TIROS-1 returned its first cloud image in April 1960. Although polar orbiting, imaging satellites that observe the whole globe twice daily have been routinely operated since the mid-1970s, a truly global constellation of imaging satellites that could observe the more rapid and smaller scale variations of clouds was formed for the first time in 1979 for the global weather experiment of the global atmospheric research program (GARP). This observing system has been maintained and improved since then. Not only has satellite technology finally provided a better view of clouds that covers a much wider range of space and timescales, but it has also made possible more detailed measurements of other cloud properties and how they change with location and time.

The importance of understanding the role of clouds and their radiative feedbacks on climate, together with the availability of a suitable satellite observing system, led to the initiation in 1982 of the International Satellite Cloud Climatology Project (ISCCP) as the first project of the World Climate Research Program (WCRP), the successor to GARP (Schiffer & Rossow, 1983). Data have been collected ever since 1 July, 1983. This article describes results from the ISCCP analysis of these satellite data.

Data and analysis method

Data

The basic measurements made by satellites are images of radiation reflected from, or emitted by, Earth in various wavelength ranges. The most common types of data are:

1. 'high' resolution images (typically with spatial resolutions from 0.01–10 km and time resolutions from $\frac{1}{2}$–12 hours) made over several narrow wavelength intervals in the solar spectrum (500–4000 nm) and the thermal infra-red spectrum (4000–12 000 nm), usually to observe changes in clouds and measure some properties of the surface,
2. 'sounder' measurements (typically with spatial resolutions from 10–50 km and time resolutions from 1–12 hours) made in the thermal infra-red and microwave parts of the spectrum to measure the temperature structure and humidity distribution in the atmosphere,
3. 'composition' and 'surface property' measurements (typically with spatial resolutions from 50–100 km and time resolutions from $\frac{1}{2}$–5 days) made in various parts of the spectrum, including the ultra-violet and microwave, to measure the abundances of other atmospheric gases and properties of the surface, such as snow and sea ice cover, and
4. 'broadband' measurements (typically with spatial resolutions from 30–2000 km and time resolutions from 1–30 days) made over the whole solar and thermal infra-red spectrum to determine the total radiation balance of Earth.

The ISCCP results are obtained from the first two types of satellite data (results from other types are discussed in other chapters of this book). Images used are made at 600 nm (visible = VIS) and at 1100 nm (infra-red = IR), which are the only measurements made by all the operational weather satellites with sufficient time resolution. Since the atmosphere is nearly transparent at these wavelengths, the measured radiation is influenced primarily by the properties of clouds and Earth's surface. Analysis results from the second type of satellite data are used to specify the temperature, water vapor and ozone in the atmosphere to remove their small effects on the images.

ISCCP images are collected from two kinds of satellites: Sun-synchronous polar orbiters and geostationary satellites. The former type flies over each location on Earth at about 850 km altitude, twice daily at about the same local times; the latter type appears to remain at the same longitude over the

equator and views a 100° latitude–longitude region of Earth every half hour from an altitude of almost 36 000 km. Currently, operating imagers have spatial resolutions ranging from 1–11 km, i.e. images can be divided into elements, called pixels, that represent areas on the surface of Earth that are 1–120 km². The polar orbiters (called NOAA satellites) are operated by the US National Oceanic and Atmospheric Administration (NOAA). Several geostationary satellites are operated: METEOSAT by the European Space Agency (ESA), GMS by the Japan Meteorological Agency (JMA), INSAT by the Indian Meteorological Department (IMD), and two GOES by NOAA.

The amount of data collected by these satellites in one year would fill more than 200 000 data tapes (at current storage densities of 6250 bpi). To reduce the data volume for ISCCP, geostationary image data are sampled to three hour intervals and all images pixels are sampled to a 25–30 km spacing. Once these data are calibrated, Earth-located and placed into a common data format, they are referred to as ISCCP Stage B3 data (Schiffer & Rossow, 1985; Rossow, Kinsella, Wolf & Garder, 1987). Fig. 1 shows an image of the global variation of IR temperatures assembled from the METEOSAT-2, GMS-2, GOES-5 (EAST), GOES-6 (WEST) and NOAA-7 images for 4 July, 1983.

Analysis of the Stage B3 data provides the information about clouds collected into the ISCCP Stage C1 and C2 data sets (Rossow et al., 1991; Rossow & Schiffer, 1991); the former provide global information every three hours and the latter provide monthly summaries.

In addition to the satellite data, several other data sets are used in the analysis to characterize each location on Earth by the type of surface (land/water/coast) (Masaki, 1976), the mean topographic altitude and its variation ('roughness') (NGDC, 1985), coverage of the ocean by sea ice (supplied by the Navy/NOAA Joint Ice Center), and coverage of the land by different vegetation types (Matthews, 1983, 1985) and by snow (supplied by NOAA).

Analysis method

The ISCCP cloud analysis (Rossow et al., 1991) is divided into three distinct steps: cloud detection, radiation analysis, and statistical analysis (Fig. 2). The first step examines the VIS and IR radiances to determine whether some clouds are present in each image pixel and divides the image data set into 'clear' and 'cloudy' populations. The second step compares the radiation measurements to those calculated with a radiative transfer model of the clouds, atmosphere and surface. The atmospheric properties are specified from other data, so the 'clear' pixels can be used to measure the properties of the

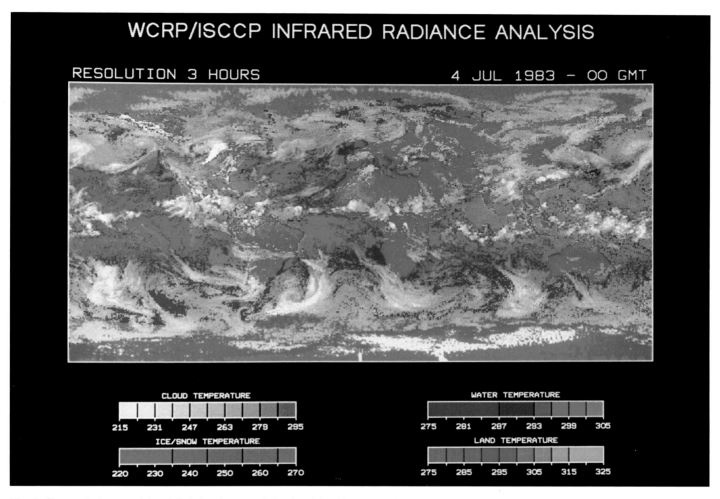

Fig. 1. Composite image of the global distribution of cloud and land/ocean surface temperatures measured by a suite of meteorological satellites (METEOSAT-2, GMS-2, GOES-5, GOES-6, NOAA-7) on 4 July 1983 at 1500 UTC. Spatial resolution is about 40 km. Color is selected by the cloud analysis method which determines whether a location is cloudy or clear.

surface. Once the atmosphere and surface are known, the properties of the clouds are retrieved from the 'cloudy' measurements. The third step summarizes the retrieved and collected information about the clouds, atmosphere, and surface and their spatial variations and maps it at a spatial resolution of about 280 km; monthly summaries of the time variations are also prepared.

Cloud detection involves a number of statistical tests of the radiation data to 'recognize' the signal that indicates the presence of clouds. The wide variety of surface and cloud properties on Earth precludes use of one or two simple tests for cloudiness (Coakley & Baldwin, 1984; Rossow *et al.*, 1985; Saunders, 1986; Minnis *et al.*, 1987). The basic assumptions that govern the separation of the data into cloudy and clear parts in the ISCCP analysis are that: 1) clouds cause more spatial variation of IR and VIS radiation than the surface, 2) clouds cause more variation of IR and VIS radiation

in time than the surface, 3) clouds are colder (less IR radiation emitted to space) and brighter (more solar radiation reflected to space) than the surface. Not all of these statements are true at the same time in one place and the valid combinations that indicate the presence of clouds vary with location, time of day, and season.

In practice, since the surface is generally (though not always) less variable than clouds (Sèze & Rossow, 1991), the VIS and IR radiation measurements associated with clear conditions are first identified by testing the magnitude of space/time variations in the radiation over scales ranging from 100–5000 km and from daily to monthly. Then, assuming that clouds are responsible for variations of the VIS and IR radiation away from those corresponding to clear conditions, a comparison of the radiation values at each location and time to the inferred clear values is used to identify clouds. Since clear conditions may also vary somewhat, only those

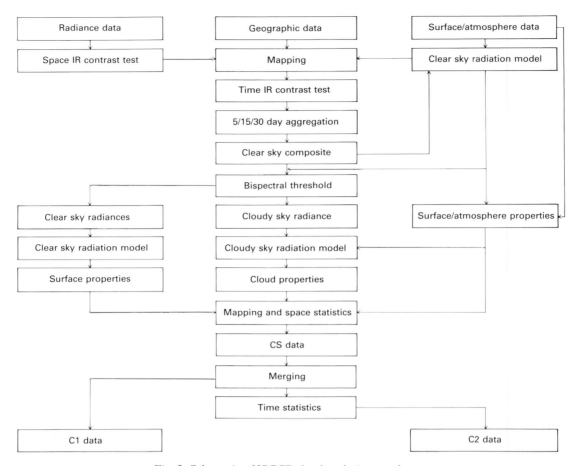

Fig. 2. Schematic of ISCCP cloud analysis procedure.

changes in radiation larger than the typical clear variations or the uncertainties in the clear radiance values can be called cloudy.

A detailed radiative transfer model, that simulates the satellite radiation observations as a function of cloud, atmosphere and surface properties, is used to retrieve quantitative information from the VIS and IR radiation measurements in each image pixel. Since only two wavelengths are analyzed, only two properties of the clouds and surface can be obtained: VIS reflectances and IR temperatures. The former is reported in terms of optical thickness and the latter in terms of both temperature and top pressure (altitude) for clouds. In addition, the fraction of the total number of image pixels that contain clouds, called 'cloud amount', is reported. Thus, the six primary quantities produced in each image pixel from the ISCCP analysis are cloud amount, cloud top temperature and pressure, cloud optical thickness, surface visible reflectance and surface temperature. At night when no VIS data are obtained, values of optical thickness and surface reflectance are not reported.

A key statistic of these results is the space/time distribution

of cloud properties that characterizes the occurrence of different types of clouds in different weather and climate situations (Sèze & Rossow, 1991). Fig. 3 illustrates how the cloudy pixels are classified by the cloud top pressure and/or optical thickness values obtained. The names of classical cloud morphological types, developed by surface observers, are associated in Fig. 3 with particular ranges and combinations of these quantities; study of these data suggests some merit in these associations, but the correspondence is only understood in qualitative terms at this time (see discussion in Warren *et al.*, 1986, 1988). The variations of the amounts of these different cloud types provides a more detailed way to describe changes in the character of cloudiness.

Limitations

There are several limitations to the ISCCP cloud information, some of which are inherent in the use of any satellite data and some of which are caused by the characteristics of current-day satellite instruments and, therefore, subject to improvement in future.

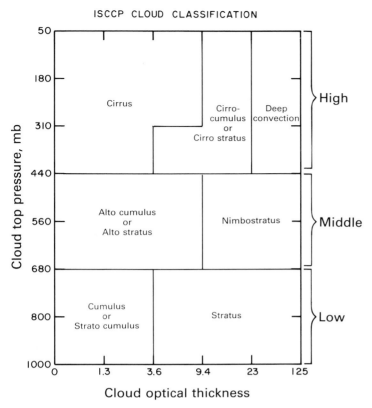

ISCCP CLOUD CLASSIFICATION

Fig. 3. Radiometric classification of clouds by their top pressure and optical thickness.

The satellite 'viewpoint' is limited in ways that complement limitations on surface observations. Most forms of radiation measured from satellites are either nearly completely insensitive to clouds (e.g. microwaves) or so sensitive that they cannot penetrate most clouds. For VIS and IR wavelengths, the satellite view is a 'top-down' view; that is, cloud layers that occur under other cloud layers cannot be observed. From the surface, higher cloud layers are obscured from view by low-level clouds. Although the majority of clouds may occur in single layers (e.g. Tian & Curry, 1989) but with variable vertical extent, there are also indications of vertical correlations of the occurrence of cloud layers (Warren, Hahn & London, 1985). Satellite-only or surface-only data are, therefore, limited in the amount of information they contain about the vertical distribution of cloud water mass.

The size of the satellite image pixels is larger than some individual clouds and smaller than others. In other words, clouds occur with a distribution of sizes and satellites do not resolve the smaller spatial scales. This is not an inherent limitation of satellite measurements (e.g. some non-military satellites have resolutions of 10 m), but it is a significant practical limit since the volume of the ISCCP image data set would amount to more than one billion data tapes per year if its resolution was 10 m! Combining the results of several analyses of the size distribution of clouds suggests, however, that, although the number of clouds with sizes below about 5 km is quite large for some cloud types (Welch *et al.*, 1988), the largest variations of the radiation caused by clouds occur at scales from 10–500 km (Zangvil, 1975; Sèze & Rossow, 1991). Nevertheless, the precise effect of partial coverage by clouds of a satellite radiometer's field of view is not completely understood. Thus, the cloud amount parameter determined by the ISCCP analysis is defined, strictly, as the frequency of occurrence of cloudiness at a spatial scale of about 5 km; the errors associated with assuming that this cloud amount is the correct fractional coverage by cloudiness are estimated to be no more than 10% (e.g. Rossow, Garder & Lacis, 1989; Rossow & Lacis, 1990) but need further study.

Variations in the satellite viewing geometry (required to image large portions of Earth) interact with the limited spatial resolution to cause the estimate of cloud amount to increase slightly for slant views of Earth. As the viewing angle of the satellite varies from near nadir to 40°–60°, the average cloud amount increases by 5–10% (Minnis, 1989). Part of this effect is caused by the variation of the pixel size projected onto the surface interacting with smaller scale cloud features (Minnis, 1989), as discussed above, and part is caused by an increased detection sensitivity for optically thin clouds. The former effect is similar to a viewing geometry effect for ground observers (McGuffie & Henderson-Sellers, 1989). This effect partially explains the artificial features in Indian Ocean cloud amounts shown in Figs. 8 and 15.

The representation of the effects of clouds on the measured radiation is limited to two parameters: optical thickness and top temperature. (Note that, in the absence of sunlight, the analysis is limited to a single parameter, cloud top temperature.) This representation is equivalent to assuming that all observed variations of radiation are explained by variations of only these two cloud properties. However, the variation of several other cloud properties can also affect the radiation; among the most important are coverage of the pixel (Rossow, 1989), cloud particle size distribution (e.g. Arking & Childs, 1985; Coakley, Bernstein & Durkee, 1987), vertical distribution of cloud water, and composition. The relative importance of these parameters is a function of wavelength; the selection of optical thickness (defined for a constant particle size distribution, composition and phase) and top temperature was governed by their predominant importance at visible and 'window' infra-red wavelengths. The estimated uncertainties in optical thickness and cloud top temperatures, associated with variations of other cloud properties, are about

15% and 3 K, respectively. The effects of smaller-scale variations on these quantities may be longer, however.

Variation of the strength of the parameter's effect with wavelength means that this limitation is not inherent in satellite observations, but can be ameliorated by making simultaneous and collocated measurements at many wavelengths. For example, Arking and Childs (1985) and Nakajima and King (1990) propose ways to measure mean cloud particle radius by adding a third wavelength to the set. Studies by Inoue (1987) and Yamanuchi et al. (1987) suggest that lower optical thickness values can be measured using two IR wavelengths. Future satellite instruments are planned that will provide information about more cloud properties.

There are some situations where even the detection of cloudiness is difficult or impossible using only VIS and IR measurements. The most significant one is low-level cloudiness in the polar regions, where the surface VIS reflectance and IR temperature are nearly the same as that for the clouds. Moreover, in some seasons and under certain viewing conditions, clouds can actually appear to be darker or warmer than the surface or both. Other such situations are very thin cirrus over very bright deserts, dust storms over such deserts, very low-level cloudiness composed of very small individual elements (e.g. 'trade-wind' cumulus), and surface fogs. Some of these ambiguous situations cannot be resolved, even with observations at more wavelengths, since the cloud is either nearly indistinguishable from the surface (thin fogs over sea ice, for instance) or the radiation measurement can have two possible values. The ISCCP results in the polar regions probably miss significant amounts of cloudiness but may be improved somewhat by analyses using the other spectral channels already available in polar orbiter imagery.

The occurrence of dust 'clouds' over deserts is a reminder that the atmosphere of Earth is, in fact, everywhere filled with suspended particulates, but the tenuous background aerosols present under 'clear' conditions are of a different composition and serve as the nuclei for the formation of the denser water clouds. Although optically thinner than most water clouds and, therefore, having less effect on the radiation balance, aerosols can have an important influence on the properties of clouds and can become more important to the climate when volcanic activity or wind-blown dust increases their abundance. Only the denser, dust storms are included in the ISCCP results. Better separation of aerosols and water clouds may be obtained using multi-spectral polarization measurements.

Scales of cloud variations

Spatial scales

Clouds vary on a range of spatial scales from about 100 m to planetary (20 000 km); however, since the magnitude of the variations increases monotonically with spatial scale, the most important variations occur at the larger scales (cf. Zangvil, 1975; Welch et al., 1988; Sèze & Rossow, 1991). This is illustrated by averaging the IR radiation variations, shown at about 40 km resolution in Fig. 1, to a resolution of 280 km (Fig. 4). Although some 'texture' (i.e. smaller scale variations) is lost, the main cloudy and clear features are still readily identified.

Fig. 5 shows the same effect in terms of the frequency of occurrence of different cloud amounts (defined by counting the fraction of the total number of 5 km-sized image pixels that contain some cloud) for 280 km-sized regions (equivalent to a latitude resolution of 2.5°) and for 2500 km-sized regions (22.5° of latitude). At the smaller scale less than half of the cloudy/clear areas have sizes smaller than 280 km (since larger cloud features have edges, some few regions would exhibit cloud amounts between 10 and 90% even if there were no clouds smaller than 280 km). However, there are almost no completely cloudy or completely clear areas with sizes as large as 2500 km. A similar study has shown that most of the cloud variation occurs at sizes > 30–50 km (Hughes & Henderson-Sellers, 1983), although there are particular types of clouds with variation concentrated in the range of 1–10 km (Welch et al., 1988).

Timescales

A similar behavior is apparent for the magnitude of cloud variations with increasing timescales. Fig. 6 shows the frequency of occurrence of cloud amounts for 280 km-sized regions when averaged over 1 day and 30 days. Again, it is found that very few regions are completely cloudy or completely clear over 30 days. Fig. 7 shows what happens when the IR temperatures are averaged over increasingly longer time periods. Averaging over smaller timescales eliminates the smaller spatial scale variations first, without affecting the larger spatial scales; however, for longer periods the motion of larger cloud systems begins to blur the larger-scale features. A remarkable feature of these images is the strong similarity of Figs. 4 and 7(b): because the spatial and temporal scales of atmospheric motions are related, the cloud variations at spatial scales ~100 km are similar to those at timescales ~1 day.

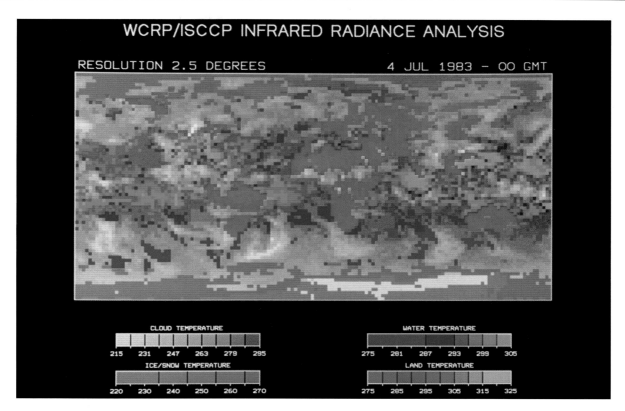

Fig. 4. Same image as in Fig. 1 but averaged to a spatial resolution of about 280 km.

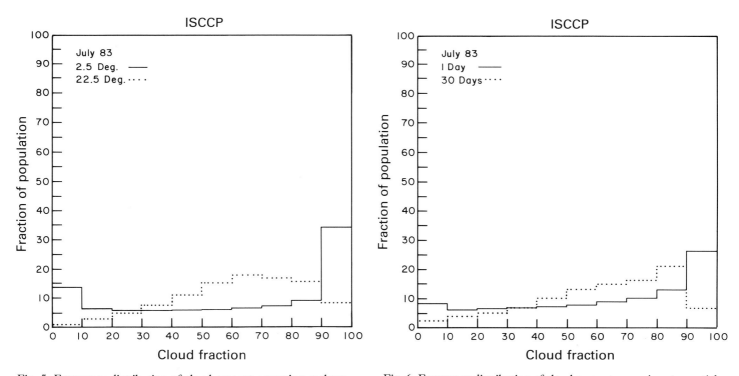

Fig. 5. Frequency distribution of cloud amount occurring at three-hour time intervals for spatial scales equivalent to 2·5° of latitude (about 280 km) and 22·5° (about 2500 km).

Fig. 6. Frequency distribution of cloud amount occurring at a spatial scale equivalent to 2·5° of latitude (about 280 km) for timescales of one day and 30 days.

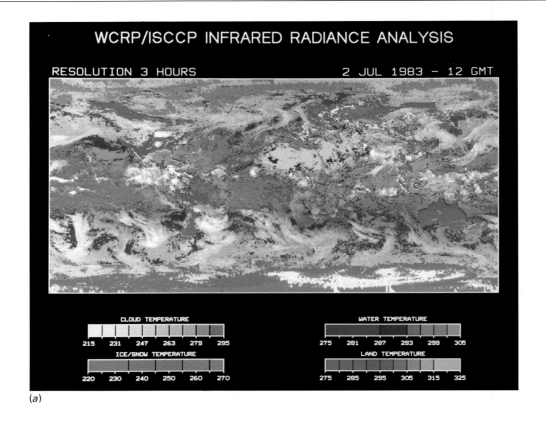

(a)

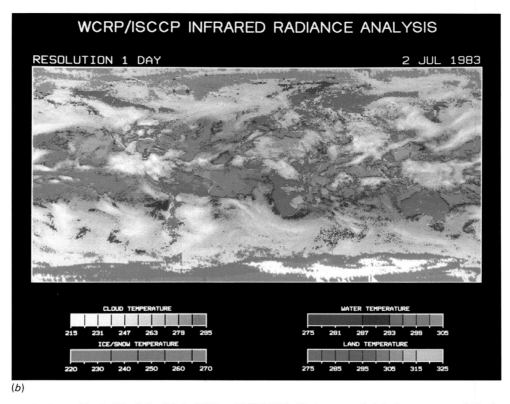

(b)

Fig. 7. (a) Composite image like in Fig. 1 for 2 July 1983 at 1200 UTC. (b) Average of eight images over whole day, 2 July 1983.

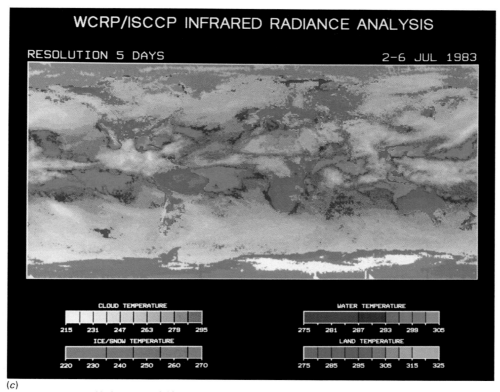

(c) Average of 40 images covering 2 July through 6 July 1983.

Variations of cloudiness

Geographic

Figures 8, 9 and 10 show the global distribution of annual mean cloud amount, optical thickness and top pressure. The cloud properties vary by roughly the same amount with both latitude and longitude, although the distribution is somewhat more uniform with longitude at higher latitudes. Particularly strong variations are clearly associated with land/water boundaries. The magnitude of these geographic variations of annual mean cloud properties are compared with the total variations (space and time) in Fig. 11.

Global cloudiness is organized roughly into three latitudinal bands, one near the equator and one in each hemisphere at higher latitudes. The tropical cloud band is formed by moving clusters of deep convective storms that exhibit a complex structure, strongly affected by the influence of the arrangement of land and water on the tropical circulation. Notable concentrations of these storms occur over India and the Indian Ocean, over the Western Pacific, off the coast of Columbia, over Brazil, off the coast of Liberia/Guinea, and over Sudan/Ethiopia. Although the deep convective towers extend higher and are denser than most other clouds on Earth, much larger areal coverage is provided by high-level mesoscale 'anvil' clouds and cirrus that form in association with the convective clouds. Thus, on average, the tropical cloud band has a smaller water density and albedo than do mid-latitude clouds, but the average cloud top altitude is higher.

The higher latitude cloud bands are composed of clouds forming in the cyclonic storm systems that dominate the mid-latitude circulation. These clouds are generally much larger in size with lower cloud top altitudes and larger (average) water densities and albedos than in the tropics. Larger cloud amounts are associated with the persistent centers of storm formation off the east coasts of Asia, North America and South America and the tracks of these storms across the Pacific and Atlantic oceans. The low latitude positions of Africa and Australia preclude formation of such storm centers. The decay of these storms upon landfall accounts for lower cloud amounts over land, although the more maritime climate of Europe is an exception.

In-between these major cloud bands are two relatively cloud-free areas associated with the transition from tropical to mid-latitude circulation regimes and the descending part of Hadley circulation. The great, cloud-free deserts all occur in this latitude band; however, the oceans have both a cloud-free area in their western parts and a very persistent, low-level cloudiness in their eastern parts. The east–west Walker

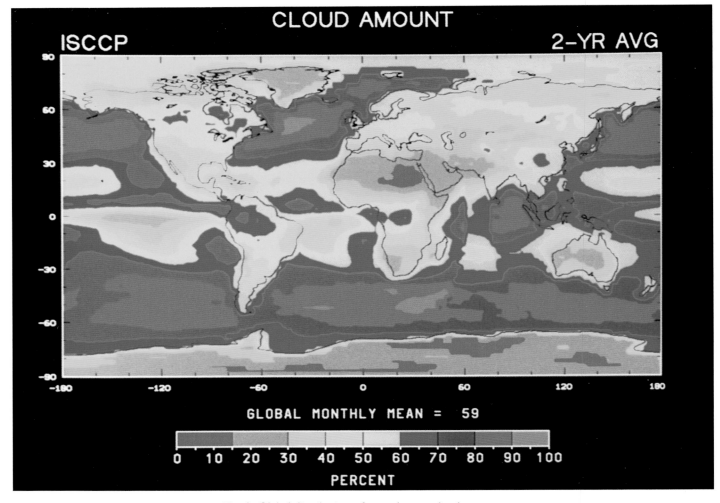

Fig. 8. Global distribution of annual mean cloud amount.

circulation in the tropics is revealed by a similar pattern of high–low cloud amount in the equatorial Pacific.

The two polar regions exhibit very different characteristics because of differences in surface topography. The North Pole is covered by the Arctic Ocean, which is almost completely enclosed by land, and is generally more cloudy, in part, because of the entry of Atlantic cyclones through the land-gap between Greenland and Europe. The South Pole is covered by the elevated plateau of Antarctica and is generally less cloudy, in part, because the high terrain blocks the passage of ocean storms.

Diurnal

One systematic small timescale variation of cloudiness that has important implications is the diurnal variation, which is illustrated in Fig. 12 for zonally and monthly averaged cloud and surface properties over ocean and land. Such systematic variations of clouds not only affect the average radiation balance of Earth by altering the interaction between clouds, sunlight and surface temperatures, but also may be caused by the same variation in radiation which changes the turbulent exchanges of energy and water between the atmosphere and the surface. This coupling between radiation, atmospheric motions and the surface characteristics leads to several different styles of diurnal variation.

Lower latitude land areas experience the largest daily variations of solar heating and consequently undergo large diurnal surface temperature variations; however, the amplitude of this variation is modulated by the evaporation of moisture and the presence of clouds. Thus, the arid, cloud-free deserts exhibit larger diurnal surface temperature variations than the moist, cloudy tropical land areas. The link of clouds to evaporating water and strong heating is revealed by a tendency of tropical land cloudiness to peak in mid-afternoon; however, local variations of winds and topography can

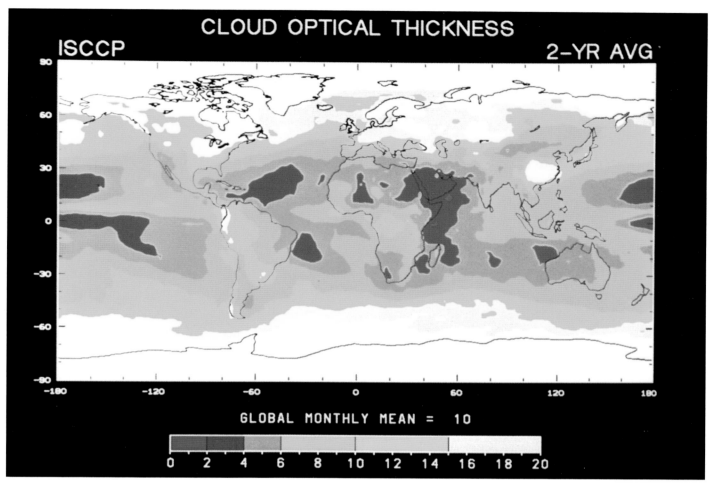

Fig. 9. Global distribution of annual mean cloud optical thickness.

shift the maximum cloudiness to other times (e.g. over the mountains in Ethiopia, maximum cloudiness occurs near midnight).

Lower latitude oceans exhibit different behavior because the surface temperature does not respond to daily variations of solar heating; rather the structure of the atmospheric boundary layer changes (e.g. Randall *et al.*, 1984). As a result of this complex balance, ocean cloudiness undergoes a diurnal variation that reaches its peak between midnight and dawn.

The much stronger planetary scale circulations at higher latitudes, especially in winter, are less sensitive to diurnal variations in radiative heating, so that diurnal cloud variations are similar but much weaker. However, mid-latitude land areas in summer are more similar to low-latitude land areas and exhibit the same peak in cloudiness in mid-afternoon. This is apparent in Fig. 12, which is for boreal summer, as a large amplitude variation in the 30°–60° latitude zone where diurnal variations of surface temperature are largest.

Synoptic

The planetary scale circulations are caused by the equator-to-pole contrast in solar heating; the atmosphere (and ocean) responds by transporting some of the excess heat near the equator to the poles. This circulation is made more complex by hydrodynamical instabilities that produce the synoptic scale wave motions, one phase of which we call storms (Lorenz, 1967). The motions in these storms produce clouds, which in turn modulate the energy exchanges that drive the storms.

Fig. 13 shows a sequence of global maps of daily cloud amount, each separated by two days, to illustrate the predominant synoptic and planetary scale variations of cloudiness that are associated with Earth's general circulation. Higher latitudes in both hemispheres contain several storm systems indicated by concentrations of cloudiness that travel slowly eastward. Although smaller storm features are apparent near the equator, their behavior is more incoherent

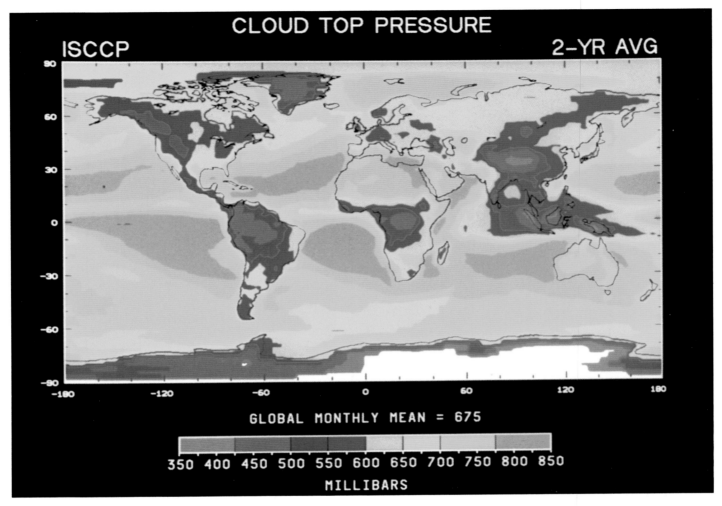

Fig. 10. Global distribution of annual mean cloud top pressure.

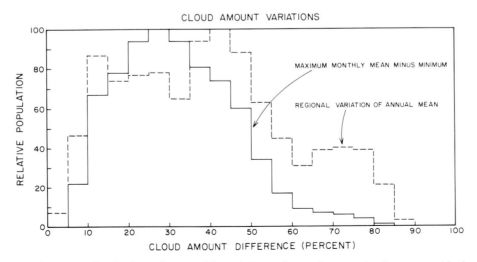

Fig. 11. Comparison of the frequency distribution of geographic variations of annual mean cloud amount with the distribution of monthly variations of cloud amount.

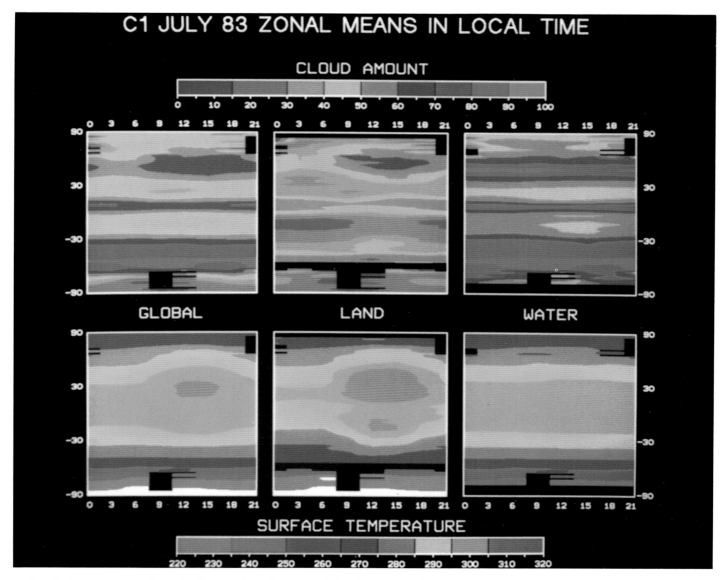

Fig. 12. Monthly mean, diurnal variations of zonally averaged cloud amounts and surface temperatures for land and ocean for July 1983.

and their slower westward drift less apparent in this display. Correlations of such maps of cloudiness reveal the characteristic timescale for mid-latitude features of a few days, whereas the tropics exhibit both a diurnal and a longer ($\approx$ 5–15 day) timescale.

Seasonal

Since Earth's rotation axis is tilted with respect to the plane of its orbit about the Sun, the latitude of maximum solar heating undergoes an annual north–south oscillation that causes a seasonal cycle of temperatures. The largest seasonal changes of solar heating occur in a band between 30°–60° in both hemispheres (Rossow & Lacis, 1990). The associated seasonal variations of the zonally averaged cloud and surface properties are shown in Fig. 14. The detailed geographic changes of cloud amount are illustrated by seasonal (three-month) average in Fig. 15. As with the diurnal variations, clouds exhibit different behavior over land and ocean, and over lower latitudes and higher latitudes.

In the tropics, the seasonal variation of surface temperature is small; the more important seasonal variation is of the cloud amount and rainfall. Over both land and ocean, the summer (wet) season is more stormy than the winter (dry) season with larger rainfall and cloud amounts; moreover, the cloud top altitudes are much larger and the cloud albedos much higher in summer. These changes are associated with a seasonal shift of the Inter-Tropical Convergence Zone (ITCZ), which is

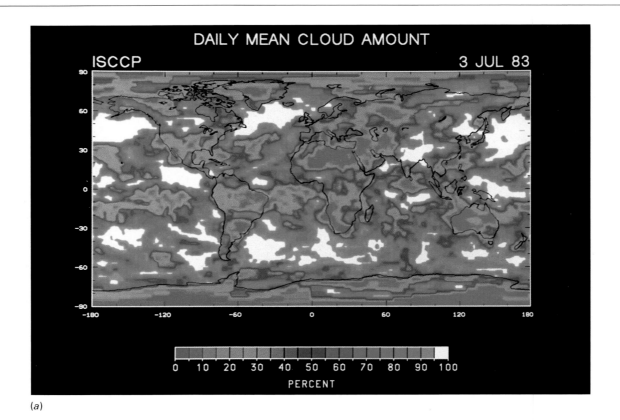

Fig. 13. Sequence of global maps of daily mean cloud amount with a two-day interval.

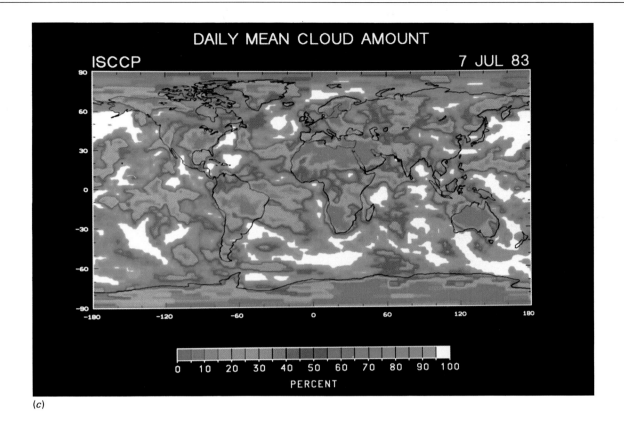

(*c*)

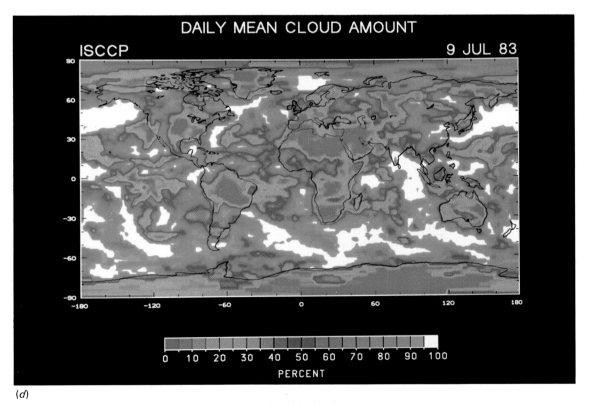

(*d*)

Fig. 13. (*cont.*)

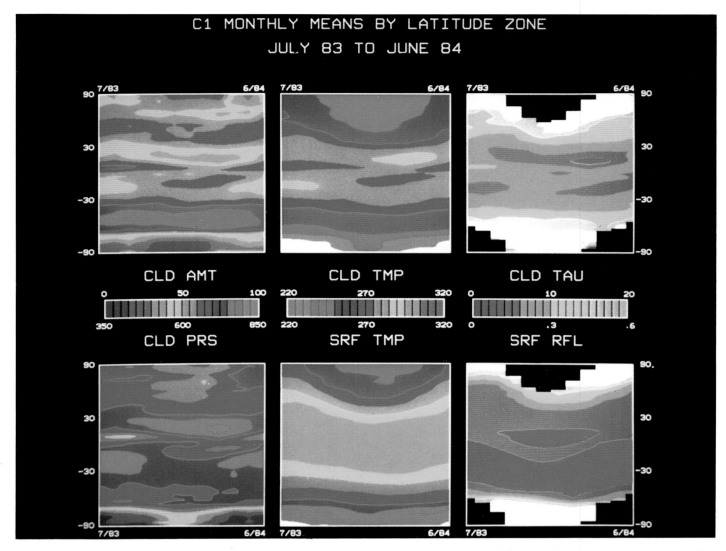

Fig. 14. Monthly variations of zonally averaged cloud amount, cloud top temperature, cloud optical thickness (tau), cloud top pressure, surface temperature and surface reflectance for July 1983–June 1984.

associated with a concentration of deep convective storm complexes that forms a near-equatorial cloud band. Over land, this cloud feature shifts in latitude as the zone of maximum solar heating shifts with seasons; however, over the ocean the storms do not actually shift position. Rather, there are actually two bands, north and south of the equator at some longitudes and a single band at others. The seasonal variation is expressed as a strengthening of summer hemisphere bands and a weakening of winter hemisphere bands. The most notable summer event is the Indian summer Monsoon (June–August): average cloud top altitudes change by more than 3 km between summer and winter (see Fig. 16).

Subtropical regions undergo a somewhat larger seasonal cycle of surface temperature, but less change in cloudiness than the tropics. Generally, subtropical land and ocean areas are cloudier in winter; however, several desert areas, the Gobi, the Gibson/Great Sandy, and the Kalahari, show the opposite behavior.

Mid-latitudes exhibit much larger seasonal variations of surface temperature; summer is generally less cloudy over both land and ocean with reduced cloud top altitudes and albedos. The stronger storms of winter produce slightly higher cloud tops and much larger cloud water densities or albedos. However, the major cause of seasonal changes in cloud top temperature in mid-latitudes, in contrast to lower latitudes, is the seasonal change of the atmospheric temperature at a constant altitude. The latitudinal position of the storms also changes with season, more so in the Northern than the Southern Hemisphere: summer storms track closer to the pole than winter storms.

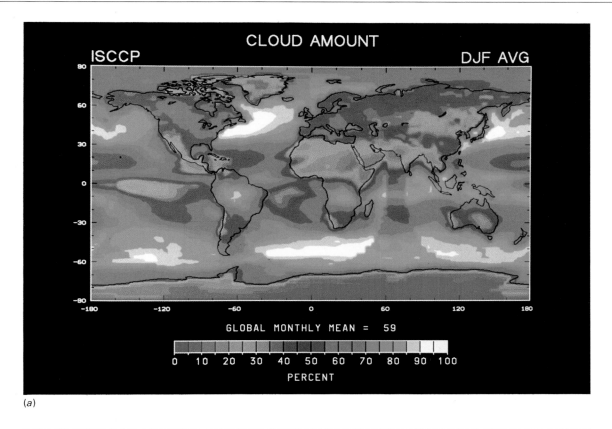

(a)

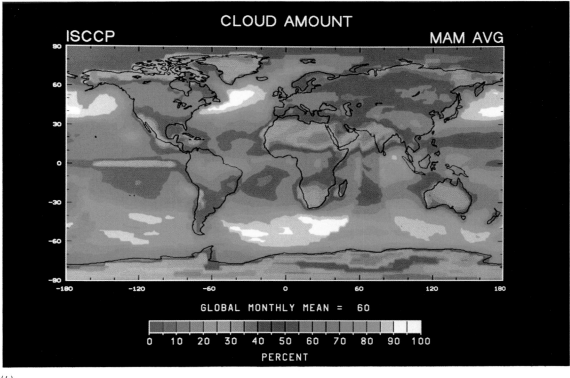

(b)

Fig. 15. Global distribution of seasonal (three-monthly) mean cloud amounts (a) for boreal winter (DJF), (b) boreal spring (MAM), (c) boreal summer (JJA) and (d) boreal autumn (SON).

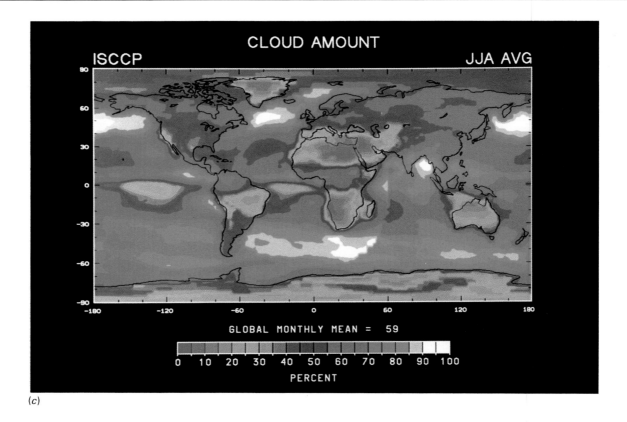

(c)

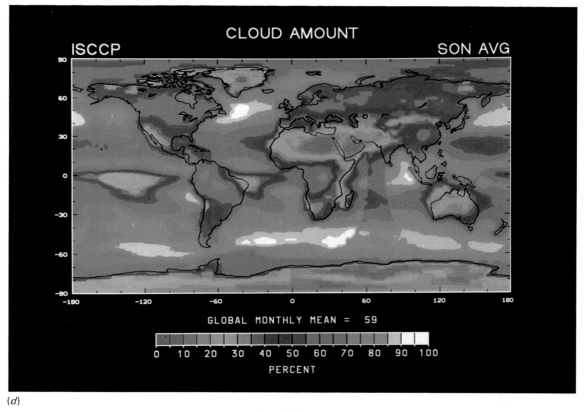

(d)

Fig. 15. (*cont.*)

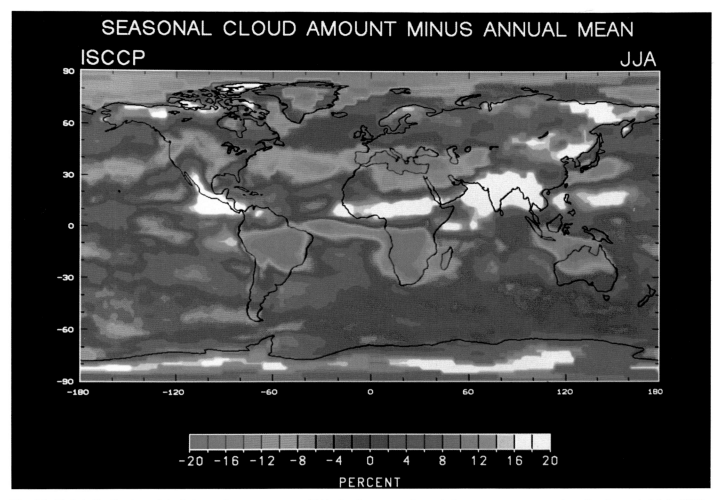

Fig. 16. Global distribution of deviations of summer–mean (JJA) cloud amounts from their two-year average values for the period July 1983–June 1985.

Examination of the frequencies of occurrence of different types of clouds, classified according to their radiative properties (Fig. 3), shows that the seasonal cloud variations are much more complex. Figs. 17 and 18 illustrate the major seasonal changes caused by the shifting of the ITCZ into and out of a region: in the dry season, mostly low-level, relatively tenuous clouds occur, whereas in the wet season, many more very high-topped and very dense clouds occur. In mid-latitudes the seasonal changes are more complex as shown in Figs. 19 and 20. The stronger storms in winter over land are composed of relatively dense clouds with middle-level tops. In summer, the large-scale storms are absent (shifted poleward), but now some smaller-scale thunderstorms occur (high tops and large albedos). Low-level tenuous clouds are also more prevalent in summer.

Inter-annual

Inter-annual variations of clouds and their properties are also complex. Fig. 21 illustrates both the seasonal and inter-annual variations of the global mean cloud amount versus the global mean surface temperature: the semi-annual cycle is explained by the combination of a larger amplitude seasonal change in the Northern Hemisphere surface temperatures, but a larger amplitude change in Southern Hemisphere cloud amount, and differences in the phase of the seasonal oscillation between the two hemispheres. Although the pattern of the seasonal variations is similar in the second year, the center of the oscillation has shifted to larger cloud amounts.

These global mean quantities and their variations are actually produced by the combination of many regional variations; Figs. 16 and 22 show the geographic deviations of mean summer and winter cloud amounts for two particular years,

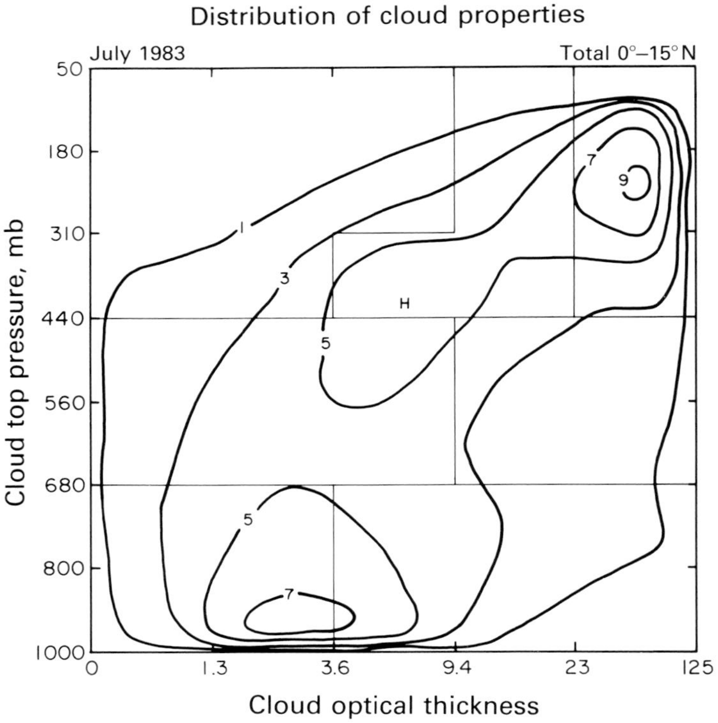

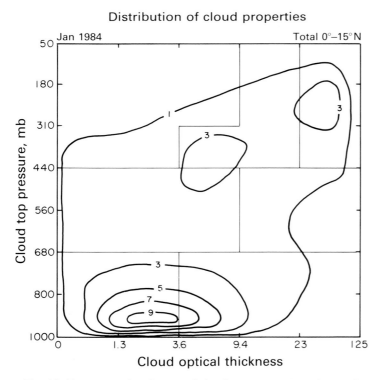

Fig. 17. Frequency distribution of cloud top pressures and optical thicknesses in the latitude zone 0°–15° N for July 1983.

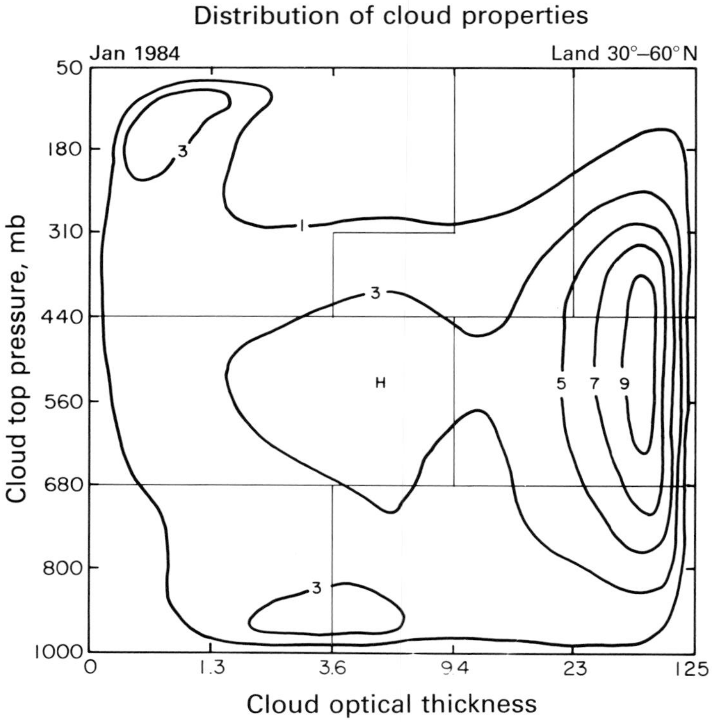

Fig. 18. Frequency distribution of cloud top pressures and optical thicknesses in the latitude zone 0°–15° N for January 1984.

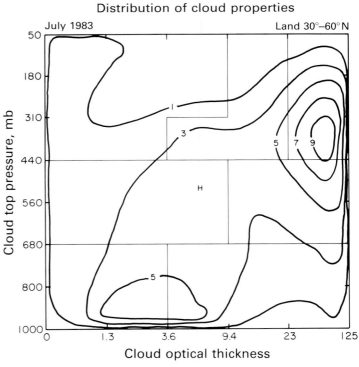

Fig. 19. Frequency distribution of cloud top pressures and optical thicknesses over land in the latitude zone 30°–60° N for January 1984.

Fig. 20. Frequency distribution of cloud top pressures and optical thicknesses over land in the latitude zone 30°–60° N for July 1983.

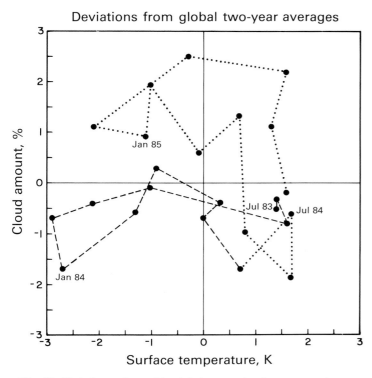

Deviations from global two-year averages

Fig. 21. Variations of monthly global mean cloud amount and surface temperature for July 1983–June 1985 expressed as deviations from their two-year global average values. Each dot is one month.

relative to their average. These regional changes are much larger in magnitude than those of the global mean values; thus, there is significant cancellation of the variations among the regions. Note especially the 'dipole' changes in Figs. 16 and 22; these are regions where the inter-annual variations are caused by a shift in the position of a large scale cloud feature, such as the ITCZ or the mid-latitude storm bands. In fact, the seasonal variation of hemisphere average cloud amount is controlled by tropical changes, while the hemisphere average surface temperature variations are controlled by higher latitude land areas. There are also 'unbalanced' changes, regions where the cloud amount decreases or increases without any apparent shift in the cloud feature; this type of change causes the inter-annual variations of the global mean values.

Conclusions

The magnitude of variations of cloudiness and cloud properties appears to grow larger from the very smallest space/timescales up to the predominant scales of atmospheric motions; however, as these variations are averaged over larger space/timescales from regional–daily to global–annual, the magnitude decreases again. The remarkable stability of the statistics of the atmospheric variations presents a severe chal-

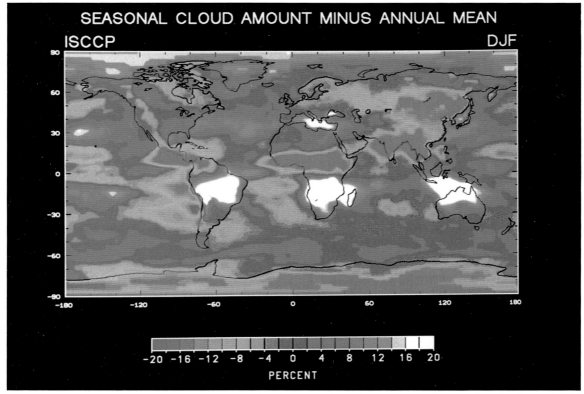

Fig. 22. Global distribution of deviations of winter–mean (DJF) cloud amounts from their two-year average values for the period July 1983–June 1985.

Monthly deviations from 2-year averages

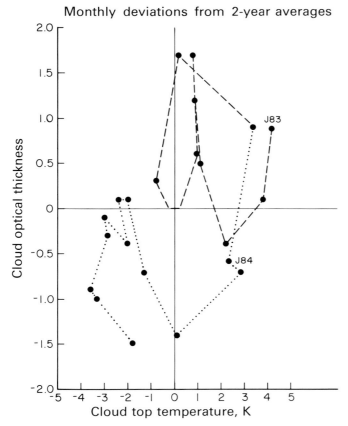

Fig. 23. Variations of monthly global mean cloud optical thickness and top temperature for July 1983–June 1985 expressed as deviations from their two-year global average values.

lenge to Earth observing systems in that they must make high precision measurements that properly sample the complete range of scales at which significant variations occur to be able to measure the very small changes associated with varying climate.

The magnitude of the cloud property variations also implies significant short-term, regional perturbations of the radiative forcing of the atmospheric and oceanic dynamics. The complexity of these perturbations is illustrated in Fig. 23 which shows the correlations between changes in the monthly, hemispheric mean cloud optical thickness and cloud top temperature. The variation of these two cloud properties affects (primarily) the solar heating and thermal cooling of Earth, respectively. The fact that these two properties do not vary in phase over the season implies a potentially complex radiative feedback on the seasonal surface temperature cycle. When examined regionally, this behavior is even more varied (Rossow & Lacis, 1990). Thus, determining the nature of the cloud–radiative feedbacks on climate changes requires that the processes that control these diurnal, synoptic and seasonal

cloud variations are understood, that they are able to be modeled, and that the resulting models are used to predict how clouds will vary with climate change.

Data availability

All ISCCP data sets are obtainable from the NOAA Satellite Data Services Division, Princeton Executive Square, Room 100, Washington, DC 20233, USA (phone: 301-763-8400; fax: 301–763–2635).

References

Arking, A. A. & Childs, J. D. (1985). Retrieval of cloud cover parameters from multispectral satellite measurements. *J. Climate Appl. Meteor.*, **24**, 322–33.

Coakley, J. A. & Baldwin, D. G. (1984). Towards the objective analysis of clouds from satellite measurements. *J. Climate Appl. Meteor.*, **23**, 1065–99.

Coakley, J. A., Bernstein, R. L. & Durkee, P. A. (1987). Effect of ship-stack effluents on cloud reflectivity. *Science*, **237**, 1020–22.

Gedzelman, S. D. (1989). Cloud classification before Luke Howard. *Bull. Am. Meteor. Soc.*, **70**, 381–95.

Hartmann, D. L., Ramanathan, V., Berroir, A. & Hunt, G. E. (1986). Earth radiation budget data and climate research. *Rev. Geophys.*, **24**, 439–68.

Heirtzler, J. R. (ed.) (1985). Relief of the Surface of the Earth. *Report MGG-2, NGDC*, National Oceanographic and Atmospheric Administration.

Hughes, N. A. (1984). Global cloud climatologies: a historical review. *J. Climate Appl. Meteor.*, **23**, 724–51.

Hughes, N. A. & Henderson-Sellers, A. (1983). The effect of spatial and temporal averaging on sampling strategies for cloud amount data. *Bull. Am. Meteor. Soc.*, **64**, 250–7.

Inoue, T. (1987). Cloud type classification with NOAA 7 split-window measurements. *J. Geophys. Res.*, **92**, 3991–4000.

Lorenz, E. N. (1967). *The Nature and Theory of the General Circulation of the Atmosphere*. WMO-No. 218. TP. 115. World Meteorological Organization, Geneva, 161pp.

Masaki, G. T. (1976). *The Wolf Plotting and Contouring Package*. GSFC Computer Program Lib. A00227, Computer Sciences Corporation, Goddard Space Flight Center, Greenbelt, MD, 187pp.

Matthews, E. (1983). Global vegetation and land use: New high resolution data bases for climate studies. *J. Climate Appl. Meteor.*, **22**, 474–87.

Matthews, E. (1985). Atlas of archived vegetation, land-use and seasonal albedo data bases. NASA Tech. Memo. 86199, 53pp.

McGuffie, K. & Henderson-Sellers, A. (1989). Almost a century of 'imaging' clouds over the whole-sky dome. *Bull. Am. Meteor. Soc.*, **70**, 1243–53.

Minnis, P. (1989). Viewing zenith angle dependence of cloudiness determined from coincident GOES East and GOES West data. *J. Geophys. Res.*, **94**, 2303–20.

Minnis, P., Harrison, E. F. & Gibson, G. G. (1987). Cloud cover over the equatorial eastern Pacific derived from July 1983 ISCCP data using a hybrid bispectral threshold method. *J. Geophys. Res.*, **92**, 4051–73.

Nakajima, T. & King, M. D. (1990). Determination of the optical thickness and effective particle radius of clouds from reflected solar radiation measurements. Part I: Theory. *J. Atmos. Sci.*, **47**, 1878–93.

Randall, D. A., Coakley, J. A., Fairall, C. W., Kropfli, R. A. & Lenschow, D. H. (1984). Outlook for research on subtropical marine stratiform clouds. *Bull. Am. Meteor. Soc.*, **65**, 1290–301.

Rossow, W. B. (1989). Measuring cloud properties from space: A review. *J. Climate*, **2**, 201–13.

Rossow, W. B. & Lacis, A. A. (1990). Global, seasonal cloud variations from satellite radiance measurements. Part II: Cloud properties and radiative effects. *J. Climate*, **3**, 1204–53.

Rossow, W. B. & Schiffer, R. A. (1991). ISCCP cloud data products. *Bull. Am. Meteor. Soc.*, **72**, 2–20.

Rossow, W. B., Mosher, F., Kinsella, E., Arking, A., Desbois, M., Harrison, E., Minnis, P., Ruprecht, E., Sèze, G., Simmer, C. & Smith, E. (1985). ISCCP cloud algorithm intercomparison. *J. Climate Appl. Meteor.*, **24**, 877–903.

Rossow, W. B., Kinsella, E., Wolf, A. & Garder, L. (1987). *International Satellite Cloud Climatology Project (ISCCP) Description of Reduced Resolution Radiance Data*. July 1985 (revised July 1987). WMO/TD-No. 58, World Meteorological Organization, Geneva, 143pp.

Rossow, W. B., Garder, L. C., Lu, P. J. & Walker, A. W. (1991). *International Satellite Cloud Climatology Project (ISCCP) Documentation of Cloud Data*. December 1988 (revised March 1991). WMO/TD-No. 266, World Meteorological Organization, Geneva, 76pp. plus three appendices.

Rossow, W. B., Garder, L. C. & Lacis, A. (1989). Global, seasonal cloud variations from satellite radiance measurements. Part I: Sensitivity of analysis. *J. Climate*, **2**, 419–58.

Saunders, R. W. (1986). An automated scheme for the removal of cloud contamination from AVHRR radiances over western Europe. *Int. J. Remote Sensing*, **7**, 867–86.

Schiffer, R. A. & Rossow, W. B. (1983). The International Satellite Cloud Climatology Project (ISCCP): The first project of the World Climate Research Program. *Bull. Am. Meteor. Soc.*, **64**, 779–84.

Schiffer, R. A. & Rossow, W. B. (1985). ISCCP global radiance data set: A new resource for climate research. *Bull. Am. Meteor. Soc.*, **66**, 1498–505.

Sèze, G. & Rossow, W. B. (1991). Time-cumulated visible and infra-red radiance histograms used as descriptors of surface and cloud variations. *Int. J. Remote Sensing*, **12**, 921–52.

Tian, L. & Curry, J. A. (1989). Cloud overlap statistics. *J. Geophys. Res.*, **94**, 9925–35.

Warren, S. G., Hahn, C. J. & London, J. (1985). Simultaneous occurrence of different cloud types. *J. Climate Appl. Meteor.*, **24**, 658–67.

Warren, S. G., Hahn, C. J., London, J., Chervin, R. M. & Jenne, R. (1986). Global Distribution of Total Cloud Cover and Cloud Type Amounts over Land. NCAR Tech. Note NCAR/TN-273 + STR, National Center for Atmospheric Research, Boulder, CO, 20pp. plus 200 maps.

Warren, S. G., Hahn, C. J., London, J., Chervin, R. M. & Jenne, R. (1988). Global Distribution of Total Cloud Cover and Cloud Type Amounts over Ocean. NCAR Tech. Note NCAR/TN-317 + STR, National Center for Atmospheric Research, Boulder, CO, 42pp. plus 170 maps.

Welch, R. M., Kuo, K. S., Wielicki, B. A., Sengupta, S. K. & Parker, L. (1988). Marine stratocumulus cloud fields off the coast of southern California observed using LANDSAT imagery. Part I: Structural characteristics. *J. Appl. Meteor.*, **27**, 363–78.

WMO (1975). *Manual on the Observation of Clouds and Other Meteors*. International Cloud Atlas, vol. 1. WMO-No. 407. World Meteorological Organization, Geneva, 155pp.

Yamanuchi, T., Suzuki, K. & Kawaguchi, S. (1987). Detection of clouds in Antarctica from infra-red multispectral data of AVHRR. *J. Meteor. Soc. Japan*, **65**, 949–62.

Zangvil, A. (1975). Temporal and spatial behavior of large-scale disturbances in tropical cloudiness deduced from satellite brightness data. *Mon. Wea. Rev.*, **103**, 904–20.

Tropical and subtropical precipitation

P. A. ARKIN AND J. E. JANOWIAK

Introduction

One of the important constituents of the Earth's atmosphere is water, which changes readily among the solid, liquid and gaseous phases at the temperatures and pressures at the surface and in the troposphere. Thus precipitation, which is the transfer of liquid or solid water from the atmosphere, after condensation, to the surface, is a relatively common phenomenon. This strongly affects the climate of the Earth by providing a sink of heat energy in some locations, through melting and evaporation, and a source in others, through condensation, thus drastically changing the manner in which the unequal distribution of solar energy over the planet is accommodated. Since liquid water is essential to life, including in particular human life, its distribution is vital to civilization. While life can survive with widely varying amounts of precipitation in the course of a year, it is quite sensitive to dramatic departures from the accustomed course of events. Because water on the ground is not stable (it can evaporate, sink into the soil or run off), and because the source of precipitation is the weather, which is highly variable in both time and space, the Earth's climate system is, and always will be, subject to droughts and floods.

One of the most significant potential dangers associated with global change is the risk that changes in the spatial and temporal distribution of temperature and precipitation will be so large and occur so rapidly that the established ecosystems will be unable to adapt. Modern human civilization uses prodigious amounts of water. In the US, for example, the per capita use of fresh water is about 1400 gallons per day (van der Leeden, 1990). The nearly universal original source of that water is precipitation. A better understanding of the current distribution of precipitation and of how it might be affected by global change is vital to the survival and the health of mankind.

Changes in the distribution of precipitation, through their relation to changes in cloudiness, cause changes in radiative forcing. Changes in atmospheric circulation can result, particularly in the tropics, from changes in the pattern of condensation of water vapor and the attendant release of latent heat of condensation. Thus precipitation is a fully interactive component of the highly non-linear global climate system. Observations of the spatial and temporal distribution of precipitation over the globe are essential to assessing, modeling and predicting global change.

Methodology

The measurement of precipitation has been one of the more challenging tasks faced by meteorologists over the years. The earliest, and still the most common, instrument used is some variation on the rain gauge, which in essence is a transparent bucket with a ruler on its side. Ideally, precipitation falling into the opening of the gauge will remain inside and collect at the bottom. In practice, of course, all sorts of things can happen, including splash either into, or out of, and collection along the sides of the gauge. In addition, the path of falling particles is altered by air flow around the collector, which may prevent the precipitation from falling into the gauge in a regular fashion.

However, the most serious drawback to rain gauges as tools for the measurement of global precipitation is that they produce what are essentially point measurements and precipitation is highly variable in space. Since it is clearly impractical to carpet the globe with gauges, various remote sensing techniques have come into use. The first of these to be applied was ground-based radar, wherein a beam of electromagnetic radiation of a frequency which is scattered or absorbed by precipitation particles more strongly than by other atmospheric constituents is used to illuminate a region, and the back-scattered signal is interpreted in terms of rain rate. Here too there are difficulties, primarily in the highly non-linear transformation from reflectivity to rain rate. Furthermore, the radar beam does not curve with the surface of the Earth, limiting its range to a few hundred kilometers, and nearer to 100 kilometers for quantitative applications. Thus complete coverage of the entire globe, particularly over the oceans, is not a practical possibility.

Attempts to estimate precipitation from satellite observations began almost as soon as such observations were available. Two principal types of methods have been attempted, measurements of frequencies which are affected by precipitating particles, and measurements of frequencies which are affected by clouds (referred to as 'direct' and 'indirect' by Arkin and Meisner, 1987). However, even the most direct of remotely sensed measurements is indirect compared to the measurements of rain gauges. The more direct methods of precipitation estimation are made using the microwave portion of the spectrum, and depend less on the establishment of an empirical relationship between clouds and rainfall and on the poorly known spatial and temporal variations in that relationship. Unfortunately, technical limitations have limited such observations to satellites in low Earth orbit and have been available only in recent years (Arkin & Ardanuy, 1989). Limited spatial and temporal sampling make the use of these observations in estimates of global precipitation difficult at the present, although this field is presently undergoing rapid evolution.

Indirect estimates of precipitation derived from observations of cloudiness have several advantages. First, the observations are routinely made from a number of satellites, including several in geostationary orbit, which are thus capable of making observations at frequent intervals. Furthermore, the operational nature of these satellites insures that the observations will be available for the long timespan necessary to study climatic phenomena. While the disadvantages of indirect methods are significant, these techniques have the necessary observational base and maturity of application to permit the derivation of temporally and spatially averaged fields of precipitation over large areas of the globe.

A great number of techniques to estimate precipitation from observations of cloudiness, in either the visible or thermal infra-red (IR) portions of the spectrum, have been developed over the last 20 years. With few exceptions, these methods were not designed for the purpose of obtaining climatic-scale estimates of precipitation over large areas, and adapting them to such a use is impractical because of their complexity, expense and/or subjectivity. A review of the techniques which have been applied to climatic-scale analyses is given by Arkin and Ardanuy (1989).

One of the simplest, and therefore most easily and widely applied, indirect techniques, is one based on a comparison of rainfall analyses derived from radar and rain gauge observations and geostationary satellite IR observations made in the eastern tropical Atlantic Ocean during the summer of 1974 for the GARP Atlantic Tropical Experiment (GATE) (Arkin, 1979, Richards & Arkin, 1981). They found that the coverage of large areas (1.5° latitude × 1.5° longitude and larger) by clouds with equivalent black body temperature of < 235 K was highly correlated with accumulated rainfall at all timescales from hourly to daily. Rainfall estimates made from just the fractional coverage of cold cloud over large areas appeared to be as accurate as those derived from more sophisticated algorithms (Richards & Arkin, 1981). An algorithm based on these results, called the GOES precipitation index (GPI), was applied to observations from the operational US geostationary satellites beginning in late 1981. Analyses of the annual cycles in estimated rainfall, its diurnal cycle, and the inter-annual variability in both, were presented by Arkin and Meisner (1987) and Meisner and Arkin (1987).

Analysis and results

The GPI technique has been used with both geostationary and polar orbiting satellite data to create a rainfall climatology for the tropics for the global precipitation climatology project (GPCP) (Arkin & Ardanuy, 1989; Janowiak & Arkin, 1990). The primary data sources for the tropical rainfall estimates are the GOES (US), GMS (Japan), and METEOSAT (European community) geostationary satellites, from which 16 class histograms of brightness temperature are collected every 3 hours for each 2.5° latitude × 2.5° longitude area in the field of view and accumulated over 5 day (pentad) periods. The fractional coverage of cold cloud (ratio of pixels with temperature < 235 K to the total number of pixels) is then determined for each area and a rainfall estimate is derived from the relationship used by Arkin and Meisner (1987). In some regions, geostationary satellite data are not available, so outgoing long-wave radiation (OLR) data from the NOAA polar orbiting satellites are used. These satellites are Sun-synchronous and view each Earth location twice each day (giving four views per day when two polar orbiting satellites are functional), giving poorer data sampling than from the geostationary satellites. Comparisons in regions where both geostationary and polar orbiting data were available showed that the resulting sampling errors were on the order of 10% or less for monthly estimates.

Fig. 1 shows the mean annual estimated rainfall over the period 1986–88. Three distinct zones of heavy rainfall stand out, located over Africa, South America, and a region from the Indian Ocean eastward to the date line. The intertropical convergence zones (ITCZ) in the Atlantic and Pacific are clearly evident. The rainiest region in the tropics is located in the eastern Indian Ocean west of Sumatra, where annual rainfall exceeds 14 mm/day. Pronounced dry regions are observed in the subtropical high pressure regions in the southern Atlantic, Pacific and Indian oceans and over the Sahara and Arabian deserts, where less than 0.5 mm/day is estimated.

This figure, as well as all other figures for seasons other

Mean annual rainfall (1986–88)

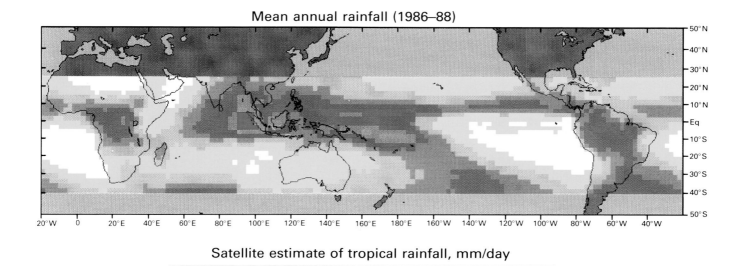

Satellite estimate of tropical rainfall, mm/day

Missing   .5   2   4   6   8   10   12   14 >14

Fig. 1. Mean annual rainfall (1986–88) as derived from satellite brightness temperatures (mm/day).

than the Northern Hemisphere summer, is truncated at 25° N, even though the data from which the estimates were made are available to 40° in both hemispheres. This rainfall estimation technique is useful primarily for convective rainfall, which is a relatively smaller portion of the total in the extratropics, and was calibrated in the tropical Atlantic. These facts make the GPI less effective as an estimate of rainfall in higher latitudes, particularly in winter and over cold land masses. This problem is more obvious in the Northern Hemisphere where much of the extratropical land masses exist, and

is particularly apparent in the Himalayas and the Tibetan Plateau during October through May, and rainfall estimates are not shown for these areas. While hints of a similar effect can be seen in far southern latitudes in Fig. 1, the extent of the problem is not so evident, and so estimates are shown for those regions for all seasons. (See the following section on Limitations for further discussion.)

The annual cycle of rainfall is depicted in Figs. 2–5, which show mean seasonal rainfall over the 3-year period. During the period December–February (DJF) (Fig. 2), the summer

Mean rainfall for December–February (1986–87 through 1988–89)

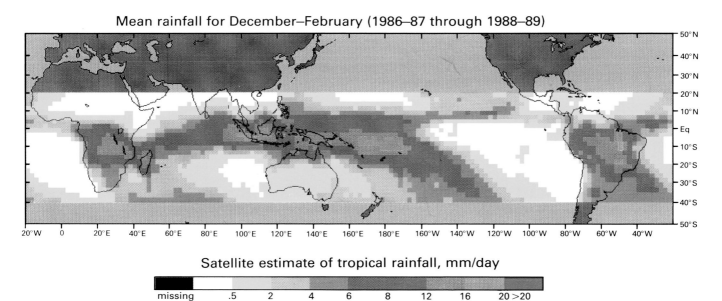

Satellite estimate of tropical rainfall, mm/day

missing   .5   2   4   6   8   12   16   20 >20

Fig. 2. Mean rainfall (1986–88) for the combined months of December, January and February.

Mean rainfall for March–May (1986–88)

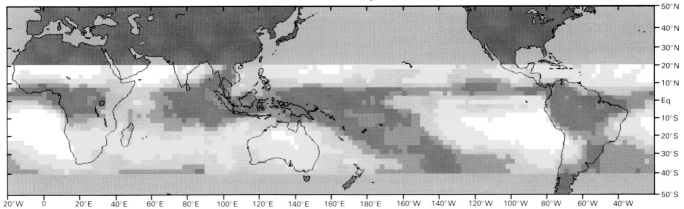

Fig. 3. Mean rainfall (1986–88) for the combined months of March, April and May.

Mean rainfall for June–August (1986–88)

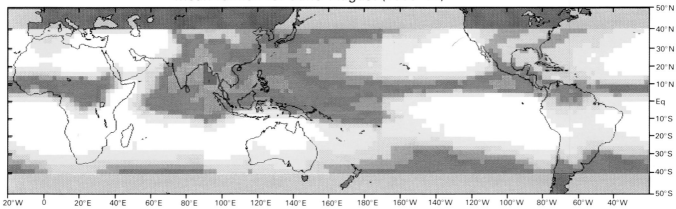

Fig. 4. Mean rainfall (1986–88) for the combined months of June, July and August.

Mean rainfall for September–November (1986–88)

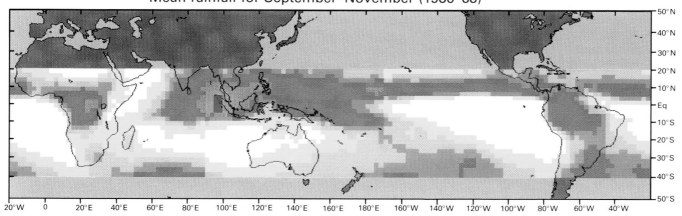

Satellite estimate of tropical rainfall, mm/day

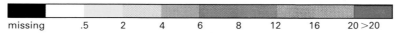

Fig. 5. Mean rainfall (1986–88) for the combined months of September, October and November.

Mean rainfall for January (1986–88)

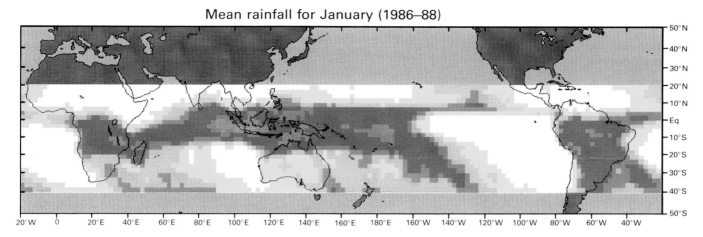

Fig. 6. Mean rainfall (1986–88) for the month of January.

Satellite estimate of tropical rainfall, mm/day

| Missing | | .5 | 2 | 4 | 6 | 10 | 15 | 20 | 25 >25 |

Mean rainfall for February (1986–88)

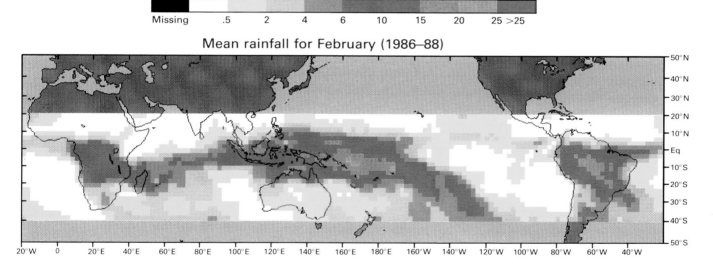

Fig. 7. Mean rainfall (1986–88) for the month of February.

season in the Southern Hemisphere, the bulk of the precipitation is south of the equator with the most intense rainfall (12–20 mm day^{-1}) observed in central southern Africa, much of Indonesia, extreme northern Australia and the western Pacific, and South America. Pronounced rainfall maxima extending toward the southeast from South America (the South Atlantic convergence zone, or SACZ), and from the central Pacific (the South Pacific convergence zone, or SPCZ) are also seen. The ITCZ in the Pacific and Atlantic oceans is relatively weak during this season. In contrast to this pattern, the majority of convection moves north of the equator during June–August (JJA), when the SPCZ and SACZ are weak while Atlantic and Pacific ITCZs are vigorous. Rainfall exceeding 20 mm day^{-1} is observed during this season in the

eastern Bay of Bengal, while the deserts in the Sahara, the Near East, southern Africa, and central and western Australia receive little, if any, rainfall. During the transition seasons (March–May (MAM) and September–November (SON)), the rainfall is generally not as intense as the other seasons and is more equally distributed between the hemispheres.

The most dramatic annual excursion of large-scale tropical convective activity is associated with the migration of the monsoon circulation between Australia and India. During February and March (Figs. 7, 8), intense convection is relegated to a zonal band from 5° N to 20° S in the central and eastern Indian Ocean and Indonesia. In the ensuing months, the intensity and extent of the convection increases as it moves northward, peaking during July–August (Figs. 12–14)

Mean rainfall for March (1986–88)

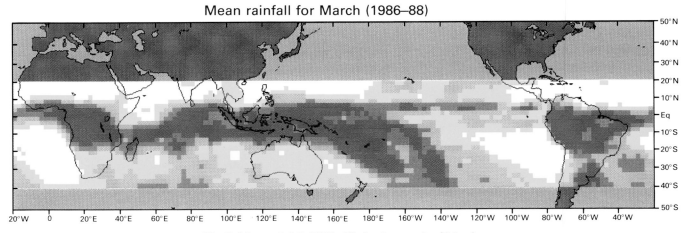

Fig. 8. Mean rainfall (1986–88) for the month of March.

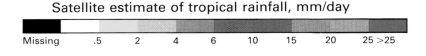

Mean rainfall for April (1986–88)

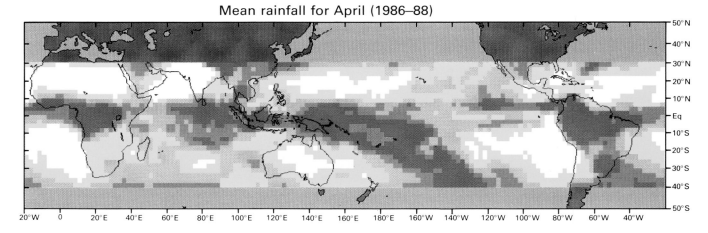

Fig. 9. Mean rainfall (1986–88) for the month of April.

when monthly rates over 25 mm/day are seen in some areas. During the remainder of the year, the convection gradually diminishes in intensity as it migrates back into the Southern Hemisphere. Similar behavior is observed over the tropical portions of Africa and South America.

Tropical rainfall patterns undergo enormous variation during the various phases of the El Niño/southern oscillation (ENSO) phenomenon (Kousky, 1984; Ropelewski & Halpert, 1987). The rainfall variation during 1986–89 is particularly striking since warm episode or low southern oscillation index (SOI) (Rasmusson & Carpenter, 1982) conditions during 1986–87 evolved into cold episode or high SOI (Ropelewski & Halpert, 1989) conditions during 1988–89. The rainfall differences over this 3–4 year period are largest over the equatorial Pacific, with large differences extending across 60° of longitude during that time. The eastern limit of equatorial convective activity in the central Pacific during the DJF 1986–87 and MAM 1987 seasons (Figs. 21–22) was about 140° W, as indicated by the estimated 0.5–2.0 mm/day rainfall rate. A large region of rainfall exceeding 20 mm/day was observed just south of the date-line and the SPCZ and SACZ were both very active. A return toward near normal conditions during DJF 1987–88 (Fig. 25) coincided with a westward shift in the eastern limit of equatorial convection in the Pacific to about 165° W. Notice also that the SPCZ was a bit weaker than during DJF 1986–87 (Fig. 21), and that the maximum rainfall south of the date-line diminished in intensity from the previous year to about 15–20 mm/day. As the cold episode

Mean rainfall for May (1986–88)

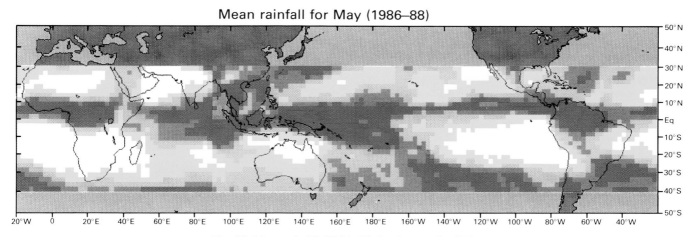

Fig. 10. Mean rainfall (1986–88) for the month of May.

Satellite estimate of tropical rainfall, mm/day

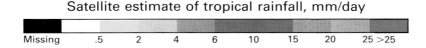

Mean rainfall for June (1986–88)

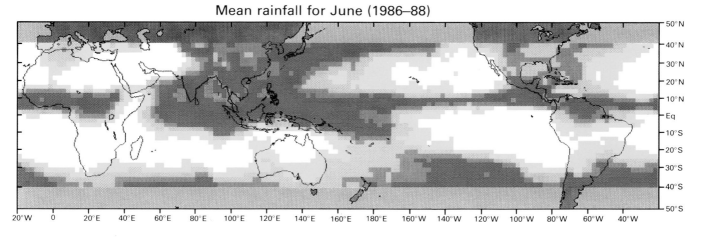

Fig. 11. Mean rainfall (1986–88) for the month of June.

conditions developed in mid-1988, the eastern limit of equatorial convection in the Pacific shifted westward until DJF 1988–89 (Fig. 29) when the dry zone extended to 160° E, a full 60° of longitude west of its position two years earlier.

Besides the central equatorial Pacific, several other regions of the world experience characteristic rainfall variations associated with the ENSO cycle. One of these regions is the Indian subcontinent, which tends to experience rainfall deficits during warm episodes and rainfall excess during cold episodes (Rasmusson & Carpenter, 1983). The JJA 1987 (Fig. 23) season in India saw rainfall rates of 10–15 mm/day over much of India, with more intense rainfall (15–20 mm/day) in the northeastern portions. In contrast, the monsoon season of JJA 1988 (Fig. 27) exhibited abundant rainfall

(15–20 mm/day) over much of the continent and extending southwestward into the Indian Ocean. In Pakistan, rainfall rates < 0.5 mm/day were estimated during JJA 1987 and increased to 2–4 mm/day during the next monsoon season.

During MAM 1989 (Fig. 30), a double ITCZ, one in each hemisphere, was observed in the eastern Pacific. In fact, during the month of March 1989 (not shown), a single ITCZ was observed in the Southern Hemisphere in this region, which is quite rare. Normally, the Pacific ITCZ is restricted to the Northern Hemisphere and is located between 2–6° N during northern winter and 10–12° N during northern summer.

Mean rainfall for July (1986–88)

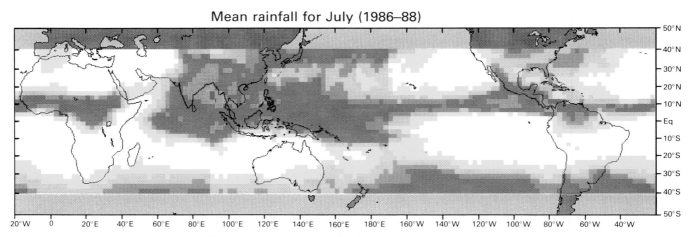

Fig. 12. Mean rainfall (1986–88) for the month of July.

Mean rainfall for August (1986–88)

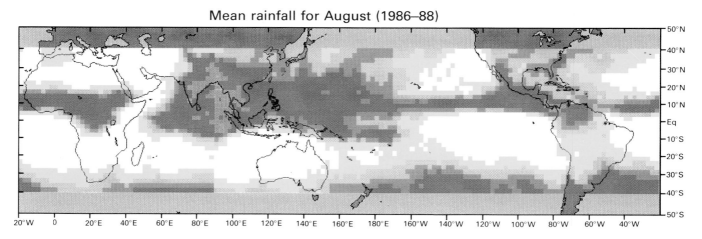

Fig. 13. Mean rainfall (1986–88) for the month of August.

Mean rainfall for September (1986–88)

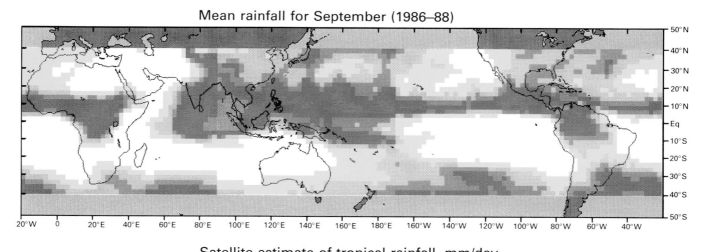

Satellite estimate of tropical rainfall, mm/day

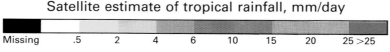

Missing   .5   2   4   6   10   15   20   25 >25

Fig. 14. Mean rainfall (1986–88) for the month of September.

Mean rainfall for October (1986–88)

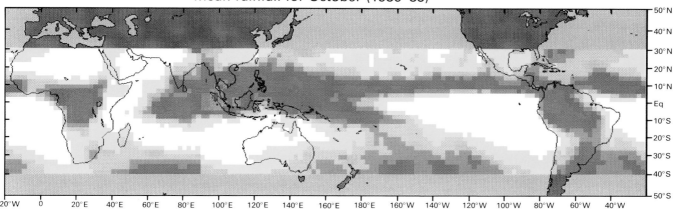

Fig. 15. Mean rainfall (1986–88) for the month of October.

Mean rainfall for November (1986–88)

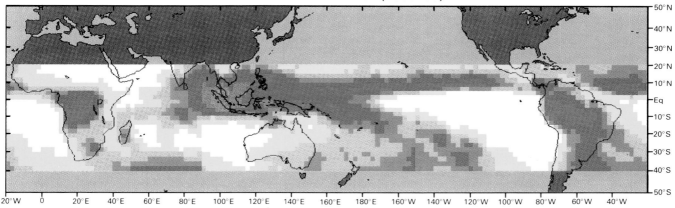

Fig. 16. Mean rainfall (1986–88) for the month of November.

Mean rainfall for December (1986–88)

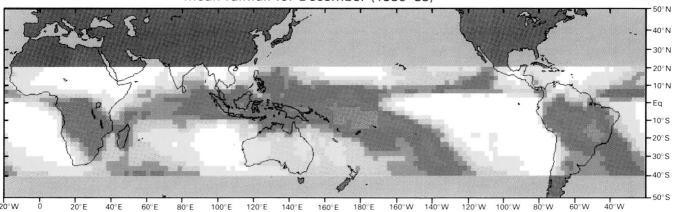

Satellite estimate of tropical rainfall, mm/day

Fig. 17. Mean rainfall (1986–88) for the month of December.

Mean rainfall for March–May, 1986

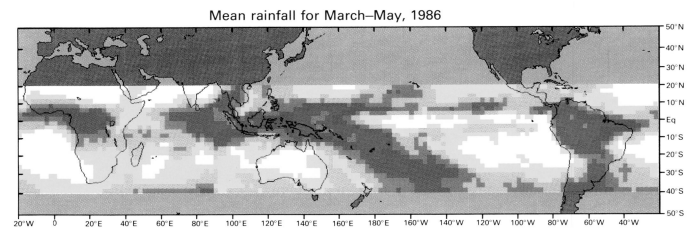

Fig. 18. Mean rainfall for the period March–May, 1986.

Satellite estimate of tropical rainfall, mm/day

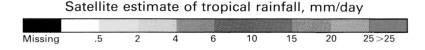

Mean rainfall for June–August, 1986

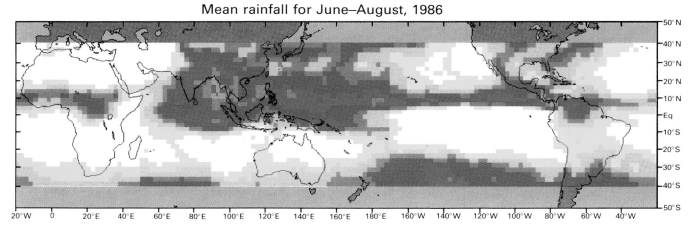

Fig. 19. Mean rainfall for the period June–August, 1986.

Limitations

While these analyses contain substantial information, their shortcomings are not inconsequential. First, the product is *not* truly precipitation; it is simply a scaled cold cloud frequency which is, at least for certain areas and times of year, highly correlated with spatially averaged accumulated rainfall. The spatial precision of estimates derived from cloudiness, however, is certainly suspect, since the expanse of cloud is often substantially greater than that of the associated precipitation.

The conversion of the measure of cloudiness to an estimate of precipitation requires a calibration coefficient. The one used here is that derived by Richards and Arkin (1981) from observations taken during GATE, which was held during one Northern Hemisphere summer in a small region of the tropical North Atlantic. The likelihood seems small that this coefficient, difficult to measure because of the scarcity of area-averaged rainfall observations, is the same in other places, years and seasons. Here, it has been assumed that the coefficient is constant. Previous studies (Arkin & Meisner, 1987) have not found strong evidence for large spatial variations in the coefficient, but their data were not capable of detecting errors of less than 30–50%. The GPCP (Arkin & Ardanuy, 1989) is engaged in an effort to determine the value of the coefficient in different places and seasons through the collection of rain gauge and radar observations.

However, while this sort of local calibration should improve

Mean rainfall for September–November, 1986

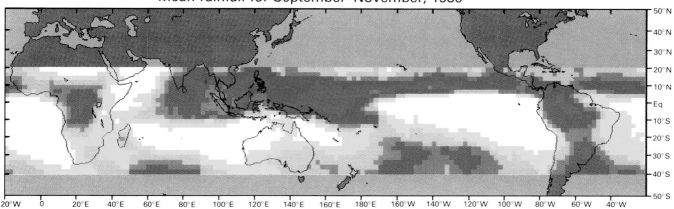

Fig. 20. Mean rainfall for the period September–November, 1986.

Mean rainfall for December, 1986 – February, 1987

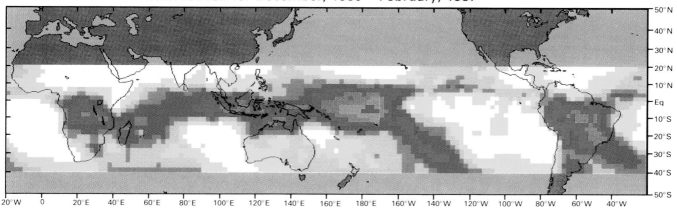

Fig. 21. Mean rainfall for the period December, 1986–February, 1987.

Mean rainfall for March–May, 1987

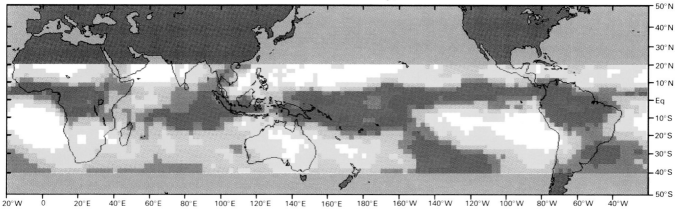

Satellite estimate of tropical rainfall, mm/day

Missing   .5   2   4   6   10   15   20   25 >25

Fig. 22. Mean rainfall for the period March–May, 1987.

Mean rainfall for June–August, 1987

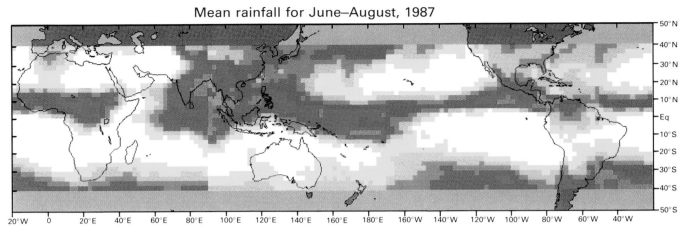

Fig. 23. Mean rainfall for the period June–August, 1987.

Mean rainfall for September–November, 1987

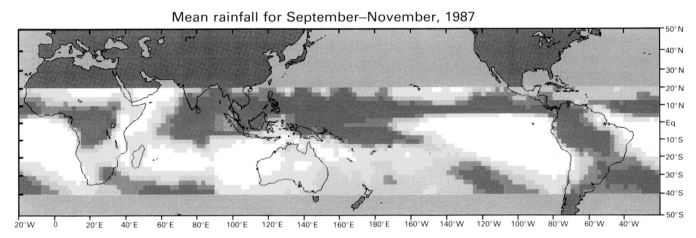

Fig. 24. Mean rainfall for the period September–November, 1987.

Mean rainfall for December, 1987–February, 1988

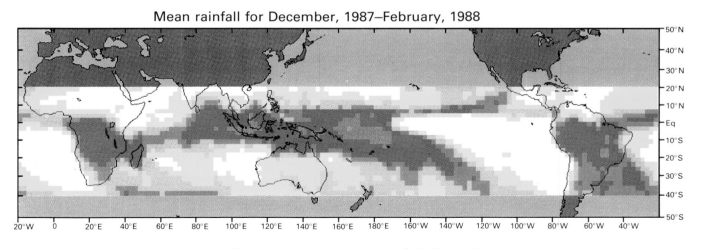

Satellite estimate of tropical rainfall, mm/day

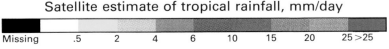

Missing   .5   2   4   6   10   15   20   25 >25

Fig. 25. Mean rainfall for the period December, 1987–February, 1988.

Mean rainfall for March–May, 1988

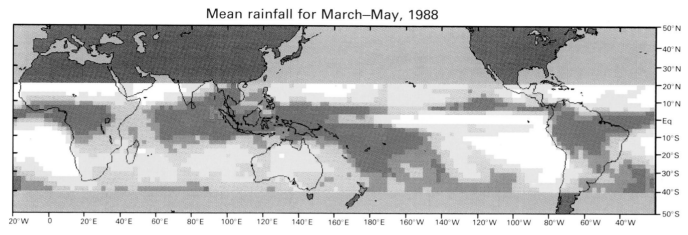

Fig. 26. Mean rainfall for the period March–May, 1988.

Satellite estimate of tropical rainfall, mm/day

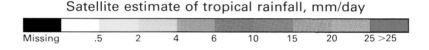

Mean rainfall for June–August, 1988

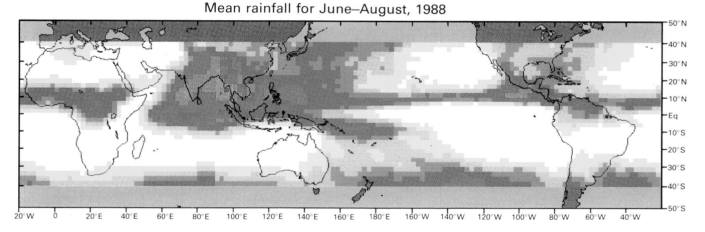

Fig. 27. Mean rainfall for the period June–August, 1988.

the estimates to some degree, it is not an adequate solution to the whole problem. Two possibilities for more complete solutions exist. The relationship between cloud cover and rainfall may be determined from a physical model of the environment in which the precipitation forms (i.e determined from a cloud model) and then calculated as a function of observed or analyzed meteorological variables. While this has substantial appeal for providing a solid physical basis for the rainfall estimation process, cloud models with sufficient validity are not yet available. Another possibility is the use of other satellite observations, such as microwave or radar (Simpson, Adler & North, 1988), to provide calibrations of the IR estimates.

Another serious limitation of IR observations in the estimation of precipitation is the requirement for these observations to discriminate between precipitating cloud and everything else using only the black body temperature. In the Tropics, this is relatively easy, since the majority of precipitation is associated with convection, and therefore with deep cold cloud, and over an underlying surface that is warm by comparison. The contrast between raining cloud and other features is therefore large. However, in higher latitudes, much precipitation is associated with less deep cloud, and thus warmer temperatures, and the underlying surface and low clouds are colder, yielding less contrast. Because of this, the GPI is not as useful in mid- and high-latitudes. It has been concluded subjectively that the estimates are reasonably useful within a zone bounded by 40° S and a seasonally adjusted northern boundary.

Mean rainfall for September–November, 1988

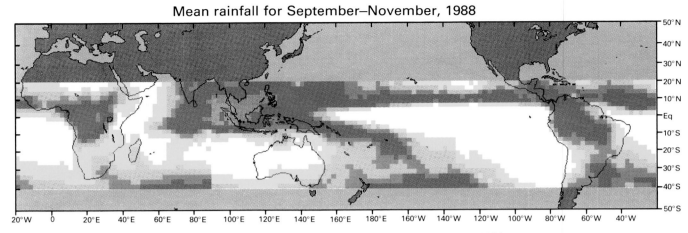

Fig. 28. Mean rainfall for the period September–November, 1988.

Satellite estimate of tropical rainfall, mm/day

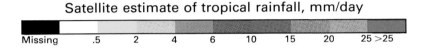

Mean rainfall for December, 1988 – February, 1989

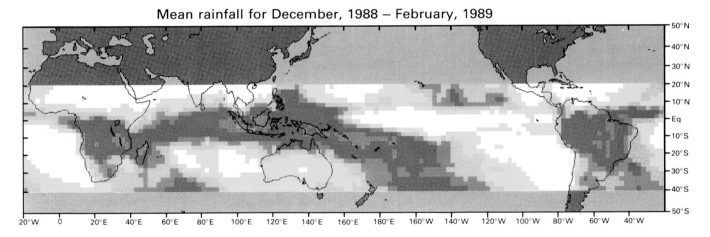

Fig. 29. Mean rainfall for the period December, 1988–February, 1989.

Conclusions

It is hoped that the reader will find the rainfall analyses presented here to be useful in defining the distribution of precipitation in the tropics and subtropics. They should provide useful information for the validation of climate models of ENSO and for the determination of fresh water fluxes as forcing for ocean models of the tropical Pacific. They might also provide guidance for the monitoring of current climatic events in the tropics by the Climate Analysis Center of the US National Weather Service.

A number of other potential applications exist for these analyses. In numerical weather prediction, a process called initialization is used to ensure that the dynamic and

thermodynamic fields are in a balanced state (Sela, 1980). Presently, initialization is carried out by determining the distribution of precipitation from a short forecast and then using that to estimate the diabatic heating. In the tropics, satellite rainfall estimates could be used to reduce errors in this process. Further, satellite-based rainfall estimates are often available more promptly than conventional observations, thus enabling more timely planning and response, e.g. for agricultural impacts. A similar application might be possible in other areas of water resource management, for example in flood forecasting, determination of optimal lake levels, and in the forcing of hydrological models of river basins.

However, for all these applications, the current state of the art is only marginally adequate. For GEWEX (the WCRP

Mean rainfall for March–May, 1989

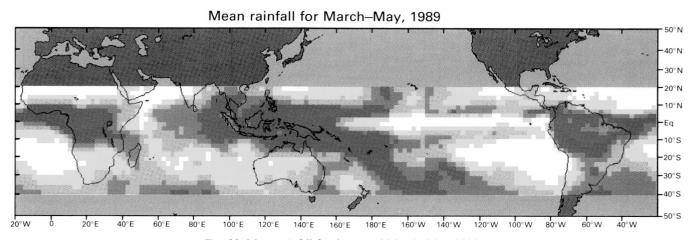

Fig. 30. Mean rainfall for the period March–May, 1989.

Satellite estimate of tropical rainfall, mm/day

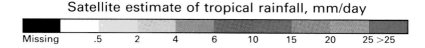

Mean rainfall for June–August, 1989

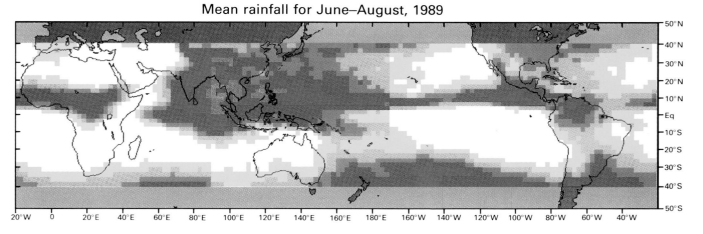

Fig. 31. Mean rainfall for the period June–August, 1989.

Global Energy and Water cycle Experiment) for example, precipitation analyses with better accuracy and more nearly global coverage will be essential. Four avenues of improvement seem to be available. Various passive microwave radiometers have been used to estimate oceanic rainfall (Rao, Abbott & Theon, 1976; Prabhakara *et al.*, 1986), and an operational instrument (the Special Sensor Microwave/Imager (SSM/I) on the US Defense Meteorological Satellite Program polar orbiting spacecraft) is now available. SSM/I data are already being used in several ways to estimate global precipitation (see Arkin & Ardanuy, 1989). Better algorithms for estimating precipitation from currently available satellite observations, both visible/IR and microwave, are certainly a possibility; the GPCP has begun an algorithm inter-

comparison program to generate data sets from which such algorithms might be derived and evaluated. New instruments, with observations more suited to the accurate estimation of precipitation, are likely to be available. For example, the Tropical Rainfall Measuring Mission (TRMM) (Simpson, Adler & North, 1988) will carry not only visible, IR and microwave radiometers in a non-Sun-synchronous orbit, but a rain radar as well. Finally, there is an opportunity to benefit from the experience of operational numerical weather prediction. Data assimilation methods have been developed to make the optimal use of observations of varying quality and type in the analysis of winds and temperatures. Similarly, by using a first guess based on the forecast of a numerical model and corrections derived from observations of all sorts, it is believed that precipitation analyses for the entire globe can be constructed.

Data availability

The precipitation data discussed in this chapter can be obtained from Lola Olsen, NASA Goddard Space Flight Center, Greenbelt, Maryland 20771, USA, from Roy Jenne, National Center for Atmospheric Research, P.O. Box 3000, Boulder, Colorado 80307 USA, or from Phil Arkin or John Janowiak, National Meteorological Centre, NOAA/NWS, Washington DC, 20233, USA.

References

Arkin, P. A. (1979). The relationship between the fractional coverage of high cloud and rainfall accumulations during GATE over the B-scale array. *Mon. Wea. Rev.*, **107**, 1382–7.

Arkin, P. A. & Meisner, B. N. (1987). The relationship between large-scale convective rainfall and cold cloud over the western hemisphere during 1982–84. *Mon. Wea. Rev.*, **115**, 51–74.

Arkin, P. A. & Ardanuy, P. E. (1989). Estimating climatic-scale precipitation from space: a review. *J. Climate*, **2**, 1229–38.

Janowiak, J. E. & Arkin, P. A. (1990). Rainfall variations in the tropics during 1986–1989 as estimated from observations of cloud top temperatures. *J. Geophys. Res.*, **96**, 3359–73.

Kousky, V. E., Kagano, M. T. & Cavalcanti, I. F. A. (1984). A review of the Southern Oscillation: oceanic–atmospheric circulation changes and related rainfall anomalies. *Tellus*, **36**, 490–504.

Meisner, B. N. & Arkin, P. A. (1987). Spatial and annual variations in the diurnal cycle of large-scale tropical convective cloudiness and precipitation. *Mon. Wea. Rev.*, **115**, 2009–32.

Prabhakara, C., Short, D. A., Wiscombe, W., Fraser, R. S. & Vollmer, B. E. (1986). Rainfall over oceans inferred from Nimbus 7 SMRR: application to 1982–83 El Niño. *J. Climate Appl. Meteor.*, **25**, 1464–74.

Rao, M. S., Abbott III, V. & Theon, J. S. (1976). Satellite-derived global oceanic rainfall atlas. NASA SP-410, Goddard Space Flight Center, Greenbelt, MD, 31pp.

Rasmusson, E. M. & Carpenter, T. H. (1982). Variations in tropical sea surface temperatures and surface wind fields associated with the Southern Oscillation/El Niño. *Mon. Wea. Rev.*, **110**, 534–84.

Rasmusson, E. M. & Carpenter, T. H. (1983). The relationship between eastern equatorial Pacific sea surface temperatures and rainfall over India and Sri Lanka. *Mon. Wea. Rev.*, **111**, 517–28.

Richards, F. & Arkin, P. (1981). On the relationship between satellite-observed cloud cover and precipitation. *Mon. Wea. Rev.*, **109**, 1081–93.

Ropelewski, C. F. & Halpert, M. S. (1989). Precipitation patterns associated with the high index phase of the Southern Oscillation. *J. Climate*, **2**, 268–84.

Sela, J. G. (1980). Spectral modeling at the National Meteorological Center. *Mon. Wea. Rev.*, **108**, 1279–92.

Simpson, J., Adler, R. F. & North, G. R. (1988). A proposed Tropical Rainfall Measuring Mission (TRMM) satellite. *Bull. Am. Meteor. Soc.*, **69**, 279–95.

van der Leeden, F. (1990). *The Water Encyclopedia.* Lewis Publishers, Chelsea, Michigan, Table 5-5, p. 307.

Tropospheric chemistry

ROBERT C. HARRISS

Introduction

The chemical composition of the troposphere, the lowest region of the atmosphere extending from the surface to about 8–15 km (depending on latitude), is changing at unprecedented rates (Intergovernmental Panel on Climate Change, 1990). Gaseous and particulate emissions from a wide variety of human activities (e.g. energy use, agricultural production, etc.) now exceed emissions from natural sources. The rate at which these air pollutants are input to the troposphere also exceeds the capacity of removal processes, resulting in an accumulation of gases: carbon dioxide, methane, chlorofluorocarbons, and nitrous oxide (Table 1). These gases contribute to the widely discussed potential for climate change due to the greenhouse effect (National Academy of Sciences, 1991).

Large-scale fires in tropical regions and combustion of fossil fuels in urban/industrial regions also produce emissions of carbon monoxide, hydrocarbons, and nitrogen oxides which, in the presence of sunlight, enhance rates of ozone formation (i.e. photochemical smog). Recent studies indicate that air pollution from urban/industrial and agricultural activities now reaches the most remote regions of the Earth

(Graedel & Crutzen, 1989; Rowland & Isaksen, 1988).

Urban air pollution is scientifically a relatively well-understood phenomena (Seinfeld, 1989). The most critical research needs for reducing the environmental threats posed by local-to-regional scale air pollution are multi-disciplinary studies on emissions reduction, and on methods for determining the costs and benefits of alternative control strategies.

Global air pollution poses many new and challenging problems, related to both monitoring of pollutant levels over the entire Earth and to the need for early detection of effects. The example of the destruction of stratospheric ozone by anthropogenic chlorofluorocarbons is the only existing case study which illustrates the likely complexities of detecting and understanding a global air pollution problem (see chapter by Schoeberl in this volume). From a scientific perspective the lessons learned have been that detecting and measuring the causes and effects of large-scale changes in atmospheric chemistry will require simultaneous, integrated measurements from ground-based, airborne, and satellite instrumentation. This chapter explores existing capabilities, and the potential, for the use of remote sensing technology in studies and monitoring of tropospheric chemistry.

Table 1. *Summary of key greenhouse gases influenced by human activities*[1]

Parameter	CO_2	CH_4	CFC-11	CFC-12	N_2O
Pre-industrial atmospheric concentration (1750–1800)	280 ppmv[2]	0.8 ppmv	0	0	288 ppbv[2]
Current atmospheric concentration (1990)[3]	353 ppmv	1.72 ppmv	280 pptv[2]	484 pptv	310 ppbv
Current rate of annual atmospheric accumulation	1.8 ppmv (0.5%)	0.015 ppmv (0.9%)	9.5 pptv (4%)	17 pptv (4%)	0.8 ppbv (0.25%)
Atmospheric lifetime[4] (years)	(50–200)	10	65	130	150

1. Ozone has not been included in the table because of lack of precise data.
2. ppmv=parts per million by volume; ppbv=parts per billion by volume; pptv=parts per trillion by volume.
3. The current (1990) concentrations have been estimated based upon an extrapolation of measurements reported for earlier years, assuming that recent trends remained approximately constant.
4. For each gas in the table, except CO_2, the 'lifetime' is defined here as the ratio of the atmospheric content to the total rate of removal. This time scale also characterizes the rate of adjustment of the atmospheric concentrations if the emission rates are changed abruptly. CO_2 is a special case since it has no real sinks, but is merely circulated between various reservoirs (atmosphere, ocean, biota). The 'lifetime' of CO_2 given in the table is a rough indication of the time it would take for the CO_2 concentration to adjust to changes in the emissions.
Source: IPCC (1990).

In the past several decades, the discovery of acid rain over most of Europe and the eastern United States, the measurement of elevated ozone in rural regions downwind of urban systems, and the discovery of increasing concentrations of carbon dioxide, methane, nitrous oxide, and chlorofluorocarbons over the entire Earth have resulted in an urgent need for continuous, large-scale observations of the chemical climate of the troposphere. Traditional ground-based, *in situ* monitoring of gas and aerosol concentrations has only been partially satisfactory for documenting the sources and dynamics regional and global variability in the chemical climate of the troposphere. The necessity of sampling remote continental and oceanic regions, and the expense of establishing a large number of high quality ground-based atmospheric chemical monitoring sites, have limited the availability of tropospheric data.

Advances in the development of remote sensing techniques for measuring tropospheric gas and aerosol constituents will resolve the problem of large-scale monitoring of the tropospheric chemical climate. In this chapter current capabilities and results from applications of remote sensing technology to studies of tropospheric chemical change will be reviewed briefly. Specific examples are used to illustrate the importance of having a diversity of sensor technologies and platforms to observe spatial and temporal variability of the tropospheric chemical climate at regional to global scales.

Methodology

The science of measuring tropospheric chemistry from airborne and space platforms is at a very early stage of development compared to stratospheric studies. Mapping the three-dimensional distribution of tropospheric gases or aerosols from space is complicated by the need to subtract any contribution from the overlying stratosphere, by the interfering effects of clouds, and other factors. The feasibility of measuring tropospheric aerosols and a few trace gas species from space has only recently been demonstrated. Measurements of tropospheric aerosols have been obtained with several existing satellite instruments, including the visible infra-red spin scan radiometer (VISSR) on NOAA geostationary environmental satellites (GOES), the advanced very high resolution radiometer (AVHRR) on NOAA polar-orbiting operational environmental satellites, and multispectral sensors on Landsat, the coastal zone color scanner (CZCS), and the stratospheric aerosol and gas experiment (SAGE). Since aerosols can form by gas-to-particle conversion processes, and can act as important sources or sinks for tropospheric gases (e.g. acids), measurements of aerosols are important to understanding global tropospheric chemistry. A detailed discussion

of satellite remote sensing of aerosols can be found in the chapter by McCormick.

Global measurements of tropospheric gases from space have been obtained by the measurement of air pollution from satellites (MAPS) project, a gas filter correlation radiometer carried on Space Shuttle flights in 1981 and 1984, by ATMOS (atmospheric molecules by spectroscopy), a high-resolution interferometer aboard SPACELAB-3 (April–May, 1985), and by SAGE II on the Earth Radiation Budget Satellite (ERBS) launched in 1984. A detailed, technical discussion of all of these instruments is beyond the scope of this paper, however, for additional information the reader should pursue Levine (1985) and numerous articles appearing frequently in the *Journal of Geophysical Research – Atmospheres*.

In this chapter, the direct measurement of carbon monoxide from space, an indirect approach for using satellite measurements to measure tropospheric ozone, and airborne laser techniques for remote sensing tropospheric ozone and aerosols will be reviewed. The airborne techniques are included because they represent the cutting edge of a new generation of instruments which will be deployed in space in future years.

The MAPS instrument and its first measurements from test flights on the space shuttle have been discussed in detail by Richle *et al.* (1986) and Newell, Reichle & Seiler (1989).

For measurements from shuttle, or a future satellite, the MAPS instrument is aimed toward the Earth and collects radiation emitted by the Earth–atmosphere system. The collected radiation is compared to a reference radiation source from a black aluminum plate which has a known spectrum and does not show losses due to absorption at any wavelength. Three detectors measure the Earth and reference radiation alternately after the radiation passes through a transparent gas cell in front of each detector which references the measurements to a specific altitude range in the troposphere.

After corrections for potential interferences by water vapor, carbon dioxide, ozone, nitrous oxide, and clouds, the current MAPS instrument is most sensitive to variations in the concentration of carbon monoxide over the altitude range of three to eight kilometers (i.e. the mid-troposphere). The next generation of MAPS is being called TRACER (tropospheric radiometer for atmospheric chemistry and environmental research) and will include capabilities for measuring both carbon monoxide and methane in the atmospheric boundary layer (0–3 km) and in the overlying free troposphere.

An indirect method for measuring tropospheric ozone from space has been developed which uses two satellite sensors measuring stratospheric ozone (Fishman *et al.*, 1990). Total ozone amounts in the atmosphere have been measured globally on a daily basis since 1979 by the total ozone mapping spectrometer (TOMS) aboard a polar orbiting satellite. The TOMS works on the principle of back-scattered ultra-violet radiation. It was observed that, in the Tropics, ozone variability in the TOMS data was primarily associated with tropospheric enhancements produced by photochemical processes associated with emissions from biomass burning. Subtracting the almost constant stratospheric component from a TOMS total column ozone measurement produces an estimate of the tropospheric residual ozone. The total ozone enhancements from tropical air pollution are typically 10–40 DU, which is well above the 2% (5–6 DU) precision of the measurement.

In the future, major new advances in studies of tropospheric chemistry from space will require measurements by laser instrumentation. The precise spectral resolution, point measurements, and high sampling rates possible with lasers will overcome some of the most serious limitations of passive optical sensors for tropospheric measurements. The airborne differential absorption lidar (DIAL) system measures gas and aerosol profiles in the troposphere and lower stratosphere (Browell et al., 1983). This multi-purpose system has the flexibility to operate in the UV for measurements of ozone or sulfur dioxide and in the near-IR for water vapor. Multiwavelength aerosol back-scatter investigations have been conducted with simultaneous measurements in the UV, visible, and near-IR. Advanced versions of the DIAL are being developed for tropospheric applications from the space shuttle and the NASA ER-2 high altitude research aircraft.

This brief review cannot cover all of the current and potential future applications of remote sensing to studies of the changing global troposphere. In this section, by example, it has been indicated that, even though the technology is in very early stages of development, a diverse array of approaches show promise.

Results

Observations from space

An interesting example of the importance of remote sensing to understanding both the sources and dynamics of global tropospheric chemical change is the study of impacts of biomass burning on tropical air chemistry. This application will be used as a case study to illustrate the following roles for remote sensing in the: 1) early detection of chemical change over remote oceanic or inaccessible continental areas where traditional ground-based air chemistry observatories cannot operate, 2) determination of regional distributions and variability of trace gases and aerosols derived from complex interactions of widely dispersed, irregular sources (i.e. fires) and synoptic meteorological systems, and 3) to illustrate the syn-

ergistic effects of an experimental design which incorporates simultaneous ground, aircraft, and space-based measurements to cover the widest possible range of both time and space scales.

The possible importance of biomass burning (i.e. fuelwood, forest, grasslands, crop residues) as a significant source of tropospheric, photochemically active trace gases was first proposed by Paul Crutzen and colleagues (Crutzen et al., 1979, 1985). Their reasoning was based on a mathematical extrapolation of a small number of analyses of gases obtained by instantaneous ground-based sampling of near-source emissions, and preliminary estimates of the amount of biomass burned annually. The first observational data which convincingly support the postulated large-scale impact of biomass burning on tropospheric chemistry have resulted from airborne measurements of gases and aerosols over the Amazon Basin, the MAPS data on the global distribution of carbon monoxide, and from satellite measurements of tropospheric ozone in the tropics.

The global distribution of carbon monoxide as observed by MAPS during October, 1984, is shown in Fig. 1. The pronounced enhancements of carbon monoxide in the mid-troposphere over the central regions of South America and Africa was a startling discovery to many atmospheric chemists. The expectation had been that carbon monoxide-rich air would be concentrated primarily in the troposphere over and downwind of major industrial centers. The combination of the *in situ* measurements and modeling with the first global 'snapshots' of carbon monoxide obtained from space, placed the idea that tropical burning might rival fossil fuel combustion as a major source of carbon monoxide on a much firmer foundation.

Satellite-derived tropospheric ozone distributions for the Tropics have added another dimension to the issue of understanding the potential impacts of fire emissions on global change. Seasonal patterns of tropical tropospheric ozone are presented in Fig. 2. The enhanced ozone over much of central South America, Africa, and over the South Atlantic Ocean during the dry season (Sept.–Nov.) is consistent with the concept that biomass burning produces precursor gas emissions which result in the production of photochemically generated ozone over and downwind of the burning areas, analogous to the formation of 'smog' commonly associated with industrialized areas (Fishman, 1991). The spatial scale of the ozone enhancement suggests a 'super-smog event', perhaps not so intense as smog produced by industrial sources, but more extensive in spatial scale. It is important to remember that this discovery required observations from space; the network of ground-based tropospheric chemical observations in the Tropics is limited, and will remain so

TROPOSPHERIC CARBON MONOXIDE

Maps experiment Oct. 5–13, 1984

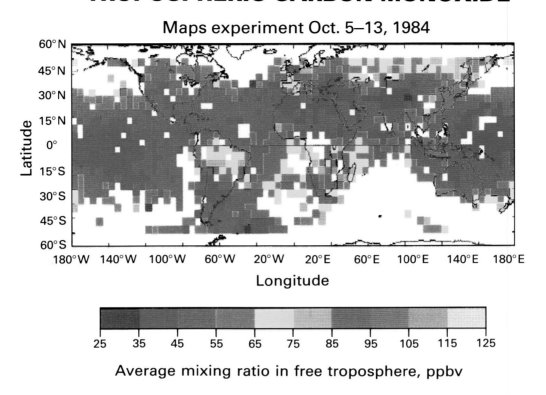

Average mixing ratio in free troposphere, ppbv

Fig. 1. Measurements of tropospheric carbon monoxide made from the space shuttle Challenger during 1984. The highest concentrations are typically associated with industrialized areas in the Northern Hemisphere and areas of agricultural development and associated biomass burning in South America and Africa. The carbon monoxide concentrations shown are for altitudes of from three to 18 kilometers. A source (e.g. in the eastern United States) may not be detected if meteorological conditions trap emissions in the atmosphere below three kilometers. Blank areas indicate interference by cloud cover.

owing to the large area of ocean and inaccessible continental terrain.

Remote sensing from aircraft

The space-based observations of large-scale enhancements of carbon monoxide and ozone over and downwind of rural regions of South America and Africa have helped to elevate the topic of biomass burning as a source of global atmospheric change to a high priority issue on the international research agenda. However, space-based remote sensing with current technology provides only part of the information necessary to quantify the role of biomass burning in global atmospheric change. Questions related to the chemistry of the emissions and atmospheric transport and dispersion processes require detailed, high resolution measurements which are not possible from space. Airborne remote sensing, carefully integrated with space-based observations and conventional ground-based data, can solve the problem. The results of airborne

lidar remote sensing of biomass burning impacts on the Amazonian atmosphere during the 1985 NASA Amazon boundary layer experiment (ABLE) illustrates the importance of airborne remote sensing to assessing the impacts of biomass burning at the regional scale (Harriss et al., 1988; Browell et al., 1988).

A collage of images illustrating tropospheric aerosol and ozone distribution derived from airborne DIAL measurements is presented in Fig. 3. These data were obtained along a flight track (~ 150 km) over the central Amazon Basin during the dry season. The data in Fig. 3(a) illustrate relative back-scattering of laser light (1064 nm) by aerosols, with the yellow and dark brown colors indicating the highest concentrations. The spatial resolution of measurement is approximately 15 m in the vertical and 20 m in the horizontal. The data in Fig. 3(b) illustrate simultaneous measurements of ozone with a vertical and horizontal resolution of 210 m and 6 km, respectively. The conversion of ozone concentrations to color plots used the scale shown above the image with yellow

SEASONAL DEPICTIONS OF TROPOSPHERIC OZONE DISTRIBUTION

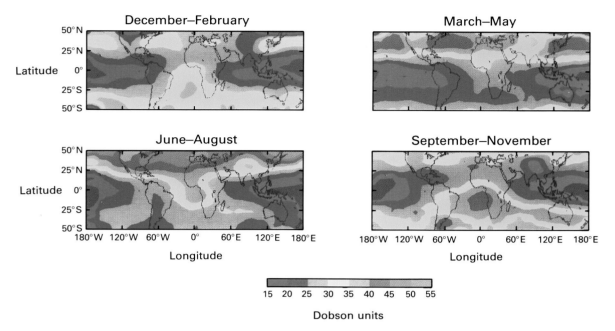

Fig. 2. Measurements of seasonal variations in total tropospheric ozone in tropical regions. The enhanced concentrations over and downwind of Africa and South America during Sept.–Nov. indicate photochemically produced ozone derived from air pollution from biomass burning in agricultural areas.

to brown colors indicating 30 to 40 ppbv (parts per billion by volume).

The use of many DIAL data sets like those shown in Fig. 3 enabled the ABLE scientific team to document the sources, transport processes, and regional impacts of biomass burning in Amazonia (Andreae *et al.*, 1988). As a first step, the lidar data were used to locate smog and haze layers for detailed *in situ* chemical measurements which provided a 'fingerprint' of the biomass burning source. Having identified the combustion source of the materials, the altitudes and horizontal extent of the layers were mapped. These data, together with concurrent satellite observations of fire locations and meteorological analyses of wind motions, indicated that the biomass burning was concentrated in a region south of the central Amazon where savannah agricultural practices and concentrated deforestation for agricultural development resulted in large-scale dry season burning.

Another feature of note in Fig. 3 is the record of atmospheric mixed layer growth over tropical rainforest documented along the flight track. At the beginning of the flight (1211 GMT, 0811 local time) the mixed layer is at the forest canopy level. By approximately 1239 GMT small cumulus clouds can be seen 0.25 km above the forest. At the end of the flight track

(1550 GMT) the atmospheric mixed layer has reached an altitude of approximately 1.25 km. The white streaks on the color plot indicate optically thick clouds which prevent penetration of laser light to lower altitudes. Repeated observations of the mixed layer at various times over different types of terrain indicated a typical growth rate of 7–10 cm s^{-1} in the late morning. Individual cumulus clouds were observed to routinely rise above the average mixed layer height to the trade wind inversion at 3.0 km (Fig. 4(*a*)). The air above the trade wind inversion (TWI) is characterized by very low backscattering. During the dry season the TWI traps both biospheric emissions and biomass burning emissions, preventing significant export of these materials to the global troposphere. Concentrations of carbon monoxide, ozone, and other atmospheric constituents increase in the Amazonian atmospheric mixed layer until the wet season begins in October–November. At the beginning of the wet season the relatively insoluble gases such as carbon monoxide and ozone are 'pumped' into the free troposphere by convective thunderstorms. In the free troposphere these gases are dispersed downwind producing the types of large-scale enhancements observed by MAPS and the tropospheric residual ozone derived from TOMS (Figs. 1 and 2).

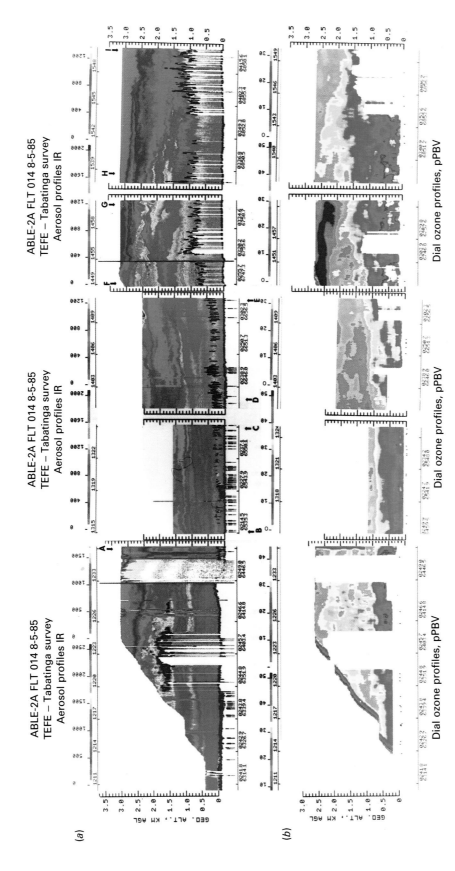

Fig. 3. (a) The vertical distribution of aerosols along a flight track over the Amazon Basin, Brazil. The high altitude aerosols (>1 km) are primarily from biomass burning emissions taking place 500–1000 km upwind of the measurements. The aerosols closest to the surface are biogenic particles and cloud droplets originating from daily heating and convection initiated at the top of the forest canopy. The atmospheric 'mixed layer' above the forest canopy level to approximately 1 km. (b) Simultaneous measurements of ozone along the flight track document a correlation of high ozone concentrations and aerosol plumes above the atmospheric mixed layer.

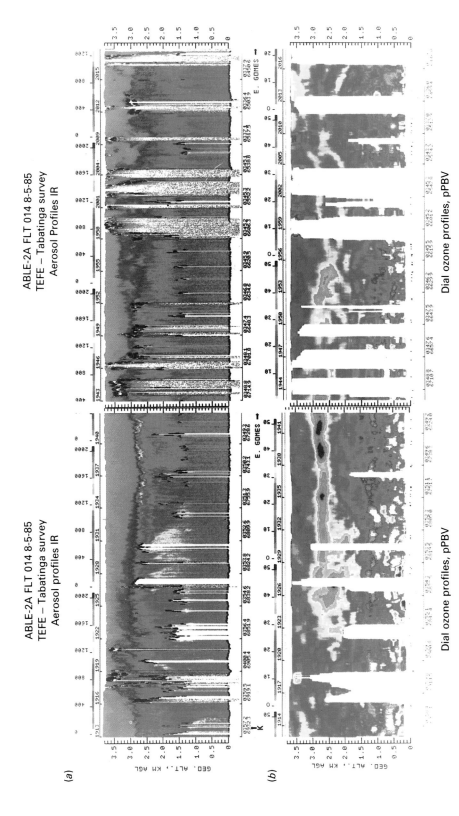

Fig. 4. (*a*) Aerosols and cloud droplets in highest concentrations identify the atmospheric mixed layer at approximately 0–1·5 km with some convective activity penetrating to the trade wind inversion at approximately 3·0 km. (*b*) A plume of high ozone concentrations is documented at 2·5 km. The association of ozone with aerosol is less pronounced than in Fig. 3, possibly due to removal of the particles by deposition during the transit to this downwind location.

This case study of the application of remote sensing to the role of biomass burning in global tropospheric change is just one of many possible applications. The reader is referred to the reference section for additional examples of how the techniques discussed in this chapter have been used to study air pollution episodes in the United States, the penetration of stratospheric air into the troposphere, and the atmospheric transport of pollutants from continents to the ocean.

Limitations

Clouds will always be a factor limiting the use of remote sensing for studies of tropospheric chemistry. However, the continued development of laser techniques for remote sensing of the troposphere from ground, aircraft, and space platforms will dramatically improve opportunities for regional and global studies of tropospheric chemical change. The high spectral resolution of lasers, which permits high selectivity for specific molecules, and the capability to achieve high sampling rates between clouds results in significant advantages for lasers compared to passive optical techniques (Killinger & Menyuk, 1987). Current disadvantages of laser techniques include their relatively high electrical power requirements and the paucity of dependable lasers in appropriate spectral regions.

Conclusions

Remote sensing measurements have made important contributions to the recognition that human activities are modifying the chemical composition of the troposphere, even in regions once considered remote. Satellite measurements of enhanced carbon monoxide and ozone over the Amazon Basin, South Atlantic Ocean, and portions of Africa indicated that biomass burning associated with tropical land clearing and agricultural activities were a likely source of these gases. An intensive scientific campaign using ground-based measurements and airborne remote sensing of ozone and aerosols confirmed the linkage between biomass burning and chemical change during the dry season in the Amazon Basin. These preliminary results have demonstrated that an experimental design which integrates ground, aircraft, and space-based measurements can add important new understanding of the degree to which human activities contribute to global environmental change.

In the near-term important advances in tropospheric chemistry can be made with the simultaneous measurements of carbon monoxide, methane and surface ecosystem characteristics from the Earth Observation System (EOS) space platform scheduled for launch in this decade. Global observa-

tions by EOS will have to be supplemented with ground-based and airborne measurements in cases where an understanding of the driving forces of chemical climate are required.

In the second generation of EOS measurements laser techniques could have a major impact on tropospheric chemistry studies by providing increased spatial resolution and accuracy for measuring tropospheric gases and aerosols. Space-based lidar could eventually become the centerpiece of a comprehensive tropospheric chemistry observing system.

Availability of data

Measurement of Air Pollution from Satellite (MAPS) data can be obtained from Dr H. G. Reichle, Mail Stop 401A, NASA Langley Research Center, Hampton, Virginia 23665 USA. Tropospheric ozone residual data determined from satellites is available from Jack Fishman, Mail Stop 401A, NASA Langley Research Center, Hampton, Virginia 23665 USA. Airborne Differential Absorption Lidar (DIAL) data can be obtained from Dr Edward Browell, Mail Stop 401A, NASA Langley Research Center, Hampton, Virginia 23665 USA.

References

Andreae, M. O., Browell, E. V., Garstang, M., Gregory, G. L., Harriss, R. C., Hill, G. F., Jacob, D. J., Pereira, M. C., Sachse, G. W., Setzer, A. W., Silva Dias, P. L., Talbot, R. W., Torres, A. L. & Wofsy, S. C. (1988). Biomass-burning emissions and associated haze layers over Amazonia. *J. Geophys. Res.*, **93**, 1509–27.

Browell, E. V., Carter, A. F., Shipley, S. T., Allen, R. J., Butler, C. F., Mayo, M. N., Siviter, J. H. Jr. & Hall, W. M., (1983). NASA multipurpose airborne DIAL system and measurements of ozone and aerosol profiles. *Appl. Optics*, **22**, 522–34.

Browell, E. V., Gregory, G. L., Harriss, R. C. & Kirchoff, V. W. J. H. 1988. Tropospheric ozone and aerosol distributions across the Amazon Basin. *J. Geophys. Res.*, **93**, 1431–51.

Crutzen, P., Delany, A. C., Greenberg, J., Haagenson, P., Heidt, L., Lueb, R., Pollock, W., Seiler, W., Wartburg, A. & Zimmerman, P. (1985). Tropospheric chemical composition measurements in Brazil during the dry season. *J. Atmos. Chem.*, **2**, 233–56.

Crutzen, P., Heidt, L. E., Krasnec, J. P., Pollock, W. H. & Seiler, W. (1979). Biomass burning as a source of atmospheric gases CO, H_2, N_2O, NO, CH_3Cl, and COS. *Nature*, **282**, 253–6.

Fishman, J. (1991). Probing planetary pollution from space. *Environ. Sci. Technol.*, **25**, 612–21.

Fishman, J., Watson, C. E., Larsen, J. C. & Logan, J. A. (1990). Distribution of tropospheric ozone determined from satellite data. *J. Geophys. Res.*, **95**, 3599–617.

Fishman, J., Minnis, P. & Reichle, H. G. Jr. (1986). Use of satellite data to study tropospheric ozone in the tropics. *J. Geophys. Res.*, **91**, 14451–14, 465.

Graedel, T. E. & Crutzen, P. J. (1989). The changing atmosphere. In *Managing Planet Earth*, W. H. Freeman & Co., NY, pp. 13–24.

Harriss, R. C. *et al.* (1988). The Amazon boundary layer experiment (ABLE 2A): dry Season 1985. *J. Geophys. Res.*, **93**, 1351–60.

Intergovernmental Panel on Climate Change (1990). *Climate Change: The IPCC Assessment*, Cambridge Univ. Press, 365pp.

Killinger, D. & Menyuk, N. (1987). Laser remote sensing of the atmosphere, *Science*, **235**, 37–45.

Levine, J. S. (ed.) (1985). *Space Opportunities for Tropospheric Chemistry Research*, NASA Conference Publication 2450, Washington, DC, 90pp.

National Academy of Sciences (1991). *Policy Implications of Greenhouse Warming*, National Academy Press, 127pp.

Newell, R. E., Reichle, H. G. Jr. & Seiler, W. (1989). Carbon monoxide and the burning earth, *Scientif. Amer.*, **260**, 82–88.

Reichle, H. G., Casas, J. C., Condon, E. P., Connors, V. S., Gormsen, B. B., Holland, J. A., Seiler, W., Sherrill, R. T. & Wallio, H. A. (1990). The distribution of middle tropospheric carbon monoxide during early October 1984, *J. Geophys. Res.*, **95**, 9845–56.

Richle, H. G. Jr., Conners, V. S., Holland, J. A., Hypes, W. D., Wallio, H. A., Casas, J. C., Gormsen, B. B., Saylor, M. S. & Heske, W. D. (1986). Middle and upper tropospheric carbon monoxide mixing ratios as measured by a satellite-borne remote sensor during November 1981, *J. Geophys. Res.*, **91**, 10865–87.

Rowland, F. S. & Isaksen, I. S. A. (eds.) (1988). *The Changing Atmosphere*, John Wiley & Sons, NY, 281pp.

Seinfeld, J. H. (1989). Urban air pollution: state of the science. *Science*, **243**, 745–52.

Global observations of lightning

STEVEN J. GOODMAN AND HUGH J. CHRISTIAN

Introduction

Lightning is one of the more spectacular responses of the atmosphere to thermodynamic and dynamic forcing and, consequently, contains useful information about the atmosphere. The processes that lead to the production of lightning are tightly controlled by updraft intensity and the formation of precipitation. Thus, lightning activity is closely coupled to storm dynamics and microphysics, and therefore, should exhibit some quantifiable relationships to the global rates, amounts, and distribution of convective precipitation and to the release and transport of latent heat from thunderstorms (Goodman et al., 1989). Lightning seems to initiate soon after the onset of strong convection, after significant cloud mass and ice have formed in the upper regions of the thunderstorm (Shackford, 1960; Goodman et al., 1988a; Dye et al., 1989; Williams, 1989). Lightning activity also tends to track the updraft in both amplitude and phase with rates increasing as the updraft intensifies and decreasing rapidly with cessation of vertical growth (Goodman, Buechler & Meyer, 1988b).

Seasonal and inter-annual observations of lightning activity in differing climatic regions can be used to increase our knowledge of the distribution, structure, and variability of thunderstorms at the local, regional, and global scale over the land and ocean. Atmospheric teleconnections associated with naturally occurring climate variations such as the ENSO (El Niño southern oscillation) and anti-ENSO (La Niña) events in the tropical Pacific often result in significant changes in the frequency and movement of storm tracks, precipitation patterns, and cloud cover in both hemispheres (Velasco & Fritsch, 1987; Ropelewski & Halpert, 1987; 1989). These climate variations will also affect the structure and characteristics of cloud systems and produce changes in the accompanying lightning activity. Recent tropical measurements near Darwin, Australia (12° S latitude) during the monsoon and monsoon 'break' periods have revealed dramatic (factor of ten) changes in lightning frequency associated with modest variations (on the order of 1 °C) in surface wet bulb temperature (Williams et al., 1992; Rutledge, Williams & Keenan, 1992). Similar results have been found for Kourou,

French Guyana (5° N latitude). This sensitive dependence appears to be systematic of the tropical atmosphere over land and has been attributed to changes in convective available potential energy (CAPE) (Keenan and Carbone, 1989; Williams et al., 1992). CAPE serves as a predictor of maximum updraft velocity which, in turn, is perhaps the most critical variable in effecting the amount of water and ice phase condensate transported to the upper regions of convective clouds where it becomes available for precipitation formation and charge separation. Ice is also of critical importance to the regulation of the Tropics by cloud–radiation feedback. Deep convection influences the planetary albedo, outgoing long-wave radiation, and upper level water vapor by populating the upper troposphere with ice particles. Lightning frequency is a sensitive indicator of the injection of ice phase condensate into the mid to upper troposphere. Therefore, variations in global lightning activity may provide one signature of changing patterns of tropical moisture and energetics.

Figs. 1 and 2 show the global spatial distribution of thunderstorm activity and its diurnal variation. More than 60 thunderstorm days per year are common in low latitudes, extending as far north as central Alabama in the southeastern US. The diurnal variation of global thunderstorm activity follows the passage of the Sun and its heating of the major convective 'chimneys' in the Tropics; i.e. Southeast Asia/Maritime Continent, Africa, and South America. The global lightning flash rate is roughly estimated at 100 s^{-1} (note the significant figures) using circa 1900 knowledge of the number of thunderstorm days. It is instructive to see how this oft referenced extrapolation was performed by Brooks (1925):

... it was estimated that each station on the average recorded the thunderstorms occurring within an area of 113 square miles surrounding the station. Many storms have a broad front and most of them drift for a longer or shorter distance while they are in progress; hence, we may enlarge this area and consider that on the average a station will record thunderstorms the centre of whose track (both as regards length and breadth) falls within area of 200 square miles surrounding the station. Thus, we can say that if we imagine the whole of the earth to be divided into segments each with an area of 200 square miles, on the average 16 thunderstorms will occur each

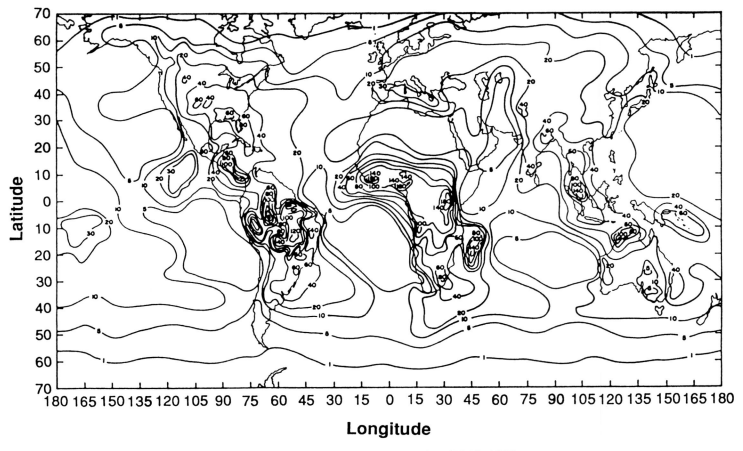

Fig. 1. Annual number of thunderstorm days (WMO, 1953).

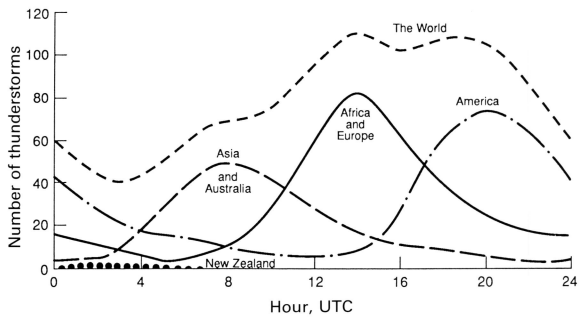

Fig. 2. Diurnal variation of global thunderstorm activity (annual mean). Time is UTC. (After Whipple & Scrase, 1936.)

year within each segment. The area of the surface of the earth is approximately 197,000,000 square miles, so that there are very nearly one million sections of area 200 square miles each, and on the whole the earth will experience 16,000,000 thunderstorms per annum or 44,000 per day.

These figures can be looked at in another way. The duration of thunderstorms is very variable, but a moderate estimate of the average duration will be about one hour. Then, again speaking in averages, there will be in progress at any one moment about 1,800 thunderstorms in different parts of the world.

What does this mean in terms of lightning flashes? During a thunderstorm at West Norwood, the late W. Marriott [Marriott, 1908] counted 98 lightning flashes in 28 minutes, which is at the rate of approximately 200 per hour. A photographic plate exposed for four minutes during a thunderstorm at Sydney, NSW shows five flashes. This is at the rate of 72 per hour, but the photograph obviously covers only a small part of the storm and we may consider that Marriott's figure of 200 per hour is approximately correct for a severe temperate or an average tropical storm. Then, 1,800 storms will give us 360,000 lightning flashes over the whole globe in an hour, or an average of 100 per second.

Marriott's representative thunderstorm average total flash rate (intracloud and ground discharges) quoted above is on the order of 3 min^{-1}. However, organized, often nocturnal, mid-latitude regional or mesoscale precipitation systems, having life-times on the order of 12 h and spatial extents of a few hundred kilometers, often produce cloud-to-ground flash rates alone in excess of 60 min^{-1} (Goodman & MacGorman, 1986). Tropical air mass thunderstorms are capable of producing peak total flash rates of 20–60 min^{-1} (Williams *et al.*, 1992; Rutledge, Williams & Keenan, 1992). Therefore, it is conceivable that the true instantaneous global flash rate is extremely variable and could possibly be much greater than 100 s^{-1}.

Methodology

Optical observations

Lightning has been observed from space since the early 1960s using both optical and radio frequency (rf) sensors (Table 1). More than a dozen satellites have flown instruments that have recorded signals from lightning (Vorpahl, Sparrow & Ney, 1970; Sparrow & Ney, 1971; Powell, 1983; Turman, 1978; 1979; Turman & Tettlebach, 1980; Turman & Edgar, 1982; Orville, 1982; Orville & Henderson, 1986). The detection of lightning from some of these satellites was an unanticipated

Table 1. *Lightning experiments from space*

Satellite Spacecraft	Launch date	Sensor	Altitude (km)	Period	Lightning power sensitivity (watts)	Footprint
Optical						
OSO 2,5	1965,1969	Photometers	600	Moonless night	~10^8	
VELA V	1970	Photodiodes	1.1×10^5	Day–night	10^{11}–10^{13}	Very wide field of view
DMSP	1970	Scanning radiometer	830	Local midnight	Sensitive	100 km
DMSP-SSL	1974	12 Photodiodes	830	Local midnight	10^8–10^{10}	700 km
DMSP-PBE 2,3	1977	2.5 mm photodiode	830	Dawn/dusk	4×10^9–10^{13}	1360 km
S81-1 (SEEP)	1982	Particle spectrometer Airglow photometers (391.4, 390.8, 630.3 nm)	230	Night	10 R	100 km
Space shuttle-NOSL	1981–1983	Photocell plus film	150	Shuttle flights STS-2, 4, 6	NA	Variable
Space shuttle-MLE	1988	Payload bay video cameras	150	STS-26, 30, 32, 34	NA	Variable
GPS-NDS	1983	Photodiodes	2×10^4	Continuous	2×10^8–2×10^{13}	Wide field of view
RF						
ARIEL-3	1967	HF radio receivers 5, 10, 15 Mhz	600	Day/night	RF	'Iris' effect
RAE-1	1968	HF radio receivers 0.2–9.18 MHz	5850			Ionosphere structure dependence
ISS-b	1978	HF radio receivers 2.5, 5, 10, 25 MHz	1100			Several hundreds of kilometers
EOS/TRMM Lightning imaging sensor	1997	CCD Array	Low earth orbit	Continuous coverage within field of view	10^8–10^{11}	450 km×450 km field of view with 3.5 km pixel resolution
Goes-Next Lightning mapper sensor (Proposed)	Late 1990's	CCD Array	Geostationary	Continuous coverage	10^8–10^{11}	10 km

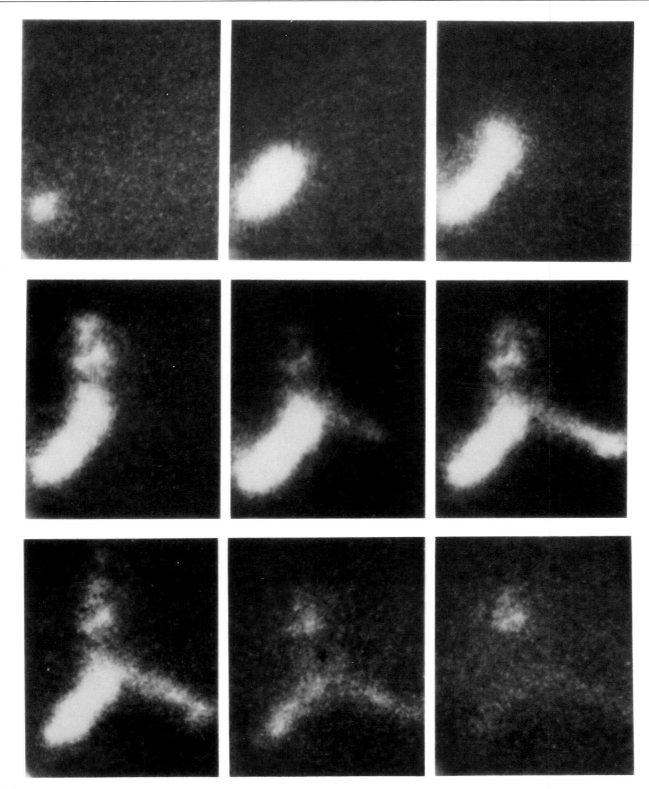

Fig. 3. Lightning photography from space shuttle taken over Brazil illuminating a 'Y'-shaped region at cloud top estimated to be in excess of 60 km on a side (From Vonnegut, Vaughan & Brook, 1983).

Fig. 4. Video images of lightning taken from the space shuttle payload bay.

bonus, while for others it was a primary research objective. Lightning observations have been made by cosmonauts and astronauts dating back to 1963. Astronauts have occasionally reported discharges having horizontal extents of many hundreds of kilometers and simultaneous lightning events occurring between widely separated storms. During 1981 the Night/day Optical Survey of Lightning (NOSL) space shuttle experiment used a small hand-held instrument package consisting of a 16 mm cine movie camera, a solar cell optical pulse detector, and a recorder that were operated by the shuttle astronauts to obtain lightning data (Fig. 3). Television cameras aboard the Space Shuttle orbiter show that even the payload bay can be illuminated by terrestrial lightning flashes (Fig. 4).

The sun-synchronous Defense Meteorological Satellite Program (DMSP) series has provided global lightning measurements using a number of different detectors (Table 1). However, the orbital period and various detector sensitivities limit the global observations of lightning to dawn, dusk, and local midnight. Although the DMSP operational linescan system (OLS) serves as the primary imaging system on the Block 5 series spacecraft, it has also unexpectedly provided the longest running global lightning data set. The dark background scene allows the OLS gain adjustment to be increased at night which causes lightning discharges (as well as city lights and fires) to saturate the OLS detector as it scans across the satellite subtrack. The lightning discharges can be seen in the archived 2.7 km (electronically smoothed from 0.6 km resolution) single-orbit visible-band positive transparency film strips as bright horizontal streaks up to 100 km across (Fig. 5).

DMSP–OLS visible (0.4–1.1 μm) and infra-red imagery (10.5–12.5 μm) are archived at the National Snow and Ice Data Center in Boulder, CO. Thousands of film strips dating back to 1973 have been manually sorted for lightning signatures which can be geolocated with date, time, and navigation information from the DMSP Block 5C and 5D series satellites (Table 2). The average total error in lightning location due to the manual digitizing, navigation, and width of the lightning streak is on the order of 100 km.

Unfortunately, the visible-band imagery is not uniformly available nor of uniform quality. There are numerous gaps in the nighttime imagery including the period from July 1980 to January 1984. The imagery from other years are far from complete (only 10–20% of the possible number of orbits) thus providing little useful climatic information. In some cases there are film strips at midnight only over the polar regions, with incomplete coverage over certain regions for months. In spite of these significant limitations and lack of alternative sources of global lightning data, the DMSP film archive represents the most comprehensive global lightning data set in existence. The DMSP–OLS data base will improve markedly in 1992 with the implementation of a digital archive of all DMSP satellite data. Initially, OLS data from the F10, and F11 satellites will be archived.

Radio frequency measurements

The early radio frequency (rf) satellite experiments (ARIEL-3, RAE-1, ISS-b) used high frequency (HF) radio techniques to detect and locate the sources of sferics from thunderstorms (Herman, Caruso & Stone, 1965; Horner, 1969). Very low frequency (VLF) receivers are not feasible for lightning mapping from space because the ionosphere is a strong reflector at low frequencies where the power density of the lightning sferic is the strongest. Furthermore, the energy that does

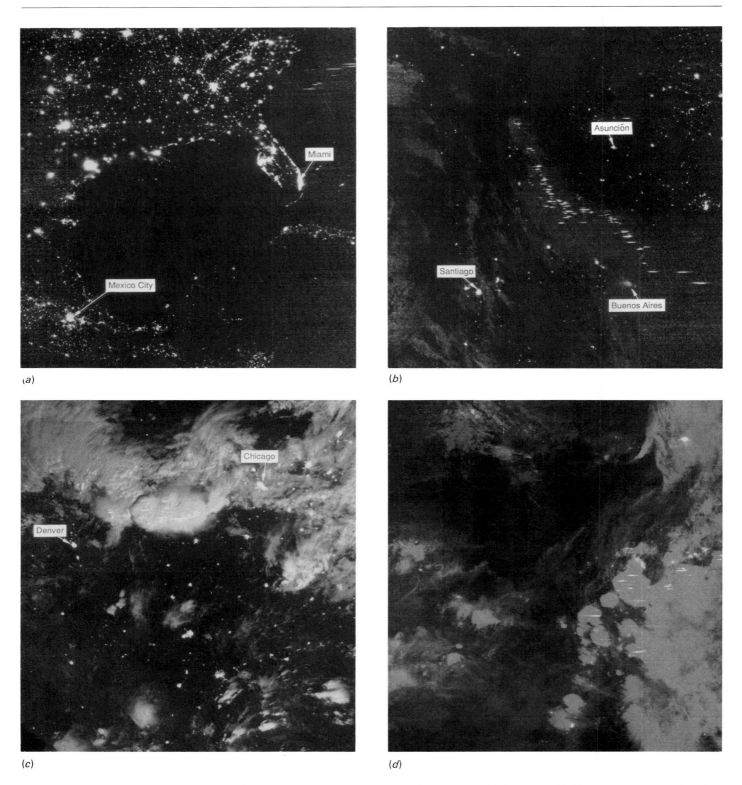

Fig. 5. DMSP–OLS series F7 satellite visible-band images with lightning streaks from the midnight pass. (a) Lightning streaks produced by individual storms off the southeast coast of the US on a dark night at 0422 UTC, 8 April 1986; (b) lightning streaks produced by a line of storms in Argentina on a partially moonlit night at 0204 UTC, 19 October, 1985; (c) lightning streaks produced by a mesoscale convective complex in the central US on a night with a full moon at 0439 UTC, 19 September 1986; (d) lightning streaks superimposed on a corresponding infrared image of the parent thunderstorms over the northwest coast of South America at 0323 UTC, 12 May 1986.

Table 2. *DMSP-OLS block 5D orbital History*

Name	Orbit	Launch date	Life (Mo.)
F1	Noon	09/11/76	24
F2	Early am	06/04/77	56
F3	Early am	04/30/78	20
F4	Noon	06/06/79	14
F5	Noon	07/14/80	0*
F6	6:30am	12/20/82	56
F7	10:10am	11/17/83	2
F8	6:35am	06/19/87	49
F9	9:30am	02/02/88	48
F10	7:42am	12/01/90	Operational**
F11	5:04am	11/28/91	Operational***

*Booster did not achieve orbit.
**F10 is precessing at rate of 44 min/yr (3 min, 50 s per month).
***F11 is precessing at rate of 20 min/yr (1 min, 40 s per month).

penetrate the ionosphere can be highly refracted and may be received at the satellite by whistler-mode propagation from the magnetic conjugate point of the Earth. In addition, geophysical processes other than lightning in the upper atmosphere can produce VLF signals resembling whistlers. Some of the earliest VLF signals attributed to lightning were received on the LOFTO-1 satellite in the early 1960s (Leiphart *et al.*, 1962).

At very high frequencies and high altitude orbits, weak lightning signals combined with man-made and galactic cosmic ray noise presents a formidable problem for unambiguous lightning detection. At HF, however, the sferics signal amplitude is well above the galactic noise background and coarse spatial estimates of lightning distributions (over many hundreds of kilometers) can be made. Elimination of interference from HF transmitters on the ground can be minimized by choosing appropriate receiver frequencies above the critical frequency of the ionosphere, where reception is possible from a limited area below the satellite. This so-called 'iris' effect describes the functional dependence of radio wave penetration through the ionosphere for a given observing frequency and critical ionosphere frequency. The critical frequency is proportional to the square root of the maximum electron density in the F-region and varies with season, time of day, and geographic location over a range of 1 to 15 MHz. All of the HF satellite measurements make use of this 'iris' effect, but only the ionospheric sounding satellite (ISS-b) experiment collected real-time information on the critical frequency to provide information on the sferic source area (Kotaki & Katoh, 1983).

Analysis and Results

Annual thunderstorm activity

One of the important links in the global atmospheric circulation is the transport of energy from the Tropics to higher latitudes. Deep convective storms within the inter tropical convergence zone (ITCZ) are the primary agents for converting latent forms of energy into internal energy, providing the driving force for poleward energy transport. Although this convective energy conversion is an important link in the general circulation and these storms may constitute a significant fraction of the total number of thunderstorms worldwide, very little is known about the heat balance and storm frequency (Houze & Betts, 1981).

Global thunderstorm activity is highly variable in space and time. Due to the lack of detailed observations, particularly in the Tropics and oceanic regions, we have mostly qualitative understanding of thunderstorm and lightning variability. A global lightning distribution, limited to local midnight only, is shown in Fig. 6 for the 12-month period October 1986 to September 1987. This climatology is based upon a sample of only 41 789 flashes derived from 2300 orbits containing horizontal streaks in the DMSP film archive of the Block 5D series F7 satellite. For a nominal flash rate of $100 \, s^{-1}$, this sample represents merely seven minutes of global activity.

Clearly, there is significantly more lightning over the land areas than over the ocean. The lack of lightning over the ocean might be attributable to the greater atmospheric instability over land which leads to more vigorous vertical motions and more energetic storms. Equatorial islands exposed to surface heating and abundant low level moisture often have vigorous afternoon thunderstorms, whereas the updrafts in oceanic storms tend to be much weaker (on the order of $5–10 \, m \, s^{-1}$ or less) (Zipser & Lemone (1980)). The stronger cloud updrafts over land transport supercooled liquid water aloft where ice and graupel particles can grow in abundance and may play a significant role in the charge separation process.

The striking absence of lightning over the Western US and Alaska at midnight illustrates the important forcing role of the diurnal cycle and topography in thunderstorm generation (Reap, 1986, 1991). Without the support of larger synoptic scale forcing, air mass thunderstorms die out by early evening. The Andes mountain range along the west coast of South America and the northern extent of the Sahel region of Africa are well delineated by the lightning activity.

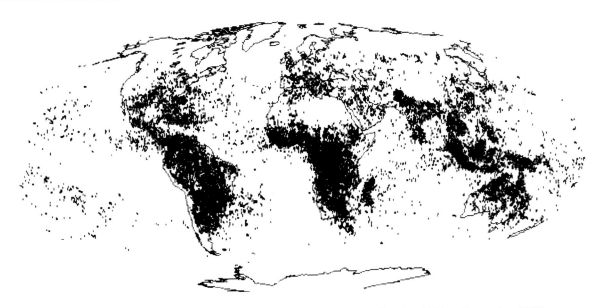

Fig. 6. Global annual distribution of DMSP–OLS lightning at midnight for the period October 1986 to September 1987.

Monthly and seasonal thunderstorm activity

Detailed monthly and seasonal distributions of the DMSP midnight lightning are shown in Figs. 7 and 8. The monthly lightning events from the archived orbits (i.e. film strips) for October 1986 to September 1987 are summarized in Table 3. The primary regions of convective activity are clearly depicted. Mid-latitude seasonal changes in lightning activity are also accompanied by the seasonal shift of the ITCZ. The ITCZ migrates from north of the equator in the Northern Hemisphere summer to south of the equator in the winter. The ITCZ migration extends as far as 15–20° north and south of the equator, reaching its northernmost point in September and southernmost point in March, also corresponding to the highest temperatures in the oceans (Byers, 1974).

Lightning frequency variations as a function of latitude show a December–February (Northern Hemisphere winter) peak between 0° and 20° S and a June–August (Northern Hemisphere summer) peak of activity between 0° and 20° N. Chen (1987) notes that the lightning activity is exactly what one would expect based on the convergence of water vapor brought about by planetary-scale divergent circulations. For example, in the tropics, local Hadley cell and east–west Walker circulations concentrate the precipitable water (and the upward vertical motions) over the three tropical continents in the same regions where Figs. 6–8 show the highest occurrence of lightning.

Lightning activity in the extratropical regions, such as the peak in the Northern Hemisphere summer, also correspond well with mesoscale and synoptic scale storm tracks. As much as 70% of the Northern Hemisphere warm season (April to September) rainfall in the major crop growing regions of the central United States, extensive flooding, and severe weather is a result of organized mesoscale circulations (Fritsch, Kane & Chelius, 1986; McAnnelly & Cotton, 1986). In the Northern Hemisphere spring, the lightning associated with storms in the Gulf Stream (best delineated in the April map) and mid-US mesoscale precipitation systems is very active. Seasonal lightning patterns also tend to highlight the global distribution of mesoscale precipitation systems (also referred to as mesoscale convective complexes or MCCs). The geographic distribution of these organized, often nocturnal, weather systems for the years 1981–1983 in the Americas and for the years 1983–1985 in and around the Asian/Maritime continents is portrayed in Fig. 9 (Velasco & Fritsch, 1987; Miller & Fritsch, 1991). MCCs can be readily identified by their persistence and extensive cold cloud shields in infra-red satellite imagery. The typical life-times of MCCs are on the order of 12 h with spatial extents of a few hundred kilometers. Although North and South American MCCs possess similar characteristics, the South American MCCs reach their maximum size nearer to local midnight (0300–0530 UTC), which provides for better sampling from the DMSP satellites. During the 1982–1983 ENSO period twice as many MCCs were produced in South America as compared to the prior year (Velasco & Fritsch, 1987).

Fig. 7. Global monthly distribution of DMSP–OLS lightning at midnight for the period October 1986 to September 1987.

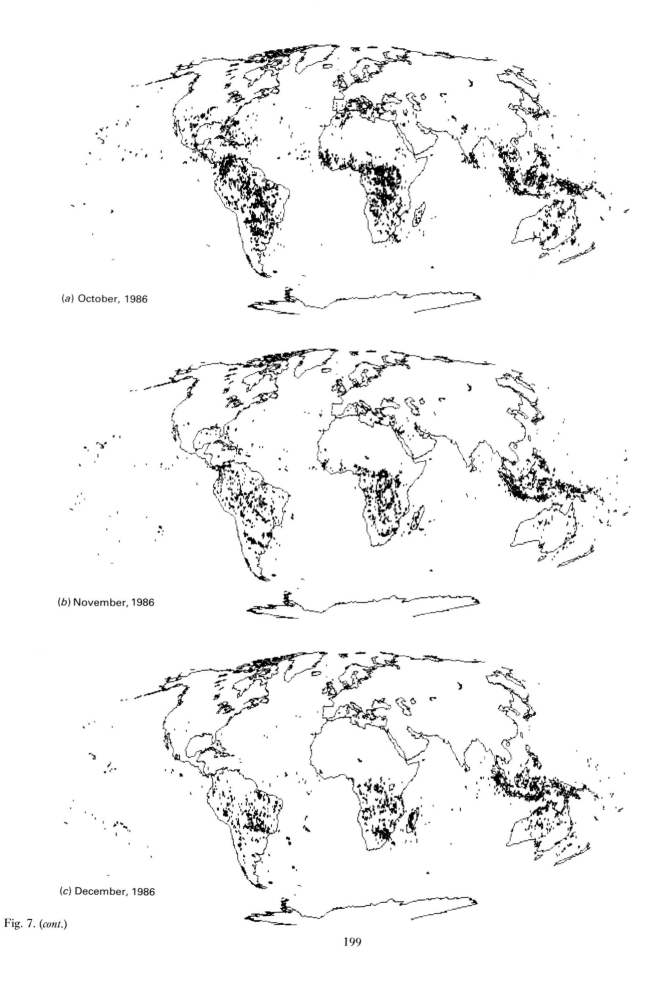

(a) October, 1986

(b) November, 1986

(c) December, 1986

Fig. 7. (cont.)

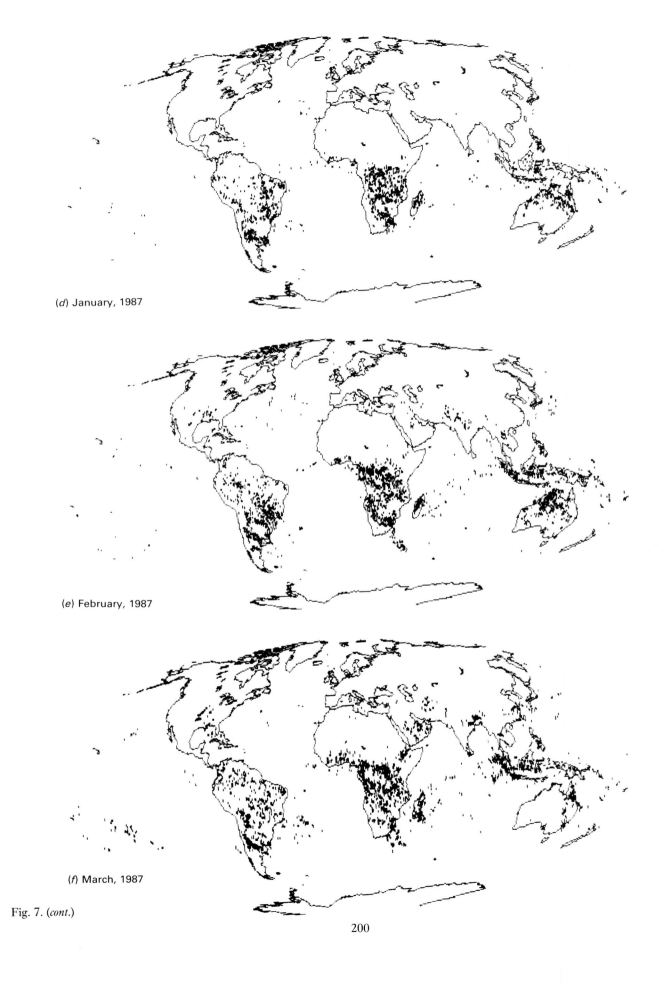

(d) January, 1987

(e) February, 1987

(f) March, 1987

Fig. 7. (cont.)

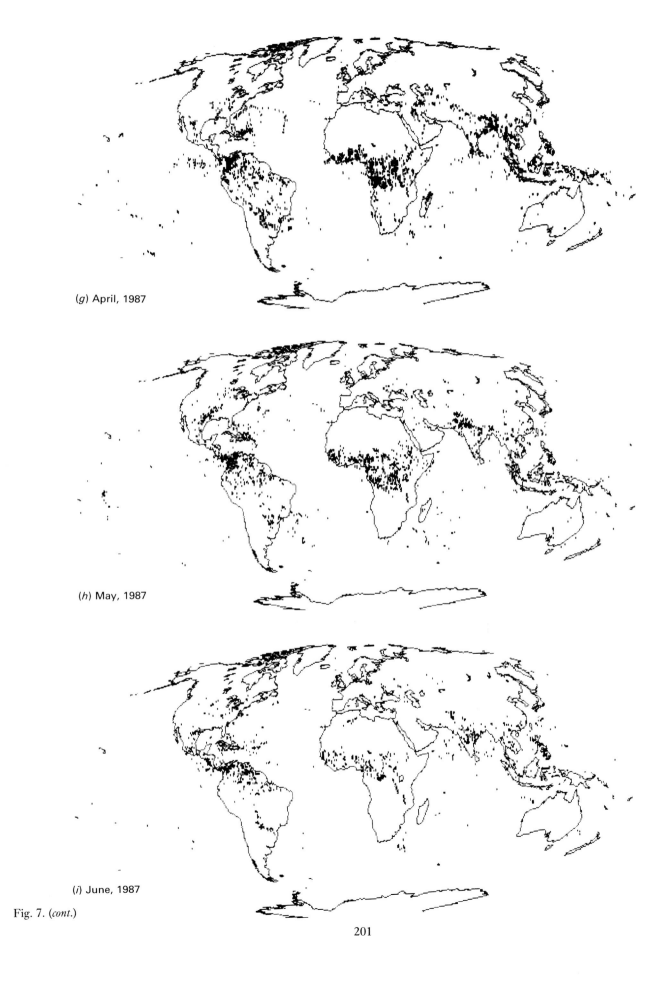

(*g*) April, 1987

(*h*) May, 1987

(*i*) June, 1987

Fig. 7. (*cont.*)

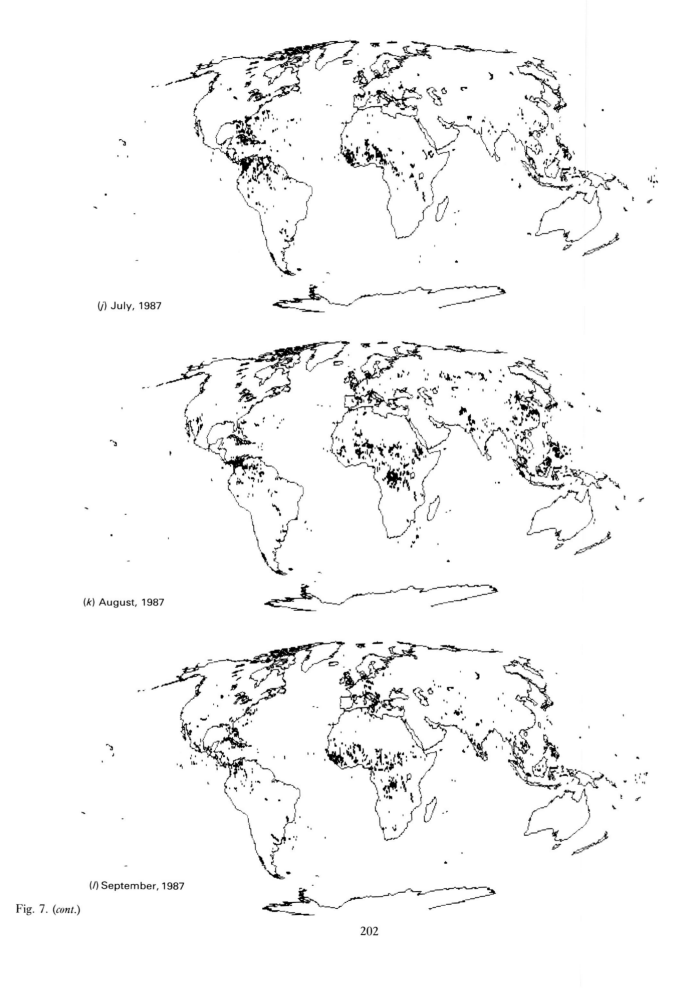

(j) July, 1987

(k) August, 1987

(l) September, 1987

Fig. 7. (cont.)

202

The world's major centers of organized mesoscale convection portrayed in Fig. 9 do not generally coincide with the thunderstorm day maxima shown in Fig. 1. The orographic and environmental interactions that initiate and sustain long-lived convective activity (most of these convective systems form downwind of north–south mountain ranges) yields a different perspective of thunderstorm activity that is not fully appreciated when considering only the number of thunderstorm days. This is because thunderstorm day statistics tend to be dominated more by the diurnal cycle alone than by large scale dynamics and give equal weight to both a day in which

perhaps only one lightning discharge occurs as well as a day in which several thousand discharges occur. For example, up to 25% of the entire annual lightning strikes at a given site within the Central US can be accounted for by the passage of a single convective complex (Goodman & MacGorman, 1986).

Inter-annual variations

The global distribution of DMSP-OLS midnight lightning and tropical rainfall for May 1986 and 1987 is shown in Figs.

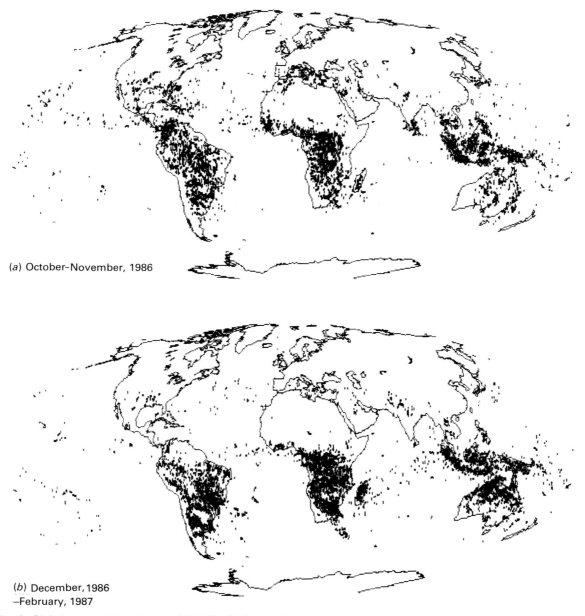

(a) October-November, 1986

(b) December, 1986
–February, 1987

Fig. 8. Global seasonal distribution of DMSP–OLS lightning at midnight for the period October 1986 to September 1987.

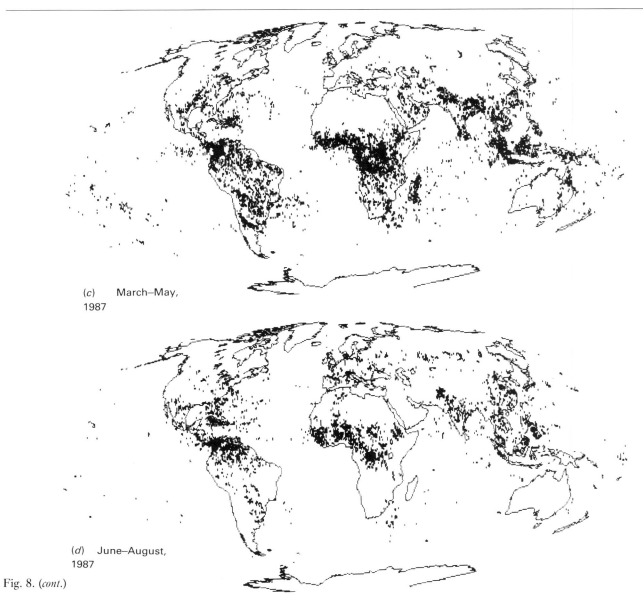

(c) March–May, 1987

(d) June–August, 1987

Fig. 8. (*cont.*)

Table 3. *DMSP–OLS lightning summary for October 1986–September 1987*

Month	Flashes	Orbits	Flashes/orbit
October	6662	246	27.1
November	3769	198	19.0
December	3214	177	18.2
January	2908	154	18.9
February	4765	203	23.5
March	4682	192	24.4
April	4514	245	18.4
May	2729	241	11.3
June	1702	126	13.5
July	1914	132	14.5
August	2952	176	16.8
September	1978	210	9.4
Total	41 789	2300	Avg. 18.2

10 and 11. The two monthly climatologies are based on nearly the same number of orbits (247 orbits for May 1986; 241 orbits for May 1987). However, 3978 flashes were detected over the Earth in May 1986 (or 16.1 flashes per orbit); nearly 50% more than the 2729 flashes (or 11.3 flashes per orbit) detected in May 1987. The period is notable for the 1986–1987 ENSO episode. This rainfall product is produced by the GOES precipitation index algorithm of Arkin and Meisner (1987) and is being provided to the WMO sponsored global precipitation climatology project (Janowiak & Arkin, 1991). This algorithm relates rainfall to the fractional coverage of cold clouds within a 2.5° latitude by 2.5° longitude area. The lightning maxima over the continents correspond to the rainfall maxima suggesting that land-based thunderstorms are major contributors to tropical continental rainfall. Due to a

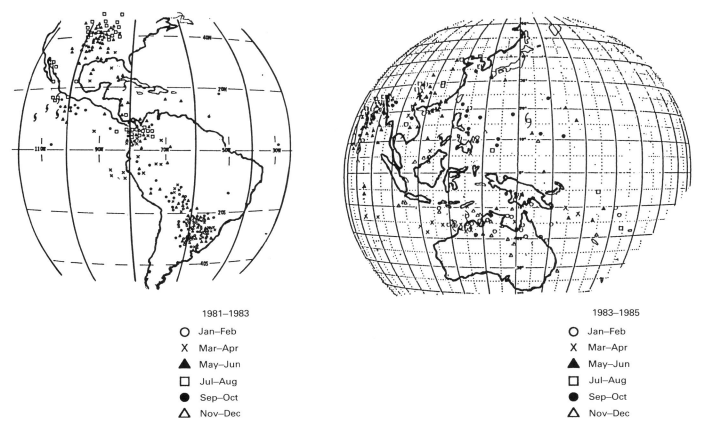

1981–1983
O Jan–Feb
X Mar–Apr
▲ May–Jun
☐ Jul–Aug
● Sep–Oct
△ Nov–Dec

1983–1985
O Jan–Feb
X Mar–Apr
▲ May–Jun
☐ Jul–Aug
● Sep–Oct
△ Nov–Dec

Fig. 9. Geographic and monthly distribution of Mesoscale Convective Complexes (MCCs) in and around the Americas (locations derived from the time of the maximum observed cold cloud shield extents (From Velasco & Fritsch, 1987); Asia and Australia (Miller & Fritsch, 1991).

lack of geostationary satellite data and less favorable equatorial crossing times for the NOAA polar orbiting satellites used to produce this rainfall product, the midnight thunderstorm (i.e. lightning) maxima over the Indian subcontinent and Pakistan seen by the DMSP–OLS is not reflected in the GPCP rainfall product. However, in May 1987, near the end of this ENSO episode, there is a less expansive region of lightning activity and lower rain rates in and around Southeast Asia and the Maritime Continent than during the same period in 1986. This result is consistent with the ENSO signal for this area of the world (Ropelewski & Halpert, 1987).

It is also of particular interest that ENSO events since the 1940s have been responsible for above normal rainfall and increased discharge of the Magdalena River at Calamar, Colombia (10°15′N, 74°55′W) during the late Spring months of May and June (Aceituno, 1988). Indeed, there is more midnight lightning activity in this region in 1987 than in 1986. Within a 10° latitude by 10° longitude region in northern Colombia (centered at 6° N, 73° W) there are 30 days (346 flashes) during May–June 1987 with observed lightning at midnight in comparison to only 23 days (240 flashes) during May–June 1986. If an analysis of additional years were to

show this same relationship, one might then anticipate a substantial increase in organized thunderstorm activity during the ENSO years.

The diabatic heating maxima (dotted) shown in Fig. 12 support the notion that latent heating due to thunderstorms and long-lived mesoscale precipitation systems over the tropical continents is an important source of tropical energetics. These vertically integrated heating rates are derived from the 7 level, 2.5° gridded European Centre for Medium Range Weather Forecasting (ECMWF) analysis for May 1987. However, it appears that the lightning and rainfall patterns in the vicinity of the South Atlantic convergence zone east of Brazil and Argentina are not as well defined in this ECMWF analysis due to the absence of upper air information over the ocean.

Comparison with other satellite lightning climatologies

Maps of the global flash frequency by season and time of day have been generated from ISS-b measurements made between June 1978 and May 1980 (Kotaki & Katoh, 1983).

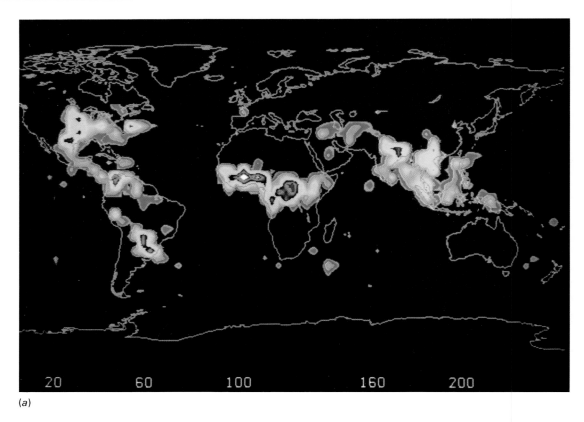

(a)

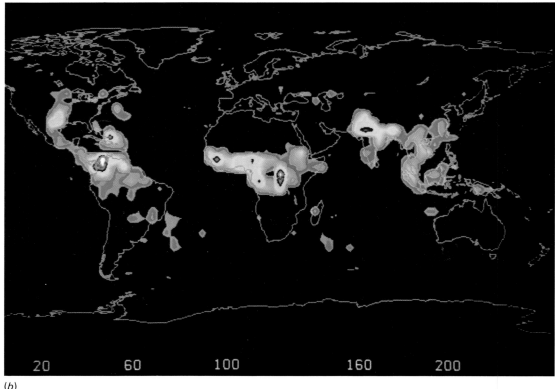

(b)

Fig. 10. DMSP–OLS lightning at midnight within geographic bins 4° latitude × 4° longitude for the months (a) May 1986 and (b) May 1987 (units of flashes per bin per month). The total region of the grid extends from 50° S–50° N latitude and from 130° W–180° E longitude.

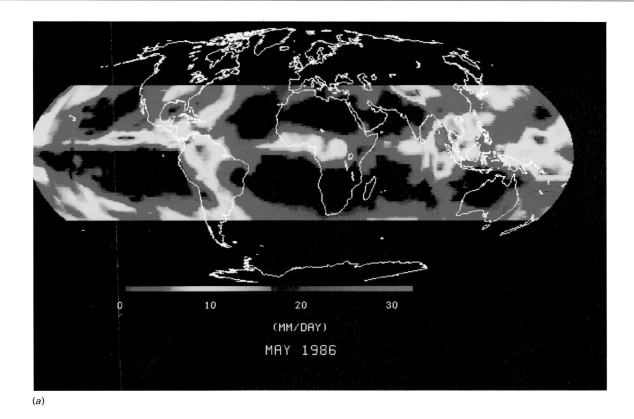

(a)

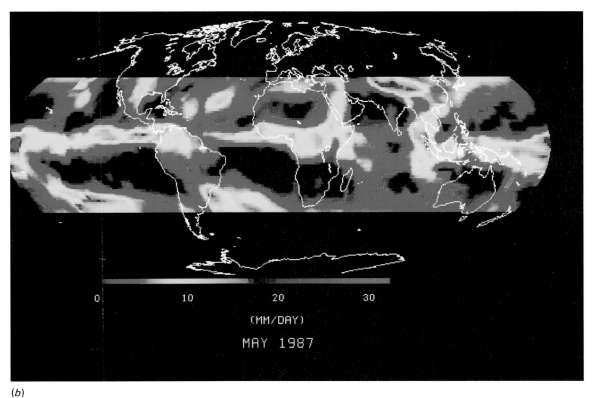

(b)

Fig. 11. Global precipitation index from infra-red channel of GOES geostationary and NOAA polar orbiting satellites for (a) May 1986 and (b) May 1987. Units are in mm/day (After Janowiak & Arkin, 1991).

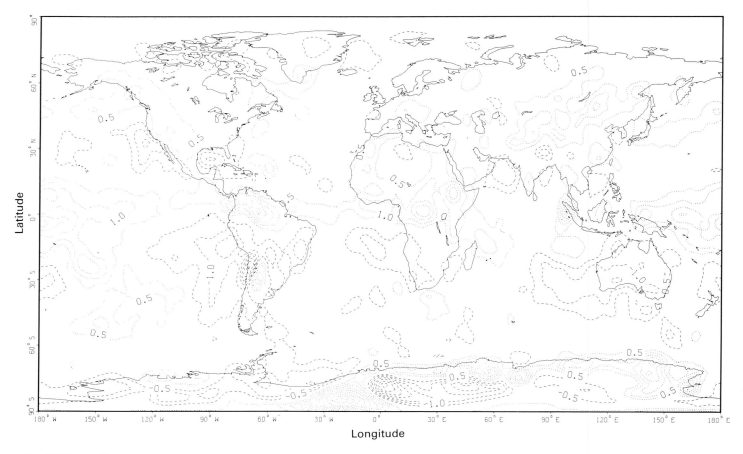

Fig. 12. Vertically integrated diabatic heating rate calculated from the residual of the dry thermodynamic equation from 7 level, 2.5° gridded ECMWF analysis for May 1987 (Christy, 1991). Values are in K/day determined from the surface pressure level to 50 hPa. Contour interval is every 0·5 K/day with positive values dotted, negative values dashed.

Approximately 125 000 observations each 20 s in duration were obtained from 1300 orbits during this period. Fig. 13 shows one of the global distributions of lightning frequency from 2200–0200 UTC during June, July and August 1978 and 1979. The number of discharges are summed over 20-second observation periods for geographic bins 10° latitude by 10° longitude in size (roughly 1.2 million square kilometers at the equator). The flash frequency is the number of discharges per bin divided by the total observation time (which ranges from 400 s (20 observation periods) in low latitudes to 800 s in high latitudes). Two maxima on the order of 5×10^{-8} km^{-2} s^{-1} occur in northern latitudes at 100° W longitude (Gulf of Mexico, South Central US) and 125° E longitude (Southeast Asia).

Fig. 14 shows a global distribution based upon a sample of 3000 flashes observed in 10° latitude by 10° longitude bins at dusk (1700 local standard time) for August 2 to September 10, 1977 with the PBE (Piggy Back Experiment) optical sensor flown on the DMSP Block 5D series satellite. The light-

ning frequency was determined by counting the number of flashes detected while the satellite subpoint was within a given bin and dividing this total by the time the subpoint was within the same area. Total sample time for each bin was about 30 min, approximately 2–4 times the observation period used to generate the ISS-b climatology. The probability of detection for the DMSP–PBE observations is believed to be no better than 2% (and perhaps much less), based on limited comparisons made with ground-based lightning measurements of small storms in Florida.

An annual and seasonal DMSP–OLS midnight climatology produced by Orville and Henderson (1986) for the 12-month period September 1977 to August 1978 is shown in Figs. 15 and 16. This earlier climatology was produced in very much the same way as the present DMSP–OLS climatology. This data base contains a sample of only 32 262 flashes derived from the DMSP film archive of the Block 5D series F1 satellite. Despite the sampling problems inherent in the DMSP midnight lightning climatologies, there are a num-

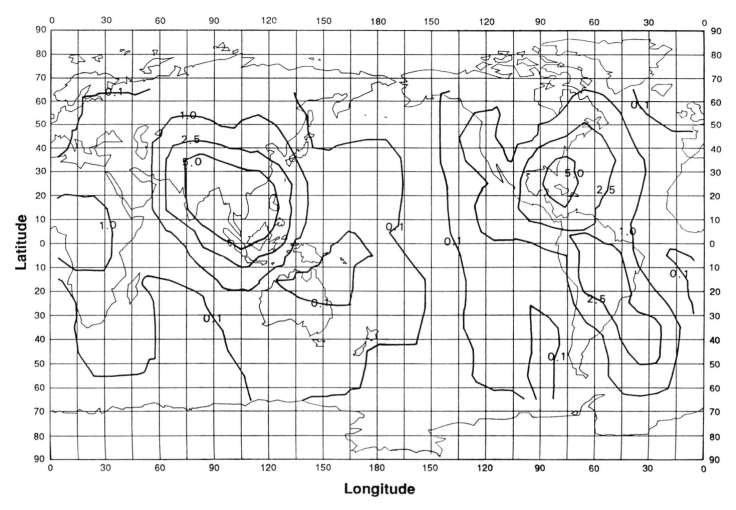

Fig. 13. Global distribution of ISS-b lightning for June–August 1978 and 1979 (2200–0200 UTC). Frequency is given in units of $10^{-7} \, \mathrm{km}^{-2} \, \mathrm{s}^{-1}$ (From Kotaki and Katoh, 1983).

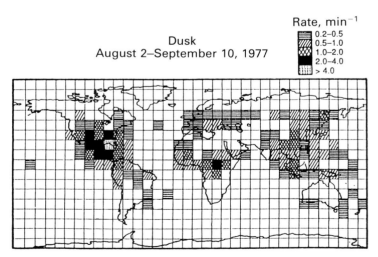

Fig. 14. Global lightning distribution of DMSP–PBE lightning at dusk (1700 local standard time) for 2 August–10 September, 1977 (From Turman, 1978).

ber of consistent features in both seasonal and spatial climatologies. The large land/ocean difference is particularly dramatic.

The two climatologies derived from the DMSP–PBE and ISS-b observations also show greater lightning activity over land than over the oceans, while their respective maxima near the Gulf of Mexico only differ by a factor of 10 (5×10^{-7} $\mathrm{km}^{-2} \, \mathrm{s}^{-1}$ for ISS-b; $5 \times 10^{-8} \, \mathrm{km}^{-2} \, \mathrm{s}^{-1}$ for PBE). Frequency variations as a function of latitude in seasonal PBE, OLS, and ISS-b maps are very similar. However, there are important differences between these global climatologies such as 1) the PBE maxima over Central Africa in August and April (not shown) also exhibited by the DMSP–OLS climatologies, but not evident in the ISS-b climatology; 2) the broad maxima in the ISS-b map over Southeast Asia extending 1000 km east of the coastline for which a corresponding maxima on the other maps can only be found over land; and 3) the lack of any demarcation of the Sahel in Northern Africa in the ISS-b

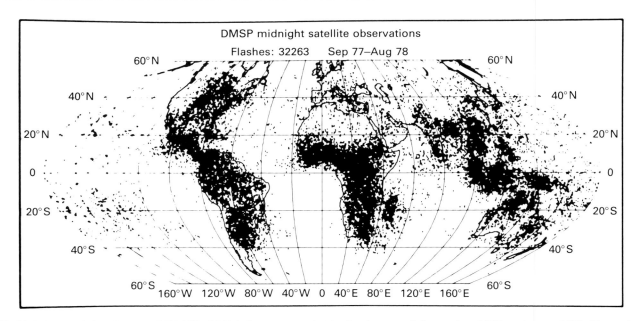

Fig. 15. Global annual distribution of DMSP–OLS lightning at midnight for the period September 1987 to August 1978 (From Orville & Henderson, 1986).

climatology, yet clearly shown by the DMSP–OLS climatologies. The higher spatial resolution DMSP–OLS product seems to have the best agreement with the thunderstorm day and mesoscale convective complex climatologies, but more comprehensive data bases will be required to reveal the finer details that are sure to exist.

Regional ground-based observations

Ground-based lightning location networks using magnetic direction finders (Krider, Noggle & Uman, 1976; Orville, 1991), time-of-arrival receivers (Lee, 1986; Lyons, 1989), and VHF radio interferometers (Richard & Auffrey, 1985; Richard et al., 1991) are in operation on a regional (> 100 km

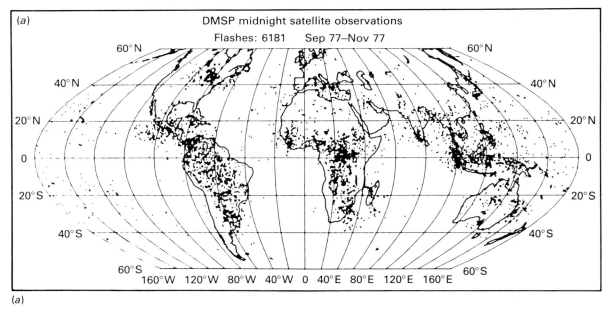

Fig. 16. Global seasonal distribution of DMSP–OLS lightning at midnight for the period September 1977 to August 1978. (a) October–November 1986; (b) December 1986–February 1987; (c) March–May 1987; (d) June–August 1987 (From Orville & Henderson, 1986).

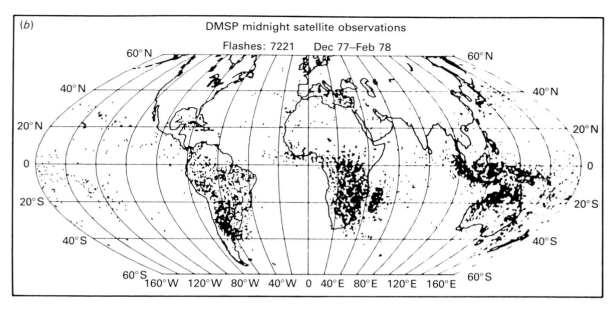

(b) DMSP midnight satellite observations
Flashes: 7221   Dec 77–Feb 78

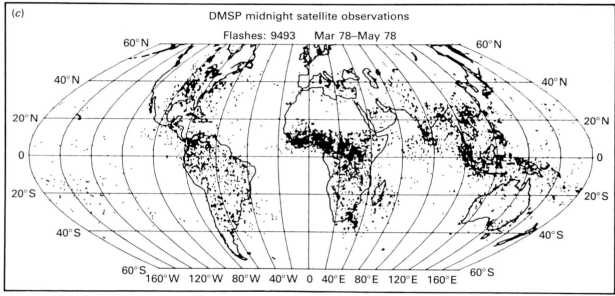

(c) DMSP midnight satellite observations
Flashes: 9493   Mar 78–May 78

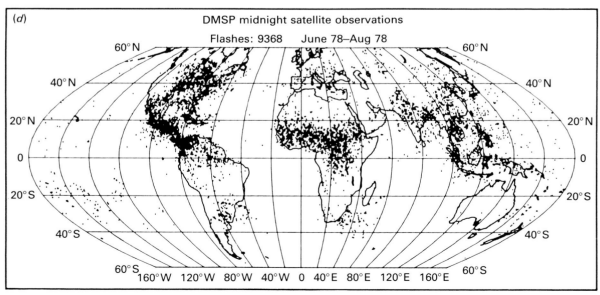

(d) DMSP midnight satellite observations
Flashes: 9368   June 78–Aug 78

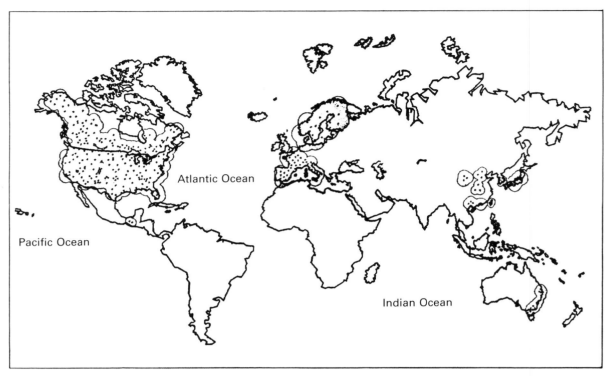

Fig. 17. Global coverage of lightning detection and location networks using magnetic direction finder techniques.

coverage) or national scale in various countries (Fig. 17). These systems provide information only obtainable from continuous observations at larger scales. These networks have been used in both scientific (lightning physics, storm characteristics, climatologies, lightning relationships with the synoptic and mesoscale environment) and in engineering (primarily utility power generating operation) studies of lightning (primarily of cloud-to-ground lightning). Regional climatologies of cloud-to-ground lightning activity can also be useful in satellite sampling strategies to ascertain the representativeness of satellite observations from a variety of orbits. Tropical rainfall sampling experiments have been conducted to examine the errors and biases of low Earth orbit observations for climatology studies (McConnell & North, 1987). It is anticipated that the ground-based networks will be used in partnership with the space-based sensors to establish flash type and relative frequency of intracloud versus ground discharges as a function of storm type and environment. When improved lightning observations are made from space, these ground based networks will also provide some measure of 'ground truth'.

Lightning and forest fires

Regional ground-based lightning location networks are presently an integral part of fire fighting operations. Lightning strikes to ground are a chief ingredient in the ignition of naturally occurring forest fire outbreaks in the western US and elsewhere (Fig. 18). For example, forest fires are often caused by lightning when the ground is dry, decayed vegetation is present, relative humidity is low, and surface winds are strong. Doubled CO_2 climate simulations to ascertain the effects of global warming predict a 25% increase in global total lightning frequency (Price & Rind, 1990). With the present limitations of the global lightning data base, we will be unable to clearly detect a 25% change in lightning activity. The various global warming simulations of cloud amounts, distributions, and structures are limited at present by coarse model spatial resolution and relatively simple convective parameterizations. Numerical simulations of the Earth's climate will improve when long-term, consistent observations of clouds are available to provide validation of model predictions and feedback to model developers.

Inter-annual variations on a regional scale

Data acquired by one of the ground-based, continuously operating national (magnetic direction finder) lightning networks further illustrates how the inter-annual variability of lightning activity can be addressed. The annual US lightning strike density for 1989 is shown in Fig. 19. More than 13.4 million lightning flashes to ground were recorded (Orville,

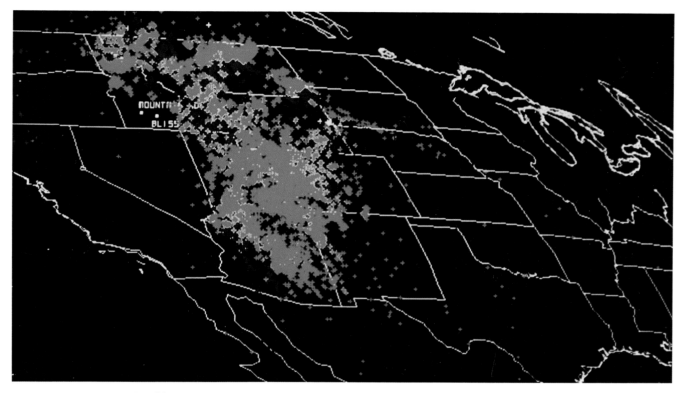

Fig. 18. Lightning activity responsible for setting off major forest fires July 7–8, 1983.

1991). This type of analysis provides a great deal of detail that is unavailable from the satellites in low Earth orbit.

This flash density map was produced by plotting the flash locations on a grid with 30 km vertical by 50 km horizontal resolution. In addition, the values were multiplied by 1.4 to correct for the average network probability of detection (estimated at 70%). It was found that some of the annual maxima were due to just a few storms, a feature alluded to earlier by Goodman and MacGorman (1986).

In climatological studies we are primarily interested in the year-to-year variations and the associated variations in synoptic weather patterns. The period 1988–1989 is particularly noteworthy as the city of Huntsville (HSV) in north Alabama consecutively experienced both its driest and wettest summers within the past 100 years (Fig. 20). Normal June rainfall at HSV is 100 mm (3.97 in). This subregion within the Tennessee Valley is contained within one of five distinct lightning ground strike maxima within the contiguous US shown in Fig. 19. Within the Tennessee Valley, lightning and rainfall data have been further analyzed within a 2° latitude × 3° longitude area (33.8–35.8° N, 86–89° W) during the period June 1986 to 1989.

The cloud-to-ground lightning in addition to the mean low-level (85 kPa) and upper-level (20 kPa) wind in the Tennessee Valley for June in the period 1986 to 1989 (Fig. 21)

shows the greatest differences between the years 1988 (4 thunderstorm days) and 1989 (17 thunderstorm days). During June 1988 the Tennessee Valley was under the influence of a ridge of high pressure in the central US, perhaps attributable to the coldest anti-ENSO (high index) episode in the past 15 years (Trenberth, Branstator & Arkin, 1988). Weak northwesterly flow with little or no vertical wind shear characterized the depth of the troposphere. A strong correlation is known to exist between cold sea surface temperature anomalies in the tropical Pacific (anti-ENSO) and above normal dryness in the south-eastern US which persists through the following Spring (Ropelewski & Halpert, 1989).

Fig. 22 shows minimal areal precipitation across north Alabama in June 1988 compared to 1986 and 1987 (10 thunderstorm days each) when the precipitation at the Huntsville, AL International Airport (HSV) was slightly above normal. June 1988 is of interest because it is the driest on record at HSV with only 4.3 mm (0.17 in) rainfall (17 lightning flashes recorded within 10 km of HSV). Interestingly, 3.8 mm of the total rainfall was recorded on the last day of the month.

June 1989 is equally noteworthy because it sets the all time June rainfall record with 380 mm (14.99 in). A total of 416 lightning flashes within a radius of 10 km of HSV were recorded during the month. In 1989 the moist low level flow from the Gulf of Mexico returned and the upper level wind of

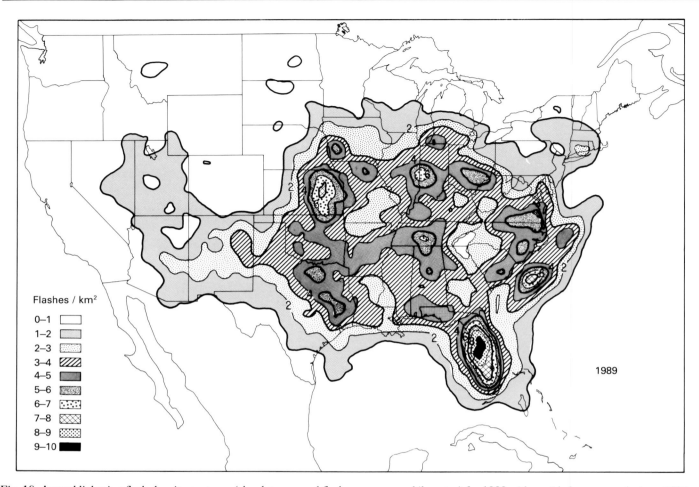

Fig. 19. Annual lightning flash density contours (cloud-to-ground flashes per square kilometer) for 1989 with a grid element resolution of 30 km in the vertical and 50 km in the horizontal (From Orville, 1991).

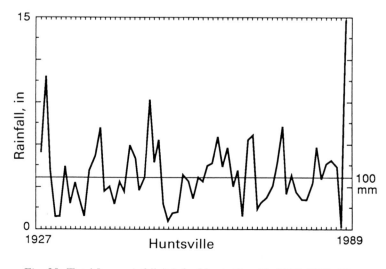

Fig. 20. Total June rainfall (in) for Huntsville, AL 1927–1989. The 30 year mean of 100 mm (3·97 in) is based on the period of record 1941–1970.

nearly 20 m s^{-1} associated with the subtropical jet stream was the strongest in the 4-year period. The 1989 mean 85 kPa wind differed from the earlier years only in direction, not in magnitude (5 m s^{-1}). Yet, deep convection was widespread in 1989 as depicted by the large number of counties having 150 or more lightning flashes per 100 km^2, which represents about 20% of the estimated mean annual lightning flash density (8 flashes km^{-2}) for this part of the US (MacGorman, Maier & Rust, 1984).

The rainfall patterns for 1986 to 1989 are in general agreement with the lightning patterns but there are some important differences as well. Some of the lightning maxima do not correspond to maxima in the rainfall pattern. This is seldom the case for individual mesoscale convective events containing deep thunderstorms. The lack of one-to-one correspondence between the gaged rainfall and lightning (r < 0.5) is partially due to the undersampling of the Cooperative Observing Network (indicated by dots in Fig. 22). An added complication to

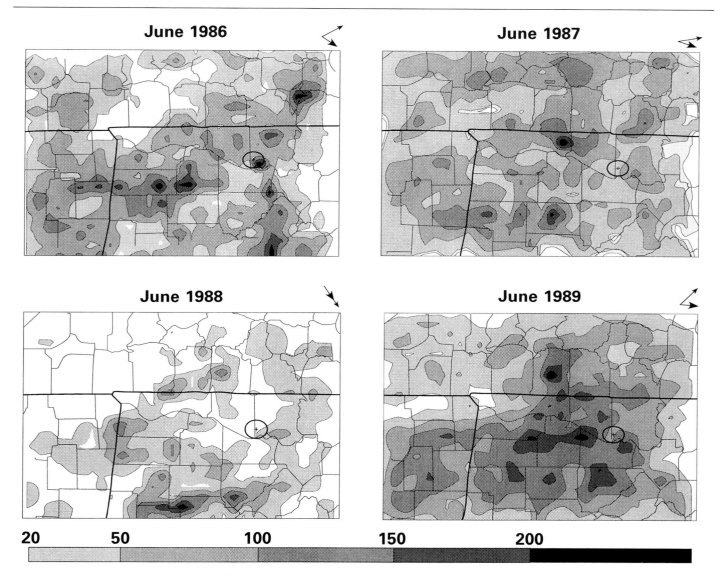

Fig. 21. Total cloud-to-ground lightning strikes for June 1986–1989 in 0·1 × 0·1° geographic bins. The mean monthly 85 kPa (long arrow) and 20 kPa (short arrow) wind directions for this region are shown above each monthly summary (from the NMC final analysis depicted in the *Climate Diagnostics Bulletin* published by NOAA). A 10 km range ring is centered at Huntsville, AL (HSV).

this picture is that intracloud lightning flashes are not detected and located by the ground-strike networks. Furthermore, the contribution of stratiform rainfall (when little or no lightning occurs) to the total rainfall amounts is a major source of variance. Stratiform rain events without lightning tend to diminish the contribution of a single intense thunderstorm.

Complete studies await the simultaneous observation of intracloud and cloud-to-ground lightning in conjunction with total rain volume. However, the lightning observations alone demonstrate a tremendous variability that, in turn, can be shown to be a direct response to changes in larger scale atmospheric forcing.

Conclusions

Observations from low Earth orbit are well suited for determining the global lightning distribution and the interactions and feedbacks between the large-scale forcing and thunderstorm occurrence. Since observations are made for short periods, complementary geostationary (continuous) observations are needed to study complete storm morphology. Detailed observations of lightning activity at the storm scale will be possible in the late 1990s with optical lightning sensors being developed as scientific payloads for the NASA Earth Observing System programme including Earth probe missions such as the Tropical Rain Measuring Mission

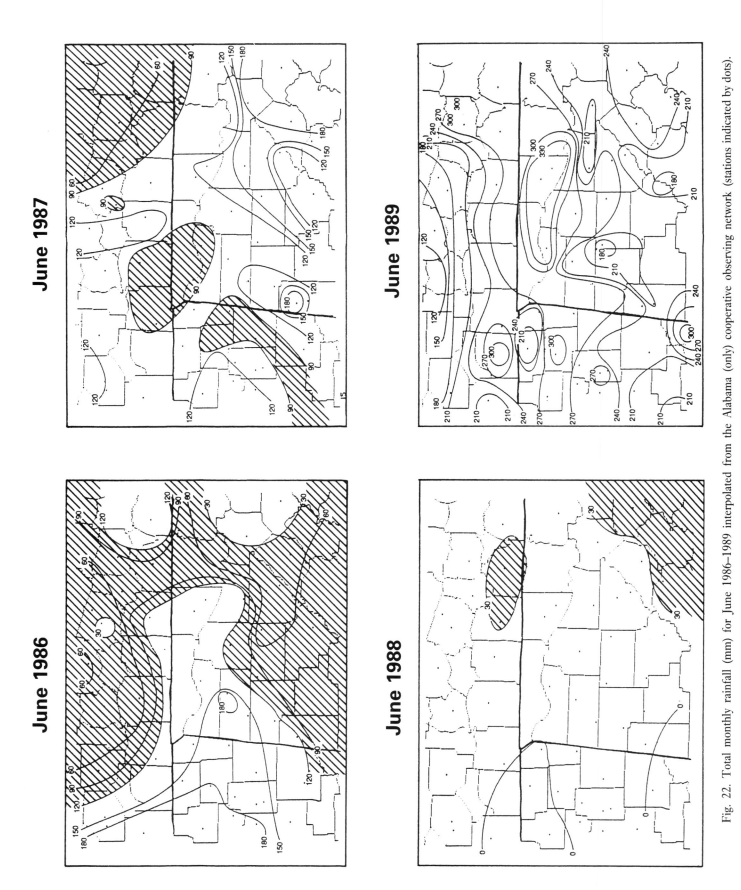

Fig. 22. Total monthly rainfall (mm) for June 1986–1989 interpolated from the Alabama (only) cooperative observing network (stations indicated by dots).

(TRMM), a geostationary platform and the NOAA GOES-next satellite series (Christian, Blakeslee & Goodman, 1989; 1992). At that time the lightning characteristics of individual clouds will be obtained simultaneously with measurements from visible and infra-red imagers, passive microwave radiometers, and active microwave radars. Such lightning observations can be readily associated with the thunderstorms that produced them, and the detection of even a single discharge is meaningful (identifying a thunderstorm) and may provide useful information on storm location, structure, physics, and electric current generation.

Global studies of the distribution of lightning and its relationship to storm microphysics and dynamics, dependence on regional climate and its variations, its relationship to precipitation and cloud type, and the incorporation of these relationships into diagnostic and predictive models of the general circulation and the hydrologic cycle are anticipated. Tropical studies of the distribution and variation in lightning activity will provide clear indications of areas of strong convection within the Walker and Hadley circulations. Heat balance in the equatorial zone can then be qualitatively accounted for if the vertical motion in the ITCZ is confined primarily to the updrafts of the individual convective cells (Riehl & Malkus, 1958). It has been estimated that 1500–5000 'hot towers' would need to exist simultaneously around the globe to account for the required vertical heat transport in the ITCZ. However, few attempts at verification have been made. The primary reason for the lack of study is that most of the deep convection in the Tropics occurs over ocean areas where observing systems are inadequate. Since lightning activity may be very sensitive to surface wet bulb temperature and atmospheric stability, changing sea surface temperature anomalies may modify the distribution and intensity of thunderstorms. Furthermore, these lightning changes should be readily observable from space.

Significant intraseasonal variability in tropical diabatic forcing has been established as has the relationship between this forcing and changes in the general circulation in mid-latitudes. Knowledge of the variability in tropical precipitation with lightning observations over periods of 5–10 days would help resolve the time and space scales of the variability in tropical forcing. The annual mean and mean annual cycle of precipitation and lightning are not fully known. Such knowledge would be valuable in understanding atmospheric teleconnections and the global balance of moist static energy.

Studies on the production, distribution, and transport of trace gases attributed to lightning and determining the contribution of lightning (and the sources of variability) to the global amount of trace gases should be feasible (Levine & Shaw, 1983; Chameides et al., 1987). The electrical coupling

of a thunderstorm to the ionosphere and magnetosphere by the generation of transient electric fields and whistler waves can be examined as well (Inan & Carpenter, 1987). Observational and modeling studies of the global electric circuit and the factors that cause it to change will be more sophisticated and detailed. Present global circuit models are quasi-steady state. New electrodynamic general circulation models with 30 min time steps are being developed and the global distribution of current sources produced by thunderstorms will be needed.

Data availability

The DMSP–OLS lightning climatology will be continued and provided to the Earth observing system data and information system (EOSDIS) distributed active archive center (DAAC) for the hydrologic cycle located at the NASA Marshall Space Flight Center in Huntsville, AL. The digital DMSP archive will continue to be located at the National Snow and Ice Data Center operated by the University of Colorado for NOAA. It is anticipated that the nighttime passes of the DMSP satellites will be provided on 8 mm tape to MSFC for digital extraction of lightning streaks.

References

Aceituno, P. (1988). On the functioning of the Southern Oscillation in the South American sector. Part I: surface climate. Mon. Wea. Rev., 116, 505–24.

Brooks, C. E. P. (1925). The distribution of thunderstorms over the globe. Geophys. Mem. London, 24, 147–64.

Chameides, W. L., Davis, D. D., Bradshaw, J., Rodgers, M., Sandholm, S. & Bai, D. B. (1987). An estimate of NO$_x$ production in electrified clouds based on NO estimates from the GTE CITE 1 fall 1983 field operation. J. Geophys. Res., 92, 2153–6.

Chen, T. (1987). Comments on 'Global distribution of midnight lightning: September 1977 to August 1978' Mon. Wea. Rev., 115, 3202.

Christian, H. J., Blakeslee, R. J. & Goodman, S. J. (1989). The detection of lightning from geostationary orbit. J. Geophys. Res. (Special Issue), 94, 13329–37.

Christian, H. J., Blakeslee, R. J. & Goodman, S. J. (1992). Lightning imaging sensor (LIS) for the Earth observing system, NASA TM-4350, available from the National Technical Information Service, Springfield, VA 22161–2171, 36pp.

Christy, J. R. (1991). Diabatic heating rate estimates from ECMWF analyses. J. Geophys. Res., 96, 5123–35.

Dye, J. E., Winn, W. P., Jones, J. J. & Breed, D. W. (1989). The electrification of New Mexico thunderstorms. Part I: Relationship between precipitation development and the onset of electrification. J. Geophys. Res., 94, 8643–56.

Fritsch, J. M., Kane, R. J. & Chelius, C. R. (1986). The contribution of mesoscale convective weather systems to the warm-season precipitation in the United States. *J. Climate Appl. Meteor.*, **25**, 1333–45.

Goodman, S. J. & MacGorman, D. R. (1986). Cloud-to-ground lightning activity in mesoscale convective complexes. *Mon. Wea. Rev.*, **114**, 2320–8.

Goodman, S. J., Buechler, D. E., Wright, P. D. & Rust, W. D. (1988*a*). Lightning and precipitation history of a microburst-producing storm. *Geophys. Res. Lett.*, **15**, 1183–8.

Goodman, S. J., Buechler, D. E. & Meyer, P. J. (1988*b*). Convective tendency images derived from a combination of lightning and satellite data. *Wea. and Forecasting*, **3**, 173–88.

Goodman, S. J., Buechler, D. E., Wright, P. D., Rust, W. D. & Nielsen, K. E. (1989). Polarization radar and electrical observations of microburst producing storms during COHMEX, *Preprints*, 24th Conf. on Radar Meteorology, March 27–31, Tallahassee, FL, Am. Meteor. Soc., Boston, 109–112.

Herman, J. R., Caruso, J. A. & Stone, R. G. (1965). Radio astronomy explorer (RAE)-1, observation of terrestrial radio noise. *Planet. Space Sci.*, **21**, 443.

Horner, F. & Bent, R. B. (1969). Measurement of terrestrial radio noise. *Proc. Roy. Soc. A.*, **311**, 527.

Inan, U. S. & Carpenter, D. L. (1987). Lightning-induced electron precipitation events observed at L 2.4 as phase and amplitude perturbations on subionospheric VLF signals. *J. Geophys. Res.*, **92**, 3293–303.

Janowiak, J. E. & Arkin, P. A. (1991). Rainfall variations in the tropics during 1986–1987. *J. Geophys. Res.*, **96**, 3359–73.

Keenan, T. D. & Carbone, R. E. (1989). A preliminary morphology of convective systems in tropical Northern Australia, *Preprints*, 24th Conf. on Radar Meteorology, March 27–31, Tallahassee, FL, Am. Meteor. Soc., Boston, 640–4.

Kotaki, M. & Katoh, C. (1983). The global distribution of thunderstorm activity observed by the ionosphere Sounding Satellite (ISS-b). *J. Atmos. and Terr. Physics*, **45**, 833.

Krider, E. P., Noggle, R. C. & Uman, M. A. (1976). A gated wideband magnetic direction finder for lightning return strokes. *J. Appl. Meteor.*, **15**, 301–6.

Lee, A. C. L. (1986). An experimental study of the remote location of lightning flashes using a VLF arrival time difference technique. *Quart. J. Roy. Met. Soc.*, **112**, 203–29.

Leiphart, J. P., Zeek, R. W., Bearce, L. S. & Toth, E. (1962). Penetration of the ionosphere by very low frequency radio signals. Interim results of the LOFTO-I experiment, *Proc. of the IRE*, **6**.

Levine, J. S. & Shaw, E. F. (1983). *In-situ* aircraft measurements of enhanced levels of N_2O associated with thunderstorm lightning. *Nature*, **303**, 312.

Lyons, W. A., Moon, D. A., Schuh, J. A., Pettit, N. J. & Eastman, J. R. (1989). The design and operation of a national lightning detection network using time-of-arrival technology. *Proceedings*, 1989 International Conf. on Lightning and Static Electricity, Sept. 26–28, Bath, England, National Interagency Coordination Group, 2B.2.1–2B.2.8.

McAnnelly, R. L. & Cotton, W. R. (1986). Meso-b-scale characteristics of an episode of meso-a-scale convective complexes. *Mon. Wea. Rev.*, **114**, 1740–70.

McConnell, A. & North, G. (1987). Sampling errors in satellite estimates of tropical rain. *J. Geophys. Res.*, **92**, 9567–71.

MacGorman, D. R., Maier, M. W. & Rust, W. D. (1984). Lightning strike density for the contiguous United States from thunderstorm duration records. US Nuc. Reg. Comm. Rept., *NUREG/CR-3759*, 44pp.

Marriott, W. (1908). (Title Unknown). *Quart. J. Roy. Met. Soc.*, **34**, 210.

Miller, D. & Fritsch, J. M. (1991). Mesoscale convective complexes in the Western Pacific region. *Mon. Wea. Rev.*, **119**, 2978–92.

Orville, R. E. (1982). Lightning detection from space. *CRC Handbook of Atmospherics*, Vol II, H. Volland, ed., pp. 79–97.

Orville, R. E. (1991). Lightning ground flash density in the contiguous United States – 1989. *Mon. Wea. Rev.*, **119**, 573–7.

Orville, R. E. & Henderson, R. (1986). Global distribution of midnight lightning: September 1977 to August 1978. *Mon. Wea. Rev.*, **114**, 2640.

Powell, J. W. (1983). Lightning research from space. *Spaceflight*, **25**, 280.

Price, C. & Rind, D. (1990). The effect of global warming on lightning frequencies, *Preprints*, 16th Conf. on Severe Local Storms, Oct. 22–26, Kananaskis Park, Alberta, Canada, Am. Meteor. Soc., Boston, pp. 748–51.

Reap, R. M. (1986). Evaluation of cloud-to-ground lightning data from the western United States for the 1983–84 summer seasons. *J. Climate Appl. Meteor.*, **25**, 785–99.

Reap, R. M. (1991). Climatological characteristics and objective prediction of thunderstorms over Alaska. *Weather and Forecasting*, **6**, 309–19.

Richard, P. & Auffray, G. (1985). VHF–UHF interferometric measurements, applications to lightning discharge mapping. *Radio Sci.*, **20**, 171–92.

Richard, P. & Auffray, G. *et al.* (1991). Localization of atmospheric discharges, a new way for severe weather nowcasting, *Preprints*, 25th Conf. on Radar Meteorology, June 24–28, Paris, France, Am. Meteor. Soc., Boston, pp. 911–15.

Riehl, H. & Malkus, J. S. (1958). On the heat balance in the equatorial trough zone. *Geophysica*, **6**, 503–37.

Ropelewski, C. F. & Halpert, M. S. (1987). Global and regional scale precipitation patterns associated with the El Niño/Southern Oscillation. *Mon. Wea. Rev.*, **115**, 1606–26.

Ropelewski, C. F. & Halpert, M. S. (1989). Precipitation patterns associated with the high index phase of the Southern Oscillation. *J. Climate*, **2**, 268–84.

Rutledge, S. A., Williams, E. R. & Keenan, T. D. (1992). The down under Doppler and electricity experiment (DUNDEE): Overview and preliminary results. *Bull. Am. Meteor. Soc.*, **73**, 3–16.

Shackford, C. R. (1960). Radar indications of a precipitation–lightning relationship in New England thunderstorms. *J. Appl. Meteor.*, **17**, 15–19.

Sparrow, J. G. & Ney, E. P. (1971). Lightning observations by satellite. *Nature*, **232**, 540.

Trenberth, K. E., Branstator, G. W. & Arkin, P. A. (1988). Origins of the 1988 North American drought. *Science*, **241**, 1640–5.

Turman, B. N. (1978). Analysis of lightning data from the DMSP satellite. *J. Geophys. Res.*, **83**, 5019.

Turman, B. N. (1979). Lightning detection from space. *Am. Scientist*, May–June, 321.

Turman, B. N. & Tettelbach, R. J. (1980). Synoptic-scale satellite lightning observations in conjunction with tornadoes. *Mon. Wea. Rev.*, **108**, 1980.

Turman, B. N. & Edgar, B. C. (1982). Global lightning distributions at dawn and dusk. *J. Geophys. Res.*, **87**, 1191.

Velasco, I. & Fritsch, J. M. (1987). Mesoscale convective complexes in the Americas. *J. Geophys. Res.*, **92**, 9591–613.

Vonnegut, B., Vaughan, O. H. Jr. & Brook, M. (1983). Photographs of lightning from the space shuttle. *Bull. Am. Meteor. Soc.*, **64**, 150.

Vorpahl, J. A., Sparrow, J. G. & Ney, E. P. (1970). Satellite observations of lightning. *Science*, **169**, 860.

Whipple, F. J. W. & Scrase, F. J. (1936). Point discharge in the electric field of the Earth. *Geophys. Memoirs (London) VIII*, **68**, 20.

Williams, E. R. (1989). The tripole structure of thunderstorms. *J. Geophys. Res.*, **94**, 13151–67.

Williams, E. R., Rutledge, S. A., Geotis, S. G., Renno, N., Rasmussen, E. & Rickenbach, T. (1992). A radar and electrical study of tropical 'hot towers'. *J. Atmos. Sci.*, **49**, in press.

Wilson, C. T. R. (1920). Investigations on lightning discharges and on the electric field of thunderstorms, *Phil. Trans. A.*, **221**, 73–115.

WMO (World Meteorological Organization) (1953). World Distribution of thunderstorm days. *WMO No. 21*, TP. 6 and supplement (1956), Geneva.

Zipser, E. J. & Lemone, M. A. (1980). Cumulonimbus vertical velocity events in GATE, Part II: Synthesis and model core structure. *J. Atmos. Sci.*, **37**, 2458–69.

PART IV

OCEANS

Ocean surface topography and circulation

C. J. KOBLINSKY

Introduction

The ocean circulation plays an important role in the Earth's climate system. For example, the ocean currents move one-third to one-half of the heat from the tropics toward the poles leading to a moderation of the climate at high latitudes. In this way, the ocean provides a memory and control function in the climate system. Similarly, dissolved gases, nutrients and other biochemical properties are all stored and transported by the sea. In order to improve the understanding and predictive capability of climate change, a quantitative understanding of the ocean circulation is required.

Ocean circulation and its variability are manifested in the sea surface topography, therefore satellite altimetry can be used to observe the circulation and describe its changes. No other instrument system is capable of providing observations of the global ocean circulation. In this chapter, a large-scale view of the sea surface topography and its variations are presented based upon measurements from the Seasat and Geosat altimeter missions. Over the past two decades these satellites, albeit limited by accuracy and duration, have provided a glimpse of the ocean circulation from space. In this decade, the joint US and French TOPEX/POSEIDON mission will observe the global ocean with unprecedented accuracy.

The altimeter measurement of the ocean circulation from space is simple in concept. Ocean currents on spatial scales exceeding the Rossby radius of deformation (10 to 100 km, depending on the latitude) and varying on times exceeding the inertial period (about 1 day, depending on the latitude) are, for the most part, the result of pressure gradients and are strongly influenced by the Earth's rotation (the Coriolis forces). The pressure gradients are manifested by deflections of the sea surface. These deflections and the Coriolis force determine the strength and direction of the flows in the same way that atmospheric flows move around high and low pressure areas.

Until the advent of satellite altimetry, observations of sea surface topography had been limited to ship- and shore-based measurements. These *in situ* observations provide only a poorly sampled picture of the sea surface topography and the structure of the circulation. Estimates of the mean global surface circulation have been constructed from historical hydrographic data (Levitus, 1982) and ship drift data (Meehl, 1982). The in-the-water measurements reveal the large scale surface circulation of the ocean as a distribution of basin scale gyres, tropical current systems spanning each ocean, and the Antarctic circumpolar current system circling the globe (Niiler, 1987).

Large-scale changes have been observed in the mean pattern of the circulation and topography. For example, a seasonal cycle in the mid-latitude circulation is caused by local surface heating resulting in a vertical variation of the surface topography of up to ± 15 cm (Pattulo et al., 1955). Seasonal variability in the tropics has been found to be caused by migrations in the wind patterns (Merle & Arnault, 1985; Busalacchi & Picault, 1983). Strong inter-annual fluctuations in sea level and surface circulation have been observed in the tropical Pacific related to the El Niño/southern oscillation (ENSO) event (Wyrtki, 1977, 1979, 1984, 1985). On interdecadal timescales, large-scale changes in surface topography and circulation have been found in the North Atlantic (Levitus, 1990) and in the Pacific (Sturges, 1987) and are predicted for the future because of the anticipated global warming (Manabe et al., 1991). On global scales, tide gauge observations have revealed that the mean level of the sea is rising at about 2 mm per year (Douglas, 1991), and models have suggested that it may accelerate to 7 mm per year in the coming century (Warrick & Oerlemans, 1990).

All in-the-water observations are plagued by inconsistencies in the reference level and insufficient coverage. Tide gauges, the standard method for directly measuring sea level change, are located on continental coastlines and the few available open ocean islands; this leads to contamination of the open ocean signal by coastal effects and undersampling. Tide gauges are not tied to a global geodetic reference frame, so that the absolute topography can not be deduced. Hydrographic observations from ships can be used to estimate the surface dynamic height in the open ocean by vertically integrating the density derived from direct temperature and salinity measurements. However, ships cannot adequately sample the global ocean because of limited resources. Furthermore, hydrographic estimates of dynamic height are referenced to a somewhat arbitrary 'level of no motion', rather than the geoid. Direct observations of currents, using drifting buoys or moored current meters, have been made at relatively few locations for extended periods of time. Satellite altimetry alleviates many of these difficulties.

The measurement of sea surface topography with a satellite altimeter is the result of differencing two large numbers, the range of the satellite from the surface and the height of the satellite from the center-of-mass of the Earth. The height of the satellite above the ocean is determined from the transit time of a radar pulse emitted from the satellite (Chelton, Walsh & MacArther, 1989). The height of the satellite above a reference ellipsoid of the Earth is determined from orbit determination procedures (Haines et al., 1990). In order to achieve a precision of 1 cm root-mean-square (rms) and an accuracy of 10 cm rms that are necessary for global change research, the technology must be accurate to one part in 10^8. In two decades, considerable progress has been made in the development of these systems to achieve this level of accuracy.

In the past few years, satellite altimeter observations have been made with sufficient precision to make preliminary estimates of the large scale and long period changes in the sea surface. The US Navy's Geosat altimeter mission was launched on March 15, 1985 and provided continuous global coverage of the ocean to the civilian community from November 8, 1986 until November, 1989 (McConathy & Kilgus, 1987). Coincidentally, dramatic improvements in modeling the Earth's gravity were achieved in preparation for the joint US (NASA) and French (Centre National d'Etudes Spatiales) TOPEX/POSEIDON ocean altimeter mission (Marsh et al., 1988, 1990). This has led to a precision of about 5 cm rms and an accuracy of less than 50 cm rms for Geosat measurements, a mission that was not designed for observing the large-scale ocean circulation. TOPEX/ POSEIDON will be the first satellite altimeter mission built with sufficient accuracy and precision to make quantitative estimates of the ocean circulation.

Methodology

The power of satellite altimeter measurements comes from the ability to obtain both mean and temporal measurements of sea surface topography on a global basis, relative to a geocentric coordinate system. The mean sea surface varies by approximately ±100 m about a reference ellipsoidal shape of the Earth. About 99% of this variation is related to the surface geopotential or geoid of the Earth. The largest high and low features in the geoid are caused by density inhomogeneities of the mantle resulting from convective processes, whereas smaller-scale structures are caused by the bottom topography and density variations in the lithosphere. Ocean circulation studies using sea surface topography examine the mean and time varying shape of the sea surface relative to the geoid.

The sea surface topography reflecting the ocean circulation varies by approximately ±1 m about the geoid. Temporal variations of the ocean surface are less than 1 m rms after tidal variations and surface gravity waves have been removed. In altimetric measurements, tides are removed by subtracting a modeled tide height (Chelton, 1988). Surface gravity waves, which constitute the visible sea level variations seen from the beach, are removed in the radar altimeter range measurement by averaging over a reflecting surface of about 2 km diameter (Chelton et al., 1989). A measure of the average surface gravity wave height within the measurement area is obtained from the rate of change of the return power in the reflected radar pulse (Chelton et al., 1989).

Methods for extracting the oceanographic signal from altimeter measurements focus on removing the geoid. At short length scales (<2500 km), the geoid is not well known and analysis techniques concentrate on removing the mean sea surface either along the ground track of the satellite for the case of repeating orbits (Cheney, Marsh & Beckley, 1983) or at locations of cross-over points between ascending and descending ground tracks for non-repeating orbits (Fu & Chelton, 1985). At longer scales (>1000 km), direct estimation of the surface topography relative to the geoid is possible by differencing independent estimates of the mean sea surface and the geoid (Marsh et al., 1990; Tapley et al., 1988).

The accuracy and precision of altimeter observations are dependent on a number of factors in the measurement system. The accuracy of satellite orbit determination procedures have increased dramatically over the past decade. Orbits for Geosat and Seasat, which were initially computed with a radial accuracy of about 2 m rms are presently about 50 cm rms (Haines et al., 1990) and limited to further improvement because of inaccurate and sparse tracking measurements. TOPEX/POSEIDON will have improved and more dense tracking observations and better dynamical models, so that the radial accuracy should approach 10 cm rms. Inaccuracies in the orbit are primarily of long wavelength, principally at once per satellite revolution (Engelis, 1987). These errors can be effectively removed at the expense of large-scale oceanographic information through high pass filtering for studies of sea surface topography at wavelengths less than 2500 km (Cheney et al., 1983; Fu & Chelton, 1985; Rosborough & Marshall, 1990), resulting in a precision of about 5 cm rms when compared with tide gauge measurements (Cheney & Miller, 1990). For studies of global-scale variations of sea surface topography, a joint inversion technique, which estimates the orbit and the surface topography simultaneously, has been able to separate the ocean signal from the orbit error with an accuracy of about 10 cm rms, derived from formal error estimates (Marsh *et al.*, 1990), and a precision of 5 cm rms, based on comparisons with tide gauge measurements (Koblinsky *et al.*, 1992).

A number of range corrections must be applied to the altimeter measurement to eliminate the effects of atmospheric refraction and the interaction between the radar pulse and the sea surface. While reasonably accurate algorithms for most of these corrections are available (Chelton, 1988; Chelton *et al.*, 1989), the necessary measurements may not be available or have sufficient precision. For example, Geosat did not make measurements of the wet troposphere refraction, and there is no coincident measure of the ionosphere refraction for Seasat, Geosat, or ERS-1. Random instrument noise affects only the shortest wavelength features (less than 50 km) and can be removed with a low-pass filter.

In the discussion that follows, estimates of global sea surface topography are described based on Geosat data from 1986 through 88 along with observations from Seasat in 1978. In order to examine the global scale sea surface mean and variations, the mean surface topography relative to the geoid has been computed on a monthly basis using a joint inversion procedure (Marsh *et al.*, 1990).

Topography and the general circulation

Three pictures of the surface circulation of the ocean are shown in Fig. 1. Two of these were derived from estimates of the surface topography. The topography estimates have been made from Geosat altimetry (Fig. 1(*a*)) and 70 years of hydrographic measurements (Fig. 1(*b*)). The surface circulation shown in Fig. 1(*c*) has been obtained from historical ship drift measurements (Meehl, 1982) and, unlike the topography estimates, includes both geostrophic and ageostrophic (surface wind driven currents) contributions.

The altimeter-derived mean dynamic topography shown in Fig. 1(*a*) was computed from two years of Geosat observations taken from 1986 through 1988. The altimeter analysis reflects many of the features in the *in situ* observations. On the largest scale, the Pacific is higher than the Atlantic because the Atlantic is composed of a higher salt content and, hence, denser water. From hydrographic data the mean height of the Pacific is about 47 cm above the Atlantic. The Geosat altimeter measured a difference of 37 cm. On smaller scales, subtropical highs in dynamic topography are found in

the western basins of all oceans, except the South Pacific. Vertical amplitudes differ somewhat in all basins between historical hydrography and altimetry. In the altimeter field relative to the historical hydrography, the South Atlantic high is stronger than the North Atlantic, the subtropical high in the western South Pacific is missing, the North Pacific high is weaker, and a high exists in the eastern Pacific.

The circulation patterns are comparable in the Northern Hemisphere. All three estimates show subpolar gyres in both the Atlantic and Pacific. The ship drift currents reveal a well-defined gyre in the Gulf of Alaska, whereas the other estimates suggest a gyre structure in the northwest corner of the Pacific. All three patterns reveal the large subtropical gyres of the North Atlantic and North Pacific. The geographic location and strength of the subtropical gyres varies among the three estimates. The North Atlantic equatorial current has apparently been smoothed out of the hydrographic data (these data have been filtered, removing wavelengths less than 2000 km with a spherical harmonic decomposition, in order to be consistent with the altimetry). The North Pacific Equatorial Current is missing in the central and eastern regions of the altimeter estimate.

In general, the tropical Pacific is considerably different in the altimetric solution. The reason for this is not apparent, anomalous sea level variations were found in the tropical Pacific because of the 1986–87 El Niño event (Miller, Cheney & Douglas, 1988). However, these were not of sufficient magnitude to cause the discrepancy shown in Fig. 1. The tropical Indian Ocean circulation varies considerably between the three estimates and may result from undersampling in the ship-based estimates and oversmoothing in the altimetric estimate. The ship drift average and the altimetric estimate are similar in the tropical Atlantic.

In the Southern Hemisphere, the Antarctic Circumpolar Current is apparent in all three representations, however the subtropical circulations vary considerably. Ship-based observations are notoriously sparse in the Southern Hemisphere, so that one can expect an oversimplification in their estimates of the mean circulation.

The lack of consistency between the three maps shown in Fig. 1 is representative of the knowledge of general circulation. All of these measurements have significant problems at the present time. Only the altimetry measurement can be expected to improve in the foreseeable future because of TOPEX/POSEIDON. Anomalous features in the Geosat altimeter mean dynamic topography could have been caused by a variety of potential error sources, including such subtleties as inaccuracies in the satellite tracking station positions or in the gravity force model that is used in the precision orbit determination. For example, errors in the tracking station

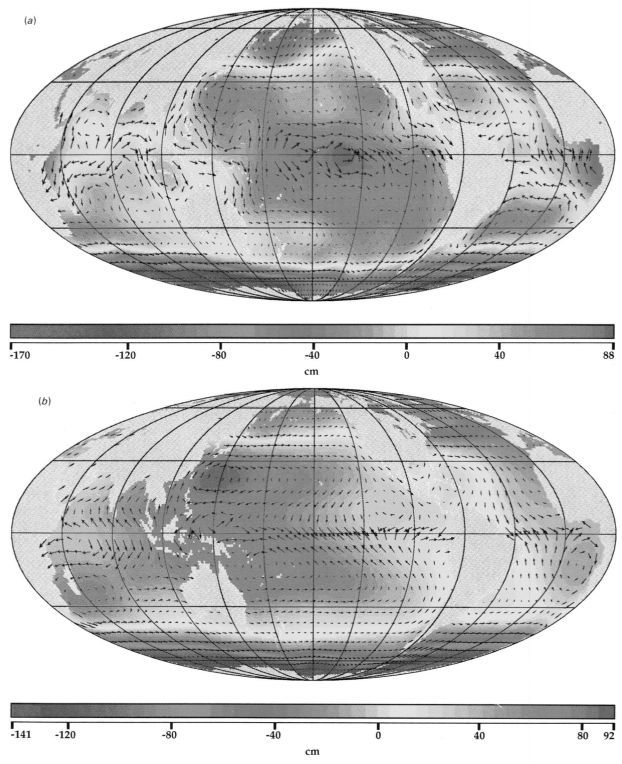

Fig. 1. The sea surface topography relative to the geoid reflects the surface geostrophic component of the ocean circulation. (*a*) An estimate of the sea surface topography relative to the geoid and the associated geostrophic circulation derived from 2 years of Geosat altimetry. (*b*) An estimate of the sea surface topography relative to a reference surface at 2250 db pressure in the ocean and the associated surface circulation derived from an average of 70 years of historical *in situ* observations (Levitus, 1982). (*c*) The mean total (geostrophic and ageostrophic) surface circulation derived from the average of historical ship drift observations (Meehl, 1982).

(c)

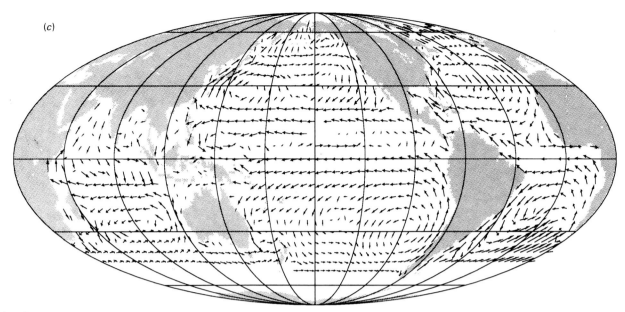

Fig. 1. (cont.)

positions lead to a bias in the center of mass and erroneous hemispheric shifts in the distribution of topography. Simulations have shown that for Geosat this error resulted in altimetric estimates of the topography being higher in the Southern Hemisphere relative to the Northern Hemisphere, when compared with hydrographic observations. Errors in the orbit force model can lead to systematic or geographically correlated orbit errors that cause anomalous highs or lows in the mean dynamic topography (Tapley & Rosborough, 1985). For Geosat the anomalously high surface topography in the eastern Pacific may be caused by this error. Both of these errors should be substantially reduced for TOPEX/POSEIDON.

Variations in sea surface topography

Mesoscale eddies

Sea level variability is dominated by short wavelengths (50 to 500 km) and time scales (10 to 100 days). These fluctuations are principally caused by the meanders of intense currents and the movement of isolated vortices or mesoscale eddies (Robinson, 1983). The mean variations in topography as determined from altimetry are shown in Fig. 2. This variability is estimated as the root-mean-square variation in time of the Geosat altimeter height measurement about the mean elevation along the altimeter groundtrack following procedures outlined by Cheney et al. (1983).

Satellite altimetry has proved to be extremely useful for providing valuable new information about the ocean mesoscale. The altimeter measurements show that eddies predominate in the western boundary currents (e.g. Gulf Stream) and Antarctic circumpolar current. Topographic steering of mesoscale structures in the Antarctic circumpolar current is found to be quite prevalent (Sandwell & Zhang, 1989; Chelton et al., 1990). Outside of these major current systems, secondary regions of eddy variability are found along the westward flow of the subtropical gyres. These less energetic regions may be caused by local instabilities of the mean flow and/or the advection of eddies from the major current systems. For example, eddies formed in the turbulent Agulhas retroflection region south of South Africa, containing water from the Indian Ocean, have been observed to traverse westward across the mid-latitude South Atlantic (Gordon & Haxby, 1990).

Seasonal modulations of eddy scale sea level variability have been found by Zlotnicki, Fu & Patzert (1989) in the subpolar gyres and may be related to fluctuations in wind forcing. Chelton et al. (1990) describe seasonal changes in the mesoscale variability of the Southern Ocean. They find that seasonal and inter-annual changes in eddy variability are quite small, except in the vicinity of western boundary currents. The seasonal variations of the Gulf Stream have been studied by Vasquez, Zlotnicki & Fu (1990) and Kelly and Gille (1990); Qiu, Kelly & Joyce (1991) have analyzed the Kuroshio. These studies indicate that there are significant annual variations in the transport of these major current systems.

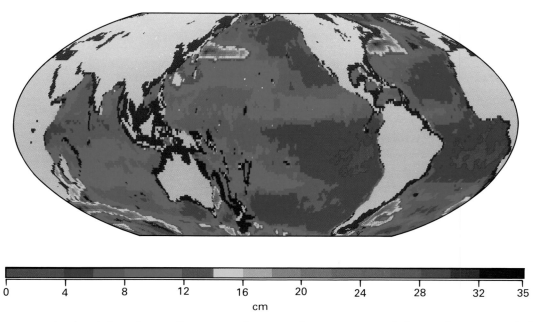

Fig. 2. The root-mean-square (rms) variation of sea surface topography averaged over two years relative to a 1 year mean derived from the Geosat altimeter data. Fluctuations of the sea surface at horizontal scales less than about 50 km, including surface waves, are not shown.

Large scale seasonal changes

Variations in topography at larger scales have been more diffi-cult to examine with Geosat data because of the large orbit errors. Monthly averaged estimates of the deviation of large scale (> 1000 km) sea surface topography from an annual mean are shown in Fig. 3. Comparisons with monthly aver-aged tide gauge measurements show that the typical dif-ference between the two observations is about 5 cm rms (Cheney & Miller, 1990; Koblinsky et al., 1992). Long-term changes, such as annual and inter-annual variations, appear to be quite consistent between the two measurements. In addition, preliminary analyses suggest that the estimates of large scale topography derived from Geosat are highly cor-related with independent estimates of surface forcing (winds, temperature and pressure), suggesting the presence of robust geophysical signals in the altimeter measurements (Wunsch, 1991b; Koblinsky et al., 1992).

A direct estimate of the annual cycle of sea level has been made from two years of monthly surface topography anomalies. Estimates of the amplitude and phase of the annual cycle are shown in Fig. 4. Multi-year averages of historical in situ data and altimeter measurements agree quite well in the mid-latitude regions.

An important signal in the seasonal variation of sea level is the expansion and contraction of the upper ocean at mid-latitudes caused by local surface heat storage (Patullo et al., 1955; Gill & Niiler, 1973). The altimeter measurements show a strong annual cycle of sea level in the mid-latitudes that is quite similar to our understanding of this phenomena from historical in situ measurements. In the oceanic winter/spring (February through June) the Northern Hemisphere ocean is below the mean throughout most of the mid-latitude region. The lowest region of topography is in the western half of each basin because of a stronger heat exchange with the continental air-mass (Gill and Niiler, 1973). In the oceanic summer/fall (August through December) the pattern is rever-sed, the upper ocean has absorbed heat and expanded. The same pattern, albeit out of phase with the Northern Hemi-sphere, can be seen in the Southern Hemisphere. The amplitude of the Northern Hemisphere mid-latitude annual cycle is much stronger than the Southern Hemisphere, con-sistent with in-the-water observations (Levitus, 1982) and atmospheric climatologies (Oberhuber, 1988). Note that secondary highs occur in offshore eastern boundary current regions, such as the California Current, suggesting summer time accelerations of these systems.

In the tropics, the seasonal variations are forced by the annual north/south migration of the trade wind systems. In the Atlantic, the annual cycle is robust and Geosat altimeter measurements are found to be very consistent with in situ measurements (Carton, 1989). In the Pacific, inter-annual variability is much stronger than the annual cycle. The two years of Geosat measurements are not long enough to separate the annual variation from the strong inter-annual changes.

The semi-annual cycle, shown in Fig. 5, has a much

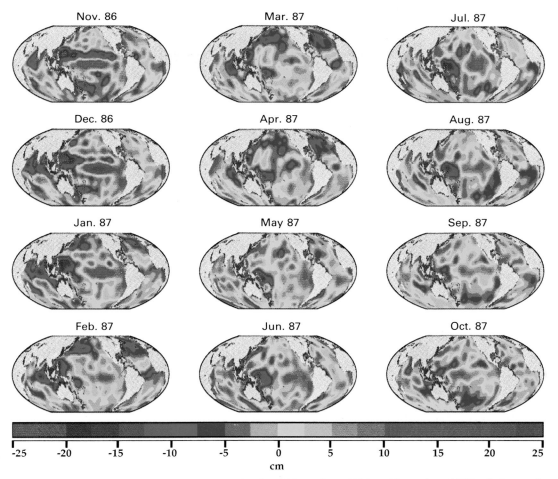

Fig. 3. The change in monthly averaged sea surface topography from November, 1986 to November, 1987 relative to the two-year mean topography shown in Fig. 1, derived from Geosat altimeter measurements. Fluctuations of the sea surface at horizontal scales less than about 1000 km are not shown.

weaker amplitude than the annual cycle. The strongest signals are found in the Tropics. There are two large amplitude areas on the east and west sides of the tropical Indian Ocean which are out of phase. These fluctuations suggest a large semi-annual fluctuation of the Indian Ocean equatorial current with a maximum flow toward the east in May and November, leading to a higher sea level in the east, and a flow toward the west in March and September. Historically, direct observations have found a strong eastward equatorial current in May, with a weaker eastward current in October, during the periods of the transitions from the south-west monsoon in summer and the north-east monsoon in winter (Knox & Anderson, 1985).

Inter-annual change

In the 1986–87 time frame, the tropical Pacific experienced an El Niño-southern oscillation (ENSO) event (Philander,

1990). The trade winds slackened in intensity and large undulations of surface topography propagated across the equatorial Pacific from west to east (Miller, Cheney & Douglas, 1988). This can be seen in the altimeter measurements shown in Fig. 3 as a high sea level in the central tropical Pacific in the fall.

An important role of altimetry in global change research will be the ability to detect large scale inter-annual changes in the ocean surface topography and circulation, including the global mean change in the level of the sea. Tide gauge observations show that long-term changes in sea level are not homogeneous and appear to have regional patterns (Barnett, 1990). The three-year Geosat mission has permitted the first view from space of these long-term patterns of the sea surface. Fig. 6 shows the change in annual average sea level between 1988 and 1987 based on Geosat measurements. Large-scale patterns of change are found between 1987 and 1988 with the dominant change occurring in the tropical Pacific.

Amplitude

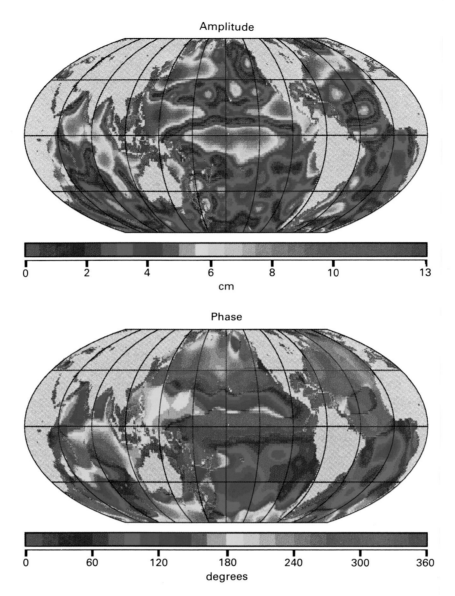

Phase

Fig. 4. The annual fluctuation of sea surface topography in terms of amplitude and phase derived from Geosat altimeter data. Fluctuations of the sea surface at horizontal scales less than about 1000 km are not shown.

One of the greatest oceanographic successes of the Geosat mission was the demonstration that altimetry could be used to monitor large-scale changes in tropical sea level. The transport of warm surface water into, and out of, the equatorial Pacific is thought to play an important role in regulating the ENSO. Although many processes are involved in this coupled atmosphere/ocean phenomena, one important indicator of the condition in the tropics appears to be the volume of upper layer water near the equator. Analyses of Pacific island tide gauge data (Wyrtki, 1979, 1985) have helped document some aspects of this water transport cycle, but the immense size of the Pacific results in undersampling by this and all other conventional measurement techniques. The long time series of Geosat measurements permitted the first Pacific basin wide synoptic view of sea level change during an ENSO event (Miller et al., 1988; Miller & Cheney, 1990). Fig. 6 shows that, in 1987, during the El Niño, the trade winds relaxed and sea level was high throughout the eastern tropical Pacific. The following year, the trade winds were strong, leading to La Niña conditions, and sea level was depressed in the eastern tropical Pacific and high in the western region.

Estimates of decadal changes in sea level from *in situ* observations have suggested the presence of basin wide changes on the order of 1 to 10 cm (Sturges, 1987; Levitus,

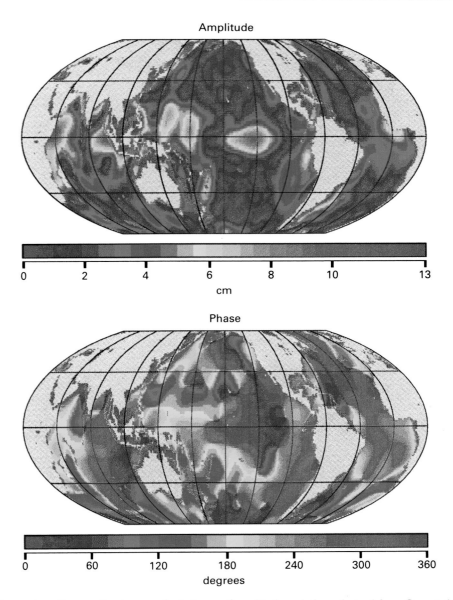

Fig. 5. The semi-annual fluctuation of sea surface topography in terms of amplitude and phase derived from Geosat altimeter data. Fluctuations of the sea surface at horizontal scales less than about 1000 km are not shown.

1990). This signal is large enough be observed with satellite altimeters. The difference between the surface dynamic topography in the summer of 1987 and the summer of 1978 is shown in Fig. 7 as derived from Geosat and Seasat altimeter data (Haines, 1991 presents a detailed discussion of the comparison of sea level estimates between Geosat and Seasat).

In the equatorial Pacific and Indian Oceans sea level is higher in the east and lower in the west in the summer of 1987 relative to 1978. In the Pacific, this is the result of the 1986–87 ENSO event. The time series of sea level that are available from tide gauges clearly show that the observed difference between 1978 and 1987 from the altimetry actually

occurred between the summers of 1986 and 1987, as a result of the ENSO event. Conditions in the summer of 1978 were very similar to the summer of 1986.

In the mid-latitude oceans, it appears that the subtropical and eastern subpolar gyres of the North Pacific have increased in height by about 10% between the summers of 1978 and 1987, whereas the western subpolar gyre has become lower than the mean. This would imply an increase in the circulation of the North Pacific subtropical and western subpolar gyres. Trenberth (1990) has suggested that the Aleutian low pressure system in the atmosphere intensified during the winters of the 1980s. This led to stronger mid-

C. J. KOBLINSKY

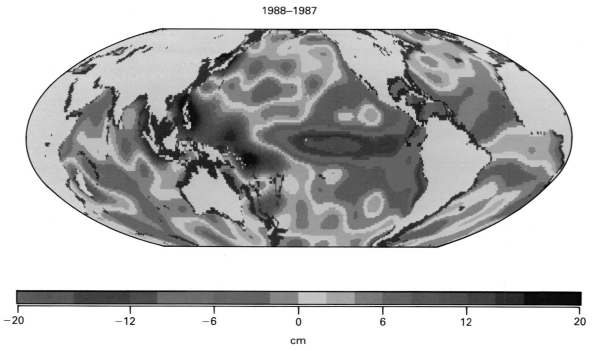

Fig. 6. The change in annual averaged sea surface topography between 1988 and 1987 derived from Geosat altimeter data. Fluctuations of the sea surface at horizontal scales less than about 1000 km are not shown.

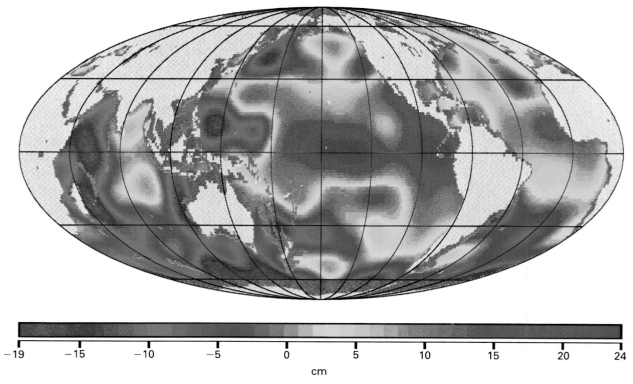

Fig. 7. The change in large-scale sea surface topography between the summer of 1987 and the summer of 1978 derived from Geosat and Seasat altimeter data.

latitude surface winds and wind stress curl and accompanying changes in sea surface temperature, implying an increase in the North Pacific ocean circulation. Comparisons with tide gauges are sparse but consistent with the differences measured by the altimeters. Unlike the tropics, some of the sea level difference appears to be consistent with a decadal change. For example, at Hawaii a gradual decrease in sea level has been observed in tide gauges between 1978 and 1987; however, shorter term inter-annual oscillations make it difficult to separate the decadal change from inter-annual variability in the isolated tide gauge measurements.

While their accuracy has been limited, Geosat and Seasat have provided an opportunity to develop the methods for measuring topographic changes over several years using satellite altimeters. Continuous and accurate (at least TOPEX/POSEIDON specifications) satellite altimeter measurements for several decades could provide the capability to detect long-term changes in the ocean climate.

The global perspective of satellite altimetry allows for a new approach to estimating the change in the mean level of the sea. Born et al. (1986) have suggested that changes in global mean sea level over the period of a year can be computed with an accuracy of a few millimeters using globally distributed altimetric measurements of sufficient accuracy. Attempts to make this computation with Seasat (Born et al., 1986) and Geosat (Nerem et al., 1992) have shown that neither of these spacecraft provided the necessary accuracy. The errors for both analyses were an order of magnitude larger than the signal. However, these studies strongly suggest that the improved accuracy provided by TOPEX/POSEIDON should be sufficient to make this measurement with the necessary precision.

Limitations

Satellite altimetry is a developing technology and a number of improvements need to be made before routine and accurate measurements of sea surface topography will be available. While estimates of the large-scale sea level variations from Geosat and Seasat appear to have some relationship to *in situ* observations over large areas, the error budget remains uncertain (Ray & Koblinsky, 1991).

The largest error in the altimeter measurement system comes from the orbit determination. This error is greatest at long wavelengths and varies slowly in time. This uncertainty has a significant impact on estimates of short-term climate change in sea level from altimetry. Removal of this error through selective filters is not a solution; the accuracy must be improved. The orbit determination process integrates a force model with direct observations of satellite position from selec-

ted sites around the Earth. The largest source of the orbit determination error has been the gravity field model of the Earth. However, recent orbital computations for Geosat show that gravity models have improved to the point where inadequacies in the satellite drag model (non-conservative forces) are becoming a significant factor.

The determination of satellite orbits with decimeter accuracy for the radial component require precise satellite tracking. At present, most satellite tracking is done from Earth with radar or laser systems. Laser tracking provides the best accuracy with errors of a few centimeters. Radar systems are more prolific and provide all weather coverage, but, until recently, they have been much less accurate than lasers. In the next decade, nearly continuous accurate satellite position determination may become a reality through the use of new tracking systems such as the French Doppler Orbitography and Radiopositioning Integrated by Satellite (DORIS), a very precise ground to satellite radar system, and the space-based US Global Positioning System. Both of these systems will be used on TOPEX/POSEIDON.

A number of corrections are made to the altimeter range measurement (Chelton et al., 1989). The path delay caused by atmospheric refraction is a concern for Geosat measurements because of the lack of simultaneous estimates for either the wet troposphere or the ionosphere. The sea state bias, which is caused by differential scattering at the surface, is not well understood, but can be estimated from altimeter measurements of the wave heights. Ocean tides are removed from the altimeter estimates based on hydrodynamical models and have an accuracy of about 10 cm rms. Atmospheric load is removed based on surface pressure forecasts that have accuracy problems in the Southern Hemisphere because of insufficient observations.

Many of the altimeter range corrections have been improved for Seasat and Geosat. For example, ancillary satellite measurements have been used to estimate the wet troposphere range delay and improved tidal estimates are being derived directly from the altimetry. Future missions will observe some corrections directly. For example, on TOPEX/POSEIDON a passive microwave sensor will observe the columnar water vapor content and the ionospheric range delay will be removed by using a two frequency altimeter.

Applications

Satellite altimetry is the first space-based instrument to provide a global and nearly synoptic measure of a significant component of the ocean circulation. It is hoped that these observations can be used to improve knowledge of the deep circulation with numerical ocean circulation models using data assimilation.

A number of basic ocean research programs have successfully utilized altimeter data. The results of these studies (for reviews see Brown & Cheney, 1983; Douglas, McAdoo & Cheney, 1987; and the edited collections of articles by Bernstein, 1982; Kirwan Ahrens & Born, 1983; Douglas & Cheney, 1990) show that altimetry is quantitatively useful for a wide variety of research, including: determination of the general circulation (Tapley *et al.*, 1988; Marsh *et al.*, 1990; Nerem *et al.*, 1990); the variations of the circulation at large spatial scales (Miller *et al.*, 1988; Chelton *et al.*, 1990; Wunsch, 1991*a*); the global mapping of eddy kinetic energy (Cheney *et al.*, 1983; Sandwell & Zhang, 1989; Zlotnicki *et al.*, 1989; Le Traon, Rouquet & Boissier, 1990; Le Traon, 1991; De Mey & Menard, 1989); measuring fluctuations in the great current systems (Chelton *et al.*, 1990; Zlotnicki, 1991; Kelly & Gille, 1990); and improving ocean predictability through the assimilation of altimeter data in numerical models (e.g. De Mey & Robinson, 1987; Malanotte-Rizzoli & Holland, 1989; Verron, 1990; Haines, 1991).

Unlike previous measurements of the level of the air–sea interface, satellite altimetry provides observations in a global coordinate system that is referenced to the geoid. Consequently, absolute determination of the ocean circulation can be made by combining altimetry, in-the-water observations, and dynamical models (Wunsch & Gaposchkin, 1980). This may be the only way to observe decadal or longer variations in the deep circulation over large regions. In the decade of the 1990s, the combination of observations and models from the World Ocean Circulation Experiment and altimeter measurements from the TOPEX/POSEIDON satellite will provide the first opportunity to test these ideas.

References

Barnett, T. P. (1990). Recent Changes in Sea Level: *A Summary, in sea Level Change*. National Academy Press, 37–51.

Bernstein R. L., ed. (1982). Seasat Special Issue I: geophysical evaluation. *J. Geophys. Res.*, **87**, 3173–438.

Born, G. H., Tapley, B. D., Ries, J. C. & Stewart, R. H. (1986). Accurate measurement of mean sea level changes by altimetric satellites. *J. Geophys. Res.*, **91**, 11775–82.

Brown, O. & Cheney, R. E. (1983). Advances in satellite oceanography. *Rev. Geophys. & Space Phys.*, **21**, 1216–30.

Busalacchi, A. J. & Picaut, J. (1983). Seasonal variability from a model of the tropical Atlantic Ocean. *J. Phys. Oceanog.*, **13**, 1564–88.

Carton, J. A. (1989). Estimates of sea level in the tropical Atlantic Ocean using Geosat altimetry. *J. Geophys. Res.*, **94**, 8029–39.

Chelton, D. B. (1988). WOCE/NASA Altimeter Algorithm Workshop, *US WOCE Technical Report No. 2*, 70pp, US Planning Office for the World Ocean Circulation Experiment (WOCE), College Station, Texas.

Chelton, D. B., Schlax, M. G., Witter, D. L. & Richman, J. G. (1990). Geosat altimeter observations of the surface circulation of the Southern Ocean. *J. Geophys. Res.*, **95**, 17877–903.

Chelton, D. B., Walsh, E. J. & MacArthur, J. L. (1989). Pulse compression and sea level tracking in satellite altimetry. *J. Atmos. & Oceanic Technol.*, **6**, 407–38.

Cheney, R. E. & Miller, L. (1990) Recovery of the sea level signal in the western tropical Pacific from Geosat altimetry. *J. Geophys. Res.*, **95**, 2977–84.

Cheney, R. E., Marsh, J. G. & Beckley, B. D. (1983). Global mesoscale variability from colinear tracks of Seasat altimeter data. *J. Geophys. Res.* **88**, 4343–54.

De Mey, P. & Menard, Y. (1989). Synoptic analysis and dynamical adjustment of Geos-3 and Seasat altimeter eddy fields in the northwest Atlantic. *J. Geophys. Res.*, **94**, 6221–30.

De Mey, P. & Robinson, A. R. (1987). Assimilation of altimeter eddy fields in a limited-area quasi-geostrophic model. *J. Phys. Oceanog.*, **17**, 2281–93.

Douglas, B. C. (1991). Global sea level rise. *J. Geophys. Res.*, **96**, 6981–92.

Douglas, B. C. & Cheney, R. E. (1990). Geosat: beginning a new era in satellite oceanography. *J. Geophys. Res.*, **95**, 2833–6.

Douglas, B. C., McAdoo, D. C. & Cheney, R. E. (1987). Oceanographic and geophysical applications of satellite altimetry. *Rev. Geophys. and Space Phys.*, **25**, 875–80.

Engelis, T. (1987). Radial orbit error reduction and sea surface topography determination using satellite altimetry. *Department of Geodetic Science and Surveying Ohio State University Report No. 377*, Columbus, Ohio, 178pp.

Fu, L.-L. & Chelton, D. B. (1985). Observing large-scale temporal variability of ocean currents by satellite altimetry: with application to the Antarctic circumpolar current. *J. Geophys. Res.*, **90**, 4721–39.

Gill, A. E. & Niiler, P. P. (1973). The theory of seasonal variability in the ocean. *Deep-Sea Res.*, **20**, 141–77.

Gordon, A. L. & Haxby, W. F. (1990). Agulhas eddies invade the South Atlantic: evidence from Geosat altimeter and shipboard conductivity-temperature-depth survey. *J. Geophys. Res.*, **95**, 3117–28.

Haines, B. J. (1991). Evaluation of Geosat and Seasat orbits and altimetry with application to observing long term sea level changes in the North Pacific. PhD Dissertation, University of Colorado, Boulder, Colorado, 165pp.

Haines, B. J., Born, G. H., Marsh, J. G. & Williamson, R. G. (1990). Precise orbit computation for the Geosat exact repeat mission. *J. Geophys. Res.*, **95**, 2871–86.

Haines, K. (1991). A direct method for assimilating sea surface height data into ocean models with adjustments to the deep circulation. *J. Phys. Oceanog.*, **21**, 843–68.

Kelly, K. A. & Gille, S. T. (1990). Gulf Stream surface transport and statistics at 69° W for the Geosat altimeter. *J. Geophys. Res.*, **95**, 3149–61.

Kirwan, A. D., Ahrens, T. J. & Born, G. H. ed. (1983). Seasat Special Issue II: scientific results. *J. Geophys. Res.*, 88, 1529–52.

Knox, R. A. & Anderson, D. L. T. (1985). Advances in the study of low-latitude ocean circulation. *Prog. in Oceanog.*, 14, 259–318.

Koblinsky, C. J., Nerem, R. S., Williamson, R. G. & Klosko, S. M. (1992). Global scale variations in sea surface topography determined from satellite altimetry. *AGU Geophysical Monograph; Sea level changes: determination and effects*, IUGG vol 11, 155–165.

Le Traon, P. Y., Rouquet, M. C. & Boissier, C. (1990). Spatial scales of mesoscale variability in the North Atlantic as deduced from Geosat data. *J. Geophys. Res.*, 95, 20267–85.

Le Traon, P. Y. (1991). Time scales of mesoscale variability and their relationship with space scales in the North Atlantic. *J. Marine Res.*, 49, 1–26.

Levitus, S. (1982). Climatological atlas of the world ocean. *NOAA Professional Paper 13*, 173pp.

Levitus, S. (1990). Interpentadal variability of steric sea level and geopotential thickness of the North Atlantic Ocean, 1970–1974 versus 1955–1959. *J. Geophys. Res.*, 95, 5233–8.

Malanotte-Rizzoli, P. & Holland, W. R. (1989). Assimilation of altimeter data into an ocean circulation model: space versus time resolution studies. *J. Phys. Oceanog.*, 19, 1507–34.

Manabe, S., Stouffer, R. J., Spelman, M. J. & Bryan, K. (1991). Transient responses of a coupled ocean-atmosphere model to gradual changes of atmospheric CO_2. Part I: annual mean response. *J. Climate*, 4, 785–818.

Marsh, J. G., Lerch, F. J., Putney, B. H., Christodoulidis, D. C., Smith, D. E., Felsentreger, T. L., Sanchez, B. V., Klosko, S. M., Pavlis, E. C., Martin, T. V., Robbins, J. W., Williamson, R. G., Colombo, O. L., Rowlands, D. D., Eddy, W. F., Chandler, N. L., Rachlin, K. E., Patel, G. B., Bhati, S. & Chinn, D. S. (1988). A new gravitational model for the Earth from satellite tracking data: GEM-T1. *J. Geophys. Res.*, 93, 6169–215.

Marsh, J. G., Koblinsky, C. J., Lerch, F. J., Klosko, S. M., Robbins, J. W., Williamson, R. G. & Patel, G. B. (1990). Dynamic sea surface topography, gravity, and improved orbit accuracies from the direct evaluation of Seasat altimetry data. *J. Geophys. Res.*, 95, 13,129–50.

McConathy, D. R. & Kilgus, C. C. (1987). The Navy Geosat Mission: an overview. *Johns Hopkins APL Technical Digest*, 8, 170–5.

Meehl, G. A. (1982). Characteristics of surface current flow inferred from a global ocean current data set, *J. Phys. Oceanog.*, 12, 538–55.

Merle, J. & Arnault, S. (1985). Seasonal variability of the surface dynamic topography in the tropical Atlantic Ocean. *J. Marine Res.*, 43, 267–88.

Miller, L., Cheney, R. E. & Douglas, B. C. (1988). Geosat altimeter observations of Kelvin waves and the 1986–87 El Niño. *Science*, 239, 52–4.

Miller, L. & Cheney, R. E. (1990). Large-scale meridional transport in the tropical Pacific Ocean during the 1986–1987 El Niño from Geosat. *J. Geophys. Res.*, 95, 17905–20.

Nerem, R. S., Tapley, B. D. & Shum, C. K. (1990). Determination of the ocean circulation using Geosat altimetry. *J. Geophys. Res.*, 95, 3163–79.

Nerem, R. S., Koblinsky, C. J., Williamson, R. G. & Klosko, S. M. (1992). Observing large-scale sea surface topography from space: part I – techniques and initial results. *J. Geophys. Res.*, submitted.

Niiler, P. P. (1987). The observational basis for large scale circulation. In *General Circulation of the Ocean*. H. D. I. Arbarbanel and W. R. Young, ed., Springer-Verlag, New York, pp. 1–54.

Oberhuber, J. M. (1988). An atlas based on the 'COADS' data set: the budgets of heat, buoyancy, and turbulent kinetic energy at the surface of the global ocean. *Max-Planck-Institut fur Meteorologie, Report 15*.

Pattulo, J., Munk, W., Revelle, R. & Strong, E. (1955). The seasonal oscillation in sea level. *J. Marine Res.*, 14, 88–155.

Philander, S. G. H. (1990). *El Niño, La Niña, and the Southern Oscillation*. Academic Press, New York.

Qiu, B., Kelly, K. A. & Joyce, T. M. (1991). Mean flow and variability in the Kuroshio Extension from Geosat altimetry data. *J. Geophys. Res.*, 96, 18491–508.

Ray, R. D. & Koblinsky, C. J. (1991). On the effectiveness of Geosat altimeter corrections, *Int. J. Remote Sensing*. 12, 1979–84.

Robinson, A. R., ed. (1983). *Eddies in Marine Science* Springer-Verlag, New York.

Rosborough, G. W. & Marshall, J. A. (1990). Effect of orbit error on determining sea surface variability using satellite altimetry. *J. Geophys. Res.*, 95, 5273–8.

Sandwell, D. T. & Zhang, B. (1989). Global mesoscale variability from the Geosat exact repeat mission – correlation with ocean depth. *J. Geophys. Res.*, 94, 17971–84.

Sturges, W. (1987). Large-scale coherence of sea level at low frequencies, *J. Phys. Oceanog.*, 17, 2084–94.

Tapley, B. D. & Rosborough, G. W. (1985). Geographically correlated orbit error and its effect on satellite altimeter missions. *J. Geophys. Res.*, 90, 11,817–31.

Tapley, B. D., Nerem, R. S., Shum, C. K., Ries, J. C. & Yuan, D. N. (1988). Determination of the general ocean circulation from a joint gravity field solution. *Geophys. Res. Lett.*, 15, 1109–12.

Trenberth, K. E. (1990). Recent observed interdecadal climate changes in the Northern Hemisphere. *Bull. Am. Meteorol. Soc.*, 71, 988–93.

Vasquez, J., Zlotnicki, V. & Fu, L.-L. (1990). Sea level variabilities in the Gulf Stream between Cape Hatteras and 50 W: a Geosat study. *J. Geophys. Res.*, 95, 17957–64.

Verron, J. (1990). Altimeter data assimilation into an ocean circulation model: sensitivity to orbital parameters. *J. Geophys. Res.*, 95, 11443–59.

Warrick, R. A. & Oerlemans, H. (1990). Sea level rise. In *Climate Change: The IPCC Scientific Assessment*, J. T. Houghton, G. J. Jenkins, and J. J. Ephraums, eds. Cambridge University Press, New York, 257–310.

Wunsch, C. (1991a). Global-scale sea surface topography from combined altimetric and tide gauge measurements. *J. Geophys. Res.*, 96, 15053–82.

Wunsch, C. (1991*b*). Large-scale response of the ocean to atmospheric forcing at low frequencies. *J. Geophys. Res.*, **96**, 15083–92.

Wunsch, C. & Gaposhkin, M. (1980). On using satellite altimetry to determine the general circulation of the oceans with application to geoid improvement. *Rev. Geophys. Space Phys.*, **18**, 725–45.

Wyrtki, K. (1977). Sea level during the 1972 El Niño. *J. Phys. Oceanog.*, **7**, 779–87.

Wyrtki, K. (1979). The response of sea surface topography to the 1976 El Niño. *J. Phys. Oceanog.*, **9**, 1223–31.

Wyrtki, K. (1984). The slope of sea level along the equator during the 1982/1983 El Niño. *J. Geophys. Res.*, **89**, 10419–24.

Wyrtki, K. (1985). Water displacements in the Pacific and the genesis of El Niño cycles. *J. Geophys. Res.*, **90**, 7129–32.

Zlotnicki, V. (1991). Sea level differences across the Gulf Stream and Kuroshio Extension. *J. Phys. Oceanog.*, **21**, 599–609.

Zlotnicki, V., Fu, L.-L. & Patzert, W. (1989). Seasonal variability in global sea level observed with Geosat altimetry, *J. Geophys. Res.*, **94**, 17959–69.

Sea surface temperature

E. G. NJOKU AND O. B. BROWN

Introduction

For centuries the surface temperature distribution of the oceans has been known to provide information on the locations of strong ocean currents such as the Gulf Stream, Somali, and Kuroshio currents. Only recently, however, has the profound role that ocean temperature plays in regulating weather and climate been understood. The oceans and atmosphere form a coupled system separated by an interface through which heat, moisture, and momentum are exchanged. The state of the ocean–atmosphere system is driven by radiation received from the Sun which causes uneven heating of the Earth's surface, in particular excess heating at the equator relative to the poles. The surface temperature gradients cause fluid motions in the atmosphere and oceans which redistribute heat towards the poles and which depend on dynamical processes that have long-term mean, seasonal, diurnal, and transient components (storms and eddies).

Sea surface temperature (SST) is an important factor in the physical processes underlying the surface energy balance, the sensible and latent heat exchanges at the air–sea interface, and the circulation of the atmosphere and oceans (Gill, 1982). The heat fluxes depend critically on SST, as does the upward long-wave radiation emitted from the ocean. Ocean circulation is influenced by the SST distribution through its effect on atmospheric circulation and surface winds, which, in turn, drive the ocean currents, and also through its effect on sea water density which contributes a buoyancy component to the ocean circulation. A major research goal is the development of an improved understanding of these processes, which can only be achieved by more precise and better sampled measurements of ocean surface parameters such as SST.

Departures from the long-term climatological mean SST, referred to as SST anomalies, are key indicators of changes in the environment. The anomalies may be transient, or cyclical (e.g. the El Niño phenomenon in the equatorial Pacific) leading to relatively short-term but potentially damaging changes in global weather patterns. Or the anomalies may indicate long-term warming (or cooling) trends with serious implica-tions for global environmental change, such as rising sea levels and desertification. Accurate, long-term measurements of SST on regional and global scales are vital for monitoring climate trends and for improving weather and climate prediction models (NRC, 1983; WCRP, 1985).

SST measurements combined with ocean chlorophyll measurements (from an ocean color sensor) may lead to improved estimates of ocean biological productivity. Nutrient-rich regions of cold water upwelling and information on the mesoscale ocean flow field can be determined from SST measurements, which thus contribute to monitoring and modeling the global phytoplankton distributions. Commercial fisheries may use these data to identify fertile fishing grounds (Laurs, Fiedler & Montgomery, 1984). Recent understanding of the importance of the oceans as a sink for atmospheric carbon dioxide (due to fixation by phytoplankton and as dissolved carbon) increases the need to understand the role of SST in influencing this process (Moore & Bolin, 1986).

Measurement of SST over the Earth's oceans has been inconsistent in the past both in space and time sampling and in quantitative accuracy. Until the late 1960s the majority of SST measurements were obtained from ships. The Northern Hemisphere was thus relatively well sampled along the commercial shipping routes while the Southern Hemisphere was poorly sampled. More recently, SST fields derived from polar-orbiting satellites and drifting buoys have provided the global coverage and spatial and temporal resolutions desired for mesoscale oceanography and climate studies, and for biological research and commercial fisheries applications. Only in recent years, however, have the satellite data approached the accuracies desired for oceanographic and climate research ($\sim$0.2 to 0.5 K).

Methodology

Satellite measurements of SST are based on techniques in which spaceborne infra-red and microwave radiometers detect thermally emitted radiation from the ocean surface (Njoku, 1990). Determining SST from satellite data therefore requires an understanding of the processes by which electromagnetic radiation is (a) emitted and reflected at the ocean surface, and (b) emitted and attenuated by the intervening atmosphere. These processes can be modeled theoretically and the received radiance expressed using equations of radiative transfer. The radiation emitted by the surface is expressed as the product of the Planck emission function, which depends on radiation wavelength and ocean temperature, and the surface emissivity which may depend on a number of surface characteristics. Since the form of the Planck function is well known, the surface temperature can be estimated if the emissivity is measured or modeled with sufficient accuracy. To minimize atmospheric effects, measurements must be made at wavelengths where the attenuation due to atmospheric constituents is small. These wavelengths occur at well-defined 'window' regions of the infra-red and microwave spectrum hence satellite SST sensors are designed to make spectral measurements at these wavelengths.

Under favorable atmospheric and surface conditions, simple linear algorithms can provide reasonably accurate SST retrievals from either infra-red or microwave measurements. The algorithm equations have the form:

$$T_S = a_o + \sum_{i=1}^{N} a_i T_i \qquad (1)$$

where T_S is the SST and N is the number of channels used in the retrieval. T_i are the observed radiometric brightness temperatures at wavelength λ_i (or channel i), and the coefficients a_i can be derived theoretically or by regression using independent *in situ* SST observations. More complex non-linear algorithms can be constructed for higher accuracy (e.g. Walton, 1988) but there are many difficulties in developing and demonstrating improved accuracy. Two major issues must be addressed: 1) natural differences between the radiation ('skin') temperature, which is sensed by satellites, and the bulk temperature, which is usually measured from ships and buoys (see 'Skin-bulk differences'); and 2) adequate ancillary data, which include atmospheric soundings and surface observations over a representative set of conditions (see 'Comparison with other data sets').

Infra-red retrievals

Satellite infra-red radiometers utilize wavelength bands at 3.5–4 μm and 10–12 μm at which atmospheric transmittance is normally greater than 80% (except in humid regions where the transmittance may decrease to 40% and varies with the distribution of water vapor). At these wavelengths the ocean

surface emissivity is high (>0.97) with a correspondingly low reflectivity (<0.03). The non-zero reflectivity, although small, causes some solar and atmospheric radiation to be reflected into the field of view of the radiometer. This must be accounted for in the SST estimation algorithms, as must the effect of variable transmittance due to water vapor. The effects of clouds are also significant since clouds are opaque to infra-red radiation and effectively mask radiation from the ocean surface. Aerosols, if present, may cause significant scattering of the infra-red emitted radiation at 3.5–4.0 μm.

SST retrievals from infra-red sensors have been produced using different methods. One approach, the multichannel sea surface temperature (MCSST), was developed for the NOAA polar-orbiting Advanced Very High Resolution Radiometer (AVHRR) (McClain, Pichel & Walton, 1985). In the MCSST procedure initial processing of the satellite radiances is performed to identify and screen out cloud- and aerosol-contaminated pixels. The remaining cloud-free radiances are used in linear algorithms of the form given in equation (1) to derive SST.

The 3.7 μm channel is not used for daytime retrievals since there is significant reflection of solar radiation by the ocean surface at this wavelength. The coefficients in the equations are derived by theoretical simulations but are fine-tuned empirically by calibrating derived SSTs against independent *in situ* measurements from drifting buoys. The use of two or more channels in combination permits retrieval of independent information, in this case the SST and a lumped correction for atmospheric emission, attenuation, and surface emissivity. Each individual pixel has a spatial sampling resolution of 4 km (for global area coverage (GAC) data), but after cloud screening and SST retrieval the data are often composited into weekly or monthly gridded products at spatial scales of 14 km or larger. These products are useful for analyses of oceanographic features such as monthly SST anomalies and mesoscale fronts and eddies, and for initializing and validating large-scale oceanographic and climate models. On smaller scales, local area coverage (LAC) data are available from the sensor at 1 km resolution and are useful for mesoscale and coastal oceanographic studies and fisheries applications. Fig. 1 shows global SST images derived from satellite infra-red observations on the NOAA-9 AVHRR during the first two weeks of January and July, 1984. Cloud-free temperature retrievals were collected into 18 km space bins and missing locations were interpolated using a Laplacian relaxation technique to generate the global, cloud-free images. The blue to red color spectrum represents increasingly warmer temperatures. Features visible in this image are described in detail in 'Global SST Variability'.

MCSST-type retrieval algorithms have also been applied

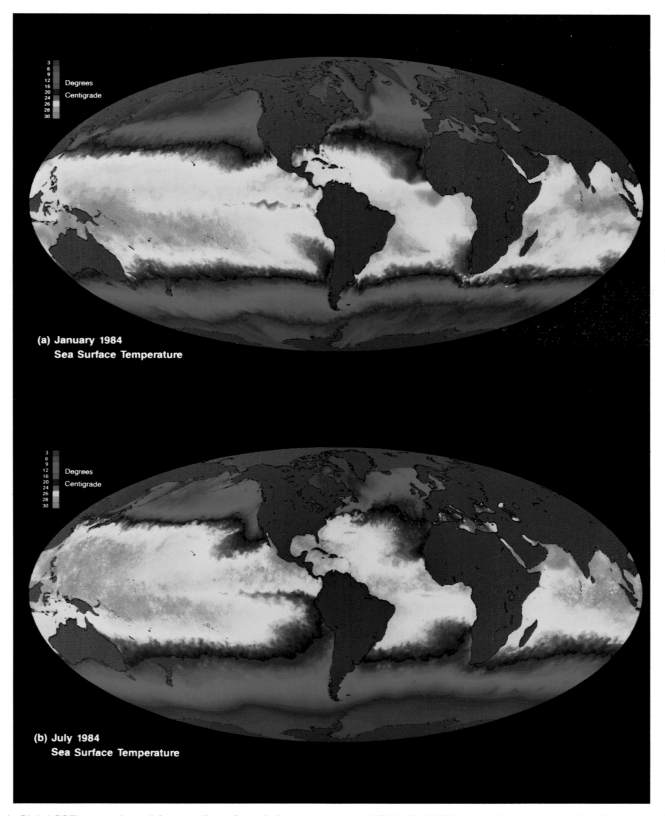

Fig. 1. Global SST images derived from satellite infra-red observations on the NOAA-9 AVHRR during the first two weeks of January and July 1984: (*a*) January 1984; (*b*) July 1984. (Images provided courtesy of G. Feldman, NASA/GSFC.)

Fig. 2. Mean global surface temperature for December 1978 (nighttime only) derived from HIRS and MSU data. (Provided by M. Chahine (JPL) and J. Susskind (GSFC).)

to data from the NOAA geostationary satellite VISSR Atmospheric Sounder (VAS) instrument, which has spectral channels similar to the AVHRR (Bates & Smith, 1985), and to combinations of AVHRR data with data from the High-Resolution Infra-red Sounder (HIRS) also on the NOAA satellites (Schluessel *et al.*, 1987).

A different approach has been developed for retrieving atmospheric and oceanographic parameters from the HIRS and Microwave Sounding Unit (MSU) instruments. The HIRS and MSU sounders are 20 and 4 channel instruments, respectively. In the HIRS/MSU approach (Susskind & Reuter, 1985) surface and atmospheric conditions (including clouds) are determined iteratively such that, when substituted into the radiative transfer equation, the resulting computed radiances match the observed radiances to within a given tolerance. The iterative scheme starts with first guess values for a set of surface and atmospheric parameters, and performs computations at each step utilizing channels sensitive to the parameters being determined (the HIRS has window channels at 3.7, 4, and 11 μm for sensing the surface). SST is one of several parameters derived simultaneously from the HIRS/MSU data using this approach. A key aspect is the ability to perform SST retrievals in partially cloud-filled scenes by reconstructing the clear-column radiances. Fig. 2 shows a global SST image derived from HIRS/MSU data. The image was derived using nighttime data only and includes both land and sea surface temperatures. (Day–night temperature differences can be quite large for land surfaces but are usually less than a few tenths of a degree in the oceans.) For a discussion of more recent work using the HIRS/MSU data please see chapter entitled 'Water vapor and temperature' by J. Susskind.

Microwave retrievals

In the microwave region of the spectrum, attenuation by water vapor and clouds is much less than in the infra-red. In fact, microwave SST retrievals can be made under complete cloud cover, although with slightly less accuracy and not under raining conditions. The atmospheric absorption windows are broad in the microwave region and precise selection of measurement bands within these windows is not critical. However, the radiometer wavelengths and polarization modes are chosen for sensitivity to SST and to provide additional information for correcting the effects of surface roughness, foam, atmospheric water vapor, and clouds. Wind-generated roughness and foam affect the ocean emissivity significantly and contribute to residual errors in the SST retrievals.

For small variations around mean values of SST and wind speed, and for non-raining conditions, the radiative transfer equations in the microwave region are approximately linear. Thus, linear equations of the form given by Equation 1 can be

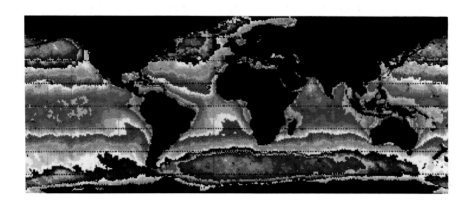

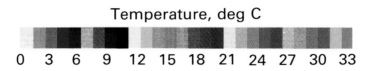

Temperature, deg C

0 3 6 9 12 15 18 21 24 27 30 33

Fig. 3. Mean global SST for February 1983 (daytime only) derived from Nimbus-7 SMMR data. (SST values close to land and sea ice are contaminated by antenna sidelobe effects.) (Image provided by P. Gloersen, NASA/GSFC.)

used to estimate SST. This approach has been applied to data from the Scanning Multichannel Microwave Radiometer (SMMR) on the Seasat and Nimbus-7 satellites (Hofer, Njoku & Waters, 1981; Wilheit et al., 1984). The SMMR radiometers operate at five wavelengths, corresponding to microwave frequencies of 6.6, 10.7, 18, 21, and 37 GHz, with vertical and horizontal polarization capability at each wavelength for a total of ten channels.

Broadly speaking, the 6.6 GHz channels are sensitive to SST, the 21 GHz channels contribute primarily a water vapor correction, and the 10.7, 18, and 37 GHz channels contribute corrections for the effects of surface roughness, foam, and clouds. The dual-polarization capability allows better discrimination of roughness and clouds. A subset of the ten channels is normally used in the SST retrievals since data from non-pertinent channels in some cases contribute more noise than SST information. In practice the selection of channels is optimized by performing a regression with simulated radiances, and the derived coefficients are fine tuned by comparison with independent in situ SST observations. Fig. 3 shows a global SST image derived from the SMMR on Nimbus-7. The data shown were taken from ascending (daytime) orbits using the calibration and processing procedure of Gloersen (1987). SST estimates close to major land and sea–ice boundaries have errors due to anomalous radiation entering the antenna sidelobes. Calibration bias errors also exist in the archived SMMR data.

However, current reprocessing of the data will result in better SST estimates. A more detailed discussion of previous SST measurements from the SMMR is given by Milman and Wilheit (1985).

Analysis and results

SST data derived from the NOAA AVHRR are used here to illustrate the annual cycles, anomalies, and global and regional characteristics of SST. Beginning in 1981 on the NOAA-7 satellite, five-channel AVHRR instruments have been launched on a continuing series of satellites up through the present date. Thus, the potential exists for a long-term, consistently analyzed satellite SST data set. As discussed earlier, NOAA generates an operational global SST product (MCSST) which is made available through the NOAA/NESDIS archives. During the past decade this product has gone through a number of algorithm improvements without reprocessing of the earlier data, resulting in some inconsistencies in the current ten-year SST record. A project has recently been initiated by NASA and NOAA, to reprocess the entire data set using consistent algorithms and to archive the data on new high-density media (SASWG, 1989).

Climatology

Before examining the satellite data, it is of interest to illustrate the long-term average features of global, monthly SST as

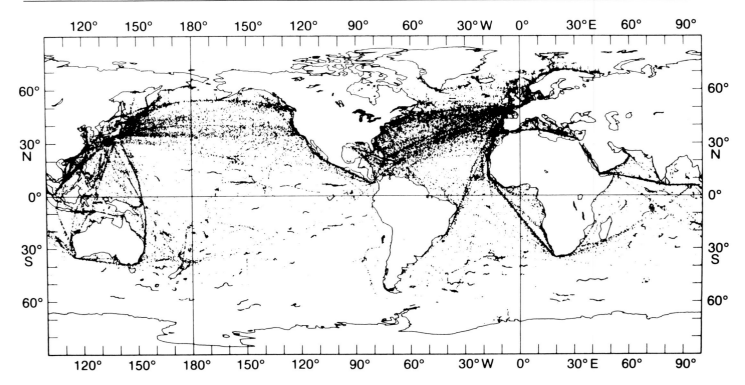

Fig. 4. Distribution of routine *in situ* (ship and buoy) SST data reported over the global telecommunications system (GTS) for October 1986. (From Reynolds, 1988.)

obtained from conventional *in situ* data, referred to as the SST climatology. The climatology represents historical average or 'normal' conditions from which one can then examine short-term deviations (i.e. differences from climatology or 'anomalies'). Fig. 4 shows a typical distribution of *in situ* SST measurements from routine ship and buoy reports. Historical data such as these are used to develop the SST climatologies, one example of which is shown in Fig. 5 derived from data provided by Levitus (1982). The figure shows the annual average surface temperature of the ocean, major features being the latitudinal variations from the equator to the poles and the warm and cold waters of circulating coastal boundary currents and upwellings. Of significance is the large warm region in the western equatorial Pacific and Indian oceans where intense atmospheric convection and precipitation take place. Because of the non-linear relationship between SST and latent heat flux, warm regions of the ocean are locations of high sensitivity of the atmospheric state to small changes in SST. It is thus important for climate purposes to make accurate SST measurements in these regions (WCRP, 1985).

Global SST variability

A number of interesting temperature patterns, indicative of the thermal response to forcing such as oceanic and atmo-

spheric circulation and solar heat input, are evident in the satellite SST images (e.g. Fig. 1). Western boundary currents such as the Gulf Stream, Kuroshio, Brazil, and Agulhas currents off the eastern shores of North America, Japan, South America, and southern Africa, respectively appear as sinuous bands of warmer waters moving poleward into the ocean interiors. One can discern the variation in these currents by noting the very different geometries, meandering, and temperature gradients among them. Shelf areas have less heat capacity due to their limited depth, and manifest greater thermal contrast than deeper waters (contrast the Yellow Sea, Sea of Japan versus warm Gulf of Mexico and a relatively shallow narrow US East coast). Arabian Sea cooling (in the western Indian Ocean) is due to the strong wind forcing of the summertime south-west monsoon.

Large scale, low frequency temporal variations are apparent in the image pair of Fig. 1. During January the Southern Hemisphere is warm while the cooler temperatures are observed in the northern temperate zone. The converse is true in July where we see the other phase of the seasonal cycle. Variations in large-scale boundary currents can be observed in the Somali, Gulf Stream, Humboldt and Agulhas current systems. Difference in response to monsoonal wind forcing is particularly apparent off north-east Africa and in the Arabian Sea. Low frequency long-wave meandering and

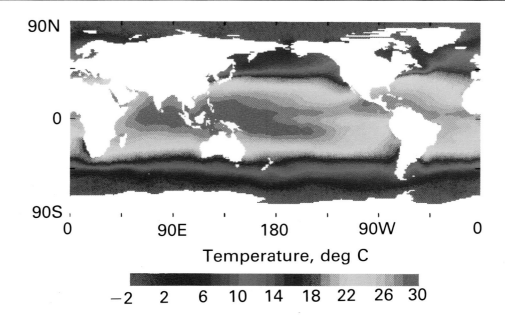

Fig. 5. Annual mean global SST (climatology) derived from historical *in situ* data (Levitus, 1982).

eddy shedding is seen in the Gulf Stream, Agulhas, Kuroshio, and Brazil current systems.

Upwelling and advection leads to large asymmetries in the subtropical thermal structure. Cold summer upwelling off California associated with southward blowing winds is seen in July while a pattern dominated by the equatorward flowing California current is observed in January. The complex connections of this system with the equatorial current system, the South Pacific eastern boundary current and Peru current can be followed in the SST. The cooler, wave-like band in the equatorial Pacific is a combination of wind-induced upwelled cold water and westward moving instability waves in the South Equatorial current system (see also a related discussion in the chapter by Lau and Busalacchi).

Asymmetric distribution of warm water is seen not only within ocean basins, but also globally with the large warm pool in the western Pacific, Indonesia, and in the eastern Indian Ocean. This leads to asymmetric along-equatorial atmospheric circulations – the Walker Cells. Variations in this pattern are associated with the El Niño/southern oscillation.

A view of the 1982/83 El Niño phenomenon in the equatorial Pacific Ocean is provided in Fig. 6 which shows SST conditions just after the peak of the El Niño (June 1983), and one year later (June 1984) when conditions had returned to normal. Features evident in June 1984 are the cold upwellings along the equator at the eastern ocean boundaries and the cold water associated with the southward currents along the eastern boundaries in the Northern Hemisphere. In June 1983 the upwelling in the eastern equatorial Pacific is virtually absent leaving anomalously warm SST in that region. The El Niño SST anomalies persist for several months and have been linked to major shifts in global weather patterns, causing increased precipitation and flooding in some areas and drought in others. Major research efforts (such as the tropical ocean global atmosphere (TOGA) program) have been initiated to understand these phenomena. Other interesting features visible in Fig. 6(*b*) include the westward-propagating waves at the northern equatorial edge of the Pacific cold tongue, which are thought to be caused by shear at the boundaries between the westward and eastward equatorial currents (Legeckis, 1986), and the meanders of the Gulf Stream flowing outward from the US east coast into the north Atlantic.

The magnitude of the differences in SST between El Niño and normal conditions is illustrated in Fig. 7. This shows conditions in the equatorial Pacific Ocean near the peak of the El Niño in December 1987 and one year later under near-normal conditions. The difference between the two years shows a broad warm zone with temperature differences exceeding five degrees centigrade at points along the equator. There are corresponding cool regions during the El Niño year, evident at higher latitudes in both hemispheres.

(a) 8/Jun/83 − 22/Jun/83

(b) 20/Jun/84 − 04/Jul/84

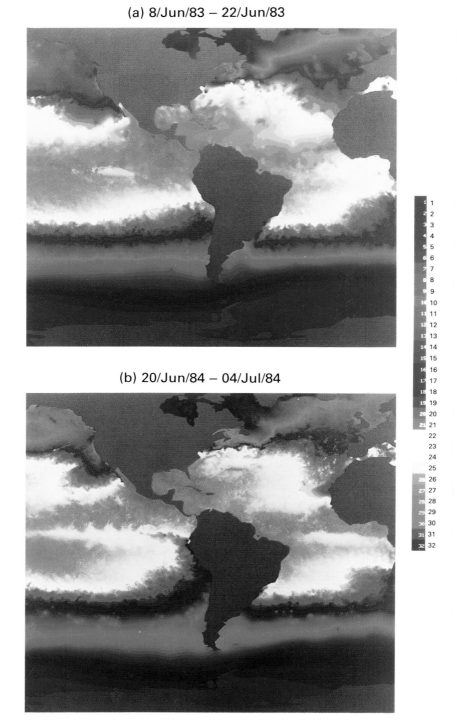

Fig. 6. Sea surface temperatures in the Atlantic and eastern Pacific oceans showing: (*a*) conditions during an El Niño (June 1983); and (*b*) normal conditions (June 1984).

Comparison with other data sets

Several studies have compared the satellite-derived SST measurements with those from *in situ* sensors deployed from ships and buoys. These studies have shown that root mean square (rms) errors in the satellite SST data may range from approximately 0.6K to 1.5K (e.g. Njoku, 1985). The AVHRR data have the highest accuracy of the satellite data analyzed to

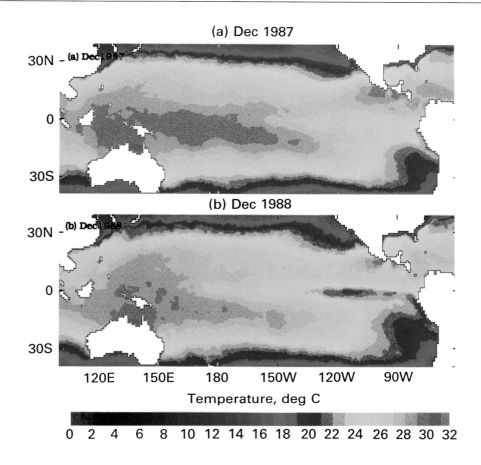

(a) Dec 1987

(b) Dec 1988

Temperature, deg C

0 2 4 6 8 10 12 14 16 18 20 22 24 26 28 30 32

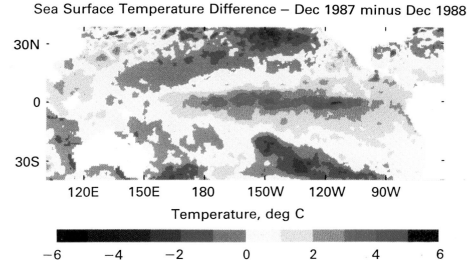

Sea Surface Temperature Difference − Dec 1987 minus Dec 1988

Temperature, deg C

−6   −4   −2   0   2   4   6

Fig. 7. Sea surface temperatures in the equatorial Pacific Ocean showing conditions during and after the 1987/88 El Niño: (a) December 1987; (b) December 1988; and (c) difference between December 1987 and December 1988.

date and are incorporated routinely in a blended ship/satellite SST product generated by the NOAA/National Meteorological Center in support of the TOGA program. The blended product has been compared to high quality drifting buoy measurements indicating an rms accuracy of approximately 0.8K (Reynolds, 1988). At the time of going to press, data from the ATSR instrument launched on the ERS-1 satellite in July 1991 had not been fully analyzed. The accuracies of SST measurements from this sensor are expected to be as good as or better than those from the AVHRR.

Unfortunately the comparison data sets are often insufficiently globally distributed to sample the full range of environmental variability. Nor do they include atmospheric soundings, surface air measurements, or radiometric estimates of the surface temperature which could be used to improve the satellite retrievals and better understand their error characteristics. Improvement of algorithms to climate accuracy (~0.25K rms) necessitates that these issues be addressed soon and in a deliberate manner.

Limitations

Retrieval algorithms

In order to make precision SST measurements from space, satellite sensors must have adequate sensitivity and must maintain stable calibration under a variety of spacecraft solar illuminations and thermal environments. The SST signals of interest are often small (i.e. a few tenths of a degree), and the retrieval algorithms must work in regions where there may be strong gradients of surface humidity and temperature. Early AVHRR MCSST algorithm retrievals indicated that volcanic aerosols from the eruption of El Chichón could bias the SST measurements anomalously low and that SST estimates in regions of high humidity (such as the western equatorial Pacific) require more than a simple linear atmospheric correction. In addition, daytime and nighttime retrievals in some cases showed differences larger than could be explained physically. Recent modifications to the algorithms using quadratic and scan-angle dependent terms, and careful analysis of calibration data, have improved the SST retrieval accuracy (McClain, 1989). A significant limitation is the inability to make AVHRR SST measurements in the presence of clouds. For some applications this can be overcome by accumulating enough samples to obtain cloud-free monthly SST composites on large spatial scales, but this is often infeasible for applications that require high resolution time series such as for tracking oceanic temperature fronts and eddies. In regions of persistent high cloudiness even monthly composites exhibit data voids. This is illustrated in

Fig. 8 which shows the global distribution of AVHRR samples on a 18 × 18 km grid for a representative month (February 1988). On this scale, large areas in the Tropics and polar regions remain unsampled. Techniques currently being developed for blending infra-red and microwave satellite SST retrievals may result in more complete global SST sampling at shorter timescales in cases where both satellite data types are simultaneously available.

Although not significantly influenced by clouds, results from the Nimbus-7 SMMR indicate that errors in the modeled dependence of microwave sea surface emissivity on windspeed may lead to anomalous SST retrievals in severe weather regions. The SMMR instrument and Nimbus-7 spacecraft and mission designs also led to data artifacts caused by calibration drifts, instrument on/off cycling, and antenna pointing stability. With careful analysis most of these problems have been understood and quantified, and are currently being removed by reprocessing the entire mission data set. Improved instrument and calibration designs will minimize these problems in future microwave sensors.

Skin-bulk differences

An important consideration in using satellites to measure SST is that satellite radiometers measure the radiative skin temperature of the upper few millimeters of the ocean (in the microwave) or upper few microns (in the infra-red). Measurements from ships and buoys, however, sample the ocean bulk at depths between 1 and 10 m. Evaporative cooling at the ocean surface can lower the skin temperature relative to the ocean bulk temperature by several tenths of a degree. Also, under conditions of low winds and high incident solar radiation, diurnal heating can raise the temperature in the upper few meters of the ocean by as much as a degree or more. Appropriate models of the air–sea interface and the upper ocean mixed layer should be considered in these cases when relating satellite measurements to ocean temperatures below the skin depth (Schluessel et al., 1987).

Applications

Atmospheric mesoscale and large-scale general circulation models can use SST fields as inputs in specifying the lower boundary condition of the atmosphere. These models are used for predicting medium and long-range weather and climate trends. Measurements of SST fluctuations in warm ocean regions (>28 °C), such as in the western equatorial Pacific, are particularly critical to the global models since the deep atmospheric convection and latent heat release in these regions is a major forcing mechanism for the global atmo-

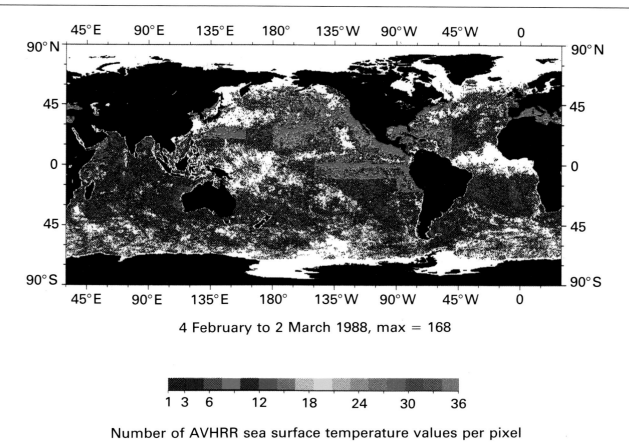

4 February to 2 March 1988, max = 168

1 3 6   12   18   24   30   36

Number of AVHRR sea surface temperature values per pixel

Fig. 8. Global sampling distribution of AVHRR data on a 18 × 18 km grid for the four-week period February 4 to March 2, 1988. (From Halpern *et al.*, 1991).

spheric circulation. SST fields are also required for initializing and validating ocean general circulation models which simulate SST variations arising from, for example, surface heat fluxes, ocean currents and eddies, and wind or shear mixing. The ocean exchanges heat with the atmosphere largely through the fluxes of sensible and latent heat, and global distributions of these fluxes can be computed using bulk parametrization formulae. SST is an important quantity in these formulae, in the direct computation of sensible heat flux and through the effect on saturation humidity at the surface in computing the latent heat flux (Liu, 1990).

Satellite SSTs can also be used to study climatological warming or cooling of the global oceans. Such trends in global or hemispheric mean SSTs are likely to be very small, thus it is essential that calibration and bias errors in the SST data be carefully analyzed and removed. A recent study by Reynolds, Folland & Parker (1989) has illustrated some of the biases inherent in the satellite data, and has shown the improvement obtained by merging satellite and *in situ* measurements into a blended SST product for climate analyses. Fig. 9 shows results of their study in which SST

anomalies derived from AVHRR, *in situ*, and a blended AVHRR/*in situ* product were averaged by hemisphere and plotted monthly from January 1982 through March 1989. The effects of volcanic aerosols from the eruption of El Chichón are visible as an erroneous cooling in the AVHRR data during 1982 and 1983. The blended product removes this anomaly and shows the two El Niño warming events in 1982/83 and 1987/88. It also indicates that, based on these data, there was no statistically significant global warming of the oceans during the period displayed.

High resolution satellite SST data gathered over the world oceans have enabled the study of a variety of mesoscale features in regions near strong current systems and within adjacent gyres. In conjunction with independent subsurface data (e.g. from expendable bathythermographs), which are needed to define the vertical structure, satellite data can be used to understand and model the structure and dynamics of such energetic features. In coastal regions, many of the eddies, fronts, and upwellings visible in the SST imagery are also associated with regions of high ocean productivity. SST data can be used with data from ocean color instruments

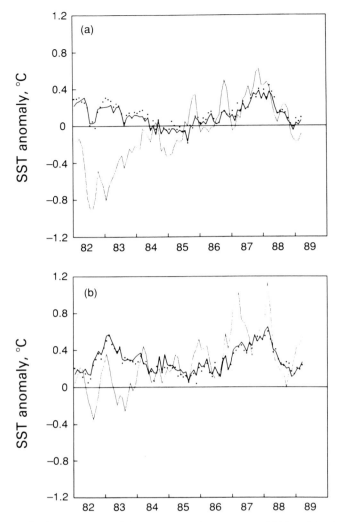

Fig. 9. Time series of SST anomalies from January 1982 to March 1989 for: (*a*) Northern Hemisphere between 0° and 60° N; and (*b*) Southern Hemisphere between 0° and 40° S. Satellite anomalies are indicated by a light line, blended anomalies by a heavy line, and *in situ* anomalies by a dotted line. (From Reynolds, Folland & Parker, 1989).

(such as the Nimbus-7 Coastal Zone Color Scanner) to map regions of high productivity and to develop models for the dynamics of the phytoplankton populations. It has been shown that these SST images are also useful for defining the distribution of marine fish habitat conditions and improving the catch of certain species such as albacore tuna. SST fisheries-aid products are thus generated routinely by NOAA and made available to the commercial fishing industry.

Conclusions

Satellite SST measurements on a global scale will continue to be available in the foreseeable future from the AVHRR sen-

sor and its follow-ons on the NOAA operational satellites. The data will be available for research analysis and will be enhanced by future sensors such as the Along-Track Scanning Radiometer (ATSR) on the ERS-1 satellite and the MODIS, MIMR, and AIRS instruments on the EOS platforms. Improvements in frequency, spatial coverage, and accuracy of SST data can thus be anticipated in the years ahead. Research is needed into improvement of surface and atmospheric data sets for long term calibration/validation activities and into techniques for quantifying the error characteristics of the SST data. Advances in methods for assimilating SST data from multiple sensors into oceanographic products and air–sea interaction models will significantly improve the benefits of these data.

Availability of data

The AVHRR MCSST data described in this paper may be obtained from the NCDC/Satellite Data Services Division, NOAA/NESDIS, Washington, DC. The HIRS/MSU SST data may be obtained from Dr Joel Susskind, Code 910.4, NASA/Goddard Space Flight Center, Greenbelt, MD. Nimbus-7 SMMR data may be obtained from the National Space Science Data Center, NASA/Goddard Space Flight Center, Greenbelt, MD. The SST Climatology may be obtained from the National Oceanographic Data Center, NOAA/NESDIS, Washington, DC. All data are available on 6250 bpi magnetic tape.

References

Bates, J. J. & Smith, W. L. (1985). Sea surface temperature: observations from geostationary satellites. *J. Geophys. Res.*, **90**, 11609–18.

Gill, A. E. (1982). *Atmosphere–Ocean Dynamics*, Academic Press, New York.

Gloersen (1987). In-orbit calibration adjustment of the Nimbus-7 SMMR, *NASA Tech. Memo. #100678*, National Aeronautics and Space Administration, Washington, DC 20546.

Halpern, D., Zlotnicki, V., Newman, J., Brown, O. & Wentz, F. (1991). An atlas of monthly mean distributions of GEOSAT sea surface height, SSMI surface wind speed, AVHRR/2 sea surface temperature, and ECMWF surface wind components during 1988, *JPL Publication 91–8*, Jet Propulsion Laboratory, Pasadena, CA 91109.

Hofer, R., Njoku, E. G. & Waters, J. W. (1981): Microwave radiometric measurements of sea surface temperature from the Seasat satellite: first results. *Science*, **212**, 1385–7.

Laurs, R. M., Fiedler, P. C. & Montgomery, D. R. (1984). Albacore tuna catch distributions relative to environmental features observed from satellites. *Deep Sea Res.*, **31**, 1085–99.

Legeckis, R. (1986). A satellite time series of sea surface

temperatures in the eastern equatorial Pacific Ocean. *J. Geophys. Res.*, **91**, 12879–86.

Levitus, S. (1982). Climatological atlas of the world ocean, *NOAA Professional Paper 13*, DOC/National Oceanic and Atmospheric Administration.

Liu, W. T. (1990). Remote sensing of surface turbulent heat flux. In *Surface Waves and Fluxes*, vol. II (G. L. Geernaert and W. J. Plant, eds.), pp. 293–309, Kluwer Academic Publishers, Dordrecht.

McClain, E. P., Pichel, W. G. & Walton, C. C. (1985). Comparative performance of AVHRR-based multichannel sea surface temperatures. *J. Geophys. Res.*, **90**, 11587–601.

McClain, E. P. (1989). Global sea surface temperatures and cloud clearing for aerosol optical depth estimates. *Int. J. Rem. Sens.*, **10**, 763–9.

Milman, A. S. & Wilheit, T. T. (1985). Sea surface temperatures from the scanning multichannel microwave radiometer on Nimbus-7. *J. Geophys. Res.*, **90**, 11631–41.

Moore, B. & Bolin, B. (1986). The oceans, carbon dioxide, and global climate change, *Oceanus*, **29**, (4).

Njoku, E. G. (1985). Satellite-derived sea surface temperature: Workshop comparisons. *Bull. Am. Met. Soc.*, **66**, 274–81.

Njoku, E. G. (1990). Satellite remote sensing of sea surface temperature. In *Surface Waves and Fluxes*, vol. II (G. L. Geernaert and W. J. Plant, eds.), pp. 311–38, Kluwer Academic Publishers, Dordrecht.

NRC (1983). *El Niño and the Southern Oscillation – A Scientific Plan*, National Academy Press, Washington, DC, 72pp.

Reynolds, R. W. (1988). A real-time global sea surface temperature analysis. *J. Climate*, **1**, 75–86.

Reynolds, R. W., Folland, C. K. & Parker, D. E. (1989). Biases in satellite-derived sea surface temperature data. *Nature*, **341**, 728–31.

SASWG (1989). Sea surface temperature products for the oceanographic scientific research community, Report of the SST archiving science working group (SASWG) (P. Cornillon, ed.), National Aeronautics and Space Administration, Code SE, Washington, DC 20546.

Schluessel, P., Shin, H.-Y., Emery, W. J. & Grassl, H. (1987). Comparison of satellite-derived sea surface temperature with *in situ* skin measurements, *J. Geophys. Res.*, **92**, 2859–74.

Susskind, J. & Reuter, D. (1985). Retrieval of sea surface temperature from HIRS2/MSU. *J. Geophys. Res.*, **90**, 11602–8.

Walton, C. C. (1988). Non-linear multichannel algorithms for estimating sea surface temperature with AVHRR satellite data, *J. Appl. Meteorol.*, **27**, 115–24.

WCRP (1985). Satellite-derived sea surface temperatures for global climate applications. *World Climate Programme Report #WCP-110*, World Meteorological Organization, Geneva, 65pp.

Wilheit, T. T., Greaves, J. A., Gatlin, J. A., Han, D., Krupp, B. M., Milman, A. S. & Chang, E. S. (1984). Retrieval of ocean surface parameters from the scanning multichannel microwave radiometer (SMMR) on the Nimbus-7 satellite, *IEEE Trans. Geosci. Rem. Sens.*, **GE-22**, 133–43.

Oceanic biological productivity

CHARLES R. McCLAIN, GENE FELDMAN AND WAYNE ESAIAS

Introduction

Microscopic green plants, called phytoplankton, form the lowest trophic level of the marine food web and play important roles in many geochemical processes. Through photosynthesis, they convert dissolved CO_2 and other dissolved nutrients into organic and other metabolic compounds which initiate additional pathways in the biogeochemical cycles of elements such as carbon, nitrogen, phosphorus, oxygen and sulfur. Each cycle consists of processes that couple the terrestrial, atmospheric and oceanic domains and includes feedback mechanisms which modulate the interactions between the various cycle components. Furthermore, cycles are intimately linked, in ways not well understood, so that perturbations in one cycle propagate into the others. A more fundamental understanding of biogeochemical cycles is essential in quantifying man's impact on the global biosphere and poses a fascinating challenge to the earth science community.

With respect to 'global change', the carbon cycle is of particular interest (Sundquist & Broecker, 1985). Fig. 1 is a simplified flow diagram of the global carbon cycle with current estimates of reservoir sizes and flux rates (Moore & Bolin, 1986). The flux pathways (arrows) represent various processes such as photosynthesis and respiration. The figure indicates that 'ocean biota' (primarily phytoplankton and zooplankton) represent a small fraction of the total carbon in the system, but that the associated fluxes are similar in magnitude to those linked with other much larger reservoirs. Thus, the relative turnover rate (flux/reservoir size) of the ocean biota component is very large compared to the others, implying that phytoplankton are a very 'active' component of the system. Indeed, phytoplankton doubling rates are on the order of once/day. Therefore, phytoplankton should respond rapidly to changes in the equilibrium of biogeochemical systems and may play an important role in the readjustment process. The recent rapid increase in atmospheric CO_2 is one case where an observable response might be expected. However, because phytoplankton concentrations and the rates of photosynthesis are controlled by environmental and physiological conditions which are, in turn, coupled to a variety of physical, chemical and other biological variables, the unambiguous identification of a response may not be straightforward.

The fixation of carbon by plants or primary productivity (Falkowski, 1980), Π, is commonly quantified in units of mg $C/m^2/day$. It is the total mass of carbon transformed from dissolved CO_2 to organic carbon integrated throughout the water column per unit area per unit time. Estimates of global primary productivity have been compiled by a number of authors based on historical data (see Berger, 1989). These composites are climatologies derived from available shipboard observations and, therefore, do not resolve seasonal and inter-annual variability or long-term trends on basin and global scales. Also, the estimates were obtained using a number of different techniques of varying accuracy (Eppley, 1989), and the data density in areas such as the Southern Hemisphere is very sparse. Much of the productivity is sustained through the recycling of nutrients within the euphotic zone and is called 'regenerated production'. Any additional production resulting from nutrient fluxes, primarily nitrate, into the euphotic zone is called 'new production' and the proportion of new production to the primary production is the 'f-ratio'. One equation for the non-dimensional f-ratio is

$$f = \Pi/1096 - \Pi^2/2.55*10^6, \qquad (1)$$

where Π is the primary productivity given in mg $C/m^2/day$ (Berger, Smetacek & Wefer, 1989). This relation is valid for values less than 1400 mg $C/m^2/day$. Assuming that the partial pressure of CO_2, pCO_2, is approximately in equilibrium with the atmosphere, any increase in phytoplankton uptake will result in a CO_2 flux into the ocean. Associated with primary production is 'export production', primarily in the form of particulate organic carbon (POC; fecal pellets and shells), which is the loss due to sinking. Export production decreases with depth as a result of: 1) oxidation of POC into dissolved organic carbon (DOC) by bacteria and 2) the increase in $CaCO_3$ solubility with depth. Sediment traps are commonly used to measure export production and have demonstrated the link between surface productivity and particle fluxes at

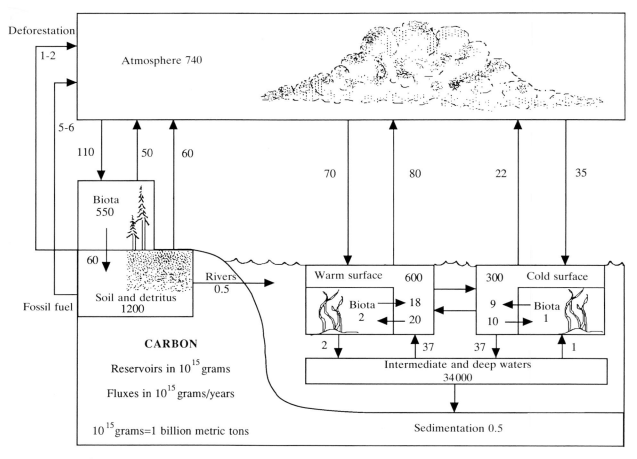

Fig. 1. Schematic of the global carbon cycle with current estimates of reservoir sizes and fluxes (redrawn from Moore & Bolin, 1986).

depth (Deuser, Muller-Karger & Hemleben, 1988). The process of CO_2 uptake in the euphotic zone and its removal to the deep ocean is referred to as the 'biological pump'. In regions where vertical processes dominate nutrient transport, new production and export production are balanced under steady-state conditions.

It has been estimated that only half of the CO_2 released into the atmosphere from the combustion of fossil fuels has remained in the atmosphere. Much of the remainder is thought by many to have been absorbed by the ocean, presumably through the actions of deep water formation and the biological pump. However, neither process is well understood and the role of the ocean in sequestering excess CO_2 is being questioned (Tans, Fung & Takahashi, 1990). An early review of the ocean's role in the fossil fuel CO_2 issue is provided in Anderson and Malahoff (1977). In order to clarify better the production and fate of biogenic materials in the ocean, the Joint Global Ocean Flux Study (JGOFS; Global Ocean Flux Committee, 1984) has been initiated. This experiment requires global long-term observations of phytoplankton biomass and other geophysical quantities,

some of which can be estimated from space-borne instrumentation. The first JGOFS field experiment was conducted in the spring of 1989 and was designed to document the onset and development of the North Atlantic spring bloom. The second field experiment will be conducted in the tropical Pacific Ocean in 1992 and a third is being planned for the Indian Ocean.

Methodology

The Coastal Zone Color Scanner mission, algorithms and processing

Because of the great variability of phytoplankton, it is not feasible to collect sufficient amounts of *in situ* data to quantify phytoplankton biomass over large time- and space scales. The Nimbus-7/Coastal Zone Color Scanner (CZCS) was designed as a one-year proof-of-concept experiment to determine if space-borne sensors could provide reasonable estimates of surface pigment concentration (chlorophyll-a plus phaeophytin) and diffuse attenuation (Hovis, 1981). Because the atmosphere produces roughly 90% of the radiation (molecular plus aerosol scattering) received by a spaceborne instrument viewing the open ocean, it was unclear if these components could be removed with sufficient accuracy to extract reliable estimates of the water-leaving radiances on which all bio-optical algorithms are based. Originally, the plan was to process 1% of the data to level-2 products (water-leaving radiances at 443 nm, 520 nm and 550 nm, aerosol radiance at 670 nm, pigment concentration and diffuse attenuation at 490 nm). However, because of the subsequent success in the development of atmospheric correction (Gordon et al., 1983a; Gordon, Brown & Evans, 1988) and bio-optical algorithms (Clark, 1981) and the sensor's extended operation (October 1978 through June 1986), a global processing effort was initiated in 1985 (Esaias et al., 1986; Feldman et al., 1989) and completed in early 1990. This data set has provided the first glimpse of global scale variability on monthly, seasonal and inter-annual time scales and the CZCS has been very useful in a number of specific process-oriented studies (McClain, Pietrafesa & Yoder, 1984; Feldman, Clark & Halpen, 1984; Abbott & Zion, 1985; Barale, McClain & Malanotte-Rizzoli, 1986; McClain et al., 1986; Muller-Karger, McClain & Richardson, 1988; Muller-Karger et al., 1989).

Photosynthetic pigments selectively absorb blue light and are neutral in the green. Water masses whose reflectance is determined by photosynthetic pigment absorption are called 'Case I' waters (Morel & Prieur, 1977). In 'Case II' water, suspended particulates and dissolved organic matter (DOM, yellow substance or *gelbstoff*) determine the reflectance. The water reflectance, $R(\lambda)$, is defined as the ratio of upwelling irradiance to downwelling irradiance just beneath the surface, $E_u(\lambda, 0)/E_d(\lambda, 0)$. Because the subsurface upwelling light field is approximately Lambertian, $E_u(\lambda, 0) \simeq \pi^* L_u(\lambda, 0)$, where $L_u(\lambda, z)$ is the upwelling subsurface radiance. The absorption peak for chlorophyll-a, the most important photosynthetic pigment, is 443 nm and the null point in the spectra between 520 and 550 nm is called the 'hinge point' as illustrated by stations C98, D10 and D23 in Fig. 2. Therefore, as concentration increases, the slope of the reflectance spectrum transitions from negative to positive in Case I water. In Case II water, the reflectance spectra are not as easily characterized. The bio-optical algorithm used in the global processing (Fig. 3) employs two empirical relationships, each relating the ratio of two water-leaving radiances (the upwelling radiances just above the air–water interface) to pigment concentration, $L_w(443)/L_w(550)$ for concentration $\leqslant 1.5$ mg/m^3 and $L_w(520)/L_w(550)$ for higher concentrations (Gordon et al., 1983a). The subsurface and water-leaving

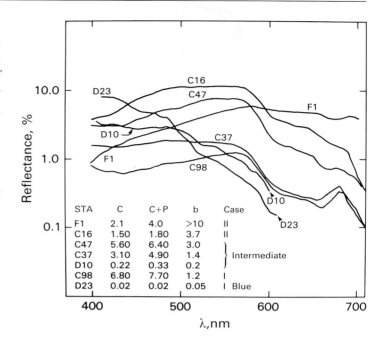

Fig. 2. Seven illustrative reflectance spectra, $E_u(\lambda, 0) / E_d(\lambda, 0)$ (redrawn from Morel, 1980). Note that the reflectance is plotted on a logarithmic scale. C and C+P are the total water column chlorophyll-a and chlorophyll-a + phaeophytin-a concentrations, respectively. b is the average scattering coefficient at 550 nm.

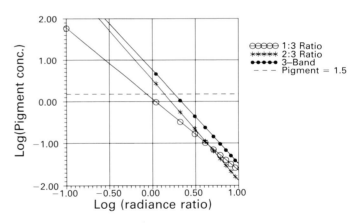

Fig. 3. Log-log plot of '2-band' and '3-band' ratio pigment algorithms. The 'Pigment = 1.5' dashed line denotes the 'switch' concentration for the 1:3 and 2:3 ratio algorithms.

radiances are proportional, and the proportionality coefficient is wavelength independent, so it cancels out in the radiance ratios. The relationships are given by

$$C_{sat} = 1.13 * [L_w(443)/L_w(550)]^{-1.71}, 0 < C_{sat} \leqslant 1.5 \text{ mg/m}^3 \quad (2)$$

and

$$C_{sat} = 3.33 * [L_w(520)/L_w(550)]^{-2.44}, 1.5 \text{ mg/m}^3 < C_{sat}. \quad (3)$$

The switch at 1.5 mg/m³ is necessary because the value of L_w (443) becomes too small to quantify accurately at greater concentrations given the digitization (8 bits) and signal-to-noise of the CZCS. A three-band algorithm also shown in Fig. 3 has been developed by Clark (Muller-Karger et al., 1990) which avoids problems with the 2-channel algorithm switching. That relationship is given by

$$C_{sat} = 5.56*[(L_w(443) + L_w(520))/L_w(550)]^{-2.252}. \quad (4)$$

While these algorithms are based on only 55 samples from stations proximate to the US, they provide reasonable estimates for much of the world ocean as documented in the process-oriented studies listed above and in others. There are, however, important exceptions, e.g. the North and Baltic Seas, and limitations which will be discussed later. The diffuse attenuation coefficient for upwelling radiance near the surface, K_u (490, 0), may be estimated using an empirical relationship developed by Austin and Petzold (1981), which, for CZCS applications, is written as

$$K_u(490,0) = 0.0883*[L_w(443)/L_w(550)]^{-1.491} + 0.022. \quad (5)$$

The final level-2 product, aerosol radiance at 670 nm, L_a (670), is obtained by assuming that L_w (670) is zero, so L_a (670) is simply the difference between the total radiance and the Rayleigh radiance. L_w (670) is approximately zero in Case I water, but it is non-zero in Case II water. An alternative algorithm by Smith and Wilson (1981) avoids the L_w (670) = 0 assumption, but only works where L_w (443) is somewhat larger than zero. In many near-shore and estuarine waters, this is not the case. When L_w (443) is small, errors in the instrument calibration and the Rayleigh correction may be equal to, or greater than, the true value, making the technique unusable.

The original volume of CZCS data (roughly 250 000 minutes of data or 125 000 two-minute scenes, Fig. 4) was reduced substantially through screening the level 0 data for cloud cover, so that only reasonably clear scenes were converted to calibrated radiance computer tapes (CRT, level 1). The screening was performed by the project scientist, Warren Hovis, shortly after the data were received. Even then, the data set filled over 30 000 1600 bpi CRTs with a final volume of approximately 700 gigabytes. The data were partitioned into scenes, usually two minutes (970 scan lines) in length. A major component of the global processing was the duplication of data from tape to write-once-read-many (WORM) optical disks which provide much greater data accessibility and media stability than magnetic tape. The processing included the creation of geophysical products in scanner coordinates (level 2) and average geophysical fields on a uniform global grid (level 3). There were three other major components to the

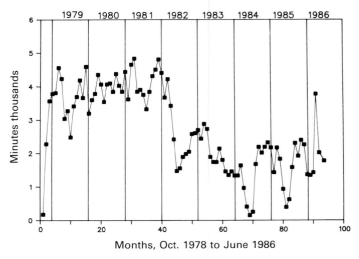

Fig. 4. Monthly total minutes of level-0 data collected by the Coastal Zone Color Scanner prior to cloud cover screening.

global processing effort: sensor calibration, quality control of the level 2 products and the archive and distribution system development. The archive is described in Feldman et al. (1989).

The CZCS lost sensitivity throughout the mission, but was temporally and spectrally erratic. A loss of sensitivity results in erroneously low estimates of total radiance measured by the sensor which can be compensated by adjusting the sensor calibration. There were several early attempts to quantify it (Gordon et al., 1983b; Hovis, Knoll & Smith, 1985; Mueller, 1985; Sturm, 1986) using both direct intercomparisons with shipboard and aircraft data and indirect or 'vicarious' methods. However, as the global processing proceeded, it became clear that a more robust calibration would be required. A rigorous vicarious calibration was developed by Robert Evans at the University of Miami. The technique assumes that the normalized water-leaving radiances ($[L_w]_N(\lambda)$; Gordon & Clark, 1981) of the central gyres did not change significantly with time. By preprocessing large quantities of data and analyzing frequency distributions of the $[L_w]_N(\lambda)$s from the central gyres for each sensor gain, the drift from nominal values was quantified which provided a means for incrementally adjusting the calibration. By the end of the mission, the degradations at 443, 520, 550 and 670 nm were estimated to be $\simeq$ 40%, 20%, 15% and 10%, respectively. This approach works well for 520 and 550 nm, but is less reliable for 443 nm because of the wide range of water-leaving radiances observed in 'clear' water (Gordon & Clark, 1981).

The quality control of the level 2 products was performed at the GSFC/Laboratory for Oceans. Some scenes were automatically rejected at tape ingest for particular problems,

Percentage

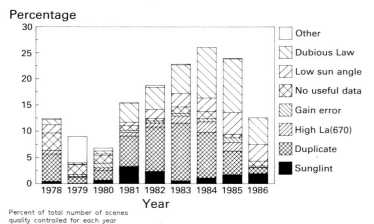

Percent of total number of scenes
quality controlled for each year

Fig. 5. Annual percentage of level-2 scenes rejected as a result of the CZCS global processing quality control effort. Rejections are quantified by rejection criteria.

e.g. missing bands. The level 2 processing also employed a land/cloud mask based on a fixed value of band 5 counts and a sensor ringing mask. Sensor ringing occurs on the downscan side of bright targets such as clouds and highly reflective land masses and results in invalid total radiances and derived products (Mueller, 1988). Special software was incorporated into the University of Miami DSP system which allowed an interactive quality control by the processing team. The procedure simultaneously displayed the daily global composites of pigment, $[L_w]_N(443)$, $[L_w]_N(550)$ and $L_a(670)$ and allowed for sequencing through each daily mosaic of scenes with the cursor. Thus, each scene was either accepted or rejected and, if rejected, one of nine rejection criteria was selected with optional comments by the investigator. The six most important categories of scene rejection, in decreasing order, were duplicate scenes, 'dubious' normalized radiances, low Sun elevation, no useful data, sunglint contamination and high L_a (670). Of nearly 62 000 scenes reviewed, over 9000 were rejected and the results are shown in Fig. 5. The duplicate scenes were due to the creation of multiple copies of the CRTs which were kept by the Nimbus Project in the tape archive. Most scenes rejected for 'dubious' normalized radiance had large areas where $[L_w]_N(550)$ was less than half the nominal value of 0.30 mW/cm².μm.sr that were not clearly the result of sunglint or atmospheric dust. Sunglint and dust both produce high L_a (670) values. Sunglint can be distinguished from dust because of the consistent pattern it produces in the center of equatorial scenes. A sunglint mask was applied in the level 2 processing, but the mask did not always cover the entire area of contamination because the sunglint pattern is wind speed dependent and the mask algorithm used a constant 6 m/s wind. The 'no useful data' classification was used when a scene was over land or com-

pletely cloud covered. Finally, scenes where the solar zenith angle was greater than 60° were rejected as 'low sun elevation' because Fresnel reflectivity for the direct solar radiation increases rapidly as zenith angles increase beyond 60°. Thus, at large solar zenith angles, the amount of light entering the water column is relatively small as are the upwelling water radiances. Also, errors in the atmospheric correction are expected to be greatest at these high zenith angles. The net result was that these scenes almost always had very high pigment concentrations which were considered to be erroneous.

Limitations

Estimation of biological primary productivity from CZCS data

The estimation of primary production from CZCS data has much appeal, but is not straightforward. To estimate primary production from CZCS data, the satellite pigment concentration must be related to total water column chlorophyll-a content which is, in turn, related to total water column primary production. The major limitations are due to the following.

1. The subsurface reflectance, $R(\lambda)$, in the visible spectrum results from absorption by water, photosynthetic pigments (primarily chlorophyll-a), ancillary pigments (Smith & Baker, 1978) and DOM (Bricaud, Morel & Prieur, 1981; Carder et al., 1989) and scattering by water and suspended particulates (Clark, Baker & Strong, 1980) and, therefore, R is not always dominated by chlorophyll.

2. The specific absorption coefficient of phytoplankton can vary by an order of magnitude (Kishino et al., 1985, 1986) and depends on cell packaging of chloroplasts, light adaptation and environmental stresses (e.g. nutrient depletion).

3. The concentration estimate derived from the CZCS, C_{sat}, is an optically weighted average over the first optical depth (Clark, 1981; Smith, 1981) of the water column and is a function of the vertical distribution of pigment concentration.

4. Subsurface maxima are common in the ocean, but are not sensed by the CZCS (Platt & Herman, 1983).

5. The relationship between chlorophyll concentration and primary production varies with species and a number of environmental and physiological condi-

tions (Smith, Eppley & Baker, 1982; Eppley *et al.*, 1985; Campbell & O'Reilly, 1988; Platt & Sathyendranath, 1988; Balch, Abbott & Eppley, 1989*a*, Balch, Eppley & Abbott, 1989*b*).

Because many substances selectively absorb light at the same wavelengths as chlorophyll, the limited number of CZCS bands does not accommodate the separation of photosynthetically active species from the others. Therefore, C_{sat} is a weighted average of all chemical species, the weight being a function of a_i, where a_i is the specific absorption coefficient. Because many of the photo-active chemical constituents are not simply dissolved, but are contained in living and nonliving particulates, a_is are often quantified in terms of bulk values with labels such as 'detritus' and 'phytoplankton', although some studies have distinguished the coefficients by phytoplankton species. In Case I water, chlorophyll and other co-varying degradation products, e.g. phaeophytin, determine the reflectance. This high correlation between chemical species allows a much higher accuracy (within ±30%; Gordon *et al.*, 1982) in pigment estimation. In Case II water, terrestrial materials, e.g. *gelbstoff* and suspended sediments, which are not necessarily correlated to chlorophyll, are important and the pigment retrievals may be grossly in error depending on the particular situation. In some coastal regions, the pigment retrievals can be quite good (Barale *et al.*, 1986; McClain *et al.*, 1988), while in others, they are poor, e.g. the Chesapeake Bay. Case II water is not necessarily synonymous with the coastal zone. For instance, coccolithopores, an open ocean phytoplankton, can have very extensive blooms which, because of their production of coccoliths (detached $CaCO_3$ platelets), produce anomalously high reflectances (Holligan *et al.*, 1983); thus, the pigment concentrations in these blooms are not quantified very well with the existing CZCS algorithms. As more data on the absorption and scattering properties are collected, better models of the water reflectance spectrum are being developed (Carder *et al.*, 1986; Gordon *et al.*, 1988; Morel, 1988).

C_{sat} is not only a composite pigment, but, being derived from the $L_w(\lambda)$s, it is also an optically weighted concentration over a portion of the upper water column from which the light is being reflected (Gordon & Clark, 1980). The depth from which 90% of the upwelling radiance originates is called the effective penetration depth, $z_{90}(\lambda)$ (Gordon & McCluney, 1975). $C_{sat}(\lambda)$ is

$$C_{sat}(\lambda) = \int_0^{z_{90}(\lambda)} C(z)f(\lambda, z)\mathrm{d}z \bigg/ \int_0^{z_{90}(\lambda)} f(\lambda, z)\mathrm{d}z \quad (6)$$

where $f(\lambda, z) = \exp[-2K(\lambda, z)]$. Thus, $z_{90}(\lambda)$ and $C_{sat}(\lambda)$ depend on the vertical distribution of the diffuse attenuation coefficient for downwelling irradiance, $K_d(\lambda, z)$, defined as

$$K_d(\lambda, z) = -\mathrm{d}(\ln E_d(\lambda, z))/\mathrm{d}z \quad (7)$$

where $E_d(\lambda, z)$ is the downwelling irradiance. In the case of the CZCS validation data set, Clark (1981) found that pigment stratification did not have a significant effect on C_{sat}.

$K_d(\lambda, z)$ can be decomposed into specific components such that

$$K_d(\lambda, z) = K_w(\lambda) + \Sigma k_i(\lambda) * C_i(z) \quad (8)$$

where K_w is the diffuse attenuation coefficient for water and k_i is the specific attenuation coefficient for each individual pigment (Smith & Baker, 1978). k_i and a_i are related by the expression (Prisendorfer, 1976)

$$k_i = [a_i(a_i + b_i)]^{1/2} \quad (9)$$

where b_i is the backscattering coefficient of the organism or particle. For most phytoplankton, coccolithopores being an exception, $a_i >> b_i$, so $k_i \simeq a_i$.

For vertically uniform distributions of diffuse attentuation, $z_{90}(\lambda) = 1/K_d(\lambda)$. Gordon and Morel (1983) provide relationships for $K_d(\lambda)$ as a function of pigment concentration which allow $z_{90}(\lambda)$ to be estimated. For example, in Case I water, $z_{90}(443)$ ranges from nearly 40 meters at 0.04 mg/m³ (the minimum concentration quantified in the global CZCS processing) to less than 1 meter at 40 mg/m³. Because $z_{90}(\lambda)$ varies substantially with λ, the integrations implicit in the radiance ratios used in the bio-optical algorithms have different limits. However, because $L_w(550)$ is insensitive to pigment concentration, the effect is primarily contained in the $L_w(443)$ and $L_w(520)$ factors.

In the open ocean, a deep chlorophyll maximum (DCM) is generally found (Cullen & Eppley, 1981; Lewis, 1987). It is not necessarily coincident to a biomass maximum or to the base of the mixed layer. Platt and Herman (1983) examined data from the Arctic, Scotian shelf and Peruvian coast and found that C_{sat} accounts for only 3–5% of the total chlorophyll in the water column. However, the percentage was fairly constant. They also found that the fraction of primary production within the effective penetration depth was even more stable at 11%. Campbell and O'Reilly (1988) analyzed the Marine Resources Monitoring, Assessment and Prediction (MARMAP) program data (over 1000 stations) from the north-east US continental shelf and slope and found the following relationship between C_{sat} and the mean concentration in the water column ($r^2 = 0.93$),

$$<C> = 0.287 + 0.685 * C_{sat} \quad (10)$$

Kuring *et al.* (1990) examined MARMAP and CZCS data from 1979 and compared C_{sat} with the *in situ* estimate of C_{sat} derived from ship data. They found the *in situ* values to be

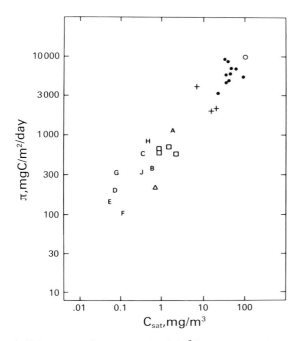

Fig. 6. Primary production, π (mgC/m²/day) data (redrawn from Eppley *et al.*, 1985). Symbols represent data from the following locations: A (Peru; June 1969), • (Peru; April 1969), + (Peru; March 1966), B (Scotia Sea), C (Panama Basin), D–G (North Pacific subtropical gyre), H (California Current), J (Lake Tahoe), Δ (Canadian Arctic, summer average), □ (Southern California bight, four seasonal averages), ○ (estimated maximum value).

roughly twice those estimated from the satellite, but could not identify a specific reason for the difference.

The correlation between C_{sat} and other mean properties of the euphotic zone provides a basis for empirical relationships between C_{sat} and total integrated primary productivity. Eppley *et al.* (1985) found that $\Pi \simeq F^* C_{sat}^{\frac{1}{2}}$ ($\langle F \rangle = 1000$) from data collected from a variety of oceanic regimes and seasons (Fig. 6). The Campbell and O'Reilly data set ($\langle \Pi \rangle = 914$ mg C/m²/day) is consistent with the Eppley *et al.* relationship although their values span a much smaller range of productivity and show a great deal of scatter. Eppley *et al.* examined data from the Southern California Bight and found that F has a strong seasonal dependence with maximal values in the summer and minimal values in the winter.

While empirical relationships are useful, they do not identify the underlying relationships between the physical environment and plant physiology which regulate primary production. Detailed models which explicitly incorporate parameters such as vertical biomass distribution, insolation, photoadaptation and other quantities are called photosynthesis–light (P–L) models. These models are somewhat different from biomass models which estimate the balance between phytoplankton, zooplankton and nutrient concentra-

tions (P–Z–N models). Satellite pigment fields have been used to qualitatively validate P–Z–N models (Wroblewski, Sarmiento & Flierl, 1988), but these models will not be discussed here. A detailed examination of several empirical and semi-analytical Π algorithms is provided in Balch *et al.* (1989*a*, *b*). One P–L model oriented towards satellite applications is described in Platt *et al.* (1988) and Platt and Sathyendranath (1988). Their approach requires certain information on the vertical distribution of biological quantities and physiological rate parameters as a function of season and location. Once oceanic regions are classified and assigned parameter values based on *in situ* observations, the modelled production can be calculated. Their initial results for five sites in the north and east Atlantic show excellent correlation to observed values over the entire range of their observation data set (0 to 2500 mg C/m²/day). However, Balch *et al.* (1989*b*) argue that the variability of the photosynthesis–light relationship is much greater than Platt *et al.* (1988) concluded.

Analysis and results

Abbott and Chelton (1990) provide a comprehensive review of the literature dealing with applications of CZCS data. Nearly all of the current literature is related to either algorithm or regional process studies. However, the CZCS data set has provided the first truly comprehensive view of the global ocean's pigment and radiance fields. Fig. 7(*a*) is the average pigment field derived from the entire 7.7-year data set. A comparison with the *in situ* composites of productivity (Berger, 1989) indicate an amazingly close correspondence in patterns. It must be noted that the sampling was extremely inhomogeneous in time and space as illustrated in Figs. 4 and 7(*b*), respectively. Fig. 7(*b*) is a map of the total number of samples used to compute the mean values in Fig. 7(*a*). These numbers are not the total number of samples actually collected by the satellite, but are the number of samples remaining after the initial cloud screening, subsampling for global processing and quality control. Sampling was highly localized because of the Nimbus experiment team's sampling priorities and solar elevation and cloud cover conditions. Other factors that limited the amount of data collected were ground station availability, tape recorder capacity, satellite power limitations and, in the latter phase of the mission, difficulties in getting the instrument to switch on. The highest value in Fig. 7(*b*) is roughly 16 000, but most values are less than 400. The greatest numbers of valid pixels were from the east (Florida to Maine) and west (Baja to Washington state) coasts of North America, the western Mediterranean Sea and the Arabian Sea. It must be mentioned that as a proof-of-concept mission,

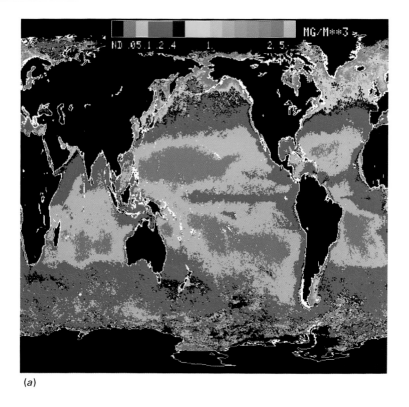

(a)

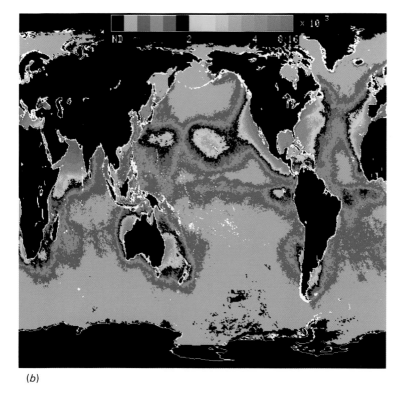

(b)

Fig. 7. (a) Overall mean CZCS pigment field for entire data set (November 1978 through June 1986) and (b) total number of valid samples processed.

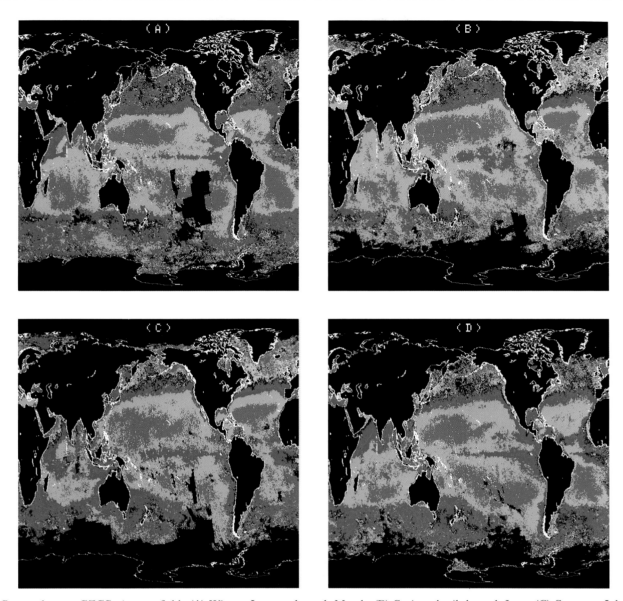

Fig. 8. Seasonal mean CZCS pigment fields (A) Winter: January through March, (B) Spring: April through June, (C) Summer: July through September, (D) Fall: October through December.

global coverage was never envisioned as a goal of the CZCS project.

The data set does provide synoptic-scale time series of surface pigment concentrations for at least those regions mentioned above. In certain instances, significant inter-annual variability (Feldman, 1986; Banse & McClain, 1986; Barale *et al.*, 1986; Brock & McClain, 1992) has been observed. For regions and periods when coverage was less dense, averaging the data into seasonal climatologies can provide a clearer picture of the seasonal cycle as in Fig. 8. Due to the uneven temporal and spatial sampling (Figs. 4 and 7(*b*)), some features in the seasonal composites are artefacts of

temporally inhomogeneous sampling coupled with inter-annual variability. None the less, the seasonal cycle is clearly demonstrated in regions like the North Atlantic Ocean (McClain *et al.*, 1990). Several interesting phenomena are depicted in Fig. 8 including 1) the relative constancy of the Southern Hemisphere compared to the Northern Hemi-sphere, 2) the higher concentrations in the north and tropical Atlantic versus the corresponding areas of the Pacific and 3) the high productivity of the Arabian Sea during the summer monsoon (Brock *et al.*, 1991).

Some very important regions, e.g. equatorial Pacific and Atlantic Oceans, had little or no data for some important periods. For instance, almost no data were collected in the equatorial Pacific during the 1982–1983 El Niño or the 1983–1984 period of pronounced inter-annual variability in the equatorial Atlantic (see *Nature*, **322**, 17 July, 1986), yet these regions are vital to our understanding of the ocean's role in the Earth's carbon budget. The lack of periodic global coverage and questions regarding the calibration, have limited what can be inferred about long-term trends in global productivity and no analyses of the CZCS data have been published thus far that attempt to do so. An analysis of this kind is complicated by the highly non-linear relationship between C_{sat} and Π. A direct computation of Π from an image of average concentration using a relationship such as that of Eppley *et al.* (1985) would not yield satisfactory results in regions where C_{sat} has significant variability. In those situations, the transformation would need to be executed on individual scenes before averaging is performed. Also, use of an image of mean pigment assumes that the sampling was adequate to estimate the true average.

Conclusions

The global processing and archival of the CZCS data has only recently made that data set generally available to the oceanographic community and extensive analyses of the data set for the estimation of primary productivity are being pursued by a number of investigators. The CZCS data has revealed a great deal about the global ocean and clearly demonstrated the feasibility of monitoring oceanic biological processes on a global scale. Also, the experience gained from the CZCS data processing has helped clarify what refinements in sensor design are needed in the next generation of instruments. Clearly, more wavelengths are needed in order to distinquish viable chlorophyll from degradation products, to improve the aerosol correction and to accommodate a more robust suite of pigment algorithms for Case II waters. Higher signal-to-noise ratios and data quantification will allow more accurate atmospheric corrections. Also, to do global science, the coverage shown in Figs. 7 and 8 is needed on a weekly basis and process-oriented studies require daily data from experiment

sites. Finally, the instrument performance must be monitored in near realtime. The only mechanism for obtaining an adequate data set to address issues of global biogeochemical cycles and global change is an *operational* ocean color satellite sensor such as SeaWiFS (Yoder *et al.*, 1988) coupled with a comprehensive calibration, validation and bio-optical algorithm development program. With large international *in situ* programs like JGOFS (joint global ocean flux study), IGBP (international geosphere–biosphere program) and WOCE (world ocean circulation experiment) already under way, the opportunity for a significant synergism between field and satellite data sets is possible for the first time. Indeed, programs like JGOFS are seriously hampered by the lack of simultaneous satellite coverage.

Availability of data

CZCS data can be obtained from NASA Goddard Space Flight Center and a number of regional archives (Feldman *et al.*, 1989). A browse capability has been developed which includes 1) software that allows the user to query a database using a number of parameters including latitude and longitude ranges and time interval to determine the scenes available which satisfy the query criteria and 2) a set of three Panasonic video disks which contain all the CZCS pigment images. The browse software can be used with or without the Panasonic player and versions are available for a variety of computers. Using the Panasonic video player allows each image that satisfies the query to be displayed and the user has the option of ordering the displayed scene before progressing to the next scene. Orders to the archive can be initiated from within the browse session provided the system is a SPAN node. Data requests may also be filed through OMNET. For information about the CZCS archive, contact DAAC User Support Office, Code 902.2, NASA/GSFC, Greenbelt, MD 20 771. Tel: (301) 286-3209. Omnet: DAAC. GSFC: SPAN, NCS; DAAC USO internet: DAAC USO QUSSD-CA.GSFC.NASA.GOV. The browse software is available at no charge.

Table 1. *Notation*

Symbol	Units	Definition
a_i	m^2/mg	Specific absorption coefficient for i_{th} optical species
b_i	m_2/mg	Specific scattering coefficient for i_{th} optical species
c_i	m^2/mg	$a_i + b_i$, specific attenuation coefficient
C	mg/m^3	Pigment concentration
C_{sat}	mg/m^3	Satellite-derived pigment concentration
$E_d(\lambda, z)$	$mW/cm^2 \cdot \mu m$	Downwelling irradiance
$E_u(\lambda, z)$	$mW/cm^2 \cdot \mu m$	Upwelling irradiance
f	dimensionless	f-ratio, ratio of new production to primary production
F	$(mg/m)^{1/2}/day$	Proportionality constant in Eppley satellite productivity relationship
k_i	m^2/mg	Specific diffuse attenuation coefficient for the i_{th} optical species
$K_d(\lambda, z)$	m^{-1}	Diffuse attenuation coefficient for downwelling irradiance
$K_u(\lambda, z)$	m^{-1}	Diffuse attenuation coefficient for upwelling radiance
$K_w(\lambda)$	m^{-1}	Diffuse attenuation coefficient for water
$L_a(\lambda)$	$mW/cm^2 \cdot \mu m \cdot sr$	Aerosol radiance
$L_u(\lambda, z)$	$mW/cm^2 \cdot \mu m \cdot sr$	Upwelling water radiance
$L_w(\lambda)$	$mW/cm^2 \cdot \mu m \cdot sr$	Water-leaving radiance above the air–sea interface
$[L_w]_N(\lambda)$	$mW/cm^2 \cdot \mu m \cdot sr$	Normalized water-leaving radiance
Π	$mg\ C/m^2/day$	Primary productivity
$R(\lambda)$	dimensionless	Reflectance
$z_{90}(\lambda)$	m	Effective penetration depth

References

Abbott, M. R. & Chelton, D. B. (1991). Advances in passive remote sensing of the ocean, U. S. National Report to International Union of Geodesy and Geophysics 1987–1990. *Contributions in Oceanography*, Am. Geophys. Union, 571–589.

Abbott, M. R. & Zion, P. M. (1985). Satellite observations of phytoplankton variability during an upwelling event, *Cont. Shelf Res.*, 4, 661–80.

Anderson, N. R. & Malahoff, A. M. (eds.) (1977). *The Fate of Fossil Fuel CO₂ in the Oceans*, Plenum Press, New York, 749pp.

Austin, R. W. & Petzold, T. J. (1981). The determination of diffuse attenuation coefficient of sea water using the Coastal Zone Color Scanner, *Oceanography from Space*, J. F. R. Gower (ed.), Plenum Press, New York, 239–56.

Balch, W. M., Abbott, M. R. & Eppley, R. W. (1989a). Remote sensing of primary production – I. A comparison of empirical and semi-empirical algorithms. *Deep-Sea Res.*, 36(2), 281–95.

Balch, W. M., Eppley, R. W. & Abbott, M. R. (1989b). Remote sensing of primary production – II. A semi-analytical algorithm based on pigments, temperature and light. *Deep-Sea Res.*, 36(8), 1201–17.

Banse, K. & McClain, C. R. (1986). Satellite-observed winter blooms of phytoplankton in the Arabian Sea. *Mar. Ecol. Prog. Ser.*, 34(3), 201–11.

Barale, V., McClain, C. R. & Malanotte-Rizzoli, P. (1986). Space and time variability of the surface color field in the northern Adriatic Sea, *J. Geophys. Res.*, 91, 12, 957–74.

Berger, W. H. (1989). Global maps of ocean productivity, *Productivity of the Ocean: Present and Past*. (W. H. Berger, V. S. Smetacek and G. Wefer, eds.), John Wiley & Sons, New York, pp. 429–55.

Berger, W. H., Smetacek, V. S. & Wefer, G. (1989). Ocean pro-ductivity and paleoproductivity – an overview, *Productivity of the Ocean: Present and Past*. (W. H. Berger, V. S. Smetacek and G. Wefer, eds.), John Wiley & Sons, New York, pp. 1–34.

Bricaud, A., Morel, A. & Prieur, L. (1981). Absorption of dissolved organic matter of the sea (yellow substance) in the UV and visible domains. *Limnol. Oceanogr.*, 26, 43–53.

Brock, J. C. & McClain, C. R. (1992). Inter-annual variability in phytoplankton blooms observed in the northwestern Arabian Sea during the southwest monsoon. *J. Geophys. Res.*, 97(C1), 733–50.

Brock, J. C., McClain, C. R., Luther, M. E. & Hay, W. W. (1991). The phytoplankton bloom in the northwest Arabian Sea during the southwest monsoon of 1979. *J. Geophys. Res.*, 96(C11), 20, 623–42.

Campbell, J. W. & O'Reilly, J. E. (1988). Role of satellites in estimating primary productivity on the northwest Atlantic continental shelf. *Cont. Shelf Res.*, 8(2), 179–204.

Carder, K. L., Steward, R. G., Paul, J. H. & Vargo, G. A. (1986). Relationships between chlorophyll and ocean color constituents as they affect remote-sensing reflectance models. *Limnol. Oceanogr.*, 31, 403–13.

Carder, K. L., Steward, R. G., Harvey, G. R. & Ortner, P. B. (1989). Marine humic and fulvic acids: Their effects on remote sensing of ocean chlorophyll. *Limnol. Oceanogr.*, 34(1), 68–81.

Clark, D. K. (1981). Phytoplankton pigment algorithms for the Nimbus-7 CZCS. In *Oceanography from Space*. (J. R. F. Gower, ed.,) Plenum Press, New York, pp. 227–37.

Clark, D. K., Baker, E. T. & Strong, A. E. (1980). Upwelled spectral radiance distributions in relation to particulate matter in sea water. *Boundary-Layer Meteor.*, 18(3), 287–98.

Cullen, J. J. & Eppley, R. W. (1981). Chlorophyll maximum layers of the Southern California Bight and possible mechanisms of their formation maintenance. *Oceanol. Acta*, 4(1), 23–32.

Deuser, W. G., Muller-Karger, F. E. & Hemleben, C. (1988). Temporal variations of particle fluxes in the deep subtropical and tropical North Atlantic: Eulerian versus Lagrangian effects. *J. Geophys. Res.*, **93**(C6), 6857–62.

Eppley, R. W. (1989). New production: history, methods, problems. In *Productivity of the Ocean: Present and Past* (W. H. Berger, V. S. Smetacek and G. Wefer, eds.), John Wiley & Sons, New York, pp. 85–97.

Eppley, R. W., Stewart, E., Abbott, M. R. & Heyman, U. (1985). Estimating ocean primary production from satellite chlorophyll: introduction to regional differences and statistics for the Southern California Bight. *J. Plankton Res.*, **7**(1), 57–70.

Esaias, W., Feldman, G., McClain, C. R. & Elrod, J. (1986). Satellite observations of oceanic primary productivity. *Eos* **67**(44), 835–7.

Falkowski, P. G. (ed.). (1980). *Primary Productivity in the Sea*. Plenum Press, New York, 531pp.

Feldman, G. (1986). Variability of the productive habitat in the eastern equatorial Pacific, *Eos*, **67**, 106–8.

Feldman, G., Clark, D. & Halpern, D. (1984). Satellite color observations of the phytoplankton distribution in the eastern equatorial Pacific during the 1982–1983 El Niño. *Science*, **226**(4678), 1069–71.

Feldman, G. *et al.* (1989). Ocean color: availability of the global data set, *Eos*, **70**(23), 634.

Global Ocean Flux Committee (1984). *Global Ocean Flux Study: Proceedings of a Workshop*, National Academy Press, Washington, DC, 360pp.

Gordon, H. R. & Clark, D. K. (1980). Remote sensing optical properties of a stratified ocean: an improved interpretation. *Appl. Opt.*, **18**, 3428–30.

Gordon, H. R. & Clark, D. K. (1981). Clear water radiances for atmospheric correction of Coastal Zone Color Scanner imagery. *Appl. Opt.*, **20**, 4175–80.

Gordon, H. R. & McCluney, W. R. (1975). Estimation of the depth of sunlight penetration in the sea for remote sensing. *Appl. Opt.*, **14**(2), 413–16.

Gordon, H. R. & Morel, A. Y. (1983). *Remote Assessment of Ocean Color for Interpretation of Satellite Visible Imagery, A Review*. Springer-Verlag, New York, 114 pp.

Gordon, H. R., Clark, D. K., Brown, J. W., Brown, O. B. & Evans, R. H. (1982). Satellite measurements of phytoplankton pigment concentration in the surface waters of a warm core Gulf Stream ring. *J. Mar. Res.*, **40**(2), 491–502.

Gordon, H. R., Clark, D. K., Brown, J. W., Brown, O. B., Evans, R. H. & Broenkow, W. W. (1983*a*). Phytoplankton pigment concentrations in the Middle Atlantic Bight: comparison of ship determinations and CZCS estimates, *Appl. Opt.*, **22**(1), 20–36.

Gordon, H. R., Brown, J. W., Brown, O. B., Evans, R. H. & Clark, D. K. (1983*b*). Nimbus-7 CZCS: reduction of its radiometric sensitivity with time, *Appl. Opt.*, **22**(24), 3929–31.

Gordon, H. R., Brown, J. W. & Evans, R. H. (1988). Exact Rayleigh scattering calculations for use with the Nimbus-7 Coastal Zone Color Scanner, *Appl. Opt.*, **27**(5), 862–71.

Holligan, P. M., Viollier, M., Harbour, D. S., Camus, P. & Champagne-Phillippe, M. (1983). Satellite and ship studies of coccolithopore production along a continental shelf edge. *Nature*, **304**, 339–42.

Hovis, W. A. (1981). The Nimbus-7 Coastal Zone Color Scanner (CZCS) program, *Oceanography from Space*. (J. R. F. Gower, ed.), Plenum Press, New York, pp. 213–25, 1981.

Hovis, W. A., Knoll, J. S. & Smith, G. R. (1985). Aircraft measurements for calibration of an orbiting spacecraft sensor. *Appl. Opt.*, **24**(3), 407–10.

Kishino, M., Okami, N., Takahashi, M. & Ichimura, S. (1986). Light utilization efficiency and quantum yield of phytoplankton in a thermally stratified sea. *Limnol. Oceanogr.*, **31**(3), 557–66.

Kishino, M., Takahashi, M., Okami, N. & Ichimura, S. (1985). Estimation of the spectral absorption coefficients of phytoplankton in the sea. *Bull. Mar. Sci.*, **37**, 634–42.

Kuring, N., Lewis, M. R., Platt, T. & O'Reilly, J. E. (1990). Satellite-derived estimates of primary production on the northwest Atlantic continental shelf. *Cont. Shelf Res.*, **10**(5), 461–84.

Lewis, M. R. (1987). Phytoplankton and thermal structure in the tropical ocean, *Oceanol. Acta*, SP, 91–5.

McClain, C. R., Pietrafesa, L. J. & Yoder, J. A. (1984). Observations of Gulf Stream-induced and wind-driven upwelling in the Georgia Bight using ocean color and infra-red imagery, *J. Geophys. Res.*, **89**, 3705–23.

McClain, C., Chao, S.-Y., Atkinson, L., Blanton, J. & de Castillejo, F. (1986). Wind-driven upwelling in the vicinity of Cape Finisterre, Spain. *J. Geophys. Res.*, **91**(C7), 8470–86.

McClain, C. R., Yoder, J. A., Atkinson, L. P., Blanton, J. O., Lee, T. N., Singer, J. J. & Muller-Karger, F. (1988). Variability of Surface Pigment Concentrations in the South Atlantic Bight, *J. Geophys. Res.*, **93**(C9), 10, 675–97.

McClain, C. R., Esaias, W. E., Feldman, G. C., Elrod, J., Endres, D., Firestone, J., Darzi, M., Evans, R. & Brown, J. (1990). Physical and biological processes in the North Atlantic during the First Global GARP Experiment. *J. Geophys. Res.*, **95**(C10), 18,027–48.

Moore, B., III & Bolin, B. (1986). The oceans, carbon dioxide, and global climate change. *Oceanus*, **29**(4), 9–15.

Morel, A. (1980). In-water and remote measurements of ocean color, *Bound.-layer Meteorol.*, **18**(2), 178–201.

Morel, A. (1988). Optical modeling of the upper ocean in relation to its biogenous matter content (Case I waters). *J. Geophys. Res.*, **93**(C9), 10,749–68.

Morel, A. & Prieur, L. (1977). Analysis of variations in ocean color, *Limnol. Oceanogr.*, **22**, 709–22.

Mueller, J. L. (1985). Nimbus-7 CZCS: confirmation of its radiometric sensitivity decay rate through 1982. *Appl. Opt.*, **24**(7), 1043–7.

Mueller, J. L. (1988). Nimbus-7 CZCS: electronic overshoot due to cloud reflectance. *Appl. Opt.*, **27**(3), 438–40.

Mueller-Karger, F., McClain, C. R. & Richardson, P. (1988). The dispersal of the Amazon water. *Nature*, **333**, 56–9.

Muller-Karger, F. E., McClain, C. R., Fisher, T. R., Esaias, W. E.

& Varela, R. (1989). Pigment distribution in the Caribbean Sea: observations from space. *Prog. Oceanog.*, **23**, 23–64.

Muller-Karger, F. E., McClain, C. R., Sambrotto, R. N. & Ray, G. C. (1990). A comparison of ship and CZCS-mapped distributions of phytoplankton in the Southeastern Bering Sea, *J. Geophys. Res.*, **95**(C7), 11,483–99.

Platt, T. & Herman, A. W. (1983). Remote sensing of phytoplankton in the sea: surface-layer chlorophyll as an estimate of water-column chlorophyll and primary production. *Int. J. Remote Sensing*, **4**(2), 343–51.

Platt, T. & Sathyendranath, S. (1988). Oceanic primary production: estimation by remote sensing at local and regional scales. *Science*, **241**, 1613–20.

Platt, T., Sathyendranath, S., Caverhill, C. M. & Lewis, M. R. (1988). Ocean primary production and available light: further algorithms for remote sensing. *Deep-Sea Res.*, **35**(6), 855–79.

Prisendorfer, R. W. (1976). *Hydrologic Optics, Volume V. Properties*. US Dept. of Commerce, 296pp.

Smith, R. C. (1981). Remote sensing and depth distribution of ocean chlorophyll. *Mar. Ecol. Prog. Ser.*, **5**, 359–61.

Smith, R. C. & Baker, K. S. (1987b). Optical classification of natural waters. *Limnol. Oceanogr.*, **23**(2), 260–7.

Smith, R. C. & Wilson, W. H. (1981). Ship and satellite bio-optical research in the California Bight, *Oceanography from Space*. (J. F. R. Gower, ed.), Plenum Press, New York, pp. 281–294.

Smith, R. C., Eppley, R. W. & Baker, K. S. (1982). Correlation of primary productivity as measured aboard ship in southern California coastal waters and as estimated from satellite chlorophyll images, *Mar. Biol.*, **66**, 281–8.

Strum, B. (1986). Correction of the sensor degradation of the Coastal Zone Color Scanner on Nimbus-7. *ESA SP-258*, 263–7.

Sundquist, E. T. & Broecker, W. S. (eds.) (1985). *The Carbon Cycle and Atmospheric CO$_2$ Natural Variations Archean to Present*, American Geophysical Union, Washington, DC, 627pp.

Tans, P. P., Fung, I. Y. & Takahashi, T. (1990). Observational constraints on the global atmospheric CO$_2$ budget, *Science*, **247**, 1431–8.

Wroblewski, J. S., Sarmiento, J. L. & Flierl, G. R. (1988). An ocean basin scale model of plankton dynamics in the North Atlantic 1. solutions for the climatological oceanographic conditions in May, *Global Biogeochem. Cycles*, **2**(3), 199–218.

Yoder, J. A., Esaias, W. E., Feldman, G. C. & McClain, C. R. (1988). Satellite ocean color – status report. *Oceanography Magazine*, **1**(1), 18–20.

Evaporation from the ocean

W. TIMOTHY LIU

Introduction

Water is the essential element for life, and evaporation is the principal mechanism to transport water from the surface of the Earth to the atmosphere. Over 70% of the Earth's surface is covered by ocean and the oceans form the largest reservoir of water on Earth. With their high specific heat and large thermal inertia, the oceans are also the largest reservoir of heat and the flywheel of the global heat engine. Since water has high latent heat, evaporation is also an efficient way to transfer the energy. Besides releasing latent heat to the atmosphere, the water transported from the ocean to the atmosphere forms clouds which absorb and reflect radiation. Water vapor is also an important greenhouse gas which absorbs more longwave radiation emitted by the Earth than the short-wave radiation from the Sun. Redistribution of clouds and water vapor changes the Earth's radiation balance and affects climate. The differential heating of the atmosphere by the ocean fuels atmospheric circulation which, in turn, drives ocean currents. Both winds and currents transport and redistribute heat and greenhouse gases. The difference between evaporation and precipitation is the fresh water flux. Heating and moistening lower the density of air; cooling and adding fresh water reduce the density of sea water. The heat and water fluxes, therefore, change both the baroclinicity and stability (horizontal and vertical density gradients) of the atmosphere and the ocean. These, in turn, modify the shears of wind and current.

Methodology

Water vapor and the latent heat are transported from the ocean surface to the atmosphere mainly by turbulence. The direct measurement of micro-scale turbulent flux posts severe demand on instrumentations (Smith, 1989). The only practical way of deriving large-scale evaporation for long periods of time is through the bulk parameterization method. The bulk parameterization formula

$$E = \varrho \, C_{\mathrm{E}} \, U \, \Delta Q$$

relates the water vapor flux (E) to some mean measurements which are more readily available, and ϱ is the surface air density. To the first approximation, the flux is assumed to be proportional to the product of wind speed (U) and sea–air specific humidity difference ($\Delta Q = Q_{\mathrm{s}} - Q$). The specific humidity at the sea–air interface (Q_{s}) is assumed to be the saturation specific humidity at sea surface temperature (T_{s}). Observations of U, T_{s} and the air specific humidity (Q) are provided by merchant ships and fishing vessels as routine meteorological reports. The dimensionless proportionality constant (C_{E}), called the transfer coefficient for water vapor, is usually determined from the slope of the linear regression between E and $U\Delta Q$ measured during field experiments. There is usually a large scatter of the data about such linear regression. In theory, C_{E} depends on the height at which U and Q are measured and also on conditions such as the roughness of the sea and the density stratification of the atmosphere. The product of E and the latent heat of vaporization is the latent heat flux. A bulk formula with a constant transfer coefficient is a simple but useful tool if one can tolerate the inaccuracy. To improve the accuracy, Liu, Kaksaros & Businger (1979) and others tried to account for the variabilities of C_{E} by deriving the flux from the similarity relation (non-dimensional humidity profile). This is equivalent to using a transfer coefficient which varies with the mean parameters.

In the past, the coefficients were determined and verified with data under moderate wind conditions, approximately between 4 to 15 m/s. Using direct measurement of E from a number of experiments, Friehe and Schmitt (1976) determined C_{E} to be 1.3×10^{-3}. Large and Pond (1982) measured the flux by a different method, and found a value of 1.15×10^{-3}. The extrapolation of these empirical values to high and low winds were controversial. At low winds, the sea surface changes from rough to smooth with different transfer processes. At high winds, breaking waves and spray provide different mechanisms of introducing water into the atmosphere. Most of the recent field experiments were directed at these extreme conditions. The value given by Liu *et al.* (1979) at a reference height of 10 m and under near neutral stability is approximately 1.3×10^{-3} at moderate winds, and the value decreases a little with increasing wind speed. At low winds, Liu *et al.* (1979) postulated that C_E increases sharply with decreasing wind speed, based on smooth flow theories. The low wind behavior is necessary to provide for buoyancy-induced turbulent transport as the mean wind vanishes. Palmer, Brankovic & Viterbo (1990) found it critical to include such behavior in the operational model of European Center for Medium Range Weather Forecasts (ECMWF) to realistically simulate observed monsoon circulation and associated rainfall. The postulation of Liu *et al.* (1979) was recently confirmed by the field measurements of Bradley, Coppin & Godfrey (1991) in the doldrums of the western equatorial Pacific. At high winds, preliminary results from an experiment in the North Sea pointed to a constant value of 1.2×10^{-3} (DeCosmo & Katsaros, 1988).

In numerical and climate studies, the bulk formula which is derived from spot measurements (i.e. approximately half hourly averages at a specific location) has to be applied to parameters averaged over a month or over grid sizes of approximately 100 km. To examine the errors introduced by the neglected variance, Esbensen and Reynolds (1981), using the parameterization model of Liu *et al.* (1979) and scalar-averaged winds, have analyzed up to 25 years of data from nine ocean weather ships. They found that the monthly averages of the latent heat fluxes do not differ significantly from averaged fluxes obtained by applying the same parameterization method to monthly mean observations. However, the ocean stations are confined to mid-latitude and subtropical locations. Liu (1988) extended the study to near-equatorial locations and found similar results. The Taylor's hypothesis (Hinze, 1959), which assumes that the time rate of change is equal to the product of an advection velocity and the spatial gradient in the direction of the advection, provides a method to relate the temporal variabilities to the spatial variabilities. These results indicate that, under general conditions, the bulk formula can be applied to average observations.

Except near coastal areas and in major shipping lanes, meteorological reports are sparse in the tropical and southern oceans. *In situ* measurements are not adequate to resolve the temporal and spatial variabilities of evaporation. Space-borne sensors would provide repeated and uniform coverage of E if the U, T_s and Q could be retrieved from satellite observations. At present, space-borne sensors can measure U and T_s but not Q. Microwave radiometers, however, can measure accurately the precipitable water (W), the column- integrated water vapor in the atmosphere (e.g. Alishouse, 1983; Chang *et al.*, 1984).

The relation between Q and W depends on the variabilities of atmospheric humidity profiles. Liu (1984) found that there

is only one dominant mode of variability in the vertical distribution of water vapor in the atmosphere on the monthly timescale and suggested the possibility of deriving monthly mean Q from W measured by space-borne sensors. A global relation between monthly mean Q and W was derived using 17 years of radiosonde reports from 46 mid-ocean meteorological stations (Liu, 1986). Hsu and Blanchard (1989) evaluated this relation with measurements taken in 13 field experiments distributed over global oceans and indicated that the relation could be used to describe not only monthly means, but also instantaneous soundings. With this Q–W relation, evaporation over global oceans can be estimated if space-borne sensors have sufficient sensitivity to monitor the variabilities of U, W, and T_s.

Satellite data

The Scanning Multichannel Microwave Radiometer (SMMR) on the Nimbus-7 spacecraft of the National Aeronautics and Space Administration (NASA), launched in 1978, provided unprecedented, simultaneous, and all-weather coverage of T_s, U and W, the three parameters required to compute evaporation as described under 'Methodology'. To demonstrate its sensitivity to climate anomalies, the distribution of these three parameters in the tropical Pacific as observed by SMMR during an El Niño Southern Oscillation (ENSO) episode in 1982–1983 are compared with those during the non-ENSO months, in Fig. 1. ENSO is one of the most dominant climate signals on timescales from a few months to a few years, involving major dislocations of atmospheric and oceanic systems. The non-ENSO distributions, hereafter referred to as 'normal' distributions, are formed by averaging 1980 and 1981 data for each calendar month. Quantitative evaluations of the parameters are given by Liu (1988).

During the October of a non-ENSO year (upper left), high values of precipitable water are found in the eastern Pacific just north of the equator where the intertropical convergence zone (ITCZ) is located, and another band is found running east–southeast from New Guinea marking the position of the South Pacific convergence zone (SPCZ). The area of highest intensity is over Indonesia. Drastic changes took place in 1982 (lower left). A very intense area was centered on the date-line at the equator. The precipitable water west of the date-line has been greatly diminished. During this time, droughts spread from southern India to Indonesia, Australia and the Philippines; floods were reported in the Line Islands and then in Columbia and Ecuador as the intense center moved east. The atmosphere is heated by the latent heat released by precipitation; anomalous precipitable water

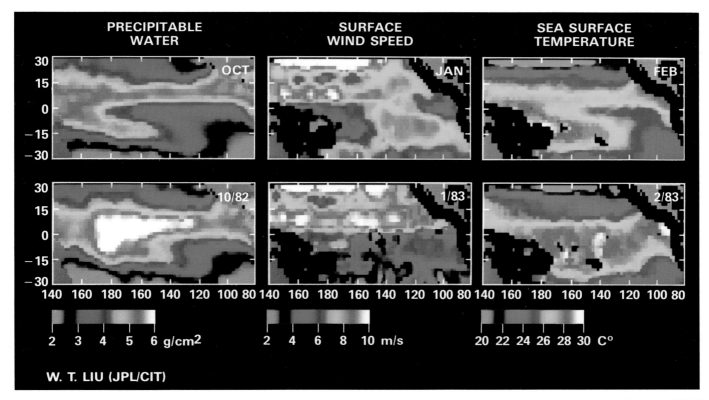

Fig. 1. Distribution of (from left to right) precipitable water, surface wind speed, and sea surface temperature derived from Nimbus/SMMR observations. In the upper row are the averages of 1980 and 1981 for a calendar month and in the lower row are the distributions during ENSO.

represents potential for anomalous heating. It is not difficult to imagine the disturbances that propagated from this 'heat explosion' and affected the climate in far-off places.

During a 'normal' January (upper center), low wind speeds due to surface convergence are found at the ITCZ and SPCZ, with high winds of the southeast trades blowing in the area wedged between them. There is a zone of low U at approximately 20° N due to the surface divergence between the westerlies to the north and the northeast trades to the south. On the equator, the winds normally blow from the east but during the ENSO episode (lower, center), anomalous west winds initially appeared west of the date-line and then moved east. A convergence center of low wind speed could be found at the eastern terminus of the anomalous westerlies, at the equator and 140° W. The wind anomalies may have excited ocean waves that changes the upper ocean thermal structure. South of the equator, the southeast trades had collapsed.

During the February of a 'normal' year, the warm water belt in the tropical Pacific is interrupted by a cold tongue due to upwelling extending from the South American coast to the eastern equatorial Pacific. During the episode, the cold tongue disappeared and surface water of over 29 °C extended

across the Pacific. The suppression of upwelling cuts off phytoplankton production, changes the entire marine ecosystem, and devastates the fishing industry.

Flux variability and oceanic response

From the description above, it is apparent that SMMR is sensitive to geographic distribution and the annual and inter-annual variations of the three parameters. With the three parameters measured by SMMR, monthly latent heat flux fields in the tropical Pacific were constructed. Shown in Fig. 2 are the time–longitude variations averaged between 2° N and 2° S, between January 1980 and October 1983, from the date-line to 90° W.

The ENSO episode is envisioned (upper left) as an apparent eastward migration, starting in June 1982, of the warm water pool marked by the 29 °C isotherm. The result is a reverse of zonal SST gradient near the date-line. At the same time, a center of organized deep convection marked by high W (upper right) also moves east from the date-line, leaving dry air behind. The seasonal cycle of U (lower left) is disrupted by the eastward migration of a low center represen-ting surface convergence associated with the organized con-

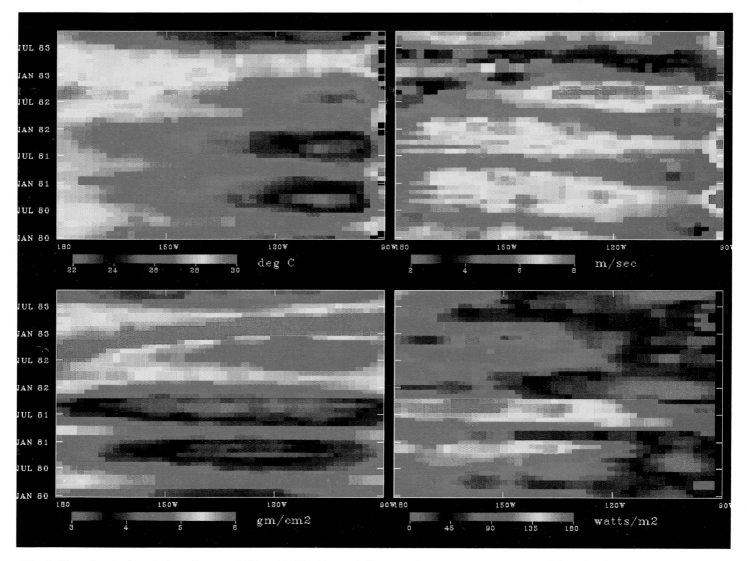

Fig. 2. Time–longitude variations (between 2° N and 2° S) of (upper left) sea surface temperature, (upper right) surface level wind speed, (lower, left) water vapor, and (lower, right) latent heat flux, derived from Nimbus/SMMR observations.

vections at the eastern terminal of anomalous westerlies. In early 1983, zonal belts of high T_s, high W, and low U stretch across the entire equatorial Pacific centered just south of the equator. Detailed evolution of these three parameters during the episode is described by Liu (1989). Despite the warm water in the central Pacific, the latent heat flux is below normal (low evaporation) during the early phase of the episode in 1982 because the higher humidity and weaker wind more than compensate for the higher T_s (lower right). It returns to normal magnitudes only briefly during March 1983.

To examine ocean's response to surface latent heat forcing, the correlation coefficient between E and the time rate of change of sea surface temperature ($\partial T_s/\partial t$) were computed at each 2° latitude by 2° longitude grid using 44 months of data from February 1980 to September 1983, as shown in color Fig. 3 (upper). The slope of the linear regression of three consecutive months of T_s is taken to be $\partial T_s/\partial t$. To isolate the large-scale coherent features and remove noise, both the E and $\partial T_s/\partial t$ fields were reconstructed from the first three empirical orthogonal functions (EOF) which, together, account for more than 80% of the variance. For 44 uncorrelated data pairs, a coefficient higher than 0.4 would be significant to 99% level. The correlation coefficient between the latent heat flux and $\partial T_s/\partial t$ is significant everywhere except in a narrow strip between 5° N and 5° S, tilting north towards Central America in the east. This area corresponds to the equatorial wave guide (Gill, 1982) where ocean

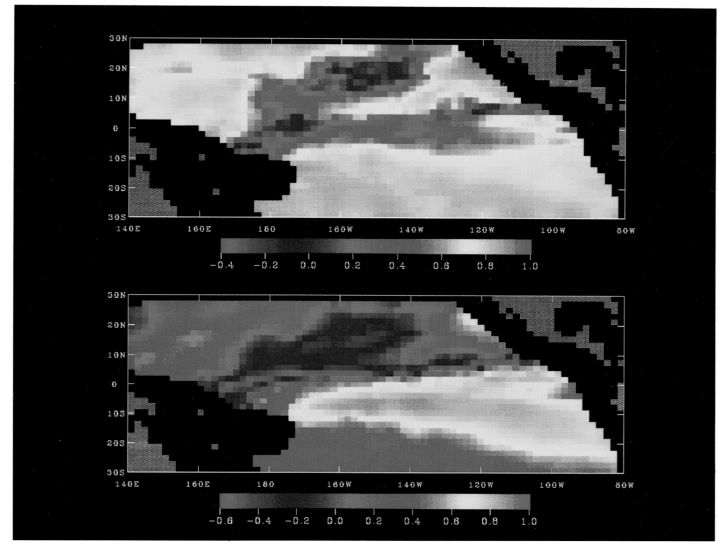

Fig. 3. Distribution of the contemporary correlation coefficients between time rate of change of sea surface temperature and latent heat flux (upper), for a 44-month period. Distribution of the contemporary correlation coefficients between anomalous time rate of change of sea surface temperature and anomalous latent heat flux (lower), for a 21-month period. The sign of latent heat flux is reversed so that it is positive when directed into the ocean.

dynamics may play a more important role than surface heating in the seasonal change of T_s and the area is also covered by the migration of the ITCZ where large cloud variability affects radiative forcing. Another exception is found in an area oriented southwest–northeast and with correlation minimum centered at 18° N and 150° W. The zonal contrast at 18° N is associated with the phase change in surface wind. In other areas, the seasonal cycles of latent heat flux are in phase with $\partial T_s/\partial t$ and are approximately three months ahead of the T_s.

The non-ENSO seasonal cycle was compiled by averaging the monthly fields of 1980 and 1981. These seasonal cycles were subtracted from the 1982 and 1983 monthly mean

fields, and the differences are referred to as 'anomalies'. These anomalies are deviations from a two-year mean, not the long-term climatological mean. Contemporary correlations were computed at each 2° latitude by 2° longitude grid point for 21 months of data (January 1982 to September 1983). For 21 pairs of uncorrelated data, a coefficient larger than 0.6 is significant to 99%. The distributions of the correlations are shown in Fig. 3 (lower). The correlation coefficients between anomalous E and anomalous $\partial T_s/\partial t$ are significant in an area which encompasses almost the entire southern tropical ocean. This area covers the normal extent of cold tropical water and is the area where intense warm anomalies were found during the 1982–1983 ENSO episode

(Liu, 1989). A sharp decrease in anomalous $\partial T_s/\partial t$ in the beginning of 1983 which led to the re-establishment of the cold tongue (Liu, 1989) coincides with a sharp decrease in latent heat flux into the ocean (higher evaporation).

Limitations

The method described under 'Methodology' and demonstrated in 'Flux variability and oceanic response' is limited by the applicability of the $Q-W$ relation. Liu, Tang & Wentz (1992) confirms early observations (Liu, 1986) that the relation fails in the western Pacific and the western Atlantic north of 35° and in a small region off the coast of Baja California during summer because of surface humidity saturation. Liu, Tang & Niiler (1991) examined the validity of the relation at various timescales through EOF analysis of humidity soundings. The validity of the $Q-W$ relation at periods shorter than a month depends on how well it accounts for high frequency variability of atmospheric humidity, and EOFs are the most efficient way of representing uncorrelated modes of variance. The first principal components (time series of the EOF coefficients) were found to correlate almost perfectly with W. The fractional variance represented by this mode increases with increasing period. It reaches approximately 90% at two weeks and decreases sharply, below one week, down to approximately 60% at the daily period. While W appears to be an adequate estimator of Q at low frequencies, more than one independent estimator is needed at periods shorter than a week.

For all the stations examined, the EOFs resemble trigonometric functions, with increasing zero crossings but accounting for fast decreasing fractional variance. To account for a larger fraction of the variance, a larger number of independent modes representing finer vertical structures are needed. However, the analysis of Liu et al. (1991) demonstrated that just the first three modes (with three broad layers) are sufficient to account for 80% to 90% of the variance. The radiances observed by atmospheric humidity sounders, such as the Advance Microwave Sounding Unit (AMSU) to be flown in the next generation of operational NOAA polar orbiters, have weighting functions (the contribution of the radiance as a function of height) peaking at various levels. Although these weighting functions are broad relative to the depth of the troposphere, they may be useful in providing the necessary additional estimators of Q and humidity profiles at high frequencies. As demonstrated by Liu et al. (1991), the high frequency surface humidity can also be estimated if the integrated water vapor in the boundary layer, instead of the entire atmospheric column, can be measured accurately by space-borne sensors. The development of an algorithm to retrieve such a parameter will be complicated by the variability of the boundary layer height. At shorter timescales, the estimation of evaporation is also aggravated by the increasing need of collocating observations from different spacecraft.

Another limitation is the accuracy of the geophysical parameters retrieved from satellite observation. For example, the main reason for limiting the application of the Nimbus/SMMR data to the tropical oceans is the latitudinal dependent errors found. Reprocessing efforts underway may mitigate the problem. The Special Sensor Microwave Imager (SSMI) on the operational spacecraft of the Defense Meteorological Satellite Program (DMSP) is providing improved U and W. However, the SSMI lacks the low frequency channels which are sensitive to T_s variation. The infra-red sensors for T_s, such as the operational Advanced Very High Resolution Radiometer (AVHRR), cannot penetrate clouds and are more susceptible to atmospheric attenuation than microwave sensors, particularly in the high humidity conditions over the tropical oceans.

The problems with the bulk formula have been discussed under 'Methodology'. It is not the optimal method for satellite data because it was designed to make use of parameters measured on ships; space-borne sensors measure radiances at various frequencies instead. Both the errors in retrieving the intermediate parameters and the uncertainties in bulk parameterization affect the accuracy of the product. A direct relation between what we need, E, and what we actually measure, the radiances, has been explored (Liu, 1990).

Data assimilation in numerical model

Atmospheric general circulation models (AGCM) can produce surface latent heat flux over global oceans by providing dynamic interpolation and quality control to different and sparse observations over the ocean. Both the National Meteorology Center of the United States and the ECMWF have started to produce surface turbulent fluxes routinely, but, it was Atlas et al. (1987) who first produced global latent heat flux by assimilating surface wind vectors measured by the microwave scatterometer on Seasat into a fourth-order general circulation model of the Goddard Laboratory for Atmospheres. In Fig. 4, the distribution of latent heat flux in August 1978 produced by this model is compared with the flux distribution computed from observations of Seasat SMMR with the method described under 'Methodology'. There are similarities in the geographic distribution, with lows in upwelling regions (low T_s), in convergence zones (low U), and at high latitudes. High values are found in subtropical oceans with lower air humidity and strong trade winds. The flux is higher in the winter hemisphere because of stronger

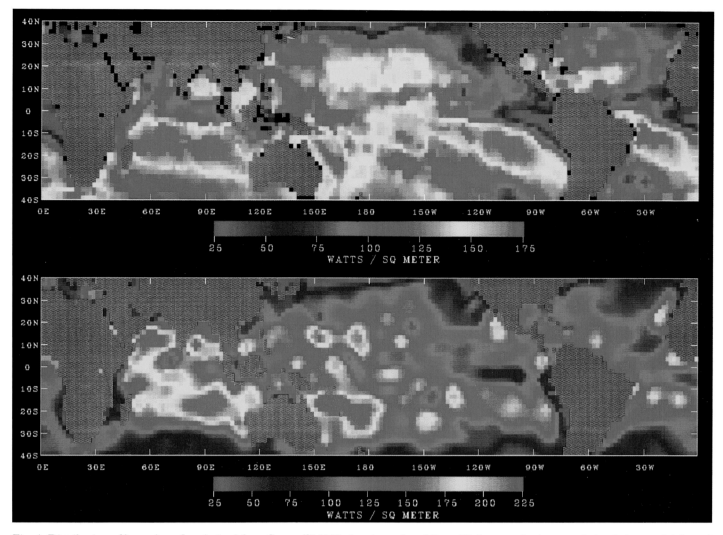

Fig. 4. Distribution of latent heat flux derived from Seasat/SMMR data (upper) and from GLA atmospheric general circulation model (lower) for August 1978.

winds. The most obvious difference is found in the Arabian Sea where the model flux is relatively high. In general, the magnitudes of the two flux sets are different because different transfer coefficients are used. Atlas *et al.* (1987) assume C_E to be equal to the transfer coefficient of momentum which increases with wind speeds.

Simonot and Le Treut (1987) examined the monthly mean E produced by the model of ECMWF from 1983 to 1985 and found that the values are systematically biased low by approximately 40 W/m². The 1983 ECMWF fluxes were compared with those computed from SMMR data by Liu (1988) and he found that ECMWF products were not adequate to capture the zonal gradient and inter-annual variability in the tropical Pacific. In 1985, the AGCM of ECMWF received several important improvements, including shallow convection, that

enhance evaporation (Barnier & Simonot, 1990). Two years later, in July 1987, SSMI was launched and the sensor is technologically an improvement over SMMR. A comparison between latent heat flux fields from the improved model and computed from the new sensor was performed. LE over global oceans were computed with the model of Liu *et al.* (1979), using U and W from SSMI and the T_s from the AVHRR. Fig. 5 (upper) shows the difference between LE computed using satellite data and using data (U, T_s and Q) from the ECMWF model, with the same coefficients. The major cause of the difference is due to Q. The difference between Q estimated from satellite data and produced by ECMWF is shown in Fig. 5 (center). The pattern of differences is almost the same as LE, but of opposite sign. To make sure that the difference is not introduced by the

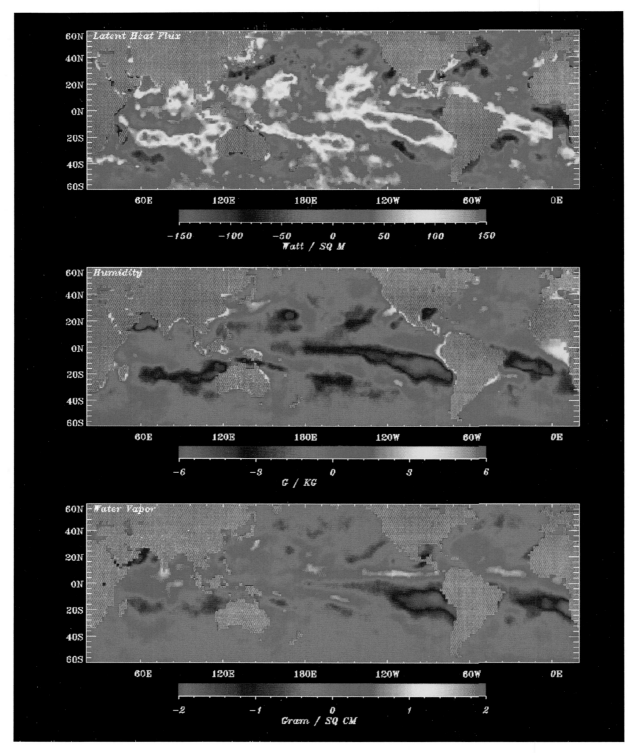

Fig. 5. Distribution of the difference between parameters derived from satellite observations and from the model at ECMWF in October 1987: (upper) latent heat flux, (center) surface level humidity, and (lower) precipitable water.

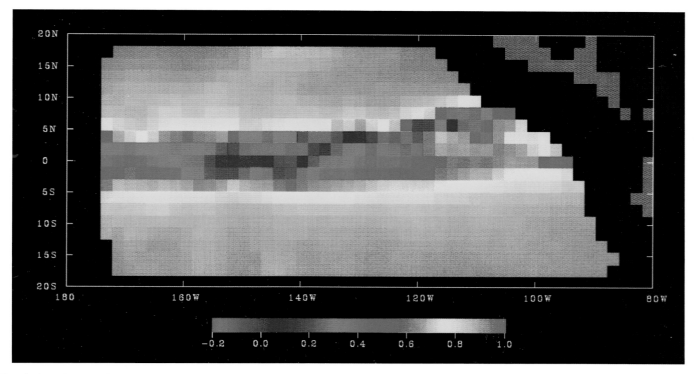

Fig. 6. Distribution of the contemporary correlation coefficients between the monthly means of time rate of change of sea surface temperature and net surface heat flux into the ocean for a 44-month period.

author's method of deriving Q from W, the difference between W measured by SSMI and W obtained by integrating the humidities at all levels produced by ECMWF model is also shown in Fig. 5 (lower). The distribution is very similar to those of Q difference; the same areas of significant difference are found. Comparisons with radiosonde data from July 1987 to July 1989 in areas of large difference were performed. At all locations, the radiosonde data are clearly in closer agreement with satellite data than ECMWF data (Liu *et al.*, 1992). In the eastern part of the southern oceans where the difference is particularly large, there are hardly any *in situ* measurements for assimilation into the model. The only data are infra-red soundings from the Tiros-N operational vertical sounders (TOVS), with coarse resolutions. The study found that neither TOVS nor ECMWF was able to reveal accurately the sharp gradient and the extent of the dry tongues in these areas.

Future application and synergism

Further understanding of ocean–atmosphere interaction and climate variability can be achieved by combining the latent heat flux with other geophysical parameters retrieved from satellite data. The following are two examples: ocean's response to surface forcing and the atmospheric hydrologic balance.

Surface forcing of the ocean

Latent heat flux is only one component of the thermal forcing on the oceans. Another important component in the tropical oceans is shortwave radiation from the Sun. Shortwave radiation computed from the observations of VISSR (Visible Infra-red Spin Scan Radiometer) on GOES-W was combined with latent heat flux computed from SMMR by Liu and Gautier (1990). The distribution of the correlation coefficient between the reconstructed (from first three EOFs) net thermal forcing (the sum of latent heat and shortwave radiation into the ocean) and $\partial T_s/\partial t$ is shown in Fig. 6, providing an unprecedentedly clear visualization of the separation of an equatorial regime from the rest of the ocean. Away from the wave-guide, the correlation is significantly positive, that indicating the surface thermal forcing is the dominant factor in change of T_s. Within the wave-guide, ocean dynamics may be the more important factor. The negative correlations infer a decrease in solar irradiance resulting from an increase in cloud cover and atmospheric convectivity, as T_s rises. Continuous monitoring of global low frequency variation of the major components of ocean surface thermal forcing is made possible recently by the operational SSMI and AVHRR, as well as the International Satellite Cloud Climatology Project (Schiffler & Rossow, 1983) which provides standardized and

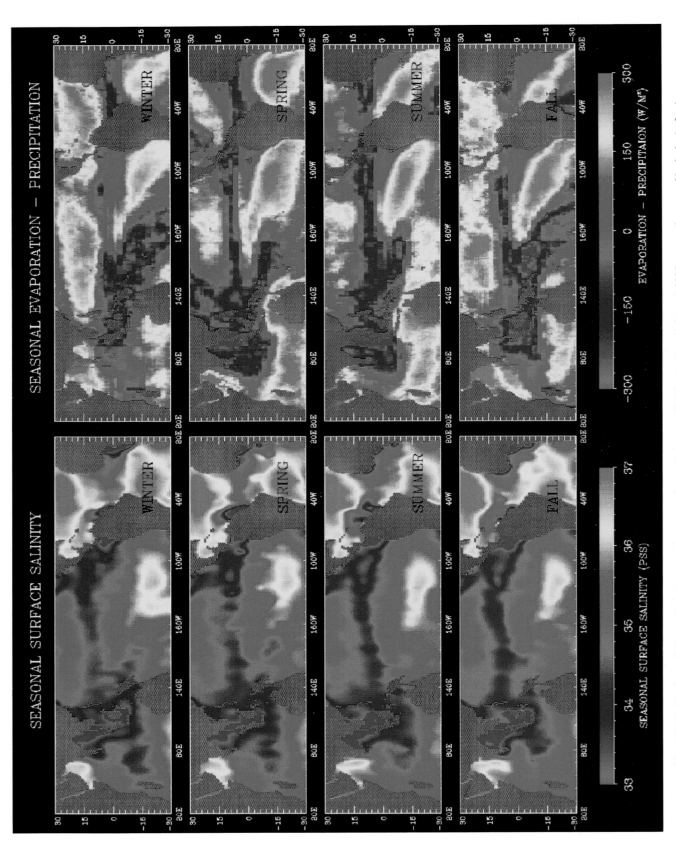

Fig. 7. Distributions of climatological seasonal mean surface salinity compiled by Levitus (left) and 1988 seasonal mean of hydrologic forcing (evaporation–precipitation) derived from satellite data. The forcing is multiplied by the latent heat of vaporization and expressed in heat flux units.

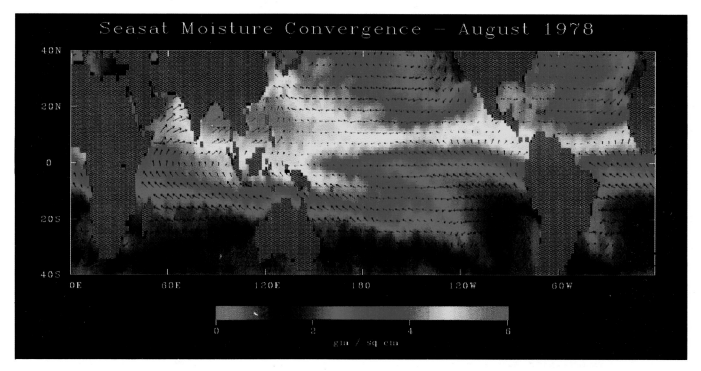

Fig. 8. Distributions of precipitable water (color image) as observed by the Seasat microwave radiometer and the surface wind vectors (dark arrows) as observed by the Seasat microwave scatterometer, during August 1978.

calibrated cloud information derived from a suite of international geostationary satellites. Improved atmospheric sounders may help to derive sensible heat flux and long-wave radiation in the future.

The difference between precipitation and evaporation is the hydrologic forcing on the ocean. The distributions of seasonal hydrologic forcing are compared with the distribution of surface salinity in Fig. 7. Seasonal surface salinity was derived by Levitus (1982) from climatological *in situ* measurements. Evaporation and precipitation fields for the corresponding seasons were from 1988 data; evaporation from SSMI and AVHRR and precipitation from the Global Precipitation Climatology Project (Arkin & Ardanuy, 1989). The geographic distributions of the forcing (left) and response (right) show strong resemblance. Areas of high evaporation largely correspond to areas of high salinity and vice versa. There are exceptions, however, that require future studies.

Atmospheric convection and hydrologic balance

By combining the W measured by the microwave radiometer and the surface wind vectors measured by the microwave scatterometer on the NASA spacecraft Seasat, the major hydrologic systems in the tropical oceans are visualized in Fig. 8. The arrows represent the surface wind vectors and show the strength of the trade winds and their convergence at the ITCZ at 10° N in the Pacific and the Atlantic and the SPCZ running east-south-east from New Guinea. The color image shows the variability of precipitable water which has high values over the ITCZ, the SPCZ and the doldrum area over the warm water pool in the western Pacific and Indian Ocean. Note the strength of the monsoon which advects moisture across the Arabian Sea to the Indian subcontinent.

The difference between local evaporation and precipitation at the surface has to be balanced by the divergence of moisture transport. As an example, the distribution, in October 1987, of each term in the balance are compared in Fig. 9. The latent heat flux (upper) and the precipitation (center) are computed in the same way as those in Fig. 7. The divergence of vertically integrated moisture transport (lower) is computed from ECMWF model data. In the areas of high water vapor, the precipitation is also high, but the evaporation is low, and the divergence is negative (convergence). In the dry areas, there is practically no precipitation, the evaporation is high and the divergence is positive. Figs. 8 and 9 demonstrate that moisture advection, corresponding to the surface branches of the local Hadley and Walker circulation, is the main force that sustains high quantities of water vapor

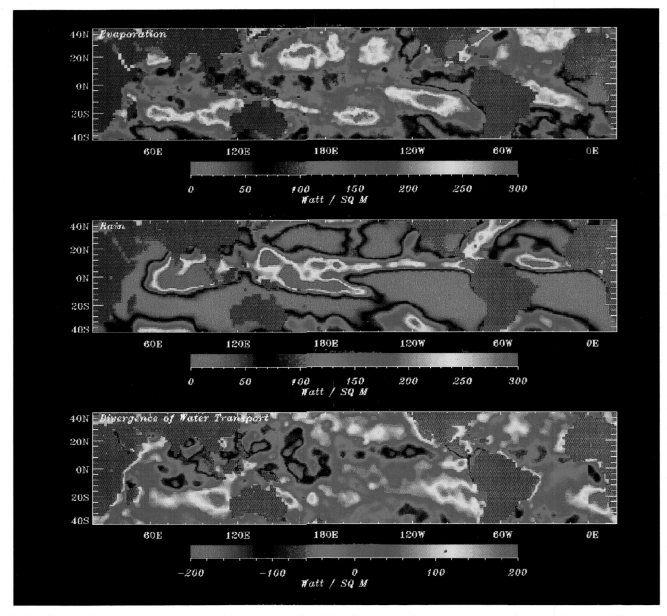

Fig. 9. Distribution of evaporation (upper), precipitation (center) and the divergence of moisture transport (lower) in October 1987. All values are multiplied by the latent heat of vaporization and expressed in heat flux units.

and precipitation in the convergence areas despite the low evaporation.

The divergence of moisture transport computed from ECMWF data is lower than the surface flux computed from satellite data in the dry regions of the eastern tropical oceans of the Southern Hemisphere. Heta and Mitsuta (personal communication, 1990) recently computed the divergence in the Pacific, using their own analysis of wind field and the W from SMMR. Their results in the dry regions, although obtained for a different time, agree with the values of surface

flux shown in Fig. 9. The discrepancy of ECMWF results is largely caused by overestimation of the atmospheric moisture as discussed under 'Limitations'.

In the future, surface wind vectors can be derived from scatterometers on ERS-1 and ADEOS. The Tropical Rain Measurement Mission (TRMM) of NASA will provide high frequency sampling of precipitation in the tropics. The microwave sounders to be launched in DMSP and NOAA satellites in the near future will help in deriving the divergence of atmospheric moisture transport. By the end of the 1990s there will be more knowledge about the hydrologic balance of the coupled ocean–atmosphere system.

Conclusion

In the past decade, spaceborne radiometers and radar altimeters have demonstrated their capability of measuring the surface signatures of ocean's responses to atmospheric wind and thermal forcing. The results of this study demonstrated that evaporation or latent heat flux at weekly and 100 km resolutions can be estimated from operational satellite data to a useful accuracy over most of the ocean. Together with wind stress from the scatterometer, precipitation from the GPCP, surface solar irradiance from ISCCP and the surface radiation budget program of the WCRP, the major ocean–atmosphere physical forcing could be monitored in the 1990s. Such data would make significant contributions to our understanding of ocean's role in climate feedback – storage and transport of heat and trace gases. Four-dimensional data assimilation by atmospheric circulation models has the potential for producing useful latent heat flux over global oceans, but the present model products still have deficiencies in the moisture fields. Methods to assimilate moisture data from spaceborne microwave radiometers are being developed.

Both the ocean and the atmosphere are turbulent fluids with non-linear interaction. Phenomena at one scale affect those at much different scales. Only space-borne sensors can provide the adequate means to observe multi-scale interactions. The synergism of different sets of satellite data is needed not only to estimate surface fluxes but is vital to unravel the complex interaction between the hydrologic and energy balance of the coupled ocean–atmosphere system. The NASA Earth Observing System is the planned endeavor to satisfy the needs of continuity and simultaneity of measurements well into the next century as the demand on accuracy and resolution increases.

Data availability

Most of the data described are available from the Physical Oceanography Distributed Active Archive Center at the Jet Propulsion Laboratory and the National Space Science Data Center at the Goddard Space Flight Center.

References

Alishouse, J. C. (1983). Total precipitable water and rainfall determinations from the SEASAT scanning multichannel microwave radiometer. *J. Geophys. Res.*, **88**, 1929–35.

Arkin, P. A. & Ardanuy, P. E. (1989). Estimating climate-scale precipitation from space: a review. *J. Climate*, **2**, 1229–38.

Atlas, R., Busalacchi, A. J., Ghil, M., Bloom, S. & Kalnay, E. (1987). Global surface wind and flux fields from model assimilation of Seasat data. *J. Geophys. Res.*, **92**, 6477–87.

Barnier, B. & Simonot, J. Y. (1990). Net surface heat flux over the north and south Atlantic in 1985–1986 from day 1 predictions of the European Center for Medium-Range Weather Forecast, *J. Geophys. Res.*, **95**, 13301–31.

Bradley, E. F., Coppin, P. A. & Godfrey, J. S. (1991). Measurement of sensible and latent heat flux in the western equatorial Pacific Ocean. *J. Geophys. Res.*, **96**, 3375–89.

Chang, H. D., Hwang, P. H., Wilheit, T. T., Chang, A. T. C., Staelin, D. H. & Rosenkranz, P. W. (1984). Monthly distributions of precipitable water from Nimbus-7 SMMR data. *J. Geophys. Res.*, **89**, 5328–34.

DeCosmos, J. & Katsaros, K. B. (1988). Surface layer fluxes of momentum, heat, and water vapor. *EOS Trans. of Am. Geophys. Union*, **69**, 1232.

Esbensen, S. K. & Reynolds, R. W. (1981). Estimating monthly averaged air–sea transfer of heat and momentum using the bulk aerodynamic method. *J. Phys. Oceanogr.*, **11**, 457–65.

Friehe, C. A. & Schmitt, K. F. (1976). Parameterization of air–sea interface fluxes of sensible heat and moisture by the bulk aerodynamic formulas. *J. Phys. Oceanogr.*, **12**, 801–9.

Gill, A. E. (1982). *Atmosphere–Ocean Dynamics*, Academic Press, Orlando, FL.

Hinze, J. O. (1959). *Turbulence*. McGraw-Hill, New York, pp. 40–41.

Hsu, S. A. & Blanchard, B. W. (1989). The relationship between total precipitable water and surface-level humidity over the sea. *J. Geophys. Res.*, **94**, 14539–45.

Large, W. G. & Pond, S. (1982). Sensible and latent heat flux measurements over the ocean. *J. Phys. Oceanogr.*, **12**, 464–82.

Levitus, S. (1982). *Climatological Atlas of the World Ocean*. NOAA Professional Paper 13, NOAA, Rockville, 173pp.

Liu, W. T. (1984). Estimation of latent heat flux with Seasat-SMMR, a case study in N. Atlantic. *Large-Scale Oceanographic Experiments and Satellites* (C. Gautier and M. Fieux, eds.), D. Reidel, Hingham, Mass., pp. 205–21.

Liu, W. T. (1986). Statistical relation between monthly precipitable water and surface-level humidity over global oceans. *Mon. Wea. Rev.*, **114**, 1591–602.

Liu, W. T. (1988). Moisture and latent heat flux variabilities in the tropical Pacific derived from satellite data. *J. Geophys. Res.*, **93**, 6749–60 and 6965–8.

Liu, W. T. (1989). The annual and inter-annual variabilities of precipitable water, surface wind speed, and sea surface temperature, over the tropical Pacific. *Ocean Air Interaction*, **1**, 195–219.

Liu, W. T. (1990). Remote sensing of surface turbulence flux. *Surface Waves and Fluxes*, vol II. (G. L. Geenaert and W. J. Plant, eds.), Kluwer Academic Press, pp. 293–309.

Liu, W. T. & Gautier, C. (1990). Thermal forcing on the tropical Pacific from satellite data. *J. Geophys. Res.*, **95**, 13209–17.

Liu, W. T., Katsaros, K. B. & Businger, J. A. (1979). Bulk

parameterization of air–sea exchanges of heat and water vapor including the molecular constraints at the surface. *J. Atmos. Sci.*, **36**, 1722–35.

Liu, W. T., Tang, W. & Niiler, P. P. (1991). Humidity profiles over ocean. *J. Climate*, **4**, 1023–34.

Liu, W. T., Tang, W. & Wentz, F. J. (1992). Precipitable water and surface humidity over global oceans from SSMI and ECMWF. *J. Geophys. Res.*, **97**, 2251–64.

Palmer, T. N., Brankovic, C. & Viterbo, P. (1990). Seasonal simulations of the summer monsoons by the ECMWF model with prescribed SST. *Intern. TOGA Scientific Conf. Proc.*, **WCP-43**, 217–28. World Climate Research Programme, Geneva.

Simonot, J. Y. & Le Treut, H. (1987). Surface heat fluxes from a numerical weather prediction system. *Clim. Dyn.*, **2**, 11–28.

Schiffler, R. A. & Rossow, W. B. (1983). The International Satellite Cloud Climatology Project (ISCCP): The first project of the World Climate Research Program. *Bull. Am. Meteor. Soc.*, **64**, 779–84.

Smith, S. D. (1989). Water vapor flux at the sea surface, *Bound. Layer Meteor.*, **47**, 277–93.

PART V

OCEAN/ATMOSPHERE COUPLING

El Niño Southern Oscillation: a view from space

K.-M. LAU AND A. J. BUSALACCHI

Introduction

The El Niño Southern Oscillation (ENSO) is the largest known global climate signal in inter-annual timescales. The phenomenon is characterized by the appearance of extensive warm surface water over the central and eastern tropical Pacific at 3–7 year intervals. This anomalous warming can have devastating socio-economic consequences. By some estimates, ENSO is responsible for thousands of weather-related disasters, dramatic changes in marine ecology over tropical islands and coastal regions, and severe economic losses due to flood, famine and crop failure in countries along the tropical and subtropical belt. In particular, the fishery industry, which is the primary national resource for countries along the South American coastal region such as Peru and Ecuador was wiped out by severe ENSOs such as the 1972–73 event.

The oceanic and the atmospheric component of ENSO had been known independently for a long time as separate phenomena. For centuries, Peruvians have used the term 'el fenomeno del Niño' in reference to the prolonged anomalous warming of coastal waters (Enfield, 1989). Walker (1923) and Walker and Bliss (1932) found a coherent global variation of barometric pressures between Indonesia/Australia and the south-east Pacific and called it the Southern Oscillation. The two phenomena were first recognized as components of a coupled ocean–atmosphere phenomenon by Bjerknes (1966, 1969). Nowadays, ENSO may be understood in the following broad sense. Under normal conditions, surface wind in the tropical Pacific blows steadily across the entire basin from east to west pushing warm surface water and raising sea level to the west while producing cold upwelling and lowering sea level in the east. Because of the favorable conditions for atmospheric convection created by warm water, the western Pacific has the highest annual rainfall amount in the world (over 2500 mm/year). As a result, there is a large surplus of rainfall over evaporation in the equatorial western Pacific region. To maintain the water balance, a large moisture flux must come from elsewhere in the tropics. When an ENSO occurs, the moisture balance in the atmosphere–ocean system undergoes dramatic changes; the easterly surface wind weakens, the warm water sloshes back to the east resulting in below normal SST and reduced convection and precipitation in the western Pacific. The basin-wide redistribution of mass and heat via equatorial processes deepens the thermocline and inhibits the upwelling of cold water along the coastal region of South America. This leads to warming of the coastal waters by up to 5 °C locally. As a result, there is a dramatic reduction in nutrients in the water leading to diminished harvests of fish and related species in the affected region. Accompanying the changes in the tropical Pacific, there is a substantial redistribution of energy in the form of large changes in patterns of precipitation, temperature, water vapor, atmospheric and oceanic circulation all over the globe. During the peak of ENSO, severe droughts are experienced in Australia, Indonesia and South Africa. Torrential rains occur in the central Pacific islands and regions along the South American coast. The extratropics are also significantly affected, with severe cold winters over the eastern part of North America, mild winters over Europe and cold wet summers over northeastern China.

Because the largest anomalies in sea surface temperature, precipitation and wind associated with ENSO occur over the tropical oceans where ground-based observations are scarce, the above picture of a coherent, global scale variation did not emerge until the late 1960s and early 1970s when weather satellites began to appear on the scene. In fact, in the seminal paper of Bjerknes (1969), the author's conclusion of large-scale, coherent variations across the Pacific was largely based on composite satellite cloudiness pictures from ESSA 3 and 5. His original depiction of the ocean–atmosphere interaction has stood up to countless follow-up observational and modeling studies. Thanks to the advent of modern satellite technology, understanding of the ENSO has progressed tremendously in the last decade. The last two ENSOs in the 1980s (1982–83 and 1986–87) are two of the most closely monitored events. A wide range of atmospheric and oceanic parameters including precipitation, water vapor, cloudiness, surface wind, surface heat and momentum fluxes, sea surface temperature and sea surface height, have been retrieved from measurements from a host of operational and research satellites. Given the lack of observations over the oceans and the need for long-term, homogeneous global coverage, there is no doubt that satellite observation will play an increasingly important role as a major source of climate data as the quest for understanding of the global climate continues. Today, remote sensing and satellite data retrieval is a burgeoning area of research. Unfortunately, retrieval of geophysical parameters from radiance data is, in general, an ill-posed mathematical problem. All retrieval schemes involve some kind of empiricism, coupled with often *ad hoc* assumptions and are therefore subject to various degrees of uncertainties. In particular for climate studies, long-term stability of satellite measurements can be problematic. Calibration of data has to be such that retrieval algorithms can be applied over a long period. However, these are issues outside the scope of this chapter. Here, the focus will be only on the application of satellite technology to the study of ocean–atmosphere interaction associated with ENSO. The assessment of retrieval techniques of specific parameters mentioned above can be found in other chapters of this book.

Remote sensing and ENSO

In the following, the status of retrieval techniques is discussed briefly for some key parameters for ENSO. These include sea surface temperature, latent heat and moisture fluxes, atmospheric columnar water vapor, clouds, radiation, precipitation, atmospheric circulation, sea surface wind stress, ocean circulation, and sea level.

Sea surface temperature

SST changes associated with ENSO are basin-wide (Pacific Ocean) and possibly global in extent (Indian and Atlantic Ocean). As discussed in the introduction, the appearance of warm water over the equatorial central and eastern Pacific is associated with anomalous weather fluctuations elsewhere in the tropics and the extratropics, due in part to the influence of SST on the large-scale atmospheric circulation. Therefore, there is no surprise that SST is the single most important parameter for ENSO monitoring, and is the key predictant in all ENSO forecast schemes (both statistical and dynamical). While the El Niño events have been known for centuries, reliable global estimates of SST were not possible until the late 1970s, when satellite data were used routinely for monitoring SST. Recently, monthly global SST fields have been retrieved from IR instruments AVHRR (Advanced Very High Resolution Radiometer) and TOVS (TIROS Operational Vertical Sounder) as well as microwave instruments

such as SMMR (Scanning Multichannel Microwave Radiometer). Microwave sensors are being used more and more to estimate SST because they can see through clouds while IR sensors cannot. The rms error from the above estimates is of the order of 1 °C (cf. Njoku & Brown, 1993). Because satellite SST estimates are often contaminated by clouds and atmospheric aerosols, the use of blended data, i.e. *in situ* plus satellite data, is preferred. Since satellites detect the 'skin' temperature (i.e. temperature of the surface layer less than a few millimeters) and *in situ* observations measure the 'bulk' temperature (i.e. temperature of the surface layer of order of meters), adjustments have to be made to correct for the bias. One such blended analysis is now being produced at the Global Sea Surface Temperature Data Center at the National Meteorological Center/Climate Analysis Center (NMC/CAC). The CAC analysis makes use of a combination of multi-channel SST analysis based on AVHRR and *in situ* measurements from ships of opportunity and drifting buoys, by way of an optimal blending procedure (Reynolds, 1988). This procedure improves the monthly rms error to 0.7–0.8 °C. For detection of ENSO signals, this is quite adequate but, for regional applications, higher order of accuracy is desirable.

Precipitation

During ENSO, large-scale SST changes are accompanied by changes in the distribution of atmospheric heat sources and sinks in the form of latent heat released in tropical rainfall. Yet, because of the complexities of rainfall processes, precipitation is perhaps the most difficult parameter to retrieve from satellite measurements. State-of-the-art space-based global, climate scale rainfall estimation techniques generally fall into two main categories, i.e. visible and IR techniques, and microwave techniques (Prabhakara *et al.*, 1986; Wu & Susskind, 1988; Arkin, 1979). Visible and IR techniques involve cloud indexing or threshold based on cloud top temperature. Using the former method, Arkin and Meisner (1987) provided precipitation estimates over the Pacific, tropical North and South America and India. The Vis/IR estimates are generally reasonable in the tropics where the precipitation is of the convective type. However, when precipitation is coming from stratiform or mixed stratiform and cumuliform clouds, these methods generally yield overestimates. While Vis/IR techniques appear to do a reasonable job for some applications, microwave techniques appear to hold the best promise for improvement of climate scale rainfall estimation from space. This is because at selected wavelengths, microwaves penetrate clouds and are absorbed or emitted by the hydrometeors themselves. Microwave methods are largely successful over ocean but can run into problems over land owing to effects of variable surface emittance. The difficulties in microwave techniques are that several parameters are needed to get a good estimate of precipitation. The relevant parameters for precipitation are: height of the rain column, drop size distribution, liquid and ice content, cloud liquid and type of rain – convective or stratiform. Present techniques provide reasonable estimates of total liquid water content and ice scattering. The remaining parameters have to be provided by models or empirical relationships. Global precipitation maps using microwave retrievals have been derived over the ocean from Nimbus-5 ESMR (Electrically Scanning Microwave Radiometer) data for about 2 years 1973–74 (Rao, Abbott & Theon, 1976). Using Nimbus-7 SMMR measurements at five frequencies in the region 6.6 to 37 GHz, Prabhakara et al. (1986) have provided rainfall estimates over the ocean during the 1982–83 ENSO. Since 1987, data from the SSM/I (Special Sensor Microwave/Imager) from the defense meteorological satellite platform (DMSP) have emerged as the key satellite data for microwave precipitation retrieval studies. Among the most serious problems facing remote sensing of rain are the scarcity of ground truth observations over the oceans and the lack of an evaluation standard. These problems hopefully will be alleviated by the Tropical Rainfall Measuring Mission (TRMM), a joint US–Japan satellite mission to be launched in 1996. A key component of TRMM is the ground truth validation program, which includes field phase observations, modeling in conjunction with satellite IR, microwave and radar measurements.

Water vapor

Much of the dynamics and thermodynamics in the tropical atmosphere which determine the structure and propagation of the entire range of tropical phenomena from mesoscale convection to ENSO are dependent on the moist static stability of the atmosphere (Lau & Peng, 1987). The moist static stability is most sensitive to the total water vapor content which is largely concentrated in the lower troposphere. Thus water vapor content and its vertical profile are important parameters for understanding the atmospheric anomalies observed during ENSO. Total water vapor can be remotely sensed in both the IR or microwave spectral regions. As with precipitation, microwave measurements give significantly better estimates over the oceans. Difference in the brightness temperatures at 21 and 18 GHz is a good measure of the strength of the absorption due to water vapor (Prabhakara, Short & Vollmer, 1985) and has been used to yield water vapor content with reasonable accuracy. Similar accuracy has been achieved

using the 18, 21, and 37 GHz channels (Chang et al., 1984). Global maps of water vapor during ENSO produced from SMMR have provided valuable information on the water vapor distribution over the tropical oceans (Prabhakara et al., 1985; Liu, 1986). Recently an innovative approach has been suggested to use the information deduced on atmospheric water vapor and rain water to infer the moisture convergence and hence re-construct the large-scale divergent circulation in the tropical atmosphere (Ardanuy, Prabhakara & Kyle, 1987; Ardanuy & Krishnamurti, 1987). Such studies provide extremely useful information about the tropical circulation anomaly crucial to understanding coupled ocean–atmosphere interactions during ENSO. At present, microwave data from SSM/I, which provides stable microwave data from 1987 to present, are widely used to provide global distribution of water vapor.

As mentioned previously, the vertical distribution of water vapor dominates the vertical moist static energy of the troposphere and hence the potential instability of the tropical atmosphere due to convection. Due to the uncertainties in present measurements, only very coarse vertical profiles can be obtained (Prabhakara et al., 1986). Up to now, the retrieved water vapor profiles are often described in terms of three basic parameters – total water vapor content, scale height of water vapor and mid-tropospheric humidity. It is obvious that much more work is needed in the techniques for determining vertical water vapor profiles. Recently moisture and heating profiles retrieved by a combination of microwave radiance data and sophisticated cloud models have demonstrated reasonable success for regional scales (Tao et al., 1990). Application of these methods to global scales is still not feasible. Simplification of the models and high resolution satellite data are required.

Clouds and radiation

The radiation at the Earth surface is a strong function of the cloud cover. While it is generally recognized that latent heat release and surface wind stress interactively drive the atmospheric and oceanic circulation anomalies during ENSO, the differential radiational surface heating caused by the movement of the massive region of cloudiness into the central Pacific could strongly modify the subsequent development of the coupled system. It has been estimated that the effect of the cloudiness gradient between the normally warm (cloudy) western Pacific and the cool (clear) eastern Pacific amounts to approximately 1 °C/month east-west heating differential averaged through the upper 100 m of the tropical ocean. This is the same order of magnitude of heating in the upper ocean that occurs during the warm phase of ENSO and therefore may play an important role in the development of ENSO (TOGA/COARE Science Report, 1990).

At present, estimates of the surface energy budget are highly uncertain because of the presence of clouds. Thus the detection of clouds, their optical properties and the way they may alter the surface heating is one of the key issues for understanding ENSO variability. Different cloud types have different impacts on the radiation balance of the Earth's climate. For example, high cirrus clouds do not significantly affect short waves but reduce the long-wave radiation to space acting as an effective 'greenhouse gas' that could warm the troposphere and the Earth surface. Low cloud will have the opposite effect of cooling the lower troposphere because of the increased radiation at the warmer cloud top. In general, the satellite cloud retrieval algorithm involves the conversion of radiance data to cloud scenes and the inference of cloud properties from the radiance values (cf. Rossow, 1993). Radiance thresholds are established to give cloud fractions for low, middle and high clouds based on radiance computed from models using observed surface temperature and climatological lapse rates. Cloud classification algorithms have been developed from both IR and UV radiances from Nimbus-7 THIR (Temperature Humidity Infra-red Radiometer) and TOMS (Total Ozone Mapping Spectrometer) respectively (Stowe et al., 1988). The ISCCP (International Satellite Cloud Climatology Project) estimates clouds from geostationary satellites (METEOSAT, GOES-E, GOES-W, GMS) relying on different combinations of visible and infrared radiances to detect clouds and to infer atmospheric and surface radiation properties (Schiffer & Rossow, 1985). These satellite estimates have provided valuable information on cloud radiation properties that are fundamental to the understanding of the ENSO phenomenon. However, there is still a long way to go before the precise role of clouds and radiation in influencing the development of ENSO can be defined.

Evaporation over the ocean

Evaporation is the process by which the atmosphere derives its moisture (latent heat) from the ocean and is a crucial parameter in the coupling between the ocean and atmosphere. Because evaporation is a complex function of a number of geophysical parameters such as sea surface temperature, surface wind speed and air–sea humidity difference, reliable estimates of these parameters have to be obtained before accurate evaporation estimates can be made. Given the recent progress in retrieving first-order parameters such as SST and water vapor, it is now possible to estimate second-order parameters such as evaporation from space

observations. Liu (1986) found a useful statistical relation between monthly mean precipitable water and surface humidity over global oceans. This relationship was used to estimate moisture and latent heat fluxes from the SMMR data to estimate the changes in evaporation over the ocean during the 1982–83 ENSO (Liu, 1988). While large uncertainties remain, these estimates represent the first attempt to derive global fields of moisture fluxes from the ocean for ENSO studies. Because in situ data from the ocean will remain scarce, satellite-based estimates of evaporation are the hope of the future. Eventually with data assimilation from general circulation models, more reliable moisture and latent heat flux estimates may be available. For more detailed discussion of evaporation over the ocean, readers are referred to Liu (1993).

Sea surface wind stress

In addition to evaporation, the other principal link between ENSO-related changes in the atmosphere circulation and those of the ocean circulation is the sea surface wind stress. The large-scale response of the tropical ocean circulation to atmospheric forcing is predominantly deterministic. The dynamic response of the ocean along the equator is tightly coupled to changes in the overlying zonal wind stress. The tropical ocean circulation away from the equator is determined to a large degree by fluctuations in the wind stress curl. Therefore understanding of changes in ocean variables such as upper-ocean currents, sea level, and heat content depends critically on ability to monitor changes in the surface wind stress. The Seasat-A satellite scatterometer, launched in June of 1978, demonstrated that the surface wind stress field could be inferred by the radar back-scatter from surface capillary waves. Although the SEASAT mission was essentially a proof of concept (the satellite failed after only three months of operation), useful information on the global momentum flux from atmosphere to ocean was obtained (Atlas et al., 1987). In the early 1980s the oceanic processes branch of NASA charged a satellite surface stress working group with identifying areas of ocean science that would experience significant advancement if another scatterometer was launched. Studies of the El Niño phenomenon were singled out as research that would benefit greatly from remotely sensed measurements of the surface wind stress (O'Brien et al., 1982).

By the time the next scatterometer was launched in 1991 on board the European space agency's Earth Resources Satellite (ERS-1) there had been a 13-year hiatus in global observations of the surface wind velocity. Another scatterometer, the NASA scatterometer (NSCAT), will follow in

1995 on the Japanese Advanced Earth Observing Satellite (ADEOS). In the interim subjective analyses of sparse shipboard observations (Goldenberg & O'Brien, 1981) and subjective analyses of satellite-derived cloud motion wind vectors (Sadler & Kilonsky, 1985) have served as the primary data sets for studies of changes to the tropical Pacific surface wind field during the 1982–83 and 1986–87 ENSO events. The inherent limitations to these data sets and the absence of scatterometer measurements have led to alternative approaches to monitoring the tropical Pacific wind field. The TOGA program has begun to implement a wind record array within ~8° of the equator across the entire tropical Pacific (Hayes, 1989). The assimilation of surface wind speeds, estimated by the SMMR and SSM/I passive microwave radiometers, into an atmospheric circulation model (Atlas & Bloom, 1989) also shows promise as another method of obtaining surface wind stress estimates going back to 1979.

Sea level and ocean circulation

Historically, the measurement of sea level has been one of the most important techniques for understanding the tropical ocean circulation (Wyrtki, 1979). Since most of the upper tropical ocean currents are in quasi-geostrophic balance, their intensity and corresponding variation are reflected as changes to the sea surface topography. Until the advent of satellite altimetry, the acquisition of sea level data had been limited to a few dozen point measurements at island and coastal stations in the tropical Pacific. The GEOSAT altimeter mission (Koblinsky, 1993) provided the first opportunity to map or monitor the variability of the global ocean circulation on seasonal timescales and longer. A particular serendipitous aspect of the GEOSAT mission was that it encompassed the 1986–87 ENSO event. This allowed the equatorial ocean wave processes that are central to the evolution of ENSO to be monitored on space and timescales never achievable before.

The application of satellite altimetry to studies of tropical ocean variability is not without difficulty. Although changes to the mass transport and heat content in the tropical Pacific are critical to climate change, the sea level expression of this upper ocean variability is only of the order of several centimeters for mean seasonal conditions and at most a few tens of centimeters during extreme El Niño events (Wyrtki & Leslie, 1980; Delcroix & Gautier, 1987). Estimation of geostrophic current variability is complicated by stringent observational accuracies required for measuring sea level slope at low latitudes. Moreover, the round-trip time of the altimeter radar pulse is a function of the medium through which it travels, and atmospheric constituents, particularly

water vapor, affect the accuracy of sea level retrievals. This is particularly important in the Tropics when the major convection zones are displaced during ENSO events. Such changes in the distribution of water vapor can induce changes in the altimeter path length retrieval comparable to the magnitude of the sea level changes of the El Niño event itself (Zimbelman & Busalacchi, 1990).

Results

The decade of the 1980s saw two warm events that occurred over the tropical Pacific (1982–83, 1986–87). The 1982–83 ENSO was the strongest event recorded in the past 50 years. By comparison, the 1986–87 ENSO was only a moderate event. Satellite observations of these two warm events have provided unprecedented space/time coverage of the evolution of two complete life cycles of the natural fluctuation of the coupled ocean–atmosphere system. In the following, some key satellite observations are highlighted for the 1982–83 and 1986–87 ENSO.

Basic features of ENSO

Fig. 1 shows the progression of SST anomalies from June 1982 through April 1983. The SST (2° × 2°, monthly) is derived from the CAC blended analysis based on AVHRR (see discussion in previous section). In June of 1982, near the onset of El Niño, a large positive SST anomaly (>1 °C) is found over the central Pacific. A new region of positive anomaly appeared over the equatorial eastern Pacific in August 1982. This anomaly continued to expand and intensify in the subsequent months. Extreme variations in SST in the eastern and central tropical Pacific Ocean, close to three standard deviations from normal conditions, were observed during this period. At the same time, large negative SST anomalies in the extra-tropical Pacific in the Northern and Southern Hemisphere were observed, indicating that not only the tropical portion but the entire Pacific Ocean may be involved. During the peak phase of ENSO (Dec 1982–Feb 1983), large areas of moderately positive (0.5° to 1.5 °C) SST anomaly were also found over the Indian Ocean. The El Niño event ends in late 1983 with a cold phase during which low SST is re-established along the coast of South America and west along the equator. The effects of these SST changes on the release of latent heat to the atmosphere are detailed in Liu (1993).

Dramatic shifts in the atmospheric convection pattern occurred accompanying the SST changes. Fig. 2 shows the monthly anomalies of outgoing long-wave radiation (OLR) during the 1982–83 ENSO. OLR is the most commonly used

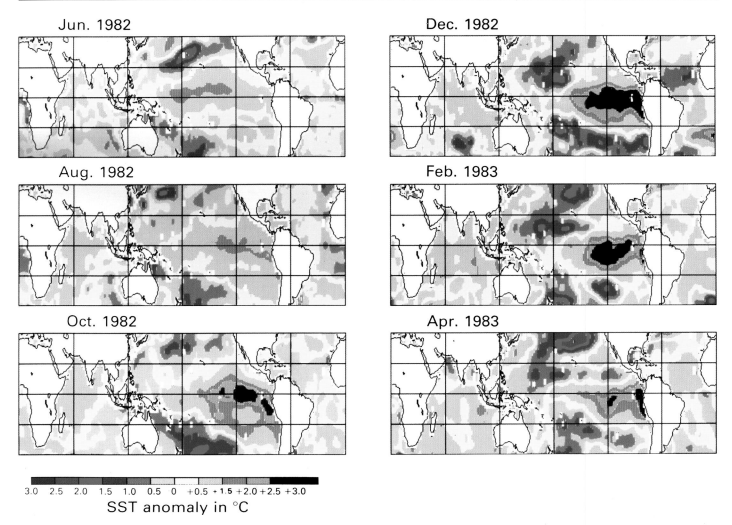

Fig. 1. AVHRR-based CAC blended analysis showing the monthly progression of sea surface temperature anomalies during the 1982–83 ENSO.

qualitative measure of tropical convection and proxy for precipitation for ENSO studies. Beginning in August 1982, the convection anomalies became very well organized. The characteristic 'dipole' anomaly pattern featuring enhanced convection (excessive rainfall) over the central Pacific and reduced convection (drought) over the maritime continent became well established by October 1982 and persisted through April 1983. From December to April, the region of enhanced convection extended into the eastern Pacific causing major floods and landslides along the coast of South America. Central America and southwestern US are similarly affected. During the same period, the Indonesian/Northern Australia region experienced record dry conditions. The maximum amplitude of the OLR anomaly was of the order of 40–50 watt m^{-2}. Although a large amount of the long-wave radiation anomaly will be compensated by short-wave

anomaly, the net radiation change due to the presence of clouds or the so-called 'cloud radiative forcing' is expected to be large and strongly impact the total energy re-distribution in the coupled ocean–atmosphere system. It can be seen from Figs. 1 and 2 that the timing of the anomalous convection and positive SST anomalies were well correlated. Anomalous convection formed first in the western Pacific but eventually coincided with the positive SST anomaly in the central and eastern Pacific. The sequence of events is largely consistent with current theories of ENSO involving coupled instability modes as well as delayed reflection of oceanic waves in a basin of finite width (Lau, 1981; Hirst, 1986; Hirst & Lau, 1990; Zebiak & Cane, 1987; Schopf & Suarez, 1988).

As discussed earlier, water vapor in the atmosphere is directly related to the dynamics of the atmospheric circulation as well as the thermal forcing from the underlying sea surface.

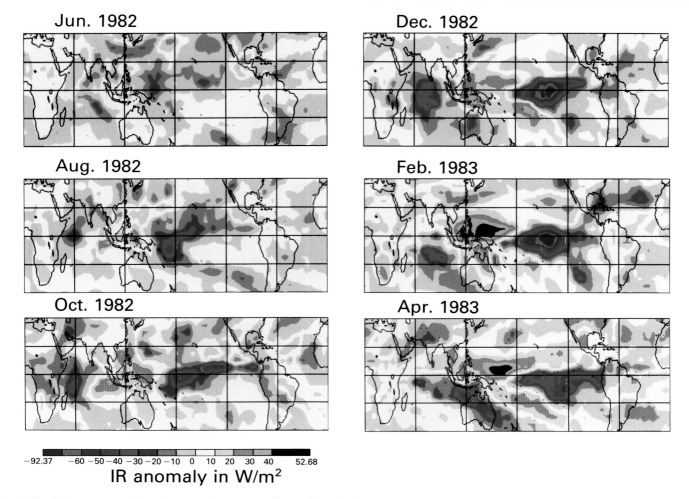

Fig. 2. Monthly mean anomalies of outgoing longwave radiation from AVHRR showing the spatial and temporal evolution of tropical convection anomalies during the 1982–83 ENSO.

Not surprisingly, during ENSO, water vapor anomalies follow very closely the variability of the SST and convection. Fig. 3 shows the monthly anomaly of water vapor retrieved from Nimbus-7 SMMR based on the brightness temperatures at 21 and 18 GHz (cf. Prabhakara *et al.*, 1985). The patterns of atmospheric moisture anomalies coincide very well with patterns of convection anomalies shown in Fig. 2. Similarly, rainfall in the form of liquid water in the atmosphere can be estimated using SMMR. An example of the retrieved seasonal rainfall anomaly for the period Mar–May of 1983 is shown in Fig. 4. The dipole anomaly similar to that shown in the OLR (Fig. 2) can be seen very clearly. Maximum seasonal mean rainfall anomalies are found to be about 10–12 mm/day. This retrieval provides for the first time a quantitative estimate of the rainfall anomalies over the oceanic regions. This is very useful for the validation of rainfall from general circulation models. Most important, because latent heat is a major component of the global heat budget, such an estimate

is extremely important in trying to understand the global energy re-distribution due to natural climate fluctuations such as ENSO.

In the ocean, theory suggests that equatorial wave processes play an important role in the readjustment of the mass and velocity fields during an El Niño event (Moore & Philander, 1977). The space/time coverage of the GEOSAT data provides the first comprehensive observational data set with which to investigate these basin-scale wave phenomena. Fig. 5 shows the GEOSAT-derived sea level time series at selected locations along the equator to track the eastward propagation (2.4–2.8 m s^{-1}) of equatorial Kelvin waves generated in response to westerly winds west of the date-line during April 1985 to April 1987 (Miller, Cheney & Douglas, 1988; Cheney & Miller, 1988). The phase speed and meridional profile of these sea level disturbances were shown to be consistent with the structure function predicted by theory (Delcroix, Picaut & Eldin, 1990). The GEOSAT data were also

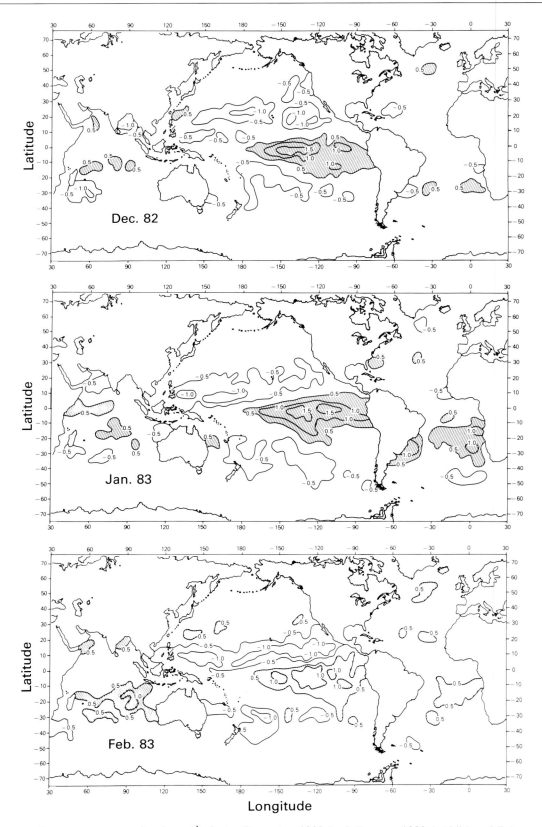

Fig. 3. Monthly maps of water vapor anomalies (g cm^{-1}) during December 1982 (top), January, 1983 (middle) and February, 1983 (bottom), based on retrieval from Nimbus-7 SMMR (from Prabhakara *et al.*, 1985).

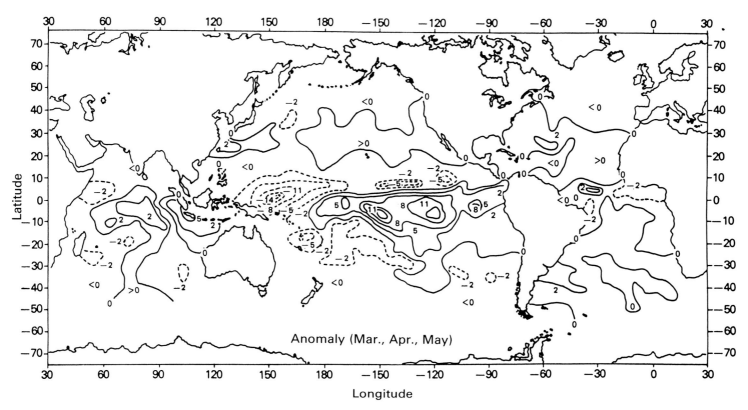

Fig. 4. Seasonally averaged rainfall anomalies inferred from SMMR for March through May of 1983. Contour intervals in units of 100 mm (from Prabhakara *et al.*, 1986).

used by Picaut *et al.* (1990) to infer changes in the zonal current field at the equator. These altimeter-derived estimates of the geostrophic flow field agreed well with the low-frequency, near-surface zonal current observed at three equatorial current meter moorings. Away from the equator, westward phase propagation of sea level features was detected in the GEOSAT data. Aspects of the phase speed, reflection at the western boundary, and meridional structure have been interpreted by Tai, White & Pazan (1989), White, Graham & Tai (1990), and Delcroix *et al.* (1990) as evidence of equatorial Rossby waves. In the past, the sparse coverage of conventional ocean measurements has prevented the detection of these planetary-scale waves.

ENSO as a multi-scale phenomenon

Thanks to the long-term, homogeneous and high resolution coverage of the tropics by weather satellites, new information regarding the evolution and possible causes of ENSO have emerged. Based on satellite radiance from AVHRR on operational NOAA satellites, Lau and Chan (1986) recently suggested that the ENSO is a multi-scale phenomena consisting of interacting low frequency (timescale of monthly or longer),

intermediate frequency (30–60 days) and possibly high frequency (less than 10 days) components. An example of the spatial and temporal variability of multi-scale structures is shown in Fig. 6, where the time–longitude sections of 5-day mean OLR anomaly along the equator during the 1982–83 ENSO, the 1986–87 ENSO and a normal period (1984–85) are shown. A quasi-regular signal featuring wave-like perturbations propagating eastward from the Indian Ocean to the central and eastern Pacific is discernible in all the sections. These features are now known to be associated with the so-called atmospheric '30–60 day' oscillation, which scientists believe to be a fundamental mode of oscillation in the tropical atmosphere. The ENSO scale anomalies can be perceived as the slow eastward migration of SST together with an envelope or ensemble of eastward propagating '30–60 day' oscillations which are, in turn, made up of even higher frequency fluctuations (Nakazawa, 1988; Lau, Nakazawa & Sui, 1990). These observations have led to new theories concerning the possible triggering of the onset of ENSO by coupled air–sea interaction in the western and central Pacific region (Lau *et al.*, 1989; Hirst & Lau, 1990).

Evidence of multi-scale features associated with ENSO can also be found in the ocean. Fig. 7 shows the high resolu-

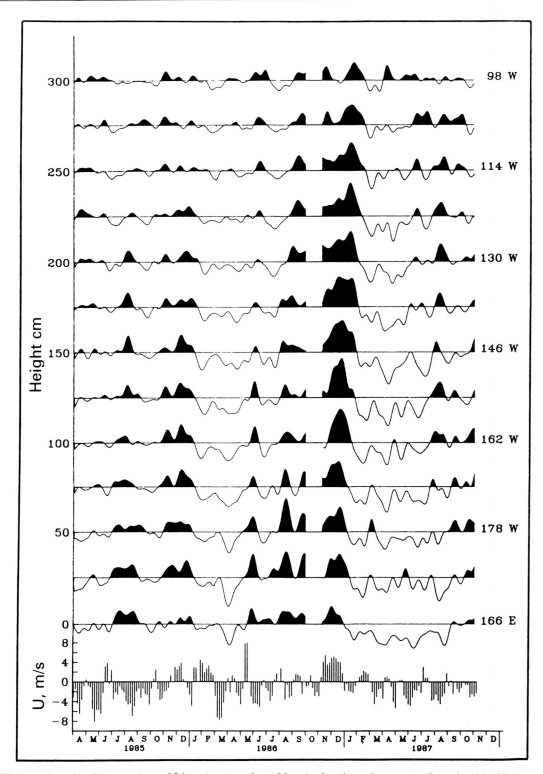

Fig. 5. GEOSAT-derived sea level time series at 13 locations in selected longitudes along the equator from April 1985 through October 1987. Also shown in the bottom is 850 mb zonal wind averaged between 5° S–5° N and 120° E–160° E (from Cheney & Miller, 1988).

(a) Long-time cross section of OLR anomaly, 1984–85

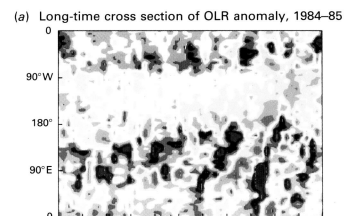

(b) Long-time cross section of OLR anomaly, 1982–83

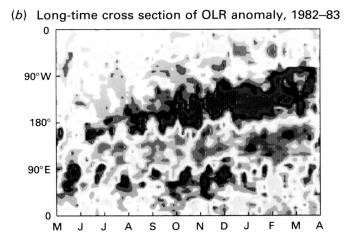

(c) Long-time cross section of OLR anomaly, 1986–87

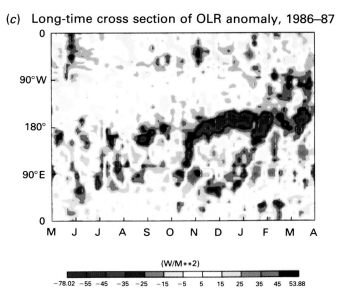

(W/M∗∗2)

−78.02 −55 −45 −35 −25 −15 −5 5 15 25 35 45 53.88

Fig. 6. Time-longitude section of AVHRR-based 5-day mean outgoing longwave radiation anomaly along the equator for (a) 1984–85, a 'normal' year, (b) the 1982–83 ENSO and (c) the 1986–87 ENSO.

tion (50 km, weekly) AVHRR-derived SST distribution in the tropical eastern Pacific during one-week periods in June and December 1982, 1983 and 1984, respectively. Notable features in June and December 1984 are the wave-like undulations along an SST front just north of the equator. The structure of these long waves was first detected in similar satellite IR imagery (Legeckis, 1977, 1986). The existence of these instability waves has been attributed to the shear present, in non-El Niño years, between the westward south equatorial current and the eastward north equatorial countercurrent (Philander, 1978). The same features have also been detected in satellite altimeter data (Musman, 1986), and are thought to cause significant equatorward eddy heat flux (Pullen, Bernstein & Halpern, 1987). During June and December of 1982 and 1983, the amplitudes of these small scale equatorial waves were substantially reduced, presumably due to the diminished shear between the above-mentioned current systems that accompanied the appearance of warm water over the tropical eastern Pacific.

Concluding remarks

By studying the spatial and temporal variabilities and the correlations among the satellite-derived geophysical fields, meteorologists and oceanographers have been able to obtain a better understanding of the causes of natural climate fluctuations, test hypotheses regarding coupled ocean–atmosphere interaction, carry out experimental short-term climate predictions and evaluate them against satellite observations. Global patterns depicted by the satellite observations have made it possible for scientists to link weather and climate anomalies in one region of the globe to another and lead to the notion of 'teleconnection' associated with inter-annual variabilities such as ENSO. To understand ENSO better, continuous long-term observations of clouds, precipitation, water vapor, SST, wind and surface fluxes by satellites are needed. Because of close coupling of these atmospheric and oceanic variables, the simultaneous and coordinated monitoring of the entire ocean–atmosphere system by different satellite instruments is paramount. In addition to satellite missions which are devoted to one class of instruments aiming at only one or two key variables, missions with multi-instrument platforms aiming at a wide range of geophysical parameters should be developed as soon as possible. The upcoming NASA Earth Observing System is a major step in this direction.

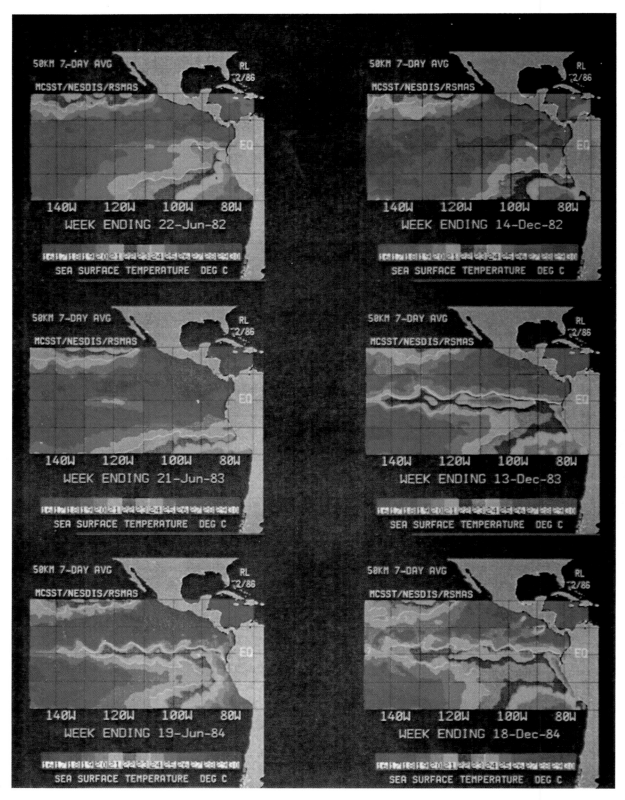

Fig. 7. Sea surface temperatures during June and December 1982–1984 at intervals of 1° C, spatial scales of 50 km and time intervals of 1 week in the eastern equatorial Pacific (from Legeckis, 1986).

References

Ardanuy, P. E., Prabhakara C. & Kyle, H. L. (1987). Remote sensing of water vapor convergence, deep convection and precipitation over the tropical Pacific Ocean during the 1982–83 El Niño. *J. Geophys. Res.*, **92**, 14204–16.

Ardanuy, P. E. & Krishnamurti, T. N. (1987). Divergent circulation inferred from Nimbus-7 ERB: Application to the 1982–83 ENSO event. *J. Meteor. Soc. Japan*, 353–71.

Arkin, P. (1979). The relationship between the fractional coverage of high cloud and rainfall accumulations during GATE over the B-scale array. *Mon. Wea. Rev.*, **107**, 1382–7.

Arkin, P. & Meisner, B. N. (1987). The relationship between large scale convective rainfall and cold cloud over the western hemisphere during 1982–85. *Mon. Wea. Rev.*, **115**, 51–74.

Atlas, R. & Bloom, S. (1989). Global surface wind vectors resulting from the assimilation of satellite wind speed data in atmospheric general circulation models. *Oceans '89 Proceedings*, September 18–21, 1989 Seattle, WA. IEEE Publication Number 89, CH2780–5, 260–5.

Atlas, R., Busalacchi, A. J., Ghil, M., Bloom, S. & Kalnay, E. (1987). Global surface wind and flux fields from model assimilation of Seasat data. *J. Geophys. Res.*, **92**, 6477–87.

Bjerknes, J. (1966). A possible response of the atmospheric Hadley circulation to equatorial anomalies of ocean temperature. *Tellus*, **18**, 820–9.

Bjerknes, J. (1969). Atmospheric teleconnections from the equatorial Pacific. *Mon. Wea. Rev.*, **97**, 163–72.

Chang, H. D., Hwang, P. H., Wilheit, T. T., Chang, A. T. C., Staelin, D. H. & Rosenkranz, P. W. (1984). Monthly distributions of precipitable water from the Nimbus-7 SMMR data. *J. Geophys. Res.*, **89**, 5328–34.

Cheney, R. E. & Miller, L. (1988). Mapping the 1986–1987 El Niño with GEOSAT altimeter data. *EOS Trans. AGU*, **69**, 754–5.

Delcroix, T. & Gautier, C. (1987). Estimates of heat content variations from sea level measurements in the central and western tropical Pacific from 1979 to 1985, *J. Phys. Oceanogr.*, **17**, 725–34.

Delcroix, T., Picaut, J. & Eldin, G. (1991). Equatorial Kelvin and Rossby waves evidenced in the Pacific Ocean through GEOSAT sea level and surface current anomalies. *J. Geophys. Res.*, **96**, 3249–62.

Enfield, D. (1989). El Niño, past and present. *Rev. Geophys.*, **27**, 159–87.

Goldenberg, S. B. & O'Brien, J. J. (1981). Time and space variability of tropical Pacific wind stress. *Mon. Wea. Rev.*, **109**, 1190–207.

Hayes, S. P. (1989). The Atlas wind and thermal structure array, in US TOGA Ocean Observation System Mid-life Progress Review and Recommendations for Continuation. Workshop report, Kaimana Beach Hotel, Honolulu, HI, March 8–10, 1989. Nova University Press, Ft. Lauderdale, Fla.

Hirst, A. C. (1986). Unstable and damped equatorial modes in simple coupled ocean–atmosphere models. *J. Atmos. Sci.*, **43**, 606–30.

Hirst, A. C. & Lau, K. M. (1990). Intraseasonal and interannual variabilities in coupled ocean–atmosphere models. *J. Climate*, **3**, 713–25.

Koblinsky, C. J. (1993). Ocean Surface Topography and circulation, This volume.

Lau, K. M. (1981). Oscillations in a simple equatorial climate system. *J. Atmos. Sci.*, **38**, 248–61.

Lau, K. M. & Chan, P. H. (1986). The El Niño Southern Oscillation and the 40–50 day oscillation: a new perspective. *Bull. Am. Meteor. Soc.*, **67**, 533–4.

Lau, K. M. & Peng, L. (1987). Origin of low-frequency (intraseasonal) oscillations in the tropical atmosphere. Part I: basic theory. *J. Atmos. Sci.*, **44**, 950–72.

Lau, K. M., Peng, L., Sui, C. H. & Nakazawa, T. (1989). Super cloud clusters, westerly wind burst, 30–60 day oscillations and ENSO: a unified view. *J. Meteor. Soc. Japan*, **67**, 205–19.

Lau, K. M., Nakazawa, T. & Sui, C. H. (1990). Observations of cloud cluster hierarchies over the tropical western Pacific. *J. Geophys. Res.*, **96**, 3197–208.

Legeckis, R. (1977). Long waves in the eastern equatorial Pacific Ocean: a view from a geostationary satellite. *Science*, **197**, 1179–81.

Legeckis, R. (1986). A satellite time series of sea surface temperatures in the eastern equatorial Pacific Ocean, 1982–1986. *J. Geophys. Res.*, **91**, 12,879–86.

Liu, W. T. (1986). Statistical relation between monthly precipitable water and surface level humidity over global oceans. *Mon. Wea. Rev.*, **114**, 1591–602.

Liu, W. T. (1988). Moisture and latent heat flux variabilities in the tropical Pacific derived from satellite data. *J. Geophys. Res.*, **93**, 6749–60, 6965–8.

Liu, W. T. (1993). Evaporation from the ocean, This volume.

Miller, L., Cheney, R. E. & Douglas, B. C. (1988). GEOSAT altimeter observations of Kelvin waves and the 1986–87 El Niño. *Science*, **239**, 52–4.

Moore, D. & Philander, S. G. H. (1977). Modeling of the tropical ocean circulation. In *The Sea*, vol. 6, pp. 316–61, Interscience, New York.

Musman, S. (1986). Sea slope changes associated with westward propagating equatorial temperature fluctuations. *J. Geophys. Res.*, **91**, 10,753–7.

Nakazawa, T. (1988). Tropical super clusters within intraseasonal variations over the western Pacific. *J. Meteor. Soc. Japan*, **66**, 823–39.

Njoku, E. G. and Brown, O. B. (1993). Sea Surface Temperature, This volume.

O'Brien, J., Kirk, R., McGoldrick, L., Witte, J., Atlas, R., Bracalente, E., Brown, O., Haney, R., Harrison, D. E., Honhart, D., Hurlburt, H., Johnson, R., Jones, L., Katsaros, K., Lambertson, R., Peteherych, S., Pierson, W., Price, J., Ross, D., Stewart, R. & Woiceshyn, P. (1982). Scientific opportunities using satellite surface wind stress measurements over the ocean. In *Report of the Satellite Surface Stress Working Group*, 153pp., Nova University/NYIT Press, Fort Lauderdale, Fla.

Philander, S. G. H. (1978). Instabilities of zonal equatorial currents. 2, *J. Geophys. Res.*, 83, 3679–82.

Picaut, J., Busalacchi, A. J., McPhaden, M. J. & Camusat, B. (1990). Validation of the geostrophic method for estimating zonal currents at the equator from Geosat altimeter data. *J. Geophys. Res.*, 95, 3015–24.

Prabhakara, C., Short, D. A. & Vollmer, B. E. (1985). El Niño and Atmospheric Water Vapor: Observations from Nimbus-7 SMMR. *J. Clim. Appl. Meteorol.*, 24, 1311–24.

Prabhakara, C., Short, D. A. Wiscombe, W. & Fraser, R. S. (1986). Rainfall over oceans inferred from Nimbus-7 SMMR: Application to 1982–83 El Niño. *J. Clim. Appl. Meteorol.*, 25, 1464–74.

Pullen, P. E., Bernstein, R. L. & Halpern, D. (1987). Equatorial long-wave characteristics determined from satellite sea surface temperature and *in situ* data. *J. Geophys. Res.*, 92, 742–8.

Rao, M. S. V., Abbott III, W. V. & Theon, J. S. (1976). Satellite-derived global oceanic rainfall Atlas (1973 and 1974). NASA Technical Report, NASA SP-410.

Rossow, W. B. (1993). Clouds, This volume.

Reynolds, R. (1988). A real time global sea surface temperature analysis. *J. Climate*, 1, 75–86.

Sadler, J. C. & Kilonsky, B. J. (1985). Deriving surface winds from satellite observations of low-level cloud motions. *J. Clim. Appl. Meteorol.*, 24, 758–69.

Schiffer, R. & Rossow, W. B. (1985). ISCCP global radiance data set: a new resource for climate research. *Bull. Am. Meteor. Soc.*, 66, 1498–501.

Schopf, P. & Suarez, M. (1988). Vacillations in a coupled ocean–atmosphere model. *J. Atmos. Sci.*, 45, 549–66.

Stowe, L. L., Wellemeyer, C. G., Eck, T. F., Yeh, H. Y. M. (1988). *Nimbus-7 Global Cloud Climatology. Part I: Algorithms and Validation.* 1, 471–84.

Tai, C. K., White, W. B. & Pazan, S. E. (1989). GEOSAT crossover analysis in the tropical Pacific. 2. Verification analysis of altimetric sea level maps with expendable bathythermograph and island sea level data. *J. Geophys. Res.*, 94, 897–908.

Tao, W. K., Simpson, J., Lang, S., McCumber, M., Adler, R. & Penc, R. (1990). An algorithm to estimate the heating budget from hydrometeor distributions. *J. Appl. Meteor.*, 29, 1232–44.

Walker, G. T. (1923). World weather I, *Mem. Indian Meteorol. Dep.*, 24, 75–131.

Walker, G. T. & Bliss, E. W. (1932). World weather V. *Mem. Royal Met. Soc.*, 4, 53–84.

White, W. B., Graham, N. & Tai, C. K. (1990). Reflection of annual Rossby waves at the maritime western boundary of the tropical Pacific. *J. Geophys. Res.*, 95, 3101–16.

Wu, M. L. & Susskind, J. (1988). Outgoing longwave radiation computed from HIRS/MSU soundings. *J. Geophys. Res.*, 95, 7579–602.

Wyrtki, K. (1979). Sea level variations: Monitoring the breadth of the Pacific, *EOS Trans. AGU*, 60, 25–7.

Wyrtki, K. & Leslie, W. G. (1980). The mean annual variation of sea level in the Pacific Ocean, *Rep. HIG-80–5*, Hawaii Inst. of Geophys. University of Hawaii, Honolulu.

Zebiak, S. & Cane, M. (1987). A model El Niño Southern Oscillation. *Mon. Wea. Rev.*, 115, 2262–78.

Zimbelman, D. F. & Busalacchi, A. J. (1990). The wet tropospheric range correction: product intercomparisons and the simulated effect for tropical Pacific altimeter retrievals. *J. Geophys. Res.*, 95, 2899–922.

PART VI

LAND

Topography

J. R. HEIRTZLER

Introduction

A good knowledge of the shape of the Earth's surface is needed for nearly every branch of the earth and environmental sciences. Whether it be on a small, laboratory scale or a large, continental scale, modeling and predictive programs increasingly require accurate, high resolution, and comprehensive topographic databases. How the topography changes with time is also important. The need for new data has become more acute since environmental concerns have increased and many studies have become global. Satellite techniques offer the possibility of providing this new data.

Engineers, land-use planners, the military and others also have an urgent need for more accurate topographic databases and are forming alliances with earth scientists to share data and technology. Topographic maps frequently form the base on which man-made or artificial terrain features are plotted in geographical information systems.

The National Aeronautics and Space Administration (NASA) has issued a report (Topographic Science Working Group, 1988) which discusses the needs of various scientific disciplines for topographic data. This need has also been recently discussed in the report of an international geodetic workshop (Mueller & Zerbini, 1988). These and other reports indicate that various aspects of remote sensing science, hydrology, geology, and geophysics are in most need of these data. With remote sensing imagery one needs to know whether strong signals are due to the strong natural reflectance that characterize certain materials or to favorable angle of reflection, therefore the slope of the surface must be known. The shape of the surface must be known to predict the drainage of water, whether flood conditions might exist, whether ground water reservoirs might be recharged, how vegetation receives water, or how erosion might be occurring or expected. In coastal areas a small change in the slope of the coast determines whether or not communities will be flooded by hurricanes, typhoons or tsunamis. A recent United Nations Environmental Programme report (1989) showed that Bangladesh, Egypt, Indonesia and some eight other countries have coasts in special danger but precise predictions of their vulnerability is hampered by lack of data on coastal morphology. A rising sea level will also affect coasts adversely, and sea level will be, at least partly, controlled by whether the volume of the polar ice sheets is increasing or decreasing, requiring repeat measurements of the topography of ice sheets. There is now a recognized need to measure the geometry of volcanoes to predict their eruptions and avoid loss of life and property.

The shape of the Earth's surface is fundamental to geology. The location and shape of mountains, ridges, plateaus, faults, batholiths, calderas, islands and many other features provide a history of the Earth. In many areas the theory of plate tectonics provides a way to relate topography to age. In geophysical studies elevation is needed to model gravity and magnetic field anomalies, seismic profiles and the rigidity of the Earth's lithosphere.

Each of these different disciplines has somewhat different requirements for topographic data. Some need great vertical and/or horizontal resolution over limited areas, some need to be assured that the reference level from one area to the next is the same, and some need frequent repeat measurements.

There are two categories for new data requirements. There is an immediate need for high resolution data (a few meters vertical resolution and a few tens of meters horizontal resolution) and for moderate resolution (a few tens of meters vertical resolution and a few hundred meters horizontal resolution). The high resolution would be needed for selected areas and the moderate resolution would be needed for all of the Earth. High resolution data are needed by hydrologists, by those studying coastal erosion and sealevel changes, volcanic phenomena, landslides, and earthquake displacements. Some of the high resolution areas would need frequent repeat measurements to study changes. The moderate resolution need not be repeated as often. Moderate resolution data are needed by those studying the flexure and rigidity of the Earth's crust, large scale crustal magnetic and gravity anomalies, and the nature of island arcs and basins. The scientific community has not expressed a more precise consensus. These databases are needed now for ongoing studies and the scientific community is anxious to see them acquired.

Table 1. *Comparison of digitally recorded remote sensing data*

Spacecraft or sensor	Nadir pixel (resolution)	Approximate area coverage	Cost per digital tape	Began operation
AVHRR GAC	4 km	3000 km strips	$80	1972
AVHRR LAC	1 km	3000 km strips	$400	1972
LANDSAT MSS	80 m	185×170 km	$1000	1972
LANDSAT TM	30 m	185×170 km	$3960	1982
SPOT Mutli-spectral	20 m	60×60 km	$1700	1986
SPOT Panchromatic	10 m	60×60 km	$1900	1986

AVHRR=Advanced very high resolution radiometer SPOT=Système Probatoire d'Observation de la Terre. There were other instruments which produced images directly of film, which recorded for short periods of time, or had limited areal coverage. Military sensors are not included here. Spectral coverage is unique to each instrument type. List of suppliers of this and other remote sensing data can be obtained, for example, from EOSAT (1986).

Digital data acquisition methods

Topographic data are kept in the form of contoured maps or in digital form as gridded elevation values for computer manipulation and display. With the multiple use of these data and the great quantity of data needed for global coverage, maps are being superseded by digital databases. As required, the digital data can be used to generate contour maps, but they can also produce various other graphic representations of terrain, such as color-coding of elevation, shaded relief images and wire-frame models. As importantly, digital data can be used in mathematical analyses.

For land areas most digital topographic data that exists today has come from digitizing contour maps or direct measurement of elevation using stereographic techniques. Contour maps are made by local government agencies using various techniques, including conventional geodetic, land surveying methods, or stereoscopic aerial photographs, whose precision may not have been recorded.

With the satellite era there has been renewed interest in creating topographic databases using satellite-based methods, including stereophotogrammetry from optical images, laser altimetry and radar techniques. Stereoscopic optical images can be obtained from satellite sensors in two ways: by using overlapping images from the same track acquired by near nadir-viewing instruments, and by using stereo pairs acquired on adjacent tracks by off-nadir-viewing, pointable instruments. The latter method is preferable because the look angle difference between a pair of images can be much greater, permitting greater vertical resolution, and because stereo coverage is not limited to regions of nadir-image overlap. On the other hand, there may be an appreciable time difference between the two images on adjacent tracks. Table 1 compares the resolution and costs of data from presently operating optical sensors.

To process these image data digitally absolute ground con-trol point elevations are required and computer processing time is intensive, even for the fastest computers. A recent comparison of various processing algorithms and the construction of special parallel-processing 'transputer' arrays suggest that the automatic processing of stereo imagery may be a practical means of obtaining topographic data for large geographic areas (for example see Muller, 1989). However, there has not been extensive experience in doing that.

Laser altimeters can give very precise height information with a small footprint along a profile, and, to a limited extent, they can be scanned to give elevation at a number of points over an area. Such methods have been used successfully from aircraft. The number of pulses from a laser transmitter is limited, although a satellite instrument can last several years transmitting pulses a few 10s of times a second and, after that period of time can provide a 1 km topographic data grid over the entire Earth. Both laser and optical remote sensing data is blocked by cloud cover.

Radar methods are being used to some extent since most radars are independent of clouds and weather. With many proposed synthetic aperture radar (SAR) instruments one can produce stereo pairs by taking images from two adjacent tracks, as with optical images. Alternatively, two radar receivers may be used in an interferometer (phase difference) arrangement on the same spacecraft, or radar can be operated in a scanning mode. All precise satellite radar methods suffer from the requirement of a large antenna (for a small footprint on the ground) and considerable power. The practical resolution for any radar method is now 100–200 meters in the horizontal directions and 10–20 meters vertically. The SEASAT and GEOSAT missions carried radar altimeters. Although they were not designed to operate over land, they have provided 1 degree square (110 × 110 km) average elevation data for all the major continents (Brenner, Frey & Zwally, 1990; Frey, personal communication). These data have a much higher resolution along track. All altimeter data

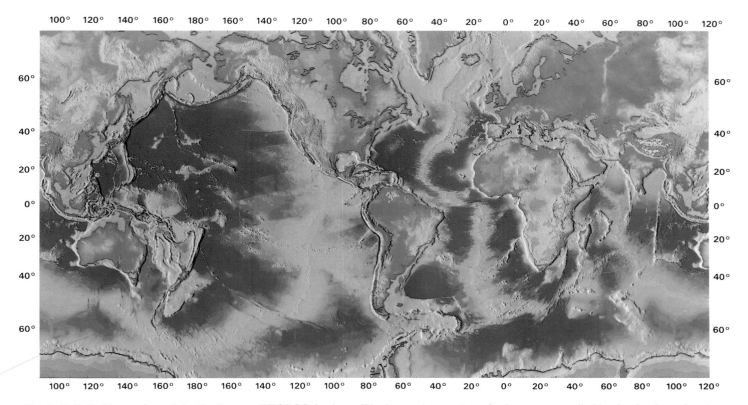

Fig. 1. Relief of the surface of the Earth using ETOPO5 database. The hue and saturation of colors are controlled by the depth or elevation. Intensity is controlled by a shaded relief calculation (after Heirtzler, 1985). In the oceans the darkest blue color shows depths to about 10·8 km below sea level, while on land the brighter reds go to heights of 5 km, and some very high elevations, such as in the Himalayas, go to about 8·7 km and are shown in light grey. Shallow water depths are also shown by light grey. The original of this figure, measuring 114 by 62 cm, and the ETOPO5 digital database from which it was made are available from the National Geophysical Data Center, 325 Broadway, Boulder, Colorado 80303–3328 USA.

from satellites have a common reference level (the geoid) so the elevations of two areas, separated by a large distance, can be directly compared.

Digital relief of the surface of the earth

The only consistent, world-wide digital data base for both land and oceans that is available is the digital relief of the surface of the Earth (ETOPO 5), distributed by the National Geophysical Data Center (NGDC) in Boulder, Colorado (Heirtzler, 1985). This database lists the average elevation and bathymetric reading for each 5 minutes of latitude and 5 minutes of longitude, or for about each 10 kilometer square. It is composed of data provided by several US national agencies or groups. Most of the land data were provided by the Defense Mapping Agency (DMA). For the seafloor the digital bathymetric data base, 5 minute (DBDB5), produced by the Naval Ocean Research and Development Activity, was used. The digital tape for ETOPO5 is distributed by the NGDC along with an atlas of three global images derived

from that digital data. Fig. 1 is a reduced copy of one of those images.

Different colors are assigned for different ranges of elevation/depths. The color scheme of this image has deeper blues for the deeper ocean depths and deeper reds for the higher elevations, although the highest elevations and the elevation/depths near zero are both shown in grey.

From the sometimes unknown and apparently disparate nature of data which went into this compilation it is hard to give a simple, meaningful description of the probable errors of the data set. For example, in the ocean areas, not every 10 kilometer square was actually measured. Rather, measurements were taken along ship's tracks by their echosounders. Although the density of ship's tracks is great in almost every part of the world, it was necessary to interpolate between readings in many cases to provide a reading for each and every 10 kilometer square. No doubt similar interpolations were applied to the land areas although the origin of the land data is even more obscure than the ocean data.

Before this data set was released it was reviewed by scientists who had expert knowledge of the topography in a part of the world. Recently this data set has been averaged into one degree squares and that compared to one degree square topographic data derived from radar ranging satellites and that comparison did not turn up any significant discrepancy. Various individual users of ETOP5 have found that the elevation of some lake surfaces, or parts of lake surfaces, is in significant error. It has also been found that some prominent topographic features are in error by a few kilometers. There has not been enough documentation of errors found through usage to make more precise comments, at this time, about the magnitude and distribution of errors.

Although this data set leaves much to be desired, it can be used to make images of the Earth that are far better than many purely artistic renditions and by its digital nature it can be used to make many quantitative descriptions of the Earth's surface.

Other topographic databases

At present there is no single agency or office which keeps a record of, archives, or distributes all the major topographic maps or digital database of the world. In the United States the Library of Congress, the US Geological Survey, and, especially, the DMA house many of these maps and the DMA is believed to have the largest digital topographic database, although not generally available to the public. The Karta Mira, produced by Eastern European mapping agencies, and the operational navigation chart (ONC) series, at 1: 1 000 000 scale, produced by western military services, are two of the more significant map series that cover the globe although the latitude and longitude of some features is known to be in error by 1 or 2 km. There are 270 ONC maps and they are for land only.

The DMA has begun to produce a digital version of the ONC sheets. These will be available to the public, at modest cost, on 30 CD-ROMs, with prototypes available in late 1989 and the series completed in late 1991. This series is called the digital chart of the world (DCW).

For less than global, but still large geographic areas, there are some other significant databases. The DMA has a digital terrain elevation data dataset available to authorized users. It covers much of the Northern Hemisphere with a resolution approaching the high resolution required by the scientific community.

Other popular topographic datasets are the 30-second, 1-minute and 3-minute data sets of the US distributed by NGDC. The 30-second data gives elevation to the nearest 20 ft and 30 seconds of latitude and longitude (about 2700 ft on the ground). The 1- and 3-minute data is derived from averaging the 30-second data. These are for the US only. The United Kingdom is extremely well mapped by the Ordnance Survey, and high quality data bases are also available for other European countries.

The management, archiving and upgrading of these large datasets is a continuing process and they are issued in consecutive versions with increasing accuracy. Most importantly, the topography itself is changing with time and the more modern datasets, or more recent versions of datasets may embody both improved accuracy and changes in the topography with time. The investigator must determine whether changes seen in new versions are real changes in the topography or are simply corrections of earlier datasets.

The future will see a great deal more effort in the acquiring and maintaining of digital topographic data sets and the application of these datasets to societal problems.

References

Brenner, A. C., Frey, H. V. & Zwally, H. J. (1990). Comparisons between Geosat and Seasat tracking over non-ocean surfaces. *Geophys. Res. Lett.*

EOSAT (1986). *Directory of Landsat-Related Products & Services*, Earth Observation Satellite Co., 4300 Forbes Blvd., Lanham, MD 20706.

Heirtzler, J. R. (ed.). (1985). Relief of the Surface of the Earth, *Report MGG-2*, National Oceanographic and Atmospheric Agency, Boulder.

Mueller, Ivan I. & Zerbini, S. (eds.). (1988). *Lecture Notes in the Earth Science, The Interdisciplinary Role of Space Geodesy*, Springer-Verlag, 300pp, New York.

Muller, Jan-Petter A. L. Real-time stereo matching and its role in future mapping systems. *Proc. Conf. Surv. Mapping*, 89, University of Warwick, 17–21 April.

Topographic Science Working Group (1988). *Topographic Science Working Group Report to the Land Processes Branch, Earth Science and Applications Division, NASA Headquarters*, Lunar and Planetary Institute, Houston, 64pp.

United Nations Environment Programme (1989). *Criteria for assessing vulnerability to sea-level rise: a global inventory to high risk areas*, Delft Hydraulics, Rept. H 838, 67pp, May.

Global vegetation mapping

J. R. G. TOWNSHEND, C. J. TUCKER AND S. N. GOWARD

Introduction

Alteration of vegetation cover, for agriculture, human settlements and other purposes is among the most pervasive and obvious impacts of human activities on the global environment. For example, in the last 300 years, there has been the net loss of forests, due to human action, of about 8 million km^2, or about 15 to 20% of the world's forested area (Turner, 1989). Changes in land cover are one of the most important sources of global environmental change and have profound implications for ecosystems, biogeochemical fluxes and climate (NRC, 1988; IGBP, 1990). For example, land cover change affects climate through factors such as albedo, evapotranspiration, and emissions of trace greenhouse gases to the atmosphere. These trace gases include methane releases from rice paddies and other wetlands, and releases of carbon dioxide, nitrous oxide, as well as other gases and particulates from biomass burning and decay of organic matter. These changes in the physical and chemical composition of the land and atmosphere in turn impact the hydrological and biogeochemical cycles of the Earth at global, regional and local scales. Many ecosystems are under considerable threat and there is a continuing decline in species and genetic diversity especially in association with the destruction of biomes in tropical areas as a consequence of anthropogenic activities. Many of these changes also impact inherent land productivity because of soil erosion and increases in nutrient leaching as land is cleared.

Because vegetation cover dynamics significantly affect the Earth's environment, quantitative information on the extent and rates of change in this cover is needed for global change research. The need for this information extends from improvement of global climate models, studies to determine the socio-economic causes and consequences of change in land cover, to research which assesses how changes in land cover alter regional and global hydrology, radiation budgets, and emissions of trace gases. Although global maps of vegetation cover have been derived through compilation of local maps based on ground survey, they provide an inadequate source of information for monitoring change at global scales (Townshend et al., 1991). Areal differences in excess of two or three fold for individual categories occur between various maps of global vegetation coverage.

Methodology

Two major series of satellites have been placed in orbit with sensors specifically designed for land applications. Both the long-lasting Landsat series and the French SPOT series have high spatial resolution multi-spectral sensors, which have produced large quantities of images for many regions of the world. However, for global studies of vegetation these observations are inappropriate because their high spatial resolution results in unmanageably high volumes of data. In addition, the relatively low temporal frequency of imaging from Landsat and SPOT has prevented use of these data sets to evaluate either seasonal variability or inter-annual variations in vegetation activity.

In order to monitor vegetation at global and continental scales, the land community has turned to data from meteorological satellites and in particular to data from the National Oceanographic and Atmospheric Administration's (NOAA) Advanced Very High Resolution Radiometer (AVHRR). This sensor has a spatial resolution as measured by its instantaneous field of view at nadir of 1.1×1.1 km. The AVHRR sensor is of particular interest for research in terrestrial vegetation, because it collects observations in both the red and the infrared parts of the spectrum. The red spectral measurements are sensitive to the chlorophyll content of vegetation and the near infrared to the mesophyll structure of leaves. Since the first is an inverse relationship and the second a direct relationship, differences between the bands and ratios between them have been found to possess useful relationships with a number of vegetative attributes, such as leaf area index, percentage vegetation cover and green leaf biomass, for specific vegetation types and the absorbed fraction of the photosynthetically active radiation (e.g. Curran, 1980). Various workers have shown that the normalized ratio (IR − Red)/(IR + Red) has a close relationship with the photosynthetic capacity of specific vegetation types (e.g. Asrar *et al.*, 1984; Sellers, 1985). This ratio, known as the normalized difference vegetation index (NDVI) has become the most commonly used remotely sensed measure of vegetation activity.

Basic AVHRR data sets

As mentioned above, AVHRR data are collected for the satellite subpoint at a basic resolution of 1.1 km. But, data at this resolution are only available for selected portions of the Earth's surface. The 1.1 km observations are only acquired for a relatively small proportion of each cycle, in sight of ground receiving stations (high resolution picture transmission (HRPT) data) or through use of on-board tape records (local area coverage (LAC) data). Global AVHRR coverage is acquired through on-board sampling and averaging of the measurements. These data, known as GAC (global area coverage), are sampled, recorded and then transmitted to Earth on a daily basis. Each GAC pixel is created by taking the first four pixels in a given row, averaging them, missing the fifth pixel, then averaging the next four and so on until the end of the scan line is reached. The next two scan lines are then skipped completely and the fourth line is then sampled and averaged in the same way as the first. Because only a fraction of each 5×3 pixel area is averaged, relating GAC pixels to specific ground areas and their properties is hindered. Other sampling schemes can readily be devised that are preferable (Justice *et al.*, 1989), but this is the scheme chosen by NOAA to produce GAC data, presumably because of engineering expediency. These data are usually quoted as having a 4 km resolution. In fact their area at the satellite subpoint is 5×3.3 km^2, which equals 16.5 km^2; even if their size is quoted in terms of the linear dimensions of a square of equivalent size the value should be quoted as 4.06 km. Moreover, their resolution off nadir is substantially greater expanding to 55.2 km^2 (12×4.6 km) at 45° off nadir (Goward *et al.*, 1991).

Although global data sets of GAC data are available from NOAA, they are not in a form readily suited for immediate use at global scales. Firstly, the data sets have not been navigated to any sort of standard map projection and consequently co-registering multi-temporal observations is difficult. Also, the ground size of pixels varies substantially due to the very large viewing swath width of the instrument. The data must be mapped in a uniform projection and resampled to assign consistent measurements to each geographic location. Currently available satellite navigational data permit location of pixels to within 7 to 8 pixels of their true location. More complex and computationally intensive methods exist to

achieve much better accuracies, but these have rarely been used.

A second major problem with both LAC and GAC AVHRR data for land investigations is the high frequency of cloud for much of the Earth's surface. Consequently, some form of automated cloud screening procedure is required. Various methods of cloud screening are available. The most commonly used method relies on the fact that the NDVI or the simple difference between the infra-red and red values for clouds produce low values when compared with cloudless land measurements. Hence, once accurately co-registered multi-temporal data sets have been generated, selection of the NDVI or simple difference between the near infra-red and red pixel value (DVI) which is highest for a given time period allows composites to be created in which cloud effects and other atmospheric effects are substantially reduced (Holben, 1986). Implementation of the two processes of remapping and compositing for existing NDVI data sets is discussed below.

GVI data sets

The most widely available global data set of the NDVI is NOAA's global vegetation index (GVI) Products. This has been produced continuously since 1982, though it is not currently available in a uniform format throughout this time period.

The GVI data set consists of a global product with a relatively coarse resolution (>15 km pixel size) with composited images representing 7 day periods. The procedure used in its generation is as follows.

1. Vegetation index maps are produced daily by mapping all daylight passes of the afternoon polar orbiter. In this mapping, only the last sensed GAC pixel of each remapped cell is retained, which means that pixels from off-nadir, back-scattered orientations are preferentially chosen. Especially in higher latitudes, this has the beneficial effect of increasing the vegetation signal in sparsely vegetated areas but the disadvantage of selecting pixels strongly affected by atmospheric scattering. This is carried out for each day so that, for each week, seven separate values of the spectral bands are available for each GVI pixel.

2. The difference between the red and near infra-red values is then calculated for each day to produce the difference vegetation index (DVI).

3. The values for each week are then selected from the date with the highest DVI to represent the seven-day period in order to reduce atmospheric effects. Unfortunately, at higher latitudes and low solar

zenith angles the largest values of the two channels and often the largest differences are selected from pixels suffering from marked back-scattering. Additionally, the seven day period is often too short so that large areas of cloud- affected pixels remain.

4. The NDVI is then calculated using the values of channels 1 and 2 selected in stage 3.

The GVI product has been made available in a number of formats. From 1982 to 1984 it was available only in a polar projection with a resolution of 13 km at the equator to 26 km at the poles. Such polar projections, although having obvious value for global snow and ice studies are especially unhelpful for global investigations of vegetation, because one has two separate images to represent the Earth and these are divided at the equator, without any simple method of recombining them. Earlier studies of global vegetation therefore usually involved remapping of the GVI product by users (e.g. Justice *et al.*, 1985; Hardy, Singh & Narracott, 1988). Channel 1 and channel 2 data were also provided. From 1985 to the present, a latitude–longitude (Plate-Caree) projection has been used with 16 km resolution at the equator to 16×8 km at $60°$ N and S. In addition to the above bands of data, channels 4 and 5 were provided to assist users in improving cloud screening; scan angle and solar zenith angle were included to assist intra-annual comparisons. Further details of the NOAA GVI product are found within Kidwell (1990) and an account of its limitations is given in Goward *et al.* (1990).

NASA/GSFC product and NASA/NOAA pathfinder data set

At NASA's Goddard Space Flight Center, the Global Inventory Monitoring and Modeling Systems (GIMMS) group has generated its own data set, using a rather different set of procedures, which overcome at least some of the limitations of the GVI. GAC data are reprojected onto an equal area projection using the on-board navigation data and they are visually checked to ensure they are properly registered. The data are resampled to give a resolution of approximately 7.6 km. Given that the basic GAC data represent areas of approximately this size at view angles of $35°$ off nadir, this means that near nadir pixels are somewhat over-sampled, whereas in those situations where pixels are selected by compositing from higher view angles, under-sampling will occur. Although no formal tests of the frequency of the latter have been carried out, they are believed to be relatively common. The DN values are converted to at-satellite reflectances using available calibration data, which is admittedly limited in amount and quality. A simple procedure for cloud detection is

applied by thresholding channel 5 temperatures. The NDVI is then calculated for each date, with zeros being included where clouds have been flagged. Composites are then generated by selecting for each pixel the highest NDVI value for a 15-day period for all continents except Africa where the period is 10 days because of operational requirements of the Food and Agricultural Organization (FAO). The resultant product is therefore substantially different from the NOAA GVI product in terms of its spatial resolution, its projection, the cloud clearing procedures and the values used to actually calculate the NDVI. Currently the product is being compiled by continent, with some minor variations in spatial resolution and compositing period between continents.

Partly arising from the NASA/GIMMS initiative, NASA and NOAA are funding the creation of a new global data set as part of the Pathfinder activity, which is concerned with the creation of long term data sets as a preliminary activity for the Earth observing system (EOS). GAC data will be reprocessed back to the start of their collection in 1981, and a consistently processed global data set for the land is being created with a resolution of 9 km. Vicarious calibration of bands 1 and 2 will be carried out as well as atmospheric correction for Rayleigh scattering and ozone. All five bands as well as the NDVI will be included in the final product.

Analysis and results

NDVI images are shown in Figs. 1 to 4 and 6 to 7. The theoretical range of the NDVI is -1 to $+1$, but in practice it varies from -0.3 for water to 0.05 for desert areas and over 0.6 for areas with the highest levels of vegetation activity. The color scale is divided into units of approximately 0.025 and changes from brown colors for the lowest values through yellow, green, red, mauve and at the highest levels to purple. Those preferring a more naturalistic rendition of the colors are referred to Goward (1990). More refined subdivision could be made, but in view of the limitations of the accuracy of the NDVI values, especially as a result of atmospheric interference, this is not warranted.

Seasonal variations in the NDVI

In Figs. 1 to 4, monthly global images are shown displaying seasonal variations in the NDVI. The data have been further composited by selecting the maximum NDVI value for each pixel from the four weeks of data, in order further to reduce cloud effects. The images are described in more detail in Justice *et al.* (1985) from which the following description is taken.

In the first global image, covering the period from 12 April

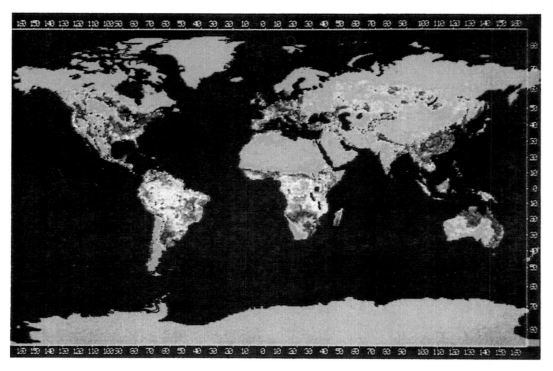

Fig. 1. Global composite of the normalized difference vegetation index for April 12 to May 15 1982 (Justice *et al.*, 1985).

to 15 May 1982 (Fig. 1), the highest NDVI values are found near the equator in the tropical rain forests and adjacent moist wooded savannahs. High values elsewhere are found only in the eastern USA, western Europe and eastern China. Low values are found not only in the desert areas but also in India, much of Canada, the west African grasslands, the north European plain and the Soviet Union. At this time remarkably high values are found in some semi-arid parts of Australia. The distribution of the NDVI clearly indicates that the index represents green-leaf vegetation activity rather than the distribution of vegetation types *per se*.

The next image, derived for the period from 14 June to 18 July 1982 (Fig. 2), shows a dramatic change especially for mid-latitude agricultural areas in the Northern Hemisphere. A belt of high NDVI values represented by the mauve and purple colors is almost continuous across the global land mass. The highest values in this belt are found in eastern North America, in western Europe and in the USSR from Latvia almost to Lake Baykal and then again in the easternmost parts of the USSR north of Vladivostok. These areas correspond to the main grain-growing areas of the Northern Hemisphere. North of these agricultural areas less dramatic changes of the NDVI are found in the northern boreal forests. In Africa, a generally northward shift of the main areas of high NDVI and a decrease in values in Angola and Mozambique can be observed. In South America, the seasonal forest

and tropical savannahs of southeast Brazil show a decrease in the NDVI, whereas the tropical rainforest areas of the Amazon remain constant with overall high values.

The third image is for the period from 13 September to 17 October (Fig. 3). Although the Northern hemisphere mid-latitude agricultural areas continue to have higher NDVI values than in the April–May image, most areas have declined significantly from the high of June–July. This arises presumably because of harvesting but also because other crops have ripened and become senescent. High values remain, however, in the eastern half of the USA, probably because of the importance of crops such as corn (maize) and soybeans which remain green until their harvesting in September and October. In contrast, the agricultural lands of Uruguay and southern Brazil show large increases in the NDVI with the onset of the Southern Hemisphere's spring. India has high NDVI values for most of its land area. This onset of greenness in fact occurred shortly after the June–July composite was obtained. In East Africa NDVI values are low, corresponding to the dry season which lasts until the onset of the short rains later in the year.

On the image for the period 13 December to 16 January (Fig. 4) high NDVI values are found throughout East Africa and across the continent to the Bie Plateau of Angola. In South America the highest NDVI values are found south of the rainforest in a zone stretching from Bolivia through Para-

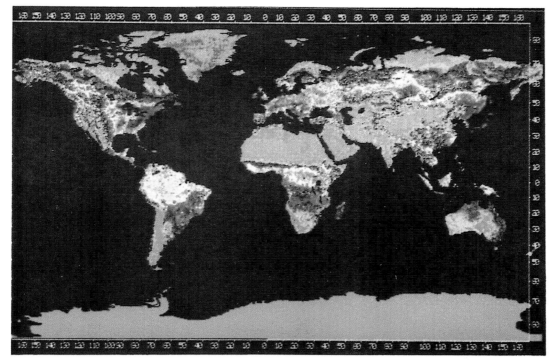

Fig. 2. Global composite of the normalized difference vegetation index for June 14 to July 18 1982 (Justice *et al.*, 1985).

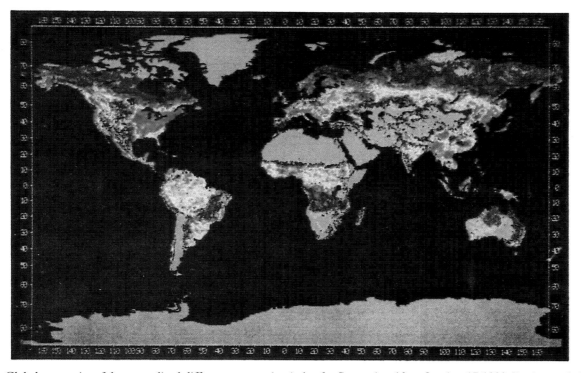

Fig. 3. Global composite of the normalized difference vegetation index for September 13 to October 17 1982 (Justice *et al.*, 1985).

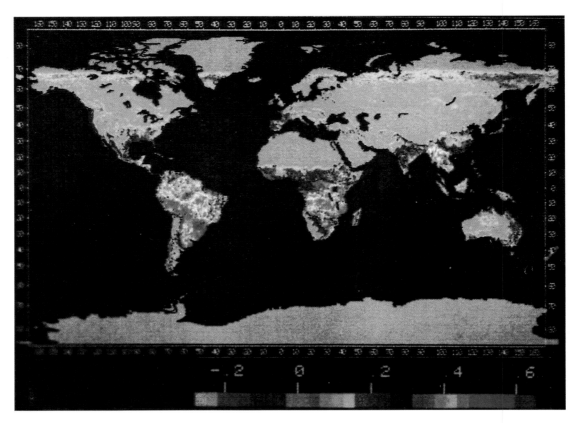

Fig. 4. Global composite of the normalized difference vegetation index for December 13 to January 16 1982 (Justice *et al.*, 1985).

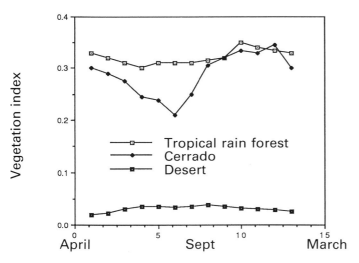

Fig. 5. Temporal profiles of the normalized difference vegetation index for selected cover types.

guay to southern Brazil and Uruguay which had high NDVI values in the previous image. This zone now also extends southward to the grain-growing areas of the pampas of Argentina and the agricultural areas of Chile.

It should be clear that in any given month the NDVI of some different vegetation types can be similar. In Fig. 5, NDVI curves are shown for different vegetation types. The desert area is different from the other two areas at all dates, but the tropical rainforest and savannah display similar values for a substantial part of the year. Also vegetation types north and south of the equator can display similar trends but be out of phase by 6 months: this is shown for example by considering in Figs. 1 to 4 savannah areas in Africa and mid-latitude agricultural areas in South America compared with North America. A failure to understand these dynamics can cause serious misunderstandings concerning vegetation discrimination with AVHRR NDVI data sets (Thomas & Henderson-Sellers, 1987; Henderson-Sellers, 1989).

Comparisons between years

In Figs. 6 and 7 part of the NASA/GSFC data set is shown for the continent of Africa for January 1984 and 1985 respectively. This data set has a resolution of approximately 8 km and has been generated somewhat differently from the NOAA/GVI product as was discussed in Methodology. Because inter-annual differences are relatively small compared with seasonal changes, only one continent is depicted in

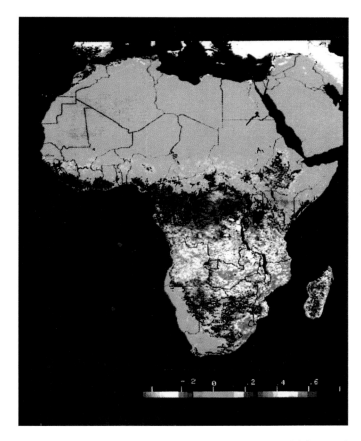

Fig. 6. Normalized difference index vegetation image of Africa with 7·6 km resolution for January 1984 (Townshend & Justice, 1986).

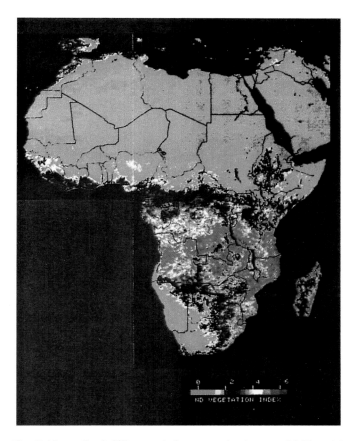

Fig. 7. Normalized difference index vegetation image of Africa with 7·6 km resolution for January 1985 (Townshend & Justice, 1986).

order that the details of change can be readily seen. The comparison is taken from Townshend and Justice (1986) from which further details can be obtained.

In making a comparison between years the first point to be made is that, although some major differences do occur, there are very considerable similarities between the years. In the January 1984 image the area of moderate NDVI values extends much further to the southwest than in the 1985 image. FAO (1984) reported deficient rains in November and December 1984 in southern Africa, resulting in an adverse effect on crops in all areas of Botswana except for the northeast border with Zambia. Comparison of the southern border between Botswana and Namibia shows clear differences between the two years. Conversely, in eastern Kenya and southern Somalia, the January 1985 image shows higher NDVI values. Within the Sudanian zone and transition to the Guinean zone, similar patterns of NDVI can be seen between the two January images, but with generally higher values for 1984. Notable examples include the Massif des Bongo (Central African Republic), the Massif del Adamaoua (Cameroun) and the border between Southern Mali and the

Ivory Coast. The generally lower values for January 1985 are most likely related to the extreme rainfall deficit throughout the Sahel during the 1984 growing season. Associated with this are the low NDVI values for the Niger Delta in Mali and the Sudd in Sudan. In contrast with the generally low NDVI values across the Sudanian zone in January 1985, the Ethiopian Highlands exhibit somewhat higher NDVI values than in January 1984. In southern Mozambique, NDVI values are markedly lower in 1984 than they are in 1985. The distribution of NDVI values can clearly be explained only through an understanding of the distribution of vegetation communities and their relationships to rainfall events in the time immediately preceding the time of imaging.

Limitations

The current NOAA GVI data product has a number of limitations some of which have been alluded to previously. Amongst these are the fact that it has been provided in two different projections and that earlier data have to be remapped to produce a continuous time series. Secondly the use of the DVI, rather than the NDVI, to produce weekly composites tends preferentially to select pixels which are from more off-nadir positions and hence are more affected by atmospheric effects. Thirdly, in many areas of the globe the weekly products are still substantially affected by clouds. Consequently it may be advisable to carry out further compositing by taking the maximum NDVI value for three or four week periods (e.g. Tucker, Townshend & Goff, 1985; Townshend & Justice, 1986). Fourthly there are dangers in using the NDVI values actually provided in the GVI product, since these are calculated from the raw digital numbers. Approximate formulae are available to convert the channel 1 and 2 values to reflectances, though these have problems as discussed below. These formulae contain offset and gain coefficients which are different for the two channels. Hence NDVIs based on DNs inevitably differ from the true NDVIs (Price, 1987). Those using the GVI data set should employ the gains and offsets, provided by NOAA, to calculate the NDVI from the calibrated values, though these coefficients are known to change after launch.

There are also a number of limitations which are found to varying degrees in both global NDVI products. The most important of these is the absence of on-board calibration for channels 1 and 2, since these were originally designed purely for imaging. Degradation of the instrument has occurred which impacts the NDVI values, though the changes in channels 1 and 2 have been partly compensatory (Holben, Kaufman & Kendall, 1990). Also the AVHRR sensors on different NOAA platforms have different gains and offsets. Consequently, inter-annual comparisons must be carried out with considerable care. The absence of calibration can be partly overcome by use of invariant ground targets, as carried out by Tucker (1989), to readjust the channel and NDVI values. The coarse resolution of the data sets in itself poses problems because of the difficulties of accurate ground location and the high spatial variability of many land areas of the Earth.

Problems also arise because of the limitations of the NDVI index itself. Soils can have a substantial influence on the index, especially where vegetation cover is sparse, and hence soil color can have a significant effect. As a consequence modifications of the index have been proposed (e.g. Huete, 1989; Major, Baret & Guyot, 1990), which help reduce, but do not eliminate the effects of the soil background. The use of other spectral bands could possibly help to reduce soil effects to a greater extent (e.g. Crist & Cicone, 1984), but currently there are no data sets with such spectral bands available at a global scale.

A final set of problems, which has to be alluded to, relates to atmospheric effects. Some of these can be eliminated, notably Rayleigh scattering, but the absorptive effects of water vapor on channel 2 and aerosols on both channels are much more difficult to reduce. In particular, channel 2 includes a major water absorption band. Variations in water vapor can cause the appearance of spurious greening in semi-arid areas unrelated to any changes in ground conditions. Aerosols will also cause variations in the NDVI, and without ground instrumentation these cannot readily be corrected.

The previously described NASA/GIMMS and NASA/NOAA Pathfinder products will correct some of these problems (see 'Methodology'). Additionally a revised global vegetation index product with the same resolution as the original one is being created at the University of Maryland from April 1983 to the present, in which corrections have been included for calibration and some atmospheric effects.

In order to overcome the limitations of spatial resolution, a proposal has been made in the framework of the International Geosphere–Biosphere Program, to combine data at a resolution of 1.1 km recorded on board the satellite with those collected by ground receiving stations in order to create a global data set with a nominal 1 km resolution every 15 days for at least a year (IGBP, 1992).

Applications

NDVI data have been used in a variety of ways to examine the vegetation of the Earth at continental and global scales. Firstly they provide an overview of the seasonal variation of vegetation activity (Tucker et al., 1985; Justice et al., 1985) as shown in the images contained within this chapter. Because the NDVI is indicative of photosynthetic activity attempts have successfully been made to relate its global annual variability to variations in CO_2 (Fung, Tucker & Prentice, 1986, Tucker et al., 1986). For similar reasons Goward and Dye (1987) were able to demonstrate empirically a direct relationship between the annual integrated NDVI and net primary productivity for a variety of cover types. The spatial variability of vegetation activity at different scales for the continent of Africa has been examined in Justice, Townshend & Kalb (1991a) where, contrary to expectations, most variability in the range 8 km to 256 km was found to lie at the coarsest rather than at the finest scales.

Using various multi-temporal data sets, the seasonal variation in NDVI values has been used to discriminate between vegetative cover types (Townshend et al., 1991). Preliminary land cover maps have been derived at continental scales by Tucker et al. (1985) for Africa and by Townshend, Justice & Kalb (1987) for South America using NOAA's GVI product with pixel sizes of approximately 15–20 km. Shimoda et al. (1986) have used the same very coarse resolution data to derive statistical estimates of global land cover types: more

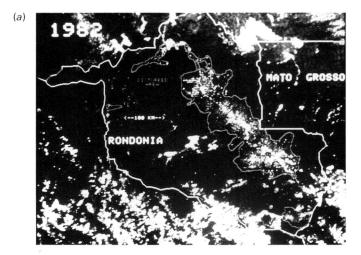

(a)

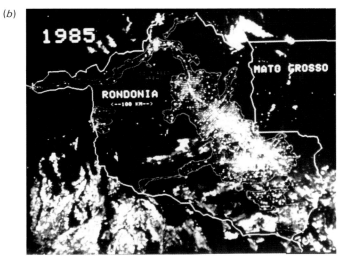

(b)

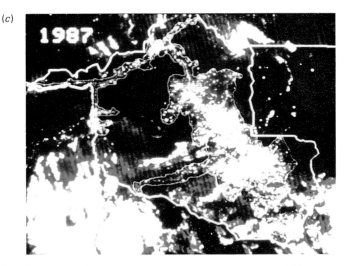

(c)

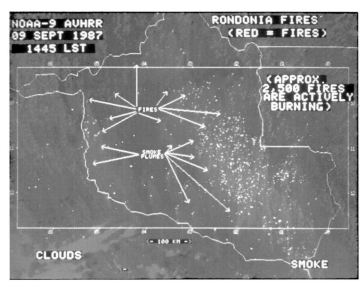

Fig. 9. Thermal image showing the large number of fires and smoke plume associated with forest clearance in the dry season in Rondonia.

Fig. 8. Images of Rondonia Brazil from 1982, 1985, and 1987. The large area of agricultural expansion can be seen in the right central part of each image. The similarly light-colored areas in the far south are natural savannah.

recently Koomanoff (1989) has produced a global map of nine basic vegetation types, using an integrated annual value of the NDVI, though without any consideration of seasonality. At a subcontinental scale Millington *et al.* (1989) used NASA/GSFC data set to stratify cover types for eight countries in southern Africa as a basis for estimating the supply of fuelwood. Integrated use of rainfall data sets derived from Meteosat data and the NASA/GSFC data set was shown to have potential for indicating variations in inherent land productivity (Justice *et al.* 1991*b*). Several studies have demonstrated the value of AVHRR data for monitoring the grasslands of semi-arid areas especially in Africa (Tucker *et al.*, 1983; Justice, 1986; Prince & Justice, 1991).

One of the most important applications of AVHRR data has been its use in the mapping of the tropical rainforest (e.g. Tucker, Holben & Goff, 1984; Malingreau, Tucker & Laporte, 1989). Specifically within Amazon rainforest data from the AVHRR dramatically illustrate the extent of forest clearance as a consequence of agricultural colonization (Fig. 8). Data from the thermal IR bands have also proved valuable in the detection of fires (e.g. Malingreau, Stevens & Fellows, 1985) associated with this clearance (Fig. 9). Comparisons between results of rates of clearance derived from AVHRR data and higher resolution Landsat data have, however, indicated that, although the former are of considerable value in indicating the location of the main areas of clearance, they are somewhat inaccurate in measuring rates of change. Consequently plans have recently been formulated by NASA to

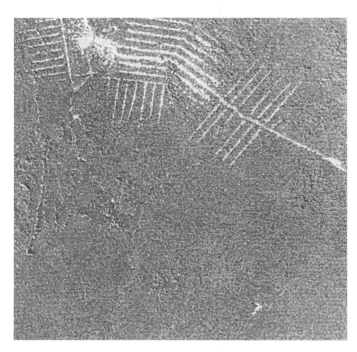

Fig. 10. Deforestation due to agricultural colonization in Rondonia Brazil shown in images from Landsat's multispectral scanner system from 1976 and 1988.

provide wall to wall coverage of Landsat data for the whole of the Earth's tropical rainforest to derive more accurate data on its extent and rate of destruction. The benefits of using higher spatial resolution Landsat MSS data can be seen in Fig. 10.

Because of the importance of quantitative information of land cover for many aspects of global change research, the International Geosphere–Biosphere Program is undertaking a pilot study on land cover change and developing procedures for creating a global land cover map at a resolution of 1 km (IGBP 1990), though the latter product is not likely to be available until the mid-1990s when comprehensive satellite data will become available (Rasool & Ojima, 1989; IGBP, 1992).

References

Asrar, G., Fuchs, M., Kanemasu, E. T. & Hatfield, J. L. (1984). Estimating absorbed photosynthetic radiation and leaf area index from spectral reflectance in wheat. *Agron. J.*, **76**, 300–6.

Crist, E. P. & Cicone, R. C. (1984). A physically-based transformation of Thematic Mapper data – the TM tasselled cap. *IEEE Trans.*, **GE-22**, 256–63.

Curran, P. J. (1980). Multispectral remote sensing of vegetation amount. *Progr. Phys. Geog.*, **4**, 175–84.

FAO (Food and Agricultural Organization) (1984). *Food Outlook Report*, 11/12. FAO, Rome.

Fung, I. Y., Tucker, C. J. & Prentice, K. C. (1986). On the applica-

bility of the AVHRR vegetation index to study the atmospheric-biospheric exchange of CO_2. *J. Geophys. Res.*, **92**, 2999–3015.

Goward, S. N. (1990). Experiences and perspective in compiling long-term data sets of landscapes and biospheric processes. *GeoJournal*, **20**, 107–14.

Goward, S. N. & Dye, D. G. (1987). Evaluating North American net primary productivity with satellite observations, *Adv. Space Res.*, **7**, 165–74.

Goward, S. N., Dye, D. G., Dulaney, W. & Yang, J. (1990). Critical assessment of the NOAA Global Vegetation Index data product. *Proceedings of the Workshop on the Use of Satellite-Derived Indices in Weather and Climate Prediction Models*. Camp Springs Maryland, US Department of Commerce, National Oceanic and Atmospheric Administration, 34–42.

Goward, S. N., Markham, B., Dye, D. G., Dulaney, W. & Yang, J. (1991). Normalized difference vegetation index measurements from Advanced Very High Resolution Radiometer. *Remote Sensing Environm.*, **35**, 257–78.

Hardy, J. R., Singh, S. M. & Narracott, A. S. (1988). Transformation of global vegetation index (GVI) data from the polar stereographic project to an equatorial cylindrical projection. *Int. J. Remote Sensing*, **9**, 583–9.

Henderson-Sellers, A. (1989). Climate, models and geography. In *Remodelling Geography* (MacMillan, B., ed.), Basil Blackwell, Oxford, pp. 117–46.

Holben, B. N. (1986). Characteristics of maximum value composite images from temporal AVHRR data. *Int. J. Remote Sensing*, **7**, 1417–34.

Holben, B. N., Kaufman, Y. J. & Kendall, J. D. (1990). NOAA-11 AVHRR visible and near-IR inflight calibration. *Int. J. Remote Sensing*, 11, 1511–19.

Huete, A. R. (1989). Soil influences in remotely sensed vegetation-canopy spectra. In *Theory and Applications of Optical Remote Sensing*. (G. Asrar, ed.) John Wiley, New York, pp. 107–41.

IGBP (International Geosphere–Biosphere Programme) (1990). *The Initial Core Projects*. International Geosphere–Biosphere Program Report No. 12, Stockholm, Sweden.

IGBP (International Geosphere–Biosphere Programme) (1992). *Improved Global Data for Land Applications: a Proposal for a new High Resolution Data Set*. International Geosphere–Biosphere Program Report No. 20, Stockholm, Sweden.

Justice, C. O. (1986). Monitoring the grasslands of semi-arid Africa using NOAA-AVHRR data. *Int. Journal of Remote Sensing*, 7, 1383–622.

Justice, C. O., Dugdale, G., Townshend, J. R. G., Narracott, A. & Kumar, N. (1991*b*). Synergism between NOAA-AVHRR and Meteosat data for studying vegetation in semi-arid west Africa. *Int. J. Remote Sensing*, 12, 1349–68.

Justice, C. O., Markham, B. L., Townshend, J. R. G. & Kennard, R. L. (1989). Spatial degradation of satellite data. *Int. J. Remote Sensing*, 10, 1539–61.

Justice, C. O., Townshend, J. R. G., Holben, B. N. & Tucker, C. J. (1985). Analysis of the phenology of global vegetation using meteorological satellite data. *Int. J. Remote Sensing*, 6, 1271–318.

Justice, C. O., Townshend, J. R. G. & Kalb, V. T. (1991*a*). Representation of vegetation by continental data sets derived from NOAA-AVHRR data. *Int. J. Remote Sensing*, 12, 999–1021.

Kidwell, K. B. (1990). *Global Vegetation Index User's Guide*. US Department of Commerce, NOAA, Camp Springs, MD.

Koomanoff, V. A. (1989). Analysis of global vegetation patterns: a comparison between remotely sensed data and a conventional map. *Biogeography Research Series, Report #890201*, Department of Geography, University of Maryland.

Major, D. J., Baret, F. & Guyot, G. (1990). A ratio vegetation index adjusted for soil brightness. *Int. J. Remote Sensing*, 11, 727–40.

Malingreau, J.-P., Stevens, G. & Fellows, C. (1985). 1982–83 forest fores of Kalimantan and North Borneo: satellite observations for detection and monitoring. *Ambio*, 14, 314–46.

Malingreau, J.-P., Tucker, C. J. & Laporte, N. (1989). AVHRR for monitoring global tropical deforestation. *Int. J. Remote Sensing*, 10, 866–7.

Millington, A. C., Townshend, J. R. G., Kennedy, P., Saull, R., Prince, S. & Madams, R. (1989). *Biomass Assessment: Woody Biomass in the SADCC Region*. Earthscan Publications, London.

NRC (National Research Council) (1988). *Toward an Understanding of Global Change: Initial Priorities for US Contributions to the International Geosphere Biosphere Program*. National Academy Press, Washington DC.

Price, J. C. (1987). Calibration of satellite radiometers and the comparison of vegetation indices. *Remote Sensing of Environm.*, 24, 15–27.

Prince, S. D. & Justice, C. O. (1991). Coarse resolution remote sensing of the Sahelian environment. *Int. J. Remote Sensing*, 12, 1113–421.

Rasool, S. I. & Ojima, D. (1989). *Pilot studies for remote sensing and data management*. Report of a meeting of the IGBP Working Group on Data and Information Systems. International Geosphere–Biosphere Program, Stockholm, Sweden.

Sellers, P. J. (1985). Canopy reflectance, photosynthesis and transpiration. *Int. J. Remote Sensing*, 6, 1335–372.

Shimoda, H., Fukue, K., Hosomura, T. & Sakata, T. (1986). Global vegetation monitoring using NOAA GAC data. *ESA Symposium on Remote Sensing for Resources Development and Environmental Management*, Enschede, 505–8.

Thomas, G. & Henderson-Sellers, A. (1987). Evaluation of satellite derived land cover characteristics for global climate modelling. *Climate Change*, 11, 313–48.

Townshend, J. R. G. & Justice, C. O. (1986). Analysis of the dynamics of African vegetation using the normalized difference vegetation index. *Int. J. Remote Sensing*, 8, 1189–207.

Townshend, J. R. G., Justice, C. O. & Kalb, V. T. (1987). Characterization and classification of South American land cover types using satellite data. *Int. J. Remote Sensing*, 8, 1189–207.

Townshend, J. R. G., Justice, C. O., Li, W., Gurney, C. & McManus, J. (1991). Monitoring global land cover: present capabilities and future possibilities. *Remote Sensing of Environment*, 35, 243–56.

Tucker, C. J. (1989). Comparing SMMR and AVHRR data for drought monitoring. *Int. J. Remote Sensing*, 10, 1663–72.

Tucker, C. J., Fung, I. Y., Keeling, C. D. & Gammon, R. H. (1986). Relationship between atmospheric CO_2 variations and a satellite-derived vegetation index. *Nature*, London, 319, 195–9.

Tucker, C. J., Holben, B. N. & Goff, T. E. (1984). Intensive forest clearing in Rondonia, Brazil, as detected by remote sensing. *Remote Sensing of Environment*, 15, 255–62.

Tucker, C. J., Townshend, J. R. G. & Goff, T. E. (1985). African land cover classification using satellite data. *Science*, New York, 227, 233–50.

Tucker, C. J., Vanpraet, C. L., Boerwinkle, E. & Easton, A. (1983). Satellite remote sensing of total dry matter accumulation in the Sengalese Sahel. *Remote Sensing of Environment*, 13, 461–9.

Turner, B. L. (1989). The human causes of global environmental change. In DeFries, R. S. & Malone, T. (eds.) *Global Change and our Common Future: Papers from a Forum*. National Academy Press, Washington DC.

Desertification

BHASKAR J. CHOUDHURY

Introduction

Deserts are territories which receive less than 120 mm of rain annually, when averaged over more than 30 years (Shmida, 1985). A definition of deserts in terms of annual rainfall is simple to obtain, and in many deserts rainfall is the only available data. The rainfall amount is highly variable on a year-to-year basis, and this variability increases as the long-term mean annual rainfall decreases (Ehleringer, 1985). However, the annual rainfall amount alone does not completely describe deserts, and there is no simple criterion by which to define deserts in either geographical or biological sense (Le Houerou, 1977; Williams & Calaby, 1985). Many deserts have high air and soil temperatures during daytime, intermittent or dried up streams, and flora and fauna display features to avoid or overcome high temperature and long periods of water scarcity. The timing, duration and amount of water available for flora and fauna are highly variable and unpredictable. There is a high spatial variability of rainfall and runoff. The soil fertility (organic matter, nitrogen, phosphorus, etc.) is generally very low in deserts and has a high spatial variability (being much higher under and around plant canopies than elsewhere). Plant biomass and productivity are generally low, being limited by both soil moisture and fertility. The plant communities have adapted to the shortages of soil water and nutrients, and stability and resilience are appropriate terms to use to describe these communities for long-term occupancy and the ability to regenerate on a given site without human intervention. Some desert surfaces are quite stable (rocky and crusted surfaces), others are unstable (shifting dunes and wind erosion). Some sand dunes and sand seas are stable. It is difficult to arrive at a single universally accepted definition of or a criterion for deserts. One has to recognize the existence of a continual geographical transition from deserts to arid to semi-arid lands. Long-term water balance calculations, which consider soil, vegetation and climate, provide a quantitative approach for delimiting the desert territories (Evenari, 1985). Nevertheless, any index or criterion based upon the water balance calculation is likely have a

geographical continuum going from deserts to arid lands, which has to be broken to delimit deserts.

The term desertification was first used by Aubreville (1949) to refer to man-induced ruination of productive land in humid and subhumid regions where annual rainfall is 700 to 1500 mm. The causes of land destruction were cutting of trees, man-made fire and cultivation, which exposed the soil for water and wind erosion. Stebbing (1937) described 'encroaching Sahara' when deforestation of the Sahelian and Sudanian zones resulted in erosion, and deposition of sand blown from the Sahara. While the term desertification has raised the public awareness of a global problem, there are no generally accepted definitions of this term (Verstraete, 1986). Dregne (1986) noted that desertification evokes a mental picture of a barren forbidding landscape like the Sahara. He points out such a grim picture does not apply to most of the land that has undergone, or is undergoing, desertification. Gbeckor-Kove (1989) defined desertification as diminution of the biological productivity of the land leading to the spatial extension of desert-like conditions of soil and vegetation into marginal areas outside the climatic desert and intensification of such conditions over a period of time. This definition emphasises events in arid and semi-arid zones bordering the deserts where the average annual rainfall is less than 500 mm. Nelson (1990) defined desertification as a process of sustained land (soil and vegetation) degradation in arid, semi-arid and subhumid areas caused at least partly by man. It reduces both resilience and productive potential of the land to an extent which can neither be readily reversed by removing the cause nor easily reclaimed without substantial capital investment. Nelson's definition accepts deterioration of both soil and vegetation, and insists that there must be some man-induced element in the process of land degradation. He characterizes the change as being sustained to exclude short-term fluctuations, caused either by man or climate. A 10-year natural recovery of productive potential under average or above average rainfall or an investment of substantial capital was considered as the dividing line between effectively reversible and irreversible situations. Lastly, Nelson's definition included areas with annual rainfall up to 800 mm (subhumid zone). Mismanagement of land by man must be recognized as an element in the desertification process.

Land degradation can, and does, occur far from any climatic desert; the presence or absence of a nearby desert has no direct relation to desertification. Also, droughts are not responsible for desertification, although it does increase the likelihood of land degradation. A well-managed land will recover from droughts with minimal alteration when rain returns. Desertification is a land degradation process involving a continuum of change from slight to very severe degradation of soil and plant resources caused by man's activities. Dregne (1986) describes four classes of desertification:

Slight: Little degradation of soil and plant cover.
Moderate: 1) 26 – 50% of plant community consists of climax species, or 2) 25 to 75% of the original top soil lost, or 3) soil salinity has reduced crop yields by 10 – 50%.
Severe: 1) 10 – 25% of plant community consists of the climax species, or 2) erosion has removed all or practically all of the original top soil, or 3) salinity has reduced crop yield by more than 50%.
Very Severe 1) Less than 10% of plant community consists of climax species, or 2) land has many sand dunes or deep gullies, or 3) salt crust has developed on soil.

The last category is often conceived as the land condition resulting from desertification. The areas of the world which are particularly threatened by desertification are generally near the perimeters of deserts. Mismanagement of semi-arid grasslands can lead to an invasion by desert shrubs, which changes the spatial and temporal patterns of soil water, nitrogen and other soil resources. These changes in the soil conditions become more favorable to further invasion by shrubs (Schlesinger et al., 1990). Although the biomass production for the grassland and the shrubland are similar, the soil becomes degraded due to erosion and the economic potential of the land is reduced. The global extent of desertification and the magnitude of the problem are not accurately known. Encroachment of moving sand dunes is highly visible and locally important, but it does not represent the entirety of desertification. The extent of southward advancement of the Sahara desert and its impact with respect to desertification have been disputed (Nelson, 1990). Desert formation and spreading is influenced by large-scale atmospheric circulation

patterns (Landsberg, 1986). Soil erosion in dry areas, which is an important element of desertification, is poorly documented.

Changes of the land surface over large areas can influence or alter climate. Vegetation, soil moisture and albedo (which determines absorption of solar radiation) influence motion of the atmosphere, rainfall and temperature (Mintz, 1984). It has been suggested that changes of the Sahel land surface might have a role in maintaining prolonged (10 to 15 years) periods of drought over this region (Nicholson, 1986, 1988). A comparative analysis of rainfall over Caribbean islands showed substantially less rainfall over the deforested islands (Anthes, 1984). In semi-arid regions, local evaporation plays a major role in causing rainfall. Thus, land degradation could have the effect of getting re-enforced through changes of climatic conditions (that is, land degradation decreases rainfall, which reduces vegetation growth).

Desertification is a complex land degradation process involving man, land, and possibly climate. Research is needed for locating, assessing and monitoring changes, such as changes in vegetation type (species composition) and fractional ground cover, soil type (texture) and land use. Remote sensing provides a way of monitoring land surface change in a quantitative and consistent fashion. Careful analysis of remotely sensed data could provide information about changes of vegetation type and cover, soil color and land use. The initial stages of desertification, which might show as changes of species composition (diversity), might not be detected by remote sensing. For desertification study, any changes in the remotely sensed data would have to be evaluated carefully in the context of the processes, as elaborated above.

Methodology

Observations in different spectral bands or wavelengths by instruments on different satellites, when properly standardized, calibrated and validated, could be quite useful for monitoring changes of land surface characteristics. These instruments measure the intensity of electromagnetic radiation reflected or emitted by the land surface and the atmosphere. The wavelength of observation ranges from the visible to the microwave (that is, from micrometer to decimeter) portion of the electromagnetic spectrum. The radiation reflected or emitted by the atmosphere must be removed from the measured intensities before one can evaluate changes of land surface. Also, changes in the time of observation or characteristics of the instruments must be considered before any changes detected by the instrument can be ascribed to changes of land surface. Furthermore, the land surface

Table 1. *Information about sensors on different satellites*

Sensor*	Satellite	Spectral range** (μm or GHz)	Spatial resolution (m or km)	Time of Data acquisition	Repeat cycle
MSR	METEOSAT	0.40–1.10 μm	2.3 km	Every 30 min	Stationary
		10.5–12.5 μm	5.0 km		
		5.7–7.1 μm	5.0 km		
MSR	GMS	0.55–0.74 μm	1.3 km	Every 3 hours	Stationary
		10.5–12.5 μm			
TM	LANDSAT (since 1982)	0.45–0.52 μm	30 m	0930 h	16 days
		0.52–0.60 μm	30 m		
		0.63–0.69 μm	30 m		
		0.76–0.90 μm	30 m		
		1.55–1.75 μm	31 m		
		2.08–2.35 μm	31 m		
		10.4–12.5 μm	120 m		
MSS	LANDSAT (since 1972)	0.5–0.6 μm	80 m	0930 h	18 days
		0.6–0.7 μm	80 m		
		0.7–0.8 μm	80 m		
		0.8–1.1 μm	80 m		
AVHRR	NOAA-7, NOAA-9 (NOAA-8)	0.57–0.69 μm	1.1 km	1430 and 0230 h	12 h
		0.71–0.98 μm	(4.0)	(1930 and 0730 h)	
		3.55–3.93 μm			
		10.4–11.3 μm			
		11.4–12.5 μm			
SMMR	Nimbus-7	6.6 GHz	145 km	1200 and 2400 h	12 h
		10.7 GHz	90 km		
		18.0 GHz	55 km		
		21.0 GHz	45 km		
		37.0 GHz	25 km		
SSM/I	F-8/DMSP	19.4 GHz	50 km	0615 and 1815 h	12 h
		22.2 GHz	45 km		
		37.0 GHz	30 km		
		85.5 GHz	15 km		

MSR: Multi-Spectral Radiometer.
TM: Thematic Mapper.
AVHRR: Advanced Very High Resolution Radiometer.
MSS: Multi-Spectral Scanner.
SMMR: Scanning Multi-channel Microwave Radiometer.
SSM/I: Special Sensor Microwave Imager.
**micrometer (μm) in the optical bands, and Gigahertz (GHz) in the microwave bands.

characteristics (such as vegetation type or fractional ground cover) are not directly measured, but may be inferred from these measurements. The crucial details of correcting the observed intensities for atmospheric radiation, instrument performance and validation against ground observations have generally not been performed in studying inter-annual variation of land surface using satellite observations (Becker, Bolle & Rowntree, 1988).

Measurements by different instruments on satellites differ not only in the spectral bands but also in the time of observation during a day, repeat (or re-visit) time of observation and the spatial resolution. The spectral, spatial and temporal characteristics of some of the instruments useful for monitoring changes of the land surface are given in Table 1. The spatial resolution ranges between 30 m to 30 km, and the repeat times of observation range between hours to 16 days.

Detailed mathematical models have been developed for interpreting visible, near-infra-red and microwave intensities observed by satellite-borne instruments in terms of land surface characteristics (Asrar, 1989; Choudhury *et al.*, 1990; Ulaby *et al.*, 1990). Physically based models provide a rational approach to quantifying land surface change using the measured intensities. Based on physical principles it can be shown that most bare soils will reflect visible radiation more than a stand of green vegetation. The effect of changing vegetation type, such as grassland into shrubland, can be detected due to differing reflectances caused by spatial heterogeneity, fractional vegetation cover and shadows cast by the shrubs. Structure and moisture within the vegetation affect the microwave radiation. While a reasonable understanding of the relationships between the measured intensities and the surface characteristics has been achieved, interpretation of many details about these measurements is still an active research area. Changes in species composition could be an initial indicator of desertification, although such changes may not initially be detected by remote sensing techniques. However, remote sensing could be extremely effective at an advanced stage of desertification and when this occurs over large areas.

A selected number of studies on land surface change using satellite observations are discussed below. These studies have used visible and near-infra-red reflectances observed by the Multispectral Scanner (MSS) and the Advanced Very High Resolution Radiometer (AVHRR) instruments on board, respectively, the LANDSAT and NOAA satellites (see Table 1). The spatial resolution of observations by these two instruments differs by about two orders of magnitude; 80 m for MSS and 4 km for the AVHRR. The MSS data are available since July, 1972, while the AVHRR data are available since February, 1979.

Several studies conducted during the last four years suggest that microwave observations can also be used for evaluating land surface change, particularly over arid and semi-arid regions (Choudhury, 1987; Becker & Choudhury, 1988; Prince & Choudhury, 1989; Choudhury, 1990). These observations are radiation intensities measured in units of temperature (Kelvin) at the wavelength of 8 mm (or at the frequency of 37 GHz) by the Scanning Multi-channel Microwave Radiometer (SMMR) and the Special Sensor Microwave Imager (SSM/I) on board the Nimbus-7 and the DMSP satellites, respectively. These intensities have been measured at orthogonal polarizations (designated as the horizontal and vertical polarizations). These observations are available for the entire globe at the spatial resolution of about 25 km from December 1978 to August 1987 by the SMMR, and from July 1987 to present by the SSM/I. Observation at any location is repeated within 3 to 6 days. Recognizing that the geolocation accuracy of the SMMR and SSM/I pixels is about 12 km, these data should not be interpreted or analyzed on a pixel-to-pixel basis. It was determined from physical principles that the difference of intensities measured at vertical and horizontal polarization (called the polarization difference or PD) should be an indicator of land surface characteristics (vegetation structure, woody biomass, moisture content within the vegetation and spatial heterogeneity). The PD values are in units of temperature (Kelvin or K). Again, from physical principles it was determined that the PD values over bare surfaces would be fairly high (25 to 35 K), and the PD value decreases with increasing vegetation or surface litter to values close to zero. Land degradation resulting in lower vegetation cover or smoother soil surface due perhaps to erosion will increase the value of PD. Apart from vegetation, the PD values are also affected by surface roughness (like mountains) and exposed water (as would be for wide rivers and swamps). These land surface data within about 50 km of coastline remain affected by water. More

details about the physical principles and satellite observations may be found in Choudhury et al. (1990) and Choudhury (1990).

Results and analysis

In this section a selected number of studies of inter-annual variation of satellite observations in relation to land surface change will be presented.

El-Shazhy, Hady & El-Kassas (1977) used visible and near-infra-red reflectances observed by the MSS to compare movement of sand dunes of Egypt with those surveyed 45 years previously. They found that the sand dune belts have moved a considerable distance. Robinove et al. (1981) used MSS observations to calculate changes in the albedo over an arid region in Utah for the period 1972 to 1976. (The albedo is defined as the ratio of solar energy reflected by the surface to solar energy incident on the surface.) They found that changes in the albedo were related to the changes in the terrain characteristics, and that these changes were due to variations in precipitation. Musick (1986) studied albedo changes using the MSS data over a semi-arid rangeland for the period 1973–1983 and found that uncertainties in instrument response posed considerable difficulty in objectively evaluating the albedo changes in relation to the land surface characteristics. Pickup and Foran (1987) found that the MSS data over semi-arid Australia for the period 1980–1984 showed little change despite changes in the ground observations.

The Sahel zone of Africa has been an area of particular concern due to repeated long-term droughts and changes in the land use patterns (Nicholson, 1983; Dregne, 1986). Courel, Kandel & Rasool (1984) found that the albedo calculated using Landsat-MSS and Meteosat-MSR data decreased from 0.3 during 1973 to 0.2 during 1979. This decrease in albedo was consistent with the ground observations of increased vegetation cover. Tucker et al. (1985) used AVHRR data to estimate biomass production for the period 1981–1984, and found that these production values are consistent with that expected from the observed rainfall patterns. Folving (1988) used MSS data for the period 1972–1986 over Oudalan province of Burkina Faso to find that approximately 9 percent of the area has changed to bare sand surface.

Several studies conducted during the past four years suggest that microwave observations at 8 mm wavelength can also be used to evaluate land surface change. Choudhury (1987) found a high correlation between PD (see 'Methodology' section) and biomass production over arid and semi-arid regions. Fig. 1 shows a color-coded image of the average PD value at any location observed between January 1979 and December

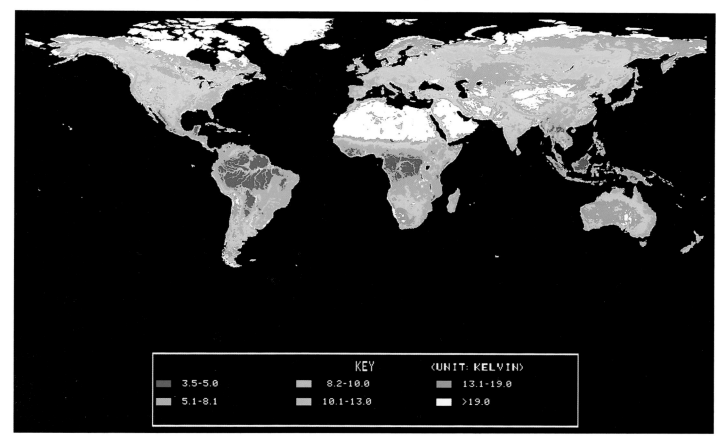

Fig. 1. Color-coded image of polarization difference at 8 mm wavelength (or 37 GHz frequency). The color scale in the image shows the magnitude of the polarization difference in units of Kelvin. At any location, all observations have been averaged for the period January 1979 to December 1986. These observations are by the Scanning Multi-channel Microwave Radiometer (SMMR) on board the Nimbus-7 satellite.

1986. This image also gives the scale for interpreting the colors in terms of the magnitude of PD, which is in units of Kelvin as has been discussed in the 'Methodology' section. Any missing pixel within the monthly global data has been filled by spatial/temporal interpolations before computing the average values shown in this figure. The PD values are about 20 K or higher over the desert regions (the Sahara, Namib, Rub Al Khali etc.), and lower than 5 K over the rainforests in Brazil, Cameroon and Indonesia. Surface roughness has the effect of decreasing the value of PD, and this effect is particularly noticeable in arid and semi-arid regions (note the distinct appearance of the Ahaggar, Adrar and Air mountains within the Sahara). The PD value over water is higher than 55 K, which allows for a clear discrimination of any land/water boundary. As a result of high PD value over water and low PD value over dense vegetation, one can see major rivers (Amazon and Congo) and swamps (Pantanal and Bananal) in the color image. Arid and semi-arid zones have PD values in the range 10–20 K. The east–west and the north–south gradients of vegetation biomass over, respectively, Australia

and sub-Saharan Africa are clearly seen. The temperate deciduous forest of the eastern United States has a lower PD value when compared to the grasslands and agricultural lands of the central great plains. In general, this color image resembles some vegetation maps.

Robinove *et al.* (1981) computed the difference in albedos observed on different dates by the MSS as a way of monitoring changes of arid lands. Following this difference approach, the annual average of PD was computed for each year from 1979 to 1986. Then, the annual average for 1979 was chosen as the base map (Fig. 2) and the difference from 1979 was computed for all other annual averages, 1980 to 1986 (Figs. 3(*a*)–3(*g*)). Thus, for example, Fig. 3(*a*) shows the difference between the annual average values of PD for 1980 and the annual average values of PD for 1979. In any one of these difference images, a positive value at any location will mean that the PD value for that location and year was higher compared to that observed at that location during 1979. Similarly, a negative value in the image will mean that the PD value was lower compared to that observed during 1979. Any random

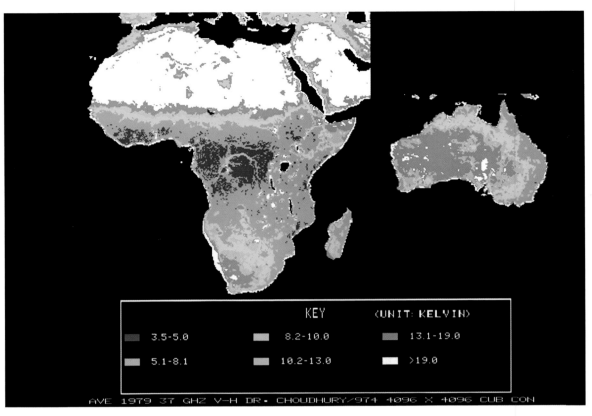

Fig. 2. This color-coded image is similar to the one shown in Fig. 1, except that the period of averaging is January 1979 to December 1979 (the annual average for 1979).

error in the PD observations is not likely to show up consistently as positive or negative differences in these images. The changes seen over the central Sahara or Rub Al Khali are most likely due to these random errors. The magnitude of the difference in Figs. 3(a) to (g) is a direct indicator of the land surface change. Consistently positive values of the difference at any location in Fig. 3(a) to (g) will mean that the PD values were consistently higher compared to that observed during 1979. The PD value is expected to increase with land degradation. Thus, land degradation with respect to the land surface condition during 1979 will appear as positive values in these figures. Particularly noticeable change in Figs. 3(a) to (g) is seen over the Sahel and the Sudan zones, the Kalahari and the Simpson desert areas. Each of these areas is known to have suffered from drought during 1979 to 1986, although the severity and the length of the drought have been variable (Nicholson, 1988). The inter-annual variation of PD values in relation to rainfall over the Kalahari area has been discussed in detail by Prince and Choudhury (1989). Although these observations suggest land degradation in these areas, to what extent these changes were caused by mismanagement of land cannot be determined from these observations. Also, the

observed inter-annual variations of PD have not yet been verified against any measured land surface changes.

Figs. 4 and 5 present in a concise way the temporal changes of the PD values for the period, January 1979 to December 1986. Fig. 4 shows the trend, that is, the slope of linear regression between PD as the dependent variable and time (month) as the independent variable. This slope is positive when the PD values have the tendency to increase with the passage of time begining January 1979. Again, the PD values will increase when vegetation cover decreases. Fig. 5 is based upon the Fourier analysis of the PD values. Here, it is recognized that temporal changes of the PD within a year will be caused by vegetation growth and senescence, which can lead to periodicities of 12 months and 6 months. The temporal variation of the PD values was fitted by a Fourier series, and the variance not explained by the 12 and the 6 month harmonics is shown in Fig. 5. This unexplained variance or the variance anomaly is an indicator of the disruption of natural periodicities of vegetation growth and senescence. Such disruption could be due to drought. Both Figs. 4 and 5 show major changes of the land surface, although it should not be concluded from these figures only

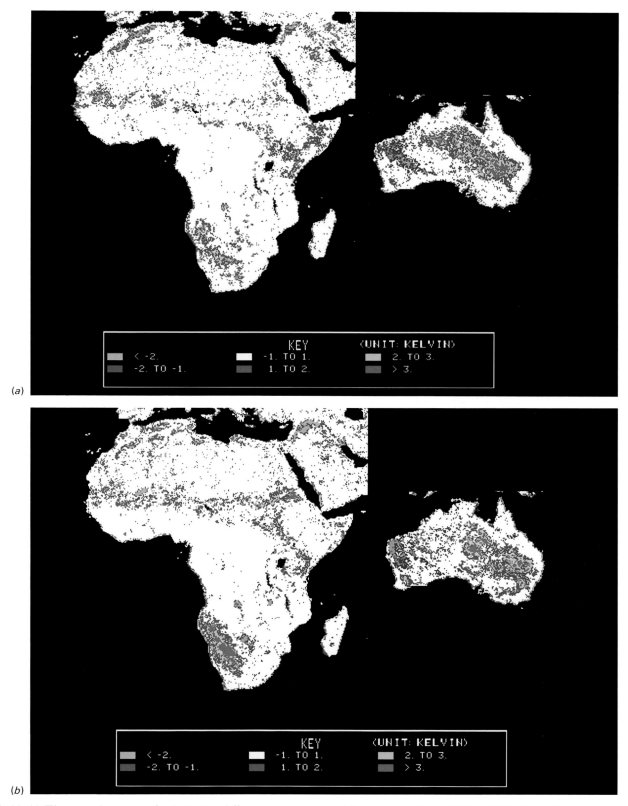

Fig. 3. (*a*)–(*g*) The annual average of polarization difference was computed for each year from 1979 to 1986. Then, the average for 1979 (as shown in Fig. 2) was subtracted from the average for the years 1980 to 1986. These difference images for each of the seven years (1980 to 1986) are shown consecutively in Figs. 3(*a*) to 3(*g*).

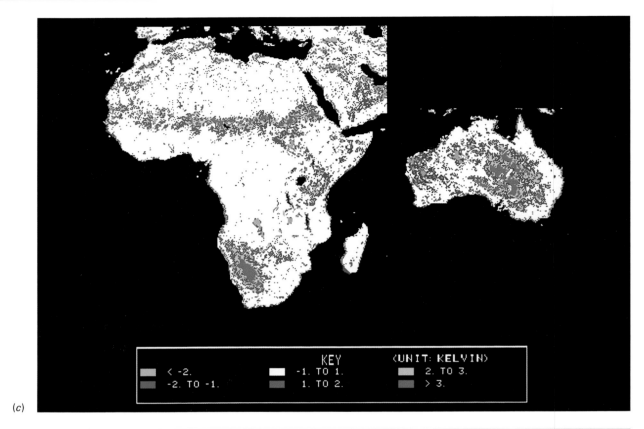

(c)

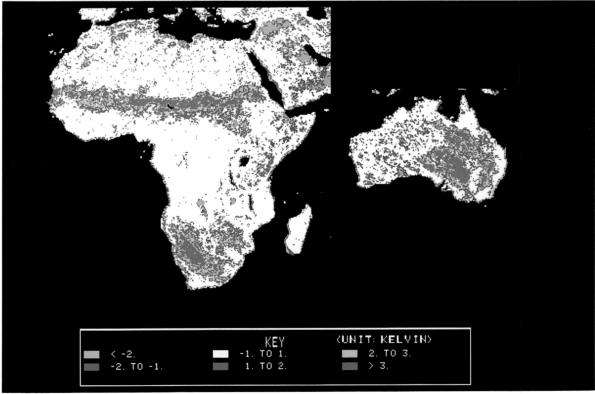

(d)

Fig. 3. (*cont.*)

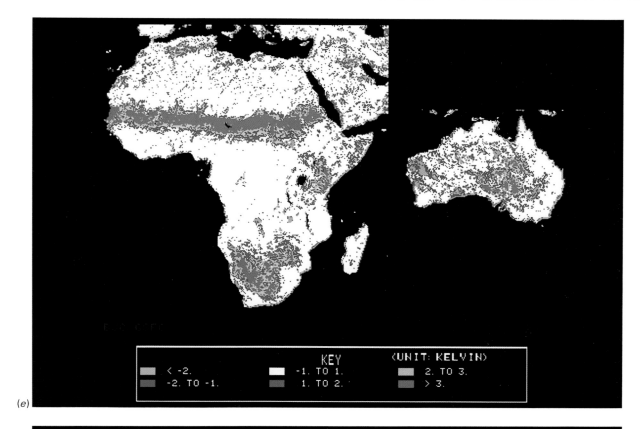

(e)

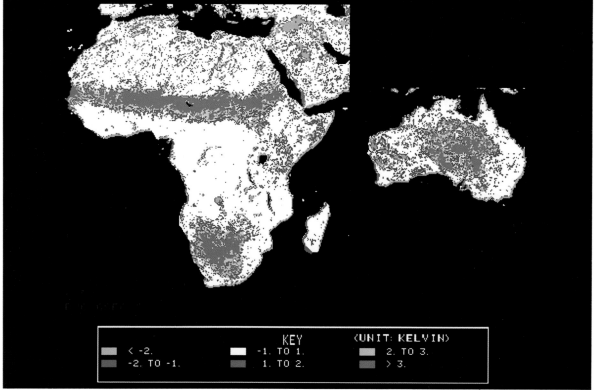

(f)

Fig. 3. (*cont.*)

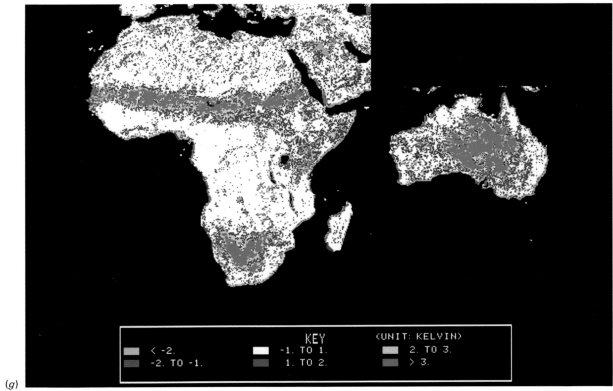

(g)

Fig. 3. (*cont.*)

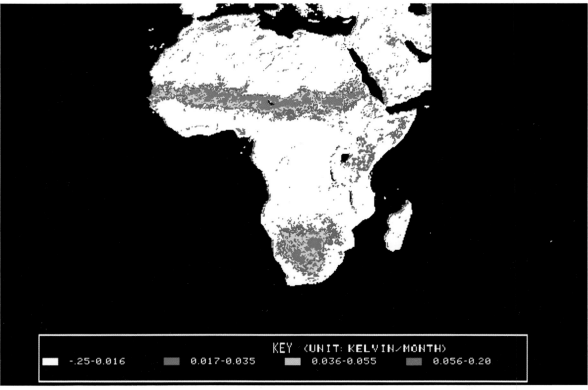

Fig. 4. The slope of linear regression between the PD values as the dependent variable and time (month) as the independent variable. The slope is positive if the PD values have the tendency to increase as a function of time starting January 1979.

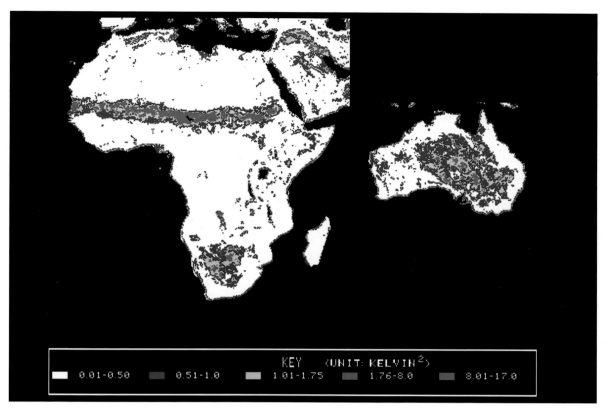

Fig. 5. The PD values for the period January 1979 to December 1986 was fitted by a Fourier series. The variance not explained by the 12 and 6 month harmonics (the variance anomaly) is shown in this Figure. Since natural periodicities of vegetation growth and senescence can almost totally be explained by 12 and 6 month harmonics, this Figure shows the areas affected by abnormalities caused by droughts or other factors.

that these changes have been caused by the mismanagement of land.

The above results are based upon 37 GHz observations by the Scanning Multi-channel Microwave Radiometer (SMMR) on board the Nimbus-7 satellite. After nearly nine years of operation, observations by the SMMR were terminated in August, 1987. Fortunately, the US Department of Navy launched an operational sensor called Special Sensor Microwave/Imager (SSM/I) on board the Defense Meteorological Satellite Program (DMSP) Block 5D-2 Spacecraft F8 in July 1987 (see Table 1). A second SSM/I was put into space in late 1989, and observations by both SSM/I are continuing. Global observations of horizontally and vertically polarized brightness temperatures are available at 19.4, 37.0 and 85.5 GHz frequencies. Being an operational sensor, it is expected that observations by the SSM/I will continue for many years to come. Consequently, these observations are highly valuable for monitoring land surface change. Fig. 6 is a color-coded global image derived from horizontally and vertically polarized brightness temperatures at 37 GHz frequency by the SSM/I for 1988. A comparison of the global images derived from the SMMR and the SSM/I shows many

similarities and differences (see Figs. 1, 2 and 6). Detailed evaluation of the SSM/I data is just begining to be performed, but the future holds considerable promise for monitoring and quantifying land surface change (perhaps, desertification) using these observations.

Limitations

Desertification is a complex land degradation process, caused at least partly by man. Satellite observations, when properly standardized, calibrated and validated, can be used to effectively document land surface change. Although satellite data spanning nearly 20 years exist, the crucial steps of calibration and validation have been difficult for these data. Effort should be directed so that these data can be used to document more precisely any sustained land surface change. Changes of species composition could be an initial indicator of desertification, but such changes at the initial stages will not be detected by remote sensing. However, remote sensing could be quite effective at an advanced stage of desertification over large areas. Any mismanagement of the land also have to be

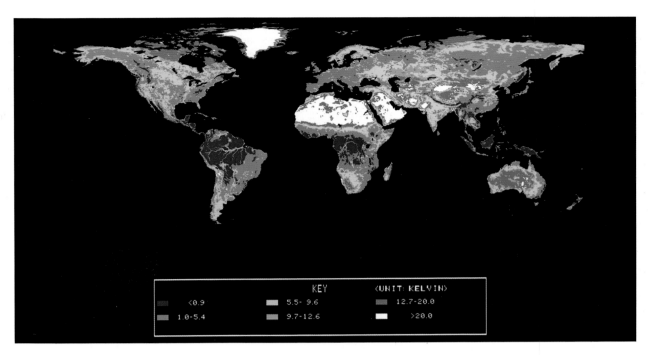

Fig. 6. Color-coded global image of the difference of vertically and horizontally polarized brightness temperatures derived from 37 GHz channel of the Special Sensor Microwave Imager (SSM/I) on board the DMSP Block 5D-2 Spacecraft F8. Global observations by this sensor are available almost daily since July 1987. All observations from January to December 1988 after automatic screening for clouds and wet soils have been averaged to produce this image. Long-term multi-frequency global monitoring for land surface change will be possible because the SSM/I has been designated to be an operational sensor by the US Department of Navy. A detailed analysis of the SSM/I observations is just beginning.

documented for a better understanding of the global extent of the desertification problem.

Conclusions

Multispectral satellite observations spanning nearly 20 years already exist, but changes observed in these data should not be ascribed to changes of land surface without proper calibration and standardization. Effort needs to be directed to calibrate, standardize and validate these data, so that they can be used to document any sustained land surface change. Mismanagement of land also has to be documented, so that climate-induced land surface change is properly identified. Microwave observations by the Scanning Multi-channel Microwave Radiometer (SMMR) on board the Nimbus-7 satellite at 8 mm wavelength for 8-year period (1979–1986) were presented as color images, which showed noticeable changes over the Sahel and the Sudan zones, Kalahari and Simpson deserts. Observations at 37 GHz are continuing today by the Special Sensor Microwave Imager (SSM/I) on board the DMSP-F8 satellite. More than a decade-long global time series at 37 GHz is available at present for monitoring and quantifying land surface change. These observations need to be validated against ground measurements, so that the observed changes can be properly interpreted in terms of changes of the land surface characteristics.

Availability of data

The monthly global data set of PD at 37 GHz for 1979–1990 has been archived for distribution. These data can be acquired by writing to: The Pilot Land Data System, Polarization Difference Vegetation Index (Microwave Vegetation Index), Code 934, Data Management Systems Facility, NASA, Goddard Space Flight Center, Greenbelt, MD 20771, USA.

References

Anthes, R. A. (1984). Enhancement of convective precipitation by mesoscale variation in vegetation covering in semi-arid regions. *J. Clim. Appl. Meteor.*, **23**, 541–54.

Asrar, G. (ed.) (1989). *Theory and Applications of Optical Remote Sensing*. John Wiley & Sons, NY.

Aubreville, A. (1949). *Climats, Fôrets et Desertification de l'Afrique Tropicale*. Societé d'Editions Geographiques et Coloniales, Paris, France.

Becker, F. & Choudhury, B. J. (1988). Relative sensitivity of normalized difference vegetation index (NDVI) and microwave polarization difference index (MPDI) for vegetation and desertification monitoring. *Remote Sens. Environ.*, **24**, 297–311.

Becker, F., Bolle, H.-J. & Rowntree, P. R. (1988). *International Land Surface Climatology Project*. ISLSCP Secretariet, Free University of Berlin, Berlin, FRG.

Choudhury, B. J. (1987). Estimates of primary productivity over the Thar desert based upon Nimbus-7 37 GHz data: 1979–1985. *Int. J. Remote Sens.*, **8**, 1885–90.

Choudhury, B. J. (1990). A comparative analysis of satellite-observed visible reflectance and 37 GHz polarization difference to assess land surface change over the Sahel zone, 1982–1986. *Climate Change*, **17**, 193–208.

Choudhury, B. J., Wang, J. R., Hsu, A. Y. & Chien, Y. L. (1990). Simulated and observed 37 GHz emission over Africa. *Int. J. Remote Sens.*, **11**, 1837–68.

Courel, M. F., Kandel, R. S. & Rasool, S. I. (1984). Surface albedo and the Sahel drought. *Nature*, **307**, 528–31.

Dregne, H. E. (1986). Desertification of arid lands. In *Physics of Desertification*, F. El-Baz and M. H. A. Hassan, eds., pp. 4–34, Martinus Nijhoff Publishers, Boston.

El-Shazly, E. M., Hady, M. A. A. & El-Kassas, I. A. (1977). Delineation of land features in Egypt by Landsat satellite images. *Proc. 6th Annual Remote Sensing of Earth Resources*, pp. 277–94, Tallahassee, FL.

Ehleringer, J. (1985). Annuals and perennials of warm deserts. In *Physiological Ecology of North American Plant Communities*, B. F. Chabot and H. A. Mooney, eds., pp. 162–80, Chapman & Hall, NY.

Evenari, M. (1985). The desert environment. pp. 1–22, In *Hot Deserts and Arid Shrublands*, M. Evenari, I. Noy-Meir and D. W. Goodall, eds., Part-A, Elsevier, NY.

Folving, S. (1988). Assessment of land/soil degradation in northern Burkina Faso. *Proc. ISLSCP International Conference*, December 2–6, 1985, pp. 843–6, Rome, Italy, ESA-SP-284, European Space Agency, Paris, France.

Gbeckor-Kove, N. (1989). Lectures on drought and desertification. In *Drought and Desertification*, pp. 41–73, WMO/TD-no. 286, World Meteorological Organization, Geneva, Switzerland.

Landsberg, H. E. (1986). Potentialities and limitations of conventional climatological data for desertification monitoring and control. *Clim. Change*, **9**, 123–8.

Le Houerou, H. N. (1977). The nature and causes of desertification. In *Desertification*, M. H. Glantz, ed., pp. 17–38, Westview Press, Boulder, CO.

Mintz, Y. (1984). The sensitivity of numerically simulated climates to land-surface conditions. pp. 79–105, In *The Global Climate*, J. Houghton, ed., Cambridge University Press, NY.

Musick, B. (1986). Temporal changes of Landsat MSS albedo estimates in arid rangeland. *Remote Sens. Environ.*, **20**, 107–20.

Nelson, R. (1990). Dryland management: the 'desertification' problem. *Technical Paper No. 116*, pp. 39, World Bank, Washington DC.

Nicholson, S. E. (1986). Sub-Saharan rainfall 1981–1984. *J. Clim. Appl. Meteor.*, **24**, 1388–92.

Nicholson, S. E. (1988). Land surface atmosphere interactions: Physical processes and surface change and their impact. *Prog. Phys. Geograph.*, **12**, 36–65.

Pickup, G. & Foran, B. D. (1987). The use of spectral and spatial variability to monitor cover change in inert landscapes. *Remote Sens. Environ.*, **23**, 351–63.

Prince, S. D. & Choudhury, B. J. (1989). Interpretation of Nimbus-37 GHz microwave brightness temperature data in semi-arid southern Africa. *Int. J. Remote Sens.*, **10**, 1643–62.

Robinove, C. J., Chavez, P. S., Jr., Gehring, D. & Holmgren, R. (1981). Arid land monitoring using Landsat albedo difference images. *Remote Sens. Environ.*, **11**, 133–56.

Schlesinger, W. H., Reynolds, J. F., Cunningham, G. L., Huenneke, L. F., Jarrell, W. M., Virginia, R. A. & Whitford, W. G. (1990). Biological feedbacks in global desertification. *Science*, **247**, 1043–8.

Shmida, A. (1985). Biogeography of the desert flora, In *Hot Deserts and Arid Shrublands*, M. Evenari, I. Noy-Meir and D. W. Goodall, eds., pp. 23–77, Part-A, Elsevier, NY.

Stebbing, E. P. (1937). The encroaching Sahara: the threat to the west African colonies. *Geograph. J.*, **86**, 506–19.

Tucker, C. J., Vanpraet, C. L., Sharman, M. J. & Van Ittersum, G. (1985). Satellite remote sensing of total herbaceous biomass production in the Senegalese Sahel: 1980–1984. *Remote Sens. Environ.*, **17**, 233–49.

Ulaby, F. T., Sarabandi, K., McDonald, K., Whitt, M. & Dobson, M. C. (1990). Michigan microwave canopy scattering model. *Int. J. Remote Sens.*, **11**, 1223–53.

Verstraete, M. M. (1986). Defining desertification: a review. *Clim. Change*, **9**, 5–18.

Williams, O. B. & Calaby, J. H. (1985). The hot deserts of Australia. In *Hot Deserts and Arid Shrublands*, M. Evenari, I. Noy-Meir and D. W. Goodall, eds., vol. A, pp. 269–312, Elsevier, NY.

Coastal change

STEPHEN P. LEATHERMAN

Introduction

The coastal zone, which represents the interface and interaction between the land and the sea, is one of the most dynamic areas on Earth. Change is occurring on all timescales, from seconds to days to centuries. In the short term, for example, more than 6000 waves per day break on open-coast beaches. These waves and resulting currents act as agents of sediment transport and coastal modification. The most dramatic changes, however, are storm generated, such as inlet creation or massive overwashing of barrier islands, but the gradual build-up of huge sand spits attests to the importance of long-term processes in sculpting the coastal landscape. Therefore, topographic base maps rapidly become outdated as the coastline is continually adjusting to a combination of natural forces and human modifications. Moreover, many of the world's coastal areas have never been properly mapped, either planimetrically or topographically, and, even when dynamic changes are absent, accurate maps or charts simply do not exist.

While field surveys can provide the most accurate information, this approach is too time consuming, prohibitively expensive, and impractical. For example, the US continental coasts are more than 20 000 kilometers long. Mapping of this huge expanse of land requires a data gathering system more appropriate for the task at hand. Remote sensing is the only possibility for obtaining time series data for such a large geographic area.

The continuance of change is virtually assured based on known physical processes, simple extrapolation of trend, and predicted climatic change. Global warming would melt land-based ice and cause the near-surface ocean waters to expand thermally; both of these factors would tend to raise sea levels in the future. It has often been pointed out that sea level rise is the most certain consequence of the greenhouse effect, and therefore sea level can be thought of as the 'dipstick' of climate change. Sea level rise will have pronounced impacts on coastal areas by causing submergence of low-lying areas and loss of wetlands as well as erosion of unconsolidated materials, particularly sandy beaches.

Sea level rise is considered the underlying driving force of shoreline changes, inducing landward retreat. This coastal response is well displayed by wave tank experiments as well as full-scale studies of the impacts of changing water levels in the Great Lakes (Hands, 1983). Unless additional supplies of sand are available to the beach system, sea level rise will throw the nearshore profile out of equilibrium. While the gradually rising water level imparts no energy itself to effect coastal change, infrequent, yet intense storms can produce the wave and current energy necessary to perform the geologic work of re-equilibration (Leatherman, 1988).

The response of coastal areas will depend upon the energy level, with the two endpoints in the spectrum being open ocean and sheltered coasts. Open ocean coasts are wave dominated and retreat largely through erosional processes (e.g. the physical removal of material from the beach). By contrast, salt marshes often occupy the intertidal zone along sheltered coasts, and submergence with the rising water level tends to be the principal coastal response in this environmental setting. As will be evident from the following discussion, both of these processes, beach erosion and coastal wetlands loss, are occurring at rates and scales that mandate the use of remote sensing technology.

Aerial photography has traditionally served as the principal medium for analysis of coastal changes (El-Ashry, 1977). The first imagery widely available for the US coasts was acquired in the late 1930s; much of this early photography for the East Coast was obtained by the US Army Corps of Engineers to document the changes wrought by the great hurricane of 1938. The quality of aerial photography greatly improved over the decades, particularly after World War II, and the availability for particular years significantly increased from the 1960s to present.

Vertical aerial photographs, with at least 60% overlap to achieve stereoscopic coverage, are still considered the mainstay for most coastal studies, especially where photogrammetric methods are employed. Satellite imagery can usually not provide the level of detail necessary for precise measurements of shoreline change because of the limitations of resolution. Landsat Multi-Spectral Scanner (MSS) data, with

79 meter pixels, is far too coarse to detect most coastal changes except in a qualitative sense or where there is an extremely rapid rate of change (e.g. erosion of Nile River delta at Rosetta, retreating more than 100 meters per year at present, Frihy, 1988). SPOT imagery can provide 10-meter pixel resolution, which is approaching the data capture level necessary to quantify many coastal changes when considered on a decadal basis. One of the most promising mapping techniques is profiling by airborne laser altimeters, in which control is provided by the Global Positioning System (GPS) of satellites. This experimental technology is still in the research and development stage, although successful profiles have been acquired of the rapidly eroding volcanic island of Surtsey, Iceland, and the southern part of Nauset Spit and Monomoy Island on Cape Cod, Massachusetts (J. Garvin, pers. comm.).

Methodology

Satellites are beginning to become a much more important source of data for coastal process studies than in the past. Part of this trend stems from the availability of decadal time series data from Landsat MSS, Return Beam Vidicon (RBV), and Thematic Mapper (TM) sensors. In a larger sense, the growing emphasis on global change analysis requires satellite data. The advantages of satellite versus airborne remotely sensed data are as follows: wider field of view (FOV)/swath width, similar solar illumination over large areas, and, of course, potential global coverage.

No single instrument is ideally suited for the acquisition of the widely varying information utilized in coastal studies. Certainly, Landsat has been the workhorse of the community, with coastal researchers largely relying upon MSS imagery. Bands 4, 5 and 7 are usually combined with color filters as false color composites to obtain clear differentiation between water and land as well as for vegetation discrimination. The 79 m pixel size limits the utility of MSS imagery, where much better resolution is typically required (e.g. shoreline-change mapping to delineate erosional/accretionary trends). The Landsat 3 RBV and the Landsat 4 and 5 TM sensors have a pixel resolution of 30 m, and precise water–land mapping capability with the TM infra-red bands has been utilized in some coastal studies. However, except for the use of a Landsat 3 RBV image mosaic as a base map for compilation of a 1:100 000 scale color geologic map of Cape Cod and the islands (Oldale & Barlow, 1986), these images have not been widely utilized by coastal geomorphologists. Landsat Thematic Mapper imagery, with a 30 m pixel resolution, has had more usage. In coastal change studies, where 30 m can be the difference between a house being high and dry on a dune or low and wet on the beachface, better resolution is always the first requirement of quantitative studies. As mentioned in the previous section, SPOT imagery, with 10 m pixels, is now approaching the resolution required for accurate time series mapping of coastal changes.

The main limitation now to further developments is the lack of a coordinated effort by coastal scientists using remote sensing technology. Without the existence of a well-funded program, academic scientists, who represent the lion's share of researchers in coastal mapping, cannot afford to purchase the expensive Landsat and SPOT satellite imagery. The cost factor has kept most potential players out of the game; even active participants are greatly limited in the use of remotely sensed data in their research by cost considerations.

Landsat and SPOT satellites cannot supply the type of imagery necessary for all coastal studies. Orbital-based radar has the obvious advantage of night operations and penetration through cloud cover and the vegetation canopy. Also, radar tends to reflect strongly from even small-scale features with particular geometries, such as marine scarps of ancient shorelines. Shuttle Imaging Radar (SIR A&B) and Seasat SAR have already been extensively utilized in investigations of earth surface processes, and this technology has much (unrealized) potential for coastal studies. Finally, satellites can provide the stable platforms in support of airborne operations through high resolution positioning both vertically and horizontally. Indeed, Global Positioning Satellites (GPS) have already found great utility in advancing surveying by providing accurate geodetic control in remote and inaccessible areas. Finally, all of these satellites are polar orbiters and therefore the same area is repeatedly imaged, providing time series information on coastal changes. Where process response studies require data with more rapid turn-around time, imagery from geostationary satellites with 'stare' and 'on-demand' capabilities can be compared to that obtained from polar orbiters.

Analysis and results

There are four principal approaches to coastal studies, depending on time frame and scale: geomorphic, historical, process, and geographic. Remote sensing can provide a unique data set on a global basis for application to each type of approach. While aerial photography and, more recently, Landsat imagery have been used extensively for such studies in the last few decades, new technology is now being tested and employed to study and map coastal landforms and processes.

Geomorphic studies

Geomorphic studies involve the use of morphological features and their spatial relationships to reconstruct evolutionary development. These studies have relied heavily upon stereopaired vertical aerial photography, and barrier islands have been a favorite subject for coastal researchers (Leatherman, 1979). In particular, beach/dune ridges can be utilized to interpret prehistorical geomorphic changes, such as spit growth, barrier progradation, or inlet breaching. For example, the southern end of Nauset Spit on Cape Cod, Massachusetts is characterized by accretionary beach ridges. This barrier has elongated at rates exceeding 100 m per year during historic time, illustrating the rate and magnitude of spit growth and longshore sand transport to this sedimentary sink.

The evolution of marine terraces as a guide to past high sea level stillstands is of particular interest to global change researchers. These ancient shorelines often represent the result of several superimposed processes. Although dominated by the postglacial global sea level rise, local or regional tectonic movements and isostatic rebound may also contribute to coastal morphology. These effects, superimposed on pre-existing structure and lithology, make understanding coastal evolution considerably more difficult than for inland regions. However, such understanding is extremely important for several reasons, including the fact that shorelines are indicators of global changes in sea level, which, in turn, are related to climate and climate change. The practical importance stems from the enormous problem of shore erosion, which is becoming an increasingly expensive proposition for US coastal states.

The study of coastal geomorphic evolution is greatly facilitated by analysis of remotely sensed data. Marine terraces, which are found in many parts of the world, are readily apparent on orbital photography (Lowman, 1968), Seasat imagery (Ford *et al.* 1984), and aircraft imagery (Fig. 1). These features are basically formed by marine abrasion, although they may also be depositional in being veneered with sediment. Several discrete scarps, although rather subdued in their morphologic expression, have been studied on the Florida Atlantic coast (Fig. 2) and Delmarva peninsula. These low relief features can also be recognized on Seasat SAR imagery.

The general nature of the processes that formed these coastal plain terraces is fairly clear (Demarest & Leatherman, 1985). The majority of those found along the Atlantic and Gulf coasts were developed during interglacial intervals, when sea level was significantly higher than at the present time. In the absence of other effects, such as local uplift, coastal terraces should, in principle, be correlative among various coastlines, but such correlations are few and tenuous (Fairbridge, 1968).

When efforts are made to understand the development of marine terraces in specific areas, problems arise rapidly. A good example is found in coastal Maine, where marine terraces are present. There are two schools of thought as to their origin. One holds that as the late Wisconsin glaciers withdrew from Maine and eastern Canada, the land rebounded almost 'instantaneously' in terms of geologic time, producing marine terraces at different elevations across the state. The other view is that early post-glacial warping was responsible for their development (i.e. a form of neotectonics). Evaluation of these two possibilities is difficult, however, because the state of mapping (available only at scales of 1:48 000 or smaller) does not give a clear view of the regional elevations and continuity of the terraces.

Correlating terraces around the world is, of course, even more difficult. In China, for example, only topographic maps at a scale of 1:250 000 are commonly available, and it is not even clear if there are multiple terraces because of the coarse contour interval of such maps.

A possible approach to the problem of studying the evolution of marine terraces through correlation is to use SIR-C imagery to map the position, continuity, distribution, and relative elevation of terraces and scarps in widely separated areas around the world. The advantages of SIR-C for this task are basically those of any orbital remote sensing technique: potential global coverage, wider FOV/swath width, and similar illumination over large areas. However, there is an additional advantage of radar over other types of satellite imagery. Many coastal areas, such as the eastern US coastal plain, are characterized by low relief, subtle expression of structure, and extensive forest cover. These are the same conditions encountered in the Canadian Shield, and SIR-B experience shows that orbital radar with suitable illumination is more effective than Landsat because of the strong azimuth highlighting (Lowman, pers. comm., 1987). The cloud penetrating ability of radar is also an advantage for coastal areas such as those in South America and Africa that are frequently cloud covered.

The potential applications of this new remote sensing technology to coastal geomorphology are enormous, but unfortunately such studies are yet to be funded. In fact, there have been no orbital experiments on SIR-A or SIR-B focussed on coastal geology, and, consequently, this general field is relatively unexplored.

Fig. 1. Radar mosaic of Cameroon, clearly showing a series of parallel beach ridges on the southern coastal plain (courtesy of Dr P. Lowman, NASA-GSFC).

Fig. 2. Landsat image of the Cape Canaveral area on the Atlantic coast of Florida. This region is characterized by north–south linear features which are beach scarps, representing earlier high stands of sea level.

Historical shoreline analysis

Shoreline changes have long been of interest to coastal geomorphologists (Shepard & Wanless, 1971; El-Ashry, 1977), and more recently this information has become of paramount concern for coastal engineers and land use planners. A significant fraction of the world's population lives within the coastal zone, with many buildings and facilities built at elevations less than three meters above sea level. Presently, many of these structures are not adequately above existing water levels or located far enough landward to ensure their survival and the safety of residents during major storm activity. This hazard has grown increasingly apparent and

serious along much of the US Atlantic and Gulf coasts, particularly the highly urbanized sandy barrier islands, as relative sea levels have risen during the twentieth century.

The general effect of sea level rise on coastal lowlands is to induce landward retreat: beaches erode and marshes are drowned. Most sandy shorelines worldwide have experienced recession during the past century (National Research Council, 1987). Such has also been the case along the US coasts; historical data indicate that about 90 percent of our sandy beaches are eroding. Accelerated sea level rise due to greenhouse-induced global warming will only increase erosion rates and exacerbate the present shoreline dilemma. Also, coastal wetlands will be lost at ever increasing rates, with many of the nation's marshes disappearing in the coming decades at the high rates of loss presently experienced in Louisiana (National Research Council, 1987).

Wetlands account for much of the land near sea level along sheltered coasts. These extensive marshes, swamps, and mangrove forests fringe most of the US coastline, particularly along the Atlantic and Gulf coasts. These areas are vital to our fisheries industry and maintenance of water quality, and are important in coastal recreation.

Salt marshes exist in a delicate balance with water levels. With gradual sea level rise (due to local subsidence or worldwide changes), marshes can generally keep pace by trapping sediments in the water column and through accumulation of their own organic material (dead stems and leaves). However, an imbalance can develop if sea levels rise significantly faster than deposition on the marsh surface, eventually resulting in waterlogging and drowning.

While wave attack at the marsh edge is an obvious mechanism of erosion, wholesale marsh losses in Louisiana and the Chesapeake Bay occur through the formation of extensive interior ponds. These shallow water bodies enlarge and coalesce at the expense of marsh vegetation in response to coastal submergence. The magnitude of such losses can be quite extensive, as shown by studies at the Blackwater Wildlife Refuge in Maryland, where over one-third of the total marsh area (about 2000 hectares) was lost between 1938 and 1979 by this process (National Research Council, 1987; Fig. 3). However, these losses are dwarfed by the wholesale drowning of coastal marshes in Louisiana where over 1.6 ha of wetlands disappear per hour. Largely because of subsidence, which averages as much as 1 cm/y, entire parishes (counties) could be lost in coming decades unless means are found to increase sedimentation on this low-lying deltaic plain.

Aerial photography, particularly false color infra-red, is presently being utilized to monitor marsh losses because of the availability of a time series record. However, Landsat can now provide a 20-year time frame, which will permit such analyses to be performed on more remote wetlands and elsewhere on a worldwide basis. Therefore, it is important that Landsat be maintained as a principal data collection means because of the emphasis on time series data that are directly comparable.

There have been a plethora of remote sensing-based studies of salt marshes (Klemas, Bartlett & Rogers, 1975), but of primary importance in global studies is the collection and analysis of process information. Such is also the case in beach erosion studies, which rely upon photogrammetric techniques to obtain quantitative data on shoreline change. Again, aerial photographs have been principally used for this purpose because of the spatial resolution requirement to obtain precise measurements.

A number of techniques are currently employed to acquire information on historical shoreline changes (Leatherman, 1983). The simplest approach utilizes enlargements of aerial photographs with shoreline changes (e.g. waterline, dune line, first line of stable vegetation) traced onto a base map. Although easy to execute and inexpensive, the quality is suspect, but adequate if only generalized trends are desired.

A recent technique for shoreline mapping uses the zoom transfer scope (ZTS), considered by many coastal specialists to represent state-of-the-art mapping. While the ZTS is efficient in removing scale differences between photographs, errors introduced by tilt cannot be fully eliminated. The method most often employed by professional photogrammetrists to construct maps is the use of stereoplotters. This photogrammetric instrument can correct for lens and atmospheric distortions as well as irregularities in airplane flight (tilt, tip, and yaw). Although very accurate, this method requires sophisticated and expensive equipment, is labor intensive, and best utilized for constructing topographic maps.

A new automated technique of shoreline mapping (metric mapping) employs computer routines to emulate photogrammetric techniques. Maps produced by this technique have been shown to meet or exceed national map accuracy standards (Leatherman & Clow, 1983). While previous mapping procedures have relied upon aerial photographs as the source material, this computerized technique allows compilation of shoreline data from all accurate information, and maps are drawn by a computer-driven plotter.

Historical shoreline changes have been influenced by natural as well as human-induced effects. Rising relative sea level tends to cause shoreline recession, except where this trend is offset by an influx of sediment (Leatherman, 1988). In some areas, it is clear that human modifications have resulted in substantial erosion. Undoubtedly the principal contributor has been the construction of jettied inlets and deepening of channel entrances for navigational purposes. Along shorelines with a high rate of longshore sediment transport, these constructed features trap sediment at the updrift jetty. If material dredged from the navigation channel is not placed on the downdrift beaches, then the amount of downdrift erosion will be equal to the reduction in transport. The present situation downdrift of the Ocean City Inlet jetties, where Assateague Island is being sand-starved and rapidly eroded (Leatherman, 1984), is indicative of this problem (Fig. 4). This prominent shoreline offset has developed entirely since jetty construction in 1934–35.

Considering the past extreme fluctuations in sea level and

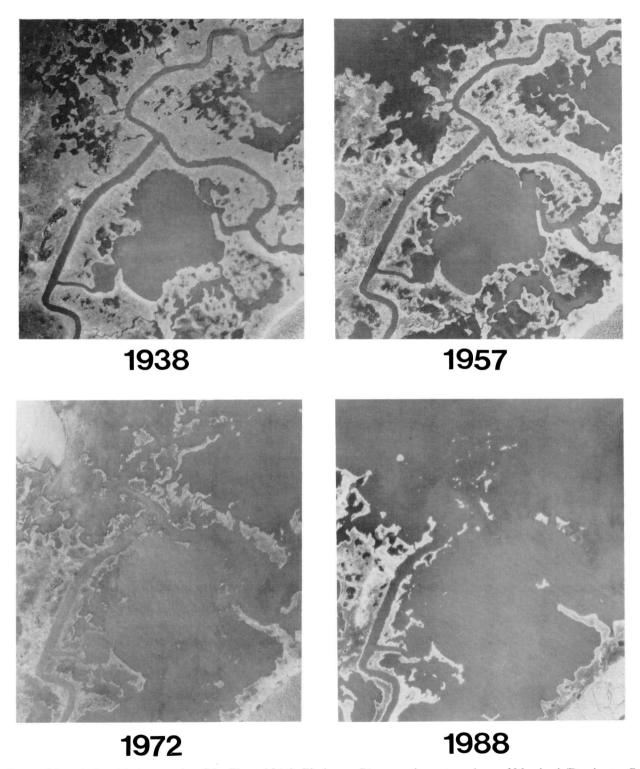

Fig. 3. Sequential vertical aerial photographs of the Big and Little Blackwater Rivers on the eastern shore of Maryland (Dorchester County), indicating progressive marsh loss as interior ponds coalesce.

Fig. 4. NASA aircraft image in 1975 of Ocean City Inlet area, Maryland, showing the offset that has developed along this barrier island shoreline since jetty construction in 1934–1935.

shoreline position on a geologic timescale, the phenomenon of erosion occurring today is dwarfed. Yet the historical rise of sea levels of approximately one foot (0.3 m) during the past century along the US East Coast is very significant when viewed within the context of the building boom that has occurred along the water's edge in the past few decades (National Research Council, 1987). Hundreds of thousands of beachfront structures (exquisite single family houses, high-rise condominiums, and elegant hotels) have been built within a few tens of meters of a retreating shoreline. In fact, beachfront property is some of the most valuable real estate in the country.

The present dilemma has resulted from the tremendous investment in coastal property at a time when most sandy beaches nationwide, and indeed worldwide, are eroding. Prior to the establishment of permanent buildings on beaches, most people took little note of the ever-changing shorelines. It was popularly envisioned that while beaches fluctuate in width from winter to summer, there was little net change. Most beaches narrow and widen on a seasonal basis, but there is a longer-term trend superimposed on these short-term fluctuations, which is largely storm driven and erosional in nature.

The effect of rising sea levels is to induce shore retreat in concert with storms, which impart the wave energy needed to transport vast quantities of sediment. A net change of less than a meter per year is often difficult to measure when the beach width naturally fluctuates by 15 meters or more seasonally, thus confusing the casual observer. However, measured over decades with accurate means of shoreline mapping (Leatherman, 1983), the trends become apparent, and rates of beach erosion can be quantified for particular areas along the coast through analysis of remotely sensed data.

Process measurements

While remotely sensed data, particularly aerial photography, have been of primary application in historical shoreline and environmental analysis, they have also played a role in process measurements (e.g. Dietz, 1963). Overwash and inlet processes in large part control barrier dynamics and serve to move the island/spit landward through time with sea level rise (Leatherman, 1981). Rates of landward transport by storm-generated overwash can be estimated from aerial photographs. Field surveys are necessary to determine the vertical dimension (thickness) of the washover deposition to facilitate volumetric calculations on a per storm basis. For example, the 1978 New England blizzard resulted in more than 8.4 m^3 of overwash sand deposition per 0.3 meters of shoreline along Nauset Spit, with depositional thickness approaching 1.5 m in some areas (Leatherman & Zaremba, 1986). This type of information is critical in determining the role of various transport processes in different environmental settings for tailoring land use and management plans.

Aircraft and satellite sensor data have also been used effectively to monitor inlet related erosional and depositional processes and patterns (e.g. El-Ashry, 1977). During the 1978 blizzard, Monomoy Island became separated into two distinct barrier sections when a new inlet was created. Landsat 3 Return Beam Vidicon (RBV) data are particularly useful for discriminating the land/water interface (Fig. 5) and for monitoring on a regular basis the sequential changes over a short-term period (Williams, 1983; Williams & Southworth, 1983).

Analysis of satellite imagery offers the opportunity to document major coastal changes that have occurred and define their relationship to both natural and human-induced causes.

Landsat-3 RBV

Landsat-1 MSS

July 1974, 1:1,000,000 scale
Monomoy Island is continuous

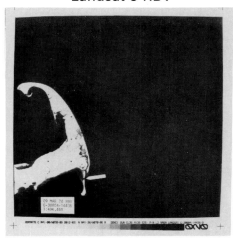

March 1978, 1:500,000 scale
500 meter rupture in Monomoy
Island

Aerial Photo (Neg)

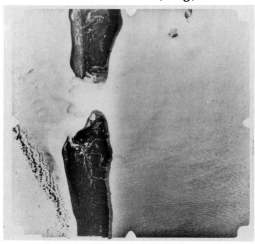

March 1978, 1:20,000 scale
Detail of Monomoy Island rupture
Low Tide

Enlarged Landsat 3 (Neg)

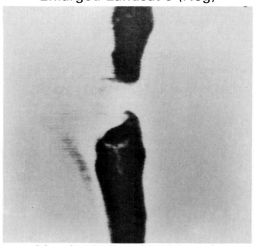

March 1978, 1:20,000 scale
Outline of Monomoy Island rupture
High Tide

Fig. 5. Landsat 1 MSS and Landsat 3 RBV images of Cape Cod, Massachusetts from July 1974 and March 1978, respectively, along with an aerial photograph from March 1978. The Landsat-3 RBV image clearly shows the inlet breach cut through Monomoy Island, Cape Cod, by the great New England blizzard of February 6–7, 1978 (from Dr R.S. Williams, Jr., USGS).

Natural disasters, such as flooding and permanent land loss in Bangladesh, result from large cyclones; orbital remote sensing can play an important role in evaluating the impacts of these storms and possible adaptive measures. Progressive coastal land loss through erosion and submergence threaten millions of people living in the low-lying deltaic areas in Bangladesh and also Egypt (UNEP, 1989). In fact, sediment starvation because of past dam building projects on the Nile River is causing severe erosion of the delta's promontories.

Rates of erosion have exceeded 100 meters per year for the past few decades (Frihy, 1988), resulting in major alterations of coastal environments as barrier beaches disappear and fresh water lakes become saline embayments. At the same time, orbital data can be used to monitor large-scale coastal accretion such as the rapid growth of the newest delta of the Mississippi River, the Atchafalaya in coastal Louisiana.

The dynamic nature of coastal areas mandates that continuous measurements be made to capture the magnitude and

Cape Cod Barrier Island topography

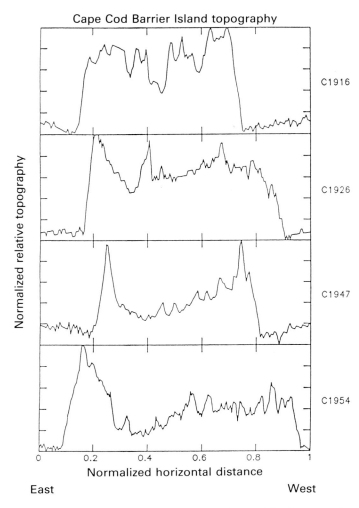

Fig. 6. Geodetic laser altimeter survey of barrier island topography across Monomoy Island, Cape Cod, Massachusetts on November 7, 1989. Vertical control is ± 15 cm, and footprints are spaced every 2 m (from Dr J. Garvin, NASA Goddard Space Flight Center).

high resolution (10 cm vertically for 1–2 meter contiguous footprints). When coupled with GPS-positioning capability, data emanating from this instrument will probably be a full magnitude better than anything else in existence.

NASA is presently supporting several airborne laser altimeter systems, and preliminary results of the first tests are available for Monomoy Island, Massachusetts (Fig. 6). The objective in the flight mission was to measure directly the topography across the hummocky barrier island dunes to infer dune evolution by means of topographic spectral analysis (Garvin, pers. comm.). This type of information is especially critical for the Federal Emergency Management Agency, which has already spent more than $1 billion in flood mapping studies and dune delineation. Also of critical importance is obtaining terrain microtopography information on coastal changes (beach erosion, dune destruction, and overwash generation) resulting from hurricane landfall. Recently, Hurricane Hugo wrought tremendous destruction throughout the Caribbean, but lack of pre- and post-storm observations have greatly hampered the scientific, engineering, and even economic assessment of this storm's impact on the coasts of St Croix, US Virgin Islands, eastern Puerto Rico, and the southeast coast of the United States.

Hugo made landfall on September 22, 1989, along the South Carolina coast, just north of Charleston, generating a maximum storm surge of 6.1 meters. While the coastal zone is reasonably well monumented so that comparative beach profiles are possible, this is a time consuming, laborious process using standard engineering techniques of transit and rod. Also, only a small portion of the entire coastal area can be assessed because the beach profile lines are widely spaced along the coast and, at best, only allow for the capture of representative changes in some areas.

Geographical analysis

In spite of limited work undertaken so far, remote sensing could also play a principal role in geographical studies of coastal areas. For example, Landsat MSS/TM or SPOT imagery could serve as an excellent data source for a global barrier island study. At present the worldwide distribution of barrier islands is only partially known. Previous studies (McGill, 1958; Gierloff-Emden, 1961; Cromwell, 1971) were based solely on available maps and charts that exhibited a wide range in data quality (due to different scales and cartographic accuracy, dates of publication, and source material used). Landsat data can provide an original, uniform data base for classification of barriers; distinct barrier types reflect forcing functions and physical factors (geologic, climatic, and oceanic). Relative barrier stability and vulnerability

rate of the sand transporting processes. Topography is of fundamental importance in coastal geomorphic research, but the overall relief is frequently small for the most dynamic landscapes – deltas and barrier islands. Therefore, high resolution and positional accuracy are required at a regional scale. Photogrammetric procedures using standard aerial photography are much too laborious to even consider, and there are positional accuracy and geometric distortion problems with radar imaging technology. Fortunately, airborne laser altimetry is presently being developed for geomorphological applications (Garvin, pers. comm.). Among the 'hot' new instruments available, the most promising are GALA (Geoscience Airborne Laser Altimeter) and SLAP (Shuttle/Scout Laser Altimeter Prototype). GALA is best suited for coastal erosion/dynamics studies, because it offers extremely

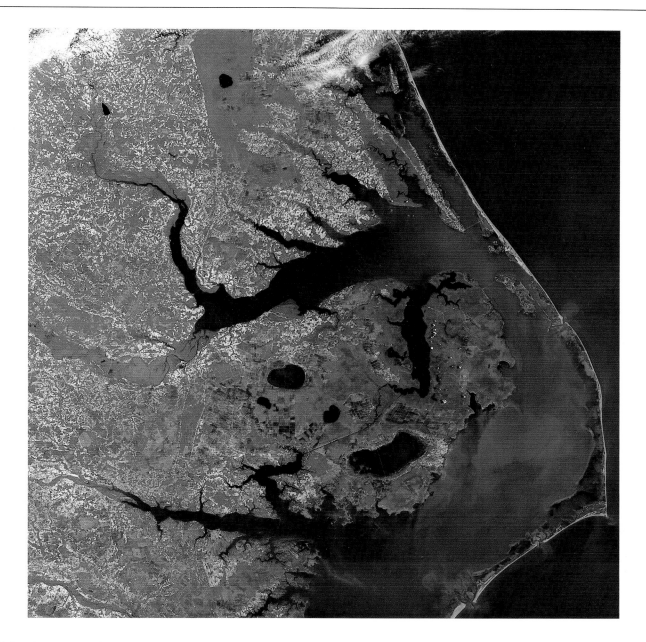

Fig. 7. Landsat images of (*a*) the outer banks of North Carolina and (*b*) the Friesan barriers along the North Sea coast, illustrating the marked differences between the narrow, elongated microtidal and short, bulbous-shaped mesotidal barrier islands, respectively.

to storms are primary considerations in the location of human development. This classification scheme would also have direct application to petroleum exploration (by obtaining knowledge on modern analogs for comparison to now buried ancient, oil-bearing barriers) as well as providing invaluable information for resource management.

In the case of barrier islands, which constitute about 15% of the world's open coast, a satellite image atlas would provide the base for a much needed improvement in the theoretical understanding and delineation of the unifying factors of bar-

rier distribution and morphology on a global basis. Microtidal and mesotidal islands vary greatly in their shape from elongated and narrow in the microtidal case (Fig. 7(*a*)) to short, bulbous barrier landforms in the mesotidal case (Fig. 7(*b*)). These characteristic shapes, illustrated here for the outer banks of North Carolina and the Friesan barriers along the North Sea, respectively, reflect differences in shoreline processes as a result of wave and tidal energy (Hayes, 1979). Mesotidal or drumstick barriers function differently from their microtidal counterparts, which tend to be more dynamic

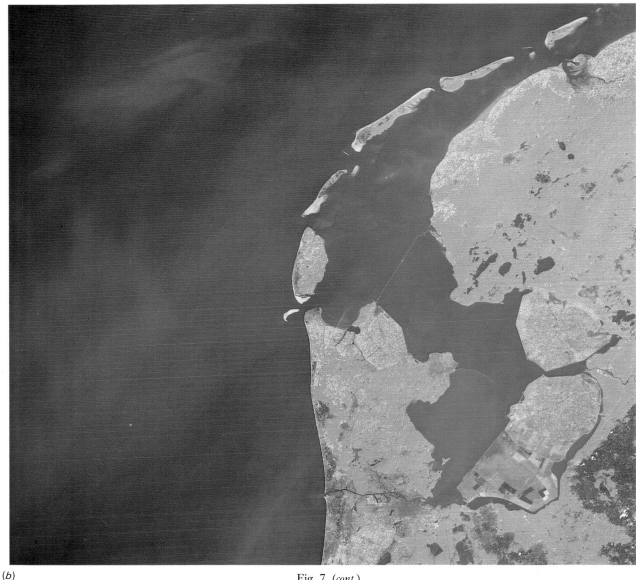

(b)   Fig. 7. (cont.)

(positionally unstable) and subject to overwash and inlet breaching. Mesotidal inlets with greater tidal ranges are more adjusted to high tides during storm conditions than microtidal barriers; the implications for human habitation should be clear. Unfortunately, we still do not even have a global inventory of these coastal features, greatly hampering further developments and analyses by coastal scientists.

Discussion and conclusions

Possible global warming and attendant sea-level rise is one of the most important subjects for coastal geomorphologists to address in the coming decades. Satellite imagery will have to play the major role in our monitoring of these on-going processes, because labor-intensive and costly field measurements can never provide the necessary data for such a global evaluation. Because water level is the principal determinant of shoreline position, more advanced techniques must be used to determine absolute sea level changes. Average relative sea level has been rising over the past century, and climatological models project accelerated sea level rise in the future due to greenhouse-induced warming. This global change has obvious ramifications for populated coastal regions, which could be inundated by increasing water levels and subjected to increased erosion.

A global survey of coastal changes could best be undertaken using a variety of EOS instruments and other satellite sensors (e.g. Landsat MSS/TM, SPOT images, and Soyuzkarta photographs). Satellite observations are particularly important for examining sea level change because of the scarcity of field measurements for remote regions (e.g. widespread mangroves in inaccessible tropical regions, where field observations are poor or lacking). Important indices of change could include coastal soil moisture and wetlands vegetation. Soil moisture could be examined with passive microwave data from the Advanced Microwave Scanning Radiometer (AMSR). Synthetic Aperture Radar (SAR) would enable observations of wetlands vegetation, particularly coastal forests, coastal salt marshes, and mangroves. Finally, for coastal plain areas with low elevational gradients, the High-Resolution Imaging Spectrometer (HRIS) could provide the resolution required to monitor the landward displacement of indicator species of vegetation over time in response to changing water levels.

Satellite observations are gradually beginning to supplant airborne imagery as the importance of coastal studies in global change research becomes more apparent. There are two major determinants of sensor utility: repetitive coverage and spatial resolution. The same area must be imaged over time for change detection and analysis. Secondly, the resolution must be sufficient to allow for detailed measurements; presently this is the major limitation in the use of digital satellite data. The ratio of potential versus realized applications of satellite instruments is still high because coastal studies are still in the infancy stage of development.

References

Cromwell, J. E. (1971). Barrier island distribution, a worldwide survey. *Second National Coastal and Shallow Water Research Conference, Abstract*, p. 50.

Demarest, J. M. & Leatherman, S. P. (1985). Mainland influence on coastal transgression: Delmarva peninsula. *Marine Geol.*, **63**, 19–33.

Dietz, R. S. (1963). Wave base, marine profile of equilibrium, and wave-built terraces: a critical appraisal, *Geol. Soc. Am.*, **74**, 971–90.

El-Ashry, M. T. (ed.). (1977). Air photography and coastal problems. *Benchmark Papers in Geology*, Hutchinson-Ross Publ. Co., Stroudsburg, PA, vol. 38, 425pp.

Fairbridge, R. W. (1968). *The Encyclopedia of Geomorphology.* Reinhold Publishing Company, New York.

Ford, J. P. *et al.* (1984). Seasat views North America, the Caribbean, and Western Europe with imaging radar. *Jet Propulsion Laboratory Publ.* 80–67, Pasadena, CA, 141pp.

Frihy, O. E. (1988). Nile delta shoreline changes: aerial photographic study of a 28 year period. *J. Coastal Res.*, **4**, 597–606.

Gierloff-Emden, H. G. (1961). Barriers and lagoons. *Petermanus Geogr. Mitt.*, **105**, 81–92.

Hands, E. B. (1983). The Great Lakes as a test model for profile response to sea level changes. In *Handbook of Coastal Processes and Erosion Control*, CRC Press, Boca Raton, FL, pp. 167–89.

Hayes, M. O. (1979). Barrier island morphology as a function of tidal and wave regime. In *Barrier Islands*, S. P. Leatherman, ed., Academic Press, New York, pp. 1–27.

Klemas, V., Bartlett, D., Rogers, R. (1975). Coastal zone classification from satellite imagery. *Photogrammetric Eng. Remote Sensing*, **41**, 499–513.

Leatherman, S. P. ed. (1979). *Barrier Islands*, Academic Press, New York, 325pp.

Leatherman, S. P. ed. (1981). Overwash processes. *Benchmark Papers in Geology*, Hutchinson and Ross Publ. Co., Stroudsburg, PA, 376pp.

Leatherman, S. P. (1983). Shoreline Mapping: a comparison of techniques. *Shore and Beach*, **51**, 28–33.

Leatherman, S. P. (1984). Shoreline evolution of north Assateague Island, Maryland. *Shore and Beach*, **52**, 3–10.

Leatherman, S. P. (1988). Beach and shoreface response to sea level rise. *Progr. Oceanog.*, **18**, 139–49.

Leatherman, S. P. & Clow, B. (1983). UMd shoreline mapping project. *Geosci. Remote Sensing Soc. Newslett., IEEE*, **22**, 5–8.

Leatherman, S. P. & Zaremba, R. E. (1986). Dynamics of a northern barrier beach: Nauset Spit, Cape Cod, Massachusetts. *Bull. Geol. Soc. Am.*, **97**, 116–24.

Lowman, P. D., Jr. (1968). *Space Panorama*, Weldflugbild, Reinhold A. Muller, Zurich, 140pp.

McGill, J. T. (1958). Map of coastal landforms of the world. *Geograph. Rev.*, **48**, 402–5.

National Research Council (1987). *Responding to Changes in Sea Level: Engineering Implications*. National Academy of Sciences Press, Washington, DC, 148pp.

Oldale, R. N. & Barlow, R. A. (1986). Geologic map of Cape Cod and the Islands. *Massachusetts: US Geological Survey Miscellaneous Investigations Series*, Map I–17.

Shepard, F. P. & Wanless, H. R. (1971). *Our Changing Coastlines*. McGraw Hill Book Co., New York, 579pp.

UNEP (1989). Criteria for assessing vulnerability to sea-level rise: a global inventory to high risk areas. *Delft Hydraulics Report H-838*, The Netherlands, 76pp.

Williams, R. S., Jr. (1983). Mini-atlas of image and related data coverage of Cape Cod, Massachusetts and environs: Introduction and photographic data of Cape Cod and environs. In *Manual of Remote Sensing*. Colwell, R. N., ed., 2nd edn., American Society of Photogrammetry, Falls Church, Virginia, vol. II, pp. 1710–14.

Williams, R. S., Jr. & Southworth, C. S. (1983). Imagery of Cape Cod and environs. In *Geological Applications, in Manual of Remote Sensing*, Colwell, R. N., ed., 2nd edn., American Society of Photogrammetry, Falls Church, Virginia, vol. II, pp. 1714–25.

Volcanoes

PETER J. MOUGINIS-MARK, DAVID C. PIERI AND PETER W. FRANCIS

Introduction

The Earth is one of the most dynamic planets in the solar system. Seen from space, its atmosphere is a turbulent montage of water vapor clouds that swirl across its blue disc in ever-changing belts of spiral storm systems. Even its solid surface is moving, as continent- and ocean-sized plates restlessly converge and diverge, alternately destroying and creating parts of the Earth's crust.

Short of giant meteorite impacts such as the one hypothesized to have caused the demise of the dinosaurs, volcanism is the most basic geological manifestation and agent of global change, varying on timescales of seconds to millions of years. For instance, in just a couple of minutes, the volcanic blast that occurred when Mt St Helens in Washington State erupted on May 18, 1980 completely devastated what was a beautiful pristine Alpine wilderness and ended nearly 60 lives. Particulates and aerosols injected into the atmosphere by such explosive eruptions can have severe short-term effects on weather and climate, as well as on technical and agricultural infrastructures. There are numerous historical records, dating back thousands of years, of major weather aberrations and crop failures associated with large explosive eruptions. At the other extreme, perennial volcanic emissions have been the major contributor to the overall development of the Earth's atmosphere and oceans, operating at a timescale that encompasses most of the history of the planet. Volcanoes thus have often induced substantive changes in the Earth's regional and global environments in the past, and will continue to do so.

Volcanoes are linked to global change in several ways, including their effects on the atmosphere, their impact upon the ecosystem, and (via the formation of new ocean floor topography and plate tectonics) on the distribution and thermal structure of the oceans. Undoubtedly, the most significant short-term (~ a few years) global effects of eruptions are related to the stratospheric injection of sulfuric acid aerosols and their impact on climate. A correlation between the sulfur mass yield and the observed surface temperature decrease following several historic eruptions has established the importance of volcanic sulfuric acid aerosols as the modifiers of climate (Sigurdsson, 1990). In his review of the global atmospheric effects of eruptions, Sigurdsson showed that volcanic gas emissions from the largest eruptions are likely to cause a drop in global surface temperatures of 1–3 °C for a few years due to the eruption of up to ~1.25×10^{11} kg of H_2SO_4 from eruptions such as the Laki fissure eruption of 1783. Because they have a higher mass yield of sulfur, basaltic fissure eruptions (typically associated with intraplate 'hot spot' eruptions such as those which occur in Iceland) have the potential to adversely affect climate to a greater extent than silica-rich magmas that are associated with island arc volcanoes, although this effect is only significant if the aerosols are injected into the stratosphere. Thus a direct link appears to exist between the tectonic setting of a volcano (e.g. island arc or intraplate hot spot), magma chemistry (i.e. the sulfur yield of different magmas), and the ability of an eruption to affect the short-term climate. Clearly, in the context of global change, volcanoes can be considered an important contributory factor to the Earth system because they introduce both mass and energy into the atmosphere and oceans, as well as onto the land surface itself.

Until recently, volcanologists have approached the study of volcanoes in a piecemeal fashion, generally focusing upon the petrology, geochemistry and structure of individual volcanoes. In fact, because of their accessibility, much of what is 'known' about mechanisms and manifestations of volcanic eruptions comes from just a few volcanoes around the world, most notably Mt Etna in Italy, and Mauna Loa and Kilauea Volcanoes on the Island of Hawaii. Global studies of volcanism, and analysis of the effects of volcanism on weather and climate, necessitate new approaches to the mapping and quantitative analysis of a diverse range of lithologic, thermal and topographic properties of volcanoes and eruption processes. Measurements of such attributes often have to be made in remote locations and in adverse weather conditions, day or night.

The most intense manifestations of the direct effects of volcanoes tend to be local. Lava flows generally only affect people if they are actually living on the volcano, as is the case

Fig. 1. Eruptions of Kilauea Volcano, Hawaii, are often more spectacular than dangerous to people, but can still cause considerable damage to property and the surrounding forests. A 200 m high fire fountain is shown in this August 1984 view of the eruption of Pu'u O'o, which is forming both an active lava flow and a vigorously convecting plume comprising ash, steam, and sulfur dioxide. (Photo: P. Mouginis-Mark.)

on Hawaii (Fig. 1) and on Mt Etna. Volcanic blasts are violent outbursts of solid volcanic material and gases, usually at elevated temperatures of several hundred degrees centigrade. If upward directed, these events often result in buoyant clouds that penetrate the stratosphere, where the volcanic products can be dispersed. If laterally directed, explosive eruptions can have severe and deadly local effects, scouring and incinerating landscapes (Fig. 2). Heavy ash falls are also associated with volcanic explosions, and may be more regional in scope. Such ash can be dispersed many hundreds of kilometers downwind, as fallout from eruption clouds. Locally, landscapes can be deeply buried by ash fallout, choking rivers and making arable land useless for years (Fig. 3). Debris flows can be triggered by eruptions, particularly where volcanoes at high altitudes have snow caps that can be melted by an eruption, sometimes with tragic results downstream. Lahars, or hot volcanic mudflows, have devastated areas at the base of volcanoes (Fig. 4). Finally, gases emitted from active volcanoes can be corrosive and even deadly. For instance, the

Island of Hawaii is routinely subjected to 'vog' or volcanic smog because of the ongoing multi-year eruption of Kilauea Volcano, Hawaii (Fig. 5).

This variety of direct effects on the environment has been studied at individual volcanoes, but quantitative data, taken in time series, are few, as are comparisons between volcanoes globally. Satellite observations offer the prospect of providing data on eruptions that may address this shortfall of information and enable the influence of volcanoes on the Earth system to be quantified. Examples of the physical processes associated with eruptions that need to be studied via satellites include the rate at which volcanic gases and aerosols are injected into the atmosphere, the thermal structure and volume of active lava flows erupted per unit time, and the deformation history of volcanic cones and craters. Data sets are emerging to address some of these topics, including high temporal resolution (every 4–6 hours) Advanced Very High Resolution Radiometer (AVHRR) visible and thermal images of eruptions, Landsat scenes of thermal anomalies at

Fig. 2. The devastation caused by the May 18, 1980 eruption of Mt St Helens included the leveling of a major portion of the surrounding forests. (Photo: P. Mouginis-Mark.)

individual volcanoes acquired over several years, and Total Ozone Mapping Spectrometer (TOMS) measurements of the dispersal of volcanic sulfur dioxide over several months. However, it will remain for improved orbital remote sensing techniques with coordinated ground observations to provide more comprehensive and perhaps definitive data. In order to study volcanoes and volcanic eruptions in the context of global change, numerous space-borne instruments must be used that not only provide the regional to global perspective of volcanoes and their eruptive products, but also collect data at many different wavelengths. Through measurements made in the ultra-violet, visible, infra-red and microwave portions of the spectrum, such attributes as the amount of sulfur dioxide released, the rapid changes in geomorphology of a volcano, the temperatures of lava flows and plumes, and the topography of a volcano can all be determined. When placed into a temporal context that considers changes on a timescale of minutes to a few years, the investigation of volcanoes via satellite observations provides a series of powerful tools for assessing the role of volcanism in global change.

Methodologies

Mapping plays a major role in the analysis of volcanoes from satellites. Different lithologies (rock types and degree of weathering) can be identified from spectral contrasts in the optical and near infra-red portion of the spectrum (such as with the Landsat Thematic Mapper and SPOT sensors), and spatial variations in surface roughness can be determined from radar back-scattering measurements. Considerable information has also been gained about remote volcanoes through photography obtained by astronauts during flights of the space shuttle (Figs. 6 and 7). However, it is in the analysis of dynamic volcanic phenomena that the spatial coverage and spectral range of orbital sensors are most valuable.

Ultra-violet

Through absorption features in the ultra-violet at two wavelengths near 0.3 μm, it has been possible to identify sulfur dioxide plumes in the stratosphere, and to track the

Fig. 3. Ash mantles a large area of the landscape following the April 1982 eruption of Galunggung, Java. (Photo: G.P.L. Walker.)

Fig. 4. Volcanic mudflows, called 'lahars', can be particularly erosive agents of the landscape surrounding a volcano. Here a road close to the volcano Sakurajima, Japan, has been almost completely removed by a fast-moving mudflow. (Photo: G.P.L. Walker.)

dispersal of major plumes around the globe. A particularly good example of this technique was the monitoring of the 1982 eruption of the Mexican volcano El Chichón (Fig. 8) using the TOMS on board the Nimbus-7 spacecraft. The El Chichón plume is the largest plume yet studied to date by a spacecraft (although the plume generated by the June 1991 eruption of Pinatubo volcano in the Philippines represents a recent second opportunity to study the dispersal of a major eruption plume). Via optical scattering of the suspended particles in the upper atmosphere, the dispersal of the plume around the circumference of the Earth was monitored via the TOMS and SAGE (stratospheric aerosol gas experiment) instruments. A dense aerosol plume from the eruption, centered at about 20° N, reached Hawaii from Mexico by April 9, and traveled to Japan by April 16, the Red Sea by April 20, and had encircled the Earth completely by 26 April. The cloud had traveled westwards at an average speed of about 20 meters per second.

As much as 3.3 million tons of gaseous sulfur dioxide were estimated from the TOMS measurements to have been injected into the stratosphere (Krueger, 1983). Within three months of the El Chichón eruption, all of this sulfur dioxide appears to have been converted to sulfuric acid, which, in the form of an aerosol, is the medium mostly responsible for the attenuation of solar radiation and for the consequent surface cooling and weather effects observed after large volcanic eruptions. El Chichón's aerosol cloud may have caused a reduction of average monthly temperatures of about 0.2 °C in June, 1982. Data from the TOMS experiment have also been used to track aerosols generated by several other major explosive eruptions such as the 1985 eruption of Nevado del Ruiz (Krueger *et al.*, 1990).

Fig. 5. Giant steam clouds containing concentrated hydrochloric acid are generated when hot lava flows enter the ocean on the flanks of Kilauea Volcano, Hawaii. These clouds have frequently been observed from orbit by astronauts on board the space shuttle, and are particularly damaging to the nearby environment due to their extreme acidity (pH < 1.0!). (Photo: C.W. Mark.)

Visible

The direct comparison of the structure of a volcano both before and after a major eruption represents a second method by which volcanic processes can be studied from orbit. In September 1988, the summit crater of Volcan Cumbres on the island of Fernandina, Galapagos, experienced a major collapse event. By happenstance, a 10 m/pixel SPOT image had been obtained of this volcano earlier that year, and on-going investigations of Fernandina permitted the acquisition of a second SPOT scene post-eruption. A direct comparison of these two images (Fig. 9) shows that the major change in the volcano was a collapse of ~one-third of the summit area, and the destruction of the summit crater lake. A small lava flow was also erupted on to the caldera floor and highly unstable inner walls characterized the interior of the crater (Fig. 10). Such satellite investigations are also possible for other volcanoes around the world, but are unlikely because of

the uncertain location and timing of eruptions: with over 600 active volcanoes worldwide, the assemblage of a data base for all of these volcanoes is both time consuming (due to cloud cover) and expensive (because the high resolution data are primarily collected by commercially operated spacecraft). Thus, it is not currently practical to obtain systematic temporal data over many volcanoes around the world, so that in most cases the temporal change caused by an eruption cannot be quantified.

Visible/Infra-red

Observations of Lascar volcano, north Chile, provide instructive examples of the volcanological applications of spaceborne visible and near infra-red data for the monitoring of an active volcano and the analysis of an explosive eruption. Lascar is a 5641 m high volcano on the crest of the Andean chain in north Chile (Fig. 11). This volcano has shown minor

Fig. 6. The tectonic setting of numerous volcanoes in Eastern Java can be seen in this excellent oblique view of a volcanic island chain, taken from the space shuttle in 1985. Beyond Java to the east are the volcanic islands of Madura, Bali, Lombok, Sumbawa, and Sumba. Space shuttle image 51B-146–051.

fumarolic activity throughout historic times, but there are no records of major eruptions. Because the volcano is located at high altitude in a remote desert region, it has been difficult to obtain useful information on the condition of the volcano. When a powerful explosive eruption took place on September 16, 1986, the first reports reached the scientific community not from the vicinity of the volcano, but from Salta in Argentina, almost 300 km distant, where ash fall was recorded.

Although neither sensor was designed specifically for the analysis of volcanoes, two aspects of Lascar's activity have been monitored, using satellite sensors with quite different spectral, spatial and temporal resolutions. Near infra-red Landsat TM images with spatial resolution of 30 m have been used to monitor radiant thermal energy from Lascar volcano on a number of occasions over a period of seven years. Evidence of previously unsuspected thermal activity at Lascar was discovered serendipitously during examination of a Landsat TM image of the area for another purpose: an

anomaly in TM bands 5 (1.55–1.75 μm) and 7 (2.08–2.35 μm) covering only about 20 pixels was revealed as a bright spot in the center of Lascar's active crater (Francis & Rothery, 1987). In a subsequent study, Rothery, Francis & Wood (1988) determined that the temperature of the anomaly was in the range 800–1000 °C, and was clearly consistent with magmatic temperatures, possibly related to hot lava within the summit crater, or high-temperature fumaroles.

In order to monitor the thermal flux from the volcano, retrospective and contemporary TM images have been acquired from 1984 to the present day, spanning the date of the 1986 eruption (Fig. 12). Prior to the 1986 eruption, the radiant thermal energy flux showed a marked decrease. Immediately after the eruption the anomaly, previously a single well-defined entity, appeared weak and fragmented into smaller centers. In subsequent months radiant thermal energy flux increased dramatically, reaching unprecedented high levels in 1988, indicating that Lascar was in an unusually

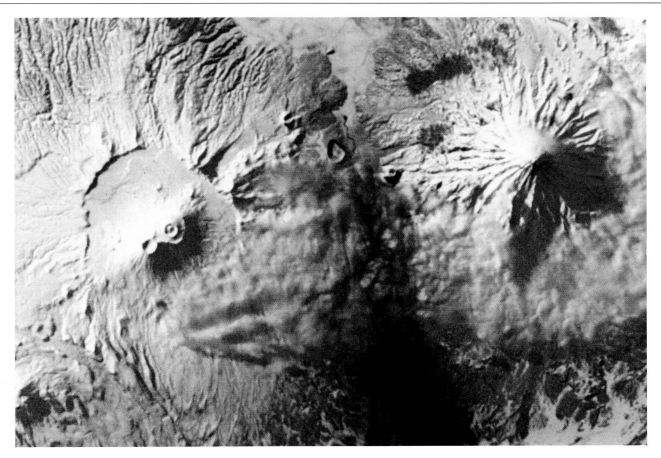

Fig. 7. Kronotska volcano in Kamchatka is one of many volcanoes that have erupted in historic times in this area. However, due to their remote location and adverse weather conditions, observations from space are often the best way to detect new activity such as the formation of a lava flow or cinder cone. Space shuttle image 61A-45–098.

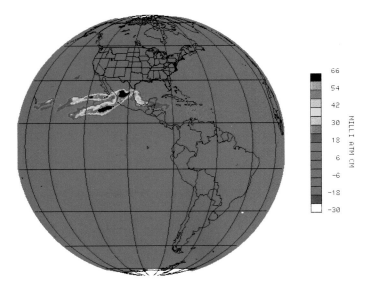

Fig. 8. TOMS image showing the dispersal pattern of the El Chichón plume on April 12, 1982, based upon the concentration of sulfur dioxide in the stratosphere. (Image courtesy of A. Krueger and L. Walter.)

active state. Field investigations revealed a growing andesitic lava dome in the summit crater. This was the first record of lava extrusion in the central Andes, and the first time that any such event had been detected exclusively by remote sensing techniques. Thermal monitoring of Lascar and other volcanoes continues using Landsat. An important research objective for many volcanoes lies in characterizing the spatial relationship of the thermal signature of different kinds of volcanic phenomena (Fig. 13), and in determining how thermal data can best be used in assessment of likely future volcanic activity.

One-kilometer resolution visible (0.55–0.75 μm) images of Lascar volcano acquired every 30 minutes from the geostationary GOES satellite were also used to monitor the downwind dispersal of the September 16, 1986 eruption cloud (Glaze *et al.*, 1989). This eruption lasted less than five minutes and produced a vulcanian eruption column that rose to a height of about 15 km, and was rapidly borne downwind. Ground observations and GOES images showed that the eruption plume formed a discrete extended slug about 2 km

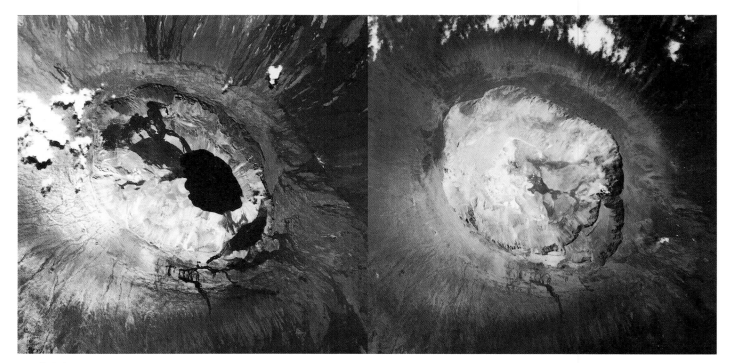

Fig. 9. This pair of 10 m resolution SPOT images of the summit caldera of Volcan Cumbres, Galapagos Islands, shows the rapid changes that accompanied the eruption in September 14, 1988. The maximum width of the caldera is ~3 km. Data were collected on April 27, 1988 (left) and October 25, 1988. (Images enhanced by H. Garbeil.)

Fig. 10. The 1988 caldera collapse at Volcan Cumbres, Galapagos Islands, produced major changes in the size and morphology of the summit area of the volcano. The haze is due to atmospheric scattering of dust formed by numerous landslides from the caldera rim. The height of the caldera wall shown here is ~1 km. (Photo: P. Mouginis-Mark.)

348

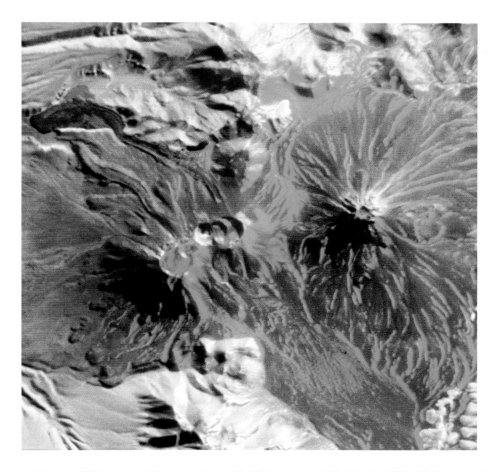

Fig. 11. Landsat Thematic Mapper (TM) image of Lascar volcano, N. Chile, acquired 11 March, 1985. TM bands 7, 5 and 2 are displayed in red, green, and blue respectively. The active crater is at the center of a nested crater chain, which is shown in an enlarged view at top left. The thermal anomaly is observed in this image as a bright red spot. The prominent lava flow northwest of Lascar is thought to have erupted in the nineteenth century, while the volcano on the right is Cerro Aguas Calientes (inactive). (Image width is equivalent to 15 km and was processed by P. Francis.)

thick at elevations between about 10 and 14 km, which passed over the city of Salta, Argentina, 285 km distant from Lascar, less than 2 hours after the eruption. The velocity of the leading edge of the cloud was derived from its position on successive GOES images (Fig. 14), and the plume's altitude was determined from shadow measurements. By 10:12am the plume had become diffused, having traveled 400 km in 3.5 hours, and covered an area greater than 100 000 km². Thermal infra-red GOES images were used to measure the plume temperature at different points along its track. The temperature at the top of the plume one hour after the eruption was −40.2 °C, corresponding to an altitude inferred from radiosonde data to be 10.6 km, significantly lower than that derived by shadow measurement. This unexpected discrepancy has focussed research on aspects of volcanic plume physics. Understanding of the ascent and dispersal of volcanic plumes will be of first importance not only for volcanological studies, but also for broader problems of atmospheric circulation and the way in which volcanic eruptions may modify atmospheric chemistry and the distribution of aerosols. The Lascar study also drew attention to a more immediate problem: the rapid downwind transport of the ash cloud could abruptly place at risk aircraft flying to and from cities such as Salta, far removed from the volcano. Incidents where large passenger aircraft have lost power in all engines and/or have had windscreens frosted by scouring after unexpectedly entering an ash cloud (such as the cloud produced by the eruption of Mt Redoubt, Alaska, in early 1990), demonstrate the major hazard that such plumes present, and the urgent need to develop means of providing rapid warning of their location (Steenblik, 1990).

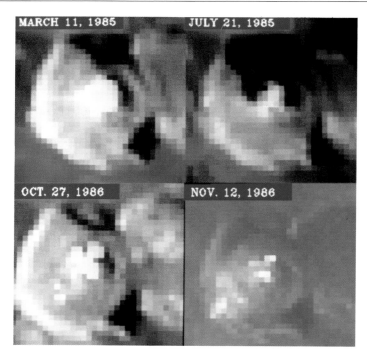

Fig. 12. Time series of four Landsat Thematic Mapper (TM) subscenes showing the temporal evolution of the thermal anomaly at the summit area of Lascar. Width of each subscene is equivalent to 1 km. Dates of acquisitions are March 11, 1985 (top left), July 21, 1985 (top right), October 27, 1986 (bottom left) and November 12, 1986 (bottom right). The major eruption of Lascar took place 41 days before the October 27 scene was obtained. (Images produced by P. Francis.)

Fig. 13. Three-dimensional projection of a June 20, 1984 Landsat TM image of M. Etna, Italy, showing an active lava flow erupting from the summit into Valle del Bove, a deep collapse depression on the volcano's eastern flank. This image was produced by convolving a digital model of the topography with a three-channel (bands 2, 5, 7) planimetric image of the scene. The active flow, orange in this

Weather satellites

The NOAA AVHRR is currently operating on three spacecraft, NOAA- 9, 10, and 11. These meteorological satellites are primarily designed for synoptic mapping of clouds and ocean surface temperatures, measuring radiance at visible/near infra-red (0.55–1.10 µm), mid-infra-red (3.55–3.93 µm) and thermal infra-red (10.3–12.5 µm). The AVHRR sensor has a spatial resolution of ~1 km. Because each satellite can observe an area on the Earth's surface twice each day (once during the day and once at night), it is possible to compile a high temporal resolution data base of dynamic phenomena. Up to six scenes of an area may be obtained each day, permitting the rate of dispersal of a volcanic plume (Fig. 15) or the advance of lava flow (Fig. 16) to be monitored. Thermal anomalies due to on-going volcanic eruptions, such as the Kupaianaha eruption in Hawaii (Fig. 16) can thus be studied with the AVHRR data to determine the evolution of a

picture, while incandescent in the IR, would appear black as visible wavelengths. IR radiance information from this image of the active lava flow can be used to determine the distribution of energy losses, and thus constrain models of flow behavior. (Figure from Pieri, Glaze & Abrams, (1990). Landsat image courtesy of Telespazio. Processed by M. Abrams.)

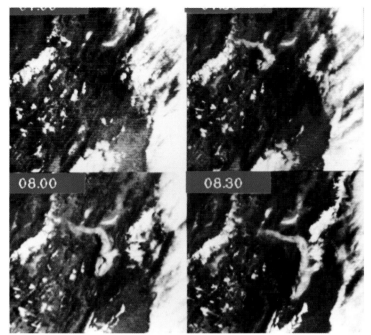

lava flow field over a period of weeks to months. The locus of surface activity has been seen to move from the Pu'u O'o and Kupaianaha vents to the mid-level break in slope (where compound lava flows occasionally break out to the surface) and at the coast where the individual flows reach the ocean. Although these Hawaii measurements do not replace the more detailed local measurements of the movement of the flows as determined on the ground, they do demonstrate the utility of using daily satellite measurements to track the large-scale motion of lava flows should they be detected on less well-monitored volcanoes.

Fig. 14. GOES images collected at 7:00am (top left), 7:30am (top right), 8:00am (bottom left) and 8:30am (bottom right) recorded the dispersal of the eruption plume from the September 16, 1986 eruption of Lascar volcano, N. Chile. Each image is ~550 km in width. (Figure from Glaze *et al.*, (1989).)

Fig. 15. AVHRR image of the volcanic plume generated from an eruption of Mt. St. Augustine (volcano denoted by asterisk) in Alaska, on March 30, 1986, showing the advantage of the synoptic coverage provided by weather satellites for the tracking of large eruption plumes. The ratio of bands 4 and 5 is displayed in red, and bands 1 and 3 are displayed in green and blue respectively. The eruption plume is orange in this image, while surrounding meteorologic clouds are yellow. (Image courtesy of W. Rose.)

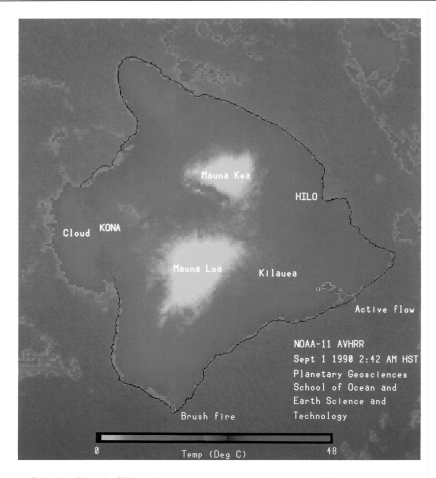

Fig. 16. Daily AVHRR images of the big Island of Hawaii are obtained by the University of Hawaii. This nighttime thermal IR scene (11·5–12·5μm) was obtained at 2:42am local time on September 1, 1990. The image has been processed to show surface temperatures between 0–48° C (see temperature bar at bottom). The active lava flow associated with an eruption of Kilauea Volcano (right of center) and a brush fire (extreme southern tip of island) were both detected in these data, which have a spatial resolution of ~1 km. Mauna Kea and Mauna Loa volcanoes appear yellow in this rendition because of their height and resultant cold temperatures. A large cloud (green) is indicated off the west coast of Kona. (Image courtesy of H. Garbeil and P. Flament.)

Synthetic aperture radar (SAR)

Optical and infra-red sensors such as the Landsat TM and AVHRR have the major disadvantage that they can only observe a volcano during cloud-free conditions. Microwave sensors such as SARs do not suffer from this limitation, and offer complementary information to the optical sensors for monitoring volcanoes. In volcanology, SARs have only been used in an exploratory manner up until now, but this situation changed with the launch of ERS-1 in July 1991. Since 1978 with the flight of the Seasat radar, SAR images of volcanoes have been used to map the distribution of lava flows, cinder cones and fault zones (Fig. 17). Starting in late 1991 with the operational phase of ERS-1, SAR data for the volcanoes in the Aleutian Islands and the Alaskan Peninsula are being obtained every 35 days (which is the repeat cycle of the space-

craft's orbit). Using radar interferometry techniques developed by Gabriel & Goldstein (1988) and Gabriel, Goldstein & Zebker (1989), topographic and deformation maps of these volcanoes will be compiled in order to search for dome growth, the formation of new lava flows or cones, or changes in summit ice cover that might be related to the onset of activity (Fig. 18).

From a pair of radar interferograms (each derived from two radar images collected from near identical orbits), it is possible to compare the surface topography of an area to investigate topographic change at a vertical scale of a few centimeters. Although this technique has not yet been applied to a volcano, Gabriel et al. (1989) have shown that swelling of agricultural fields in California due to irrigation can be detected. Instead of soil swelling due to variable moisture content, change on a volcano may be due to the intrusion of a magma

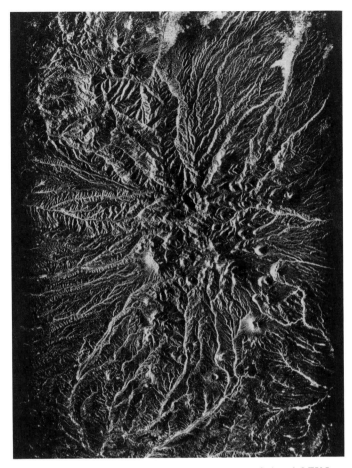

Fig. 17. The eroded summit of the volcano Kuh'e Sahand, NW Iran was imaged by the SIR-A radar experiment, flown on the Space Shuttle in November 1981. Numerous parasitic cones are visible on the flanks of the main volcano. The area shown here is ~50 × 70 km in extent and the illumination direction is from the left. (Image obtained on data take 35/36 and is courtesy of A. Richardson.)

body close to the surface. Other volcanic phenomena may also be detected by this radar interferometric technique: new lava flows, cones or collapse craters would be sufficiently different that successive radar images could not be used to construct the interferogram. Thus new volcanic landforms could readily be distinguished from areas that had remained the same between observations.

Limitations

In the context of global change, the analysis of volcanoes, and particularly those in eruption, is limited by several factors that are facets of the orbital characteristics of the spacecraft and the sensor performance. Of the numerous factors that face the remote sensing volcanologist at the present time, the lack of areal coverage, viewing conditions (cloud cover and avail-

able daylight), insufficient temporal resolution, and spectral coverage, are the most pressing.

Lack of areal coverage at sufficient spatial resolution

Many volcanoes produce plumes that extend downwind for hundreds to thousands of kilometers, requiring synoptic data coverage. Targeting high resolution sensors such as Landsat and SPOT can rarely be done sufficiently rapidly to obtain data for transient volcanic phenomena, and swath widths of these high spatial resolution instruments are typically <100 km. Conversely, weather satellite sensors (e.g. AVHRR, GOES and TOMS) do not provide the spatial resolution that is required to accurately map lava flows, volcanic vents and small gas plumes even though they have swath widths in excess of 1000 km.

Viewing conditions

Many active volcanoes are located in tropical or high latitude parts of the world. Areas such as Indonesia, the Aleutian Islands and Central America possess many active volcanoes that are frequently subjected to considerable cloud cover. In addition, high latitude volcanoes experience very short periods of daylight and low angles of illumination during winter months, making optical imaging difficult for a significant portion of the year. Imaging radars, such as those of the European Space Agency (ERS-1), Japan (JERS-1), and Canada (RadarSat) offer considerable improvement in our ability to map volcanoes and to detect topographic change via radar interferometry, but nevertheless these methods will not be applicable for thermal studies or for the tracking of eruption plumes because of their wavelength range.

Temporal coverage

Most sensors in low Earth orbit provide at best only a very coarse data base by which to study temporal changes on a volcano. Many of the phenomena of interest to the volcanologist have timescales of a few hours to weeks, so that the relatively narrow angle, high-resolution coverage provided by, for instance, Landsat (once every 18 days) and SPOT (~5 times every 14 days) may not be adequate even if cloud-free acquisitions can be obtained. Frequent (every 4–6 hours) synoptic low-resolution coverage can be obtained from instruments like the advanced very high resolution radiometer (AVHRR) operating upon several NOAA satellites. However, the ~1 km spatial resolution of this instrument is insufficient to investigate the advance of lava flows, which might advance

Fig. 18. Topographic model of Mt Shasta, California, constructed from radar data collected by the SIR-B radar experiment in October 1984. Topographic information from future orbital radars will be used to investigate slopes and volume changes on remote volcanoes. (Image courtesy of M. Kobrick.)

by a few tens to hundreds of meters per day. More promising for temporal studies would be sensors placed in geostationary orbit (e.g. NOAA GOES satellites), which can return data every 30 minutes. The utility of current systems for volcanology, however, is likewise compromised by the 1 km spatial resolution of the GOES instruments. Thus there remains a key gap in our knowledge of the rapidly changing physical processes associated with eruptions: insufficient data at high temporal resolution are available to study volcanic phenomena at a spatial scale of tens to a few hundreds of meters.

Spectral coverage

Though a variety of multi-spectral instruments have been placed into Earth orbit over the past two decades, the spectral coverage of these instruments has been optimized for a variety of non-volcanic applications. For instance, the dynamic range of the Landsat TM is too small to obtain thermal radiometric observations of high temperatures ($\sim$500–1000 °C), and the spatial resolution of the AVHRR (1.1 km) is insufficient to resolve the detailed characteristics of active lava flows and lava ponds. In addition, spectral bands are usually too widely spaced to provide adequate radiometric sampling of hot targets at more than one wavelength, inhibiting estimation of the extent and temperature of heat sources that are smaller than one pixel in area (e.g. Matson & Dozier, 1981; Pieri et al., 1990). For thermal radiometry of volcanoes, there is thus a need for additional infra-red bands between $\sim$1.6–2.5 μm with dynamic range adequate to observe both molten rock and the surrounding targets at ambient temperatures.

For atmospheric observations, while current UV instruments (e.g. TOMS) provide valuable synoptic information on the presence, amount, and global dispersion of stratospheric SO_2 and aerosols, there is presently no way to obtain spatial information with an adequate signal-to-noise ratio on tropospheric emissions from major sulfur-emitting volcanoes such as Mt Etna. In order to observe volcanic SO_2 in the tropos-

Temperature

25   30   35   40   45   50

Fig. 19. This temperature map of La Solfatara, a small geothermally active caldera in the town of Pozzuoli, near Naples, Italy, was produced from IR images generated by the airborne Thermal Infra-red Multispectral Scanner (TIMS). Temperatures in the scene range from 25–50° C and hot areas are associated with solfataric and geyser activity. Such data are of the type that will be acquired by the ES Advanced Spaceborne Thermal Emission and Reflection radiometer (ASTER), from orbit. (Figure from Bianchi *et al.* (1990), courtesy of A. Kahle.)

phere from discrete sources, UV imaging spectrometry in the range 0.3–0.4 μm will be required at a spatial resolution of ~20–40 m. Other volcanic gases such as HF, HCl, and CO could also be measured in the spectral range 2.38–2.40 μm, 3.36–3.43 μm, and 4.59–4.76 μm respectively.

Future directions in satellite volcanology

Over the next decade, a major effort in remote sensing in volcanology in the context of global change will be one of 28 interdisciplinary investigations for the Earth Observing System (EOS), due to be launched by NASA starting in 1998

(Mouginis-Mark *et al.*, 1991). This volcanological investigation will include both long-term and short-term monitoring of selected volcanoes, the detection and analysis of precursor activity associated with eruptions, and the monitoring of on-going eruptions. The data collected by EOS will allow two aspects of volcanism to be addressed. First, it will further knowledge of the distribution of volcanic landforms, their temporal evolution, and the nature of the potential hazards posed by individual volcanoes. Secondly, it will provide a means of documenting the compositions, flux rates and total atmospheric budgets of gases, particulates and aerosols injected into the atmosphere by volcanoes, both in the immediate

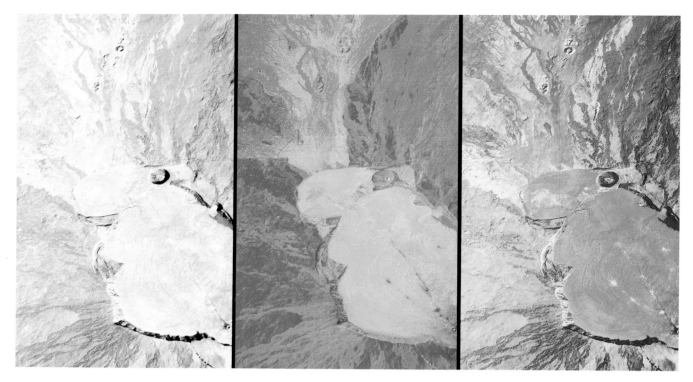

Fig. 20. Three views of the summit of Mauna Loa volcano, Hawaii, derived from TIMS data. The crater is filled with lava from the 1984 eruption, which breached a section of its northeast wall (top right of each image). Natural color (left), principal component (center) and decorrelation stretch (right) images such as these are a great aid to mapping lithologic boundaries on volcanoes such as Mauna Loa, where the rock chemistry is quite uniform between different eruptions. (Image courtesy of H. Garbeil.)

vicinity of the volcano, and on a hemispheric scale. A variety of instruments, including the thermal infra-red ASTER instrument will fly on EOS. ASTER data collected in the 8–12 μm region will permit the distribution of 'cool' volcanic targets such as fumaroles ($<\sim100$ °C) to be mapped (Fig. 19) as well as aid in the mapping of volcanic lithologies (Fig. 20).

Prior to the launch of EOS, existing polar orbiting remote sensing satellites such as Landsat 5, SPOT and meteorological satellites will continue to provide valuable data. It will also be possible to use experiments flown on the space shuttle and other satellites to collect data on volcanoes. Three radar systems (ERS-1, JERS-1 and Radarsat) are being flown between 1991 and 1994, and the space shuttle will carry the third Shuttle Imaging Radar (SIR-C) experiment in 1994. From the shuttle, volcanoes in Hawaii, the Galapagos Islands, the Indian Ocean and the Andes will be imaged. From ERS-1, the topography and morphology of volcanoes in the Aleutian Islands will be investigated.

Atmospheric studies will also continue to be an important part of volcanology investigations from satellites even before EOS is launched. Although the primary objective of TOMS instrument on Nimbus-7 is the measurement of ozone, TOMS has successfully been used since 1978 to study the

SO_2 released into the stratosphere by major eruptions. A series of TOMS instruments is planned for launch starting with the Soviet Meteor-3 spacecraft in 1991, followed by a NASA dedicated Earth probe satellite in 1993, and the Japanese ADEOS satellite in 1995. The third stratospheric aerosol gas experiment (SAGE III) which will measure the stratospheric aerosol concentration, will either fly on an Earth probe-class satellite in the mid-1990s or will be part of an EOS platform. The SeaWIFS, which is an 8-band VNIR radiometer, is scheduled for launch in late 1993 and may provide the first opportunity to search for shallow marine eruptions, based on the resultant discoloration of the sea surface.

Most satellite investigations of volcanic eruptions have, by virtue of the rare occurrence of major eruptions during the timeframe when orbital sensors have been flying, concentrated on the relatively small eruptions. With the exceptions of the 1982 eruption of El Chichón and the 1991 eruption of Mt Pinatubo, volcanoes have been only small-scale perturbations to the Earth system over the last decade, and there have been no eruptions of extensive lava flows comparable to those produced during the 1783 eruption of Laki in Iceland. It is highly likely, however, that during the

356

coming years other major explosive eruptions will occur that will inject major amounts of particulates, aerosols and gases into the stratosphere, where they may adversely affect a significant portion of the globe. Stratospheric aerosols resulting from volcanic eruptions have been implicated in a variety of anomalous weather and short-term climatic events, including the infamous 'Year without a summer' in North America following the eruption of Tambora in 1815, and even the more recent El Niño event which followed the El Chichón eruption of 1982. Comparable events will almost certainly occur in the future.

While such direct linkage, as in the case of El Niño events and volcanic eruptions, is not without controversy, there are very well-documented occurrences of crop failures and anomalous atmospheric effects from, for instance, the ancient Chinese scientific archives from as long ago as 5000 BC. These documented effects correlate well with high acidity layers deposited in the Greenland ice sheet at precisely the same times (Rampino, Self & Stothers, 1988). One of the goals of the volcanology community over the coming years is therefore to investigate these linkages between the solid Earth and the other components of the Earth system. In order to make these connections, a data base has to be developed that provides the spatial, spectral and temporal coverage appropriate for studying eruptions whenever and wherever they occur around the world. Concurrent with the establishment of this data base, quantitative methods for assessing the influence of, for example, volcanic aerosols on sea surface temperature and the impact of volcanic ash on ecosystems need to be developed. One of the goals of the Earth Observing System is to build such a data base, and to refine the methodologies and understanding of the physical basis of these analyses (Mouginis-Mark et al., 1991).

In the longer term, there is also the need for satellites dedicated to volcanological research. A low-Earth orbital satellite with a high spatial (<~50 m/pixel) and spectral resolution imager in the range 0.3–4.0 μm would allow systematic monitoring of thermal and atmospheric emissions over several dozen of the world's most active volcanoes every day. Additional measurements of active volcanoes could also be obtained from a geostationary platform, where a similar high spectral and spatial resolution instrument could provide the temporal coverage necessary for the detection and continuous monitoring of eruptions.

References

Bianchi, R., Casacchia, R., Coradini, A., Duncan, A. M., Guest, J. E., Kahle, A., Lanciano, P., Pieri, D. & Poscolieri, M. (1990). Remote sensing of Italian volcanos, *Eos*, **71**, 1789–91.

Francis, P. W. & Rothery, D. A. (1987). Using the Landsat Thematic Mapper to detect and monitor active volcanoes: an example from the Lascar volcano, northern Chile, *Geology*, **15**, 614–17.

Gabriel, A. K. & Goldstein, R. M. (1988). Crossed orbit interferometry: theory and experimental results from SIR-B. *Int. J. Rem. Sen.*, **9**, 857–72.

Gabriel, A. K., Goldstein, R. M., & Zebker, H. A. (1989). Mapping small elevation changes over large areas: Differential radar interferometry. *J. Geophys. Res.*, **94**, 9183–91.

Glaze, L. S., Francis, P. W., Self, S. & Rothery, D. A. (1989). The Lascar September 16 1986 eruption: satellite investigations *Bull. Volcanol.*, **51**, 149–60.

Krueger, A. J. (1983). Sighting of El Chichón sulfur dioxide clouds with the Nimbus-7 Total Ozone Mapping Spectrometer. *Science*, **220**, 1377–9.

Krueger, A. J., Walter, L. S., Schnetzler, C. C. & Doiron, S. D. (1990). TOMS measurement of the sulfur dioxide emitted during the 1985 Nevado del Ruiz eruptions. *J. Volcanol. Geotherm. Res.*, **41**, 7–15.

Mackenzie, J. S. & Ringrose, P. S. (1986). Use of Seasat SAR imagery for geological mapping in volcanic terrain: Askja Caldera, Iceland. *Int. J. Rem. Sen.*, **7**, 181–94.

Matson, M. & Dozier, J. (1981). Identification of subresolution high temperature sources using a thermal IR sensor. *Photogram. Eng. Rem. Sen.*, **47**, 1311–18.

Mouginis-Mark, P. J. *et al.* (1991). Analysis of active volcanoes from the Earth Observing System. *Rem. Sen. Environ.*, **36**, 1–12.

Pieri, D. C., Glaze, L. S. & Abrams, M. J. (1990). Thermal radiance observations of an active lava flow during the June 1984 eruption of Mount Etna. *Geology*, **18**, 1018–22.

Rampino, M. R., Self, S. & Stothers, R. B. (1988). Volcanic winters. *Ann. Rev. Earth Planet. Sci.*, **16**, 73–99.

Rothery, D. A., Francis, P. W. & Wood, C. A. (1988). Volcano monitoring using short wavelength infra-red data from satellites. *J. Geophys. Res.*, **93**, 7993–8008.

Sigurdsson, H. (1990). Assessment of the atmospheric impact of volcanic eruptions. In *Global Catastrophes in Earth History*. Sharpton, V. L. and Ward, P. D., eds., *Geol. Soc. Am. Special Paper*, **247**, 99–110.

Steenblik, J. W. (1990). Volcanic ash: A rain of terra. *J. Airline Pilots Assoc.*, **59**, (6), 9–15.

PART VII

CRYOSPHERE

Snow cover

J. L. FOSTER AND A. T. C. CHANG

Introduction

Quite apart from its natural beauty, snow is an important component of the Earth's climate, significantly impacting global weather and vital to the water supply in many areas. In the Northern Hemisphere, during winter the land area that is whitened by snow more than doubles. After being deposited on the surface, snow subsequently serves as a source of water vapor input to the atmosphere through the processes of sublimation and evaporation and as a source of water to the soil and river systems when melting occurs. It also markedly changes the albedo and the radiation balance and may reduce the solar energy available to heat the surface and lower atmosphere by more than 50%. Therefore, snow cover represents a changing atmospheric output that is a function of variability in the Earth's climate, and is also a boundary condition that affects meteorology and climate through the changes that it makes in the radiation balance and the water vapor input to the atmosphere.

Unusually heavy snow accumulations in late winter or early spring may delay the arrival of expected increases in air temperature, and in addition, late season heavy snow can cause extensive flooding. Conversely, the absence of normal snow cover can cause acute water deficits in the many regions that rely on snowmelt as a water source (Hall, 1988).

Until recently, the only way to study snow has been from ground-based observations where data collection may be hazardous. While field measurements are still needed, satellites are now providing valuable data that cover large areas and increasingly longer time periods. In order to study and comprehend the climatic and economic impact of snow cover, it is necessary to have long-term data bases of various snow parameters. Since 1966, continental snow cover extent has been monitored on a weekly basis using NOAA satellites in the visible and near infra-red wavelengths, thus providing a data base with spatial and temporal continuity (Matson, Ropelewski & Varnadore, 1986). But to obtain quantitative information concerning the volume of snow, snow depth as well as snow extent must be known. The Scanning Multichannel Microwave Radiometer (SMMR) on board the Nim-

bus-7 satellite has been acquiring passive microwave data since 1978. This instrument has the capability of providing global estimates of snow depth and area by using an algorithm derived from microwave radiometric observations of snow. Through the use of satellite data, an improved understanding of the role of snow in global climate and hydrology processes is being developed.

Methodology

It is the large contrast between the dielectric properties of water and those of most solids that make the use of microwave radiometric techniques important for problems related to water resources. The dielectric constants of water, ice and snow are so drastically different that even a little melting causes a strong microwave response (Jones, 1983). In addition, the dielectric constant of snow is usually lower than that of dry soil so that there is sufficient contrast in brightness temperature (the temperature thermally emitted by an object inferred from the blackbody exitance over a specified wavelength band) between snow and snow-free surfaces to permit snowfields to be monitored (NASA, 1982).

An electromagnetic wave emitted from the underlying ground surface propagates through the snowpack and is scattered by the randomly spaced snow grains into all directions. Consequently, when the wave emerges at the snow/air interface, its amplitude has been attenuated. The dry snow absorbs very little energy from the wave and therefore also contributes very little in the form of self-emission. When the snowpack grows deeper, the wave suffers more scattering loss, and the transmission through the snowpack is further reduced, and so less radiation reaches the sensor resulting in a lower brightness temperature (Foster et al., 1984). This is the basis for developing algorithms to estimate snow depth.

Currently several algorithms are available to evaluate and retrieve snow cover and snow depth parameters for specific regions and specific seasonal conditions. A straightforward method to relate microwave radiometric data to snow cover and snow depth is to examine the difference between the brightness temperature observed for snow-covered ground

361

and that for snow-free ground (Hallikainen & Jolma, 1987). The monthly snow cover and snow depth maps presented here were generated by using a difference algorithm, one developed by Chang, Foster & Hall (1987) which assumes dry snow conditions, a snow density of 0.30 g/cm and a snow grain size of 0.35 mm for the entire snowpack. The difference in brightness temperature between the SMMR 37 GHz and 18 GHz channels is used to derive snow depth for a uniform snowfield. This is expressed as follows:

$$SD = 1.59 \, (T18_H - T37_H)$$

where SD is snow depth in centimeters, H is horizontal polarization, T is brightness temperature in degrees kelvin, and 1.59 is a constant derived by using the linear portion of the 18 and 37 GHz responses to obtain a linear fit of the difference between the 18 GHz and 37 GHz frequencies. If the 18 GHz T is less than the 37 GHz T, the snow depth is zero and no snow cover is assumed.

An evaluation of the various algorithms that have been derived shows that only algorithms including the 37 GHz channel provide adequate agreement with the manually measured snow depth and snow water equivalent values. It may also be noted that the difference $(T18_H - T37_H)$ often gives better results than the 37 GHz channel alone. Use of the 18 GHz channel helps to partly eliminate the effects of the snow and ground temperatures and the atmospheric quantities (integrated water vapor and clouds) on changes in T (Foster, Hall & Chang, 1987).

Analysis and results

Data collected by the Nimbus-7 SMMR of snow cover and snow depth for the Northern Hemisphere are presented here in a map format (Figs. 1–10). The microwave maps are based on average brightness temperatures for a 5-day period near the middle of each month and displayed on color-coded polar stereographic projection. The brightness temperature data are placed into $\frac{1}{2}°$ latitude by $\frac{1}{2}°$ longitude grid cells uniformly subdividing maps according to the geographic coordinates of the center of the field of view of the radiometers (Parkinson *et al.*, 1987). A template was made to mask data over oceans and bays so that only microwave data for land areas are displayed.

Twenty eight color increments in various shades of blue, green, yellow, red and violet represent different snow depth observations. Each color shade corresponds to a depth of about 3 cm. The shallowest depth used is 3 cm and the deepest is 84 cm. Theoretically it is possible to distinguish snow depths of about 2 cm, but in actuality it is probably not feasible to differentiate between depths of less than about 5

cm. However, it should be kept in mind that these values are not meant to be indicative of a given locale, but are integrated over the entire $\frac{1}{2}°$ by $\frac{1}{2}°$ microwave pixel. So even though, for instance, a given point may have a depth of 100 cm, it is unlikely that 100 cm of snow will cover a complete pixel. Ice cap regions such as Greenland are infinitely thick to microwaves and are shown in pink, which represents the deepest snow detectable with the algorithm used here.

Snow cover patterns and distributions

As seen from the microwave brightness temperature maps (Fig. 1–10), the snow cover becomes established first in northeastern Siberia and in northern Alaska between mid-September and mid-October. A shallow layer of cold air forms above the snow surface in response to radiative losses resulting from the increase in albedo of the expanding snow cover (Lydolph, 1977). If the snow cover forms early and becomes deep and extensive, then the air above the snowpack is likely to be colder than if the snow cover is late forming and does not cover as extensive an area. The refrigerated air overlying the snowpack is transported southward during the late fall and winter, cooling much of the continent.

In October and November the snowpack increases in extent and begins to thicken, as indicated by the brighter colors (lower brightness temperatures) in the tiaga and tundra zones. By this time, the Siberian High has become well developed as a result of the extreme surface cooling and the constant feeding of fresh Arctic air into central Asia. This high is generally large enough to effectively prevent the incursion of maritime air or air from other source regions into the continental interior. By December the snow covered area has expanded well into southern Russia and into the northern US. From December through March the snowpack continues to increase in depth in the interior regions.

In March, with increasing solar insolation, the snowline begins a rapid retreat northward, and by mid-April the snowpack is typically confined to boreal forest and tundra areas. Because moisture is often scarce, much of the snow-covered areas in the steppes and plains of interior Eurasia and North America is quite shallow (< 15 cm) and thus these areas melt quickly in early spring. The snowpack, as seen from the microwave maps, shows a fairly constant regression poleward from March through June. However, since the storm tracks migrate north as spring progresses, it is not unusual for the snowpack to build in some areas north of about 60° latitude throughout April. The snowpack recedes rapidly northward between mid-April and mid-May and by mid-June most of the remaining snow lies along the Arctic coasts adjacent to the still very cold Arctic Ocean.

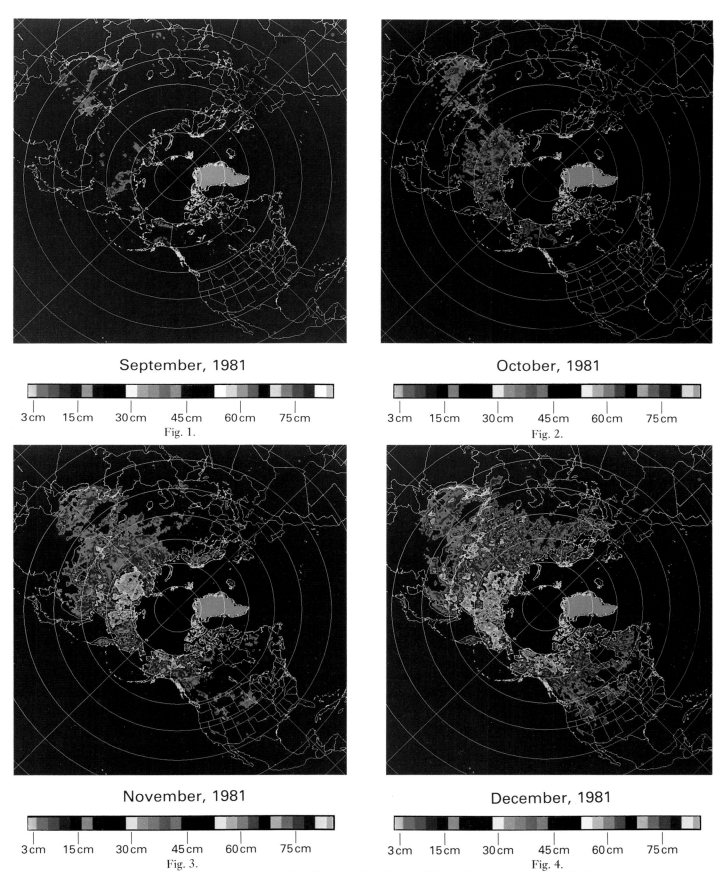

September, 1981

3 cm	15 cm	30 cm	45 cm	60 cm	75 cm

Fig. 1.

October, 1981

3 cm	15 cm	30 cm	45 cm	60 cm	75 cm

Fig. 2.

November, 1981

3 cm	15 cm	30 cm	45 cm	60 cm	75 cm

Fig. 3.

December, 1981

3 cm	15 cm	30 cm	45 cm	60 cm	75 cm

Fig. 4.

Figs. 1–10. Monthly snow depth and snow cover maps of the Northern Hemisphere (September–June) for the 1981–82 snow season as derived from the Nimbus-7 SMMR.

363

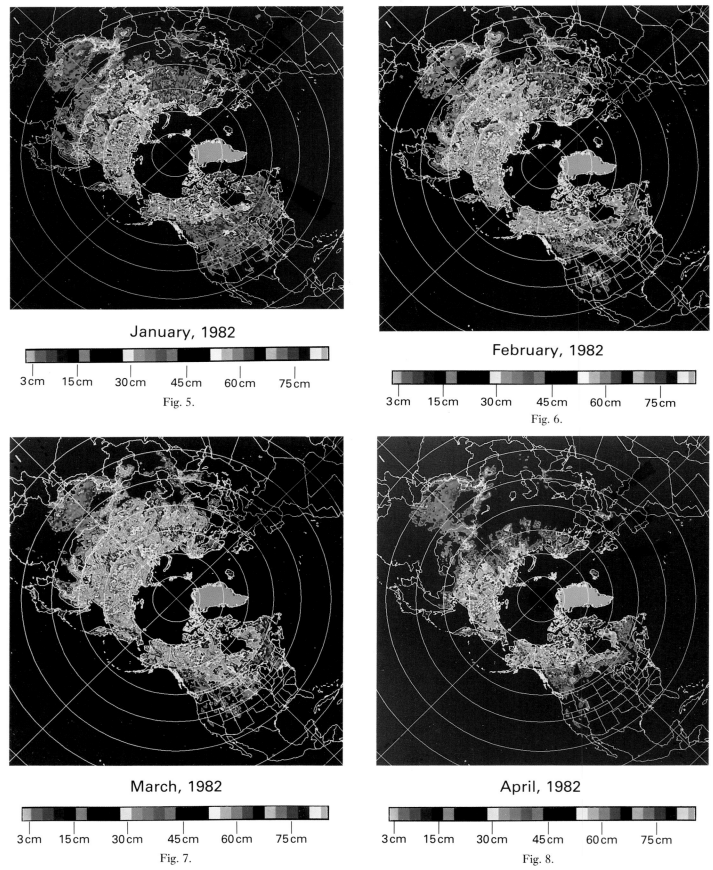

January, 1982

3cm 15cm 30cm 45cm 60cm 75cm

Fig. 5.

February, 1982

3cm 15cm 30cm 45cm 60cm 75cm

Fig. 6.

March, 1982

3cm 15cm 30cm 45cm 60cm 75cm

Fig. 7.

April, 1982

3cm 15cm 30cm 45cm 60cm 75cm

Fig. 8.

Figs. 1–10. (*cont.*)

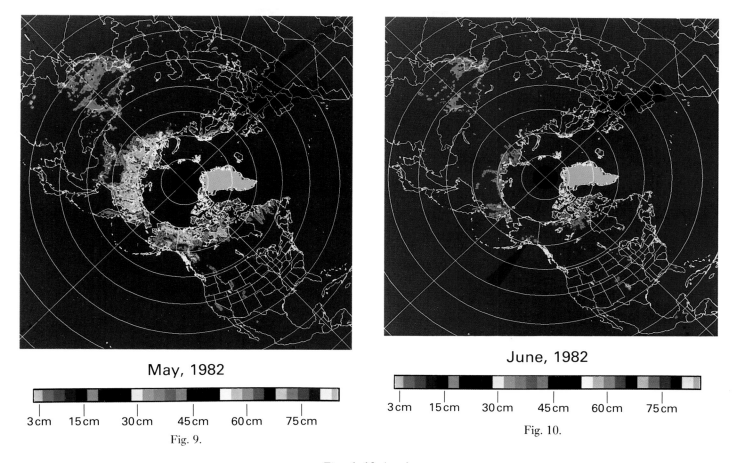

May, 1982

3 cm   15 cm   30 cm   45 cm   60 cm   75 cm

Fig. 9.

June, 1982

3 cm   15 cm   30 cm   45 cm   60 cm   75 cm

Fig. 10.

Figs. 1–10. (*cont.*)

Comparison with other data sets

Plots of seasonal and annual variability in snow extent have been produced from NOAA data as well as SMMR data, but the error bands are lacking for both products. The SMMR and NOAA products agree fairly well but the SMMR data produces consistently lower (an average of about 10%) snow cover area estimates than does the NOAA data. The error in the SMMR derived snow depths is more difficult to assess because there is no reliable data set that is sufficiently dense spatially against which to compare the SMMR derived snow depths on a hemispheric and monthly basis. The only other data set available to derive global snow depth is a data set produced by the RAND Corporation. The monthly averaged RAND snow depth data set was constructed by using climatological averages from meteorological station data. Preliminary comparisons between the SMMR and the RAND data sets for snow depth in the Northern Hemisphere indicate that the data sets are comparable. For the month of March, for example, the snow mass is 290×10^{16} g and 364×10^{16} g as determined from the SMMR and RAND data sets

respectively. The error bands are unknown and may be large; however this SMMR temporal data set is the only source of monthly snow depth currently available (Chang, Foster & Hall, 1990).

Trends

Fluctuations of snow depth and extent can be viewed in part as consequences of the varying large-scale circulation. There is a large amount of natural variability in snow extent and snow depth (Fig. 11). This variability is imperfectly known due to the relatively short period of record, and several decades or more of such data may be needed in order to discern if a trend exists. But no sustained trend in snow cover is observable from the NOAA data (1966–present) or from the shorter SMMR snow cover and snow depth record (1979–1987) (Figs. 12–20). However, indirect evidence indicates that changes in cryospheric features may already be in progress. A 2 °C to 4 °C rise in permafrost temperature has been measured in northern Alaska over the last 100 years, and melt water from small valley glaciers has apparently con-

Northern Hemisphere

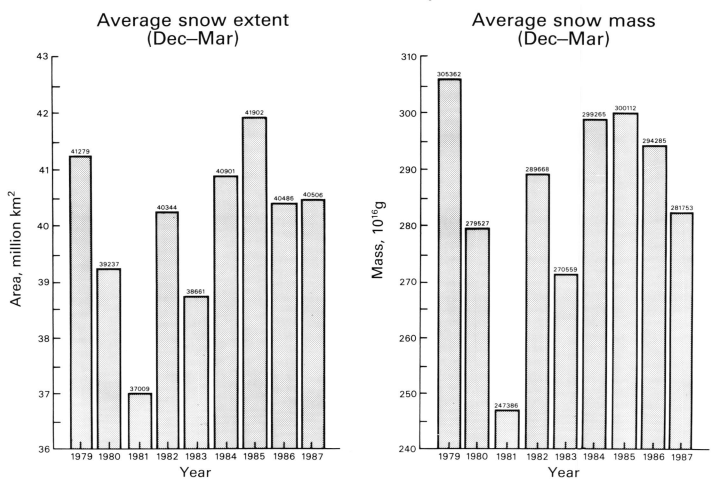

Fig. 11. Bar graphs showing the extent and mass of snow in the Northern Hemisphere (1979–1987) as derived from the Nimbus-7 SMMR.

tributed up to 50% of the observed rise in sea level since about 1900. Even though satellite snow cover records are too short at present to determine definite trends, continued monitoring is essential and may provide an early indication of the onset of a warming signal or some other climatic fluctuation.

When interpreting the SMMR data to see if trends exist it is, of course, essential to know if the sensor has been stable over the period of record. As determined over large ocean areas, it appears that both the 37 GHz channel and the 18 GHz channel have warmed up by about 2 K between 1979 and 1987. However, because both channels have drifted in synchrony, the effects of the drift on the difference in brightness temperature is considered to be inconsequential.

The establishment of the microwave snow data set has permitted a quantitative assessment to be made of changes in global snow mass, and has demonstrated that considerable

seasonal and inter-annual variability exists. The Special Sensor Microwave Imager (SSM/I) on board the Defense Meteorological Satellite Program (DMSP), launched in June of 1987, is continuing the snow measurements made by SMMR until it lost its ability to scan in the summer of 1987. The SSM/I operates at four frequencies (19.35, 22.24, 37.00 and 85.00 GHz) and provides near global coverage every day. It is hoped that the SSM/I will operate without interruption or malfunction until the next generation of microwave sensors can be launched on the Earth Observation System (EOS) in the late 1990s.

Limitations

There are, as expected, complications which arise when trying to apply an algorithm based on average snow conditions to specific regions where the climate, snowpack structure and

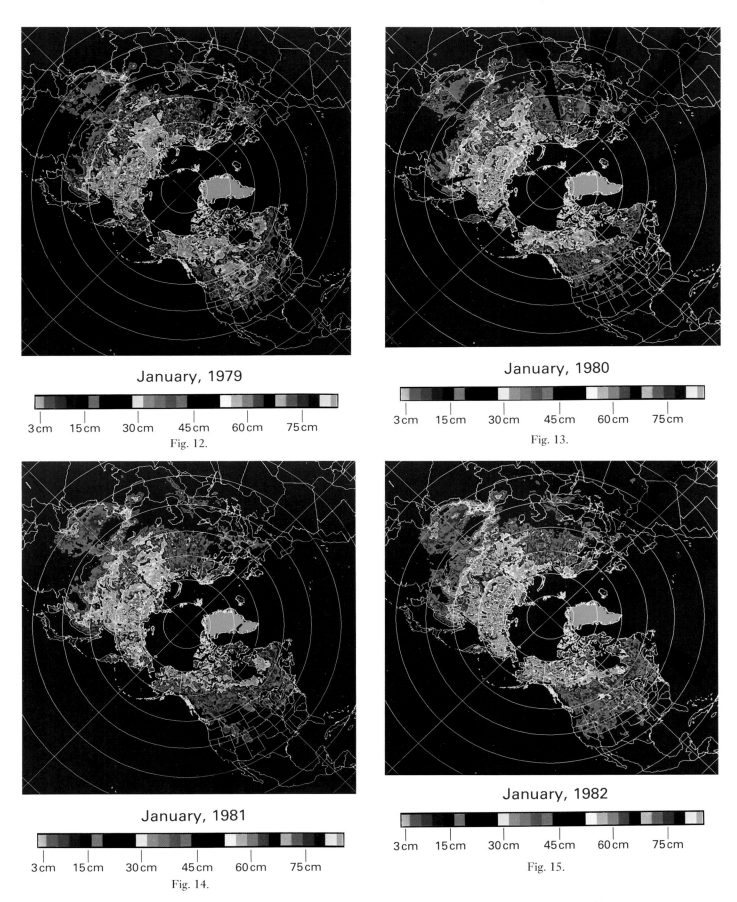

January, 1979

3 cm 15 cm 30 cm 45 cm 60 cm 75 cm

Fig. 12.

January, 1980

3 cm 15 cm 30 cm 45 cm 60 cm 75 cm

Fig. 13.

January, 1981

3 cm 15 cm 30 cm 45 cm 60 cm 75 cm

Fig. 14.

January, 1982

3 cm 15 cm 30 cm 45 cm 60 cm 75 cm

Fig. 15.

Figs. 12–20. Snow depth and snow cover maps of the Northern Hemisphere for the month of January (1979–1987) as derived from the Nimbus-7 SMMR.

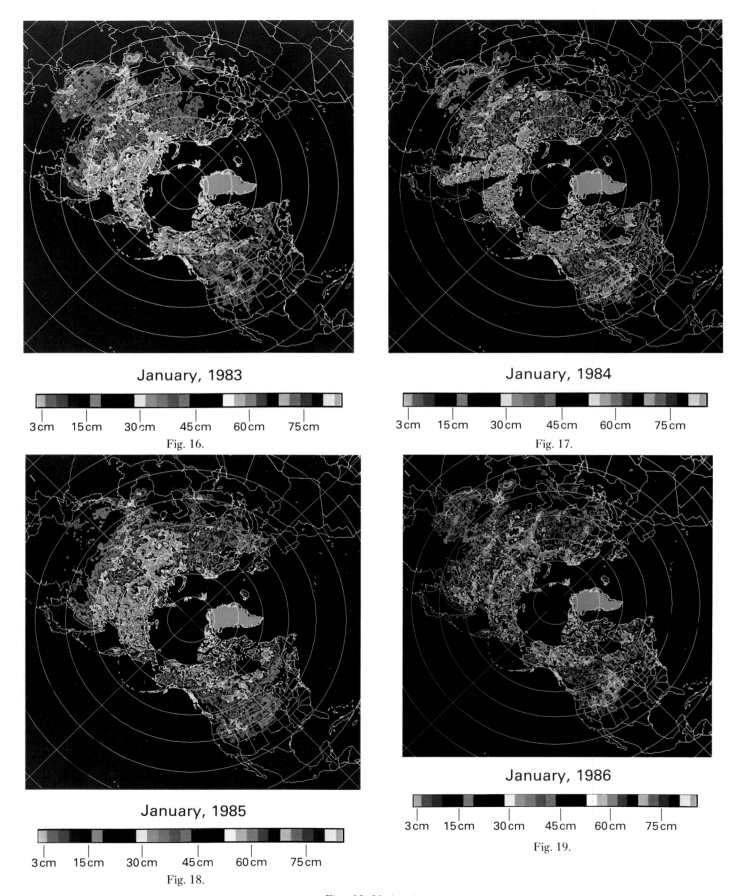

January, 1983

3 cm   15 cm   30 cm   45 cm   60 cm   75 cm

Fig. 16.

January, 1984

3 cm   15 cm   30 cm   45 cm   60 cm   75 cm

Fig. 17.

January, 1985

3 cm   15 cm   30 cm   45 cm   60 cm   75 cm

Fig. 18.

January, 1986

3 cm   15 cm   30 cm   45 cm   60 cm   75 cm

Fig. 19.

Figs. 12–20. (*cont.*)

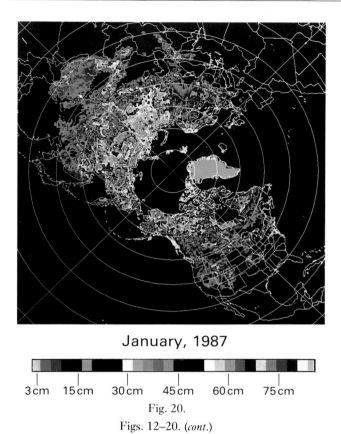

January, 1987

3cm   15cm   30cm   45cm   60cm   75cm

Fig. 20.

Figs. 12–20. (*cont.*)

vegetation may differ. Studies using radiative transfer modeling and SMMR data have demonstrated that snowpack structure significantly influences the microwave emission. Depth hoar, at the base of some snowpacks, consists of large snow grains (can exceed 5 mm) which are effective scatterers of microwave radiation at the 37 GHz and 18 GHz frequencies, causing a reduction in the microwave brightness temperatures (Hall, Chang & Foster, 1986). Additionally, in forested areas the greater emission from the trees may overwhelm the emission from the underlying ground. Thus the microwave brightness temperature of the snowpack is higher than if no trees were present. This is a major source of error in estimating the snowpack thickness in the dense boreal forest of eastern Canada (Foster *et al.*, 1991). Also, shallow, dry snow (< 5 cm) is nearly transparent to microwave radiation at 37 GHz which results in underestimates of snow extent and snow depth in the vicinity of the snow boundary. The 85 GHz channel on the SSM/I is capable of providing improved snow information in areas where the snow is less than about 10 cm. In some areas such as the Tibetian Plateau in southwestern China the snow depth is over-estimated using the global algorithm. This is because the atmosphere above the plateau, which in some areas is over 4750 m high, is relatively thin. At sea level the algorithm was tuned to minimize the atmospheric effects. But with increasing altitude (thinner atmosphere) the brightness temperatures recorded by the 37 GHz channel are colder relative to the 18 GHz channel. As a result of the larger difference in brightness temperature between the two channels, the derived snow cover is greater than is actually the case. These problems are currently being addressed and will lead to 'fine tuning' or adjusting of the global algorithms.

Applications

Although the microwave snow products are not yet being used in an operational mode, several ongoing studies point out the potential uses of the microwave snow data set. Snow cover and snow depth derived from microwave data are being used as inputs to general circulation models (GCMs) because SMMR data provide more realistic rather than climatologically prescribed global values of snow and the scale of the SMMR data is compatible with typical grid scales used in GCMs. Also, satellite microwave data have been used to evaluate the average areal water equivalent of snow in the Colorado River Basin in the western US. It has been shown that, even with the coarse resolution of the SMMR data (25 km at 37 GHz), the microwave approach can be used to obtain information about the snow water equivalent in some mountainous watersheds (Rango *et al.*, 1989). Additionally, there is a potential for using passive microwave data to detect areas of winterkill which results when grain planted in the fall, such as winter wheat, is damaged or killed because there was insufficient snow cover to insulate the young plants from subfreezing temperatures. Winterkill is most often experienced in the Great Plains of the US and Canada and in the Russian Steppes. Microwave maps of North America and Eurasia are useful for discerning areas of meager snow cover, and thus may be used as an indirect means to assess winterkill losses. SMMR data have also been used in conjunction with Lageos satellite data to compute the snow load excitation of the annual wobble of the Earth's rotation axis. The build-up and disappearance of snow excites polar motion producing a shift in the position of the rotation axis relative to a fixed geographic axis. It has been found that the snow-load excitation has an amplitude that is some 30% of the total annual wobble excitation, representing a significant geophysical contribution (Chao *et al.*, 1987).

Availability of data

The SMMR snow data set can be obtained in digital form from the Pilot Land Data System (PLDS) User Support Office at NASA/Goddard Space Flight Center: PLDS

USO/GSFC, Code 902.2, NASA/Goddard Space Flight Center, Greenbelt, Maryland USA 20771, (301) 286–9761.

References

Chang, A. T. C., Foster, J. L. & Hall, D. K. (1987). Nimbus-7 SMMR derived global snow cover parameters, *Ann. Glaciol.*, **9**, 39–44.

Chang, A. T. C., Foster, J. L. & Hall, D. K. (1990). Satellite estimates of Northern Hemisphere snow volume, *Rem. Sens. Lett.*, **11**, 167–72.

Chao, B., O'Connor, W. P., Chang, A. T. C., Hall, D. K. & Foster, J. L. (1987). Snow-load effect on the Earth's rotation and gravitational field, 1979–1985, *J. Geophys. Res.*, **92**, 9415–22.

Foster, J. L., Hall, D. K., Chang, A. T. C. & Rango, A. (1984). An overview of passive microwave snow research and results, *Rev. Geophys.*, **22**, 195–208.

Foster, J. L., Hall, D. K. & Chang, A. T. C. (1987). Remote sensing of snow, Eos Trans. AGU, 68, 681–4.

Foster, J. L., Chang, A. T. C., Hall, D. K. & Rango, A. (1991). Detection of snow water equivalent in boreal forests using microwave radiometry. *Arctic.* **44**, (1) 147–52.

Hall, D. K. (1988). Assessment of polar climatic change using satellite technology. *Rev. Geophys.*, **6**(21), 26–39.

Hall, D. K., Chang, A. T. C. & Foster, J. L. (1986). Detection of the depth-hoar layer in the snowpack of the Arctic coastal plain of Alaska, USA, using satellite data, *J. Glaciol.*, **32**, 87–94.

Hallikainen, M. & Jolma, P. (1987). Development of algorithms to retrieve the water equivalent of snow cover from satellite microwave radiometer data. *Rep. ESA SP-254*, 611–16, Eur. Space Agen., Zurich.

Jones, E. B. (1983). Snowpack ground-truth manual. *NASA Contractor Report 170584*.

Kukla, G., Barry, R. G., Hecht, A. & Wiesnet, D. (1985). Snow-Watch '85, Recommendations. *Glaciological Data GD-18*, Snow Watch '85, pp. 1–18.

Lydolph, P. E. (1977). Climates of the Soviet Union, *World Survey of Climatology*, vol. 7, Elsevier Publishing, 1977.

Matson, M., Ropelewski, C. F. & Varnadore, M. S. (1986). *An Atlas of Satellite-derived Northern Hemisphere Snow Cover Frequency*, Natl. Weather Serv., Washington, DC.

NASA (1982). Plan of research for snowpack properties remote sensing (PRS) recommendations of the Snowpack Properties Working Group, Goddard Space Flight Center, Greenbelt, Md.

Parkinson, C. L., Comiso, J. C., Zwally, H. J., Cavalieri, D. J., Gloersen, P. & Campbell, W. J. (1987). Arctic sea ice, 1973–1976: satellite passive-microwave observations, *NASA Spec. Publ.*, *SP-489*, 296pp.

Rango, A., Martinec, J., Chang, A., Foster, J. & van Katwijk, V. (1989). Average areal water equivalent of snow on a mountain basin using microwave and visible satellite data, *IEEE Trans.*, **GRS-27**, 740–5.

Global sea ice coverage

CLAIRE L. PARKINSON AND PER GLOERSEN

Introduction

Sea ice, ice that forms from the freezing of sea water, extends over a large and varying portion of the polar regions and affects both the overlying atmosphere and the underlying oceans in several important ways. For instance, it is a strong insulator, restricting exchanges of heat, mass, and momentum between ocean and atmosphere; it has a much higher short-wave albedo than does open water, so that the absorption of solar radiation at the Earth's surface is considerably reduced in the presence of a sea ice cover; and it tends to reject salt during freezing and aging, altering the salinity and density content of the upper ocean. At times, the salt rejection leads to deep convection and bottom water formation, thereby affecting water circulations throughout the oceans. In addition to its importance to the climate system, sea ice also provides a surface for polar animals, obstructs shipping activities, modifies submarine acoustics, and occasionally serves as a platform for oil drilling operations. It is thus a vital constituent of the polar regions (Fig. 1) from many different perspectives. More detail on the varied impacts of the sea ice cover can be found in Barry (1983) and in Parkinson *et al.* (1987).

The harshness of the polar environment has traditionally made sea ice a very difficult variable for which to obtain consistent long-term data sets. Satellite technology now eliminates the disadvantages of the harsh environment, although some ground observations are still essential for validating and properly interpreting the satellite observations. Satellite data for limited regions have been obtained from visible and near infra-red instruments since the 1960s, often with a resolution allowing the identification and tracking of individual ice floes (e.g. Fig. 2). These data can be very valuable for detailed regional studies, allowing, for instance, the determination of ice-floe shapes and sizes and the calculation of ice velocities (e.g. DeRycke, 1973; Dey, Moore & Gregory, 1979; Dey, 1981; Ito & Muller, 1982). However, the visible and near infra-red data are limited in their usefulness for large-scale, long-term climate studies because 1) the data have a resolution that, for all practical purposes, is too fine to allow global data coverage, 2) sea ice is obscured in the event of overlying clouds, and 3) the visible data are unobtainable during periods of darkness.

The advent of satellite passive microwave imagery in the early 1970s allowed for the first time the routine monitoring of global sea ice distributions. Although certain important aspects of the ice, such as ice thickness, were and still are unobtainable from satellites, the spatial pattern of sea ice distributions can be determined readily from the passive microwave data because of the significant contrast between the emissivities of sea ice and sea water at microwave wavelengths, sea ice having the higher values. This emissivity contrast allows not only the determination of sea ice distributions but, more quantitatively, the calculation of sea ice concentrations (spatial percentage coverages, in units of percent) and sea ice extents (areas covered by ice, in units of square kilometers). Furthermore, the microwave data are not restricted by darkness or by non-precipitating clouds, so that meaningful data can be obtained for all seasons of the year and all hours of the day. In addition, the data have coarse enough resolution to allow routine global monitoring and yet adequate resolution for identifying major changes in the sea ice cover and performing climate analyses.

The first passive microwave imager successfully launched into space was the Electrically Scanning Microwave Radiometer (ESMR) on board the Nimbus-5 satellite, launched in December 1972. This single-channel instrument was a cross-track scanner with incidence angle varying from 0° to 50°, and it recorded horizontally polarized radiation at a wavelength of 1.55 cm. At that wavelength, open water has an emissivity of approximately 0.44 whereas sea ice has much higher emissivities, generally within the range 0.80–0.98. The ESMR data have been used to determine and map global sea ice distributions and concentrations at a grid spacing of approximately 30 km. Although the spatial resolution of the microwave radiances varies significantly depending on the swath position of the instrument scan, ranging from approximately 30 km for data collected at nadir to as high as 100 km for data from the outer beam positions, in general the data used in the calculations are restricted to inner beam positions, yielding resolu-

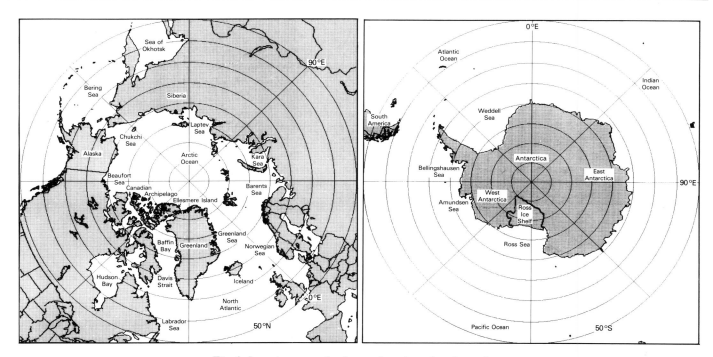

Fig. 1. Location maps for the north and south polar regions.

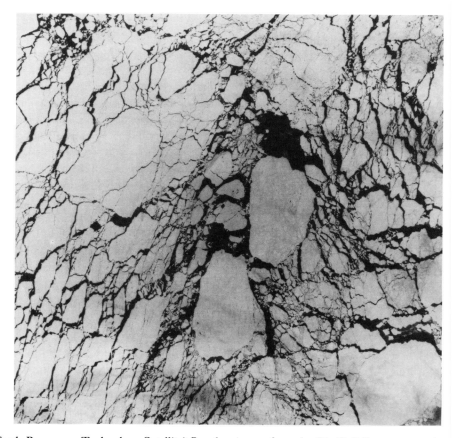

Fig. 2. Sample ERTS (Earth Resources Technology Satellite)/Landsat image from the Weddell Sea, at approximately 77° S and 40° W, on November 17, 1973.

tions of 30–50 km. An exception comes for the area poleward of 85° latitude, for which data coverage is limited to the outer beam positions and hence those positions are used in the calculations. The ESMR instrument transmitted high-quality data for most of the period 1973–1976, and monthly averages of the resulting data have been analyzed and compiled in two atlases of the sea ice cover, one for the south polar region (Zwally et al., 1983) and one for the north polar region (Parkinson et al., 1987).

In October 1978 a more advanced microwave instrument, the Scanning Multichannel Microwave Radiometer (SMMR), was launched on board the Nimbus-7 satellite. In contrast to the ESMR, which scanned the surface across the satellite track and had a wide range of incidence angles, the Nimbus-7 SMMR was a conical scanner with a constant incidence angle of 50°. The conical scanner permits the acquisition of both vertically and horizontally polarized data, and indeed the Nimbus-7 SMMR had 10 channels, receiving and transmitting both polarized components at wavelengths of 0.81, 1.4, 1.7, 2.8, and 4.6 cm. The spatial resolution of the data is dependent upon the wavelength and varies from approximately 30 km for the 0.81 cm channels to approximately 150 km for the 4.6 cm channels (Gloersen & Barath, 1977). The multi-channel nature of the SMMR led to reduced error bars for the calculated sea ice concentrations and additionally allowed the determination, for the wintertime ice cover in the Arctic, of the concentrations of two primary ice types: ice that has not undergone a summer melt period, termed 'first-year ice', and ice that has undergone a summer melt period, termed 'multiyear ice' (Cavalieri, Gloersen & Campbell, 1984). Unfortunately, the Nimbus-7 orbit and the 780 km width of the SMMR swath did not allow SMMR data coverage poleward of about 84.6° latitude, eliminating a 5.4° latitude region in the central Arctic Ocean and an equivalently sized region on the Antarctic continent. Also, the SMMR instrument was generally operated on an every-other-day basis, rather than continuously. An atlas presenting monthly averages of sea ice concentrations derived from the SMMR data and analyzing the SMMR sea ice data set has been produced by Gloersen et al. (1992). The atlas includes Northern and Southern Hemisphere monthly average total ice concentration images for each month November 1978 through August 1987, plus Arctic multiyear ice concentrations for the winter months and, in an appendix, derived monthly average sea ice temperatures for each hemisphere. The ice concentration algorithm, issues of calibration, instrument drift, and validation, and many aspects of the sea ice cover revealed by the SMMR data are all discussed in detail (Gloersen et al., 1992).

SMMR data coverage continued through mid-August 1987, by which time the Defense Meteorological Satellite Program (DMSP) had, in June 1987, launched a special sensor microwave imager (SSMI). The seven-channel DMSP SSMI incorporates the conical scanning design, with a constant incidence angle of 53°. The SSMI measures dual-polarized radiation at wavelengths of 0.35, 0.81, and 1.55 cm and singly polarized radiation at 1.35 cm. The DMSP orbit and the 1394 km swath width of the SSMI allow data coverage everywhere equatorwards of 87.6° north and south latitude. Details on the SSMI instrument can be found in Hollinger et al. (1987), and a discussion and validation of sea ice concentrations derived from the SSMI data can be found in Cavalieri et al. (1991). Plans exist for a continuing sequence of DMSP SSMI instruments. Furthermore, a Multifrequency Imaging Microwave Radiometer (MIMR) is planned for the Earth Observing System near the end of the 1990s. It thus appears likely that passive microwave data coverage of the polar regions will continue on an uninterrupted basis indefinitely into the future, providing a lengthening sea ice data set for climate studies.

Satellite active microwave imaging is also proving extremely valuable for sea ice research. Synthetic Aperture Radar (SAR) emits microwave energy and measures the reflected signal. This active microwave technique shares with passive microwave imaging the advantages of being able to obtain measurements of the Earth's surface through clouds and during periods of darkness. SAR data have much finer resolution than passive microwave data, so that they are less appropriate for routine global coverage but can be used for identifying individual ice floes and carrying out the types of detailed studies also possible with visible and near infra-red imagery, although with the major advantage of not being hindered by cloud or darkness. SAR instruments have flown on NASA's Seasat in 1978, on the European Remote Sensing Satellite (ERS-1), launched in 1991, and on the Japanese Earth Resources Satellite (JERS-1), launched in 1992. A SAR instrument is also planned for the Canadian Radarsat scheduled for launch in 1995. The Seasat SAR data have been used in several sea ice studies (e.g. Fu & Holt, 1982; Leberl et al., 1983; Lee & Yang, 1987; Carsey & Pihos, 1989), and plans exist for extensive use of the ERS-1 SAR data, JERS-1 data, and the anticipated Radarsat data. The SAR capabilities and results, however, will not be elaborated here, because of the emphasis in this chapter and book on large-scale, repeated observations appropriate for climate studies. The coarser resolution of the passive microwave data, and the resultant feasibility of routine global monitoring on the order of every few days, makes the passive microwave data much more applicable than the active microwave data for long-term, global studies. Hence the concentration in the remainder of this chapter will be on the passive microwave data and the results obtained from them.

Methodology

The large contrast in the microwave emissivities of sea ice and liquid water is the crucial factor making satellite passive microwave measurements so valuable for sea ice studies. With a single channel of microwave information, as from the Nimbus-5 ESMR, approximate sea ice concentrations can be calculated in locations where the ice and water emissivities can realistically be accepted as constants, by assuming a linear relationship between the observed microwave brightness temperature, T_B, and the brightness temperatures of the ice and water. ('Brightness temperature' is a variable frequently used to represent the intensity of microwave radiation thermally emitted by an object. It is given in units of temperature, made appropriate because of the approximate proportionality between emitted radiation at microwave wavelengths and the physical temperature of the radiating layer.) Labelling the ice and water emissivities as ε_I and ε_w and the physical temperatures of the ice and water as T_I and T_w, then the respective brightness temperatures are $\varepsilon_I T_I$ and $\varepsilon_w T_w$, and the approximate ice concentration, C, is:

$$C = \frac{T_B - \varepsilon_w T_w}{\varepsilon_I T_I - \varepsilon_w T_w} \quad (1)$$

In the case of horizontally polarized radiation at a wavelength of 1.55 cm, as received and transmitted by the ESMR, a constant value of 0.44 is appropriate for ε_w in Equation 1. However, ε_I varies with such conditions as the age of the ice, its surface salinity, and its air and liquid-water contents. In much of the Southern Ocean and many of the peripheral seas of the Arctic, sea ice is predominantly first-year ice and has an emissivity of approximately 0.92. In such locations, Equation 1 can be used to calculate ice concentrations from the ESMR data, with ε_w and ε_I set at 0.44 and 0.92, respectively. In the central Arctic Ocean, on the other hand, much of the multiyear ice has a lower microwave emissivity, due in part to radiation scattering within air pockets remaining after brine drainage has occurred in the freeboard layer of the ice during the summer melt season. This complicates the determination of ice concentrations from the single-channel ESMR data in regions with a mixture of ice types (Campbell et al., 1976) and leaves an ambiguity in the determination of ice concentrations (see Carsey (1982) and Parkinson et al. (1987) for details).

To adjust for this ambiguity in the presence of a mixture of ice types, the single variable ice concentration scale used in mapping ice concentrations in regions with predominantly one ice type is replaced by a nomogram incorporating both ice concentration and multiyear ice fraction. In the nomogram, a sample of which is given in the following section (see Fig. 5), the scale on the horizontal axis is for the fraction of multiyear ice, while lines of equal total ice concentration slope downward across the face of the nomogram, reflecting the fact that as the fraction of multiyear ice increases, a given brightness temperature will correspond to a higher total ice concentration (because the emissivity of multiyear ice is closer to that of open water than the emissivity of first-year ice is). For a known fraction of multiyear ice, the nomogram associates with each color a range of total ice concentrations covering about 4%, as in the case of the corresponding single variable ice concentration scales (e.g., see Figs. 4, 7, 8). However, when the fraction of multiyear ice is unknown, then the range in ice concentration values associated with a given color can be greatly increased. For example, referring to the nomogram in Fig. 5 in the next section, deep green signifies total ice concentrations ranging anywhere from 44% for regions of no multiyear ice to 58% for regions where all the ice is multiyear ice. This shows the effect that the ambiguity produced by having a mixture of ice types has on increasing the error bars for the ice concentrations calculated from the ESMR data.

The ambiguities inherent in calculating sea ice concentrations with single-channel data can be reduced or even eliminated by using multichannel data and appropriate geophysical algorithms. Cavalieri et al. (1984) and Gloersen and Cavalieri (1986) have used the 0.81 and 1.7 cm channels of the SMMR to calculate total ice concentrations and multiyear ice concentrations based on the following polarization ratio (PR) and spectral gradient ratio (GR):

$$PR = \frac{T_B(V,1.7) - T_B(H,1.7)}{T_B(V,1.7) + T_B(H,1.7)} \quad (2)$$

$$GR = \frac{T_B(V,0.81) - T_B(V,1.7)}{T_B(V,0.81) + T_B(V,1.7)} \quad (3)$$

where $T_B(V, \lambda)$ and $T_B(H, \lambda)$ are the brightness temperatures at wavelength λ (given in centimeters in Equations 2 and 3) for vertically and horizontally polarized radiation, respectively. The PR values for water significantly exceed those for ice; and in wintertime GR is distinctly positive for water, negative for multiyear ice, and near zero (slightly negative) for first-year ice. These contrasts allow the calculation of ice concentrations C and wintertime multiyear ice concentrations C_M, as detailed in Gloersen et al. (1992). The results for the Northern Hemisphere are:

$$C = \frac{2091.92 - 5054(PR) - 8744(GR) - 1600(PR)(GR)}{1648.2 + 7735.6(PR) - 4112.2(GR) - 10\,200(PR)(GR)} \quad (4)$$

$$C_M = \frac{-690.38 + 14\,990(PR) - 27\,579(GR) - 43\,260(PR)(GR)}{1648.2 + 7735.6(PR) - 4112.2(GR) - 10\,200(PR)(GR)} \quad (5)$$

The multiyear ice calculations produce meaningful values only when the ice surface is dry, as a wet surface obscures the first-year/multiyear contrast. Thus the multiyear ice calculations are not reliable during summer or at anytime near the seaward ice edge. In the case of the Southern Hemisphere, because of the limited amount of ice that experiences summer melt and then survives into the winter with the microwave signatures typical of Arctic multiyear ice, multiyear ice concentrations are generally not calculated. However, the same GR/PR-based algorithm is used in the calculation of total ice concentrations, although with coefficients corresponding to 'Type A' and 'Type B' ice, terms left intentionally ambiguous to avoid, in the absence of appropriate *in situ* data, identifying them explicitly with specific geophysical ice types. The labels 'Type A' and 'Type B' are meant simply to refer to two types of ice in the Southern Ocean with distinctly different microwave signatures. The formulations for total ice concentrations, C, and Type B ice concentrations, C_B, for the Antarctic are:

$$C = \frac{2301.95 - 5648(PR) - 9422(GR) - 1473(PR)(GR)}{1950.5 + 6585.7(PR) - 417.6(GR) - 5052.8(PR)(GR)} \quad (6)$$

$$C_B = \frac{-569.75 + 15{,}142(PR) - 29{,}096(GR) - 44{,}808(PR)(GR)}{1950.5 + 6585.7(PR) - 417.6(GR) - 5052.8(PR)(GR)} \quad (7)$$

Fig. 3 presents plots of the relationship between GR, PR, and the total and multiyear ice concentrations for the Arctic and the relationship between GR, PR, and the total and Type B ice concentrations for the Antarctic.

Alternative algorithms for the calculation of ice concentrations from the multi-channel SMMR data also exist (e.g. Svendsen *et al.*, 1983; Swift, Fedor & Ramseier, 1985; Comiso, 1986), but the Cavalieri *et al.* (1984) algorithm has been widely applied and is the one used, in the revised form of Equations 2–7, to generate the SMMR ice concentration images for the SMMR sea ice atlas of Gloersen *et al.* (1992) and for Figs. 4, 6, and 7 in the next section.

Analysis and results

The ESMR data have been compiled into 3-day composites and monthly averages and mapped onto polar stereographic projections gridded into a 293×293 format enclosing the $50°$ latitude circle. The resulting pixel size is approximately 30×30 km. The SMMR data have been compiled into daily composites (every other day) and monthly averages and mapped with several different projections and grids. The projection used here for the SMMR data is equal-latitude and pole-

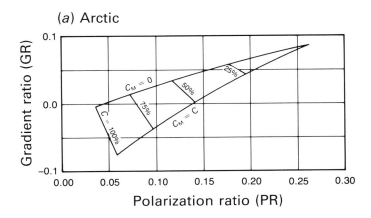

(a) Arctic

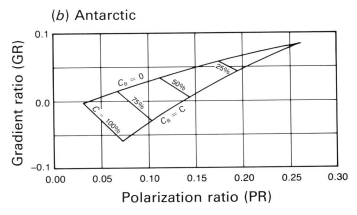

(b) Antarctic

Fig. 3. (*a*) Relationship between the gradient ratio, polarization ratio, sea ice concentration, C, and multiyear ice concentration, C_M, in the Arctic, based on Equations 4 and 5. (*b*) Relationship between the gradient ratio, polarization ratio, sea ice concentration, C, and Type B ice concentration, C_B, in the Antarctic, based on Equations 6 and 7.

centered, and the grid is a 461×461 square grid, again enclosing the $50°$ latitude circle.

The ice-concentration maps have been color-coded for easy visualization, although the reader is cautioned that the color scales are not identical for the ESMR and SMMR products. In all cases, land areas are artificially masked, open ocean appears as light blue, and 22 shades of blue, green, yellow, brown, and red represent sea ice concentrations ranging from 12% (for the SMMR data) or 14% (for the ESMR data) to 100%. Each color shade corresponds to an ice concentration increment of 4%. In most instances, the sea ice edge is easily identifiable on the maps, as it generally occurs at a fairly sharp transition from the light blue of open ocean to the yellows, browns, and reds of the sea ice cover. The gridded sea ice concentrations have also been integrated to obtain time series of the area of sea ice coverage in each of several regions in the Arctic and Antarctic, as well as in the north and south polar regions as a whole (Zwally *et al.*, 1983; Parkinson

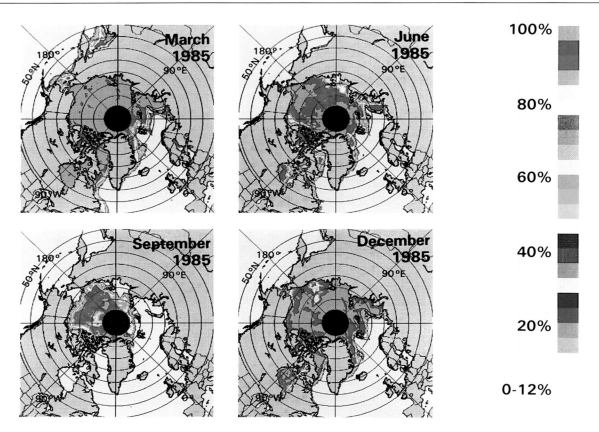

Fig. 4. Monthly average sea ice concentrations for the north polar region for March, June, September, and December 1985, from the data of the Nimbus-7 SMMR. The black circular area in the midst of the Arctic Ocean signifies missing data.

et al., 1987; Parkinson & Cavalieri, 1989; Gloersen *et al.*, 1992).

Arctic sea ice distributions

The passive microwave data reveal that sea ice extent in the Northern Hemisphere typically ranges from a minimum of approximately 8×10^6 km^2 in September to a maximum of approximately 15×10^6 km^2 in March (Parkinson & Cavalieri, 1989). In September ice covers much of the central Arctic Ocean and portions of the Canadian Archipelago and the Greenland Sea. By the end of October ice covers almost the entire Arctic Ocean and Canadian Archipelago, and extends well south along the east coast of Greenland. The ice cover expands rapidly during the next two months, with most of Baffin Bay and the Kara Sea ice covered by the end of November, and Hudson Bay and the northern Bering Sea ice covered by the end of December. Expansion continues at a slower rate in January and February, with the ice by the March maximum generally covering almost the entire Arctic Ocean, Canadian Archipelago, Kara Sea, Baffin Bay, and Hudson Bay, plus large portions of the Sea of Okhotsk, Ber-

ing Sea, Greenland Sea, Davis Strait, and Barents Sea. Retreat generally proceeds slowly in March and April, when it tends to be most pronounced in the Sea of Okhotsk. By mid-May noticeable retreat has also occurred in the Bering Sea and at the open-water ice edge in the North Atlantic vicinity. By mid-June major openings appear in the ice cover of the remaining regions, and by mid-July most of the ice of Hudson Bay, Davis Strait, and Baffin Bay has disappeared. By August the ice cover is close to its September minimum, with significant coastal openings around much of the Arctic Ocean and little or no ice remaining in most of the peripheral seas and bays. Fig. 4 shows the seasonal cycle of the sea ice cover in the Northern Hemisphere for 1985, a fairly typical year in the 1970s and 1980s.

The strong spatial asymmetry in the wintertime sea ice cover (Fig. 4) is caused by a variety of geographic, oceanographic, and atmospheric factors, a fact that can be illustrated by the contrasting cases of Hudson Bay and the southern Barents Sea. Hudson Bay tends to be fully ice covered in winter in spite of being situated in lower latitudes (52–65° N) than many regions that are free of ice throughout the year. This is in large part due to the positioning of Hudson Bay in

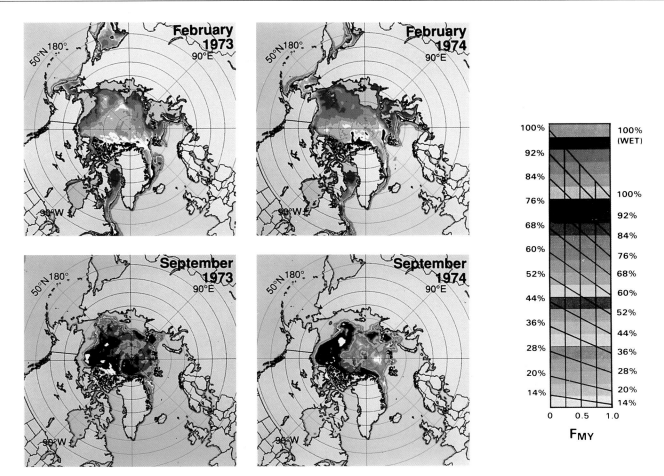

Fig. 5. Monthly average February and September sea ice concentrations for the north polar region for 1973 and 1974, from the data of the Nimbus-5 ESMR. See text for discussion of the nomogram, made necessary by the ambiguities in determining ice concentrations from single-channel data in regions with a mixture of ice types. F_{MY} is the fraction of multiyear ice, whereas the values listed on each side of the nomogram are total ice concentrations, with lines of equal total ice concentration sloping downward across the face of the nomogram. (Rearranged from Parkinson *et al.*, 1987.)

the midst of the North American continent, making it subject to colder winters and warmer summers than oceanic regions at the same latitudes, and to the fact that its openings to warmer waters are very limited. In contrast, the southern Barents Sea tends to remain free of ice even in the midst of winter (Fig. 4) in spite of its high latitudes (70–75° N). This results largely from the warm water advected into the Barents Sea by the north-flowing Norwegian Current.

The Northern Hemisphere ice cover exhibits prominent inter-annual variations in each month, and these are illustrated in Fig. 5 with February and September ice concentration images for 1973 and 1974. A few highlights of specific examples of the inter-annual differences visible in Fig. 5 will be mentioned, although others are clearly visible as well. In February 1973 sea ice covered almost the entire Sea of Okhotsk, whereas in February 1974 only half the sea was ice covered; and in February 1973 a large extension of ice

occurred eastward from the main ice field of the Greenland Sea, whereas this extension did not exist in February 1974. In contrast, February ice coverage in the Bering Sea was greater in 1974 than in 1973. For analysis of the inter-annual contrasts in the Sea of Okhotsk and the Bering Sea and comparison with atmospheric pressure fields, the reader is referred to Parkinson (1990) and Cavalieri and Parkinson (1987). Many other inter-annual differences in both the ice distributions and the ice concentrations are apparent from the two February images of Fig. 5, as are noticeable inter-annual consistencies, such as the full ice coverage in Hudson Bay, the absence of ice in most of the Barents Sea, and the extension of ice along the entire east coast of Greenland (Fig. 5).

The September images of Fig. 5 show inter-annual differences in late summer that are comparable to the winter inter-annual differences shown in the February images. For instance, the ice had retreated far more from the northeast

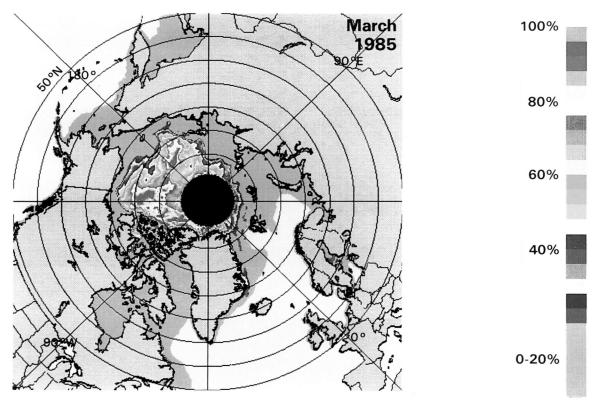

Fig. 6. Monthly average multiyear ice concentrations for the Arctic for March 1985, from the data of the Nimbus-7 SMMR. Medium blue signifies areas with first-year ice but no multiyear ice concentrations as high as 20%, and light blue signifies open water.

coast of Alaska in September 1973 than in September 1974 but far less from the northeast coast of Siberia. Among the consistencies in the Septembers of these two years is the persistence of ice along the north coasts of Greenland and the Canadian Archipelago and along the northern half of the east coast of Greenland (Fig. 5).

Because the SMMR data have been used to calculate wintertime multiyear ice concentrations as well as total ice concentrations, a sample multiyear ice concentration image is included for March 1985 (Fig. 6). The March 1985 image shows high multiyear ice concentrations north of Greenland and the Canadian Archipelago, where the ice cover is known to be frequently highly concentrated and ridged (Bourke & Garrett, 1987). Although the multiyear ice concentrations have larger error bars than the total ice concentrations and have been less thoroughly validated with *in situ* data, the possibility of routinely determining multiyear ice coverage from the multi-channel SMMR and SSMI data is considered a major advance over the possibilities available with the single channel ESMR data. In particular, because multiyear ice is quasi-conservative in the Arctic Basin during the winter season, its distribution can be used to infer patterns of ice motion, as done by Zwally and Walsh (1987). In a later study,

Walsh and Zwally (1990) compare SMMR multiyear ice concentrations with model calculations, finding the simulated concentrations of multiyear ice to be slightly higher than the SMMR-derived values, although finding good agreement between the simulated and observed total coverage of multiyear ice. Arctic multiyear ice concentration images for all winter months of the SMMR record are included in the SMMR atlas of Gloersen *et al.* (1992).

Antarctic sea ice distributions

The sea ice cover of the Southern Hemisphere, unconstrained by land along its equatorward perimeter, experiences a seasonal cycle having a much greater amplitude than that of the ice cover in the Northern Hemisphere. In the Southern Hemisphere, the ice extent typically ranges from a minimum of approximately 4×10^6 km^2 in February, only half the minimum in the Northern Hemisphere, to a maximum of approximately 20×10^6 km^2 in September, which exceeds by about 5×10^6 km^2 the maximum in the Northern Hemisphere. In February, the Southern Hemisphere ice is concentrated in the Weddell, Bellingshausen, Amundsen, and eastern Ross seas, with only a narrow fringe of ice exist-

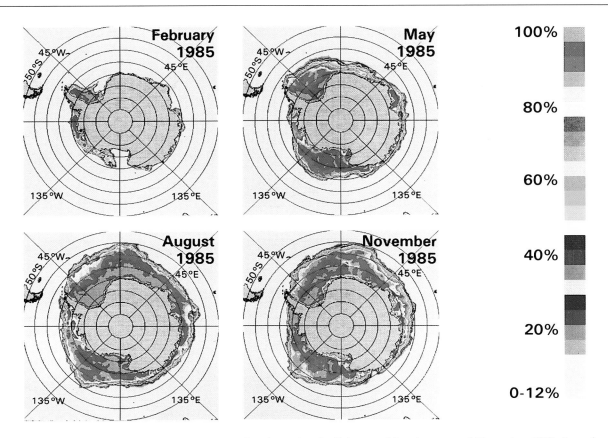

Fig. 7. Monthly average sea ice concentrations for the south polar region for February, May, August, and November 1985, from the data of the Nimbus-7 SMMR.

ing around most of the rest of the Antarctic continent (Fig. 7). Late summer expansion of the ice cover is generally most noticeable in the eastern Ross Sea, and early autumn expansion is most noticeable in the entire Ross Sea and the central and eastern Weddell Sea. By May the ice cover has expanded northward to about 65° S in the Ross Sea and around much of the eastern portion of the continent, while lagging somewhat in the Bellingshausen and Amundsen seas and extending outward to near 60° S in the western Weddell Sea. Growth continues around the continent for the next 3–4 months, although with temporary intervals of decay in individual localities. At maximum ice coverage, the ice surrounds the Antarctic continent and at most longitudes extends equatorward to between 55° and 65° S. At this time, the ice edge is generally farthest north in the eastern Weddell Sea near the Greenwich meridian and farthest south in the western Bellingshausen Sea. Decay of the ice proceeds slowly in early Spring but then very rapidly from October to January. A primary anomaly in the generally southward retreat of the ice edge occurs in the Ross Sea, where a large polynya consistently opens off the coast of the Ross Ice Shelf in November or December and then expands northward, contributing

to a local decay of the ice pack from the south to the north. By January the western Ross Sea is nearly free of ice, although considerable ice remains to the east. Fig. 7 shows the seasonal cycle of the sea ice cover in the Southern Hemisphere for 1985; full sets of monthly images for the ESMR and SMMR Southern Hemisphere data sets can be found in Zwally *et al.* (1983) and in Gloersen *et al.* (1992), respectively.

The asymmetry in the typical Antarctic growth/decay cycle, with the spring/summer decay occurring more rapidly (September to February) than the fall/winter growth (February to September), contrasts with the more symmetric growth/decay cycle typical in the Arctic, where ice extent minima and maxima tend to be about six months apart, occurring in September and March (see previous section). Gordon (1981) suggests that the contrast between the Northern and Southern Hemispheres reflects fundamental differences in the heat budgets of the sea ice in the two regions. In particular, the rapid decay of the Antarctic ice is likely related to significantly greater upwelling of relatively warm deep water than occurs in the Arctic, as the atmosphere-to-ocean heat flux alone appears insufficient to account for the observed rate of melting, especially during the period of most rapid

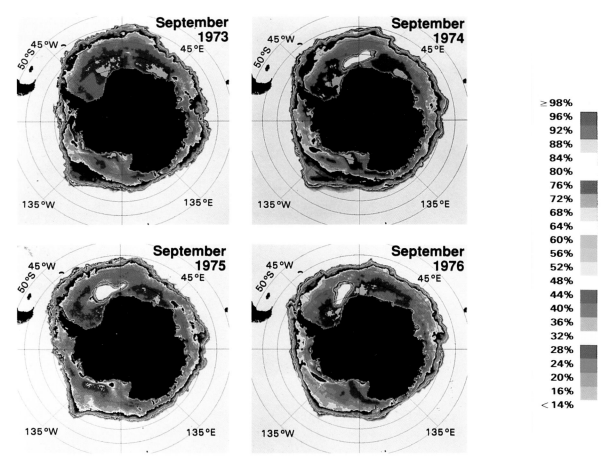

Fig. 8. Monthly average September sea ice concentrations for the south polar region for 1973, 1974, 1975, and 1976, from the data of the Nimbus-5 ESMR. (Rearranged from Zwally *et al.*, 1983.)

melt, from mid-November to mid-January (Gordon, 1981).

Similarly to the ice in the Northern Hemisphere, the sea ice cover in the Southern Hemisphere experiences noticeable inter-annual variations. These are illustrated in Fig. 8 with September ESMR images for each of the four years 1973–1976. One of the most striking inter-annual contrasts apparent in these images is the occurrence at about 0° E and 67° S of a large open water region (the Weddell polynya) in 1974–1976 and its absence in 1973. Over the three winters of its existence, there was a noticeable westward shift in the location of the polynya, accompanied by a change in shape (Fig. 8). This open water region has been the topic of much discussion in the past two decades (e.g. Gordon, 1978; Carsey, 1980; Martinson, Killworth & Gordon, 1981; Parkinson, 1983; Zwally *et al.*, 1983; Lemke, 1987; Gordon & Huber, 1990) and highlights not only the inter-annual variability of the sea ice cover but also remaining uncertainties regarding generating mechanisms for major polynyas and the relative importance of oceanic, atmospheric, and internal ice proces-

ses. The polynya has not reoccurred since 1976 at even close to the size and duration experienced in 1974–1976.

Limitations

There are several important limitations of the satellite passive microwave data for sea ice studies, among the most important being the limitations due to coarse resolution, the limitations due to imperfect algorithms, the limitations due to the specific satellite orbits, and the limitations due to the brevity of the satellite record. Each of these will be discussed in turn.

Resolution

The approximately 30 km spatial resolution of the satellite passive microwave data, although appropriate for climatic and other large-scale studies, is too coarse to allow identification of individual ice floes and hence to track floes or determine floe shapes and sizes. Other satellite data can be used for such determinations, however, and those data, from Landsat, Synthetic Aperture Radar (SAR), and other high resolution instruments, can complement the satellite passive microwave record by providing a high degree of detail in select local areas. The reader is referred to Hall and Martinec (1985) for an overview of the uses of these higher resolution data for sea ice studies, as well as an overview of the properties of the sensors. Another problem aggravated by the coarse resolution of the passive microwave data is the issue of land contamination, whereby the ice concentration calculations often lead to a spurious indication of ice in near coastal open water areas because of the existence of land (with high brightness temperatures generally at or above the brightness temperatures of ice and well above the brightness temperatures of open water) within the field of view of the sensor (e.g. see the discussion in Parkinson & Cavalieri, 1989).

Algorithms

The algorithms used to convert from the radiances transmitted by the satellite passive microwave sensors to the desired geophysical sea ice parameters entail several simplifications and uncertainties. Snow cover, temperature, moisture, surface salinity, air bubbles, and meltponding all have effects on the microwave emissions of the ice surface and yet generally are not explicitly incorporated in the algorithms. Also, atmospheric constituents and processes alter the amount of microwave radiation received by the satellite, and these are only partially accounted for in the calculations. All such complications can lead to errors in the calculated ice concentrations. Taking all the various uncertainties into consideration, accuracy estimates for the calculated sea ice concentrations are 15–25% for the ESMR data (Zwally et al., 1983; Parkinson et al., 1987) and 5–9% for the SMMR data (Cavalieri et al., 1984; Steffen & Maslanik, 1988). The highest uncertainties (about 25%) for the ESMR data occur in situations with an unknown mixture of first-year and multiyear ice. In the case of multiyear ice concentrations calculated from the SMMR data, the precision is estimated to be 13–25% (Cavalieri et al., 1984). The algorithm used for calculating ice concentrations from the SSMI data has the same basic formulation as the SMMR algorithm, although with different coefficients. A study recently completed for validating the SSMI data in the Beaufort and Chukchi seas (Cavalieri et al., 1991) has found good correspondence between sea ice concentrations derived from the satellite passive microwave data and those determined from coincident aircraft data, but less satisfactory results for the multiyear ice concentrations. The SSMI algorithm appears to overestimate multiyear ice con-

centrations by about 9%, while the mean differences between total ice concentrations obtained from the SSMI and those obtained from the aircraft range from −3% to +5% (Cavalieri et al., 1991).

Orbits

Although the orbit of the Nimbus-5 satellite allowed global data coverage by the ESMR instrument, the orbits of subsequent satellites carrying passive microwave sensors have instead allowed near-global but not fully global coverage. Due to the orbit of the Nimbus-7 satellite and the swath of the SMMR, there are no data from the Nimbus-7 SMMR for the region poleward of 84.6° latitude. Due to the orbit of the DMSP satellite and the swath of the SSMI, there are no data from the DMSP SSMI for the smaller region poleward of 87.6° latitude. The affected region in the Southern Hemisphere is located over the Antarctic continent; but in the Northern Hemisphere it is in the midst of the Arctic Ocean, leaving a pole-centered circular region of missing data on the Northern Hemisphere sea ice maps from the SMMR and SSMI data.

Record length

One of the major limitations of current satellite passive microwave data sets for use in climate studies is the fact that the satellite passive microwave record only began in December 1972, making the record too short for establishing a long-term climatological data base or for resolving many climate issues. This is clearly a limitation that can be overcome, but only with time and with continued satellite coverage.

Conclusions

Satellite passive microwave data are allowing an improved knowledge of sea ice distributions, including their seasonal, regional, and inter-annual variabilities, and an improved understanding of the role of sea ice in the global climate system. Such data have provided the ability to determine global sea ice distributions and approximate ice concentrations on a routine basis, with a frequency of every few days and a spatial resolution of approximately 30 km. Thus the seasonal cycle and inter-annual variations in the sea ice cover can be examined even in regions with no in situ observations, and changes in the sea ice cover can be monitored easily. Furthermore, the large-scale passive microwave data are complemented by much finer resolution data from visible, infra-red, and active microwave sensors, which can be used both to validate the passive microwave data and to examine individual regions in much greater detail. Although the global sea ice record is still too short for a long-term climatological data base, such a data base will eventually become possible as the satellite passive microwave record is extended. Now that the basic technology is developed and its value proven, it is hoped that satellite passive microwave instruments will be maintained indefinitely into the future.

The four-year ESMR data set, averaged over both three-day and monthly time periods, and the nine-year SMMR data set can be obtained in digital form from the National Snow and Ice Data Center (NSIDC) in Boulder, Colorado. SSMI data are being compiled and routinely added to the NSIDC archives as well. As passive microwave data are collected in the late 1990s and beyond from the Earth Observing System (EOS), these will be available from the EOS data and information system (EOSDIS).

References

Barry, R. G. (1983). Arctic Ocean and climate: perspectives on a century of polar research. *Ann. Assoc. Am. Geog.*, **73**, 485–501.

Bourke, R. H. & Garrett, R. P. (1987). Sea ice thickness distribution in the Arctic Ocean. *Cold Regions Sc. Tech.*, **13**, 259–80.

Campbell, W. J., Gloersen, P., Webster, W. J., Wilheit, T.T. & Ramseier, R. O. (1976). Beaufort Sea ice zones as delineated by microwave imagery. *J. Geophys. Res.*, **81**, 1103–10.

Carsey, F. D. (1980). Microwave observation of the Weddell polynya. *Monthly Weather Rev.*, **108**, 2032–44.

Carsey, F. D. (1982). Arctic sea ice distribution at end of summer 1973–1976 from satellite microwave data. *J. Geophys. Res.*, **87**, 5809–35.

Carsey, F. D. & Pihos, G. (1989). Beaufort-Chukchi seas summer and fall ice margin data from Seasat: conditions with similarities to the Labrador Sea. *IEEE Trans.*, **GRS-27**, 541–51.

Cavalieri, D. J. & Parkinson, C. L. (1987). On the relationship between atmospheric circulation and the fluctuations in the sea ice extents of the Bering and Okhotsk seas. *J. Geophys. Res.*, **92**, 7141–62.

Cavalieri, D. J., Gloersen, P. & Campbell, W. J. (1984). Determination of sea ice parameters with the Nimbus-7 SMMR. *J. Geophys. Res.*, **89**, 5355–69.

Cavalieri, D. J., Crawford, J. P., Drinkwater, M. R., Eppler, D. T., Farmer, L. D., Jentz, R. R. & Wackerman, C. C. (1991). Aircraft active and passive microwave validation of sea ice concentration from the Defense Meteorological Satellite Program Special Sensor Microwave Imager. *J. Geophys. Res.*, **96**, 21,989–2,008.

Comiso, J. C. (1986). Characteristics of Arctic winter sea ice from satellite multispectral microwave observations. *J. Geophys. Res.*, **91**, 975–94.

DeRycke, R. J. (1973). Sea ice motions off Antarctica in the vicinity of the eastern Ross Sea as observed by satellite. *J. Geophys. Res.*, **78**, 8873–9.

Dey, B. (1981). Monitoring winter sea ice dynamics in the Canadian Arctic with NOAA-TIR images. *J. Geophys. Res.*, **86**, 3223–35.

Dey, B., Moore, H. & Gregory, A. F. (1979). Monitoring and mapping sea-ice breakup and freezeup of Arctic Canada from satellite imagery. *Arctic Alpine Res.*, **11**, 229–42.

Fu, L. & Holt, B. (1982). *Seasat Views Oceans and Sea Ice with Synthetic-Aperture Radar*, JPL Publication 81–120, Jet Propulsion Laboratory, Pasadena, California, 200pp.

Gloersen, P. & Barath, F. T. (1977). A scanning multichannel microwave radiometer for Nimbus-G and SeaSat-A. *IEEE J.*, **OE-2**, 172–8.

Gloersen, P. & Cavalieri, D. J. (1986). Reduction of weather effects in the calculation of sea ice concentration from microwave radiances. *J. Geophys. Res.*, **91**, 3913–19.

Gloersen, P., Campbell, W. J., Cavalieri, D. J., Comiso, J. C., Parkinson, C. L. & Zwally, H. J. (1992). *Arctic and Antarctic Sea Ice, 1978–1987: Satellite Passive-Microwave Observations*, NASA SP–511, National Aeronautics and Space Administration, Washington, DC.

Gordon, A. L. (1978). Deep Antarctic convection west of Maud Rise. *J. Phys. Oceanog.*, **8**, 600–12.

Gordon, A. L. (1981). Seasonality of Southern Ocean sea ice. *J. Geophys. Res.*, **86**, 4193–7.

Gordon, A. L. & Huber, B. A. (1990). Southern Ocean winter mixed layer. *J. Geophys. Res.*, **95**, 11,655–72.

Hall, D. K. & Martinec, J. (1985). *Remote Sensing of Ice and Snow*. Chapman and Hall, London, 189pp.

Hollinger, J., Lo, R., Poe, G., Savage, R. & Peirce, J. (1987). *Special Sensor Microwave/Imager User's Guide*, Naval Research Laboratory, Washington, DC, 177pp.

Ito, H. & Muller, F. (1982). Ice movement through Smith Sound in northern Baffin Bay, Canada, observed in satellite imagery. *J. Glaciol.*, **28**, 129–43.

Leberl, F., Raggam, J., Elachi, C. & Campbell, W. J. (1983). Sea ice motion measurements from SEASAT SAR images. *J. Geophys. Res.*, **88**, 1915–28.

Lee, M. & Yang, W. (1987). Image-analysis techniques for determination of morphology and kinematics in Arctic sea ice. *Ann. Glaciol.*, **9**, 92–6.

Lemke, P. (1987). A coupled one-dimensional sea ice-ocean model. *J. Geophys. Res.*, **92**, 13,164–72.

Martinson, D. G., Killworth, P. D. & Gordon, A. L. (1981). A convective model for the Weddell polynya. *J. Phys. Oceanog.*, **11**, 466–88.

Parkinson, C. L. (1983). On the development and cause of the Weddell polynya in a sea ice simulation. *J. Phys. Oceanog.*, **13**, 501–11.

Parkinson, C. L. (1990). The impact of the Siberian High and Aleutian Low on the sea ice cover of the Sea of Okhotsk. *Ann. Glaciol.*, **14**, 226–9.

Parkinson, C. L. & Cavalieri, D. J. (1989) Arctic sea ice 1973–1987: seasonal, regional, and interannual variability. *J. Geophys. Res.*, **94**, 14,499–523.

Parkinson, C. L., Comiso, J. C., Zwally, H. J., Cavalieri, D. J.,

Gloersen, P. & Campbell, W. J. (1987). *Arctic Sea Ice, 1973–1976: Satellite Passive-Microwave Observations*, NASA SP-489, National Aeronautics and Space Administration, Washington, DC, 296pp.

Steffen, K. & Maslanik, J. A. (1988). Comparison of Nimbus-7 Scanning Multichannel Microwave Radiometer radiance and derived sea ice concentrations with Landsat imagery for the North Water area of Baffin Bay. *J. Geophys. Res.*, **93**, 10,769–81.

Svendsen, E., Kloster, K., Farrelly, B., Johannessen, O. M., Johannessen, J. A., Campbell, W. J., Gloersen, P., Cavalieri, D. & Matzler, C. (1983). Norwegian Remote Sensing Experiment: Evaluation of the Nimbus-7 Scanning Multichannel Microwave Radiometer for sea ice research. *J. Geophys. Res.*, **88**, 2781–91.

Swift, C. T., Fedor, L. S. & Ramseier, R. O. (1985). An algorithm to measure sea ice concentration with microwave radiometers. *J. Geophys. Res.*, **90**, 1087–99.

Walsh, J. E. & Zwally, H. J. (1990). Multiyear sea ice in the Arctic: model- and satellite-derived. *J. Geophys. Res.*, **95**, 11,613–28.

Zwally, H. J. & Walsh, J. E. (1987). Comparison of observed and modeled ice motion in the Arctic Ocean. *Ann. Glaciol.*, **9**, 136–44.

Zwally, H. J., Comiso, J. C., Parkinson, C. L., Campbell, W. J., Carsey, F. D. & Gloersen, P. (1983). *Antarctic Sea Ice, 1973–1976: Satellite Passive-Microwave Observations*, NASA SP-459, National Aeronautics and Space Administration, Washington, DC, 206pp.

Ice sheets

R. H. THOMAS

Introduction

Most of the fresh water on Earth occurs as vast ice sheets in Greenland and Antarctica, with more than 90% of the ice in Antarctica (Fig. 1). These ice sheets influence global climate through their high albedo and elevated topography, and they store a long and detailed record of past climatic and atmospheric conditions in the annual layers of snow deposited in regions where surface melting seldom occurs.

Perhaps the most critical aspect of the polar ice sheets is their potential for affecting global sea level. If the entire Antarctic ice sheet were to melt, sea level would rise by some 70 meters. Fortunately, air temperatures over Antarctica are so low that even the climate warming anticipated for a doubling of carbon dioxide is unlikely to cause significant surface melting over most of the ice sheet. By contrast, large areas of the Greenland ice sheet experience periods of intense melting each summer, and climate warming will probably enlarge these areas and increase the rates of melting. However, much depends on the seasonal signal of the climate warming because a warmer atmosphere contains more water vapour which may lead to increased snowfall and a larger ice sheet (Fig. 2).

At this time, despite more than four decades of sustained international field investigations costing several hundreds of millions of dollars, we still know very little about either of the polar ice sheets. It is not even known whether they are growing bigger or smaller, and it certainly cannot be predicted what they will do in response to a warmer climate. Research in the past has been hampered by the vast size of the ice sheets, their remoteness, and the harshness of the polar environment. However, the advent of airborne and satellite remote sensing has allowed the making of measurements over very large areas without regard to severe weather conditions or the long polar night, but there is still a long way to go.

The uncertainty in estimates of ice-sheet mass balance is equivalent to an uncertainty of $\pm$ 3 mm per year in the rate of change of global sea level. This means that even the high estimates of more than 2 mm per year sea level increase during the recent past (Peltier & Tushingham, 1989) could be entirely caused by wastage from the polar ice sheets. Moreover, the various processes that determine the mass balance (snow accumulation; surface melting; ice-stream and glacier discharge; and ice-shelf/ocean interactions) are not well enough understood for credible models to be constructed that could predict responses to possible future changes in climate.

These processes can all be investigated using remotely sensed data. In every case, *in situ* measurements are also needed, but the remotely sensed data provide the broad area context needed to interpret and to extrapolate the localized measurements. Moreover, satellite radar- and laser-altimetry offer the only practical means for measuring ice thickening/thinning rates over entire ice sheets. Relevant existing satellite data include: high-resolution images from Landsat, Système Probatoire d'Observation de la Terre (SPOT), and Synthetic Aperture Radar (SAR); medium-resolution visible and infrared images, such as those obtained by weather satellites; course-resolution passive microwave imagery; and radar-altimetry data. Although a laser altimeter and ranging system (the geoscience laser ranging system, or GLRS) is planned for NASA's Earth Observing System (EOS), for most of the next decade laser altimeters and radio-echo sounders (for measuring ice thickness) will be limited to aircraft operations.

A variety of remote-sensing techniques can be applied to ice-sheet investigations, using energy with wavelengths ranging from microns to meters. Here, attention will be focussed on those techniques that can be applied from satellites, but mention will also be made of airborne techniques that complement satellite sensors. These sensors will be reviewed under the broad classifications of imaging sensors and instruments for measuring ranges.

Imaging sensors

Imaging sensors can be subdivided according to their spatial resolution: tens of kilometers for microwave radiometers and scatterometers; on the order of one kilometre for visible and infra-red scanners on weather satellites; and meters to tens of

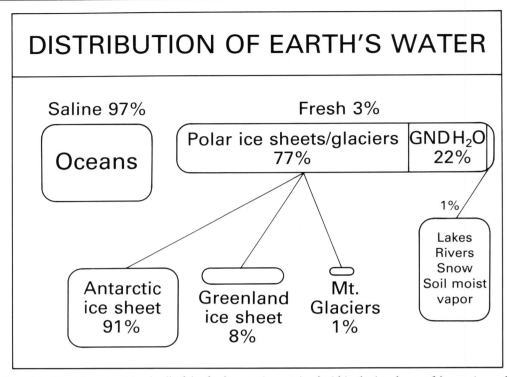

Fig. 1. The distribution of the Earth's water. Nearly all of the fresh water is contained within the ice sheets of Antarctica and Greenland. (Figure provided by H.J. Zwally.)

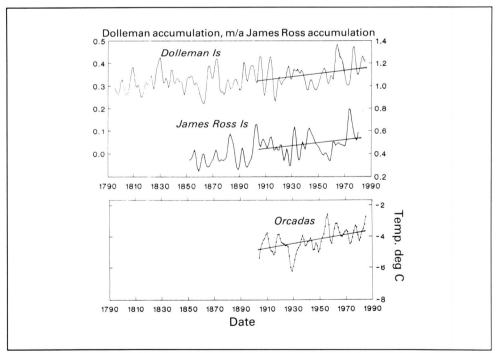

Fig. 2. Temperature and accumulation rates in the Antarctic peninsula. Surface temperatures from station measurements, and snow-accumulation rates from ice-core analysis (composited from data presented by Peel, in press). These measurements reveal significant increases in both surface temperature and snow accumulation during the past 80 years. Note that the left ordinate in the upper graph refers to Dolleman Island, and that on the right refers to James Ross Island. Shorter temperature records from Dolleman Island and other stations suggest an increase in this warming trend since 1950, with temperatures increasing by about 0·06° C per year and precipitation by approximately 6 mm water equivalent per year (from Peel *et al.*, 1988; and private communication from D.A. Peel, June 1990).

meters for high-resolution imagers such as Landsat, SPOT, and SAR.

Coarse-resolution microwave instruments

Methodology

This class of instruments includes microwave radiometers, such as the single-frequency Electrically Scanning Microwave Radiometer (ESMR), and the Scanning Multi-channel Microwave Radiometer (SMMR) and Special Sensor Microwave/Imager (SSM/I), and scatterometers, such as the Seasat-A Satellite Scatterometer (SASS), the Active Microwave Instrument (AMI) aboard ERS-1, and NASA scatterometer (NSCAT) planned to fly aboard Japan's Advanced Earth Observing System (ADEOS) mission. Apart from a hiatus in 1977–1978, there is almost continuous passive microwave coverage of the polar ice sheets since 1973, but at present there is only a limited scatterometer data set obtained by Seasat during 1978 and from AMI on ERS-1 since 1991.

Radiometers measure the intensity of radiation, within some prescribed frequency band and polarisation, from a particular picture element (pixel), of the observed surface, which is viewed at some known viewing angle. Images are obtained by sequentially measuring the radiance from a series of pixels. At optical frequencies, the measured radiation comprises energy that is primarily reflected from the surface, but passive microwave radiation is almost entirely emitted by the surface. Scatterometers measure the intensity of microwave energy that is back-scattered from a surface illuminated by radar emissions from the sensor. With present-day instruments, spatial resolution for both passive microwave and scatterometer data is on the order of tens of kilometres, and almost total coverage of the polar ice sheets, except for a circular region around each Pole, can be acquired every day, regardless of weather conditions.

Ice and liquid water have very distinct microwave emission and back-scatter signatures, with back-scatter strongly affected by surface conditions such as wetness and roughness, and both back-scatter and emission determined, progressively more at longer wavelengths, by conditions beneath the surface. Moreover, different ice samples can have distinct signatures, partly because of temperature differences and partly because of differences in texture, the distribution of air bubbles, and impurity content. Snow density, grain size, surface roughness, depth hoars, and the degree of wetness all influence the back-scattered and radiated energy, and they influence it differently at different wavelengths. Thus, by measuring with an appropriate suite of wavelengths, the ice

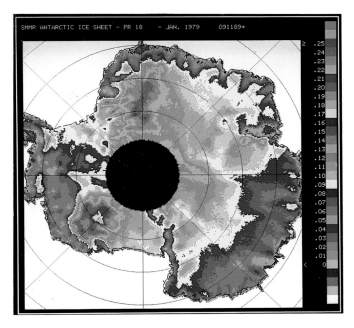

Fig. 3. Regions of surface melting derived from passive microwave measurements. This image shows the polarization ratio (PR) at 18 GHz (defined as the difference between vertically and horizontally polarized brightness temperatures divided by their sum) obtained from SMMR data taken over Antarctica in January, 1979. Small amounts of liquid water in the snow significantly reduce the PR, and the blue areas in this image are in locations likely to undergo summer melting. More research is needed before melt zones can confidently be delineated from passive microwave data, but there is considerable promise in this approach. (Image provided by D. Cavalieri and K. Jezek.)

cover can be classified according to its surface and near-surface properties.

Analysis and results

Microwave emissivity increases markedly with snow wetness, and it should be possible to use passive microwave data to indicate the time of onset of melting and the total extent of summer melting on the ice sheets (Fig. 3). Both of these parameters are likely to be strongly affected by any significant climate change, particularly if it is enhanced at high latitudes. This is an area of research that has hitherto been neglected, and it is strongly recommended that data from ESMR, SMMR, and SSM/I be analyzed to extract the melt-zone signal and to establish the foundation for a long time series of such information. This is particularly important over Greenland because climate models predict a major amplification in greenhouse warming at high northern latitudes (Hansen et al., 1984).

Examination of passive microwave images of Antarctica

reveals an intriguing similarity between some of the patterns of microwave brightness temperature and patterns of snow accumulation, and there have been attempts to explain this theoretically (Zwally, 1977), and to make use of the observations to deduce snow accumulation over large areas of the ice sheet (Rotman, Fisher & Staelin, 1982). However, many other parameters affect microwave emissivity, and considerable research is required before it can be confidently stated whether such analysis is viable.

Back-scattered energy, measured by a scatterometer, comprises both a surface reflection determined principally by surface roughness, and energy that has penetrated the surface layers of the ice sheet and has suffered multiple reflections from ice grains, hoarfrost layers, etc, before being reflected back towards the spacecraft. The few existing measurements over ice sheets have received little attention, and it cannot be assessed what might be learned from them, but it is highly likely that they will complement the passive microwave data.

Limitations

The principal limitations of passive microwave and scatterometer data over ice sheets are the coarse resolution and the need for an improved understanding of how to interpret them. However, the coarse resolution does have some advantages. The measurements give an indication of average conditions over each individual pixel, and the resulting data sets are compact enough to be analyzed on desk-top computers, bringing them into the reach of any investigator. At present, spatial resolution is from approximately 10 km, for scatterometer and 86 GHz passive microwave data, to about 50 km for 19 GHz data. Future sensors, slated for operation at the turn of the century, will have a significantly higher resolution.

Medium-resolution visible and infra-red sensors

Methodology

Since 1972, instruments of this type have provided continuous coverage of the globe, primarily to monitor weather conditions. An earlier series of weather satellites, beginning in 1962, provided analogue images of clouds and the Earth surface, but data quality was poor. The Advanced Very High Resolution Radiometer (AVHRR), currently operating aboard NOAA weather satellites, is a scanning radiometer operating at five frequencies in the visible, near infra-red, and thermal infra-red with a spatial resolution of between 1 and 4 km and a very wide swath, providing total coverage of the globe every day. The Optical Line Scanner (OLS) aboard

weather satellites of the Defense Meteorological Satellite Program spacecraft obtains similar data, with less spectral, but slightly better spatial resolution.

Despite their comparatively low resolution, these low-cost data show great promise for mapping large regions to provide the broad areal context for the more detailed, but also more costly and more localised information obtained by higher resolution instruments such as Landsat. Moreover, the thermal infra-red bands offer the potential for synoptic, cloud-free measurements of ice-surface temperatures.

Analysis and results

As a result of a cooperative effort between NOAA and the UK National Remote Sensing Centre, a mosaic has been compiled of Antarctica (Merson, 1989) using AVHRR images with minimal cloud cover (Fig. 4). A great deal of information on the morphology of the ice surface is contained within this mosaic, and detailed analyses of AVHRR data from major ice streams draining the Siple Coast region of West Antarctica into the Ross Ice Shelf have shown that many important features can be identified (Bindschadler & Vornberger, 1990; Casassa et al., 1991). These include: crevasse patterns associated with intense deformation within the ice; surface undulations caused by subglacial relief; the boundaries between the fast-moving ice streams and intervening ice domes and ridges; the location of grounding lines where the ice becomes thin enough to float; apparent streamlines across the ice shelf, which contain a 'memory' of past ice flow directions; and ice rises, where the ice shelf is locally grounded on shoaling seabed.

Currently, estimates of surface temperature on the polar ice sheets are based on observations at a few meteorological stations and data buoys, and on temperatures measured in shallow boreholes in the ice sheets, the temperature at 10 meters depth providing a good indication of the average annual air temperature at the borehole site. Analysis of satellite thermal infra-red data gives results that are broadly consistent with the surface observations (Fig. 5), but they have not been validated rigorously.

Limitations

The major limitation of this type of data is its dependence on cloud-free and, for the visible, sunlit conditions. Moreover, reliable techniques are needed to distinguish clouds from snow. This is particularly important if the thermal infra-red data are to be used to derive ice surface temperatures.

New AVHRR instruments, and the Along Track Scanning Radiometer (ATSR) aboard ERS-1, include a 1.6 micron

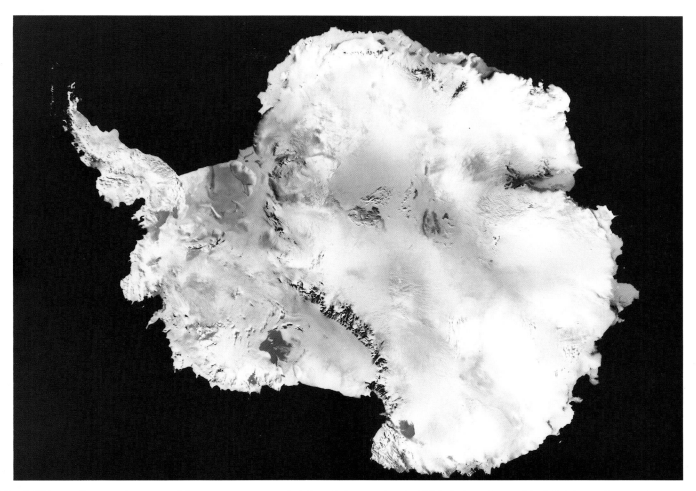

Fig. 4. This satellite mosaic image of Antarctica was compiled from 1-km resolution AVHRR data obtained by NOAA weather satellites. (The image was produced by the National Remote Sensing Centre, UK.)

channel to help discriminate clouds from snow. Moreover, the ATSR is better calibrated than earlier thermal infra-red radiometers and obtains measurements to correct for errors introduced by the atmosphere.

High-resolution imagers

Methodology

Higher resolution visible and infra-red data are currently obtained by Landsat and by the French Système Probatoire d'Observation de la Terre (SPOT) satellite, both of which are operated as subsidized commercial enterprises. Multi-Spectral Scanner (MSS) data, with a pixel size of 79 meters, have been acquired since 1972. Thematic Mapper (TM) data have been acquired since 1983. Pixel size for the six visible, near infra-red, and infra-red TM bands is 30 m, and that for the thermal infra-red band is 120 m. The swath width for both MSS and TM data is 185 km, and potential coverage extends to approximately 82.5° latitude.

SPOT obtains data similar to Landsat, but with a pixel size of 20 m for multi-spectral data, and 10 m for the panchromatic. Both modes have a swath width of 60 km. The SPOT orbit covers similar latitude limits to Landsat, but SPOT has an ability to view obliquely, extending coverage to about 85° latitude. This capability also permits stereo viewing from different spacecraft positions, and hence reconstruction of surface topography to an elevation accuracy of approximately 10 meters.

High-resolution microwave images are obtained by the Synthetic Aperture Radar (SAR), which discriminates individual resolution cells according to their range and the Doppler shift in frequency of the reflected radiation, caused by spacecraft motion. Spatial resolution is on the order of meters to tens of meters. Data are acquired at extremely high rates (on the order of 100 Mbit/s), and they are transmitted

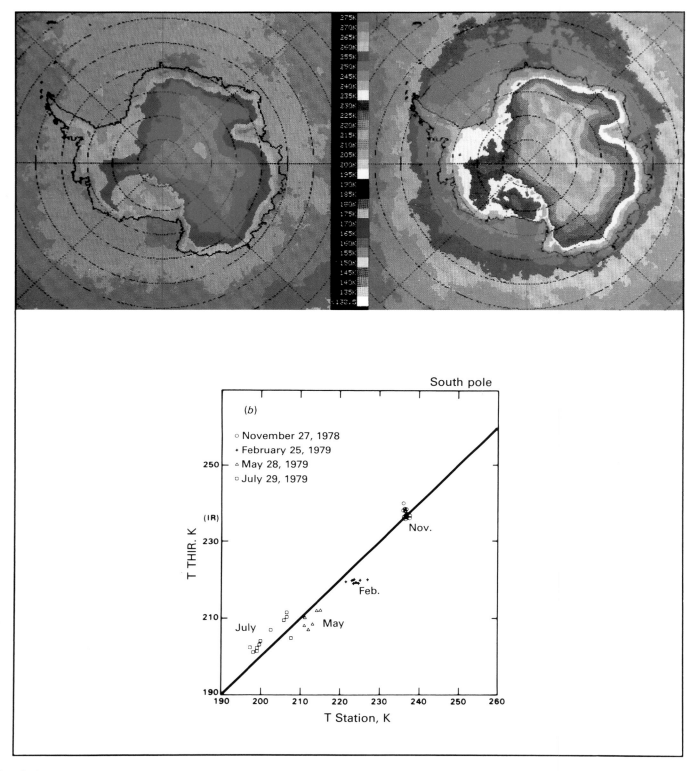

Fig. 5. Average surface temperatures over Antarctica for January (left) and August (right) 1979. These estimates were derived by J. Comiso (personal communication) from satellite thermal infra-red data. The lower plot provides a comparison between the satellite-derived estimates and surface measurements at the South Pole (Comiso, 1983).

immediately to ground receiving stations within view of the spacecraft. Future SAR missions will also be capable of recording some of the data aboard the spacecraft for later transmission.

In addition to providing high-resolution information at frequencies which complement those in the visible and infrared, SAR data have the major advantage of being unaffected by clouds or darkness. Moreover, radar wavelengths penetrate snow and ice to detect shallow subsurface features. A SAR produces high-resolution digital images with intensity proportional to radar back-scatter. Correction for distortions induced by surface topography yields geocoded images with locations for each of the image pixels.

Extensive SAR coverage was first obtained in 1978 by NASA's Seasat, which operated for only 3 months. A few images were obtained over Greenland, but none over Antarctica. Analysis of the Seasat and airborne SAR data indicate that melt zones on the ice sheet can be identified along with melt features such as lakes and streams. The next opportunities for large-scale acquisition of SAR data at high latitudes will be provided by a series of non-US satellites that are planned to operate through most of the 1990s.

Analysis and results

Accurate maps, particularly ones giving a pictorial indication of the terrain, are important for almost all ice-sheet research. Their usefulness in planning and conducting field investigations, as well as in the interpretation of field measurements, cannot be overstated. Mapping from high-resolution images now involves sophisticated registration and mosaicking techniques that minimize position errors and provide maps that are excellently suited to most research requirements (Swithinbank, 1988). These can be produced at considerably less expense than conventional aerial photography. Both the MSS and the TM images are adequate for mapping, but clearly, the TM and SPOT data provide greater detail.

With the high resolution of such data, the image itself becomes a valuable source of information for glaciological studies, and many excellent examples are included in Swithinbank, 1988. In regions where other measurements are available, the image data can be combined with those measurements (e.g. surface deformation, velocity, ice thickness, surface winds and temperatures, optical leveling, etc) to extend correlations to areas where there are no *in situ* data.

The digital images allow enhancement of subtle features that have minimal contrast, and examination of various combinations of the different frequency bands. Such analysis has revealed the presence of surface features ranging from subtle undulations associated with ice flow over mountainous terrain

to crevasses and melt-water lakes. Quite subtle topographic relief on ice-sheet surfaces is readily discernible in images that were obtained with a low sun angle, and this information can be used to reconstruct relative surface topography, to delineate glacier catchment basins, and to identify ice streamlines. US and European investigators are making extensive use of Landsat and SPOT images to map the Siple Coast region and the Filchner/Ronne ice shelf system in Antarctica, and to investigate a variety of glaciological aspects, including ice motion, tributary ice streams and glaciers, and areas of grounded ice within the ice shelf. This work is a major aid in the planning and interpretation of the field measurements.

Apparent streamlines can be identified in the imagery almost entirely across the major ice shelves. Accurate mapping of streamlines is particularly important, because they can be compared with independent measurements of ice velocity. Differences reveal non-steady-state conditions, and comparisons along a complete flowline provide an insight into past behaviour of the ice-sheet–ice-shelf system. The images can also be used to investigate the albedo of the ice-sheet surface. The causes for variability in the albedo are not fully understood, but they are probably associated with factors such as surface melting, snow grain size and orientation, or surface features such as sastrugi, which are indicative of local winds.

Comparison of sequential images of the same region provide information on changes that have occurred during the time interval between imaging. These include ice motion, ice-shelf advance or retreat, iceberg calving, crevasse patterns, grounded regions within ice shelves, and extent of summer melting. This technique has been widely used to estimate glacier velocity by tracking the location of large crevasses in the images (for example, Lucchitta & Ferguson, 1986). Results from analysis of Landsat imagery from the Stancomb Wills Glacier are shown in Fig. 6.

In an attempt to make better use of Landsat coverage, NASA and the USGS are collaborating with other SCAR nations to complement the existing collection of images with new acquisitions (Ferrigno & Molnia, 1989). The resulting data set will enable compilation of maps depicting the various morphological features of overflown parts of the ice sheets (latitudes lower than about 82.5°), and these will represent a particularly valuable resource for planning field investigations and for helping to interpret other data. However, the many images of Antarctica were collected over a period of about 15 years (Williams, Ferrigno & Kent, 1984; Swithinbank, 1988), and our next major goal should be to initiate a long-term program of data acquisition that will provide almost simultaneous coverage of the large terrestrial ice sheets every decade. This would permit the systematic monitoring of

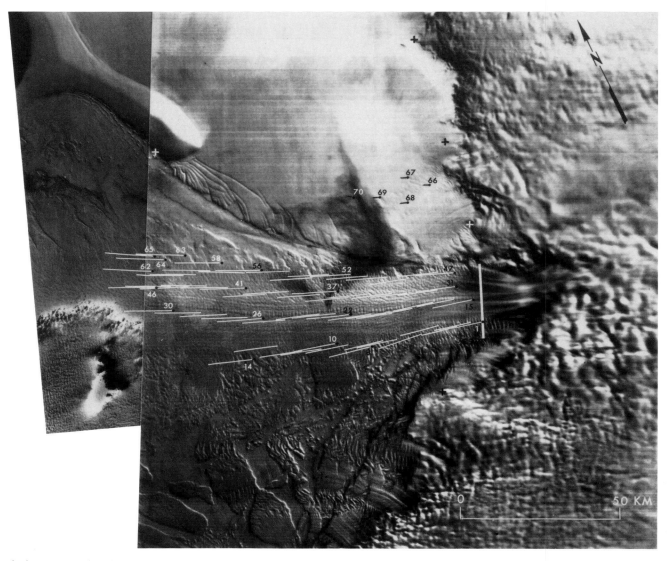

Fig. 6. Antarctic outlet-glacier velocities obtained by comparing two sets of Landsat images. The image depicts the Stancomb-Wills glacier Tongue of the Brunt Ice Shelf, Weddell Sea. Movement vectors were obtained by tracing crevasse patterns on Landsat images acquired 12 years apart. Paper print copies of the images were optically matched under a stereoscope. The heavy white baseline is about 10 km west of the grounding line, and glacier movement is to the left. The velocities range from approximately 950 m/year, close to the baseline, to about 1·2 km/year 100 km downstream (Lucchitta *et al.*, 1990). They show excellent agreement with a velocity of 1·3 km/year measured 30 km further downstream (Thomas, 1973).

changes in the areal extent and surface features of the ice sheets that will be needed by the US global change research program. Images from SPOT and from optical sensors aboard other spacecraft will complement those from Landsat, but systematic coverage of large areas is more easily achieved by Landsat, with its broader swath.

The few SAR images that have been acquired over the ice sheets give an indication of potential glaciological applications (Bindschadler, Jezek & Crawford, 1987), and the SAR is expected to have a mapping and change-detection capability similar to that of Landsat and SPOT, with the added advantage of all-weather operation.

Limitations

Landsat and SPOT data suffer from two major limitations: cloud cover and cost. For most glaciological applications, frequent coverage by this type of data is not required, so cloud

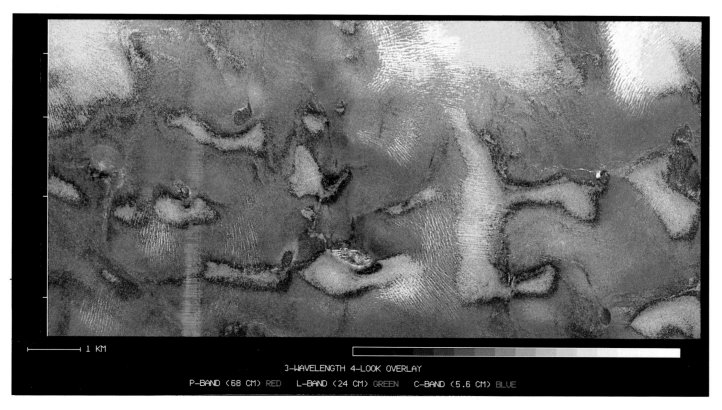

Fig. 7. A SAR image of the ablation region in southwest Greenland. This image was obtained by the Jet Propulsion Laboratory (JPL) airborne polarimetric, multifrequency SAR. The orange-colored areas are regions with strong backscatter at the longer, P-band wavelengths (68 cm), and the blue areas have strong backscatter at the shorter, C-band wavelengths (5·6 cm). This 12-km wide image was obtained in August 1989 from an area of considerable summer melting, with surface melt streams and ponds, the very dark features in the image. Many of the ponds can also be identified in Seasat SAR imagery of the same area, obtained in 1978, and there appears to have been little change in their positions during the intervening 11 years (Jezek *et al.*, 1991). The fingerprint-like bright returns are strongest at the longer wavelengths, suggesting they are associated with subsurface features, but their cause is unknown at this time. (Image provided by J. Crawford, JPL)

cover is not a serious problem. However, the images are expensive, particularly in digital form. Fortunately, both Landsat and SPOT provide a guarantee that purchased images will be almost cloud free. Moreover, these images are significantly less costly than equivalent coverage by air photography. Approximately 100 cloud-free Landsat images would provide complete coverage of the coast of Antarctica; about 500 cloud-free Landsat images would provide total coverage of the continent down to 82.5° S latitude.

For SAR, limitations include high power consumption, high data rate, and complex data-processing techniques, including geometric rectification of the images to provide a true orthogonal view. In addition, swath width is generally narrow (75–100 km) but, by the mid-1990s, Canada's Radarsat will acquire coarser-resolution SAR data within a 500 km swath. All of the upcoming SAR missions will have either no onboard SAR storage or only a limited recording capacity. Consequently, broad areal coverage of both Greenland and Antarctica will require suitably placed receiving stations. Arc-

tic coverage will be provided by stations in Sweden, Scotland, Norway, Canada, and Alaska, but there may still be gaps in data acquisition over Greenland. In the Antarctic, there will be a Japanese station at Shōwa and a German receiver at the Chilean General Bernardo O'Higgins research station on the northwest coast of the Antarctic Peninsula. This will leave a major gap in the Ross Sea sector, and the National Science Foundation is considering the possibility of establishing a receiving station at McMurdo research station in time to acquire data from Radarsat in the mid-1990s.

Techniques have been developed for producing digital mosaics of SAR images, and these will assist in mapping applications. However, much work remains to be done on interpretation of the radar back-scatter that is recorded by the SAR. At present, a SAR image of, for example, an ablation region on the Greenland Ice Sheet can be looked at (Fig. 7), and the amount of information that the image apparently contains is impressive, but cannot be quantified.

Ranging instruments

Ranging instruments include: radar altimeters, which provide accurate measurements of surface topography beneath the spacecraft; laser altimeters, and laser-ranging devices that precisely measure the distance between the spacecraft and targets on the ice surface; and radio-echo sounders that measure ice thickness.

Radar altimeters

Methodology

Satellite radar altimeters operated aboard NASA's GEOS-3 (1975–1978) and Seasat (July–October, 1978), and the US Navy's Geosat (1985–1989). These instruments were designed to measure ranges to the ocean surface at intervals of approximately 700 m along the orbit track. They transmitted short radar pulses and measured the time delay until receipt of the reflected pulse. Excellent results are obtained over the oceans, where the measured range changes slowly along the orbit track, and the precision of a range measurement, averaged from one second's data, is on the order of 10 cm or less. Moreover, because the altimeter illuminates several square km of the ocean, the altimeter-derived range automatically averages the effects of waves; and it provides a means for measuring ocean wave height from the shape of the return pulse.

Over the sloping and undulating surfaces of the polar ice sheets, the servo-tracking circuit in the altimeter is not sufficiently agile to follow rapidly changing ranges, and the altimeter frequently loses track of the return pulse. In this respect, the more agile tracker of the Geosat altimeter represented a major improvement over Seasat, and it acquired more continuous records over the Greenland and Antarctic ice sheets.

Analysis and results

Because of the sloping and undulating surface, altimeter-derived ranges measured over ice sheets have significant errors, and each return pulse waveform must be retracked to give a range precision over smoother portions of the ice sheets on the order of 30 cm, while over rougher portions it is more commonly on the order of a few meters. These corrected data provide the best available information for mapping ice sheet topography over the vast areas of Greenland and Antarctica as far north or south as the orbital inclination of the spacecraft permits.

Results from Seasat data over Greenland have been

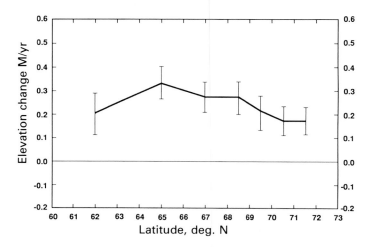

Fig. 8. Greenland ice sheet surface-elevation change derived from comparison of Geosat and Seasat radar-altimetry data. The rate of thickening of the ice sheet is plotted against latitude. The error bars are estimates of standard deviation, assuming the errors in each orbit-crossover comparison are independent (after Zwally, 1989).

published in atlas form (Bindschadler et al., 1989), and the corrected ranges and derived ice surface elevations are available from the National Snow and Ice Data Center (NSIDC). Data from GEOS-3 are not sufficiently accurate to warrant reprocessing, but all the over-ice Geosat data are being reprocessed by NASA. The resulting data sets provide the basic information necessary for many glaciological requirements, such as delineating catchment basins, deducing flowlines, calculating ice-flow driving stresses, and setting boundary conditions for theoretical models, as well as for the production of topographic maps.

A major potential application of satellite altimetry data is measurement of ice thickening/thinning rates. Errors in individual estimates of surface elevation are on the order of a meter or more, and this is inadequate for detecting changes at a specific location. A careful study (Lingle, Brenner & Zwally, 1990) of the extensive data set obtained during the first 18 months of the Geosat mission, indicates that errors are largely random, apart from a slope-induced error, which should remain almost constant at a given location on the ice sheet. Consequently, comparison of data obtained at the locations where one set of orbits crosses a later set should provide an indication of the thickening/thinning rate of the ice sheet. Such an analysis has been applied to the Greenland Ice Sheet (Fig. 8), and indicates that the higher elevation parts of the ice sheet south of 72° N, thickened by approximately 1.6 meters between 1978 and 1986 (Zwally et al., 1989). If this is correct, then it has important ramifications, and a high priority should be given to continuing this type of systematic analysis, and to extending it to higher latitudes using data from ERS-1.

Zwally's (1989) discussion of the Zwally *et al.* (1989) observations focussed on apparent trends in Greenland ice-surface elevation during the first 18 months of the Geosat mission, and he concluded that these trends were consistent with the longer-term trend implied by the Geosat/Seasat comparison. However, the inferred ice thickening rates of 20 cm/year are very large, and they are not supported by conclusions from indirect mass balance calculations. Errors in the Zwally *et al.* (1989) estimates depend heavily on the accuracy of the Seasat and Geosat orbits, and on the depth of penetration of the radar signal into the ice-sheet surface. Douglas *et al.* (1990) challenged these estimates, suggesting that the Geosat data could also be interpreted to indicate ice-sheet thinning. In a response, Zwally (1990) stressed that these arguments did not invalidate the conclusion of ice thickening based on Seasat/Geosat intercomparison, in which the calculated orbits for the two satellites had been reduced to a common datum by comparing measurements made over the ocean. However, satellite orbits over the ice sheets retain unknown errors, and confirmation of ice-sheet thickening must await additional measurements from future spacecraft or airborne instruments, for which accurate knowledge of platform location should be a first priority.

Some of the energy radiated by a radar altimeter undoubtedly penetrates the ice surface, and reflects back to the spacecraft from layers beneath the surface. This introduces additional, unknown errors to the measured ranges. The degree of penetration probably depends on surface snow and ice conditions, so that altimetry data obtained in different seasons might indicate an apparent change in surface elevation caused solely by seasonal changes in radar penetration. Nevertheless, this effect is unlikely to explain the 1.6 meter difference observed by Zwally *et al.* (1989).

Lingle *et al.*'s (1990) error analysis indicates that radar-altimetry data may also be useful to detect elevation changes in the Greenland ablation area. Here, although errors of individual altimeter measurements can be very large (tens of meters), they appear to be independent, and therefore amenable to reduction by taking averages over sufficiently large areas. This is an important development because of the possibility that the more steeply sloping ablation areas may undergo significantly increased melting, and consequently thinning, as a result of climate warming.

Other potential applications include: mapping ice cliff margins of the Antarctic ice sheet (Thomas, Martin & Zwally, 1983); and investigating ice surface characteristics such as sastrugi roughness, crevasse intensity, and surface wetness (Partington *et al.*, 1989).

Limitations

Each corrected radar altimeter range is measured to the closest surface within the altimeter footprint, with the effects of minor undulations (like sastrugi) averaged out. Consequently, over a sloping surface, the measured range is to a point that is not directly beneath the spacecraft. Corrections for this slope-induced error can be applied where the slope is constant over large distances, but it is very difficult to correct for the effects of the large undulations that are commonly found on the polar ice sheets. This translates to an elevation error that can be on the order of many meters. Moreover, useful data cannot be acquired over slopes that exceed half the angular beam width of the radar antenna (i.e. slopes steeper than about 1:70). This restriction applies to approximately 10–15% of the Greenland and Antarctic ice sheets, and predominates in the coastal regions where ice velocities are highest, and scientific interest is most pronounced.

Because of the large radar footprint, and because of radar penetration into the surface snow and firn, the ice-sheet surface reconstructed from radar altimetry data represents a smoothed approximation to the actual surface. The effect of surface slope is to bias this envelope above the real surface, whereas the effect of radar penetration into the ice is to bias the envelope below the real surface. The bias and the degree of smoothing are determined by local surface slopes, the properties of the surface snow and firn, and by characteristics of the altimeter and its tracking system. It is important to understand this relationship in order to make effective use of the data, particularly if this involves intercomparison of data from different instruments.

Coverage by both Geosat and Seasat extends to 72° latitude, while GEOS-3 reached only to 65°, and there is a clear need to extend coverage nearer the poles. ERS-1, launched in July 1991, makes considerable progress in this direction, reaching 82° latitude.

Laser altimeter and ranging instruments

Methodology

A satellite laser altimeter operates with a very narrow beam, so that its footprint on the ice sheet surface is just a few tens of meters in diameter. Consequently, a laser altimeter measures ranges to more clearly defined positions on the Earth's surface than does a radar altimeter, so long as both the satellite position and the laser pointing direction are accurately known. The net result is an improved capability to measure thickening/thinning rates. This means that changes averaged over large areas can be detected over shorter periods, and patterns of change can be discriminated at a far higher spatial resolution than with a radar altimeter. Moreover, useful measurements can be made over the ice sheet margins, where surface slopes are too large for existing radar altimeters.

A laser altimeter was used on Apollos 15–17 to measure elevation profiles of the lunar surface in 1971–1972, and the first major satellite laser altimeter mission will be the Mars Observatory Laser Altimeter (MOLA), launched in 1992. If this mission is successful, then by the mid-1990s the surface topography of Mars will be better mapped than many parts of the Earth. The earliest opportunity for satellite laser altimetry over the Earth's polar ice caps will be provided by the Geoscience Laser Ranging System (GLRS), planned for inclusion within the Earth Observing System (EOS) with a launch near the turn of the century. The GLRS is designed to operate as an altimeter and to measure ranges to remote targets. The altimeter mode will provide measurements of average surface elevation within footprints some tens of meters in diameter, spaced at intervals of a few hundred meters along track. The prime application of these data will be to measure rates of ice sheet thickening/thinning.

Pending launch of a satellite laser altimeter, there are plans for airborne laser altimeter surveys over the Greenland ice sheet, with Global Positioning System (GPS) receivers aboard the aircraft, to provide the very accurate navigation required to measure the height of the aircraft above the ellipsoid, to identify the ground track, and to direct the aircraft as nearly as possible along repeat tracks.

The ranging mode of GLRS is primarily for studies of crustal motion, but it can be applied over ice to measure ice strain rates over very large distances. Current specifications call for measurement of the relative position of retroreflectors to accuracies of millimeters to centimeters. Repeated measurements to targets planted in the surface of an ice sheet will provide accurate estimates of ice velocity and strain rate over distances of tens to hundreds of km, and over short time periods.

Analysis and results

Airborne laser altimeter measurements over a glacier in Iceland are shown in Fig. 9. The aircraft ground speed was approximately 100 meters per second, and the laser pulse rate was 200 Hz, yielding a range measurement every 50 cm along the glacier. Ranges were measured to the highest portion of the approximately 1 meter spot illuminated by the laser, with a precision of 10 cm or better. The derived surface elevations shown in Fig. 9 have been adjusted for the aircraft altitude calculated from GPS data, and the horizontal nature of the

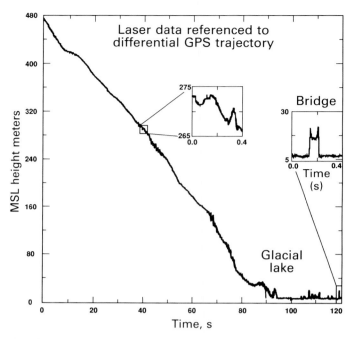

Fig. 9. Airborne laser-altimetry measurements over Breidamerkurjokul Glacier in Iceland. The position of the aircraft was fixed using global positioning system (GPS) receivers. A highly detailed, accurate surface-elevation profile of the terminus of the broad outlet glacier was obtained in less than two minutes of flight time. (Figure provided by W. Krabill, NASA Wallops Flight Facility.)

proglacial lake surface is a measure of their consistency; the vertical spikes on the lake surface are produced by icebergs and a suspension bridge spanning the river that drains melt water from the glacier into the north Atlantic Ocean. Enlargements of the horizontal scale show the remarkable detail that can be achieved with this technique, with small-scale undulations on the glacier, and even the twin suspension cables of the bridge being mapped.

Laser ranging from a satellite to targets positioned on the ice surface will provide frequent measurements of ice strain rates and, by including targets on rock outcrops, accurate estimates of ice motion. The ranging measurements also yield the elevation of the target above the Earth ellipsoid, while the laser altimeter measures the elevation of the snow surface above the ellipsoid. Consequently, a time series of both ranging and altimeter measurements will provide estimates of snow accumulation rates at all target sites.

Limitations

The major limitations of satellite laser altimetry are: the requirement for cloud-free conditions; the requirement for very accurate knowledge of the laser pointing direction; and

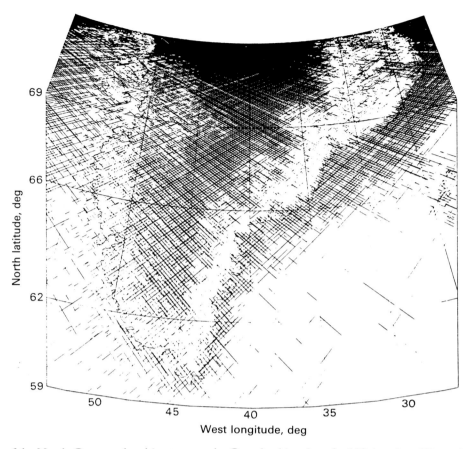

Fig. 10. Ground tracks of the Navy's Geosat radar altimeter over the Greenland ice sheet for 110 data days. Discontinuities in tracks represent locations where the altimeter lost track of the reflected signal because of very rapid variations in the range to the ice surface or excessive smearing of the return pulse by sloping terrain. The extremely dense coverage is a result of the long time interval between repeating satellite orbit tracks (Zwally *et al.*, 1987).

the confinement of data acquisition to only the orbit track of the spacecraft. However, these are not serious obstacles to the application of this technique. Ice sheets change sufficiently slowly to permit repeated attempts until data are acquired in all but the most persistently cloud-covered regions; the requirement for accurate knowledge of the laser pointing direction represents a significant technical challenge, but by no means an insurmountable one; and even a few detailed and accurate surface-elevation profiles across the major ice sheets would represent far more information than we can ever hope to obtain using surface-based surveying techniques. In reality, a remarkably dense coverage of orbit tracks can be achieved by placing the satellite into a non-repeating orbit (Fig. 10).

For laser ranging from a satellite, the major limitations are likely to be associated with the retroreflectors. They should be low-cost; they must be capable of remaining above the snow surface for many years (preferably more than a decade); they need to be constructed in a way that minimizes snow and hoar-frost deposits on the retroreflector, and they should

preferably be designed for deployment from an airplane. Taken together, these requirements represent quite a tall order, but they can probably be met. Moreover, retroreflectors deployed on ice sheets are unlikely to be affected by one of the major hazards anticipated at lower latitudes – interference by vandals and trophy hunters.

Radio-echo sounding for measuring ice thickness

At frequencies of tens to hundreds of kHz (wavelengths of a few meters), fresh-water ice is almost transparent to radio waves, and techniques have been developed for measuring ice thickness from the surface and from aircraft by measuring the time delay of reflected pulses of radio energy transmitted by downward-looking antennae. Reflections come from the upper surface of the ice, from the bottom interface (over rock or seawater), and from internal layers that are probably asso-

Fig. 11. Detection of changes in glacier thickness by airborne laser altimetry. This artist's impression shows how a scanning laser could be used to measure repeat surface profiles of a glacier, with the airplane navigated by real-time GPS data to within less than 100 meters of a previous flight path. (Figure provided by W. Krabill, NASA Wallops Flight Facility.)

ciated with small density variations or with layers rich in volcanic dust.

This powerful technique has provided estimates of ice thickness over much of Antarctica and Greenland with an accuracy on the order of 10 meters. Most of this information resulted from a systematic program of airborne surveys during the 1970s. Unfortunately, aircraft navigation at high latitudes was imperfect at this time, and many of the flight lines may have significant position errors. Moreover, additional surveys during the 1980s have been confined to specific regions, and there are still parts of the Antarctic ice sheet where thickness measurements are sparse. Because of the broad beam width associated with the comparatively long wavelengths used for radio-echo sounding, the technique is ill suited to operation aboard a satellite.

Conclusions

If all the ice in Greenland and Antarctica were to melt, sea level would rise by some 75 meters. Fortunately, even under the most extreme predictions of climatic warming, such melt-

ing would take several thousand years. Nevertheless, even a small mass imbalance could change sea level enough to have severe consequences for many densely populated coastal regions.

At present, sea level appears to be rising by 1 or 2 mm per year, and only some of this increase can be explained by expansion of a possibly warming ocean. Some of the rest may be caused by melting of small glaciers (see the chapter by Williams & Hall, 1993), but very little is known about what is happening to the ice sheets of Greenland and Antarctica. What is known is based on measurements from just a few locations, and these measurements suggest that the ice is *thickening* at many of those locations.

So where is the water coming from to raise sea level? The ice sheets are truly vast. Antarctica is bigger than the United States, and in those huge areas where little or no information is available, almost anything might be happening. Particularly important are the marginal regions of the ice sheets, where the surface slopes are steepest and ice velocity and surface melting rates are highest. Within these regions, detailed studies have been made at only a very few locations.

The only way to improve knowledge significantly is to make accurate measurements over entire ice sheets by remote sensing from satellites and aircraft. The major components of ice-sheet mass balance that can potentially be measured from space are snow accumulation, surface temperature, surface melting, ice motion, and changes in ice volume. Of these, measurement of changes in ice volume is a direct indication of the mass balance and is the objective with highest priority. However, the other measurements are important in that they provide insight into the processes affecting the mass balance, and this insight will be needed if we are to assemble models that realistically predict the ice sheet contribution to sea level change in a warmer world.

Required sensors include: radar altimeter (to measure changes in surface elevation over the smoother, near-horizontal portions of the ice sheets); laser altimeter (to measure elevation changes over the rest of the ice sheets, and to measure elevation profiles entirely across the big ice sheets with a precision significantly better than can be achieved with radar altimeters); SAR and Landsat (to measure changes in ice-sheet areal extent, and ice velocity on large ice streams and glaciers); SAR, scatterometer, and passive microwave (to map regions of summer melting); thermal infra-red (for ice surface temperatures); and the laser ranger (to measure ice velocities and strain rates and, together with the laser altimeter, to measure snow-accumulation rates).

Apart from the laser instruments, all these sensors will be available during most of the next decade, with appropriate data systems either already in existence or under development. The lack of a satellite laser altimeter until the turn of the century will seriously delay full assessment of the ice-sheet contribution to sea level rise. Consequently, the use of an airborne scanning laser altimeter, together with GPS navigation is strongly recommended, to make an early start on measuring the mass balance of individual ice streams and glaciers (Fig. 11).

Data availability

Details on how to obtain the various data sets referred to in this chapter can be found in Appendices I and II of Thomas (1991).

References

Bindschadler, R. A., Jezek, K. C. & Crawford, J. (1987). Glaciological investigations using the synthetic aperture radar imaging system. *Ann. Glaciol.*, 9, 11–19.

Bindschadler, R. A., Zwally, H. J., Major, J. A. & Brenner, A. C. (1989). Surface topography of the Greenland Ice Sheet from satellite radar altimetry. *NASA Special Publication No. 503*, Washington, DC 20546.

Bindschadler, R. A. & Vornberger, P. L. (1990). AVHRR imagery reveals Antarctic ice dynamics. *EOS*, 71 (23), 741–2.

Casassa, G., Jezek, K. C., Turner, J. & Whillans, I. M. (1991). Relict flow stripes on the Ross ice shelf. *Ann. Glaciol.*, 15, 132–8.

Comiso, J. C. (1983). Sea ice effective emissivities from satellite passive microwave and infra-red observations. *J. Geophys. Res.*, 88 (C12), 8686–704.

Douglas, B. C., Cheney, R. E., Miller, L., Agreen, R. W., Carter, W. E. & Robertson, D. S. (1990). Greenland ice sheet: is it growing or shrinking? *Science*, 248, 288.

Ferrigno, J. G. & Molnia, B. F. (1989). Availability of Landsat, Soyuzkarta, and SPOT data of Antarctica for ice and climate research. *Antarctic J.*, 24 (4), 15–18.

Hansen, J., Lacis, A., Rind, D., Russell, P., Fung, I., Ruedy, R. & Lerner, J. (1984). Climate sensitivity: Analysis of feedback mechanisms. In *Climate Processes and Climate Sensitivity*, J. Hansen and T. Takahashi, eds., American Geophysical Union, Washington, DC, pp. 130–63.

Jezek, K. C., Crawford, J. P., Bindschadler, R., Drinkwater, M. R. & Kwok, R. (1991). Synthetic aperture radar observations of the Greenland ice sheet. *Proceedings of the JPL Airborne Science Workshop*, Pasadena, Ca., June 1990, M. Kobrick, ed., pp. 21–8.

Lingle, C. S., Brenner, A. C. & Zwally, H. J. (1990). Satellite altimetry, semivariograms, and seasonal elevation changes in the ablation zone of west Greenland. *Ann. Glaciol.*, 14, 158–63.

Lucchitta, B. K., Ferrigno, J. G. & Williams, Jr. R. S. (1990). Monitoring the dynamics of the Antarctic coastline with Landsat images. *Abstracts of the International Symposium on Glaciers–Oceans–Atmosphere Interactions*, Sept. 24–29, 1990, Leningrad, USSR, pp. 123–4.

Lucchitta, B. K. & Ferguson, H. M. (1986). Antarctica: measuring glacier velocity from satellite images. *Science*, 234, 1105–8.

Merson, R. H. (1989). An AVHRR mosaic image of Antarctica. *Int. J. Rem. Sens.*, 10, 669–74.

Partington, K. C., Ridley, J. K., Rapley, C. G. & Zwally, H. J. (1989). Observations of the surface properties of the ice sheets by satellite radar altimetry. *J. Glaciol.*, 35 (120), 267–75.

Peel, D. A., Mulvaney, R. & Davison, B. M. (1988). Stable-isotope/air temperature relationships in ice cores from Dolleman Island and the Palmer Land Plateau, Antarctic Peninsula. *Ann. Glaciol.*, 10, 130–6.

Peel, D. A. (1992). Ice-core evidence from the Antarctic Peninsula region. In *Climate since 1500 A.D.* R. S. Bradley and P. D. Jones, eds., Unwin Hyman, in press.

Peltier, W. R. & Tushingham, A. M. (1989). Global sea level rise and the Greenhouse Effect: might they be connected? *Science*, 244, 806–10.

Rotman, S. R., Fisher, A. D. & Staelin, D. H. (1982). Inversion for physical characteristics of snow using passive radiometric observations. *J. Glaciol.*, 28, 179–85.

Swithinbank, C. (1988). Antarctica, with sections on the 'dry valleys' of Victoria land, by T. J. Chinn, and Landsat images of Antarctica, by Williams, R. S. Jr. & Ferrigno, J. G., A volume in the series *Satellite Image Atlas of Glaciers of the World*, Williams, R. S. Jr. & Ferrigno, J. G., eds., USGS Professional Paper 1386–B, U.S. Government Printing Office, Washington, DC, 278 pp.

Swithinbank, C., Brunk, K. & Sievers, J. (1988). A glaciological map of Filchner-Ronne ice shelf. *Ann. Glaciol.*, **11**, 150–5.

Thomas, R. H. (1973). The dynamics of the Brunt Ice Shelf. *Br. Antarctic Survey Sci. Rep.*, No. 79, 45pp.

Thomas, R. H. (1991). *Polar Research from Satellites*, Joint Oceanographic Institutions, Washington, DC, 91pp.

Thomas, R. H., Martin, T. V. & Zwally, H. J. (1983). Mapping ice-sheet margins from radar-altimetry data. *Ann. Glaciol.*, **4**, 283–8.

Williams, R. S. Jr. and Ferrigno, J. G. (1981). In *Satellite Image Atlas of Glaciers of the World*. Williams, R. S. Jr. and J. G. Ferrigno, eds. USGS Professional Paper 1386-B, US Government Printing Office, Washington, D.C. 278pp.

Williams, R. S. Jr, Ferrigno, J. G. & Kent, T. M. (1984). Index map and table of optimum Landsat 1, 2 and 3 images of Antarctica: *USGS Open-File Report 84–573*.

Williams, R. S. Jr. & Hall, D. K. (1993). Glaciers, This volume.

Zwally, H. J. (1977). Microwave emissivity and accumulation rate of polar firn. *J. Glaciol.*, **18**, 195–215.

Zwally, H. J. (1989). Growth of Greenland Ice Sheet: interpretation. *Science*, **246**, 1589–91.

Zwally, H. J. (1990). Greenland ice sheet: is it growing or shrinking? (Reply) *Science*, **248**, 288–9.

Zwally, H. J., Major, J. A., Brenner, A. C. & Bindschadler, R. A. (1987). Ice measurements by Geosat radar altimeter. *Johns Hopkins APL Tech. Digest*, **8** (2), 251–4.

Zwally, H. J., Brenner, A. C., Major, J. A., Bindschadler, R. A. & Marsh, J. G. (1989). Growth of Greenland Ice Sheet: measurement. *Science*, **246**, 1587–9.

Glaciers

RICHARD S. WILLIAMS, JR. AND DOROTHY K. HALL

Introduction

A glacier is a multi-year surplus accumulation of snowfall in excess of snowmelt on land and resulting in a mass of ice at least 0.1 km² in area that shows some evidence of movement in response to gravity (Meier, 1974). A glacier may terminate on land, or it may terminate in water (Fig. 1). Glaciers are classified as continental ice sheets (> 50 000 km², Armstrong et al., 1973), ice caps (Fig. 2), ice fields, outlet glaciers (from ice sheets, ice caps, and ice fields) (Fig. 3), valley glaciers, mountain glaciers, glacierets, ice shelves, and rock glaciers (Unesco, 1970a; Sugden & John, 1976; Müller et al., 1977).

At present, the estimated volume and area of glacier ice on Earth is 32 950 000 km³ and 15 812 780 km², respectively (covering about 10.7% of the land area and 3.1% of the Earth's surface). Antarctica contains about 30 110 000 km³ and 13 586 380 km²; Greenland contains about 2 600 000 km³ and 1 726 400 km². Altogether, the Greenland ice sheet represents 7.9% of the total volume of glacier ice, and the Antarctic ice sheet and associated ice shelves represent 91.4% of the volume. The Greenland and Antarctic ice sheets account for 99.3% of the volume and 96.8% of the area of glaciers (Table 1). All of the other glaciers on Earth, found on every continent except Australia, account for only 0.7% of the total volume of glacier ice. Glacier ice is the largest reservoir of fresh water on Earth (77%) and the second largest reservoir of total water (2.15%) after the oceans, which contain 97.2% of the Earth's water (Table 2).

Glaciers play a major role in the global hydrologic cycle, especially the volumetric transfer of water between glacier ice and the oceans (Allison, 1981; Williams, 1990; Warrick & Oerlemans, 1990). The approximate maximum sea level rise potential (see definition, Table 1) for the Antarctic ice sheet, Greenland ice sheet, and smaller glaciers (ice caps, ice fields, valley glaciers, etc.) is 73.4 m, 6.5 m, and 0.6 m, respectively. During the most recent glacial maximum, about 18 000 years BP (before present) in the late Wisconsinan, the volume of glacier ice on the Earth was 2.5 times greater than that of today, and the area of the Earth covered by glacier ice was about 3 times that of today (Flint, 1957, 1971). Sea level was

also about 125 m lower (Fairbanks, 1989), so 8% more land was above sea level. The present land area is 29.1% of the Earth's surface. During 'Ice Age' maxima the land surface comprised 37.1% of the Earth's surface. During the last glacial minimum, about 120 000 years BP, the volume of glacier ice on the Earth was less than that of today. Sea level rose about 6 m beyond present-day sea level; recent research by Koerner (1989) suggests that the Greenland ice sheet nearly disappeared during the last interglacial. The Greenland ice sheet, therefore, is likely to be the primary contributor to sea level rise during an interglacial. Whether or not it is presently contributing to the sea level rise is not known (Reeh, 1985).

During the Pleistocene Epoch, when the land area covered by glacier ice was about triple that of today, the Earth's albedo was higher. Additionally, a greater expanse of land was covered by seasonal snow and contributed to a higher albedo. Thus, the cold climate was enhanced because less solar radiation was absorbed by the Earth's surface. The albedo of snow and ice is a crucial climatic parameter that has a significant effect upon the Earth's climate.

Unlike snow cover and sea ice, both of which vary seasonally, the total area covered by glacier ice changes slowly over time. All glaciers respond to climate change either by increasing or decreasing their total mass; changes in mass balance eventually result in a glacier's terminus or margin (for ice caps and ice sheets) advancing or retreating. Generally speaking, smaller glaciers respond more rapidly to changes in climate, although even large glaciers, such as ice sheets, ice caps, and ice fields, because they are actually aggregates of many independent glaciers, can also show annual or decadal changes along their margins. Glacier movement and changes in mass balance often occur on a timescale that is compatible with the lifespan of humans; annual- and decadal-scale changes in a glacier's terminus or margin and decadal-scale changes in volume may be measured in the field (ground-based observations), on oblique and vertical aerial photographs, or by satellite sensors (space-based observations). Measurement of changes in relative volume of glaciers by satellite sensors requires data delineating changes in area (from images) and in elevation (radar and laser altimetry or

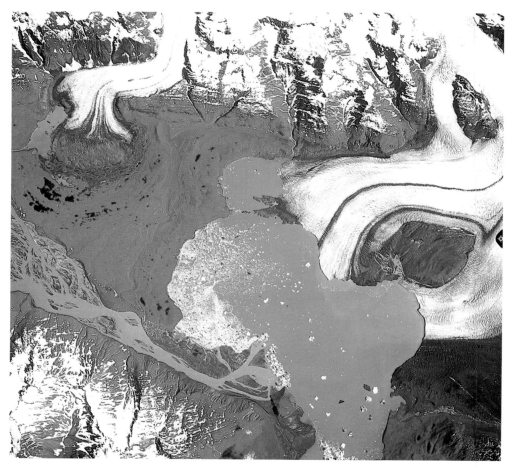

Fig. 1. NASA high-altitude, false-color infrared aerial photograph of the Alsek River and part of the terminus of the Alsek Glacier, southeast of Yakutat, Alaska, acquired from a U-2 aircraft on 21 June 1978 from an altitude of 19.8 km. EROS Data Center, Accession No. 578002618 ROLL, frame 4898.

satellite photogrammetry). Satellite altimetric measurements are still in the experimental stage. Measurement of changes in the area and relative volume of the Earth's glaciers can play an important role in the assessment of global climate change.

Ice sheets are continental in areal extent and several thousand meters thick; they exist today only in Antarctica and Greenland (see the chapter by Thomas, this volume). Antarctica has numerous fringing ice shelves (floating ice sheets) and two large ones, the Ross Ice Shelf and the Ronne/Filchner Ice Shelves, both in West Antarctica. Ice caps are dome-shaped masses of ice that flow radially from highland areas and usually have lobate or valley-glacier-like outlet glaciers on their margins. They are located principally in Iceland, Svalbard (Norwegian possession), on some of the Russian Arctic islands, northeastern Canada, China, Norway, and South America. Ice caps are of special interest because of their rapid response to climate change. Ice fields are similar to ice caps, except that they do not have sufficient thickness to

cover the terrain completely. They are located principally in southern South America (Fig. 4), Alaska, northeastern Canada, and Svalbard, and also have numerous valley-glacier-like outlet glaciers flowing from their margins. Valley glaciers usually originate in a well-defined catchment area called a cirque, a bowl-shaped hollow at a mountain divide. A mountain glacier occupies a cirque, niche, or crater and includes ice aprons on a mountain slope or groups of small units.

Ice sheets, ice caps, ice fields, and smaller glaciers have up to four facies that can be delineated on the basis of snow and ice density and wetness: dry-snow, percolation, wet-snow, and the ice facies (Benson, 1962; Benson & Motyka, 1979). Within the dry-snow facies, the glacier experiences negligible melting. The dry-snow facies exists only on the Antarctic ice sheet, in the northern interior and higher elevations of the Greenland ice sheet, and near the summits of the world's highest mountains (Paterson, 1981). The percolation facies is

402

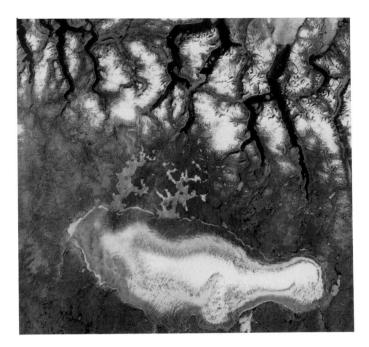

Fig. 2. Landsat 1 MSS image (10380–16182); 7 August 1973) of the 140-km long Barnes ice cap, Baffin Island, Northwest Territories, Canada. (NASA image courtesy of Canada Centre for Remote Sensing.)

Fig. 3. Landsat 2 MSS image (20204–16513; 14 August 1975) of numerous outlet glaciers from the ice field on Bylot Island, Northwest Territories, Canada. Small ice caps and associated small outlet glaciers can also be seen on neighboring Baffin Island. (NASA image courtesy of Canada Centre for Remote Sensing.)

Table 1. *Estimated present-day area* and volume* of glaciers and maximum sea level rise potential*

Geographic region	Area (km²)	Percent	Volume (km³)	Percent	Maximum sea level rise potential (m)**	Source for area and volume
Ice caps, ice fields, valley glaciers, etc.	500 000	3.22	240 000	0.7	0.6	Untersteiner (1975)
Greenland	1 726 400	10.9	2 600 000	7.9	6.5	Holtzscherer and Bauer (1954) and Weidick (in press)
Antarctica	13 586 380	85.9	30 110 000	91.4	73.4***	Drewry and others (1982)
East Antarctica	10 153 170		26 039 200		64.8	
West Antarctica	1 918 170		3 262 000		8.0	
Antarctic Peninsula	446 690		227 100		0.5	
Ross Ice Shelf	536 070		229 600		0.01	
Ronne-Filchner ice shelves	532 200		307 300		0.1	
Totals	15 812 780	100.0	32 950 000	100.0	80.5	

*Modified from Table 1 in Swithinbank (1985). **Sea level rise potential (in meters) [defined as the maximum sea level rise expected if all glacier ice were to melt in a specified geographic region based on a density of 0.9 for glacier ice (Robin, 1967), an ocean area of 3.62×10^6 km² (National Geographic Society, 1990), and 400 km³ of glacier ice melted to raise sea level 1 mm.] ***The total volume of glacier ice in Antarctica is 30 110 000 km³. For the calculation of sea level rise potential, only the grounded parts of the Antarctic ice sheets (including ice rises within the ice shelves) are used or a total grounded-ice volume of 29 377 700 km³. The total grounded ice volume includes 25 921 700 km³ for East Antarctica, 3 222 700 km³ for West Antarctic, and 183,700 km³ for the Antarctic Peninsula. The volume of ice rises on the Ross Ice Shelf and the Ronne-Filchner ice shelves are 5 100 km³ and 44 600 km³, respectively.

so named because localized melting occurs, and water percolates through the surface layers of snow before refreezing. Ice lenses and layers develop beneath the glacier surface. In the wet-snow facies, all snow deposited since the end of the previous summer becomes wet throughout by the end of the melt season. The ice facies extends from the firn line (the highest elevation to which the snow line recedes during summer) to the terminus of the glacier. The production of meltwater is the main ablation process here. Satellite images can be used to define the ice facies and the snow facies (combined

Table 2. *Estimated percentage by volume of the Earth's water supply (modified from US Geological Survey, 1976)*

'Reservoir'	Percentage of total water supply by volume
Surface water	
Freshwater lakes	9×10^{-3}
Saline lakes and inland seas	8×10^{-3}
Average in stream channels	1×10^{-4}
	Subtotal 1.71×10^{-3}
Subsurface water	
Vadose water (includes soil moisture)	5×10^{-3}
Ground water within upper 0.8 km of the Earth's crust	3.1×10^{-1}
Ground water (deeper than 0.8 km)	3.1×10^{-1}
	Subtotal 6.25×10^{-1}
Other	
Atmosphere	1×10^{-3}
Glacier ice	2.15
Oceans	97.2
	Subtotal 99.351
	Total 100

Fig. 4. Oblique color satellite photograph of most of the Southern Patagonian ice field along the crest of the Andes Mountains on the common border of Chile and Argentina, southern South America. Numerous outlet glaciers extend into fjords on the west and lakes on the east. Many of the lakes extend along valleys occupied by valley glaciers when the ice field expanded manyfold during the Pleistocene Epoch. The photograph was taken on 10 March 1978 from the Salyut-6 spacecraft by Soviet cosmonauts G.M. Grechko and Yu. V. Romanenko, as part of a series of glaciological research experiments designed by Vladimir M. Kotlyakov, glaciologist and Director, Institute of Geography, Russian Academy of Sciences. It is one of about 40 satellite photographs acquired of glaciers in the region (Denisov *et al.*, 1987; Williams, 1987*b*).

wet-snow, percolation, and dry-snow facies) (Williams, Hall and Benson, 1991) (Fig. 5).

Small glaciers, although they are just 0.7% of the total volume of the Earth's glaciers, still represent a significant reservoir of water (National Research Council, 1985; Table 1). According to Meier (1984, 1985), mass loss of small glaciers, from the ice facies and from meltwater runoff from the wet-snow facies, is the most probable source of about 50 percent of the 10–20 cm of sea level rise that has occurred during the past century. Although there have been few long-term, *in situ* measurements of small glaciers worldwide, geologic and historic evidence has shown that, in general, the world's small glaciers have retreated for 100 years or more, essentially at the end of a prolonged period of cooling popularly referred to as the 'Little Ice Age'. Grove (1988) provides a comprehensive review of the historical, geological, and glaciological evidence for the 'Little Ice Age' climatic fluctuation.

Methodology

Glaciers may be studied *in situ* and/or by airborne and satellite-borne remote-sensing methods (Williams, 1983*a*). Beginning in the early 1970s, the study of glaciers by satellite sensors became an important method of studying changes in areal extent, terminus position, and glacier dynamics (Williams, 1985, 1986*a, b*). The Landsat satellite series was first launched in July 1972 with a multispectral scanner system (MSS) and a return beam vidicon (RBV) camera on-board. The MSS eventually imaged most of the world's glaciers

under cloud-free conditions (Williams, 1986*a*; Williams & Ferrigno, 1991); it passed over the same spot on the Earth's surface, between about 81° N and S latitudes, every 18 days. In 1982, the thematic mapper (TM) sensor was flown on Landsat 4; it was launched with a 16-day repeat cycle.

Aerial photography has been invaluable for assessing glacier changes as well as for locating glaciers prone to rapid terminus change. Synthetic aperture radar (SAR) data have also been obtained of glaciers, and SAR sensors provide images through cloud cover. The Seasat satellite operated for a few months in 1978 and obtained SAR data of some of the world's glaciers. These data may be compared with Landsat data (Fig. 6) (Hall & Ormsby, 1983) and aerial photographs to enhance one's ability to interpret surface (Fig. 7) and near-surface features (NASA, 1989).

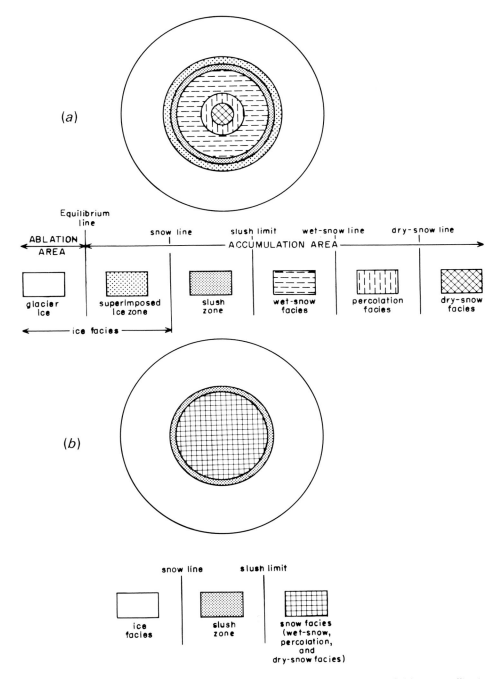

Fig. 5. Schematic diagram of glacier facies. A. Field-identifiable facies. B. Facies identifiable on satellite images.

Ground observations

Using guidelines promulgated by the International Association of Scientific Hydrology (IASH), under the sponsorship of the United Nations Educational, Scientific, and Cultural Organization (Unesco), glaciologists from all over the world have standardized field observations of glacier fluctuation and glacier mass balance measurements (Unesco, 1969, 1970a, b, Østrem & Brugman, 1991). Kasser (1967, 1973), Müller (1977), Haeberli (1985), and Haeberli and Müller (1988) published a series of reports on glacier variation, first under the auspices of the Permanent Service on the Fluctuation of Glaciers (PSFG) and later under the World Glacier Monitoring Service (WGMS) in Zürich, Switzerland. The PSFG is

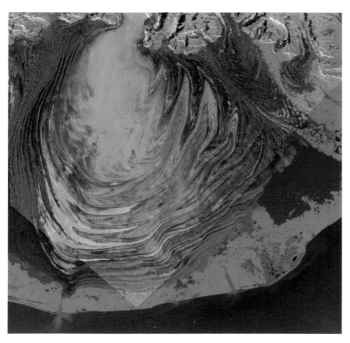

Fig. 6. Landsat MSS bands 5 and 7 (21 675–19 482, 24 August 1979) of the Malaspina Glacier, southeastern Alaska, combined with Seasat SAR data (05520270); 3 August 1978. (From Hall & Ormsby, 1983.)

Fig. 7. Oblique aerial photograph of the southeastern part of the Malaspina Glacier showing the prominent contorted moraines that have resulted from periodic surges. Photograph no. 425 taken by Austin Post, US Geological Survey, on 15 August 1969. (Photograph courtesy of US Geological Survey Photographic Library.)

now a part of the WGMS; WGMS also assumed responsibility for operating the Unesco-sponsored Temporary Technical Secretariat for the world glacier inventory project to compile a basic inventory of all the world's glaciers (International Association of Hydrological Sciences, 1980; Haeberli *et al.*, 1989*a, b*). Müller and others (1977), and Müller (1978) provided a standardized methodology and set of data sheets for compiling a world glacier inventory based on field observations and interpretation of aerial photographs. Scherler (1983) prepared additional instructions and special data sheets for using Landsat and other types of satellite imagery to compile glacier inventories of remote glacierized regions or regions where adequate maps or aerial photographs are lacking. Swithinbank (1983) broadened the perspective of the glacier inventory project to include the Greenland and Antarctic ice sheets.

The six volumes published by PSFG and WGMS cover the years 1959–1985 and are compilations of glaciological data submitted by correspondents in various countries to the PSFG and the WGMS. Wood (1988*a*) used part of this extensive database to analyze trends in global alpine glaciers from 1960 to 1980. He concluded that, during the 20-year period, alpine glaciers shifted from a primarily recessionary mode to a mixed one, and that many temperate glaciers were readvancing, from 7% of observed glaciers in 1960 to 55% in

1980. He also recommended that satellite images be used to augment ground observations, especially in glacierized regions where only a few, if any, glaciers are monitored on an annual basis. In a related paper, Wood (1988*b*) argued for a systems research approach to investigations of global climate change. During the 1980s, however, many temperate glaciers that had been advancing began to retreat again.

Glacier fluctuation data are based on direct field observations made by scientists or trained laymen, from analysis of vertical or oblique aerial photographs, or by analysis of satellite images. An outstanding example is the Icelandic glacier-observation program, started in 1950, in which trained lay people, often local farmers or sheepherders in remote areas, form the network of observers. They report on unusual glaciological phenomena, such as glacier surges and jökulhlaups (glacier outburst floods), and make annual measurements of glacier advance or recession. Oddur Sigurdsson (1988) collates observations made by various observers, combines them in tabular form and accompanying text, and publishes the compilation in the Icelandic glaciological research journal *Jökull* each year (Sigurdsson, 1988). He also forwards the tabular information to the WGMS for inclusion in their publications.

Worldwide, only a few mass balance measurements of glaciers are made each year because of the high cost and labor-intensive nature of such measurements. Long-term mass balance measurements have been made by the US Geological Survey on South Cascade Glacier, Washington, since 1958, on the Gulkana Glacier in the central Alaska Range since 1965, and on the Wolverine Glacier in the Kenai Mountains, Alaska, since 1968. In most glacierized regions, mass balance data are collected for scientific reasons, generally as part of a glaciological/meteorological research station run by a university. These studies generally operate only for a few years. However, there are notable exceptions, such as the Blue Glacier research on Washington's Olympic Peninsula operated by the California Institute of Technology and the University of Washington since 1957. Also, the longest continuous mass balance research program in the world is on Storglaciären in northern Sweden, operated by the University of Stockholm. When glacier meltwater flows into reservoirs used for hydroelectric power generation, such as in Norway and Switzerland, the mass balance data have economic value, and well-designed, national programs to collect such data are in operation.

Aerial observations

The labor-intensive nature of ground observations only permits a few glaciers to be monitored annually. Airborne remote sensing technology has been used since the 1930s as a means of acquiring data on glacier fluctuation on a regional basis. Vertical aerial photographs are often the most useful data available of glaciers for any given area, and, if aerial photographs are available for different dates, areal and volumetric changes in glaciers can be monitored (Haakensen, 1986).

In most cases, vertical aerial photographs, with sufficient overlap to achieve stereoscopic coverage, are acquired to support topographic mapping programs based on aerial photogrammetric methods tied to photo-identifiable ground-control points established by geodetic surveys. For example, aerial photography has been combined with precision ground surveying to measure rate of ice loss from glaciers that are melting because of volcanic heat flux (Benson & Follett, 1986). Østrem and Tvede (1986) discussed the use of sequential maps of glaciers to provide climatological information.

Vertical aerial photographs are usually acquired by a national mapping agency and archived in a central data center. In the United States, the US Geological Survey's National Mapping Division is the responsible agency for the acquisition of aerial photographs used to support national mapping requirements. The central archive is the EROS

Data Center (EDC) in Sioux Falls, South Dakota. During the past decade, a consortium of several federal agencies has supported a national high-altitude aerial photographic acquisition program in the conterminous United States. Both black-and-white and color–infrared vertical aerial photographs are reacquired of each area routinely. In the late 1970s, a NASA U-2 aircraft was used to acquire color–infrared aerial photographs of much of Alaska (Fig. 1).

For most years, the US Geological Survey's Water Resources Division schedules aerial surveys of glaciers in the Pacific Northwest and Alaska to acquire, on an annual basis, an oblique and/or vertical aerial photographic record of the position of glacier termini. This is attained at the end of the ablation period, which is the optimum time to acquire aerial photographs of glaciers for mass balance studies. For temperate glaciers in the Northern Hemisphere, early September is the approximate end of the ablation period and the beginning of the accumulation period.

The spatial resolution of Landsat TM and SPOT images is adequate to provide information relating to the position of glacier termini, except that the images are not acquired routinely. The high cost of purchasing the data often precludes extensive time-series analysis on a routine basis. Both vertical aerial photographs and satellite images must be acquired under cloud-free conditions and near the end of the ablation period.

Other types of airborne remote-sensing data exist, such as SAR or multispectral scanner images. Unless such data are acquired as part of a major program, however, the data are often difficult to locate, and typically reside in the offices of the project scientist responsible for the investigation. Some of the available coverage of the United States is discussed in Williams (1983b).

Satellite observations

The launch of the first Landsat spacecraft in July 1972 revolutionized the study of glacier fluctuations. It also permitted the comparative analysis of Landsat images of glaciers and related glacial landforms on a global basis for the first time (Williams, 1986a). Analysis of changes in area and changes in position of glacier termini became possible over much of the world (Fig. 8) (Williams, 1985). MSS images (and a few RBV images) from Landsats 1 and 2 provided nearly complete coverage of the land areas of the planet to about 81° N and S latitude. Landsat 3 provided MSS images and RBV images with improved pixel resolution (about 30 m for the Landsat 3 RBV versus 80 m for Landsat 1 and 2 MSS and RBV and Landsat 3 MSS images) of selected areas. Landsats 4 and 5 provided (and continue to provide) MSS images (80 m pixels)

Fig. 8. Landsat TM image acquired on 16 September 1986 (50929–20093) of the Mt. Wrangell area showing changes in the termini of the MacKeith Glaciers (unofficial names), which began to advance around 1964. Arrows show that the termini advanced about 190 m between 1973, when an MSS image was acquired (1422–20212; 18 September 1973) and 1986, when the TM image was acquired. The yellow lines represent the termini positions determined from the MSS data.

and TM images (30 m pixels) of selected areas. Since the commercialization of the Landsat program, data for regions that provide no profitability are not acquired on a systematic basis, even though such regions may be important scientifically. All Landsat data are archived at the EDC, Sioux Falls, South Dakota, or by data centers operated by foreign Landsat receiving stations. Older (>2 years old) Landsat MSS data are sold by the EDC; all other Landsat data are marketed by EOSAT Corporation, the private company designated by the US Congress, as the sole distributor of Landsat data.

The French Satellite Pour l'Observation de la Terre (SPOT) has, since 1986, acquired panchromatic (10 m pixel) and multispectral (20 m pixel) images of the Earth's surface, and these are also useful for glacier studies. SPOT images are archived at the primary data center in Toulouse, France, although SPOT images can also be obtained from regional archives at several foreign locations.

The Russian space program has also acquired a large number of photographs and multispectral scanner images by manned (Williams, 1987*b*) and unmanned spacecraft. Both photographic and image data of selected areas are made available to all users through Soyuzkarta, a marketing agency operated by Russia. Ferrigno and Molnia (1989) discussed Landsat, SPOT, and Soyuzkarta coverage of Antarctica. Fig. 4 is a color satellite photograph of the Southern Patagonian ice field in southern South America taken during one of the Salyut-6 missions in 1978 (Denisov *et al.*, 1987).

Seasat and Shuttle Imaging Radar (SIR) missions acquired SAR images of selected areas. Ford and others (1980) and Hunting Geology and Geophysics, Ltd. (no date) compiled a 1:500 000 scale Seasat SAR mosaic of most of Iceland, including all of its ice caps and smaller glaciers. ERS-1, which was launched by the European Space Agency in 1991, is currently acquiring SAR images of many areas and is discussed in the section 'future sensors'.

Analysis and results

Inter-annual changes in the distribution of the glacier facies on a particular glacier or ice sheet are indicative of a mass balance change. For example, expansion of the ablation area over a period of years is indicative of a negative mass balance on a particular glacier. Changes in the boundaries between the other facies upglacier will also take place. Some of the glacier facies boundaries are visible if Landsat MSS and TM data are used (Crabtree, 1976; Hall *et al.*, 1987; Williams, 1987*a*; Williams, Hall & Benson, 1991). Changes in glaciers should be analyzed in concert with other climate variables, such as areal extent and concentration of sea ice, diurnal and seasonal temperatures, seasonal precipitation and whether solid or liquid, sea level change, etc., to develop an improved understanding of the total Earth system's response to global environmental change.

Studies of satellite-derived reflectances of glaciers reveal a distinct boundary at the snowline (Krimmel & Meier, 1975) which, if measured at the time of maximum melt, is coincident with the equilibrium line. The location of the equilibrium line can be used to measure mass balance change, when satellite data are used (Østrem, 1975; Østrem and Haakensen, 1992). Landsat TM data may be used to measure the reflectance of snow and ice features (Dozier, 1989), and results show that varying reflectances may characterize individual facies because of different grain size and wetness characteristics within the facies (Hall *et al.*, 1987). Reflectance of snow and ice may be measured by use of Landsat TM data after corrections for atmospheric effects have been made (Dozier, Schneider & McGinnis, 1981; Dozier, 1984 and 1989; Hall *et al.*, 1989). These Landsat-derived reflectances of snow and ice represent realistic reflec-

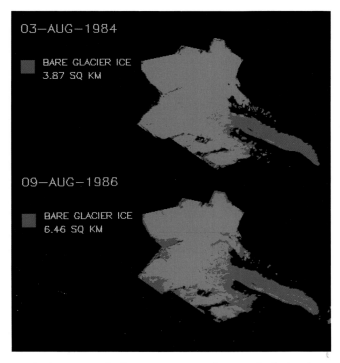

03–AUG–1984

■ BARE GLACIER ICE
3.87 SQ KM

09–AUG–1986

■ BARE GLACIER ICE
6.46 SQ KM

Fig. 9. Inter-annual changes in area of exposed glacier ice on Pasterze Glacier, Austria, from analysis of Landsat images acquired on 3 August 1984 and 9 August 1986.

tances that have been shown to compare well, under some circumstances, with reflectances measured *in situ* (Hall *et al.*, 1989).

It is important to use reflectance values to be able to measure changes in glacier reflectance accurately. This is because analysis of changes in tone on photographic products may be misleading and may preclude an accurate interpretation of facies boundaries and thus changes in facies boundaries or mass balance over time.

Work done on the Pasterze Glacier of the Grossglockner Mountain system of glaciers in the eastern Alps of Austria shows that the glacier's recession is accompanied by an expansion of the ablation area of the Pasterze Glacier basin (Hall *et al.*, 1987 and 1989), as seen in Fig. 9. Because the ablation area has a lower reflectance than the accumulation area, it is easily distinguished. Other work (Williams *et al.*, 1991) has shown that TM reflectances on Brúarjökull, an outlet glacier of the Vatnajökull ice cap, Iceland (Williams, 1987*a*), reveals boundaries that appear to delineate the ice facies and slush zone. Through analysis of the reflectance of the various facies within a glacier, as measured by use of TM digital data, one can infer mass balance change if data are acquired at the end of the melt season, and over a period of years. Münzer and Bodechtel (1980) also experimented with

analysis of digitally enhanced Landsat images of Vatnajökull.

The ability of SAR to penetrate cloud cover enables the imaging of some glaciers that are almost continually cloud covered. While visible data are excellent for analysis of glacier surface conditions such as flow lines, ogives, and large crevasses, penetration through the surface layers of snow with SAR may reveal boundaries of the glacier facies that are not visible from the surface (NASA, 1989). These transition areas are covered by snow and firn and thus are not visible to sensors operating in the visible and near infra-red parts of the electromagnetic spectrum.

Until the advent of the Landsat and other satellite remote-sensing programs, glaciologists had no means of measuring and monitoring fluctuations of glaciers on a global basis. This lack of knowledge has been (and still is) a special problem in polar regions, where the greatest mass of glacier ice exists (Robin Drewry & Squire, 1983; Thomas, 1991).

Landsat images permit decade-scale glacier changes to be monitored from an initial baseline of glacier terminus or margins and areal extent (Williams & Ferrigno, 1988*a*, *b*). Ice caps in Iceland and in Svalbard and the Antarctic ice sheet have been the focus of a number of investigations with Landsat images. Williams (1983*c*) reviewed the use of satellite images to study Iceland's glaciers. Landsat images and maps formed the basis of an analysis on how best to compile a glacier inventory of Iceland (Williams, 1986*b*). Dowdeswell (1984, 1986), Dowdeswell and Cooper (1986), and Dowdeswell and McIntyre (1987) used Landsat images of ice caps in Svalbard in conjunction with airborne radio-echosounding surveys to better define the surface and subsurface morphology of these large ice caps.

Antarctica is covered with 2514 Landsat nominal scene centers (grid-point intersections of Landsat orbits (251) and rows (119)). As a result of the large number of Landsat scenes of Antarctica, properly indexing the images suitable for glaciological investigations is a monumental problem (Williams & Ferrigno, 1988*b*, *c*). Williams *et al.* (1982), Swithinbank and Lucchitta (1986), and Lucchitta *et al.* (1987) discussed the use of Landsat images, in photographic and digital format, for mapping and glaciological studies. Because of the association of many 'blue ice' areas (bare glacier ice) with meteorites in Antarctica, Landsat images have proven to be useful in the identification and mapping of such areas (Williams, Meunier & Ferrigno, 1983). Areal changes in the coastal margins of Antarctica have been monitored and measured by Colvill (1977), Ferrigno and Gould (1987), Williams and Ferrigno (1988*a*), and Ferrigno *et al.* (1990).

Through the use of satellite image time-lapse techniques, the average velocity of glacier flow can be calculated. Williams *et al.* (1974) measured the average velocity of Skeidarárjökull, one of Vatnajökull's outlet glaciers, at 655 m a^{-1} from two Landsat images acquired 11 months apart. Williams *et al.*, (1982) calculated an average velocity of 2.2 km a^{-1} for the Pine Island Glacier, a tidal outlet glacier in West Antarctica. Lucchitta and Ferguson (1986), MacDonald *et al.* (1990), and Lucchitta *et al.* (1990*a*, *b*) have measured the average velocity of more than 15 outlet glaciers in Antarctica. From flow lines discernible on outlet glaciers, ice streams, and ice shelves in Antarctica, Crabtree and Doake (1980), McIntyre (1983, 1985), and Simmons (1986) examined the dynamics of outlet glaciers and ice streams. Bindschadler and Scambos (1991) used a new analytical technique with Landsat TM images to determine the velocity field of 'Ice Stream E', one of the five major ice streams that flows into the east side of the Ross Ice Shelf, Antarctica. Thomas (see companion chapter 'Ice Sheets' in this book) provides additional information about satellite remote sensing of the Antarctic and Greenland ice sheets.

Response of glaciers to climate change

Wastage of small glaciers (including ice caps) has contributed to the rise in sea level during the past century. Melting of the Greenland and Antarctic ice sheets does not appear to have been a factor in sea level rise over the last century, although the present state of mass balance of both ice sheets is unknown (National Research Council, 1985). About two-thirds of the calculated glacier contribution to sea level rise is thought to be from meltwater originating from glaciers in the mountains bordering the Gulf of Alaska, the high mountains of central Asia, and glaciers in the Patagonian Andes (Meier, 1984, 1985). Mid-latitude glaciers will likely continue to be contributors to sea level rise, because they are closest to decay (Kuhn, 1985). Glacier shrinkage has been most pronounced since the late 1800s in the temperate mid-latitudes and somewhat less pronounced in the high latitudes; however, mass balance data are very sparse (National Research Council, 1985). Mayo and Trabant (1984) found that from 1965 through 1976, Wolverine Glacier in Alaska underwent a small, net thinning over the 11-year period; however, since 1977, as the regional climate has warmed, the glacier thickened because of increased snow accumulation (Mayo, March & Trabant, 1988). Other glaciers located in the central Alaska Range, such as the Gulkana and the Black Rapids Glaciers, have also increased in mass since 1980.

Global warming could produce a mixture of glacier growth and glacier thinning with non-synchronous advances and non-synchronous retreats worldwide (Mayo & Trabant, 1984). Warmer air in the lower troposphere may permit more moisture to be retained and thus released as precipitation. Eventually, however, if global temperatures increase, glaciers will recede.

Applications

Environmental considerations and glaciological hazards

In many regions of the world, glaciers are an important source of water, especially during the summer. Glaciers tend to maintain the flow of streams during the hot summer months, when water is most needed for irrigation and recreation. As glaciers shrink, this seasonally important water source diminishes (Meier & Tangborn, 1961; Post *et al.*, 1971).

Although most of the Earth's glaciers are located in remote areas, well away from population centers, there are four types of hazards associated with glaciers that can damage or destroy fixed facilities (e.g. dams, roads and railroads, buildings, etc.), sink or damage ships, or cause loss of life. The four types of hazards are 1) slow (advance or retreat) and fast (surge) movement, 2) jökulhlaups, 3) iceberg discharge, and 4) rapid ice break-offs. Switzerland, for example, because of the occurrence of glaciers and population located in intermontane valleys and high relief areas typical of many alpine villages, has a high risk of hazards associated with glaciers: glacier advance, ice avalanches, and jökulhlaups (Haeberli *et al.*, 1989*c*).

The advance or retreat rate of a glacier terminus or margin is normally relatively slow, a few meters to a few tens of meters per year. In temperate latitudes, glacier termini have been in a general state of recession since the end of the 'Little Ice Age', or since the late 1800s. During the latter part of the twentieth century, however, many temperate glaciers began to readvance (Wood, 1988*a*) probably in response to heavier snowfalls in the winter and cloudier, cooler summers; during the 1980s, however, most of the glaciers that were advancing began to retreat again. Although a slowly readvancing glacier may eventually overrun fixed facilities, such as dams and roads, the main danger, in the case of slow advance or recession, is the creation of glacier-dammed lakes in tributary valleys during an advance, or the failure of an ice dam during recession. The resulting flood is called a jökulhlaup.

Jökulhlaups, or glacier outburst floods, are the largest flood events known to occur on Earth. For example, jökulhlaups in Iceland occur either as the result of the failure of dams of ice-dammed lakes (Thorarinsson, 1940) (Fig. 10) or as the result of subglacial geothermal or volcanic activity (Thorarinsson, 1957, 1958; Björnsson, 1975, 1976). Landsat images (Thorarinsson *et al.*, 1974; Williams & Thorarinsson, 1974;

Fig. 10. RBV image of part of a Landsat 3 RBV image (30157–11572-A; 9 August 1978) showing ice-dammed Grænalón, a proglacial lake which is the source of annual jökulhlaups (glacier-outburst floods). A distributary glacier from the Skeiðarárjökull outlet glacier, on the southern margin of the Vatnajökull ice cap (Iceland's largest at 8300 km²), forms the ice dam. (NASA image courtesy of the USGS EROS Data Center.)

Williams *et al.*, 1974, 1975; Williams, 1976; Rist, 1974; Björnsson, 1975; Tómasson, 1975) have been used to monitor and document phenomena related to jökulhlaups in Iceland. Jökulhlaups from partial emptying of the Grímsvötn caldera in the Vatnajökull ice cap, southwestern Iceland, following lifting of an ice dam, have been measured at 1×10^4 m³ s⁻¹ by Rist (1974). In the past, discharges of 5×10^4 m³ s⁻¹ from Grímsvötn were usual (Thorarinsson, 1957). Thorarinsson (1957) also estimated peak discharge during short-lived jökulhlaups from the eruption of Katla under the Mýrdalsjökull ice cap to have exceeded 2×10^5 m³ s⁻¹.

The 18 May 1980 catastrophic eruption of Mount St Helens, Washington, included a jökulhlaup component in the debris flow that coursed down the Toutle and Cowlitz River valleys (Brugman & Post, 1981). All of the glacier-capped volcanoes of the Cascade Mountains, as well as other ice-capped volcanoes throughout the world (for example, South America, Iceland, Jan Mayen (Norway), Canada, Alaska, Antarctica, Africa, Turkey, Iran, New Zealand, and Kamchatka) have a potential for jökulhlaup events. The 1985 eruption of Nevado del Ruiz, Colombia, also included a substantial jökulhlaup component, from partial melting of the summit ice cap, in the debris-charged floods that swept down

river valleys on its flanks (Naranjo *et al.*, 1986). As a result, more than 25 000 lives were lost in the town of Armero (Lowe *et al.*, 1986; Herd, 1986).

In Alaska, occasional jökulhlaups occur that are caused by subglacial geothermal or volcanic activity (Benson & Motyka, 1979), but the vast majority of glacier outburst floods are caused by the failure of ice-dammed lakes (Post & Mayo, 1971; Sturm & Benson, 1985, 1989; Sturm, Beget & Benson, 1987). The Hubbard Glacier, a tidewater glacier, moved forward rapidly in the spring of 1986, creating a temporary ice dam that blocked the mouth of Russell Fiord on 29 May 1986 (Fig. 11). The water level in the newly formed lake rose rapidly from runoff of melting snow and ice in the nearby mountains. Incoming freshwater floated on top of the salt water, jeopardizing marine mammals that thrive in salt water but were trapped in the lake. On 8 October 1986, failure of the ice dam (Mayo, 1988) resulted in an enormous jökulhlaup as 'Russell Lake' drained catastrophically (about 5.4 km³ total volume of water released) into Disenchantment Bay. Mayo (1988) estimated the peak discharge at 1×10^6 m³ s⁻¹. Jökulhlaups from the northwestern United States have been documented by Richardson (1968).

A surging glacier is a type of glacier in which the normal flow suddenly increases ten to one thousand times the normal rate. The terminus advances suddenly on the order of several kilometers or more over a period of a few months (Meier & Post, 1969; Clarke *et al.*, 1986). An increase in length of 25 percent may result (Clarke *et al.*, 1986). A surging glacier can be a hazard if it occurs near fixed structures. Sudden advances may engulf parts of highways, railroads, dams, or other structures and create ice-dammed lakes in tributary valleys (Krimmel *et al.*, 1976; Meier, 1976; Post *et al.*, 1976).

Post (1969) reviewed the geographic distribution of surge-type glaciers in North America. Of the thousands of glaciers examined on aerial photographs, 204 showed evidence of present or past surge-type flow. Although the non-random geographical distribution of surge-type glaciers would indicate environmental influences, no obvious control mechanisms have been identified (Post, 1969; Clarke *et al.*, 1986). Large numbers of surge-type glaciers are found in several well-defined areas. Many additional surge-type glaciers have been identified by use of Landsat imagery. Wavy or contorted medial moraines are produced as converging glaciers move differentially during a surge phase, when the forward velocity is high, as in the case of the Black Rapids Glacier, Klutlan Glacier (Fig. 12), or the southeastern part of the Malaspina Glacier (Figs. 6 and 7). Because of the characteristic medial moraine pattern, one can locate surge-type glaciers by using both Landsat MSS (Meier, 1976) and TM imagery (Fig. 13). The Landsat database should prove useful as an historical

Fig. 11. Enlargement of Landsat TM false-color image (50924–19513); 11 September 1986) of the terminus of the Hubbard Glacier, a tidewater glacier, after it advanced forward to close off the mouth of Russell Fiord, southeastern Alaska. The ice dam was only temporary, failing on 8 October 1986 and unleashing a major jökulhlaup into Disenchantment Bay (Mayo, 1988). Landsat and SPOT images can be used to periodically monitor the position of many glacier termini to determine whether an advance or recession has taken place between image acquisition dates (Mayo, 1988). (NASA image courtesy of the USGS EROS Data Center.)

base to study the surge histories of glaciers since 1972, when Landsat 1 was launched. Svalbard, a glacierized archipelago in the North Atlantic Ocean belonging to Norway, probably has more surging glaciers than any other region on Earth. Liestøl (1992) noted that 86 glaciers in Svalbard were observed to have surged since the end of the 19th century. Thorarinsson (1964, 1969) reviewed the history of glacier surges in Iceland; Williams and others (1974) discussed the surge of Eyjabakkajökull, an outlet glacier from the Vatnajökull ice cap as recorded in a time-lapse manner on sequential Landsat images.

It is not known why some glaciers are prone to surging and why others are not (Meier & Post, 1969). A detailed examination of the non-random distribution of surging glaciers, done by Clarke et al. (1986) and by Wilbur (1988), underscored the complexity of the distribution problem. However, Kamb and others (1985) have shown that water volume, distribution, and flow at the base of the Variegated Glacier, Alaska, changed dramatically at the start of the surge, and that basal lubrication was necessary for the high rates of speed attained during the surge phase. High basal water pressure causes a great increase in basal sliding by reducing friction and increasing basal cavitation (Kamb et al., 1985).

Tidewater glaciers terminate in ocean water; they experience a unique cycle of advance and rapid retreat that is independent of short-term climate change (Austin Post, pers. comm., 1991). There is also a seasonal pattern of fluctuation superimposed on a long-term trend (Meier, 1985). In the ablation season, the glacier retreats as icebergs calve, while in the winter, when calving rates slow, the glacier moves forward. When the amount of ice supplied in the accumulation area equals the amount of ice lost through calving, the glacier is in equilibrium. However, when glacier velocity is less than the calving rate, the terminus of the glacier will retreat, and icebergs will be released. The rate of iceberg calving is dependent upon the water depth at the grounded terminus of tidewater glaciers (Post, 1977). If the glacier terminates in shallow water, the rate of iceberg calving is low, but in deep water the rate is high. In the case of the Columbia Glacier in south-eastern Alaska (Fig. 14), the water is deeper toward the land and thus a retreat to the deeper water area causes an accelerated retreat (Meier et al., 1980). Of the 52 tidewater glaciers in the area, Columbia Glacier is the last to undergo a rapid retreat (Fig. 15) (Meier & Post, 1987).

Examples of satellite remote sensing studies of glaciers

Areal and velocity changes

Areal changes in glaciers can be measured by use of Landsat MSS and TM data. Satellite data have been available to measure changes in some glaciers over a period of two decades. These measurements may be compared with measurements made on the ground and on aerial photographs. Measurements using an 18 September 1973 Landsat MSS image registered digitally to a 16 September 1986 TM image reveal that the center lobes of the Ahtna and the MacKeith Glaciers (both flow north from Mt Wrangell) have advanced approximately 190 m during the 13-year period (Fig. 8). This measurement is consistent with the average

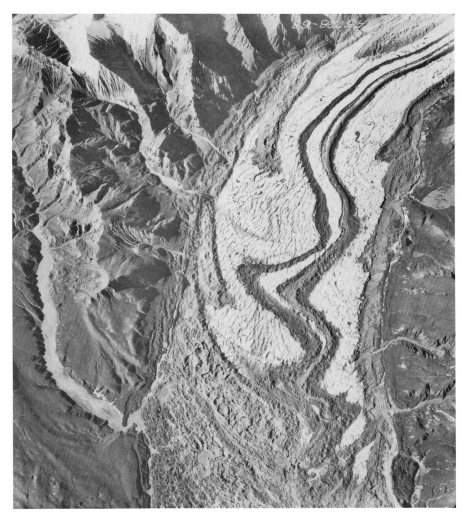

Fig. 12. Contorted medial moraines on the Klutlan Glacier, an 89-km long surging glacier in southwestern Yukon Territory, Canada. (Vertical aerial photograph no. A15728–63 courtesy of the National Air Photo Library, Canada.)

15 m a^{-1} advance that has been measured by precision surveying and photogrammetry on the center lobe of MacKeith Glacier during this period (Sturm, 1983). Landsat digital data show that all of the other termini of glaciers emanating from Mt Wrangell appear to be stationary. While movement of the termini may have occurred on some glaciers, debris-laden termini are difficult to distinguish from the surrounding moraine and outwash plain; thus, image or digital data may not be able to discern movement of the terminus. The advance of the glaciers flowing north from Mt Wrangell is thought to be due to increased geothermal activity near the summit of Mt Wrangell (Motyka, 1983) and not due to short-term climate change (Benson & Follett, 1986; Sturm, 1983; Sturm *et al.*, 1991).

In situ analysis of the Harvard and Yale Glaciers in College Fjord in southern Alaska shows that the Harvard Glacier has advanced an average of about 40 m a^{-1} since 1910. The adjacent Yale Glacier has retreated an average of about 80 m a^{-1} during that same time period. Analysis of a 15 August 1973 Landsat MSS scene and a 1 August 1985 TM scene shows a maximum terminus advance on the Harvard Glacier of about 27 m a^{-1}. A maximum retreat of the terminus of the Yale Glacier of 138 m a^{-1} has also been measured by use of the same satellite data. The behavior of these tidewater glaciers, which are adjacent and at the head of the same fjord, are in the same climatic setting, and are flowing from an interconnecting snow and firn field, provides a striking example of non-climatic controls on glacier flow (Sturm *et al.*, 1991).

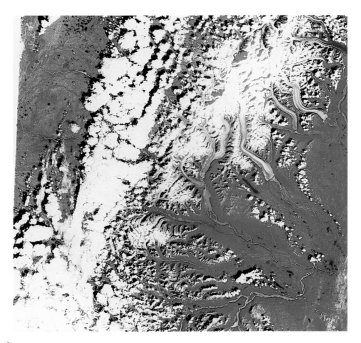

Fig. 13. Landsat 1 MSS false-color infra-red image (1033–21020; 25 August 1972) of valley glaciers in the Mt. McKinley region, Alaska. Three surging glaciers, easily identified by the wavy (contorted) medial moraines, can be identified: the Yentna Glacier and the Lacuna Glacier on the left, and the Tokositna Glacier on the right (Meier, 1976). (NASA image courtesy of the USGS EROS Data Center.)

Fig. 14. Oblique aerial photograph of Columbia Glacier, Alaska, in July 1976, before it began a catastrophic retreat as predicted by the US Geological Survey (Meier and others, 1980). (Photograph by Larry R. Mayo, US Geological Survey.)

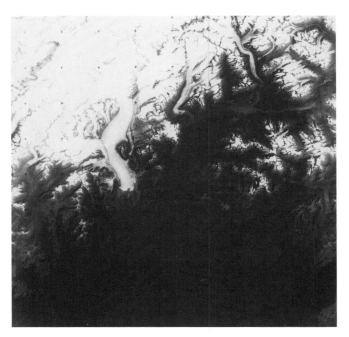

Fig. 15. Landsat 3 RBV (30174–20290-D) image of the Columbia Glacier, Prince William Sound, Alaska, on 26 August 1978. A rapid retreat of the Columbia Glacier began in the early 1980s, several years later than expected from field measurements carried out in the late 1970s and from predictions made by Meier and others (1980). On the Landsat image, the terminus has retreated from its terminal moraine at the head of the fjord. Note the large embayment that has formed in the central part of its terminus. (NASA image courtesy of the USGS EROS Data Center.)

Global glacier inventory

The realization that one element of the Earth's cryosphere, its glaciers, was amenable to inventorying and areal change monitoring with Landsat images led to the decision, in 1978, to prepare the 11-volume US Geological Survey Professional Paper, *Satellite Image Atlas of Glaciers of the World* (Professional Paper 1386-A-K), in which Landsat 1, 2, and 3 MSS and RBV images are used to inventory the areal occurrence of glacier ice on our planet within the spacecraft's orbital coverage (Ferrigno & Williams, 1980; Williams & Ferrigno, 1981, 1990). Between 1979 and 1981, optimum Landsat images (minimum snow cover and cloud cover for each glacierized region) were distributed to an international team of 54 scientists (from 25 nations, representing 42 different institutions), who agreed to author a chapter or subchapter of the Professional Paper concerning either a geographic area or a glaciological topic. In addition to analyzing images of a specific geographic area, each author was asked to summarize up-to-date information about the glaciers within the area and to compare the present areal distribution of glaciers with reliable historical information about their past extent (for example, from published maps, reports, and photographs). Because of the limitations of Landsat images for delineating or monitoring small glaciers in some geographic areas (for example, inadequate spatial resolution, lack of suitable seasonal coverage, or complete absence of coverage), information on areal distribution is sometimes derived from ancillary sources.

Four volumes ('chapters') have been published: Chapter B, Antarctica (Swithinbank, 1988), Chapter H, Glaciers of Irian Jaya, Indonesia, and New Zealand (Allison & Peterson, 1989), Chapter G, Glaciers of the Middle East and Africa (Kurter *et al.*, 1991), and Chapter E, Glaciers of Europe (Rott *et al.*, 1992), seven more chapters remain to be published. When the 'Atlas' is completed, it will provide an accurate regional inventory of the areal extent of glaciers on our planet within a relatively short time (1972 to 1982). This global 'snapshot' or 'benchmark' of glacier extent already is being used for comparative analysis with previously published maps and aerial photographs and with new maps, satellite images, and aerial photographs to determine the areal fluctuation of glaciers in response to natural or culturally induced changes in the Earth's climate.

Future sensors

Detailed analysis of glacier dynamics, reflectance, and movement requires good (preferably 30 m or better) pixel resolution. Sensors operating in the reflective and microwave parts of the electromagnetic spectrum are especially useful for glacier studies.

Early in 1993, Landsat 6 will be launched with an enhanced thematic mapper (ETM) sensor on-board (seven bands with 30 m pixels, one panchromatic band with 15 m pixels); Landsat 6 will be operated by the EOSAT Corporation. The final design of Landsat 7 has not yet been determined (as of December 1992). It will likely be launched in late 1997, probably carry an ETM, and possibly include a high-resolution multispectral stereoscopic imager (HRMSI). The ETM will operate in the visible, near-infrared, short-wave infrared, and long-wave infrared bands of the electromagnetic spectrum. The HRMSI will have a pointing and stereoscopic capability, a three-day revisit time, and spectral bands in the visible and near-infrared parts of the spectrum. In addition, Landsat 7 will be made available to all users at the cost of filling user requests. This policy change should be a major benefit to the global environmental change research community of scientists, and, in particular, glaciologists who will use the historic Landsat image data set, in comparison with future Landsat data, to monitor decade-scale glacier changes. As proposed, Landsat 7 will have improved spatial

resolution (5 m pixels) and radiometric resolution relative to previous Landsat sensors.

SAR sensors are also planned to be flown by the European Space Agency (ESA) and by the Canadian government in the future. Two spacecraft now carry SARs in near-polar orbits. The first European Remote Sensing (ERS-1) satellite was placed in a Sun-synchronous orbit in 1991 and carries a C-band (5.25 GHz) SAR. The first Japanese Earth Resources Satellite (JERS-1) was placed in orbit in 1992 and carries an L-band (1.275 GHz). The Canadian Radarsat will have a C-band (5.3 GHz) SAR on-board, and ERS-2, to be flown by ESA, will have a SAR on-board that is similar to that which is currently operating on ERS-1.

In addition to the use of satellite radar altimeters to produce profiles of the Greenland (Brooks *et al.*, 1978; Zwally *et al.*, 1983 & 1989; Zwally, 1989; & Bindschadler *et al.*, 1989) and Antarctic (Brooks, 1982; Brooks & Norcross, 1983; Brooks *et al.*, 1983) ice sheets, ice caps, and smaller glaciers, satellite laser altimeters will provide very accurate profiles (Zwally *et al.*, 1981), especially when coupled with accurate ephemeris information (James B. Garvin, pers. comm., 1991). The Geodynamics Laser Altimeter System (GLAS), to be orbited on an EOS polar-orbiting platform, will provide high-resolution altimetric profiles of the Greenland and Antarctic ice sheets. A modification of the Mars orbiting laser altimeter (MOLA) is being considered for use if one of the Earth Probe series of satellites to acquire accurate laser terrain profiles of the Earth (James B. Garvin, pers. comm., 1991.

Limitations

The primary limitation to analyzing long-term changes in glaciers on a global basis is the lack of systematic and repetitive data acquisition. The second limitation is the current cost of satellite data, even if the data were being acquired and archived (Williams, 1991). During the early years of the Landsat program, Landsat MSS and TM data were acquired systematically and repetitively and made available to scientists and other users at the cost of reproduction and distribution, just as the US Government does for most forms of publically available data, such as aerial photographs, maps, and reports. Since commercialization of the Landsat program, MSS and TM data are no longer acquired systematically and repetitively, and, except for MSS data older than 2 years, newer MSS data and all TM data, even if available of areas of interest, are priced beyond the project budgets of most academic and governmental global environmental change research program scientists.

Cloud cover and seasonal snow cover also limit the number of Landsat scenes that are suitable for analysis to a small number for many glacierized regions. For example, in the compilation of Landsat images for each of the glacierized areas addressed in US Geological Survey Professional Paper 1386, *Satellite Image Atlas of Glaciers of the World*, it took 10 years of systematic and repetitive (every 18 days) acquisition to achieve an optimum Landsat image dataset of the glaciers of Canada (minimum snow cover, no cloud cover) used in the Canada subchapter of Chapter J, 'Glaciers of North America'. Thus, the seasonal acquisition of all available data is imperative to compensate for cloud-cover problems. In addition, it is sometimes important to have data acquired during different seasons.

The Landsat data archive represents the primary source of satellite data in the study of areal changes in glaciers from space, especially the near-global dataset of the land areas achieved by Landsat 1. The Landsat 1 and the Landsats 2–5 datasets are crucial for global environmental change studies and should be maintained indefinitely in a stable storage media. Unfortunately, a sizable fraction of the early Landsat data in digital format (computer compatible tapes) has been lost because of lack of funding for permanent storage. With the advent of the EOS in the late 1990s, one component of NASA's 'Mission to Planet Earth' program and the largest single budget and programmatic element of the US Global Change Research Program (Committee on Earth and Environmental Sciences, 1990, 1991), the 30-year historic, retrospective, and discontinuous Landsat dataset, will be invaluable for decadal-scale determinations of areal changes in glaciers, but the data must be accessible to all researchers in terms of cost and availability. It is vitally important during the pre-EOS decade and during EOS operation that Landsat once again be dedicated to the systematic and repetitive acquisition of images of all the land areas, because no sensor currently proposed or under development for EOS will meet Landsat image parameters (area covered by a single image, availability of broad spectral bands, repeat cycle, Equatorial-crossing time, and pixel resolution). One proposal made by Williams (1991) is for Landsat to be made an integral part of NASA's 'Mission to Planet Earth' program and continued indefinitely as an Earth Probe satellite.

A specific limitation of Landsat data for detection of changes of glaciers is the difficulty in measuring the terminus position of retreating valley and outlet glaciers on land (Hall, Bayr & Kovalick, 1988). As a glacier thins and retreats, glacial debris that was within or on the surface of the ice is freed, and the terminus assumes a reflectance similar to the surrounding lateral and terminal moraines and the outwash plain. The retreating terminus may be difficult to distinguish spectrally from the surrounding terrain both on aerial and satellite remote-sensing data; even with direct field observation it is often difficult to determine the precise location of the

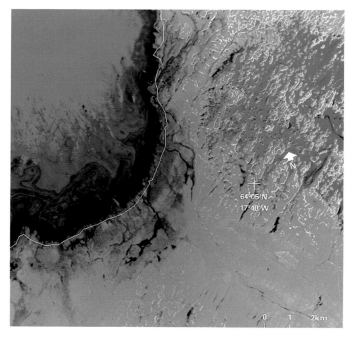

Fig. 16. Thematic mapper subscene (51242–11530) acquired on 26 July 1987 by the eastern margin of Sidjujökull in the southwestern part of Vatnajökull, Iceland, showing the 22 September 1973 position of the ice front (yellow line) as drawn from Lansat multispectral scanner digital data (1426–12070); the ice front retreated 456–827 m as measured using Landsat data (from Hall, Williams & Bayr, 1992).

terminus. However, in many cases it is still possible to measure terminus retreat as seen in Fig. 16 (Hall, Wiliams & Bayr, 1992). Conversely, glaciers with an advancing terminus are usually easy to delineate with Landsat digital data, as long as the amount of the advance is spatially resolvable by the satellite sensor.

Improvement could be achieved in distinguishing the terminus of a debris-covered glacier if stereoimages were available, because there are generally major morphological distinctions between a glacier, its terminal and lateral moraines, the outwash plain, and the surrounding terrain. Stereoimages of glacierized regions are needed to be able to map accurately glaciers in areas of high relief. One of several designs recommended for Landsat 7 is an orbital mapping satellite capable of producing convergent, 20 m pixel multi-spectral and 10 m or 5 m pixel panchromatic stereoimages along the orbital tract of the spacecraft (Itek Optical Systems, 1981; Light, 1990; Colvocoresses, 1991). The study of global variations in glaciers and other dynamic landforms and land-cover, such as dunes, forested regions, barrier islands, etc., would benefit greatly from having three-dimensional Landsat images available for analysis and photogrammetric measure-ments on the same basis as today's two-dimensional analysis of spectral and textural characteristics of images.

References

Allison, I., ed. (1981). Sea level, ice, and climatic change. Proceedings of the symposium (7–8 December 1979) held during the 17th General Assembly of the International Union of Geodesy and Geophysics, Canberra, Australia. *International Association of Hydrological Sciences. Association Internationale des Sciences Hydrologiques Publication No. 131*, 471pp.

Allison, I., & Peterson, J. A. (1989). Glaciers of Irian Jaya, Indonesia (H-1), and Chinn, T. J., 1989, Glaciers of New Zealand (H-2). In Williams, R. S., Jr., and Ferrigno, J. G., eds. *Satellite Image Atlas of Glaciers of the World. US Geological Survey Professional Paper 1386-H (Glaciers of Irian Jaya, Indonesia, and New Zealand)*, 48pp.

Armstrong, T., Roberts, B. & Swithinbank, C. (1973). *Illustrated Glossary of Snow and Ice*. 2nd edn., Cambridge, Scott Polar Research Institute, 60pp.

Benson, C. S. (1962). Stratigraphic studies in the snow and firn of the Greenland ice sheet. *Snow, Ice, and Permafrost Research Establishment (SIPRE), US Army Cold Regions Research and Engineering Laboratory (CRREL) Research Report No. 70*, 93pp. (Published version of C. S. Benson's PhD Dissertation (1960). Division of Geological Sciences. California Institute of Technology, Pasadena, California 213pp.)

Benson, C. S. & Motyka, R. J. (1979). Glacier–volcano interactions on Mt. Wrangell, Alaska. In *1977–78 Annual Report of the Geophysical Institute*, University of Alaska, Fairbanks, pp. 1–25.

Benson, C. S. & Follett, A. B. (1986). Application of photogrammetry to the study of volcano–glacier interactions on Mount Wrangell, Alaska, *Photogram. Eng. Rem. Sens.* **52** (6), 813–27.

Bindschadler, R. A. & Scambos, T. A. (1991). Satellite-image-derived velocity field of an Antarctic ice stream. *Science*, **252** (5003), 242–6.

Bindshadler, R. A., Zwally, H. J., Major, J. A. & Brenner, A. C. (1989). Surface topography of the Greenland ice sheet from satellite radar altimetry. *National Aeronautics and Space Administration, Special Publication*, SP-503, 105pp.

Björnsson, H. (1975). Explanation of jökulhlaups from Grímsvötn, Vatnajökull, Iceland. *Jökull*, **24** (1974), 1–26.

Björnsson, H. (1976). Subglacial water reservoirs, jökulhlaups and volcanic eruptions. *Jökull*, **25** (1975), 1–14.

Brooks, R. L. (1982). Satellite altimeter results over East Antarctica. *Annals of Glaciology*, **3**, 32–5.

Brooks, R. L., and Norcross, G. A. (1983). Ice sheet surface features in southwestern Greenland from satellite radar altimetry. *NASA Contractor Report 156887*, February, 22p.

Brooks, R. L., Campbell, W. J., Ramseier, R. O., Stanley, H. R. & Zwally, H. J. (1978). Ice sheet topography by satellite altimetry. *Nature*, **274** (5671), 539–43.

Brooks, R. L., Williams, R. S., Jr., Ferrigno, J. G. & Krabill, W. B. (1983). Amery Ice Shelf topography from satellite radar altimetry. In Oliver, R. L., James, P. R., and Jago, J. B., eds. *Antarctic Earth Science. Proceedings of the Fourth International Symposium on Antarctic Earth Sciences* (16–20 August 1982),

University of Adelaide, South Australia, Australian Academy of Science, Canberra, pp. 441–5.

Brugman, M. M. & Post, A. (1981). Effects of volcanism on the glaciers of Mt. St Helens. *US Geological Survey Circular 850-D* (Hydrologic effects of the eruptions of Mt. St Helens, Washington, (1980)), pp. D1–D11.

Clarke, G. K. C., Schruck, J. P., Ommanney, S. C. L. & Collins, S. G. (1986). Characteristics of surge-type glaciers, *Journal of Geophysical Research*, **91** (B7), 7165–80.

Colvill, A. J. (1977). Movement of Antarctic ice fronts measured from satellite imagery. *Polar Record*, **18** (115), 390–4.

Colvocoresses, A. P. (1991). Landsat 7 – A challenge to America. In *Technical Papers, 1991 American Congress on Surveying and Mapping-American Society for Photogrammetry and Remote Sensing Annual Convention*, vol. 3, Remote Sensing, pp. 78–82.

Committee on Earth and Environmental Sciences (1990). Our changing planet: the FY 1991 research plan. The US Global Change Research Program. *A Report by the Committee on Earth and Environmental Sciences*, Federal Coordinating Council for Science, Engineering, and Technology, Office of Science and Technology Policy, Executive Office of the President, 169 pp. (with a 79 pp. appendix).

Committee on Earth and Environmental Sciences (1991). Our changing planet: the FY 1992 US Global Change Research Program. *A Report by the Committee on Earth and Environmental Sciences, Federal Coordinating Council for Science, Engineering, and Technology, Office of Science and Technology Policy, Executive Office of the President*, A Supplement to the US President's Fiscal Year 1992 Budget, 90pp.

Crabtree, R. D. (1976). Changes in the Mýrdalsjökull ice cap, south Iceland: Possible uses of satellite imagery. *Polar Record*, **18** (112), 73–6.

Crabtree, R. D. & Doake, C. S. M. (1980). Flow-lines on Antarctic ice shelves: *Polar Record*, **20** (124), 31–7.

Denisov, L. V., Nosenko, G. S., Grechko, G. M., Ivachenko, A. S. & Kotlyakov, V. M. (1987). Glaciological studies and experiments from the Salyut-6 orbital space station, translated from Issledovaniye Zemli iz Kosmosa, 1980, **2** (1), 25–34; Williams, R. S., Jr., and Tamberg, N. eds., *Polar Geography and Geology*, **11** (1), 12–24.

Dowdeswell, J. A. (1984). Remote sensing studies of Svalbard glaciers: PhD dissertation, University of Cambridge, Jesus College, Cambridge, England, 250pp.

Dowdeswell, J. A. (1986). Drainage-basin characteristics of Nordaustlandet ice caps, Svalbard. *Journal of Glaciology*, **32** (110), 31–8.

Dowdeswell, J. A. & Cooper, A. P. R. (1986). Digital mapping in polar regions from Landsat photographic products: a case study. *Annals of Glaciology*, **8**, 47–50.

Dowdeswell, J. A. & McIntyre, N. F. (1987). The surface topography of large ice masses from Landsat imagery: *Journal of Glaciology*, **33** (113), 16–23.

Dozier, J. (1984). Snow reflectance from Landsat-4 Thematic Mapper: *IEEE Transactions*, **GE-22**, 323–8.

Dozier, J. (1989). Spectral signature of alpine snow cover from the

Landsat Thematic Mapper. *Remote Sensing of Environment*, **28**, pp. 9–22.

Dozier, J., Schneider, S. & McGinnis, D. F. (1981). Effect of grain size and snowpack water equivalence on visible and near infrared satellite observations of snow. *Water Resources Research*, **17**, 1213–21.

Drewry, D. J., Jordan, S. R. & Jankowski, E. (1982). Measured properties of the Antarctic ice sheet: surface configuration, ice thickness, volume and bedrock characteristics. *Annals of Glaciology*, **3**, 83–91.

Fairbanks, R. G. (1989). A 17,000-year glacio-eustatic sea level record: influence of glacial melting rates on the Younger Dryas event and deep-ocean circulation. *Nature*, **342** (6250), 637–49.

Ferrigno, J. G. & Williams, R. S., Jr. (1980). Satellite image atlas of glaciers. *World Glacier Inventory, Proceedings of the Riederalp (Switzerland) Workshop, IAHS-AISH Publication No. 126*, International Association of the Hydrological Sciences, pp. 333–41.

Ferrigno, J. G. & Gould, W. G. (1987). Substantial changes in the coastline of Antarctica revealed by satellite imagery. *Polar Record*, **23** (146), 577–83.

Ferrigno, J. G. & Molnia, B. F. (1989). Availability of Landsat, Soyuzkarta, and SPOT data of Antarctica for ice and climate research. *Antarctic Journal of the United States*, **24** (4), 15–18.

Ferrigno, J. G., Williams, R. S., Jr., Lucchitta, B. K. & Molnia, B. F. (1990). Recent changes in the coastal regions of Antarctica documented by Landsat imagery [abs.]. In *Abstracts, International Conference on the Role of the Polar Regions in Global Change*, University of Alaska, Fairbanks, Alaska (11–15 June 1990), p. 24.

Flint, R. E. (1957). *Glacial and Pleistocene Geology*. John Wiley and Sons, Inc., New York, 553pp.

Flint, R. F. (1971). *Glacial and Quaternary Geology*. John Wiley and Sons, Inc., New York, 892pp.

Ford, J. P., Blom. R. G., Bryan, M. L., Daily, M. I., Dixon, T. H., Elachi, C. & Xenos, E. C. (1980). Seasat views North America, the Caribbean, and western Europe with imaging radar. California Institute of Technology, Jet Propulsion Laboratory, Pasadena, California, *JPL Publication 80–67*, 141pp.

Grove, J. M. (1988). *The Little Ice Age*. New York, Routledge, 498pp.

Haakensen, N. (1986). Glacier mapping to confirm results of mass balance measurements. *Annals of Glaciology*, **8**, 73–7.

Haeberli, W. (1985). Fluctuations of glaciers. 1975–1980: International Hydrological Programme. Compiled for the Permanent Service on the Fluctuation of Glaciers (IUGG-FAGS/ICSU), *United Nations Educational, Scientific, and Cultural Organization, International Association of Hydrological Sciences*, vol. 4, 265pp.

Haeberli, W. & Müller, P. (1988). Fluctuations of glaciers. 1980–1985. *Unesco, IAHS, UNEP Global Environmental Monitoring System (GEMS), International Hydrological Programme, United Nations Educational, Scientific, and Cultural Organization, International Association of Hydrological Sciences, United Nations Environment Programme*, vol. 5, 290pp.

Haeberli, W., Bösch, H., Scherler, K., Østrem, G. & Wallén, C. C. (1989a). World glacier inventory. Status 1988: Compiled by the World Glacier Monitoring Service, Global Environmental Monitoring Systems (GEMS) and the International Hydrological Programme, *United Nations Educational, Scientific, and Cultural Organization, International Association of Hydrological Sciences. United Nations Environment Programme*, 438pp. (in four appendices, A–D).

Haeberli, W., Müller, P., Alean, J. & Bösch, H. (1989b). Glacier changes following the Little Ice Age – A survey of the international data base and its perspectives. In Oerlemans, J., ed. *Glacier Fluctuations and Climatic Change*. Kluwer Academic Publishers, pp. 77–101.

Haeberli, W., Alean, J.-C., Müller, P. & Funk, M. (1989c). Assessing risks from glacier hazards in high mountain regions: Some experiences in the Swiss Alps. *Annals of Glaciology*, **13**, 96–102.

Hall, D. K. & Ormsby, J. P. (1983). Use of SEASAT Synthetic Aperture Radar and LANDSAT multispectral scanner subsystem data for Alaskan glaciology studies. *Journal of Geophysical Research*, **88** (C3), 1597–607.

Hall, D. K., Bindschadler, R. A., Ormsby, J. P. & Siddalingaiah, H. (1987). Characterization of snow and ice zones on glaciers using Landsat Thematic Mapper data. *Annals of Glaciology*, **9**, 104–8.

Hall, D. K., Bayr, K. J. & Kovalick, W. M. (1989). Determination of glacier mass balance using thematic mapper data. *Proceedings of the Eastern Snow Conference*, Lake Placid, New York, 7–9 June 1988, pp. 192–96.

Hall, D. K., Chang, A. T. C., Foster, J. L., Benson, C. S. & Kovalick, W. M., (1989). Comparison of *in situ* and Landsat derived reflectance of Alaskan glaciers. *Remote Sensing of the Environment*, **28**, 23–31.

Hall, D. K., Williams, R. S., Jr. & Bayr, K. J. (1992). Glacier recession in Iceland and Austria observed from space, *Eos. (Transactions, American Geophysical Union)*, **73** (12), pp. 129, 135 and 141.

Herd, D. G. (1986). The 1985 Ruiz volcano disaster: *Eos (Transactions, American Geophysical Union)*, **67** (19), 457–60.

Holtzscherer, J. J. & Bauer, A. (1954). Contribution à la Connaissance de l'Inlandis du Groenland [Contribution to the knowledge of the Greenland ice sheet]. *International Association of Scientific Hydrology, Publication no. 39*, pp. 244–96.

Hunting Geology and Geophysics, Ltd., no date, Seasat-1 radar mosaic [of] Iceland: 1:500,000-scale mosaic constructed by Hunting Surveys, Ltd., Borehamwood, Hertfordshire, England, for the Royal Aircraft Establishment (European Space Agency-Earthnet), from Seasat SAR data acquired by the Royal Aircraft Establishment receiving station, Oakhanger, England. Survey mode optical correlation of the SAR data by the Environmental Research Institute of Michigan.

International Association of Hydrological Sciences (1980). World glacier inventory: Proceedings of the Workshop at Riederalp, Switzerland (17–22 September 1978), Organized by the Temporary Technical Secretariat for the World Glacier Inventory, *IAHS-AISH Publication No. 126*, 351pp.

Itek Optical Systems (1981). Conceptual design of an automated mapping system (Mapsat). Final Technical Report to the US Geological Survey, Reston, VA; Report No. 81–8449A–1 (12 January 1981), variously paginated by sections.

Kamb, B., Raymond, C. F., Harrison, W. D., Engelhardt, H., Echelmeyer, K. A., Humphrey, N., Brugman, M. M. & Pfeffer, T. (1985). Glacier surge mechanism: 1982–1983 surge of Variegated Glacier, Alaska: *Science*, **227** (4686), 469–79.

Kasser, P. (1967). Fluctuations of glaciers. 1959–1965: *United Nations Educational, Scientific, and Cultural Organization, International Association of Scientific Hydrology*, 1, 52pp.

Kasser, P. (1973). Fluctuations of glaciers. 1965–1970: International Hydrological Programme, Compiled for the Permanent Service on the Fluctuation of Glaciers (IUGG-FAGS/ICSU), *United Nations Educational, Scientific and Cultural Organization, International Association of Hydrological Sciences*, vol. 2, 357pp.

Koerner, R. M. (1989). Ice core evidence for extensive melting of the Greenland ice sheet in the last interglacial. *Science*, **244** (4907), 964–8.

Krimmel, R. M. & Meier, M. F. (1975). Glacier applications of ERTS images: *Journal of Glaciology*, **15** (73), 391–402.

Krimmel, R. M., Post, A. & Meier, M. F. (1976). Surging and non-surging glaciers in the Pamir Mountains, USSR. In *ERTS-1, A New Window on Our Planet* (Williams, R. S., Jr., and Carter, W. D., ed., US Geological Survey Professional Paper 929, pp. 178–9.

Kuhn, M. (1985). Reactions of mid-latitude glacier mass balance to predicted climatic changes. In *Glaciers, Ice Sheets, and Sea Level: Effects of a CO_2-Induced Climatic Change* (Report of a Workshop Held in Seattle, Washington, September 13–15, 1984), Polar Research Board, National Research Council, Washington, DC, National Academy Press, pp. 248–54.

Kurter, A. (1991). Glaciers of Turkey (G-1), Ferrigno, J. G., 1991, Glaciers of Iran (G-2), and Young, J. A. T., and Hastenrath, S. L., 1991, Glaciers of Africa (G-3). In Williams, R. S., Jr., and Ferrigno, J. G., eds. *Satellite Image Atlas of Glaciers of the World. US Geological Survey Professional Paper 1386-G (Glaciers of Middle East and Africa)*, 70pp.

Liestl, O. (1992). Glaciers of Svalbard, Norway. In Chapter E, Glaciers of Europe: *US Geological Survey Professional Paper 1386-E, Satellite Image Atlas of Glaciers of the World* (Williams, R. S., Jr., and Ferrigno, J. G., ed.), *in press*.

Light, D. (1990). Characteristics of remote sensors for mapping and earth science applications. *Photogrammetric Engineering and Remote Sensing*, **56** (12), 1613–25.

Lowe, D. R., Williams, S. N., Leigh, Henry, Connor, C. B., Gemmell, J. B. & Stoiber, R. E. (1986). Lahars initiated by the 13 November eruption of Nevado del Ruiz, Colombia. *Nature*, **324** (6092), 51–3.

Lucchitta, B. K. & Ferguson, H. M. (1986). Antarctica: Measuring glacier velocity from satellite images. *Science*, **234** (4780), 1105–8.

Lucchitta, B. K., Bowell, Jo-Ann, Edwards, K. L., Eliason, E. M. & Ferguson, H. M. (1987). Multispectral Landsat images of Antarctica. *US Geological Survey Bulletin*, 1696, 21pp.

Lucchitta, B. K., Ferrigno, J. G., MacDonald, T. R. & Williams, R. S., Jr. (1990*a*). The velocity field of Antarctic outlet glaciers [abs.]. In *Abstracts, International Conference on the Role of the Polar Regions in Global Change*, University of Alaska, Fairbanks, Alaska (11–15 June 1990), p. 153.

Lucchitta, B. K., Ferguson, H. M., Schafer, F. J., Ferrigno, J. G. & Williams, R. S., Jr. (1990*b*). Antarctic glacier velocities from Landsat images. *Antarctic Journal of the United States*, **24** (5), 106–7.

MacDonald, T. R., Ferrigno, J. G., Williams, R. S., Jr. & Lucchitta, B. K. (1990). Velocities of Antarctic outlet glaciers determined from sequential Landsat images. *Antarctic Journal of the United States*, **24** (5), 105–6.

Mayo, L. R. (1988). Hubbard Glacier near Yakutat, Alaska – The ice damming and breakout of Russell Fiord/Lake, 1986; *in* US Geological Survey, National water summary 1986 – Hydrologic events and ground-water quality. *US Geological Survey Water-Supply Paper 2325*, pp. 42–9.

Mayo, L. R. & Trabant, D. C. (1984). Observed and predicted effects of climate change on Wolverine Glacier, southern Alaska. In *The Potential Effects of Carbon Dioxide-induced Climate Changes in Alaska*, School of Agriculture and Land Research Management, University of Alaska Miscellaneous Publication 83–1, pp. 114–23.

Mayo, L. R., March, R. S. & Trabant, D. C. (1988). Wolverine Glacier, southern Alaska, surface altitude measurements show continuing growth. In 1988 *Arctic Science Conference Proceedings, AAAS Arctic Division and University of Alaska Geophysical Institute*, 7–10 October 1988, pp. 123–4.

McIntyre, N. F. (1983). The topography and flow of the Antarctic ice sheet. PhD dissertation, University of Cambridge, England.

McIntyre, N. F. (1985). The dynamics of ice-sheet outlets. *Journal of Glaciology*, **31** (108), 99–107.

Meier, M. F. (1974). Ice sheets and glaciers: 15th edn., *Encyclopedia Britannica*, pp. 175–86.

Meier, M. F. (1976). Monitoring the motion of surging glaciers in the Mount McKinley massif, Alaska. In *ERTS-1, A New Window on Our Planet* (Williams, R. S., Jr. and Carter, W. D., editors), *US Geological Survey Professional Paper 929*, pp. 185–87.

Meier, M. F. (1984). Contributions of small glaciers to global sea level. *Science*, **226** (4681), 1418–21.

Meier, M. F. (1985). Mass balance of the glaciers and small ice caps of the world. In *Glaciers, Ice Sheets, and Sea Level: Effects of a CO_2-Induced Climatic Change* (Report of a Workshop Held in Seattle, Washington, September 13–15, 1984), Polar Research Board, National Research Council, Washington, DC, National Academy Press, pp. 138–44.

Meier, M. F. & Tangborn, W. V. (1961). Distinctive characteristics of glacier runoff. In *Geological Survey Research 1961. US Geological Survey Professional Paper 424-B*, pp. B-14-B-16.

Meier, M. F. & Post, A. (1969). What are glacier surges? *Canadian Journal of Earth Sciences*, **6** (2), 807–17.

Meier, M. F. & Post, A. 1987, Fast tidewater glaciers. *Journal of Geophysical Research*, **92** (B9), 9051–8.

Meier, M. F., Rasmussen, L. A., Post, A., Brown, C. S., Sikonia, W. G., Bindschadler, R. A., Mayo, L. R. & Trabant, D. C. (1980). Predicted timing of the disintegration of the lower reach of Columbia Glacier, Alaska. *US Geological Survey Open-File Report 80–582*, 47pp.

Motyka, R. J. (1983). Increases and fluctuations in thermal activity at Mt. Wrangell, Alaska. PhD dissertation, University of Alaska at Fairbanks.

Müller, F. (1977). Fluctuations of glaciers. 1970–1975. International Hydrological Programme, Compiled for the Permanent Service on the Fluctuation of Glaciers (IUGG-FAGS/ICSU). *United Nations Educational, Scientific, and Cultural Organization, International Association of Hydrological Sciences*, 3, 269pp.

Müller, F. (1978). Instructions for the compilation and assemblage of data for a world glacier inventory. Supplement: Identification/glacier number: Temporary Technical Secretariat for World Glacier Inventory. *International Commission on Snow and Ice, International Association of Hydrological Sciences, United Nations Environment Programme, United Nations Educational, Scientific, and Cultural Organization*, 7pp. (with appendix).

Müller, F., Caflisch, T. & Müller, G. (1977). Instructions for compilation and assemblage of data for a world glacier inventory: Temporary Technical Secretariat for World Glacier Inventory. *International Commission on Snow and Ice, International Association of Hydrological Sciences, United Nations Environment Programme, United Nations Educational, Scientific, and Cultural Organization*, 19pp. (with appendix).

Münzer, U. & Bodechtel, J. (1980). Digitale Verarbeitung von Landsat-Daten uber Eis- und Schneegebieten des Vatnajökull (Island) [Digital processing of Landsat data over ice and snow areas of Vatnajökull (Iceland)]. *Bildmessung und Luftbildwesen*, **48**, 21–8.

Naranjo, J. L., Sigurdsson, H., Carey, S. N. & Fritz, W. (1986). Eruption of the Nevado del Ruiz volcano, Colombia, on 13 November 1985: Tephra falls and lahars. *Science*, **233** (4767), 961–3.

NASA (1989). Science plan for the Alaska SAR facility program, NASA, Jet Propulsion Laboratory, Pasadena, CA. *JPL Publication 89–14*, 87pp.

National Geographic Society (1990). *Atlas of the World*. 6th edn., 138pp.

National Research Council (1985). Glaciers, ice sheets, and sea level: effects of a CO_2-induced climatic change: Report of a Workshop Held in Seattle, Washington, September 13–15, 1984, Ad hoc Committee on the Relationship Between Land Ice and Sea Level. *Committee on Glaciology, Polar Research Board, Commission on Physical Sciences, Mathematics, and Resources, National Academy Press*, Washington, DC, 330pp.

Østrem, G. (1975). ERTS data in glaciology – an effort to monitor glacier mass balance from satellite imagery. *Journal of Glaciology*, **15** (73), 403–14.

Østrem, G. & Tvede, A. (1986). Comparison of glacier maps – a source of climatological information? *Geografiska Annaler*, **68A** (3), 225–31.

Østrem, G. & Brugman, M. (1991). Glacier mass-balance measurements. A manual for field and office work. National Hydrology Research Institute, Saskatoon, Saskatchewan and Norwegian Water Resources and Energy Administration, Oslo. NHRI Science Report No. 4, 224pp.

Østrem, G. & Haakensen, N. (1992). Glaciers of Norway. In Chapter E, Glaciers of Europe: US Geological Survey Professional Paper 1386-E, *Satellite Image Atlas of Glaciers of the World* (Williams, R. S., Jr., and Ferrigno, J. G., eds.), pp. E63–E109.

Paterson, W. S. B. (1981). *Physics of Glaciers*. 2nd edn., New York, Pergamon Press, 380pp.

Post, A. (1969). Distribution of surging glaciers in western North America. *Journal of Glaciology*, **8** (53), 229–40.

Post, A. (1977). Reported observations of icebergs from Colombia Glacier in Valdez Arm and Columbia Bay, Alaska, during the summer of 1976. *US Geological Survey Open-File Report 77–235*, 7pp.

Post, A. & Mayo, L. R. (1971). Glacier dammed lakes and outburst floods in Alaska. *US Geological Survey Hydrologic Investigations Atlas*, HA-455, 3 map sheets, 10pp.

Post, A., Richardson, D., Tangborn, W. V. & Rosselot, F. L. (1971). Inventory of glaciers in the North Cascades, Washington. In Glaciers in the United States *US Geological Survey Professional Paper 705-A*, 10pp.

Post, A., Meier, M. F. & Mayo, L. R. (1976). Measuring the motion of the Lowell and Tweedsmuir surging glaciers of British Columbia, Canada. In *ERTS-1, A New Window on Our Planet* (Williams, R. S., Jr. and Carter, W. D., eds.), *US Geological Survey Professional Paper 929*, pp. 180–4.

Reeh, N. (1985). Greenland ice-sheet mass balance and sea-level change. In *Glaciers, Ice Sheets, and Sea Level: Effects of a CO_2-Induced Climatic Change* (Report of a Workshop Held in Seattle, Washington, September 13–15, 1984), Polar Research Board, National Research Council, Washington, DC, National Academy Press, pp. 155–71.

Richardson, D. (1968). Glacier outburst floods in the Pacific Northwest: *US Geological Survey Professional Paper 600-D*, pp. D79–86.

Rist, S. (1974). Jökulhlaupaannáll 1971, 1972 og 1973 [Jökulhlaup annals 1971, 1972, and 1972]. *Jökull*, **23** (1973), 55–60.

Robin, G. deQ. (1967). *Glaciology: Annals of the International Geophysical Year*, vol. 41, 239pp.

Robin, G. deQ., Drewry, D. J. & Squire, V. A. (1983). Satellite observations of polar ice fields. *Philosophical Transactions, Royal Society of London, Series A*, **309** (1508), 447–61.

Rott, H., Scherler, K. E., Reynaud, L., Barbero, R. S. & Zanon, G. (1992). Glaciers of the Alps (E-1); Serrat, D. & Ventura, J. (1992). Glaciers of the Pyrenees, Spain and France (E-2); Østrem, G. & Haakensen, N. (1992). Glaciers of Norway (E-3); Schytt, V. (1992). Glaciers of Sweden (E-4); Liestøl, O. (1992). Glaciers of Svalbard, Norway (E-5); Orheim, O. (1992). Glaciers of Jan Mayen, Norway (E-6). In Williams, R.

S., Jr. & Ferrigno, J. G., eds. *Satellite Image Atlas of Glaciers of the World. US Geological Survey Professional Paper 1386–E (Glaciers of Europe)*, 164pp.

Scherler, K. E. (1983). Guidelines for preliminary glacier inventories. *Temporary Technical Secretariat for the World Glacier Inventory, Global Environment Monitoring System, United Nations Environment Programme, United Nations Educational, Scientific, and Cultural Organization*, 16pp.

Sigurdsson, O. (1988). Jöklabreytingar [Glacier variations] 1930–1960, 1960–1980, 1980–1986, og 1986–1987. *Jökull*, **38**, 91–7.

Simmons, D. A. (1986). Flow of the Brunt Ice Shelf, Antarctica, derived from Landsat images, 1974–85. *Journal of Glaciology*, **32** (111), 252–4.

Sturm, M. (1983). Comparison of glacier flow of two glacier systems on Mt. Wrangell, Alaska. MS dissertation, University of Alaska at Fairbanks.

Sturm, M. & Benson, C. S. (1985). A history of jökulhlaups from ice-dammed Strandline Lake, Alaska. *Journal of Glaciology*, **31** (109), 272–80.

Sturm, M., Beget, J. & Benson, C. (1987). Observations of jökulhlaups from ice-dammed Strandline Lake, Alaska: implications for paleohydrology. In Mayer, L. and Nash, D., eds. *Catastrophic Flooding*. London, Allen and Unwin, pp. 79–94.

Sturm, M. & Benson, C. (1989). Jökulhlaups from Strandline Lake, Alaska: With special attention to the 1982 event. *Alaska Division of Geological and Geophysical Surveys, Report of Investigations*, R. I. 88–10.

Sturm, M., Hall, D. K., Benson, C. S. & Field, W. O. (1991). Glacier-terminus fluctuations in the Wrangell and Chugach Mountains, resulting from non-climatic controls. Journal of Glaciology, 37(127), 348–356.

Sugden, D. E. & John, B. S. (1976). *Glaciers and Landscape. A Geomorphological Approach*. New York, John Wiley and Sons, 376pp.

Swithinbank, C. (1983). Towards an inventory of the great ice sheets. *Geografiska Annaler*, **65A** (3–4), 289–94.

Swithinbank, C. (1985). A distant look at the cryosphere. *Advances in Space Research*, **5** (6), 263–74.

Swithinbank. C. & Lucchitta, B. K. (1986). Multispectral digital image mapping of Antarctic ice features. *Annals of Glaciology*, **8**, 159–63.

Swithinbank, C. (1988). Antarctica, *with sections on* the 'Dry Valleys' of Victoria Land, by Chinn, T. J., and Landsat images of Antarctica, by Williams, R. S., Jr. and Ferrigno, J. G. In Williams, R. S., Jr. and Ferrigno, J. G., eds., *Satellite Image Atlas of Glaciers of the World: US Geological Survey Professional Paper 1386-B*, 278pp.

Thomas, R. H., (1991). *Polar Research from Satellites*. Washington, DC, Joint Oceanographic Institutions, Inc., 91pp.

Thomas, R. H., Martin, T. V. & Zwally, H. J. (1983). Mapping ice-sheet margins from radar altimetry data. *Annals of Glaciology*, **4**, 283–8.

Thorarinsson, S. (1940). The icedammed lakes of Iceland with particular reference to their values as indicators of glacier oscillations. *Geografiska Annaler*, **21** (3–4), 216–42.

Thorarisson, S. (1957). The jökulhlaup from the Katla area in 1955 compared with other jökulhlaups in Iceland. *Jökull*, **7**, 21–5.

Thorarinsson, S. (1958). The Öræfajökull eruption of 1362: *Acta Naturalia Islandica*, **2** (2), 100pp.

Thorarinsson, S. (1964). Sudden advances of Vatnajökull outlet glaciers 1930–1964: *Jökull*, **14**, pp. 76–89.

Thorarinsson, S. (1969). Glacier surges in Iceland, with special reference to the surges of Brúarjökull. *Canadian Journal of Earth Sciences*, **6** (4, pt. 2), 875–82.

Thorarinsson, S. Saemundsson, K. & Williams, R. S., Jr. (1974). ERTS-1 image of Vatnajökull: Analysis of glaciological, structural, and volcanic features. *Jökull*, **23** (1973), 7–17.

Tómasson, H. (1975). Grímsvatnahlaup 1972, Mechanism and sediment discharge: *Jökull*, **24** (1974), 27–39.

Unesco (1969). Variations of existing glaciers. A guide to international practices for their measurement. *Paris, United Nations Educational, Scientific, and Cultural Organization, International Association of Scientific Hydrology, Technical Papers in Hydrology*, No. 3, 19pp.

Unesco (1970a). Perennial ice and snow masses. A guide for compilation and assemblage of data for a world inventory. *Paris, United Nations Educational, Scientific and Cultural Organization, International Association of Scientific Hydrology, Technical Papers in Hydrology*, No. 1, 59pp.

Unesco (1970b). Combined heat, ice and water balances at selected glacier basins. A contribution to the International Hydrological Decade. *Paris, United Nations Educational, Scientific and Cultural Organization, International Association of Scientific Hydrology, Technical Papers in Hydrology*, No. 5, 20pp.

Untersteiner, N. (1975). Sea ice and ice sheets and their role in climatic variations. In *The Physical Basis of Climate and Climatic Modelling, Global Atmospheric Research Project (GARP) Publication Series No. 16*, World Meteorological Organization/International Council of Scientific Unions, pp. 206–24.

US Geological Survey (1976). Water of the world. *US Geological Survey General Interest Publication*, INF-68–7, 20pp.

Warrick, R. & Oerlemans, J., eds. (1990). Sea level rise. In Houghton, J. T., Jenkins, G. J., and Ephraums, J. J., eds. *Climate Change. The IPCC Scientific Assessment. Intergovernmental Panel on Climate Change, Report Prepared for IPCC by Working Group 1*, Cambridge University Press, pp. 257–81.

Weidick, A. Greenland. In Williams, R. S. Jr. and Ferrigno, J. G., eds. *Satellite Image Atlas of Glaciers of the World: U.S. Geological Survey Professional Paper 1386-C, in press*.

Wilbur, S. (1988). Surging versus non-surging glaciers: a comparison using morphometry and balance. MS dissertation, University of Alaska at Fairbanks.

Williams, R. S., Jr. (1976). Vatnajökull ice cap, Iceland. In *ERTS-1, A New Window on our Planet* (Williams, R. S., & Carter, W. D., eds.), *US Geological Survey Professional Paper 929*, pp. 188–93.

Williams, R. S., Jr. (1983a). Remote sensing of glaciers. In Geological applications (Williams, R. S., Jr., author-editor), *Manual of Remote Sensing*, 2nd edn. (Colwell, R. N., ed.-in-chief), v. II,

Interpretation and Applications (Estes, J. E., and Thorley, G. A., eds.) Falls Church, VA, American Society of Photogrammetry, pp. 1852–66.

Williams, R. S., Jr., author-editor. (1983*b*). Geological applications, ch. 31. In Colwell, R. N., editor-in-chief, *Manual of Sensing*, 2nd edn., v. II, *Interpretation and applications* (Estes, J. E., and Thorley, G. A., eds.): Falls Church, VA, American Society of Photogrammetry, pp. 1667–953.

Williams, R. S., Jr. (1983*c*). Satellite glaciology of Iceland. *Jökull*, **33**, 3–12.

Williams, R. S., Jr. (1985). Monitoring the area and volume of ice caps and ice sheets: Present and future opportunities using satellite remote-sensing technology: In *Glaciers, Ice Sheets, and Sea Level: Effects of a CO_2-Induced Climatic Change (Report of a Workshop Held in Seattle, Washington, September 13–15, 1984)*, Polar Research Board, National Research Council, Washington, DC, National Academy Press, pp. 232–40.

Williams, R. S., Jr. (1986*a*). Glaciers and glacial landforms; ch. 9. In Short, N. M., and Blair, R. W., Jr., eds. *Geomorphology from Space. A global Overview of Regional Landforms*. National Aeronautics and Space Administration Special Publication, SP-486, pp. 521–96.

Williams, R. S., Jr. (1986*b*). Glacier inventories of Iceland: evaluation and use of sources of data. *Annals of Glaciology*, **8**, 184–91.

Williams, R. S., Jr. (1987*a*). Satellite remote sensing of Vatnajökull, Iceland. *Annals of Glaciology*, **9**, 127–35.

Williams, R. S., Jr. (1987*b*). Background to the Soviet glaciological studies from the Salyut-6 orbital space station. *Polar Geography and Geology*, **11** (1), 1–11.

Williams, R. S., Jr., author-editor (1990). Cross-cutting example: sea level change; In *Our Changing Planet: The FY 1991 research plan. The US Global Change Research Program: A Report by the Committee on Earth and Environmental Sciences, Federal Coordinating Council for Science, Engineering, and Technology*, Office of Science and Technology Policy, Executive Office of the President, pp. 121–23.

Williams, R. S., Jr. (1991). Landsat: The key space-based component of the US Global Change Research Program for the 1990s. In *GSA Forum* (Molnia, B. F., ed.); *Issue: The Future of US Civilian Satellite Remote Sensing: GSA Today*, **1** (3), p.56 and p.67.

Williams, R. S., Jr. & Thorarinsson, S. (1974). ERTS-1 image of Vatnajökull area: general comments. *Jökull*, **23** (1973), 1–6.

Williams, R. S., Jr. & Ferrigno, J. G. (1981). Satellite image atlas of the Earth's glaciers; In Deutsch, Morris, Wiesnet, D. R., and Rango, Albert, eds., *Satellite Hydrology: Proceedings of the Fifth Annual William T. Pecora Memorial Symposium on Remote Sensing*, Sioux Falls, SD (10–15 June 1979), Minneapolis, American Water Resources Association, pp. 173–82.

Williams, R. S., Jr. & Ferrigno, J. G. (1988*a*). Documentation on satellite imagery of large cyclical or secular changes in Antarctic ice sheet margin (abs.): *Eos (Transactions, American Geophysical Union)*, vol. 69, no. 16, p. 365.

Williams, R. S., Jr. & Ferrigno, J. G. (1988*b*). Landsat images of Antarctica. In Williams, R. S., Jr. and Ferrigno, J. G., eds., *Satellite Image Atlas of Glaciers of the World. US Geological Survey Professional Paper 1386-B*, p. B139–B278.

Williams, R. S., Jr. & Ferrigno, J. G. (1988*c*). Index map showing optimum Landsat 1, 2, and 3 images of Antarctica; Plate 1. In Williams, R. S., Jr. and Ferrigno, J. G., eds. *Satellite Image Atlas of Glaciers of the World*: US Geological Survey Professional Paper 1386-B, 1:10,000,000.

Williams, R. S., Jr. & Ferrigno, J. G. (1990). Satellite monitoring of areal changes in the glacier component of the Earth's cryosphere [abs.]. In *Abstracts, International Conference on the Role of the Polar Regions in Polar Change*, University of Alaska, Fairbanks, Alaska (11–13 June 1990), p. 13.

Williams, R. S., Jr. & Ferrigno, J. G. (1991). *Cold Beauty: Rivers of Ice: Earth*, vol. 1, (1), pp. 42–9.

Williams, R. S., Jr., Bödvarsson, Á., Fridriksson, S., Pálmason, G., Rist, S., Sigtryggsson, H., Sæmundsson, K., Thorarinsson, S. & Thorsteinsson, I. (1974). Environmental studies of Iceland with ERTS-1 imagery. In *Proceedings of the Ninth Symposium on Remote Sensing of Environment*, Environmental Research Institute of Michigan, Ann Arbor, Michigan, vol. 1, p. 31–81.

Williams, R. S., Jr., Bodvarsson, A., Rist, S., Sæmundsson, K. & Thorarinsson, S. (1975). Glaciological studies in Iceland with ERTS-1 imagery [abs.]. *Journal of Glaciology*, **15** (73), 465–6.

Williams, R. S., Jr., Ferrigno, J. G., Kent, T. M. & Schoonmaker, J. W., Jr. (1982). Landsat images and mosaics of Antarctica for mapping and glaciological studies. *Annals of Glaciology*, **3**, 321–6.

Williams, R. S., Jr., Meunier, T. K. & Ferrigno, J. G. (1983). Blue ice, meteorites, and satellite imagery of Antarctica. *The Polar Record*, **21** (134), 493–6.

Williams, R. S., Jr., Hall, D. K. & Benson, C. S. (1991). Analysis of glacier facies using satellite techniques. *Journal of Glaciology*, **37** (125), pp. 120–8.

Wood, F. B., Jr. (1988*a*). Global alpine glacier trends, 1960s–1980s. *Arctic and Alpine Research*, **20** (4), 404–13.

Wood, F. B., Jr. (1988*b*). The need for systems research on global climate change. *Systems Research*, **5** (3), 225–40.

Zwally, H. J. (1989). Growth of Greenland ice sheet: interpretation. *Science*, **246** (4937), 1589–91.

Zwally, H. J., Thomas, R. H. & Bindschadler, R. A. (1981). Ice-sheet dynamics by satellite laser altimetry. *National Aeronautics and Space Administration Technical Memorandum 82128*, May, 11pp.

Zwally, H. J., Bindschadler, R. A., Brenner, A. C., Martin, T. V. & Thomas, R. H. (1983). Surface elevation contours of Greenland and Antarctic ice sheets. *Journal of Geophysical Research*, **88** (C3), 1589–96.

Zwally, H. J., Brenner, A. C., Major, J. A., Bindschadler, R. A. & Marsh, J. G., (1989). Growth of Greenland ice sheet: measurement. *Science*, **246** (4937), 1587–9.

PART VIII

HUMAN-INDUCED CHANGES

Indications and effects
of human activities

JAMES L. FOSTER AND CLAIRE L. PARKINSON

For many millennia, human activities have resulted in noticeable impacts on local environments, including the effects of building villages and cities, clearing forests, excavating minerals, damming and diverting rivers, and using the atmosphere, oceans, lakes, and rivers for waste disposal. These impacts have by now reached the level of affecting the Earth's environment as a whole and are no longer confined to isolated local changes, as the combination of current energy-utilizing technology, urbanization, and population growth imposes formidable demands on the global system (Wolman, 1990). Some of the major impacts of human activities have been discussed and illustrated in previous chapters. These previously discussed impacts include the ongoing deforestation of the tropical rain forests (Townshend, Tucker & Goward, 1993) and the destruction of the stratospheric ozone layer, especially in the south polar region, through the insertion into the atmosphere of chlorofluorocarbons (Schoeberl, 1993). This chapter provides illustrations of the use of remote sensing to depict or monitor several additional ways in which humans have changed and are changing the environment. The chapter differs from many of the previous chapters in that it is not intended to highlight specific data sets and their uses for recording the state of specific variables but instead is intended to illustrate the visibility from space of various consequences of human activities not already discussed in previous chapters.

Data sources

Almost all space-borne sensors aimed toward the Earth reveal something that can be related in some way to human activities. The particular cases selected for illustrative purposes here are from visible imagery of the United States Air Force Defense Meteorological Satellite Program (DMSP), visible, near infra-red, and thermal infra-red imagery from the Landsat Thematic Mapper (TM), visible, near infra-red, and thermal infra-red imagery from the NOAA Advanced Very High Resolution Radiometer (AVHRR), and visible photography taken from the United States Space Shuttle. Details on the DMSP, Landsat TM, and NOAA AVHRR can be found in the chapters by Goodman & Christian (1993), Williams and Hall (1993), and Townshend, Tucker & Goward (1993), respectively, so that only some summary comments will be made here.

The DMSP spacecraft orbit the Earth at an altitude of approximately 800–900 km. Relative to the Earth, the orbital plane of the satellite rotates in a Sun-synchronous fashion, so that time of day during data collection does not vary. The orbits are chosen so that data collection occurs either at dawn and dusk or at noon and midnight local time. Visible and infra-red data are collected on the DMSP satellites through an Operational Linescan System (OLS). The OLS has several modes of operation, using a solid state detector in daylight hours and a photomultiplier tube at night. The photomultiplier tube is located at the focal plane of a 13.3 cm telescope that scans the Earth's surface cross track at constant angular resolution. DMSP visible and infra-red data are stored with pixel resolutions of both 2.8 km and 0.6 km.

Landsat satellites also orbit the Earth in a sun-synchronous mode. The Thematic Mapper, first launched on the Landsat 4 satellite in July 1982, images the Earth in seven wavelength bands, bands 1–3 being within the visible portion of the electromagnetic spectrum (approximate wavelength ranges of 0.45–0.52 micrometers, 0.52–0.60 micrometers, and 0.63–0.69 micrometers, respectively), band 4 being within the near infra-red portion (0.76–0.90 micrometers), bands 5 and 7 being within the middle infra-red portion (1.55–1.75 micrometers and 2.08–2.35 micrometers, respectively), and band 6 being within the thermal infra-red portion (10.40–12.50 micrometers). The spatial resolution is 30 m for bands 1–5 and 7 and 120 m for the thermal infra-red band 6 (Hall & Martinec, 1985).

The orbits for the NOAA satellites are near-polar and Sun-synchronous, although at a higher altitude than the Landsat orbits. The NOAA data coverage is more frequent but at a poorer resolution than Landsat. The AVHRR provides daily coverage in either four or five wavelength bands, depending on the specific instrument, with a spatial resolution of approximately 1.1 km at nadir. The bands include a visible, near infra-red, and middle infra-red band (bands 1, 2, and 3, respectively) plus either one or two thermal infra-red bands (band 4 on the even numbered NOAA satellites and bands 4 and 5 on the odd numbered NOAA satellites) (Hall & Martinec, 1985).

Space Shuttle photography of the Earth's surface has been a part of the United States Space Shuttle program since the inaugural launch of the Shuttle *Columbia* in April 1981. Most Shuttle flights are at an altitude of about 275 km, with an orbit that allows coverage only between latitudes 30° N and 30° S, so that the mid-latitude and polar regions of the Earth are generally not seen, but tropical regions can be repeatedly viewed on any given mission. Advances in photographic digitization have allowed computer rectification of shuttle photographs, with a consequence that the level of information obtainable from such photographs can be comparable to that in Landsat imagery (Helfert & Lulla, 1989).

Population and urbanization

Many of the primary threats now confronting the world derive from the escalating global population (Tickell, 1990), estimated at 5.3 billion people in 1990 and rising by nearly a billion people every decade (King, 1990; Haub, 1990). Fortunately the rate of growth has begun to decline in many countries, but still the global population increases every three years by roughly the combined populations of the United States and Canada (Ehrlich & Ehrlich, 1988), and it is projected that, by the year 2000, the 11 largest metropolitan areas will each have over 13 million people (Wolman, 1990). As global population increases, not only does the cumulative impact of humans on the environment grow, but the vulnerability of humans to various changes, climatic or otherwise, increases as well. In many countries coastal regions are expected to experience particularly rapid growth, and this means that, if predictions of climate warming prove correct, the probable associated rise in sea level will imperil a proportionately larger number of inhabitants. Furthermore, in the face of existent population pressures, few societies any longer have the option to avoid the damage they have done to one locality simply by migrating to a pristine locality elsewhere.

Although some success has been achieved in increasing global food production to keep pace with the increasing population, this success is attributable largely to a few major grain growing areas, especially the Great Plains of the United States and Canada. Deficits in other areas, such as the Sahel region of Africa, have not been overcome (Tickell, 1990). Moreover, on a global scale, continued increases in food production to feed the growing population will probably mean clearing more land for agricultural purposes, with resultant environmental changes.

A first-order determination of large-scale population pat-

Fig. 1. Nighttime DMSP visible image of the eastern United States, November 11, 1987. Lights from urban areas are enhanced but somewhat blurred as a result of an unusually heavy early season snowfall which affected most of the northeastern United States. Direct and indirect light (reflection off the snow) are sensed by the photomultiplier tube on the DMSP satellite. (Courtesy of Hank Brandli.)

terns can be made from nighttime satellite visible imagery. Many of the world's most heavily populated regions are illuminated by the bright lights of cities and towns; and indeed the distribution of lights visible in nighttime satellite imagery, especially for developed countries, often approximates the distribution of population. Figs. 1 and 2 illustrate

Fig. 2. Nighttime DMSP visible image of Europe, North Africa, and the Middle East.

this for the eastern United States and for Europe, North Africa, and the Middle East, respectively, using visible imagery from the Defense Meteorological Satellite Program (DMSP). The heavily populated eastern seaboard of the United States from Boston southward to Washington, DC appears ablaze in Fig. 1, this Boston-to-Washington corridor being one of several megalopolises around the world that show up prominently on nighttime imagery. Major European cities including Paris, London, and Moscow are clearly visible on Fig. 2, as is the more linear feature of lights along the Nile River, reflective of the swelling population of the fertile Nile Valley. The prominence with which human population centers are apparent on these images contrasts sharply with the views that would have been obtained a century or more ago if satellites had been available to image the Earth at that time. Nighttime images taken from space at visible wavelengths in the nineteenth century would have revealed very little, if any,

presence of human activity. The invention of electric lighting combined with the escalating population has radically changed that situation, as Figs. 1 and 2 graphically attest. It has been estimated that by the late 1970s, in the United States alone the total power sent skyward at night in the form of visible light was approximately 50 million watts (Croft, 1978).

Nuclear accidents, highlighting the example of Chernobyl, 1986

The escalating global population, increased industrialization, and heightened expectations of citizens around the world for a better quality of life have brought with them rising needs for energy of many different forms. Unfortunately, no energy source has yet been found that is perfect in all respects, and many have significant inherent dangers that must be weighed

427

against costs and other factors. In the case of nuclear energy, a major benefit is the lack of environmental damage under normal operating conditions. However, a major disadvantage is the seriousness of the possible consequences in the event of a major accident. Such an accident occurred at the Chernobyl nuclear power facility in the former Soviet Union in the spring of 1986.

On the morning of April 26, 1986, there was a devastating nuclear meltdown at the Chernobyl facility, about 90 miles northeast of Kiev. A graphite reactor at the facility went out of control during experimental tests that had purposely eliminated the option of flooding the reactor with water from the nearby safety pond. The facility experienced a thermal nuclear meltdown and a series of hydrogen explosions that vaporized about 50 tons of nuclear fuel into the atmosphere and ejected about 70 additional tons. Lethal doses of gamma radiation continued to be emitted from the reactor for several days; dozens of people died agonizing deaths within weeks of the accident as a direct result of their overexposure to the radiation, and tens of thousands of additional people were subjected to dangerously high doses of radiation, with potential serious health consequences for the rest of their lives. Radiation levels on the roof of the reactor building were 2000–15 000 roentgens per hour, compared to a maximum permissible level for a nuclear power plant of 5 roentgens per *year* as set by the World Health Organization (Medvedev, 1990). An estimated 50–60 million curies of radioactivity were injected into the atmosphere, including 3 million curies of cesium-137, with a half-life of 30 years and the potential of causing cancer of the breast, lung, colon and other organs two or more decades after its absorption (Boly, 1991).

The radioactive material emitted at the Chernobyl facility was transported by wind over much of the low and middle atmosphere of the Northern Hemisphere (Pudykiewicz, 1988). With low level wind flow from the southeast at the time of the accident, the radioactive cloud reached Scandinavia within the first 24 hours. A portion of the cloud then moved southwest over Poland, southern Germany, Austria, and northern Italy, remaining confined basically to Europe until the end of April. Another portion of the cloud moved southeast from Scandinavia, back over the Soviet Union, and was subsequently transported by westerly wind flow across Asia, with the 850 mb flow arriving at Japan on May 3. During the first week of May, the radioactivity reached the Arctic and eastern Canada (moving north and west from Europe), and by the end of May had reached most portions of the Northern Hemisphere (Pudykiewicz, 1988).

The Chernobyl accident provides an example of a situation for which satellite technology enabled the remote monitoring of a dangerous event occurring in a country from which very

little information was initially available. For illustrative purposes, Landsat 5 Thematic Mapper (TM) imagery of the Chernobyl region has been obtained for June 6, 1985, ten months prior to the accident; for April 29, 1986, three days after the accident; for December 2, 1986, seven months after the accident; and for May 11, 1987, a year after the accident (Fig. 3). The four images of Fig. 3 are false-color composites from the data of Bands 2, 4, and 7 of the Landsat TM instrument. TM Band 2 records information at the green wavelengths of visible radiation (0.52–0.60 micrometers); Band 4 records information at near infra-red wavelengths (0.76–0.90 micrometers); and Band 7 records information at middle infra-red wavelengths (2.08–2.35 micrometers) (Hall & Martinec, 1985).

The color choices for the false-color composites from the three Landsat bands were selected so as to give the imagery an approximately natural appearance (J. Barker and L. Wanchoo, personal communication, 1991). Most noticeably, vegetation appears green. Water, particularly the Pripyat River at the top of the images and the reactor's cooling pond covering much of the lower right of the images, appears black. The white rectangle near the center of each image encompasses the four nuclear reactors.

Several consequences of the Chernobyl nuclear explosion can be seen in Fig. 3. The red spot within the rectangle of the April 29, 1986 image indicates unusually high Band 7 values, in the middle infra-red wavelengths. This spot is believed to be located directly over the faulty reactor, and the high Band 7 values suggest considerable heat still being generated three days after the accident. Richter *et al.* (1986) calculate from the Landsat TM imagery an estimated reactor surface temperature of 1000–1300 K on April 29; this compares with an estimated interior reactor temperature of 2500 K on the date of the accident (Richter *et al.*, 1986, from T. Ewe). The dark line proceeding southwestwards from the red dot marks the central path of material ejected from the explosion (J. Barker and L. Wanchoo, personal communication, 1991). This ejected material extended in a fairly straight line for a distance of about 100 m from the reactor and included highly radioactive graphite and nuclear fuel.

At the bottom of the white rectangle in Fig. 3(a) are two small rectangular ponds, identifiable by their black coloring. Although both ponds survived the initial explosion, as is clear from Fig. 3(b), the western pond, immediately south of the reactor, became highly contaminated and was consequently drained (Fig. 3(d)). Another artificial, human-effected change brought on by the explosion and visible in the Landsat imagery is the widening of several of the roads during the clean-up operations, in order to facilitate removal of the radioactivity from the vicinity. This widening is particularly

Fig. 3. Landsat 5 TM images of the vicinity of the Chernobyl nuclear power plant on the following dates: (*a*) June 6, 1985, (*b*) April 29, 1986, (*c*) December 2, 1986, and (*d*) May 11, 1987. The images are color composites using TM bands 2, 4, and 7, and have been cropped to show a 7·6 × 7·6 km area. The images are oriented with north at the top. (Courtesy of John Barker and Lalit Wanchoo.)

visible within the boxed-off square to the southwest of the power plant (Figs. 3(*c*) and 3(*d*) versus Figs. 3(*a*) and 3(*b*)). The road that passes through the square boxed area with a prominent bend had been the main road from Pripyat (farther north) to Kiev (farther south). A new road constructed through the forests to the south, providing a route with a lower risk of radioactivity, is apparent on the May 11, 1987 image (Fig. 3(*d*)). Also visible in the lower portion of the May 11 image is a sizable barren area to the west of the major cooling pond and to the northeast of the just mentioned road

through the southern forests (Fig. 3(*d*)). The barren area had earlier been forested (Figs. 3(*a*), 3(*b*), and 3(*c*)), but the forests were cleared between December 2, 1986 and May 11, 1987, in order to remove highly contaminated vegetation.

Gas flares

Gas flares (Fig. 4) are among the most conspicuous features on nighttime visible imagery of the Earth (e.g. center of Fig. 5) other than centers of population. These fires are often

Fig. 4. Ground-based photograph of a gas flare in north Africa. The photograph was taken by D. F. Cupp and appeared originally in the May 1969 issue of *National Geographic*. (From Croft, 1978.)

purposely set to burn off waste gas, especially in conjunction with oil field operations, when large volumes of gas typically rise to the Earth's surface as the oil is pumped. This waste gas must be disposed of in some fashion, and in remote areas it is often considered more economical to burn the gas than to transport it to a buyer. The wasted energy can be considerable; in fact it has been estimated that 3% of all hydrocarbons are burned in waste gas flares (Croft, 1978, from R. Rotty).

Although the practice of burning waste gas has been known for some time, its widespread extent was not realized until revealed by satellite observations. The DMSP satellites have been particularly useful in this regard (e.g. Fig. 5). The OLS photomultiplier tube on board these satellites measures the average brightness over areas of approximately 3 km^2. The contribution of a single flare to the average brightness depends both on the intrinsic brightness of the flare and on the percentage of the observed area that the flare occupies, so that both these properties affect the clarity with which it shows up on the DMSP imagery. The large areas frequently covered by gas flares result in part from the practice of spreading the fire laterally to ensure complete combustion. Usually this is done by dispensing gas from a series of stand-

pipes placed in a row 50 m or more in length (e.g. Fig. 4). Gas flares are set in many parts of the world, with the greatest numbers being in the vicinity of the Persian Gulf. In the Gulf region the gas flares are prominent enough to be visible in the DMSP satellite imagery even under conditions of bright moonlight.

Oil well fires, highlighting the example of the Kuwaiti oil fields, 1991

In January and February 1991, war in the Persian Gulf region produced considerable environmental damage as a result of oil well fires, oil and gas pipeline ruptures, and exploding projectiles. One of the most severe environmental consequences of the war was the damage from the fires intentionally set at the Kuwaiti oil fields by the Iraqi troops. The regional environmental pollution and changes to the regional weather as a result of the oil well fires have been significant. Smoke plumes from the Kuwaiti oil fields extended for tens of thousands of km^2, polluting and blackening the skies over much of the eastern Arabian peninsula. Presumably this smoke was a significant factor in Bahrain's experiencing in

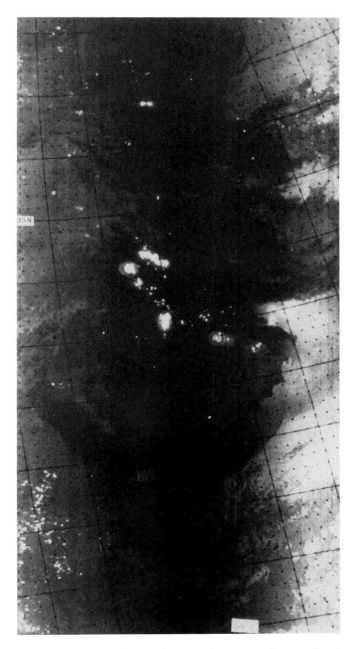

Fig. 5. Nighttime DMSP visible image showing gas flares and agricultural fires in the Middle East and vicinity. The lights in the lower left are from agricultural fires in Sudan and Ethiopia, while the brighter lights in the center of the image are from gas flares along the northwest coast of the Persian Gulf.

1991 its coldest May in 35 years, with average temperatures approximately 4 °C below normal (Simarski, 1991).

A phalanx of satellites was primed for observations over the Persian Gulf region during the Gulf War. In addition to satellite observations for military purposes, Landsat, the French Système Probatoire d'Observation de la Terre (SPOT) satellite, NOAA, DMSP, and Meteosat all were utilized to sense remotely the ecological damage being done to the land, air, and sea in and around occupied Kuwait. In late February, near the end of the war, hundreds of oil well fires were burning. It has been estimated that between 3 and 6 million barrels of oil were burned daily as a result of the sabotage (American Geophysical Union, 1991) and that the oil well fires contributed about 1.5% of the global annual production of carbon dioxide. On a regional scale, the fires produced significant amounts of carbon monoxide, methane, hydrocarbons, nitrogen oxides, and particulates (American Geophysical Union, 1991, quoting J. S. Levine).

Fig. 6 is a ground-based photograph which shows the veil of dense smoke produced by the burning oil wells. Air temperatures beneath the smoke plumes were reported by military personnel and news media correspondents to be about 7 °C cooler than in adjacent areas free of smoke. Even at midday, flashlights were frequently needed to read ordinary maps.

Fig. 7 provides a NOAA-11 image illustrating the visibility with which the Kuwaiti oil well fires showed up on high-resolution satellite imagery. Several oil well fires appear in red at the top of the image, and the resultant smoke plumes appear in black, stretched prominently across the center of the image and extending downwind of the fires themselves by approximately 300 km. Clearly such satellite imagery can help in the monitoring and tracking of contaminants spewed into the atmosphere.

In addition to the oil well fires, other environmental damage produced during the Persian Gulf War included massive oil spills, some of which resulted from bombing raids and others of which are thought to have been purposely caused by the Iraqi military. These oil spills fouled the waters in the Persian Gulf along the coasts of Kuwait, Saudi Arabia, Bahrain, and Qatar during and after the Gulf War. The World Conservation Monitoring Centre in London estimates that as many as 400 million gallons of oil may have leaked into the Gulf, which would be an order of magnitude more than the Exxon–Valdez oil spill discussed in the next section.

Oil spills, highlighting the example of the Exxon–Valdez, 1989

Major oil spills join nuclear accidents, gas flares, and oil well fires as examples of energy-related phenomena visible from space. Ever since large quantities of oil were first transported by ship, concerns have existed over the potential environmental damage in the event of a major spill, and indeed these fears

Fig. 6. Ground-based photograph of oil well fires at the Kuwaiti oil fields in late February 1991. (Courtesy of *Space News*. Photograph by Doug Pensinger.)

have sadly been realized in several instances at various locations around the world. One of the most publicized and ecologically damaging oil spills in the United States occurred in Prince William Sound off the coast of Alaska on March 24, 1989. Over 11 million gallons of crude oil spilled into the water from the hull of a grounded tanker, the *Exxon–Valdez*. Attempts at containment of the oil were in large part ineffectual. Winds and currents battering the shores and coastal waters spread the slick more than 500 km from the grounding site, and marine life was devastated by the floating sludge.

Satellite images of the affected region were obtained shortly after the *Exxon–Valdez* grounding. In particular, imagery of the oil spill was obtained by the NOAA AVHRR, the SPOT Panchromatic Scanner, the SPOT Multispectral Scanner (MS), and the Landsat Thematic Mapper (TM). These data have been digitally analyzed by Stringer *et al.* (1992) in order to distinguish spectral signatures related to the oil.

Fig. 8 is a Landsat TM image showing Prince William Sound on April 7, 1989, two weeks after the oil spill occurred. This image is a color composite produced with the middle infra-red band 5 as red, the near infra-red band 4 as green,

and the visible band 1 as blue. The data have been adjusted by various digital analysis techniques, including application of an algorithm to minimize sensor noise that might confuse the depiction of the oil signature. Landsat TM images have relatively high spatial resolution (30 m for optical bands and 120 m for the thermal infra-red band) but provide a swath of only about 180 km, approximately one-tenth the width of the AVHRR swath (Stringer *et al.*, 1992). The oil spill is visible on Fig. 8 in the magenta colored filament features. As can be seen, by the time of the image (approximately 12:30 Alaskan Standard Time, April 7, 1989), some of the floating oil remained in Prince William Sound but much of it had moved into the Gulf of Alaska (Fig. 8).

Satellite images of the *Exxon–Valdez* oil spill were compared by Stringer *et al.* (1992) to daily maps showing the distribution of the oil from aircraft and other observations. They were also compared with oceanographic measurements of salinity, temperature, and chlorophyll obtained from aboard the University of Alaska research vessel the *Alpha Helix* in April, May, and June. The apparent temperature range of the oil is 1.5–2.4 °C, which is generally colder than the surrounding water. The low

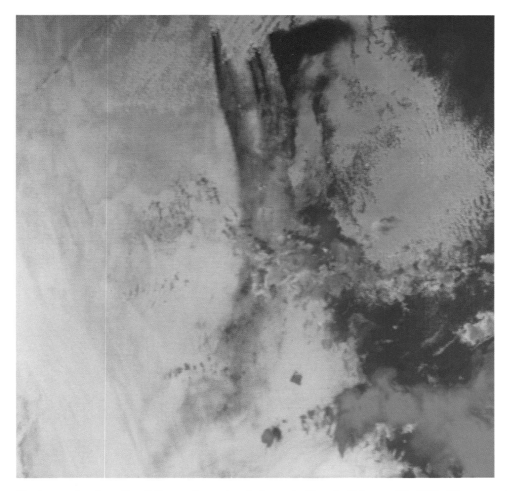

Fig. 7. NOAA-11 satellite image showing oil well fires and associated plumes in Kuwait, February 21, 1991. The two major plumes are more than 300 km long. Burning oil wells appear red, smoke plumes black, desert tan, and clouds green. (Courtesy of D. R. Cahoon, Jr.)

apparent temperature is most likely a result of a lower emissivity of the oil rather than of a lower kinetic temperature. Analysis of the TM image reveals the temperature anomaly as an assemblage of filament structures or windrows of oil. These filaments were most prominent on TM bands 5 and 7, although showed up also on bands 1 and 4. Satellite imagery has proven superior to aircraft data in depicting the size, shape, and precise positions of the windrows; however, these images have not proven satisfactory in recording sheen (Stringer *et al.*, 1992).

Stringer *et al.* (1992) list four criteria necessary for satellite imagery to be useful during the active phase of oil spill monitoring and clean-up: 1) availability to field operations on a near real-time basis, 2) high enough resolution for detecting windrows, 3) repeat coverage every one or two days, and 4) penetration through clouds. At present, satellite imagery tends not to be available in the timely manner necessary for assisting the work crews in limiting the environmental

damage. AVHRR imagery was occasionally available to the crews at Prince William Sound within eight hours of the satellite pass, and it proved somewhat useful; but the AVHRR data have insufficient resolution for many of the clean-up needs. In contrast, if the high resolution Landsat TM or SPOT data had been available within a day, these could have significantly aided clean-up operations. The requirement for repeat coverage every one or two days with a satellite instrument providing a spatial resolution adequate to detect oil may be achieved in the near future. Specifically, the pointable multispectral scanners on SPOT allow high resolution data to be obtained, and with two functioning SPOT satellites the data coverage poleward of 60° latitude should be more than adequate. The last criteria, cloud penetration, can be accomplished with microwave sensors (Stringer *et al.*, 1992). At present, passive microwave sensors have too coarse a resolution to be practical for monitoring oil spills; however, active sensors should be able to allow the identification of oil with

Fig. 8. Computer-enhanced Landsat TM image of Prince William Sound (center) and the Gulf of Alaska (left), April 7, 1989, two weeks after a major oil spill occurred in Prince William Sound from the *Exxon-Valdez* oil tanker. Much of the oil had washed onto shore by the time of the image, but the oil still at the water's surface is visible as the magenta colored filament features both in Prince William Sound, and, even more so, downstream in the Gulf of Alaska. (Courtesy of Ken Dean and William Stringer, Northern Remote Sensing Laboratory, University of Alaska.)

sufficient resolution to map and monitor major oil spills at a useful level of detail.

Forest fires, highlighting the example of Yellowstone National Park, 1988

Forest fires, whether ignited by humans or otherwise, can spread over vast areas, with both the fires themselves and the devastation produced from them becoming visible from space-based sensors. While fire is generally the principal agent of destruction at the site itself, the associated smoke can travel thousands of kilometers and have much farther ranging consequences. The smoke, composed of minute ash and carbon particulates, can damage many man-made and natural surfaces as well as effectively attenuating the incoming solar radiation, thereby obscuring the Sun and causing reduced visibility. If the fires are massive enough, noticeable temporary cooling from the smoke is possible (Warren & Clarke,

1990). In the event of extreme cases, such as the extensive fires predicted in various nuclear-war scenarios, the cooling from the smoke may be severe (Warren & Wiscombe, 1985). In the less extreme case of the Kuwaiti oil well fires during the 1991 Persian Gulf War referred to earlier (e.g. Fig. 7), regional cooling has been mentioned as a possible consequence of the fires' smoke.

Visible imagery from satellites frequently reveals the approximate location of forest fires by the resultant smoke patterns. Such imagery, however, generally does not show the fire itself, which is obscured by the smoke. The locations of the fires can be pinpointed by use of satellite sensors with medium and thermal infra-red channels, highlighting the hot spots in the image area. Satellite data can also allow monitoring of various effects of fires, such as the effects on atmospheric chemistry. A preliminary study by Watson, Fishman & Reichle (1990) demonstrates that tropical biomass burning plays a major role in atmospheric chemistry both near the

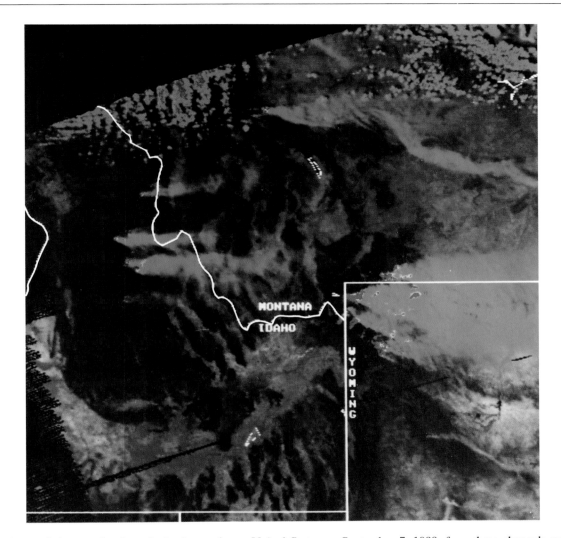

Fig. 9. Forest fires and the associated smoke in the northwest United States on September 7, 1988, from three channels on the NOAA-9 AVHRR: a broadband visible channel (band 1), a near infra-red channel (band 2), and a thermal infra-red channel (band 3). Fires are apparent near Glacier National Park, Montana, toward the top of the image, in several national parks in Idaho, and especially in Yellowstone National Park in northwest Wyoming. The color-enhanced image shows the active fires as red and the smoke as light blue.

source of the burning and throughout the tropics. Measurements from the Total Ozone Mapping Spectrometer (TOMS) and the Measurement of Air Pollution from Satellites (MAPS) instruments have revealed a clear seasonal cycle in the atmospheric ozone and carbon monoxide amounts in the tropics, a seasonal cycle believed to be caused by extensive seasonal biomass burning and the subsequent transport of the smoke trace gas constituents by the prevailing winds.

To illustrate the use of satellite remote sensing in monitoring forest fires, Fig. 9 shows several major forest fires burning in and around Yellowstone National Park in the western United States during the summer of 1988. The unusually low regional rainfall during that summer, combined with relative humidities that were often under 10%, provided the extreme

conditions which led to one of the largest conflagrations in the United States during the twentieth century. More than a third of Yellowstone National Park (itself 9000 km²) was burned. Most of the fires in the park were triggered by lightning, but human carelessness contributed to a number of the blazes (Jeffery, 1989) and National Park policy played a role in how much of the park was affected.

From the 1880s through the 1970s, National Park policy in the United States had been to extinguish all fires as soon as possible. As a result, 90 years of deadfall (fallen trees not burned) was available to kindle any fire that might begin, so that the forest was in effect primed to be incinerated once a major fire ignited. The policy of extinguishing all fires was revised in the early 1970s, partly in recognition of both the

Fig. 10. Photograph taken from the United States Space Shuttle of the Himalayan region of Nepal, India, and Tibet, May 1989. Sources of the smoke are individual fires burning in subtropical rainforests. (NASA STS *Atlantis* photograph S30–84–014.)

dangers from the increasing deadfall and the well-tested recuperative powers of nature. The new policy is to extinguish all human-caused fires immediately but to extinguish fires ignited naturally only in the event that life or property become threatened. As a result, the fires of 1988 were allowed to gain momentum in the early stages. The dry conditions, however, continued for an abnormally long period, and this combined with the 90 years of deadfall led to an enormous conflagration, with 9500 fire fighters eventually called in. By the end, after rains finally came, nearly 4050 km² of Yellowstone had been damaged, compared with only 600 km² of the park having been burned in the 116 years prior to 1988. Nevertheless, in spite of the enormous extent of the damage, natural regeneration of the forest began almost immediately. In fact, many bird and mammal species actually benefited from the fires, due to the increased open area (Jeffery, 1989).

Fig. 9 shows not only the forest fires in Yellowstone (in northwestern Wyoming) but also forest fires in several

National Parks in eastern Idaho and western Montana. The color-enhanced NOAA-9 image shows the fires in red, from the hot spots identified by a thermal infra-red channel of the AVHRR, and the smoke in light blue, from the band 1 visible channel of the AVHRR. The distribution of the smoke and its position in relation to the generating fires gives a striking confirmation of the prevailing westerly wind direction.

Although many forest fires are due to lightning or other natural causes, and others are due to human carelessness, still others are set quite deliberately either for clearing the land or in conjunction with slash and burn agricultural practices. In fact, the prominent points of light visible over savannah areas of northeastern Africa in the lower left of Fig. 5 are from numerous agricultural fires set as part of an intentional slash and burn seasonal growth cycle. Extensive agricultural burning in the cultivated areas of many undeveloped countries is clearly visible from space, although burning is by no means the only, or sometimes even the most important, means of

Fig. 11. Photograph taken from the United States Space Shuttle on September 7, 1985, showing sediment-laden and turbid waters of the Mahajamba Bay on Madagascar Island, resulting from extreme erosion due to deforestation. Annual erosion may exceed 250 tons of soil per hectare. (NASA STS *Discovery* Photograph 51–39–42.)

clearing the land. In some areas of the Tropics, notably in the Brazilian rainforest, powered machines are doing an increasing percentage of the damage (Croft, 1978; Foster, 1983).

Fig. 10 illustrates how clearly the smoke from agricultural fires can be seen on photography taken from the United States Space Shuttle. This photograph shows fires in the foothills of the Himalayas, where the forest is being removed to give way to agricultural development. The extensive amount of similar purposeful deforestation occurring in the Tropics is detailed in the chapter on vegetation (Townshend, Tucker, & Goward, 1993). In addition to the deforestation itself, several of the secondary effects of fires are also visible from space, such as the increased sediment load in rivers due to upstream erosion in deforested areas (e.g. Fig. 11).

Contrails

When a jet aircraft passes overhead, a white condensation trail, called a contrail, often marks the path of the jet. Con-

trails result from the condensation of water vapor produced by the combustion of fuel within the jet engine. Hot, moisture-laden air from the engine mixes with much colder air outside the aircraft, resulting in saturation of the cooled exhaust air and consequent condensation. The frequent occurrence of contrails demonstrates the relative ease with which artificial clouds can be produced in very cold air (Miller & Thompson, 1975). The persistence of a contrail can serve as an indicator of the temperature and amount of moisture present at the altitude of the jet aircraft: with sufficient moisture, contrails may stretch across the sky for some time after the passage of the jet, but in a very dry atmosphere the contrail will evaporate almost immediately. With the increase in the number of operating jet aircraft, contrails have become increasingly visible across the skies, and on a small scale they may play a role in altering the local energy budget. Their effect is similar to that of cirrus clouds, allowing shortwave energy to pass through with relatively little absorption, but absorbing within the condensed ice crystals a higher percent-

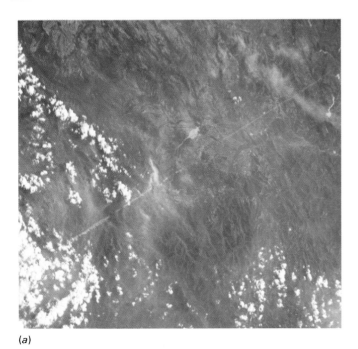

(a)

(b)

age of the longwave energy emitted by the Earth. Some evidence exists for increased cloud cover over heavily traveled air routes. In fact, it has been estimated that contrails from high altitude jet aircraft have resulted in a 5–10% increase in high-level cirrus clouds and a concomitant increase in the frequency of cloudy days in parts of the mid-western United States (Changnon, 1981).

While easy to see from the ground, contrails cannot always be readily observed from weather satellites because of their limited width. However, meteorological spacecraft, such as the NOAA and DMSP satellites, and Earth resources spacecraft, such as Landsat, have all revealed the occurrence of contrails (Carleton & Lamb, 1986; Joseph *et al.*, 1975). Fig. 12 illustrates the visibility of contrails from space with a photograph over the Canta Bricka Mountains of northern Spain taken from the Space Shuttle *Columbia* and a thermal infra-red image over the mid-western United States taken from a DMSP satellite. The long contrail diagonally crossing Fig. 12(*a*) reflects the atmospheric conditions at the altitude of the jet, indicating sufficient water vapor to maintain the contrail over this distance, approximately 100 km, whereas the numerous contrails in the left center of Fig. 12(*b*) reflect the heavy air traffic in this region of the United States. In a study on jet contrails from high-resolution (0.6 and 1.0 km) DMSP imagery, Carleton and Lamb (1986) find infra-red wavelengths to be preferable to visible wavelengths for the detection and analysis of contrails, because of the greater discrimination on the infra-red imagery between cirrus-level features and features from the lower troposphere and the surface. They find contrails to be consistently identifiable on the DMSP imagery and readily distinguished from natural cirrus cloud, due to their linearity, short length, and random orientation with respect to the clouds.

Ship stack effluents and cloud reflectivity

Whereas contrails directly mark the path of the jet producing them, ships at sea may leave indirect tracks in the atmosphere that are also visible from satellite imagery. Such tracks result from man-made aerosols released from the ships. These aerosols, just like aerosols from other sources, can serve as nuclei around which cloud droplets and ice crystals rapidly form and expand. Although the small size of the aerosols makes the direct interactions with solar and terrestrial radiation fairly weak, the much larger cloud droplets formed

Fig. 12. (*a*) Photograph of a contrail over the Canta Bricka Mountains of northern Spain taken from the United States Space Shuttle *Columbia* on August 10, 1989. (NASA STS *Columbia* photograph S28–97–006.) (*b*) DMSP thermal infra-red image showing a maze of contrails embedded in a cirrus cloud deck over southern Michigan, western Ohio, and eastern Indiana. Lakes Huron and Erie are visible in the upper right portion of the image, and Lake Michigan is visible under the cloud deck in the upper left of the image. (From the DMSP image archive at the World Data Center A for Glaciology (Snow and Ice); courtesy of James DeGrand, Ohio State University.)

$(1\text{km})^2$ NOAA-9 AVHRR 2227Z 3 Apr 1985

Composite
0.63 μm and 0.89 μm
reflectivities

3.7 μm radiance

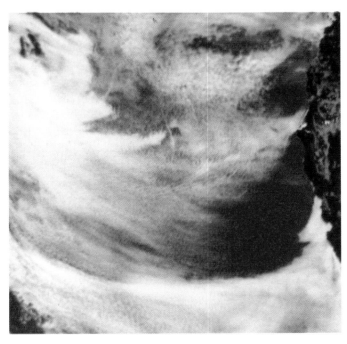 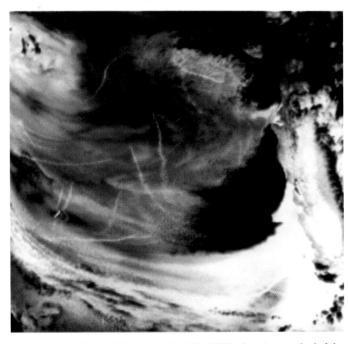

Fig. 13. NOAA-9 AVHRR images of the Pacific Ocean region off the west coast of the United States on April 3, 1985, showing tracks left by ship stack effluents. The image on the right is from the 3·7 micrometer channel and the image on the left is a composite from the 0·63 micrometer and 0·89 micrometer channels. (Courtesy of Michael King.)

around the aerosols can have much stronger radiative interactions (Coakley, Bernstein & Durkee, 1987). In fact, although the net results of man-made aerosols on the Earth's radiation budget are by no means certain, it has been estimated that they may be comparable in magnitude but opposite in sign to the effects of increased carbon dioxide (Twomey, Piepgrass & Wolfe, 1984).

Aerosols released by ships at sea have been observed to generate cloud lines in regions otherwise devoid of clouds and noticeable ship-track signatures within pre-existing shallow-layer stratus clouds (Conover, 1966; Radke, Coakley & King, 1989). Such cloud lines and ship-track signatures are at times clearly observable in visible and infra-red satellite imagery, although this tends to be true only after extended periods of stagnant conditions. Under normal conditions, the pollution is dispersed over broad scales and hence becomes less apparent (Coakley, Bernstein & Durkee, 1987). None the less, the limited satellite observations available of ship tracks do reveal the increases in cloud reflectivity resultant from the ship effluents. The observed changes in cloud radiance properties produced by the aerosols, such as an increased ratio of scattering to absorption and increased cloud reflectivity, suggest that droplet sizes in ship tracks are less than those in the surrounding cloud but total concentrations of both droplets and particles are substantially greater than those in the surrounding clouds. Both of these facts have been confirmed with *in situ* aircraft data (Radke, Coakley & King, 1989).

Fig. 13 illustrates the observability of ship tracks on NOAA-9 AVHRR imagery. Numerous tracks from ship stack effluents are prominent on the 3.7 micrometer image of Fig. 13 and a few are barely visible on the coincident 0.63 and 0.89 micrometer composite image for the same area. Clearly the 3.7 micrometer channel is preferable for studying ship stack effluents, although the 0.63 and 0.89 micrometer composite would be preferable for various other cloud studies.

Vanishing or deteriorating seas and lakes, highlighting the example of the Aral Sea

From the narrow linear features of contrails and ship tracks, requiring high resolution imagery to be resolved from space, we turn to the much larger and non-linear features of seas and lakes. Many of the world's seas and lakes are currently undergoing severe shrinkage due to human activities. Among these, perhaps the most prominent, because of its size and the extent of the shrinkage, is the Aral Sea (Fig. 14) in the former Soviet Union. The Aral Sea had been one of the largest inland bodies of water on the Earth's surface but over the past few decades it has been rapidly disappearing (Figs. 15–16). The rivers which once fed the Aral no longer do so, as their waters have been diverted for irrigation and other uses. As a consequence, the delicate balance between inflow into the sea and evaporation from it has been broken, with the result that a sea which was the world's fourth largest inland water body in the middle of the twentieth century could be disappearing in a timespan not much longer than a single generation. If so, this would be the first instance in historic times that such a large body of water has disappeared so rapidly. Increasing the tragedy, the sea is being transformed into a barren land unable to sustain almost any form of life other than a small bushy plant called Solianka (Nasar, 1989; Ellis & Turnley, 1990).

The damage to the Aral Sea has resulted from an otherwise successful effort by the former Soviet Union to become self-sufficient in cotton production. The waters of the rivers feeding the Aral have been diverted for irrigating cotton fields and, to a lesser extent, rice fields. As of 1989, of the two major rivers that had fed the sea, the Syr Darya had failed to reach the Aral in the previous 18 years and the Amu Darya had been drained sufficiently so that its waters now only occasionally reached the Aral (Nasar, 1989). Although the Soviet goal of cotton self-sufficiency was first enunciated in 1918, the most massive irrigation projects were not begun until the 1950s, and the damage to the Aral was not widely apparent until about 1960. At that time the area of the sea was 65 000 km^2; but by 1990 only 37 500 km^2 remained, over 40% of the sea's area having disappeared (Ellis & Turnley, 1990). From another perspective, as recently as 1965 the fishing center of Muynak bordered the sea, but by 1990, without having moved, it was 20 miles from the shore (Ellis & Turnley, 1990). Compounding the horror of the shrinking area, the reduced input of fresh water and the continued evaporation of the existent water have meant that the Aral has become saltier, with the average salinity increasing from about 10 grams per liter in 1960 to about 30 grams per liter in 1989 (Micklin, 1991).

Consequences of the rapidly retreating sea include the desert of salt and sand left behind as the sea recedes, the increase in damaging sand and dust storms, and the lack of life within the sea itself. Of the 24 native species of fish in the Aral earlier in this century, none remained by 1990 (Ellis & Turnley, 1990). Over the past few decades especially, the land has been poisoned with fertilizers, the drinking water has been seriously polluted with pesticides, fertilizers, and salts, and the air is plagued by dust from the drying sea. Some experts fear that the health hazards are rapidly making the Aral Sea vicinity uninhabitable. Incidence of hepatitis, jaundice, and typhoid have been soaring, as have rates of intestinal cancer, throat cancer, infant mortality, and many varieties of respiratory diseases (Nasar, 1989). Even cotton production has finally been hurt, as the salts lessen the fertility of the soils (Ellis & Turnley, 1990).

If, as expected, the Aral continues to shrink, environmental problems related to it will almost certainly worsen. Early in the next century the remnant of the Aral is expected to be reduced in area to under 5000 km^2 and to have an average water salinity 4–5 times that of the open ocean. At that point the Aral is likely to be a lifeless depression, essentially an overblown version of the Dead Sea (Ellis & Turnley, 1990). Some projections suggest that the Aral will be completely dried up by the year 2010 (Nasar, 1989), although others suggest that the sea will shrink to 4000–5000 km^2 and stabilize at that level (Ellis & Turnley, 1990). Fortunately, a much brighter possibility also exists, as the problem is receiving widespread attention and corrective policies are being established. In particular, irrigation systems are being made more efficient, canals are being built to direct some of the used waters to the sea, and the area set aside for cotton production is being reduced (Ellis & Turnley, 1990).

In this age of increased environmental awareness it is possible that potential future environmental tragedies of the magnitude of the Aral Sea shrinkage can be avoided or at least greatly reduced. Space observations have a tremendous potential to contribute. In the case of the Aral Sea, considerable damage had occurred before space observations were available to monitor it. However, the monitoring of the size and shape of a large body of water from space is so straightforward, especially if the region is viewed repeatedly with the same instrument, that no comparable shrinkage of any sea should occur in the future without its being apparent through space observations at a much earlier stage, when, presumably, a reversal of the damage would be more feasible.

Unfortunately, the Aral Sea is not the only body of water rapidly shrinking or otherwise degenerating because of either natural or human activities. Notable additional examples include Lake Chad in central Africa and the Sea of Galilee in Israel, both of which have experienced noticeable water loss

Fig. 14. Photograph of the Aral Sea taken from the United States Space Shuttle on August 6, 1985. (NASA STS *Challenger* photograph 51F-36–59.) The whitish area along the southeastern border of the sea is sand and salt exposed due to the lowering of the water level.

Fig. 16. NOAA 11 daytime visible image (0937 GMT) of the Aral Sea taken on September 6, 1990. Note the shrinkage of the sea and the enlarged islands when compared with Fig. 15.

over the past few decades. The desiccation of Lake Chad might be in large part associated with natural cyclic fluctuations in rainfall rather than human intervention, and some welcome reversal of the drying trend of the 1970s and early 1980s is apparent from the size of the lake revealed by images from the Space Shuttle *Discovery* in 1989, showing a noticeable rebounding of the lake area in its northern portion (Lulla *et al.*, 1989; Mohler, Helfert & Giardino, 1989). In the case of the Sea of Galilee, several years of drought conditions plus overuse by the surrounding communities have lowered the water level to its lowest recorded position. This inland lake, which lies more than 200 m below sea level and supplies Israel with a third of its water needs, may be irrevocably damaged by salinization if the water level continues to drop.

Conclusions

Space observations provide a tremendous potential for monitoring changes in the Earth's environment. The previous chapters of this book have illustrated this with a wide variety of examples and variables from each of four major spheres: the atmosphere, hydrosphere, cryosphere, and lithosphere.

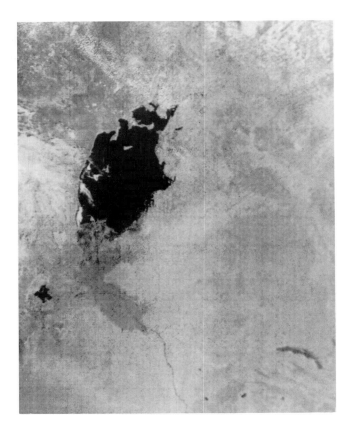

Fig. 15. DMSP daytime visible image (0743 GMT) of the Aral Sea taken on August 10, 1973. Resolution is 0·6 km. (The large, elongated dark area south of the Aral Sea is the irrigated flood plain associated with the Amu Darya river entering from the center bottom of the image.) (Courtesy of Don Wiesnet.)

This chapter has looked at a few additional examples, where the changes have been at least in part due to human activities. These have ranged from accidental oil spills, nuclear meltdowns, and shrinking seas to quite intentional agricultural burning and urbanization. Although some of the examples have had little known effect beyond their visibility, others have been clearly deleterious to one aspect or another of the environment.

In view of the widespread changes that human populations are causing to the environment and the increased awareness of this, it is quite timely that space-borne sensors are now available to reveal and monitor the changes that are occurring. The information that these sensors reveal can contribute to policy decisions that will help reverse those ongoing changes that are detrimental and perhaps help limit additional detrimental changes in the future. Of course not all changes due to humans are negative; and the hope is that in the decades ahead space-borne sensors in addition to monitoring environmental damage will also be recording and monitoring major environmental improvements resulting from increased human awareness and concern.

References

American Geophysical Union (1991). Burning Kuwait oil wells, *EOS*, **72** (14), 153.

Boly, W. (1991). Chernobyl five years after: Life in the wasteland, *In Health*, May/June, 60–70.

Carleton, A. M. & Lamb, P. J. (1986). Jet contrails and cirrus cloud: A feasibility study employing high-resolution satellite imagery, *Bull. Am. Meteorol. Soc.*, **67**, 301–9.

Changnon, S. A. (1981). Midwestern cloud, sunshine, and temperature trends since 1901: Possible evidence of jet contrail effects, *J. Appl. Meteorol.*, **20**, 496–508.

Coakley, J. A., Jr., Bernstein, R. L. & Durkee, P. A. (1987). Effect of ship stack effluents on cloud reflectivity, *Science*, **237**, 1020–2.

Conover, J. H. (1966). Anomalous cloud lines, *J. Atmos. Sci.*, **23**, 778–85.

Croft, T. (1978). Nighttime images of the Earth from space, *Sci. Am.*, **239**, 86–98.

Ehrlich, P. R. & Ehrlich, A. H. (1988). Population, plenty, and poverty, *Nat. Geog.*, **174** (6), 914–45.

Ellis, W. S. & Turnley, D. C. (1990). The Aral: A Soviet sea lies dying, *Nat. Geog.*, **177** (2), 73–93.

Foster, J. (1983). Observations of the Earth using nighttime visible imagery, *Proc. Int. Soc. Opt. Eng.: Opt. Eng. for Cold Environm.*, **414**, 187–93.

Goodman, S. & Christian, H. (1993). Lightning, this volume.

Hall, D. K. & Martinec, J. (1985). *Remote Sensing of Ice and Snow*. Chapman and Hall, London, 189pp.

Haub, C. (1990). 2050: Standing room only? *The Washington Post*, July 8, C3.

Helfert, M. R. & Lulla, K. P. (1989). Monitoring tropical environments with Space Shuttle photography, *Geocarto Int.*, **1**, 55–67.

Jeffery, D. (1989). Yellowstone: The Great Fires of 1988, *Nat. Geog.*, **175** (2), 255–73.

Joseph, J. H., Levin, Z., Mekler, Y., Ohring, G. & Otterman, J. (1975). Study of contrails observed from the ERTS 1 satellite imagery, *J. Geophys. Res.*, **80** (3), 366–72.

King, G. W. (1990). *Statistical Abstract of the United States 1990*, US Department of Commerce, Washington, DC, 991pp.

Lulla, K., Helfert, M., Whitehead, V., Amsbury, D., Coats, M., Blaha, J., Buchli, J., Springer, R., Bagian, J. & Evans, C. (1989). Earth observations during Space Shuttle flight STS-29: *Discovery's* voyage to the Earth, 13–18 March 1989, *Geocarto Int.*, **4** (4), 67–74.

Medvedev, G. (1990). *The Truth About Chernobyl*. English translation by E. Rossiter, Basic Books, 274pp.

Micklin, P. P. (1991). The water management crisis in Soviet central Asia. *The Carl Beck Papers*, #905, Center for Russian and East European Studies, University of Pittsburgh, Pittsburgh, 120pp.

Miller, A. & Thompson, J. (1975). Observations of the atmosphere, *Elements of Meteorology*, C. E. Merrill Publishing, Columbus, Ohio, 23–45.

Mohler, R. R. J., Helfert, M. R. & Giardino, J. R. (1989). The decrease of Lake Chad as documented during twenty years of manned space flight, *Geocarto Int.*, **1**, 75–9.

Nasar, R. (1989). How the Soviets murdered a sea. *The Washington Post*, June 4, B3.

Pudykiewicz, J. (1988). Numerical simulation of the transport of radioactive cloud from the Chernobyl nuclear accident, *Tellus*, **40B**, 241–59.

Radke, L. F., Coakley, J. A., Jr. & King, M. D. (1989). Direct and remote sensing observations of the effects of ships on clouds, *Science*, **246**, 1146–9.

Richter, R., Lehmann, F., Haydn, R. & Volk, P. (1986). Analysis of Landsat TM images of Chernobyl. *Int. J. Rem. Sens.*, **7**, 1859–67.

Schoeberl, M. R. (1993). Stratospheric ozone depletion, this volume.

Simarski, L. T. (1991). Global impact unlikely from Kuwait fires, *EOS*, **72** (27), 289–90.

Stringer, W. J., Dean, K. G., Guritz, R. M., Garbeil, H. M., Groves, J. E. & Ahlnaes, K. (1992). Detection of petroleum spilled from the M. V. *Exxon–Valdez*, *Int. J. Rem. Sens.*, **13**(5), 799–824.

Tickell, C. (1990). Climate change and world affairs, *EOS*, **67** (17), 425.

Townshend, J., Tucker, J. & Goward, S. (1993). Global vegetation and deforestation, this volume.

Twomey, S. A., Piepgrass, M. & Wolfe, T. L. (1984). An assessment of the impact of pollution on global cloud albedo, *Tellus*, **36B**, 356–66.

Warren, S. & Clarke, A. (1990). Soot in the atmosphere and snow surface of Antarctica, *J. Geophys. Res.*, **95** (D2), 1811–16.

Warren, S. & Wiscombe, W. (1985). Dirty snow after nuclear war, *Nature*, **313**, 467–70.

Watson, C., Fishman, J. & Reichle, H., Jr. (1990). The significance of biomass burning as a source of carbon monoxide and ozone in the southern hemisphere tropics, *J. Geophys. Res.*, **95** (D10), 16443–50.

Williams, R. & Hall, D. (1993). Glaciers, this volume.

Wolman, M. G. (1990). The impact of man, *EOS*, **71** (52), 1884–6.

Future directions

Introduction

This book has illustrated the many types of global data sets that are now becoming available from the investment in Earth-orbiting satellites. Many of these data sets provide time series of geophysical information that can be used quantitatively in numerical computer models. This is a marked advance over the situation in the early days of remote sensing (1960s and early 1970s), when the data were poorly calibrated and only used qualitatively. Naturally, different disciplines in the environmental sciences have reached different degrees of sophistication in using remotely sensed data, a fact that is amply illustrated by the material in this book. Meteorologists, because of the importance of temperature profiles in the atmosphere, the requirement for global data and the fact that the data can come from a single instrument, have been the most numerous and sophisticated users of remotely sensed data. This sophistication builds on earlier, more qualitative use of cloud data for tracking storms and therefore checking weather forecasts, as well as use of ground-based weather radar data for precipitation estimation. Oceanographers have recently been using remotely sensed data to provide upper boundary conditions for ocean circulation models, supplementing the earlier cruise and *in situ* data that was mainly used for process studies, as the demand for global and basin ocean circulation models has grown. The use of remotely sensed data for land studies started very early, in conjunction with geological and land use surveys, as a result of the improved cartographic fidelity of satellites such as ERTS (Landsat). But, because of the complexity of the problem, such studies have not progressed very rapidly into quantitative applications. Remotely sensed data have been used extensively by individuals and small groups to study the cryosphere, including global sea ice coverage, the Greenland and Antarctic ice sheets, and individual mountain glaciers. However, most traditional glaciologists have yet to participate actively in analyzing remotely sensed data.

This diversity in the level of development of the use of remotely sensed data is reflected in this atlas. As time goes on, developments both in the scientific questions that are being asked and in the computational and instrument advances that are being made will probably reduce the disciplinary differences. The remainder of this chapter will briefly review some of these expected developments.

Data handling and assimilation

Among the complications in producing time series of remotely sensed data for large areas are the problems of storing data and processing them in a consistent and timely fashion. The recent development of optical disc technology, allowing random access to large quantities of data, and of graphics workstations able to display the results easily, has greatly accelerated the generation of the types of data products described in this book. It is hard to produce ten years of data products when it may take several years simply to read and process the data. Now that access to the new, faster, more convenient technology is becoming more widespread, it is likely that many more derived data sets will become available.

A particularly nice example of the possibilities for the generation of global derived data sets is represented by the Wetnet project of the University of Wisconsin and NASA's Marshall Space Flight Center. A group of investigators who are working mainly in the United States with passive microwave observations are distributing quick-look SSM/I data on a daily basis and calibrated and gridded observations every two weeks. The recipients then process the data for such variables as rainfall rate and sea ice concentration and return the gridded products to the central archive at Marshall Space Flight Center. All participating investigators can then access each others' products for intercomparison and further analysis. This test project will provide experience with interactive data set production and cataloguing, which will be very useful for future, far more ambitious projects such as EOSDIS, described in the next section.

Many of the derived data sets described in this book can be checked for consistency using physical principles, such as conservation of energy and momentum, and need also to be compared to conventional observations, such as from radiosondes. A technique known as assimilation has been developed in numerical weather prediction (NWP) to allow atmospheric sounding data to be used in global NWP models. Such a technique has been widely suggested as a basis for making consistent data sets for climate studies and for synthesizing different data sets together, again for climate studies (WMO, 1989).

Data assimilation systems can use and interpret data in processes represented within a numerical model, whether a one-component model or a fully coupled atmosphere, ocean and land surface model (Hollingworth, 1989). There are already operational data assimilation schemes for short- and medium-range weather forecasts (up to ten days ahead), which have rather complete atmospheric process representation. Climate models clearly also need thorough representation of coupled ocean–atmosphere–land surface processes.

A central aim of data assimilation in atmospheric simulations is to resolve the conflicts between observations and the predicted atmospheric state. A similar statement can be made for data assimilation in ocean or land surface simulations, although here the atmospheric case will be concentrated on for illustrative purposes. Accurate numerical weather prediction generally requires a good understanding of the laws of the atmosphere, a good *a priori* estimate of the current state of the atmosphere, and some general information about observational and model errors (Hollingworth, 1989). Data input into NWP includes *in situ* ship, aircraft and satellite data. However, even in the unusual event of having very high-quality and spatially dense data, there is always insufficient information to describe completely the state of the atmosphere without information from earlier observations and an understanding of the laws governing atmospheric motion. In the assimilation process, the numerical forecast models are used to interpolate between the observations in order to produce a four-dimensional description of the state of the atmosphere. Early assimilation methods used linear interpolation (e.g. Bengtsson *et al.*, 1982), but more recent techniques have taken into account various non-linearities in the equations (e.g. Lorenc, 1986), making them considerably more sophisticated. All assimilation techniques are of course limited by the sophistication of the model description and by truncation caused by the numerical techniques used. Consequently, great care has to be used not to attribute spurious accuracy to the model results.

The ways in which remotely sensed radiometric data can be related to geophysical quantities are usually inverse methods; that is, it is possible to estimate a radiance without ambiguity from (say) an atmospheric profile of temperature observations, but it is not possible to produce an unambiguous description of the way temperature varies with height in the atmosphere from one radiometric observation. Knowledge of earlier atmospheric states is used to reduce this ambiguity in numerical weather prediction. The technique most often used is to estimate a satellite radiance from knowledge of the state of the atmosphere at earlier times, predicted forward to the time of the satellite observation. The observations are compared to the model predictions for the locations where the observations are available, and the model calculations are then adjusted throughout the model grid using maximum likelihood techniques to get the 'best' estimate of the current state of the atmosphere, taking account of the error structure of the observations and of the model results (Eyre, 1989).

Similar but more heuristic techniques have been suggested for other data types, for instance to calibrate soil-vegetation-atmosphere transfer models (e.g. Camillo, O'Neill & Gurney, 1986). The features of the assimilation technique in numerical weather prediction that make the technique so attractive for the future are not just that it gives a consistent basis for incorporating remotely sensed data into numerical models, but also that this is done in real time using large quantities of global data, as necessitated by the constraints of weather prediction. Such techniques will be used increasingly, not just in numerical weather prediction, but also to synthesize the many available data sets, including those described in this book, into inferences about our planet.

Future observations

Although there are many derived large-scale data types described in this book, and additional types of remotely sensed data that have been used in regional experiments or in solid Earth geophysics, there are still large and obvious gaps in the types of observations that can be made, and considerable limitations to their accuracy. Furthermore, the effective combination of different types of data is still only in its initial stages, as described in the previous section, yet environmental scientists are being urgently requested to provide improved predictions of future global and regional changes.

This challenge has led environmental and space agencies to propose a suite of new satellites to help fill some of the observational gaps. These satellites and a brief description of their sensors are given in the Appendix, together with a list of existing satellites and sensors. While many of the details of future satellites and times of launch will undoubtedly change, several features about this list are notable. Firstly, the European Space Agency, the National Space Development Agency of Japan, and the Canadian Space Agency are becoming increasingly involved in providing environmental science data, not just meteorological data. The sources of future data will thus be far more international than at present, with the current strong bias toward the United States as the centre for satellite technology. Furthermore, the types of observation are becoming more diverse. For instance, satellites such as ERS-1 and ERS-2 of the European Space Agency will make fairly routine observations of oceanographic variables for input into oceanographic circulation models, complementing the continuing atmospheric and resource mapping observations. There is also a realisation of the need to use many of the observations together, which is driving various space agencies to propose satellite platforms that can carry many different instruments. This can be seen particularly in the ongoing planning for the Earth Observing System (EOS) (e.g. NASA, 1988). Advances are also apparent on the scale of individual instrument technologies, such as in the increased detail obtainable with the new active microwave synthetic aperture radars in contrast to passive microwave instruments and in the increased precision of the upcoming laser altimeters over the existing radar altimeters.

Very important aspects of satellite planning now and in the future are the data management and information systems that will quality-control the data and make them available in a usable form to the research community. Such a data system is so prominent a feature of EOS that it is proposed that the data system termed EOSDIS will absorb over half the total funds for the project. An early consequence of EOSDIS will be the general availability of many of the data types described in this book. The exact architecture of EOSDIS is not yet fully articulated, and the implementation of similar data systems outside the United States is even less well defined.

However, it is apparent that sophisticated data distribution systems providing free or low cost data access for research purposes are a prerequisite for the success of future satellite missions.

References

Bengtsson, L., Kanamitsu, M., Kallberg, P. & Uppala, S. (1982). FGGE 4-dimensional data assimilation at ECMWF, *Bull. Am. Meteor. Soc.*, **63**, 29–43.

Camillo, P. J., O'Neill, P. E. & Gurney, R. J. (1986). Estimating soil hydraulic parameters using passive microwave data, *IEEE Trans.* **GE-24**, 930–6.

Eyre, J. (1989). Inversion of cloudy satellite sounding radiances by non-linear optimal estimation: I. theory and simulation for TOVS, *Quart. J. Roy. Meteor. Soc.*, **115**, 1001–26; II application of TOVS. *Quart. J. Roy. Meteor. Soc.*, **115**, 1027–38.

Hollingworth, A. (1989). The role of real-time four-dimensional data assimilation in the quality control, interpretation and synthesis of GEWEX data, *WMO WCRP-25*, Appendix D, Geneva, Switzerland, p. 13.

Lorenc, A. (1986). Analysis methods for numerical weather prediction, *Quart. J. Roy. Meteor. Soc.*, **112**, 1177–94.

NASA (1988). From pattern to process: The strategy of the Earth Observing System, *NASA Tech. Memo 86129*, 140pp.

WMO (1989). Global Energy and Water Cycle Experiment (GEWEX), Report of First Session of the JSC Scientific Steering Group for GEWEX, WCRP-25, WMO/TD 321, Geneva, Switzerland, 28pp.

Appendix: Operational and research satellites for observing the earth in the 1990s and thereafter

RENNY GREENSTONE AND BILL BANDEEN

US OPERATIONAL SATELLITES

NOAA Weather satellites – 1980s–1990s

Objectives: operational weather data

Orbit: Sun-synchronous, 833 to 870 km, 7:30 am and 1:30 pm equator crossing times

Table 1.

| Payload: | 8 | 9 | 10 | 11 | 12 | | | | | | | |
NOAA	E	F	G	H	D	I	J	K	L	M	N	0–Q
Advanced very high resol. rad. (AVHRR)	X	X	X	X	X	X	X	X	X	X	X	VIRSR
High resolution IR sounder (HIRS)	X	X	X	X	X	X	X	X	X	X	X	IRTS
Stratospheric sounding unit (SSU)		X		X		X	X					
Microwave sounding unit (MSU)	X	X	X	X	X	X	X					
ARGOS data collection and position system	X	X	X	X	X	X	X	X	X	X	X	X
Space environment monitor (SEM)	X		X		X	X	X	X	X	X	X	X
Solar backscatter UV exp. (SBUV) (p.m. orbit only)		X		X		X		X		X		SBUV/ TOMS
Earth radiation budget experiment (ERBE)		X	X									
Search and rescue (S&R)	X	X	X	X		X	X	X	X	X	X	X
Advanced microwave sounding unit (AMSU)								X	X	X	X	MTS/ MHS
Planned or actual launch year	83	84	86	88	91	91	93	94	96	97	99	2001-
Equator crossing time (am or pm)	am	pm	am	pm	am	pm	am	pm	am	pm	am	pm

Instrument description

AMSU: 15 bands, 24 to 90 GHz, 5 bands, 89 to 183 GHz, 15 km res., all-weather temperature profiles

ARGOS data collection and position location system: 3 bands, 137.77 MHz, 136.77 MHz, 401 MHz; platform location and sensor data relay

AVHRR: 5 bands, 0.58–12.5 μm, 1 km/4 km res., 2200 km swath, temperature of clouds, sea surface, and land

ERBE: Earth's radiation loss and gain

HIRS/2: 20 bands 0.7–15 μm, atm sounding, temperature and moisture profiles, 17 km res., 2200 km swath

IRTS: infra-red temperature sounder, improved HIRS

MHS: microwave humidity sounder (humidity component of AMSU)

MSU: 4 bands, 50.3 to 57.9 GHz, atmospheric sounding

MTS: microwave temperature sounder (temperature component of AMSU)

S and R: location of beacons on airplanes, ships, etc, in distress and alert to international rescue organizations

SBUV: 12 bands, 255–340 nm, solar spectrum, O_3 profiles, Earth radiance spectrum

SEM: 3 instruments, solar protons, alpha particles, and 'e' flux density

SSU: 3 bands, atm sounding, temperature profiles

TOMS: total ozone mapping spectrometer, 6 bands, 306–360 nm

VIRSR: visible and infra-red scanning radiometer, improved AVHRR, 7 spectral bands, 0.605–12.5 μm

GOES – Geostationary operational environmental satellite weather satellite system – 1975–1990s

Objectives: operational weather data, cloud cover, temperature profiles, real-time storm monitoring, severe storm warning

Orbit: geostationary at east and west longitudes

Payload: visible and infra-red spin-scan radiometer (VISSR), VISSR atmospheric sounder (VAS), data collection system (DCS), space environment monitor (SEM)

　　　　1–5 inactive
　　　　6, G failed
　　　　7 operational
　　　　I through M operational: new 3-axis-stabilized system under development with payload similar to that on present spin-stabilized spacecraft except that the sounder and imager will be separate instruments

Instrument description

DCS: random access from buoys, balloons, and platforms
SEM: solar protons, alpha particles, and 'e' flux density
VAS: 12 bands, 0.55–0.70 μm, 3.9–14.7 μm, day/night cloud cover, atmospheric temperature and water content
VISSR: 2 bands, 0.55–0.70 μm, 10.5–12.6 μm, 0.9 km res. visible, 8 km res. IR, sensitivity of 0.4 – 1.4 K, day/night cloud cover, Earth/cloud radiance temperature measurements

DMSP – Defense meteorological satellite program – 1970s–1990s

Objective: operational weather data for DoD
Orbit: Sun-synchronous, 720 km, equator crossing time as desired
Payload: operational linescan system (OLS), multispectral IR radiometer (MIR), microwave temperature sounder (MTS), space environment sensor (SES), and special sensor microwave Imager (SSM/I) 20 inactive, latest, DMSP 502–4, launched 3 February 1988

Instrument description

MIR: 9.8 and 12.0 μm bands, 13.4–15.0 μm (CO_2), 18.7–28.3 μm ($H_{92}O$), vertical temperature profiles
MTS: 50–60 GHz, seven-band scanning microwave temperature sounder
OLS: 0.4–1.1 μm, 10–13 μm, 0.56 km/2.78 km res., global cloud cover
SES: charged-particle monitor
SSM/I: 19.35, 37.0, 85.5 GHz, dual polarization, 22.23 GHz vertical polarization; 16×23 km res. at 19 GHz, 1400 km swath; precipitation, water vapor, soil moisture, wind speed over ocean, and sea-ice morphology

ERTS/LANDSAT, 1972–1990s

ERTS (Earth resources technology satellite) 1972–1974[a]*Landsat 1975–1990s*[b].

Objectives: agriculture, forestry, and range resources; land use and mapping; geology; coastal oceanography and marine resources; water resources; environment

Orbits: Sun-synchronous, 913 km (circular), descending node, 9:00 am (Landsats 1, 2) – 9:30 am (Landsat 3) 18 day repeat
Sun-Synchronous, 705 km (circular), descending node, 9:45 am (Landsats 4, 5, and 6), 16-day repeat

Table 2.

Payload:	1	2	3	4	5	6
Landsat	A	B	C	D	D'	
Return-beam Vidicon (RBV)	X	X	X[c]			
Multispectral scanner (MSS)	X	X	X[d]	X	X	
Thematic mapper (TM)				X	X	X[e]
Data collection system (DCS)	X	X	X			
Planned or actual launch year	72	75	78	82	84	92

Payload: multispectral scanner (MSS), thematic mapper (TM). Landsat 1, 2, and 3 are inactive, 4 and 5 are operational, and 6 is under development

Instrument Description

DCS: real-time data relay system
MSS: 4 bands, 0.5–0.6 μm, 0.6–0.7 μm, 0.7–0.8 μm, 0.8–1.1 μm, 80 m res., 185 km swath
RBV: 3 cameras (coincident FOVs); 0.475–0.575 μm, 0.580–0.680 μm, and 0.698–0.830 μm, 80 m res.; ground coverage/ frame = 185×185 km
TM: 7 bands, 0.45–0.52 μm, 0.52–0.60 μm, 0.63–0.69 μm, 0.76–0.90 μm, 1.55–1.75 μm, 2.08–2.35 μm, 30 m res., 10.4–12.5 μm, 120 m res., 185 km swath
Notes:
(a) ERTS 1, launched on 23 July 1972, was redesignated Landsat 1 on 13 January 1975.
(b) A decision to transfer the responsibility for the operational aspects of earth-resources satellites from NASA to NOAA was made in 1979. NOAA assumed operational responsibility for Landsat 4 on 31 January 1983.
(c) On Landsat 3, only 2 cameras (side-by-side FOVs); panchromatic: 0.505–0.750 μm (40 m res); ground coverage/ frame = 183×98 km.
(d) On Landsat 3, a 5th band was added, 10.4–12.6 μm (240 m res.).
(e) On Landsat 6, an 'Enhanced TM' (ETM) will be flown, incorporating a 0.5–0.9 μm panchromatic 8th channel with 15-meter resolution and a 2-level gain setting.

US RESEARCH SATELLITES

UARS – Upper atmosphere research satellite, September 1991 launch

Objective: coordinated measurement of major upper atmospheric parameters
Orbit: 57° inclination; 600 km altitude

Payload: Cryogenic limb array Etalon spectrometer (CLAES). Halogen occultation experiment (HALOE), High resolution Doppler imager (HRDI), improved stratospheric and mesospheric sounder (ISAMS), microwave limb sounder (MLS), particle environment monitor (PEM), solar/stellar irradiance comparison experiment (SOLSTICE), solar-UV spectral irradiance monitor (SUSIM), wind imaging interferometer (WINDII), active cavity radiometer irradiance monitor (ACRIM)

Instrument description:

ACRIM: solar constant monitor
CLAES: global synoptic measurement of nitrogen and chlorine ozone-destructive species, minor constituents, temperature
HALOE: stratospheric species concentrations, HCl, HF, CH_4, CO_2, O_3, and H_2O
HRDI: atmospheric wind velocities for upper troposphere and above
ISAMS: atmospheric temperature and species concentration
MLS: vertical profiles of O_3 and O_3-related species, inferred pressure
PEM: charged-particle-entry measurements for atmosphere
SOLSTICE: solar irradiance from 115 to 430 nm
SUSIM: solar flux changes over 120 to 400 nm range
WINDII: wind velocities above 80 km

TOPEX/POSEIDON – ocean topography experiment, August 1992 launch

Objectives: ocean topography, ocean-current signatures
Orbit: 1334 km, 63.13° inclination, 10-day repeat

Payload and instrument description

GPS (global positioning system): precise orbit determination
LRA (laser retroflector array): precise orbit determination
TMR (TOPEX microwave radiometer): atmospheric composition, Earth radiation budget at 18, 21, and 37 GHz
TOPEX: 2 bands, Ku – 13.5 GHz, C – 5.3 GHz, 2-cm precision, atmospheric correction provided by onboard microwave radiometer (TMR)

ERBS – Earth radiation budget satellite – October 1984

Objective: determine Earth's radiation budget on regional, zonal, and global scales
Orbit: 56° inclination, 610 km

Instrument description:

ERBI(NS): Non-scanner portion of instrument, 1100 km res., full disk view
ERBI(S): Scanning portion of instrument, 50 km res.

Nimbus Satellite Program – 1964–1978

Objectives: develop and test advanced remote sensors for meteorological, oceanographic, and environmental research.
Orbit: Sun-synchronous, 940 to 1300 km, approximately noon equator crossing times

Payloads: During the period 1964–1978, seven Nimbus satellites carrying more than 40 cameras, scanning radiometers, atmospheric sounders, ozone mappers, radiation budget systems, ocean color sensors, data-collection-and-location systems, etc, were orbited. The data from these sensors significantly advanced our knowledge of the earth–atmosphere system. In addition, many of these sensors, after being proven on Nimbus missions, were adapted for flight on the NOAA Operational Satellites. The data from Nimbus-7, launched in October 1978, was used extensively in the global weather experiment, 1978–1979 [Originally known as the First GARP (Global atmospheric research program) global experiment (FGGE)]. The Solar backscatter ultra-violet/total Ozone mapping spectrometer (SBUV/TOMS) on Nimbus-7 played a major role in the study of global ozone and the 'ozone hole' over Antarctica. As of this writing, the Nimbus-7 TOMS is still reading out good data.

US SHUTTLE PAYLOADS

ATLAS (Atmospheric laboratory for applications and science): ATLAS is a series of Shuttle experiments scheduled for flight on an approximately annual basis for a period approaching a decade, starting in March 1992.

Objectives: provide information on solar activity and the trace-constituent concentration of the upper atmosphere over a long period of time such that inter-annual variability and long- term trends may be studied. There is a 'core' of instruments which will be the same on the ATLAS missions, and there are additional instruments unique to several of the flights. ATLAS 1 and 2 will provide correlative measurements and complementary science to UARS.

Core instrument description

ACR (active cavity radiometer): measures solar constant with technique similar to SOLCON (allowing for intercomparison)
AEPI (atmospheric emissions photometric imaging experiment): measures optical emissions from the upper atmosphere/ionosphere and from the Space Shuttle environment. Makes auroral measurements.
ALAE (atmospheric lyman-alpha emissions): uses onboard hydrogen and deuterium cells to measure thermospheric/exospheric H and D concentrations, as well as Lyman-alpha amounts in the interplanetary medium.
ATLAS-1 special instrument description:
ATLAS-3 will be flown with the German SPAS-CRISTA payload, which will have two instruments:
ATLAS-3A special instruments description:
ATMOS (ATMOSpheric trace molecule spectroscopy) – infra-red instrument works at occultation (sunrise, sunset) and measures a wide variety of species with good vertical resolution
CRISTA (cryogenic infra-red spectrometers and telescopes for the atmosphere): this is an infra-red instrument with three independent telescopes directed towards the limb. Because of

the angular separation of the telescopes, information on small-scale variability in the atmosphere should become available.

ENAP (energetic neutral atom precipitation): measures very faint nighttime emissions due to flux of energetic neutral atoms in the thermosphere.

FAUST (far ultra-violet space telescope): a wide field-of-view, far ultra-violet (130–180 nm) instrument, studies extended and point sources.

GRILLE (grille spectrometer): infra-red absorption spectrometer similar in goal to ATMOS. Has emission mode for mesospheric/thermospheric OH.

ISO (imaging spectrometric observatory): spectrometer to make low-light observations of both day and night side of the Earth, primarily for airglow emissions. Covers five spectral ranges from 30–1300 nm.

MAHRSI (middle atmosphere high resolution spectrograph investigation) measures the dayglow in the 190–320 nm spectral region to study OH and NO in the mesosphere and thermosphere (40–150 km region). Vertical resolution will be 2 km.

MAS (millimeter-wave atmospheric sounder): measures millimeter-wave emission from the atmosphere to determine stratospheric temperature, ozone, and chloride monoxide (ClO)

SEPAC (space experiments with particle accelerators): Performs experiments on and in the Earth's ionosphere.

SOLCON (measurement of the solar constant): measures solar constant with two-channel instrument, allowing for correction of degradation of instrument surfaces.

SOLSPEC (SOLar SPECtrum): measures solar irradiance from 180 to 3000 nm using three double spectrometers and an onboard calibration device.

SSBUV (shuttle solar backscatter ultra-violet experiment): uses UV backscatter in nadir to measure vertical profiles of ozone in the stratosphere and into the lower mesosphere.

SUSIM (solar ultra-violet spectral irradiance monitor): measures solar UV flux as a function of wavelength.

SIR-C/X-SAR-shuttle imaging radar

The SIR-C/X-SAR flights, in 1994, 1995, and 1996 provide the next evolutionary steps in NASA's spaceborne imaging radar (SIR) Program in preparation for the Eos SAR planned for launch later in the decade.

Objectives

1. Conduct geoscience investigations that require the observational capabilities of orbiting radar sensors alone, or in conjunction with other sensors, that will lead to a better understanding of the surface conditions and processes on the Earth;

2. Explore regions of the Earth's surface that are not well characterized because of vegetation, cloud, or sediment cover in order to better understand surface conditions and processes on a global scale; and

3. Incorporate this new knowledge into global models of land and ocean surface and subsurface processes operating on the Earth and other planets.

SIR-C/X-SAR will provide data required for studies of:
- vegetation extent, biomass, and condition
- soil moisture and snow properties
- recent climate change and tectonic activity
- ocean-wave spectra

Instrument description

SIR-C operates at L-band (wavelength = 24 cm) and C-band (wavelength = 5.6 cm). Its polarization modes are HH (horizontally polarized transmission, horizontally polarized reception), HV (horizontally polarized transmission, vertically polarized reception), VH (vertically polarized transmission, horizontally polarized reception) and VV (vertically polarized transmission, vertically polarized reception). SIR-C will not only provide images of the magnitudes of HH, VV, and cross-polarized returns, it will also provide images of the relative phase difference between HH, VV, VH, and HV returns and will allow derivation of the complete scattering matrix of the scene on a pixel-by-pixel basis. From the scattering matrix every polarization configuration (linear, circular, or elliptical) can be generated by ground processing.

The X-SAR sensor, provided by Germany and Italy, will acquire data at X-band (wavelength = 3 cm) in VV polarization. Thus, the combined SIR-C/X-SAR capability will yield measurements of the Earth's surface and cover at a variety of frequencies. A steerable antenna allows acquisition of data at a variety of incidence angles.

Digital correlation to full resolution will result in images with resolution of approximately 25 m (bandwidth = 20 MHz), and 40 m (bandwidth = 10MHz). The SIR-C swath width will depend on the mode, look angle, resolution (bandwidth), signal quantization level, and the surface being imaged. Generally, swath widths for calibrated data will range from 15–65 km, and swath widths for mapping mode will range from 40–90 km.

MAPS – Measurement of air pollution from satellites – 1981–1996

Objective: measure global distribution of CO in the troposphere

Instrument description

MAPS instrument uses gas-correlation technique to measure vertical distribution of CO.

US EOS AND EARTHPROBE SATELLITES

The US EOS and Earthprobe satellites are designed to make observations particularly related to climate and the hydrological cycle.

EOS AM-1 (launch 6/98)

Ceres measures longwave and shortwave infra-red radiation to determine Earth's radiation budget.

Modis-N provides global observations of land, atmosphere and ocean properties.

MISR provides multiangle data for top of atmosphere and surface albedoes.

ASTER provides high spatial and spectral resolution data of visible and infra-red radiation.

MOPITT provides column amounts of CO and CH_4 and vertical profiles of CO.

EOS PM-1, PM-2 (launch 12/2000 and 12/2005)

Ceres – as AM-1

Modis-N – as AM-1

AIRS is a high spectral resolution, multispectral IR atmospheric sounder.

AMSU-A is a microwave sounder to estimate atmospheric temperature.

MHS is a microwave sounder to estimate atmospheric humidity.

EOS AM-2 (launch 6/2003)

As AM-1, except ASTER is replaced and MOPITT is replaced by EOSP, an instrument for measuring atmospheric aerosols.

TRMM – TROPICAL RAINFALL MEASUREMENT MISSION

Microwave radiometer

Rain radar

AVHRR

CERES

BRAZIL

BRESEX – Brazilian remote sensing experiment

Objective: Earth resources

Orbit: Sun-synchronous, 650 km, 35-day repeat

Instrument description

Multispectral pushbroom imager, CCD scanner, 40-m resolution

SSR-1, 2 – Brazilian remote sensing satellites-1, 2, 1993–1994 launch

Objectives: oceans, land

Orbit: Sun-synchronous, 650 km

Instrument description

SSR Camera scans electronically

Canada

RADARSAT – Canadian radar program – 1994–2000, one/two satellite series

Objectives: multi-mode from high resolution, narrow swath to lower resolution, wide swath studies of Arctic areas, agriculture, geology, forestry, water resources, and ocean characteristics.

Orbit: dawn-dusk, approx. 800 km altitude, 24-day repeat cycle

Payload: synthetic aperture radar (SAR)

Instrument description

SAR, C Band, HH (may be changed to VV), within 500 km accessibility swath: 1500 km, 100×100 m resolution SCANSAR; 7 approx. 100 km swaths, 25×30 m resolution; 40 km, nominally 10×10 m resolution; 4–6 experimental swaths (outside the accessibility swath) 80–100 km, 25×30 m resolution.

PEOPLES' REPUBLIC OF CHINA (PRC)

ERS (PRC) – Earth resources satellite

Objective: land research

Orbit: Sun-synchronous, 400 km

Launch date: January 1989

Instrument description

MS (PRC) multispectral scanner

CBERS-1, -2 – China Brazil Earth resources satellite-1, 1992–1994 Launch

Objective: Earth resources cartography

Orbit: Sun-synchronous, 98.5°, 778 km

Instrument description

CCD Camera

IR-MSS

EUROPEAN SPACE AGENCY (ESA) OPERATIONAL SATELLITES

METEOSAT-3 – Geosynchronous weather satellite. European Space Agency

Objective: operational weather data

Orbit: geostationary, 0°, launched June 1988

Payload: 3 bands, 0.4–1.1 μm, 2.5 km res., 5.7–7.1 μm, 5 km, res., 10.5–12.5 μm, 5 km res.

Instrument description

DCS: random access data collection from buoys, balloons, and platforms

MOP-1 (Meteosat operational programme-1) was launched March 1989

MOP-2 was launched March 1991

MOP-3 launched 1992

VIRR: temperature of clouds, sea surface, and land.

ESA RESEARCH SATELLITES

ESA polar-orbit Earth observation mission M-1 (EPOP M-1), 1997 Launch

Objective: Earth science research
Orbit: Sun-synchronous, 800 km, 10:00 am equator crossing, descending node

Instrument description

AATSR: advanced along-track scanning radiometer, high-precision SST retrieval and land-surface bi-directional measurements, 10 channels in visible and near IR, 0.47–12.0 μm, 500 m/1 km res., 500 km swath

ARGOS+: operational system, provides platform location and sensor data from fixed and mobile platforms from anywhere in the world.

ASCATT: active microwave system to measure ocean surface vector winds in the range from 4 m/s to 20 m/s, 2 m/s accuracy, 50 km res., two 500 km swaths

CERES: two broadband scanning radiometers; one in a crosstrack mode and one with rotating scan plane. Three channels on each scanner will be a total channel (0.2 to > 100 μm), SW channel (0.2 to 3.5 μm) and a LW channel (6–25 μm). Nadir field of view about 25 km

GOMOS: global ozone monitoring by occultation of stars, nighttime only, plus observations of interacting species H_2O, NO_2, NO_3, ClO, BrO, and OClO and aerosols, 2 km vertical res.

IRTS: infra-red temperature sounder, 21 km res., 20 bands, 0.69–14.95 μm, profiles water vapor and ozone

IASI: infra-red atmospheric sounding interferometer

LR: laser retroreflector, provides altitude correction for RA-2, using ground-based lasers

MERIS: medium-resolution imaging spectrometer designed to operate in very narrow bands (5–20 nm) in the visible/near-IR part of the spectrum, 400–1050 nm, with medium resolution, 250 m/1000 m res., tuned to ocean/meteorological/climate applications, has design option for tilt capability

MHS: operational microwave radiometer instrument for humidity sounding, 5 channels, 15 km res.

MIPAS: Michelson interferometer for passive atmospheric sounding, four spectral bands, 4.15–14.6 μm, measures chemical species and temperatures in the middle atmosphere and upper troposphere, 3 km vertical res.

MTS: operational microwave radiometer instrument for temperature sounding, water vapor precipitation, sea ice, snow cover, ocean wind stress, 21 channels, 23.8–60.8 GHz, 15 km/45km res.

PRAREE: precise range and range rate equipment to determine satellite positions to within millimeters

RA-2: radar altimeter for topographic mapping of ocean, ice, and land, 13.8 GHz center frequency

S&R: international cooperative search and rescue system

SCIAMACHY: scanning imaging absorption spectrometer for atmospheric cartography, measures tropospheric and stratospheric chemical species, temperatures, and aerosols, daylight only, 1 km vertical res. The following gases are to be measured: tropospheric O_3, O_2, O_4, N_2O, HCHO, CO, CO_2, CH_4, H_2O, and possibly SO_2, and stratospheric O_3, O_2, NO, NO_2, NO_3, CO_2, CH_4, H_2O, ClO, OClO, BrO, and possibly HCHO and CO. In addition are aerosols, cloud top heights, and stratospheric clouds

SEM: operational space environment monitor to measure and predict solar events

VIRSR: visual IR scanning radiometer, 7 bands, 0.6–12.5 μm, clouds, SST, vegetation, snow, and ice, 1 km res.

ESA polar orbit Earth observation mission N-1 (EPOP N-1), 1999 launch

Objectives: Earth science research
Orbit: Sun-synchronous, 705 km, 10:00 am equator crossing

Instrument description

A-SAR: C-band synthetic aperture radar for all-weather surface observations, 30 m res., 5.3 GHz

ALT-2: an adaptive pulse-limited radar altimeter designed to operate over land and ice as well as ocean. A dual-frequency radar altimeter, including a passive microwave radiometer mode for humidity correction.

APAFO: particles and fields measurements, incorporating GOS, IPEI, and XIE

ATLID: atmospheric lidar

AURIO: auroral observations

HRIS: high resolution imaging spectrometer

HRTIR: pushbroom radiometer

LISA: infra-red interferometer for the investigation of stratospheric composition.

MERIS: imaging spectrometer designed to operate in very narrow bands in the visible/near-IR part of the spectrum with medium resolution, tuned to ocean/meteorology/climate applications.

VHROI: very high resolution optical instrument

ERS-1 – ESA first remote sensing satellite, July 1991 Launch; ERS-2 in 1994; (European Program)

Objectives: all-weather land and ocean sensing, coastal ocean, ice studies, global weather, land use
Orbit: Sun-synchronous, 780 km, 10:30 am equator crossing time, 3-day repeat cycle
Payload: active microwave instrument (AMI), along track scanning radiometer (ATSR)

Instrument description

AMI: SAR: C band 5.3 GHz, 30 × 30 m res., 100 km swath, provides ice sheet mapping, ocean wave patterns, land cover information, Scatterometer (wind mode): 3 beam C-band, VV polarization, 500 km swath, 50 km res., range 4 m/s–24 m/s, accuracy 2 m/s or 10%. Scatterometer (wave mode): 5 km × 5 km image every 200 km; Altimeter: Ku band (12.5 GHz), 10 cm precision – land, 40 cm precision – ocean, 1.2 m diameter antenna

ATSR: Infra-red radiometer, 1.6, 3.7, 11, and 12 μm bands, 1 km res., 50 km swath (global sea surface temperature (SST) and microwave sounder, 23.8 and 36.5 GHz (atmosphere integrated water content),

GOME: global ozone monitoring experiment (will be added for flight on ERS-2, will measure ozone and related upper atmosphere trace gases)

LRR: laser retroreflector (precise orbit determination), used with ground-based laser ranging stations

PRARE: precision range and range-rate experiment

RA (ERS-1): radar altimeter (ocean topography; ocean waves, ice sheet topography, ocean ice, ocean surface winds)

FRENCH OPERATIONAL SATELLITE

SPOT – Système Probatoire d'Observation de la Terre, 1986 launch with follow-on in 1990

Objectives: operational land use and inventory monitoring system
Orbit: Sun-synchronous, 10:30 am node, 2.5-day repeat
Payload: SPOT

Instrument description

(Version number in parentheses)
DORIS (2, 3, 4, 5): dual Doppler receiver (precise orbit determination)
HRV (1, 2): high resolution visible imager (land surface topography and composition)
HRVIR (3, 4, 5): improved high-resolution visible imager
SPOT: 3 bands 0.5–0.6 μm, 0.6–0.7 μm, 0.78–0.9 μm, 20 m res. color mode, panchromatic mode (0.51–0.73 μm), 10 m res., 60 km × 60 km viewing area, swath of 950 km centered around nadir, stereoscopic images
VMS (3, 5): vegetation monitoring sensor

GERMAN RESEARCH SATELLITE

ATMOS – German Atmospheric and Environmental Research Satellite – 1996 Launch

Objective: Earth science research
Orbit: 781 km, Sun-synchronous, 3-day repeat, 11:00 am node
Payload: advanced millimeter-wave atmospheric sounder (AMAS), Michelson interferometer for passive atmospheric sounding (MIPAS), scanning imaging absorption spectrometer for atmospheric chartography (SCIAMACHY), and reflective optics system imaging spectrometer (ROSIS). (Payload intended to serve as predecessor to EOS-era instruments.)

Instrument description

AMAS: passive microwave limb emission sounder; operates in the spectral region between 62 and 206 GHz; provides day and night measurements of temperature, ClO, O_3, H_2O, and CO in the middle atmosphere.

MIPAS: passive limb emission sounder; operates in the spectral region between 4.5 and 15 micrometers; provides day and night measurements of many trace gases in the stratosphere and cloud-free regions of the upper troposphere.

ROSIS: nadir-looking imaging spectrometer with narrow spectral channels in the visible and near-IR regions

SCIAMACHY: uses differential absorption spectroscopy of solar and lunar radiation in the region between 240 nm and 2400 nm to measure trace gases in the troposphere and stratosphere; views in occultation, nadir, and limb-scattering modes

INDIAN OPERATIONAL SATELLITES

INSAT Indian operational weather satellite, 1982–1991 launch

Objective: operational weather data
Orbit: geostationary
Payload: very high resolution radiometer (VHRR), 0.55–0.90 μm, 2.75 km res., 10.5–12.5 μm, 11 km res., IB – operational, IC, ID, IIA, IIB – proposed

IRS: Indian operational remote sensing mission, 1988–1995 launch

Objective: Earth resources
IA – operational, IB – development, IC, ID – proposed
Orbit: 904 km Sun-synchronous, 22-day repeat
Payload: linear imaging self scan (LISS), 0.45–0.52 μm, 0.52–0.60 μm, 0.65–0.69 μm, and 0.76–0.90 μm, all 73 m res., 148 km swath

ITALIAN RESEARCH SATELLITE

LAGEOS-2: laser geology satellite-2, 1991 launch

Objective: detect tectonic plate motions
Orbit: 52°, 6000 km

Instrument description

PLCR: Laser beam from ground reflects off retroreflectors on spacecraft

JAPANESE OPERATIONAL SATELLITES

GM – geosynchronous meteorological satellite – Japan, 1977 launch will follow-on

Objective: operational weather data
Orbit: geostationary, 140° E
Launch Dates: GMS-3 – 8/84, GMS-4 – 9/89, GMS-5 – 1/94

Instrument description

DCS: relays environmental data from ground
SEM: space environmental monitor
VISSR: visible and infra-red spin-scanning radiometer, 2 bands (0.5–0.75 μm, 1.25 km res.; 10.5–12.5 μm, 5 km res.)

JAPANESE RESEARCH SATELLITES

ADEOS – advanced Earth observation satellite

Objective: Earth science research
Orbit: Sun-synchronous, 800 km, 10:30 am equator crossing time
Launch date: February 1995

Instrument description

AVNIR: Advanced visible and near-IR radiometer (NASDA), five bands, 0.40–0.92 μm, 16 m res., (8 m res. in panchromatic band), 80 km swath

ILAS: improved limb atmospheric spectrometer, performs solar occultation measurements in the IR, 4.1–6.9 and 7.3–11.8 μm, measures stratospheric ozone and related species, O_3, HNO_3, NO_2, H_2O, CO_2, N_2O and CH_4, 2 km vert. res.

IMG: interferometric monitor for greenhouse gases, eight bands, 3.3–14 μm, profiles of CH_4, N_2O, CO, O_3, and CO_2

NSCAT: NASA scatterometer (NASA)

OCTS: ocean color and temperature scanner (NASDA), 12 channels, 0.41–12.0 μm, 700 m res.

POLDER: polarization and directionality of the Earth's reflectances (CNES), seven channels, 435–880 nm, 5 km res.

RIS: retroreflector in space, laser beam absorption with reflector in space, measures ozone, chlorofluorocarbons, and other trace gases; measures profiles of H_2O, O_3, and CO_2 (Japanese Environmental Agency)

TOMS: total ozone mapping spectrometer (NASA)

ADEOS-2 (Japanese Polar Platform), 1998 Launch, follow-on to ADEOS

Objective: Earth science research, particularly hydrologic circulation
Orbit: Sun-synchronous, 800 km
Launch date: February 1998

Instrument description

ADALT (advanced radar altimeter): two-frequency radar altimeter

AMSR (advanced microwave scanning radiometer): multifrequency microwave radiometer measures precipitation rate, water vapor, cloud water, SST, snow and ice extent, and sea wind speed

E-LIDAR (experimental Lidar): measures aerosols, clouds by Mie scattering, measures water vapor profiles by DIAL technique, measures ice sheets and sea level

GLI (global imager): monitors biological and physical processes and stratospheric ozone, 20 bands, UV to thermal IR, 1 km res., 1800 km swath

IMB (investigation of micro-biosphere): multiband optical radiometer for measurement of ecology with high spatial resolution, VIS to near IR, 100–1000 km swath

(D)PR (precipitation radar): 3-D measurement of rain rate, 8 km res., 400 km swath

SLIES (stratospheric limb infra-red emission spectrometer): interferometer spectrometer to measure species from limb and nadir, 2 km vert. res.

TERSE (tunable Etalon remote sounder of Earth): monitors tropospheric species (CH_4, H_2O, N_2O, and CO_2), 500 km swath

TOMUIS (3-D ozone mapper with ultra-violet imaging spectrometer): uses UV back-scatter, 1500 km swath

JEOS – Japanese 55° Platform, 2000 launch

Payload: AVHRR, LIS, CERES (2), SAGE III – all from US, plus AMSR, PR (precipitation radar), and ILAS

MOS – Marine observation satellite

MOS-1: 2/87; MOS-1B; 2/90
Objective: color and temperature of sea surface
Orbit: Sun-synchronous, 909 km, 10 am node, 17-day repeat
Payload: multispectral electronic self-scanning radiometer (MESSR), visible and thermal IR radiometer (VTIR), microwave scanning radiometer (MSR)

Instrument description

MESSR: 4 bands, 0.5 to 1.1 μm, 50 m res., 100 km swath

MSR: 2 bands, 23.8, and 31.4 GHz, 317 km swath

VTIR: 4 bands, 0.5–0.7 μm, 6.0–7.0 μm, 10.5–11.5 μm, 11.5–12.5 μm, 1 km/3 km res., 500 km swath

JERS-1 – Japanese Earth Resources Satellite-1 – 1992 launch

Objective: Earth resource exploration, coastal monitoring
Orbit: Sun-synchronous, 568 km, 10:30–11:00 am equator crossing time
Launch date: February 1992
Payload: synthetic aperture radar (SAR), optical sensor (OPS) can produce stereo images in the VNIR

Instrument description

SAR: L-band, 1.275 GHz, 18 m res., 75 km swath

OPS: 4 VNIR bands (stereo), 0.52~0.86 μm; 4 SWIR bands, 1.6~2.40 μm, 18 × 24 m res., 75 km swath

CIS OPERATIONAL SATELLITES

METEOR-2 – operational weather satellite – 1977

Objective: operational weather data

Orbit: 900 km polar orbit, 2-day repeat, 2100 – 2600 km swath
Payload: 3 channels: 0.5–0.7 μm, 2 km res., 0.5–0.7 μm, 1 km res., 8–12 μm, 8 km res.

Cosmos oceanographic research series

	Cosmos −1076	Cosmos −1151	Cosmos −1766	Cosmos −1869
Launch dates:	2/79	1/80	7/86	7/88
Orbit inclination:	82.5°	82.5°	82.5°	82.5°
Orbit altitude:	634 km	650 km	662 km	663 km

Instrument descriptions for Cosmos 1766 and 1869

DGTS: Data gathering and transmitting system; ocean surface winds, waves, ice, dynamics, and SST; 2.1 km res.

MSU-M: Measures ocean color and dynamics, four spectral bands at 0.55, 0.65, 0.75, and 0.95 μm, 1 km res.

SLR: Side-looking radar

TFPMS: Nadir-viewing three-frequency panoramic microwave spectrometer; three bands at 0.8, 1.35, and 8.5 GHz with 85, 20, and 7 km res.

Almaz – operational radar satellite – 1991

Objective: all-weather surface imaging, measure soil moisture and roughness, 15-meter res.

CIS RESEARCH SATELLITES

Meteor-priroda – Environmental Satellite – 1993 launch

Objective: operational environmental, land use, and inventory determination

Orbit: 650 km polar orbit

Launch date: June 1980

Payload: MSU-M: 0.5–0.6 μm, 0.6–0.7 μm, 0.7–0.8 μm, and 0.8–1.1 μm, all 1 km res., 1930 km swath

MSU-S: 0.5–0.7 μm and 0.7–1.0 μm, 240 m res., and 1380 km swath

MSU-SA: 0.5–0.6, 0.6–0.7 μm, 0.7–0.8 μm, and 0.8–1.0 μm, all 170 m res., 600 km swath

Fragment: 0.4–0.8 μm, 0.5–0.6 μm, 0.6–0.7 μm, 0.7–1.1 μm, 1.2–1.3 μm, 1.5–1.8 μm, and 2.1–2.4 μm, similar to thematic mapper, all 80 m res. and 85 km swath

MSU-VA: 0.5–0.7 μm, 0.7–0.8 μm, and 0.8–1.0 μm, all 30 m res., 30 km swath

METEOR-3 ENVIRONMENTAL SATELLITE – 1991 launch

Objective: ozone monitoring

Instrument description:

SCARABE: scanning radiation budget sensor (France provided), four channels, 0.5–12.5 μm, 2500 km swath

TOMS: total ozone mapping spectrometer (US provided); FOV = 3.1 km; also images clouds and surface along track in VIS

Index

Entries are filed in word by word order. Alphabetization of subentries ignores prepositions such as 'in' or 'and'. Instruments, satellites and programs have as a rule been entered under their acronyms and in full. Further information on these, and on future research, may be found in the Appendix, which is not indexed.

special sensor microwave imager, *see*
    SSS/I
species change 314, 315
spectroscopy of the atomosphere using far
    infra-red emission (SAFIRE) 56
SPOT (Système Probatoire d'Observation
    de la Terre)
    coastal studies 328, 336, 339
    glaciers 407, 408, 415
    human environmental impact 431, 432,
        433
    vegetation cover 301
    volcanological studies 343, 345, 353
SSBUV (shuttle solar back-scatter U–V)
    experiment 45–6, 54–5
SSM/I (special sensor microwave/imager)
    evaporation data 270, 271, 273–4, 275
    global precipitation estimation 179, 283
    ice sheets 387
    land surface changes 316, 323, 324
    sea ice 373, 378, 381, 382
    snow measurements 366
    Wetnet project 445
    wind data 129–38, 285
SSU (stratospheric sounding unit) 45
Stancomb Wills Glacier 391
stereoimages of glacierized regions 416
stereophotogrammetry 298
stereoplotters 323
storms
    and clouds 151, 156, 159, 161
    and coastal change 327, 334
    and lightning 191–3
    and snow cover 362
    see also thunderstorms
stratosphere 39–86
    composition 41–57
    meteorology 41–57
    temperatures 41–57, 70–1, 79–86
    trace constituents 43, 44, 45, 46, 54–6;
        see also stratospheric aerosols
    warming events 50–2
    water vapor 89
    winds 43, 44, 46, 49–52, 54–6
stratospheric aerosol and gas experiment, *see*
    SAGE
stratospheric aerosol measurement (SAM I)
    686
    SAM II 68–75
stratospheric aerosols 67–76
    increased background 70–1, 74–5
    polar stratosphere 70–2
    seasonal behavior 72–4
    trend 74–5

volcanic effects on 45, 67, 70–5, 86, 341,
    344, 354–6
stratospheric and mesopheric sounder
    (SAMS) 45, 46; *see also* ISAMS
stratospheric sounding unit (SSU) 45
stratospheric wind infra-red limb sounder
    (SWIRLS) 56
Sudan 307, 313, 318, 324
sulfur dioxide
    stratospheric 67
    tropospheric 45
    volcanic emissions 343–4, 354–5, 356
sulfuric acid, stratospheric 67, 341, 344
sunspot 'deficit' effect 11, 13
surface radiation budget (SRB) 33; and
    ENSO 283–4
Svalbard 402, 409, 412
Sweden 47–8, 407
SWIRLS (stratospheric wind infra-red limb
    sounder) 56
Switzerland 407, 410
synthetic aperture radar, *see* SAR
Système Probatoire d'Observation de la
    Terre, *see* SPOT

Tamboura eruption, Indonesia 357
teleconnection patterns 35, 191, 291
televison and infra-red observational
    satellite, *see* TIROS
temperature anomalies, atmospheric 81–6;
    see also sea surface temperature;
    thermal anomalies
temperature humidity infra-red radiometer
    (THIR) 284
temperatures, *see also* tropospheric
    temperatures
Tennessee Valley 213–15
TES (tropospheric emission
    spectrometer) 56
thematic mapper sensors, *see* TM sensors
thermal anomalies, volcanic 342, 346–7,
    350, 354
THIR (temperature humidity infra-red
    radiometer) 284
Thule, Greenland 53
thunderstorms
    and cloudiness 159
    and greenhouse gases 185
    and lightning 191–3, 197–217
    radio frequency measurements 195–7
    and temperature anomalies 81, 182
    variations: annual activity 197;
        diurnal 31, 191–3, 197; inter-
        annual 204–8, 213–73; monthly and

seasonal 198–204; *see also* lightning;
    storms
Tibetan Plateau 33–5, 369
tidal gauges 223, 225, 231
tidewater glaciers 412, 413
TIROS (televison and infra-red
    observational satellite) 20, 141
TIROS N series
    evaporation data 273
    stratospheric data 79, 89–90, 94–5
TIROS operational vertical sounder
    (TOVS) 90, 127, 273
TM (thematic mapper) sensors
    coastal studies 328
    glaciers 404, 407–9, 411, 412–13, 415
    human environmental impact 425, 428,
        432, 433
    ice sheets 389–91
    volcanological studies 343, 346, 354
TOGA (tropical ocean global atmosphere)
    program 243, 246, 284
TOMS (total ozone mapping
    spectrometer) 45, 48, 54, 59, 62
    biomass burning 183, 435
    cloud classification 284
    vocanological studies 343, 344, 353, 354
TOMS-ADEOS 54, 65
TOMS-METEOR 54, 62
TOMS-version-6 59
TOPEX/POSEIDON 223, 224, 227, 233,
    234
topographic databases and maps 297–300
total ozone mapping spectrometer, *see*
    TOMS
TOVS (Tiros operational vertical sounder
    system) 90, 127, 273
trace gases
    and forest fires 435
    and land cover changes 301
    and lightning 217
    ocean's role in storage and transport of
        277
    stratospheric 41–57
    tropospheric 182
    see also chlorofluorocarbons; greenhouse
        gases
TRACER (tropospheric radiometer for
    atmospheric chemistry and
    environmental research) 182
trade wind inversion (TWI) 185
tropical biomass burning 183–8, 434–5
tropical current systems 223, 225, 227–8;
    see also El Niño
tropical energetics 191, 205, 217, 289